import statement p. 53

java.awt p. 54

javabook p. 53

ActionListener p. 199

Button p. 605
TextField p. 618
Frame p. 605
Dialog p. 636
MenuItem p. 620
MenuBar p. 620
Menu p. 620

super p. 562

null p. 206

layout manager p. 197

protected p. 659

insets p. 779

actionPerformed p. 613

action event p. 611
mouse event p. 626
window event p. 614

Class Declaration Summary

```java
import java.awt.*;

import javabook.*;

class SampleDialog extends JavaBookDialog implements ActionListener
{
    private    TextField    editBox;
    private    Button       button;
    private    Frame        myOwner;

    public SampleDialog(Frame owner)
    {
        //set the properties of the dialog
        super(owner);
        setTitle("Sample Dialog");
        setResizable(false);
        setLayout(null);
        myOwner = owner;

        //create and add GUI objects to the dialog
        editBox = new TextField("");
        button = new Button("CLEAR");
        add(editBox);
        add(okButton);

        //set the dialog as an action listener
        okButton.addActionListener(this);
    }

    protected void adjustSize()
    {
        addNotify();

        Insets inset = getInsets();

        setSize(inset.left + inset.right + 150,
                inset.top + inset.bottom + 100);

        editBox.setBounds (inset.left + 30, inset.top + 25, 150, 20);
        button.setBounds(inset.left + 75, inset.top + 155, 50, 25);
    }

    public void actionPerformed(ActionEvent event)
    {
        //tell the owner frame the value entered by the user
        myOwner.valueEntered(editBox.getText() );

        editBox.setText("");        //clears the entry
    }

}
```

An Introduction to Object-Oriented Programming with Java™

C. Thomas Wu
Naval Postgraduate School

 McGraw-Hill

Boston   Burr Ridge, IL   Dubuque, IA   Madison, WI   New York   San Francisco   St. Louis
Bangkok   Bogotá   Caracas   Lisbon   London   Madrid
Mexico City   Milan   New Delhi   Seoul   Singapore   Sydney   Taipei   Toronto

McGraw-Hill Higher Education

*A Division of The **McGraw-Hill** Companies*

AN INTRODUCTION TO OBJECT-ORIENTED PROGRAMMING WITH JAVA
Published by McGraw-Hill, an imprint of The McGraw-Hill Companies, Inc. 1221 Avenue of the Americas, New York, NY, 10020. Copyright © 2001, 1999, by The McGraw-Hill Companies, Inc. All rights reserved. No part of this publication may be reproduced or distributed in any form or by any means, or stored in a data base or retrieval system, without the prior written consent of The McGraw-Hill Companies, Inc., including, but not limited to, in any network or other electronic storage or transmission, or broadcast for distance learning.

Some ancillaries, including electronic and print components, may not be available to customers outside the United States.

This book is printed on acid-free paper.

2 3 4 5 6 7 8 9 0 DOC/DOC 0 9 8 7 6 5 4 3 2 1 0

ISBN 0-07-239684-9

Vice president/Editor-in-Chief: *Kevin T. Kane*
Publisher: *Thomas Casson*
Executive editor: *Elizabeth A. Jones*
Developmental editor: *Emily J. Gray*
Senior marketing manager: *John T. Wannemacher*
Media technology producer: *Christopher Styles*
Project manager: *Scott Scheidt*
Production supervisor: *Michael R. McCormick*
Designer: *Pam Verros*
Supplement coordinator: *Rose M. Range*
Typeface: *10/12 Times Roman*
Printer: *R. R. Donnelley & Sons Company, Crawfordsville*

Library of Congress Cataloging-in-Publication Data

Wu, C. Thomas.
     An introduction to object-oriented programming with Java / C. Thomas Wu. -- 2nd ed.
       p.   cm.
     ISBN 0-07-239684-9 (softcover: alk. paper)
     1. Object-oriented programming (Computer science)   2. Java (Computer program language)   I. Title.
QA76.64.W78 2001
005.13'3 dc--21   00033914

To my family

Contents

Preface   xiii

New Features in the Second Edition   xiv

Major Features   xv

Supplement Materials   xxiv

Book Organization   xxv

Acknowledgments   xxvii

0 Introduction to Computers and Programming Languages   1

0.1   A History of Computers   2

0.2   Computer Architecture   5

0.3   Programming Languages   11

0.4   Java   13

0.5   Exercises   14

1 Introduction to Object-Oriented Programming and Software Development   15

1.1   Classes and Objects   16

1.2   Messages and Methods   18

1.3   Class and Instance Data Values   23

1.4   Inheritance   26

1.5   Software Engineering and Software Life Cycle   29

1.6   Having Fun with Java   31

1.7   Exercises   34

2

Java Programming Basics   37

2.1   The First Java Application   38

2.2   Program Components   48

2.3   Edit–Compile–Run Cycle   59

2.4   The javabook Package   61

2.5   Sample Program: Displaying Messages   62

2.6   The First Java Applet   66

2.7   Exercises   77

3

Numerical Data   83

3.1   Variables   84

3.2   Arithmetic Expressions   92

3.3   Constants   98

3.4   The Math Class   100

3.5   InputBox   103

3.6   OutputBox   106

3.7   Sample Program: Loan Calculator   113

3.8   Numerical Representation (Optional)   124

3.9   Exercises   128

4

Defining Instantiable Classes   139

4.1   Defining Instantiable Classes   140

4.2   Instantiable Classes and Constructors   152

4.3   Visibility Modifiers: public and private   157

4.4   Local Variables, Return Values, and Parameter Passing   162

4.5   Loan Calculator Program with an Instantiable Class   167

4.6   Exercises   181

5

Processing Input with Applets   191

5.1   Placing GUI Objects on Applets   192

5.2   Adding ActionListener to an Event Source   199

5.3   Absolute Positioning of GUI Objects   206

5.4   The Button Class   208

5.5   Converting Text to a Numerical Value   210

5.6   Sample Program: Finding Body Mass Index (BMI)   213

5.7   Running an Applet as an Application   223

5.8   Exercises   224

6

Selection Statements   229

6.1   The if Statement   230

6.2   Boolean Expressions and Variables   238

6.3   Nested-if Statements   242

6.4   ListBox   249

6.5   The switch Statement   252

6.6   Sample Program: Drawing Shapes   258

6.7   Exercises   280

7

Repetition Statements   289

7.1   The while Statement   290

7.2   Pitfalls in Writing Repetition Statements   294

7.3   The do–while Statement   299

7.4   ResponseBox   303

7.5   The for Statement   308

7.6   Nested-for Statements   312

7.7   The Format Class   316

7.8   Loan Tables   322

7.9   Sample Program: Hi-Lo Game   325

7.10   Recursive Methods (Optional)   338

7.11   Exercises   343

8

Characters and Strings   355

8.1   Characters   356

8.2   Strings   359

8.3   Primitive versus Reference Types   370

8.4   StringBuffer   379

8.5   Passing Objects as Parameters   384

8.6   Returning an Object from Methods   389

8.7   Sample Program: Word Play   392

8.8   Exercises   404

9

Arrays   411

9.1   Array Basics   412

9.2   Arrays of Objects   421

9.3   Passing Arrays to Methods   431

9.4   MultiInputBox   436

9.5   Self-Referencing Pointer   439

9.6   Sample Development: The Address Book   446

9.7   Two-Dimensional Arrays   463

9.8   Vectors   470

9.9   Exercises   476

10

Sorting and Searching   481

10.1   Searching   482

10.2   Sorting   488

10.3   Heapsort   495

10.4   Sample Program: Sorting an AddressBook   509

10.5   Exercises   515

11

File Input and Output   519

11.1   File and FileDialog Objects   520

11.2   Low-Level File I/O   525

11.3   High-Level File I/O   532

11.4   Handling Exceptions   539

11.5   Object I/O   544

11.6   Sample Class: Saving an **AddressBook** Object   548

11.7   Exercises   556

12   Reusable Classes and Packages   559

12.1   Object Categories   560

12.2   Method Overriding and Overloaded Methods   562

12.3   Sample Classes: Reusable **EggyPeggy** and **HiLo**   569

12.4   Package Organization   595

12.5   Exercises   597

13   GUI Objects and Event-Driven Programming   603

13.1   Placing Buttons on a Frame   605

13.2   Handling Events   611

13.3   Placing **TextField** Objects on a Frame   618

13.4   Menus   620

13.5   Handling Mouse Events   626

13.6   Other GUI Objects   634

13.7   Sample Program: A Simple Calculator   639

13.8   Exercises   652

14   Inheritance and Polymorphism   657

14.1   Defining Classes with Inheritance   658

14.2   Using Classes Effectively with Polymorphism   662

14.3   Inheritance and Member Accessibility   666

14.4   Inheritance and Constructors   672

14.5   Abstract Superclasses and Abstract Methods   676

14.6   When and When Not to Use Inheritance   682

14.7   Sample Program: Computing Course Grades   684

14.8   Exercises   704

15

Class Roster Maintenance Program   709

15.1   Method Call Sequence Diagram   710

15.2   Problem Statement   711

15.3   Overall Planning   712

15.4   Step 1 Development: Program Shell with Menus   716

15.5   Step 2 Development: Create a New Roster   722

15.6   Step 3 Development: Add Students   729

15.7   Step 4 Development: Delete Students   737

15.8   Step 5 Development: Edit Student Names   740

15.9   Step 6 Development: Edit Test Scores and Compute Grades   746

15.10 Step 7 Development: Display Student Information   753

15.11 Step 8 Development: Storing Grade Rosters   765

15.12 Step 9 Development: Finalize and Improve   775

15.13 The **StudentNameDialog** Class   776

15.14 The **TestScoreDialog** Class   786

15.15 Exercises   791

16

Recursive Algorithms   797

16.1   Basic Elements of Recursion   798

16.2   Directory Listing   799

16.3   Anagram   801

16.4   Towers of Hanoi   805

16.5   Quicksort   809

16.6   When Not to Use Recursion   815

16.7   Exercises   817

The **javabook** Package   819

Preface

We have made a number of improvements in this second edition of the book, but the main objectives remain the same. This book is intended as an introductory text on object-oriented programming, suitable for use in a one-semester CS1 course, and assumes no prior programming experience from the students. Those who already have experience in traditional process-oriented programming languages such as C, BASIC, and others also can use this book as an introduction to object-oriented programming, graphical user interface, and event-driven programming. The two main objectives of this book are to teach

- Object-oriented programming.
- The foundations of real-world programming.

Object-orientation has become an important paradigm in all fields of computer science, and it is important to teach object-oriented programming from the first programming course. Teaching object-oriented programming is more than teaching the syntax and semantics of an object-oriented programming language. Mastering object-oriented programming means becoming conversant with the object-oriented concepts and being able to apply them effectively and systematically in developing programs. The book teaches object-oriented programming, and students will learn how to develop true object-oriented programs.

The second objective of this book is to prepare students for real-world programming. Knowing object-oriented concepts is not enough. Students must be able to apply that knowledge to develop real-world programs. Sample programs in many introductory textbooks are too simplistic. Students rarely encounter sample programs in other textbooks that define more than three classes. But in real-world projects, programmers must use many classes from the libraries and define many classes of their own. In this book, we teach students how to use classes from the class libraries and how to define their own classes. For example, the sample program from Chapter 15 defines 10 classes and uses numerous classes from the existing class libraries.

New Features in the Second Edition

We would like to take this opportunity to thank the adopters of the first edition. We especially appreciate numerous suggestions and encouraging words from the adopters and their students. For the second edition, we focused on improving the strengths of the first edition and incorporating as many suggestions as possible. Because all the suggestions cannot be bound into a single hardcopy of a book, we tried to accommodate varying needs of the adopters by placing materials on our websites. Please see the section on supporting materials for more details on the website contents.

Before we get into the features of the book, we will first highlight briefly what's new with the second edition:

1. **Use of javadoc comments**. Except for the early chapters, all sample code and programs are documented in the standardized javadoc style. The updated javabook classes are also fully documented using the javadoc comments. The HTML documentation files for the javabook classes, generated from the javadoc comments, are available from our websites.

2. **Two-color pages**. We received many accolades for our illustrations in the first edition. We improved them further by using the second color and adding a 3-D appearance. We characterize our style of explaining hard-to-grasp concepts with informative and visually appealing diagrams and figures as *visual teaching*. We believe visual teaching is the most appropriate way to teach introductory programming.

3. **New and improved javabook classes**. Two new classes are added to the javabook package: Clock and SimpleInput. The Clock class provides basic clock functions such as reading the current time, getting today's date, and providing stopwatch functions. Using the stopwatch functions, the programmer can record easily the running time of a program. For example, they can be used conveniently to compare the running time of different sorting algorithms. The second new class, SimpleInput, provides non-GUI-based input routines. A number of

adopters requested the functionality of InputBox for the non-GUI environment. We added this class to answer their request. In addition to the two new classes, we made a number of minor improvements to the existing classes.

4. **Swing-based** javabook **classes**. With the advent of the Swing classes in the Java 2 platform, the Swing-based version of the javabook package is implemented. The direct benefits of using the Swing classes include the simplified implementation of several javabook classes and new functionality such as placing an icon on a MessageBox object. Information on the Swing-based javabook classes can be found at our websites. Whether to use the original javabook or the Swing-based javabook depends on the extent that the instructor covers Swing classes in the course. Even if Swing classes are not covered in the course, Swing-based javabook can be used if the instructor does not plan to get into the internal workings of the javabook package.

5. **Additional topics**. Although we feel the detailed coverage of the collection classes belongs to a CS2 book, we received requests from the adopters to include a discussion on Vector. We concur with them that it is desirable to introduce the convenience and power of the Vector class to the CS1 students. The Vector class is described in Chapter 9. Another new topic we included in the second edition is heapsort. After moving the sorting algorithms from the old Chapter 15 to the new Chapter 10, we added heapsort to strengthen the chapter with a nonrecursive $N\log_2 N$ sorting algorithm. Heapsort serves as a great example of a clever use of an array for storing heap nodes.

6. **Improved supporting materials**. We improved the existing supporting materials and added many new ones. Please read the Supporting Materials section on page xxiv for a detailed information on what's available from our websites.

Major Features

There are many pedagogical features that make this book unique among the introductory textbooks on object-oriented programming. We will describe the major features of this book.

Feature 1   Java

We chose Java for this book. Unlike C++, Java is a pure object-oriented language, and it is an ideal language to teach object-oriented programming because Java is logical and easy to program. Java's simplicity and clean design make it one of the most easy-to-program object-oriented languages. Java does not include any complex language features that could be a roadblock for beginners in learning object-oriented concepts. Although we use Java, we must emphasize that this book is not about Java programming. As this book is about object-oriented programming, we do not cover every aspect of Java. We do, however, cover enough language features of Java to make students competent Java programmers.

Feature 2   The javabook Package

We provide a class library (a *package* in Java terminology) called javabook that includes a number of classes we use throughout the book. We wrote a series of articles in 1993 on how to teach object-oriented programming in the *Journal of Object-Oriented Programming* (Vol. 6, No. 1; Vol. 6, No. 4; and Vol. 6 No. 5). The core pedagogic concept we described in the series is that one must become an object user before becoming an object designer. In other words, before being able to design one's own classes effectively, one first must learn how to use predefined classes. The use of javabook is based on this philosophy.

There are many advantages in using the javabook package:

1. ***It shows students how real-world programs are developed.*** We do not develop practical programs from scratch. Instead, we use predefined classes whenever possible. One of the major benefits of object-oriented programming is the enhanced programmer productivity by reusing the existing classes. Students will get hands-on experience of code reuse by using classes from the javabook package.

2. ***It minimizes the impact of programming language syntax and semantics.*** The use of javabook classes lets students concentrate on learning concepts instead of the Java language features. We have seen many cases where novice programmers started out with a well-designed program, yet ended up with a very poorly constructed program. Often, because they do not understand the programming language fully, their design is not translated into a syntactically and semantically correct program. When they encounter an error while developing a program, instead of correcting the program code, they change their program design. Using predefined classes minimizes the impact of programming language because these predefined classes hide the complexity of underlying programming language. Students will have a much easier time implementing their program design into a working program code using the javabook classes.

3. ***It allows students to write useful programs from very early on, which helps to sustain the students' initial interest and motivation to learn.*** Without using predefined classes, students must learn far too many details of programming language before they can start writing interesting and practi-

cal programs. But before they reach that point, many of them would lose interest in programming, drowning in the boring details of language syntax and semantics. Using the predefined classes from the standard Java libraries such as java.awt from the beginning, however, is not practical because these classes require programming sophistication that beginning students do not possess. Easy-to-use and intuitive predefined classes such as the javabook classes are more appropriate for beginning programmers.

4. ***It provides a necessary foundation before students can start designing their own classes.*** The ultimate goal of learning object-oriented programming is to master the skills necessary for designing effective classes. But before being able to design such classes, students must first learn how to use existing classes. Again, teaching how to use the standard Java classes to novice programmers from the beginning is not pedagogically sound because the majority of the classes from java.awt, java.io, and others are not easy enough for beginning programmers to use. We designed the javabook classes with novice programmers in mind.

5. ***You can customize the* javabook *package to meet your needs.*** For example, there is a class called MainWindow in the package that serves as a top-level window of a program. You can easily extend this class to display your school's logo when this window appears on the screen. Or you can add a help menu that will list your T.A.'s office and phone numbers. You can extend other javabook classes as well. The javabook package also can be a training ground for your graduate or upper-division undergraduate students. By designing classes for the javabook package used by hundreds of beginning students, they will learn first hand what it takes to make classes reliable and truly reusable.

One concern raised about the use of javabook is whether the students would be able to write programs without using the javabook package. The answer is, of course, yes. The javabook package is not an end, but a means for students to learn the standard package. It is a stepping stone, a kind of training wheel for the standard packages. In addition to the javabook classes, we cover many classes from the standard Java packages such as java.awt and java.io.

The source code of all javabook classes is provided, and students are encouraged to study them as they are practical examples of reusable classes. After finishing Chapter 13, students can understand almost all of the javabook classes. We say "almost" because some of the classes in javabook are implemented using the standard classes that are not explained in the book. If the students take time to look up these standard classes in a reference manual, then they should be able to understand the javabook classes 100 percent.

Feature **3**

Full-Immersion Approach

We adopt a full-immersion approach in which students learn how to use objects from the first program. It is very important to ensure that the core concepts of object-oriented programming are emphasized from the beginning. Our first sample program from Chapter 1 is this:

```
/*
    Program FunTime

    The program will allow you to draw a picture by
    dragging a mouse (move the mouse while holding the left mouse
    button down; hold the button on Mac). To erase the picture and
    start over, click the right mouse button (command-click on Mac).
*/

import javabook.*;

class FunTime
{

    public static void main(String[ ] args)
    {
        SketchPad    doodleBoard;
        doodleBoard = new SketchPad();
        doodleBoard.setVisible( true );
    }

}
```

This program captures the most fundamental notion of object-oriented programming. That is, an object-oriented program uses objects. As obvious as it may sound, many introductory books do not really emphasize this fact. In the program, we use a SketchPad object called doodleBoard that allows the user to draw a picture. Almost all other introductory textbooks begin with a sample program such as

```
/*
    Hello World Program
*/

class HelloWorld
{
    public static void main(String args[])
    {
        System.out.println("Hello World");
    }
}
```

or

```
/*
    Hello World Applet
*/
import java.applet.*;
import java.awt.*;

public class HelloWorld extends Applet
{
    public void paint( Graphics g)
    {
        g.drawString("Hello World", 50, 50);
    }
}
```

Both programs have problems. They do not illustrate the key concept that object-oriented programs use objects. The first program does indeed use an object System.out, but the use of System.out does not illustrate the object declaration and creation. Beginners normally cannot differentiate classes and objects. So it is very important to emphasize the concept that you need to declare and create an object from a class before you can start using the object. Our first sample program does this.

Another problem with the System.out program is that no real window-based programs use it for output. Some textbooks not only use System.out in their first program, they rely on System.out almost exclusively for program output. This is not real-world programming. In this book, we use System.out only to output data for verification purposes while developing programs.

The second HelloWorld program is an applet, which, as its name suggests, is a mini-application with a very specific usage. Although applets are fun, teaching applets exclusively is a problem because students will learn only a very limited view of programming. We will discuss more on applications versus applets later in the preface.

Another major problem with these two programs is that they are not adaptable to real-world situations. In contrast, our first sample program can be a main program of a commercial application by replacing SketchPad with another class, say, WordProcessor. In fact, our second sample program from Chapter 2 is this: (Note: This is the first program we actually explain line by line.)

```
/*
    Program MyFirstApplication

    The first sample Java application.
*/

import javabook.*;
```

```
class MyFirstApplication
{
    public static void main(String args[])
    {
        MainWindow mainWindow;
        mainWindow = new MainWindow();//create and
        mainWindow.setVisible( true );//display a window
    }
}
```

The structure of this program is identical to the structure of the first sample program. Our second sample program reinforces the concept that we program by using objects and by changing objects, we create a different program.

Feature 4   Illustrations

We believe a picture is worth a thousand words. Difficult concepts can be explained nicely with lucid illustrations. We use *object diagrams* to show the relationships among objects and classes. Diagrams are an important tool for designing and documenting programs, and no programmers will develop real-world software applications without using some form of diagramming tools. We use simple and informal diagrams, but the diagrams we use in this book are modeled after the industry standard object diagrams. After becoming comfortable with the object diagrams in this book, students are well prepared to study more formal object-oriented design methodology. For those who would like to introduce formal object diagrams, we have UML diagrams for the sample programs and javabook classes available for viewing and downloading from our websites.

This book includes numerous illustrations that are used as a pedagogic tool to explain core concepts such as inheritance, difference between private and public methods, and so forth. Notations used in the object diagrams are used consistently in all types of illustrations. Figure 1 is one example from Chapter 2, and there are over 230 such illustrations and diagrams in this book. Other representative illustrations can be found on pages 90, 165, 243, 378, 387, 428, 498, 669, and 724.

In addition to object diagrams, we use *method call sequence diagrams* that indicate the sequence of method calls such as the one shown in Figure 15.1 on page 711. The method call sequence diagrams are very useful in showing the flow of messages. We use method call sequence diagrams extensively in documenting an advanced sample program in Chapter 15.

Feature 5   Incremental Development

We teach object-oriented software engineering principles in this book. Instead of dedicating a separate chapter for the topic, we interleave program development principles and techniques with other topics. Every chapter from Chapter 2

FIGURE 1   Correspondence between message sending as represented in the object diagram and in the actual Java statement.

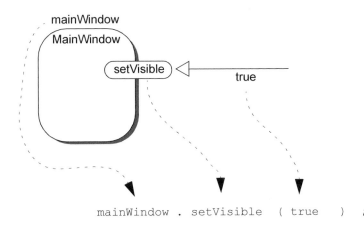

to Chapter 14 includes at least one sample program to illustrate the topics covered in the chapter, and we develop the program using the same design methodology consistently. Chapter 15 is the case study chapter in which we develop a substantially large program for the CS1 standard.

One major problem with many of the other introductory programming books on the market today is that they teach a two-decade-old structured programing, which just does not work with object-oriented programs. This book really teaches a software design methodology that is conducive to object-oriented programming. All sample programs in this book are developed by using a technique we characterize as incremental development. The incremental development technique is based on the modern iterative approach (some call it a spiral approach), which is a preferred methodology of professional object-oriented programmers.

Beginning programmers tend to mix the high-level design and low-level coding details, and their thought process gets all tangled up. Presenting the final program is not enough. If we want to teach students how to develop programs, we must show the development process. An apprentice will not become a master builder just by looking at finished products, whether they are furniture or houses. Software construction is no different. It is often the case with other textbooks that a single chapter is dedicated to showing software development. This is not enough. We must show the development process more than just once. In this book, we develop every sample program incrementally to show students how to develop programs in a logical and methodical manner.

Source code of all sample programs at every step of development is available from our websites. However, we do not encourage students to simply fol-

Preface

low the development presented in the book and read the source code. We encourage students to actually build the sample programs following the development steps presented in the book. This is the surest and quickest way for the students to truly master the software development.

Feature **6**   **Design Guidelines, Helpful Reminders, and Quick Checks**
Throughout the book, we include design guidelines and helpful reminders. Almost every section of the chapters is concluded with a number of Quick Check questions to make sure that students have mastered the basic points of the section.

Design guidelines are indicated with a pencil icon like this:

> *Design a class that implements a single well-defined task. Do not overburden the class with multiple tasks.*

Helpful reminders come in different styles. The first style is indicated with a thumbtack icon like this:

> *Watch out for the off-by-one error (OBOE).*

The second style is Dr. Caffeine's monologue:

> **Dr. Caffeine**
> *On occasions, programming can be very frustrating because no amount of effort on your part would make the program run correctly. You are not alone. Professional programmers often have the same feeling, including this humble self. But, if you take time to think through the problem and don't lose your cool, you will find a solution. If you don't, well, it's just a program. Your good health is much more important than a running program and a good grade.*

The third style is a dialogue between Dr. Caffeine and his honor students Ms. Latte or Mr. Espresso. Ms. Latte and Mr. Espresso appear in alternate chapters.

> **Dr. & Ms.**
> **Ms. Latte:**   *I appear in the odd-numbered chapters and ask great questions.*
>
> **Dr. Caffeine:**   *That's right, and your questions are insightful and helpful to other students.*

> **Dr. & Mr.**
> **Mr. Espresso:**   *I appear in the even-numbered chapters and also ask questions.*
>
> **Dr. Caffeine:**   *Yes, and I like your questions, too.*

When we have materials related to the topic covered in the book on our Web sites, we indicate this availability with the following icon:

The document that explains the Swing classes is available from our website at www.drcaffeine.com/additionaltopics.

Quick Check questions appear at the end of the sections with the following banner:

Quick Check

1. Who are the two honor students of Dr. Caffeine?
2. Name the purpose of the pencil and thumbtack icons.

Feature 7   **Graphical User Interface and Event-Driven Programming**
Since modern real-world programs are GUI-based and event-driven, we cannot skirt around them if we want to teach the foundation of real-world programming. Some may feel that GUI-based and event-driven programs are difficult topics for the beginning students to master. Although they are not trivial, we believe they can be made approachable to the beginning students by presenting the topics piecemeal. We cover in depth GUI-based and event-driven programming in Chapter 13. However, students will start writing GUI-based programs exclusively from Chapter 2 using the javabook classes and learn the rudiments of event handling in Chapter 5. By the time they reach Chapter 13, they are well prepared to absorb the topics. (For this reason, it is preferable to cover Chapter 5, but as we explain later, you may skip the chapter if you do not wish to cover applets.)

Feature 8   **Applications and Applets**
We teach both Java applications and applets, but we put emphasis on developing applications. Some introductory books rely heavily or exclusively on applets, but the use of applets is limited. We don't write applets exclusively in the real world, and an introductory programming book should not teach just applets. At the same time, we should not shy away from teaching applets. We should teach both. Although the use of applets is limited, writing applets is generally fun for students, and we can use applets as an effective pedagogic tool. In this book, we use applets to introduce the basics of event handling and GUI-based programming in Chapter 5.

Although we cover applets and recommend that instructors teach them, we organize the book so the instructors can skip the coverage on applets without losing the continuity.

Supplement Materials

All supplement materials are available from our websites at www.mhhe.com/
wu2 and www.drcaffeine.com. The website www.drcaffeine.com is under the author's control, so it will be updated more frequently than the one maintained by
McGraw-Hill. Materials available from our websites include

1. **Source code for all sample programs and the javabook classes.**
   For all sample programs, source code at every development step is
   available. Both byte code and source code are available for the javabook classes. Documentation for the javabook package in HTML format, generated from the javadoc comments, is also available.

2. **Additional software packages**. The Swing-based javabook classes
   are available for those who wish to use new Java GUI objects. For
   those who wish to put more "fun" into programming exercises, we
   provide the Turtle class that implements the Logo turtle. The Turtle
   class and the supporting classes are contained in the galapagos package.

3. **Additional topics**. To satisfy the varying needs of instructors, we
   place additional topics on our websites. Some of the topics available
   include

   - Swing classes
   - Linked lists and dynamic allocation
   - Different sample programs

   We will try our best to put out new topics periodically.

4. **Hand outs on how to use Java compilers**. We have step-by-step instructions on how to edit, compile, and run the programs using the
   plain JDK compiler and commercial compilers such as Symantec Visual Cafe, Borland JBuilder, Metrowerks CodeWarrior, and others.

5. **Solutions to the Quick Check and selected chapter exercises**. Solutions to the Quick Check exercises are available to everybody. At
   present, we limit the solutions to the chapter exercises to the instructors only. Instructors can download the solutions and make them
   available to their students if they wish.

6. **Transparency masters.** PowerPoint slides are available in animated
   and nonanimated versions. Both versions of the slides can be viewed
   online via a web browser. Adopters of the book also can download
   and edit the slides to customize them for their courses.

7. **Chapter notes and suggestions for teaching**. This material is available to the instructors who adopt the textbook.

McGraw-Hill Online Learning Center

The book's Online Learning Center at www.mhhe.com/wu2 is a "digital cartridge" that contains the book's pedagogy and supplements. As students read the book, they can go online to take self-grading quizzes, access the source code, and review PowerPoint slides for the relevant chapter. There is also an instructor's portion of the Online Learning Center, which contains PowerPoint slides, source code, and password-protected solutions organized by chapter for easy reference.

Book Organization

There are 17 chapters in this book. There are more than enough topics for one semester. Basically the chapters should be covered in linear sequence. Chapter 0 can be skipped or assigned as an outside reading if you want to jump right into programming. If you do not wish to cover applets, then you can skip Chapter 5 altogether. Section 3.8 on numerical representation and Section 7.10 on recursive methods are optional and can be skipped.

In the following, we will give a short description for each chapter:

- **Chapter 0** is an optional chapter. We provide background information on computers and programming languages. This chapter can be skipped or assigned as an outside reading if you wish to start with object-oriented programming concepts.

- **Chapter 1** provides a conceptual foundation of object-oriented programming. We describe the key components of object-oriented programming and illustrate each concept with a diagrammatic notation. The first sample program we present in this chapter is a fun drawing program.

- **Chapter 2** covers the basics of Java programming and the process of editing, compiling, and running a program. We introduce both application and applet in this chapter. We also introduce two classes—MainWindow and MessageBox—from the javabook package. The last section of the chapter that covers an applet can be skipped if you do not cover applets.

- **Chapter 3** introduces variables, constants, and expressions for manipulating numerical data. We explain the standard Math class from java.lang and introduce and use two more classes—InputBox and OutputBox— from the javabook package. These classes handle the input and output of an application program. The optional section explains how the numerical values are represented in memory space.

- **Chapter 4** teaches how to define instantiable classes. The key topics covered in this chapter are constructors, visibility modifiers (public and private), local variables, parameter passing, and value-returning methods. By the end of Chapter 4, students will have a basic understanding of how to use classes from the packages and how to define their own (simple) classes.

- **Chapter 5** covers applets. We teach how to process input with applets. GUI objects Label, TextField, and Button from the java.awt package are introduced. This chapter provides a first glimpse of event handling that serves as a nice foundation for a fuller coverage of GUI objects and event-driven programming in Chapter 12. We recommend instructors cover this chapter, but we understand some prefer not to cover applets. If that is the case, this chapter can be skipped without any loss of continuity.

- **Chapter 6** explains the selection statements if and switch. We cover boolean expressions and nested-if statements. To illustrate the use of selection statements, the ListBox class from the javabook package is introduced and used in the sample program.

- **Chapter 7** explains the repetition statements while, do–while, and for. We introduce two more classes—ResponseBox and Format—from the javabook package and use them in the sample program. The optional last section of the chapter introduces recursion as another technique for repetition.

- **Chapter 8** covers nonnumerical data types: characters and strings. Both the String and StringBuffer classes are explained in the chapter. Using these objects, we explain the difference between primitive and reference data types. We also explain how the objects are passed as parameters to methods and how they are returned from the methods.

- **Chapter 9** teaches arrays. We cover arrays of primitive data types and of objects. Arrays are objects in Java, and we reiterate how objects are passed to methods using arrays as an example in this chapter. The self-referencing pointer this is introduced here. We describe how to process two-dimensional arrays and explain that a two-dimensional array is really an array of arrays in Java. The Vector class from the java.util package is introduced and explained at the end of the chapter.

- **Chapter 10** presents searching and sorting algorithms. Both N^2 and $N\log_2 N$ sorting algorithms are covered. You may skip the mathematical analysis of searching and sorting algorithms depending on the students' background.

- **Chapter 11** explains the file I/O. Standard objects such as File and File-Dialog objects from java.awt and java.io are explained. We cover all types of file I/O, from a low-level byte I/O to a high-level object I/O. This coverage of object I/O is unique among the introductory textbooks. As a part of file processing, we introduce exception handling in this chapter.

- **Chapter 12** explores reusable classes and describes package organization. In the chapter, we show how to classify objects into four categories as an aid to designing classes. As an illustration of how a class can be made reusable, we will convert the earlier sample classes into reusable classes.

- **Chapter 13** covers event-driven programming and GUI objects. The GUI objects we explain in this chapter are Button, Menu, Dialog, Frame, and Applet. GUI objects introduced in Chapter 5 are also used in this chapter. We will also teach the processing of mouse events.

- **Chapter 14** discusses inheritance and polymorphism and how to use them effectively in program design. The effect of inheritance for member accessibility and constructors is explained. We also explain the purpose of abstract classes and abstract methods.

- **Chapter 15** is a case study chapter. We will use the techniques learned in the book to develop a large program. The program uses objects from both the javabook and standard Java packages in addition to the 10 classes we design for the program. No other introductory textbooks include a sample program that is composed of as large a number of classes as this sample program.

- **Chapter 16** covers recursion. Because we want to show the examples where the use of recursion really shines, we did not include any recursive algorithm (other than those used for explanation purposes) that really should be written nonrecursively.

Acknowledgments

First, I would like to thank the following reviewers for their comments, suggestions, and encouragement.

Lewis Barnett	University of Richmond
Peter Biggs	Brigham Young University
Allen Brookes	Linfield College

Edward Chow	University of Colorado, Colorado Springs
Stephanie Crouch	Texas A & M University
Ann Ford	University of Michigan
Homer C. Gerber	University of Central Florida
Michael Hoffhines	Maui Community College
Lily Hou	Carnegie Mellon University
Faisal Kaleem	Florida International University
Saroja Kanchi	Kettering University
Alan Kaplan	Clemson University
Chung Lee	California State Polytechnic University at Pomona
John Lowther	Michigan Technical University
Keith B. Olson	Montana Tech of the University of Montana
John Phillips	Dodge City Community College
Bina Ramamurthy	SUNY at Buffalo
Arturo Sanchez-Ruiz	University of Massachusetts, Dartmouth
Nan C. Schaller	Rochester Institute of Technology
Zhong Shao	Yale University
Lou Steinberg	Rutgers University
Deborah Trytten	University of Oklahoma
Allen Tucker	Bowdoin College
Paul Tymann	Rochester Institute of Technology
John D. Tvedt	The Catholic University of America
Ming Wang	Embry-Riddle Aeronautical University
Barbara Williams	North Hennepin Community College

First and foremost, I thank the instructors and their students who used the first edition. I would like to thank all those who took time to comment on the book and detect the errors. I thank Andy Duncan and Chris Steketee especially for reporting all those errors. I thank Chris Eagle for the all-around help I received in implementing the Swing version of the javabook classes. I thank Jim Skrentny of the University of Wisconsin, Madison and his graduate students for finding errors in the final manuscript.

I thank my friends at McGraw-Hill. On the production side, I thank Scott Scheidt and Pam Verros. On the sales side, I thank John Wannamacher and all the sales reps for what they're doing to sell the book. On the editorial side, I thank Emily Gray and Betsy Jones. When I speak to the editors from other publishing companies, they frequently ask me, "Are you happy with your editorial staff?" or some variation of it. My answer is invariably yes. Writing a textbook is a hard work and often a real drudgery, but it was always a pleasure to deal with Betsy and Emily.

Finally, I would like to thank my family for their love and support. Thank you, Mari and Iris.

Introduction to Computers and Programming Languages

OBJECTIVES

After you have read and studied this chapter, you should be able to

- State briefly a history of computers.
- Name and describe four major components of the computer.
- Convert binary numbers to decimal numbers and vice versa.
- State the difference between the low-level and high-level programming languages.

Introduction

Before we embark on our study of computer programming, we will present some background information on computers and programming languages in this optional chapter. We provide a brief history of computers from the early days to present and describe the components found in today's computers. We also present a brief history of programming languages from low-level machine languages to today's object-oriented languages.

0.1   A History of Computers

Mankind has evolved from a primitive to a highly advanced society by continually inventing tools. Stone tools, fire powder, wheels, and other inventions have changed the lives of humans dramatically. In recent history, the computer is arguably the most important invention. In today's highly advanced society, computers affect our lives 24 hours a day: your class schedules are formulated by computers, your student records are maintained by computers, your exams are graded by computers, your dorm security system is monitored by computers, and numerous other functions that affect you are controlled by computers.

Charles Babbage

Difference
Engine

Although the first true computer was invented in the 1940s, the concept of a computer is actually more than 160 years old. Charles Babbage is credited with inventing a precursor to the modern computer. In 1823 he received a grant from the British government to build a mechanical device he called the *Difference Engine,* intended for computing and printing mathematical tables. The device was based on rotating wheels and was operated by a single crank. Unfortunately, the technology of the time was not advanced enough to build the device. He ran into difficulties and eventually abandoned the project.

Analytical
Engine

But an even more grandiose scheme was already with him. In fact, one of the reasons he gave up on the Difference Engine may have been to work on his new concept for a better machine. He called his new device the *Analytical Engine*. This device also was never built. His second device also was ahead of its time; the technology did not yet exist to make the device a reality. Although never built, the Analytical Engine was a remarkable achievement because its design was essentially based on the same fundamental principles of the modern computer. One principle that stands out was its programmability. With the Difference Engine, Babbage would have been able to compute only mathematical tables, but with the Analytical Engine he would have been able to compute any calculation by inputting instructions on punch cards. The method of inputting programs to computers on punch cards was actually adopted for real machines and was still in wide use as late as the 1970s.

Ada Lovelace

The Analytical Engine was never built, but a demonstration program was written by Ada Lovelace, a daughter of the poet Lord Byron. The programming language Ada was named in honor of Lady Lovelace, the first computer programmer.

In the late 1930s John Atanasoff of Iowa State University, with his graduate student Clifford Berry, built the prototype of the first automatic electronic calculator. One innovation of their machine was the use of binary numbers. (We discuss binary numbers in the next section.) At around the same time, Howard Aiken of Harvard University was working on the *Automatic Sequence-Controlled Calculator,* known more commonly as MARK I, with support from IBM and the U.S. Navy. MARK I was very similar to the Analytical Engine in design and was described as "Babbage's dream come true."

MARK I

MARK I was an electromechanical computer based on relays. Mechanical relays were not fast enough, and MARK I was quickly replaced by machines based on electronic vacuum tubes. The first completely electronic computer, ENIAC I (*Electronic Numerical Integrator and Calculator*), was built at the University of Pennsylvania under the supervision of John W. Mauchly and J. Presper Eckert. Their work was influenced by the work of John Atanasoff.

ENIAC I

ENIAC I was programmed laboriously by plugging wires into a control panel that resembled an old telephone switchboard. Programming took an enormous amount of the engineers' time, and even making a simple change to a program was a time-consuming effort. While programming activities were going on, the expensive computer sat idle. To improve its productivity, John von Neumann of Princeton University proposed storing programs in the computer's memory. This *stored-program* scheme not only improved computation speed but also allowed far more flexible ways of writing programs. For example, because a program is stored in the memory, the computer can change the program instructions to alter the sequence of the execution, thereby making it possible to get different results from a single program.

stored-program

generations of computers

We characterized these early computers with vacuum tubes as *first-generation computers*. *Second-generation computers,* with transistors replacing the vacuum tubes, started appearing in the late 1950s. Improvements in memory devices also increased processing speed further. In the early 1960s, transistors were replaced by integrated circuits and *third-generation computers* emerged. A single integrated circuit of this period incorporated hundreds of transistors and made the construction of minicomputers possible. Minicomputers are small enough to be placed on desktops in individual offices and labs. The early computers, on the other hand, were so huge, they easily occupied the whole basement of a large building.

Advancement of integrated circuits was phenomenal. Large-scale integrated circuits, commonly known as *computer chips* or *silicon chips*, packed the power equivalent to thousands of transistors and made the notion of a "computer on a single chip" a reality. With large-scale integrated circuits, *microcomputers* emerged in the mid 1970s. The machines we call *personal computers* today are descendants of the microcomputers of the 1970s. The computer chips used in to-day's personal computers pack the power equivalent to several millions of transistors. Personal computers are *fourth-generation computers*.

Early microcomputers were isolated, stand-alone machines. The word *personal* describes a machine as a personal device intended to be used by an individual. However it did not take long to realize there was a need to share computer resources. For example, early microcomputers required a dedicated printer. Wouldn't it make more sense to have many computers share a single printer? Wouldn't it also make sense to share data among computers, instead of duplicating the same data on individual machines? Wouldn't it be nice to send electronic messages between the computers? The notion of networked computers arose to meet these needs.

network

Computers of all kinds are connected into a *network*. A network that connects computers in a single building or in several nearby buildings is called a *local area network* (LAN). A network that connects geographically dispersed computers is called a *wide area network* (WAN). These individual networks can be connected further to form interconnected networks called *internets*. The most famous internet is simply called the *Internet*. The Internet makes the sharing of worldwide information possible and easy. The hottest tool for viewing information on the Internet is a *web browser*. A web browser allows you to view *multimedia information* consisting of text, audio, video, and other types of information. We will describe how Java is related to the Internet and web browsers in the last section of the chapter.

Internet

> *If you want to learn more about the history of computing, there is a wealth of information available on the Web. You can start your exploration from* http://www.yahoo.com/Computers_and_Internet/History. *For a nice slide show on the evolution of computing machines, visit* http://www.computer-museum.org. *For more information on the pioneers of computers, visit* http:www.comlab.ox.ac.uk/archive/other/museums/computing.html.

Quick Check

1. Who was the first computer programmer?
2. Who designed the Difference and Analytical Engines?
3. How many generations of computers are there?

0.2   Computer Architecture

A typical computer today has five basic components: RAM, CPU, storage devices, I/O (input/output) devices, and communication devices. Figure 0.1 illustrates these five components. Before we describe the components of a computer, we will first explain the binary numbering system used in a computer.

FIGURE 0.1   A simplified view of an architecture for a typical computer.

Binary Numbers

To understand the binary number system, let's first review the decimal number system in which we use 10 digits: 0, 1, 2, 3, 4, 5, 6, 7, 8, 9. To represent a number in the decimal system, we use a sequence of one or more of these digits. The value that each digit in the sequence represents depends on its position. For example, consider the numbers 234 and 324. The digit 2 in the first number represents 200, whereas the digit 2 in the second number represents 20. A position in a sequence has a value that is an integral power of 10. The following diagram illustrates how the values of positions are determined:

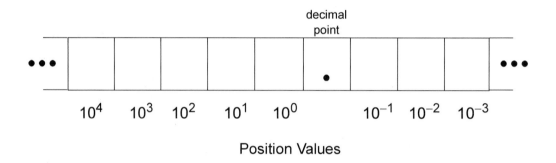

The value of a decimal number (represented as a sequence of digits) is the sum of the digits multiplied by their position values, as illustrated below:

$$= 2 \times 10^2 + 4 \times 10^1 + 8 \times 10^0 + 7 \times 10^{-1}$$

$$= 2 \times 100 + 4 \times 10 + 8 \times 1 + 7 \times 1/10$$

$$= 200 + 40 + 8 + 7/10 = 248.7$$

In the decimal number system, we have 10 symbols, and the position values are integral powers of 10. We say that 10 is the *base* or *radix* of the decimal number system. The binary number system works the same as the decimal number system but uses 2 as its base. The binary number system has two digits (0 and 1) called *bits*, and position values are integral powers of 2. The following diagram illustrates how the values of positions are determined in the binary system:

base-2 numbers

bits

Position Values

The value of a binary number (represented as a sequence of bits) is the sum of the bits multiplied by their position values, as illustrated below:

binary-to-decimal conversion

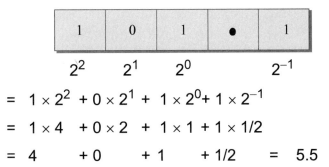

$$= \; 1 \times 2^2 \; + 0 \times 2^1 \; + \; 1 \times 2^0 + 1 \times 2^{-1}$$

$$= \; 1 \times 4 \quad + 0 \times 2 \quad + \; 1 \times 1 + 1 \times 1/2$$

$$= \; 4 \qquad + 0 \qquad + 1 \qquad + 1/2 \quad = \quad 5.5$$

So the binary number 101.1 is numerically equivalent to the decimal number 5.5. This illustration shows how to convert a given binary number to the decimal equivalent. How about converting a given decimal number to its binary equivalent?

We will show you how to convert a decimal number (only the whole numbers) to the equivalent binary number. The basic idea goes something like this:

decimal-to-binary conversion

1. Divide the number by 2.

2. The remainder is the bit value of the 2^0 position.

3. Divide the quotient by 2.

4. The remainder is the bit value of the 2^1 position.

5. Divide the quotient by 2.

6. The remainder is the bit value of the 2^2 position.

7. Repeat the procedure until you cannot divide any further, that is, the quotient becomes 0.

The following diagram illustrates the conversion of decimal number 25.

Division #5	Division #4	Division #3	Division #2	Division #1

$$
\begin{array}{ccccc}
0 & 1 & 3 & 6 & 12 \\
2\overline{)\ 1} & 2\overline{)\ 3} & 2\overline{)\ 6} & 2\overline{)\ 12} & 2\overline{)\ 25} \\
0 & 2 & 6 & 12 & 24 \\
\hline
1 & 1 & 0 & 0 & 1
\end{array}
$$

$$2^4 \qquad 2^3 \qquad 2^2 \qquad 2^1 \qquad 2^0$$

$$16 \ + \ 8 \ + \ 0 \ + \ 0 \ + \ 1 \ = 25$$

The binary system is more suitable for computers than the decimal system because it is far easier to design an electrical device that can distinguish two states (bits 0 and 1) than 10 states (digits 0 through 9). For example, you can represent 1 by turning the switch on and 0 by turning the switch off. In a real computer, 0 is represented by electrical voltage below a certain level and 1 by electrical voltage at or above this level.

RAM

Random access memory (RAM) is a repository for both program instructions and data manipulated by the program during execution. RAM is divided into *cells* with each cell having a unique address. Typically, each cell consists of 4 *bytes*, and a single byte in turn consists of 8 *bits.* Each bit, which can be either on or off, represents a single binary digit. RAM is measured by the number of bytes it contains. For example, 16 megabytes (Mb) of RAM contain $16 \times 2^{20} =$ 16,777,216 bytes. We use the term *mega* (M), which is 10^6, to represent the value 2^{20}, because 1 kilo (K) $= 10^3 = 1000$ is a close approximation to $2^{10} = 1024$, and $10^6 = 10^3 \times 10^3 \approx 2^{10} \times 2^{10} = 2^{20}$. With 4 bytes to a cell, 16 Mb of RAM contain 4,194,304 cells. In 1998, a typical computer has anywhere from 32 Mb to 64Mb of RAM. In contrast, the first Macintosh computer introduced in 1984 came with 128 kilobytes (Kb) of RAM ($128 \times 2^{10} = 131,072$ bytes).

byte

CPU

The *central processing unit* (CPU) is the brain of a computer. The CPU is the component that executes program instructions by fetching an instruction (stored in RAM), executing it, fetching the next instruction, executing it, and so on until it encounters an instruction to stop. The CPU contains a small number of *regis-*

ters, which are high-speed devices for storing data or instructions temporarily. The CPU also contains the *arithmetic-logic unit* (ALU), which performs arithmetic operations such as addition and subtraction and logical operations such as comparing two numbers.

clock speed

    CPUs are characterized by their clock speeds. For example, in the Intel Pentium 200, the CPU has a clock speed of 200 megahertz (MHz). A *hertz* is a unit of frequency equal to one cycle per second. A *cycle* is a period of time between two on states or off states. So 200 megahertz equals 200,000,000 cycles per second. The fastest CPU for commercially available personal computers was around 200 MHz in 1997. But by the beginning of 1998, many vendors started selling 300 MHz machines. And in a mere six months, by the middle of 1998, the top-of-the-line personal computers were 400 MHz machines. Now at the beginning of the millennium, we begin to see computers with 733 MHz CPU being advertised and sold. The increase of the CPU speed in the last 20 years is truly astonishing. The clock speed of the Intel 8080, the CPU introduced in 1974 that started the PC revolution, was a mere 2 MHz. In contrast, the clock speed of the Intel Pentium Pro-200 introduced in 1995 was 200 MHz. Table 0.1 lists some of the Intel processors.

I/O Devices

Input/output (I/O) *devices* allow communication between the user and the CPU. Input devices such as keyboards and mice are used to enter data, programs, and commands in the CPU. Output devices such as monitors and printers are used to display or print information. Other I/O devices include scanners, barcode readers, magnetic strip readers, digital video cameras, and musical instrument digital interface (MIDI) devices.

Storage Devices

Storage devices such as disk and tape drives are used to store data and programs. Secondary storage devices are called *nonvolatile memory*, while RAM is called *volatile memory*. *Volatile* means the data stored in a device will be lost when the power to the device is turned off. Being nonvolatile and much cheaper than RAM, secondary storage is an ideal medium for permanent storage of large volumes of data. A secondary storage device cannot replace RAM, though, because secondary storage is far slower in data access (getting data out and writing data in) compared to RAM.

    The most common storage device today for personal computers is a disk drive. There are two kinds of disks: hard and floppy (also known as diskettes). Hard disks provide much faster performance and larger capacity, but are normally not removable, that is, a single hard disk is permanently attached to a disk drive. Floppy disks, on the other hand, are removable, but their performance is far slower and their capacity far smaller than hard disks. As the standard floppy

TABLE 0.1   A table of Intel processors. For some CPUs, more than one type with different clock speeds are possible. In such case, only the fastest clock speed is shown. For more information on Intel CPUs, visit http://www.intel.com/intel/museum and http://www.intel.com/pressroom/kits/processors/quickref.htm.

	CPU	Date Introduced	Clock Speed (MHz)
	4004	11/15/71	0.108
	8008	04/01/72	0.200
1970s	8080	04/01/74	2
	8088	06/01/79	8
	80286	02/01/82	12
1980s	80386SX	06/16/88	16
	80486DX	04/10/89	25
	Pentium	03/22/93	66
	Pentium Pro	11/01/95	200
1990s	Pentium II	05/07/97	300
	Pentium II Xeon	06/29/98	400
	Pentium III	10/25/99	733

disks can store only up to approximately 1.44 Mb, they are becoming less useful in today's world of multi-megabyte image and sound files. Hard disks can store a huge amount of data, typically ranging from 4.3 Gb (gigabyte; giga = 10^9) to 13.5 Gb for a standard desktop PC in 1999. Some new breeds of disk drives use removable disks, typically ranging in capacity from 100 Mb to 1 Gb, with performance that rivals nonremovable hard disks.

Compact discs (CDs) also are very popular today for storing massive amounts of data, approximately 660 Mb. Many software packages you buy today—computer games, word processors, and others—come with a single CD. Before the CD became a popular storage device for computers, some software came with more than 20 floppy diskettes. Because of its massive storage capacity, the current trend is for computer vendors to get rid of printed manuals altogether by putting the manuals on the CD.

Communication Devices

A communication device connects the personal computer to a network. The most common communication device for computers at home and small offices is the *modem*. A modem, which stands for *modulator-demodulator*, is a device that converts analog signals to digital and digital signals to analog. By using a modem, a computer can send to and receive data from another computer over the phone line. The most critical characteristic of a modem is its transmission speed, which is measured in *bits per second* (bps). A typical speed for a modem sold in 1999 ranges from 14,400 bps to 56,000 bps. To connect a computer to the Internet, you would not want to use anything slower than a 28,800 bps modem. Under an ideal condition (no line noise or congestion), a 28,800 bps modem can transfer a 1Mb file in about 5 minutes. Frequently, though, the actual transfer rate is much lower than the possible maximum.

A communication device for connecting a computer to a LAN is a *network interface card* (NIC). An NIC can transfer data at a much faster rate than the fastest modem. For instance, a type of NIC called *10BaseT* can transfer data at the rate of 10 Mbps over the network.

Quick Check

1. Name five major components of a computer.
2. What is the difference between volatile and nonvolatile memory?
3. What does the acronym CPU stand for?
4. How many bytes does the 64Kb RAM have?
5. Which device connects a computer to the Internet using a phone line?

0.3   Programming Languages

Programming languages are broadly classified into three levels: machine languages, assembly languages, and high-level languages. Machine language is the only programming language the CPU understands. Each type of CPU has its own machine language. For example, the Intel Pentium and Motorola PowerPC understand different machine languages. *Machine-language* instructions are binary coded and very low level—one machine instruction may transfer the contents of one memory location into a CPU register or add numbers in two registers. Thus we must provide many machine-language instructions to accomplish a simple task such as finding the average of 20 numbers. A program written in machine language might look like this:

machine
language

machine code

```
10110011 00011001
01111010 11010001 10010100
10011111 00011001
01011100 11010001 10010000
10111011 11010001 10010110
```

assembly
language

One level above machine language is *assembly language*, which allows "higher level" symbolic programming. Instead of writing programs as a sequence of bits, assembly language allows programmers to write programs using symbolic operation codes. For example, instead of 10110011, we use MV to move the contents of a memory cell into a register. We also can use symbolic, or mnemonic, names for registers and memory cells. A program written in assembly language might look like this:

assembly code

```
MV      0,    SUM
MV      NUM,  AC
ADD     SUM,  AC
STO     SUM,  TOT
```

assembler

Since programs written in assembly language are not recognized by the CPU, we use an *assembler* to translate programs written in assembly language into machine-language equivalents. Compared to writing programs in machine language, writing programs in assembly language is much faster, but not fast enough for writing complex programs.

high-level
languages

High-level languages were developed to enable programmers to write programs faster than when using assembly languages. For example, FORTRAN (FORmula TRANslator), a programming language intended for mathematical computation, allows programmers to express numerical equations directly as

high-level code

```
X = (Y + Z) / 2
```

COBOL (COmmon Business Oriented Language) is a programming language intended for business data processing applications. FORTRAN and COBOL were developed in the late 1950s and early 1960s and are still in use. BASIC (Beginners All-purpose Symbolic Instructional Code) was developed specifically as an easy language for students to learn and use. BASIC was the first high-level language available for microcomputers. Another famous high-level language is Pascal, which was designed as an academic language. Since programs written in a high-level language are not recognized by the CPU, we must use a compiler *compiler* to translate them into assembly language equivalents.

The programming language C was developed in the early 1970s at AT&T Bell Labs. The C++ programming language was developed as a successor of C in the early 1980s to add support for object-oriented programming. Object-oriented programming is a style of programming gaining wider acceptance today. Although the concept of object-oriented programming is old (the first object-oriented programming language, Simula, was developed in the late 1960s), its significance wasn't realized until the early 1980s. Smalltalk, developed at Xerox PARC, is another well-known object-oriented programming language. The programming language we use in this book is Java, the newest object-oriented programming language, developed at Sun Microsystems. We describe Java in the next section.

0.4   Java

Java is a new object-oriented language that is receiving a wide attention from both industry and academia. Java was developed by James Gosling and his team at Sun Microsystems in California. The language was based on C and C++ and was originally intended for writing programs that control consumer appliances such as toasters, microwave ovens, and others. The language was first called Oak, named after the oak tree outside of Gosling's office, but the name was already taken, so the team renamed it Java.

applet

application

Java is often described as a *Web programming language* because of its use in writing programs called *applets* that run within a web browser. That is, you need a web browser to execute Java applets. Java is receiving phenomenal attention today because of applets, a feature unique to Java. Applets allow more dynamic and flexible dissemination of information on the Internet, and this feature alone makes Java an attractive language to learn. However, we are not limited to writing applets in Java. We can write Java applications also. A Java *application* is a complete stand-alone program that does not require a web browser. A Java application is analogous to a program we write in other programming languages. Although we cover both applets and applications in this book, we place more emphasis on Java applications because our objective is to teach the fundamentals of object-oriented programming that are applicable to all object-oriented programming languages.

We chose Java for this textbook not only for its relevance to the Internet but also for its clean design. The language designers of Java took a minimalist approach; they included only features that are indispensable and eliminated features that they considered excessive or redundant. This minimalist approach makes Java a much easier language to learn than other object-oriented programming languages. Java is an ideal vehicle for teaching the fundamentals of object-oriented programming.

0.5   Exercises

1. Visit your school's computer lab or a computer store and identify the different components of the computers you see. Do you notice any unique input or output devices?

2. Visit your school's computer lab and find out the CPU speed, RAM size, and hard disk capacity of its computers.

3. Convert the following binary numbers to decimal numbers:

    a. 1010

    b. 110011

    c. 110.01

    d. 111111

4. Convert the following decimal numbers to binary numbers:

    a. 35

    b. 125

    c. 567

    d. 98

5. What is the maximum decimal number you can represent in 4 bits? 16 bits? N bits?

6. If a computer has 48 Mb of RAM, how may bytes are there?

7. How do high-level programming languages differ from low-level programming languages?

8. Consider a hypothetical programming language *Kona*. Using Kona, you can write a program to compute and print out the sum of 20 integers entered by the user as

    ```
    let sum = 0;

    repeat 20 times [
        let X = next input;
        add X to sum;
    ]

    printout sum;
    ```

    Is Kona a high-level language? Why or why not?

Introduction to Object-Oriented Programming and Software Development

Introduction

Before we begin to write actual programs, we need to introduce a few basic concepts of *object-oriented programming*, the style of programming you will learn in this book. The purpose of this chapter is to give you a feel for object-oriented programming and to introduce a conceptual foundation of object-oriented programming. You may want to refer back to this chapter as you progress through the book.

> *Those of you who have some experience in programming, whether object-oriented or non-object-oriented, will probably find many similarities between Java and the programming languages you already know. This similarity may accelerate your learning process, but in many cases what seems to be similar at first may turn out to be quite different. So please do not jump to any conclusions about similarity prematurely.*

Dr. Caffeine

Another purpose of this chapter is to introduce the software development process. To be able to write programs, knowing the components of object-oriented programs is not enough. You must learn the process of developing programs. We will provide a brief description of the software development process in this chapter.

1.1   Classes and Objects

object

class

instance

The two most important concepts in object-oriented programing are the class and the object. In the broadest term, an *object* is a thing, both tangible and intangible, that we can imagine. A program written in object-oriented style will consist of interacting objects. For a program to maintain bank accounts for a bank, we may have many Account, Customer, Transaction, and ATM objects. An object is comprised of data and operations that manipulate these data. For example, an Account object may consist of data such as account number, owner, date opened, initial balance, and current balance and operations such as deposit, transfer, and withdrawal. We will use the diagram shown in Figure 1.1 throughout the book to represent an object.

Almost all nontrivial programs will have many objects of the same type. For example, in the bank program we expect to see many Account, Customer, and other objects. Figure 1.2 shows two Customer objects with the names Jack and Jill and one Account object with the name SV129.

Inside a program we write instructions to create objects. For the computer to be able to create an object, we must provide a definition, called a *class*. A class is a kind of mold or template that the computer uses to create objects. An object is called an *instance* of a class. An object is an instance of exactly one class. An instance of a class *belongs to* the class. The two Customer objects Jack and Jill

FIGURE 1.1   A graphical representation of an object.

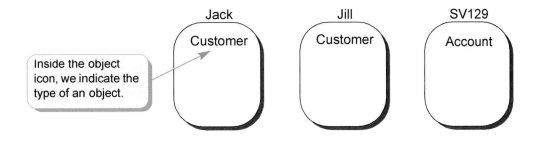

FIGURE 1.2   Two **Customer** objects with the names **Jack** and **Jill** and one **Account** object with the name **SV129**.

are instances of the Customer class. Once a class is defined, we can create as many objects of the class as a program requires.

A class must be defined before you can create an instance (object) of the class.

Figure 1.3 shows a diagram that we will use throughout the book to represent a class. Figure 1.4 shows two classes and five objects. Notice that we include the class names of the objects to identify clearly the classes to which they belong.

Quick Check

1. Draw an object diagram for a Person class and two Person objects Ms. Latte and Mr. Espresso.
2. What must be defined before you can create an object?

FIGURE 1.3   A graphical representation of a class.

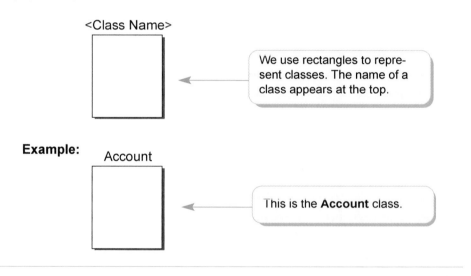

1.2   Messages and Methods

In writing object-oriented programs we first define classes, and while the program is running, we create objects from these classes to accomplish tasks. A task can range from adding two numbers to computing an interest payment for your college loan to calculating the reentry angle of a space shuttle. To instruct a class or an object to perform a task, we send a *message* to it. For example, we send a message new to the Account class to create an instance (an Account object), and then we may send a message deposit to this Account object to deposit $100.

message

FIGURE 1.4   Two classes, **Account** and **Customer**, with two **Account** objects and three **Customer** objects.

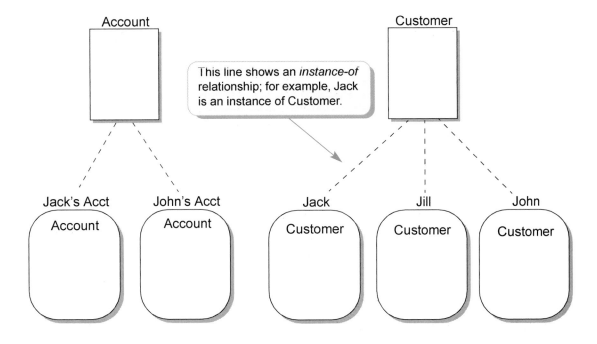

For a class or an object to process the message it must be programmed accordingly. You cannot just send a message to any class or object. You can send a message only to the classes and objects that understand the message you send to them. For a class or an object to process the message it receives, it must possess a matching *method*, which is a sequence of instructions a class or an object follows to perform a task. A method defined for a class is called a *class method,* and a method defined for an object is an *instance method*.

method

class and instance methods

Let's look at an example of an instance method first. Suppose a method called deposit is defined for an Account object and instructs the object to deposit a given amount to the account. With this method defined, we can send the message deposit to an Account object, along with the amount to be deposited. A value we pass to an object is called an *argument* of a message. Notice that the name of the message we send to an object or a class must be the same as the method's name. In Figure 1.5 we represent the sending of a message.

argument

The diagram shown in Figure 1.5 illustrates one-way communication, that is, an object carries out the requested operation (it deposits the given amount) but does not respond to the message sender. In many situations we need two-

Ms. Latte: *Dr. Caffeine, the difference between the class and the object is unclear to me. Could you explain the difference?*

Dr. Caffeine: *Sure thing. Have you ever seen a print made from a woodcut by Hiroshige, the 19th-century Japanese artist?*

Ms. Latte: *Yes, as a matter of fact, I think I have. The one I saw is a print from the series titled "Fifty-Three Stations of Tokaido."*

Dr. Caffeine: *Very good. For those of you who haven't, you can view his works at **http://j-entertain.co.jp/bellquiz/quizhome.html**. Anyway, an object is like a print, and a class is like a woodcut. Once you have a woodcut, you can make as many prints as you wish. Just like a woodcut and its many prints, there's one class, but many objects from that class.*

Ms. Latte: *Just as a print cannot exist without a woodcut, an object cannot exist without a class from which it is created?*

Dr. Caffeine: *Yes, precisely. And just as people appreciate prints more than they appreciate the woodcut itself, objects are more predominant in programs, but classes are as indispensable as woodcuts are.*

FIGURE 1.5   Sending the message **deposit** to an **Account** object.

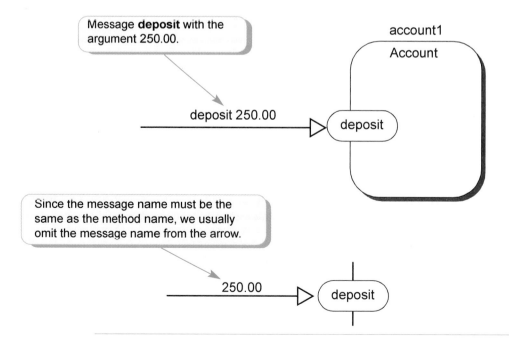

way communication, in which an object responds by returning a value to the message sender. For example, suppose we want to know the monthly fee charged for an account. We can define a method getMonthlyFee that returns the monthly fee. The diagram in Figure 1.6 shows a method that returns a value to the message sender. Instead of returning a numerical value, a method can report

FIGURE 1.6   The result **monthly fee** is returned to the sender of the message.

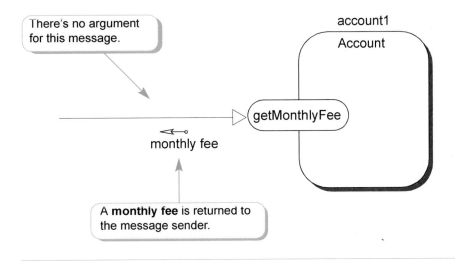

back the status of the requested operation. For example, we can define a method deduct to return the status fail if subtracting the passed amount would result in a negative balance.

Have you ever left a message on the wrong person's answering machine by mistake? When the machine said, "Hi, I cannot come to the phone right now, but if you leave your message...," You answered, "Hi. It's me. Please come to SP105 right now." Of course, nothing happens, because the receiver of your message does not recognize it.

Similarly, you cannot send a message to a class or an object unless it is programmed to handle the message; that is, it must contain a matching method. Sending a message to a class or an object is the way to execute the matching method, and if there's no matching method, nothing happens (actually, an error will occur).

Dr. Caffeine

Now let's look at an example of class methods. The class method getAverageBalance shown in Figure 1.7 returns the average balance of all Account objects. A method such as getAverageBalance that deals with collective information about the instances of a class is usually defined as a class method. So you define an instance method for a task that pertains to an individual instance and a class method for a task that pertains to all instances.

FIGURE 1.7   The average balance of all **Account** objects is returned by the class method
getAverageBalance.

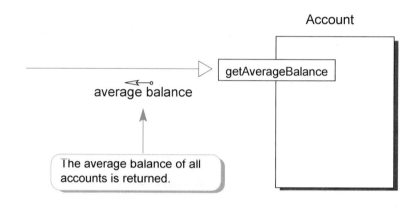

Notice how we use different icons for representing class methods (rectangles) and instance methods (rectangles with rounded corners). Since the class definition is the place we define the methods its instances possess, we need to attach both class and instance methods to the class icon. Dotted lines represent instance methods; the dotted lines indicate that you cannot send instance messages to the class itself. Figure 1.8 summarizes the drawings used for representing a class, an instance, and their methods.

Quick Check

1. Draw an object diagram of an Account object with instance methods deposit and withdraw.

2. Which message do you send to a class to create an instance of the class?

FIGURE 1.8   Graphical representation for classes and objects.

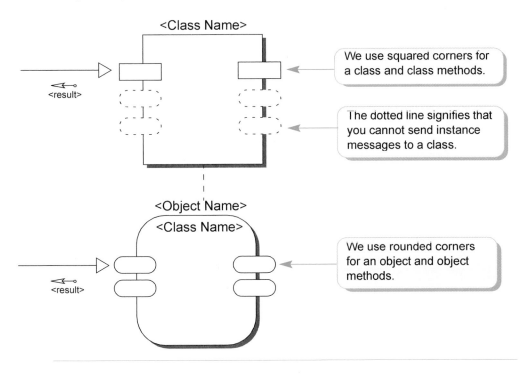

1.3   Class and Instance Data Values

The method deposit of an Account object instructs the object to deposit a given amount to the current balance. But where does the object keep the current balance? Remember that an object is comprised of data values and methods. Analogous to defining class and instance methods, we need to define class and instance data values. For example, we define an *instance data value* current balance for Account objects to record the current balance. Figure 1.9 shows three Account objects with their data values current balance. Notice that they all have the same data value current balance. All instances of the same class will possess the same set of data values. The actual dollar amounts for current balance, as the diagram illustrates, differ from one instance to another. Items such as opening balance and account number are other possible instance data values for Account objects.

A *class data value* is used to represent information shared by all instances or to represent collective information about the instances. For example, if every

instance data value

class data value

FIGURE 1.9   Three **Account** objects possess the same data value **current balance**, but the actual
dollar amounts differ.

account must maintain a minimum balance, say $100, we can define a class data
value minimum balance. An instance can access the class data values of the
class to which it belongs, so every Account object can access the class data value minimum balance. Figure 1.10 shows how we represent a class data value.

To appreciate the significance of a class data value, let's see what happens if
we represent minimum balance as an instance data value. Figure 1.11 shows
three Account objects having different dollar amounts for the current balance
but the same dollar amount for the minimum balance. Obviously, this duplication of minimum balance is redundant and wastes space. Consider, for example,
what happens if the bank raises the minimum balance to $200. If there are 100
Account objects, then all 100 copies of minimum balance must be updated. We
can avoid this by defining minimum balance as a class data value.

*variable and
constant data
values*

There are two types of data values: those that can change over time and
those that cannot. A data value that can change is called a *variable* and one that
cannot change is a *constant*. Figure 1.12 illustrates how we represent and distinguish between variables and constants. We use a lock icon for constants to indicate that they cannot change. Notice that we now have four kinds of data values:
class variables, class constants, instance variables, and instance constants.

Quick Check

1. What is the difference between a constant and a variable?
2. Draw an object diagram of a Person object with three instance vari-
    ables name, age, and gender.

FIGURE 1.10 Three **Account** objects sharing information (**minimum balance** = $100) stored as a class data value.

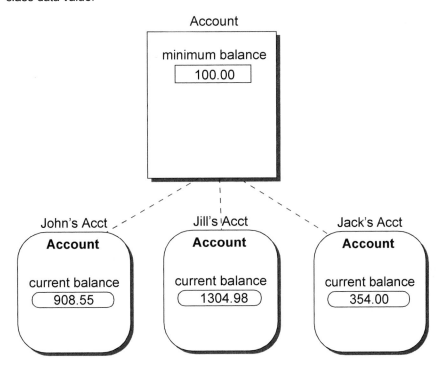

FIGURE 1.11 Three **Account** objects duplicating information (**minimum balance** = $100) in instance data values.

FIGURE 1.12   Graphical representations for four types of data values: class variable, class constant, instance variable, and instance constant.

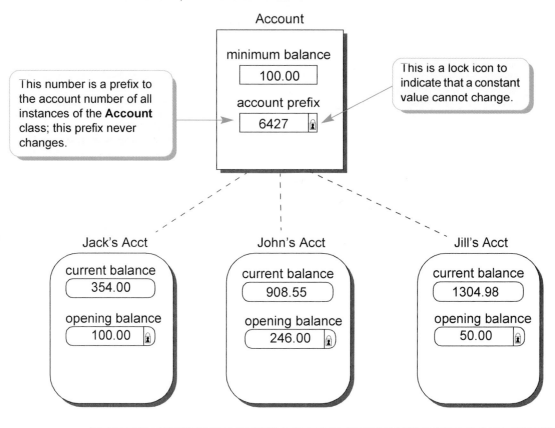

1.4   Inheritance

When we used the Account class and its instances to illustrate object-oriented concepts, some of you were probably thinking about checking accounts, while others may have been thinking about savings accounts. We did not distinguish between the two in the examples. When you look at the problem a little more carefully, you will realize that in fact these two types of accounts are different, even though they share many features.

In general, using only a single class to model two or more entities that are similar but different is not good design. Let's study why this is the case using the Account class. Suppose the bank requires you to maintain different minimum balances for savings and checking accounts. How could we model this situation using only a single class? We could choose one of two possible solutions:

(1) make minimum balance an instance variable or (2) set up two class variables minimum savings balance and minimum checking balance. Both solutions have major drawbacks. Solution 1 duplicates the same value, which we already mentioned is a very poor programming technique. Solution 2 complicates the processing of withdrawals because we need to determine the type of account and then use the corresponding minimum balance. Determining whether a given object is either a savings or a checking account requires additional processing and a data value.

If using a single class for modeling two or more entities is not good design, then should we design a separate class for each distinct type of entity? For the preceding example, we would define two classes: Savings Account and Checking Account. This alternative design is not a good one either, because we would end up duplicating methods. For example, if the ways we deduct the amount of a withdrawal from a savings account and the check amount from a checking account are the same, then we will have to define identical methods for both classes, duplicating the same code. Thus the problem we identified with data value duplication may also occur with method duplication.

So both alternatives have problems. In object-oriented programming, we actually use a mechanism called *inheritance* to design two or more entities that are different but share many common features. First we define a class that contains the common features of the entities. Then we define classes as an extension of the common class inheriting everything from the common class. We call the common class the *superclass* and all classes that inherit from it *subclasses*. We also call the superclass an *ancestor* and the subclass a *descendant*. For the bank example, we can define a superclass Account and then define Savings and Checking as subclasses of Account. We represent the superclass and its subclasses as shown in Figure 1.13. Notice that we draw arrows from each subclass to its superclass because a subclass can refer to items defined in its superclass, but not vice versa.

A subclass will inherit everything from its superclass. We cannot say we want a subclass to inherit 50 percent of its superclass. However, it is possible for a subclass to override inherited components. For example, the Account class defines a class variable minimum balance of $100.00, but the Savings class overrides this value with the amount $250.00. Other inherited components also can be overridden. For example, the Checking class may override the inherited method deduct by adding instructions applicable to instances of the class (e.g., charge $1.00 for every withdrawal after more than 10 checks are drawn in any given month). Also, a subclass can add methods and data values to those inherited from its superclass. The Checking class may add a new instance variable to keep track of the number of checks issued in a month.

Inheritance is not limited to one level. A subclass can be a superclass of other classes, forming an inheritance hierarchy. Consider the example shown in

inheritance

superclass and
subclass

FIGURE 1.13 A superclass **Account** and its subclasses **Savings** and **Checking**.

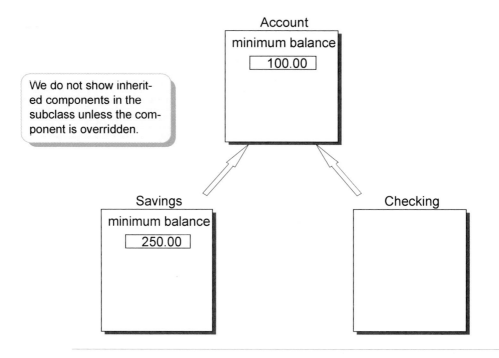

Figure 1.14. Inheritance is very powerful, and if used properly, we can develop complex programs very efficiently and elegantly. The flip side of using a very powerful tool is that if you are not careful, you can misuse it and end up in a far worse situation than if you did not use it. We will discuss inheritance and how to use it properly throughout this book.

Quick Check

1. If Class A inherits from Class B, which is a superclass? Which is a subclass?

2. Draw an object diagram that shows Class A is inheriting from Class B.

3. What are the other names for superclass and subclass?

4. If we have Animal, Insect, and Mammal classes, which one will be a superclass?

FIGURE 1.14   An example of inheritance hierarchy among different types of accounts.

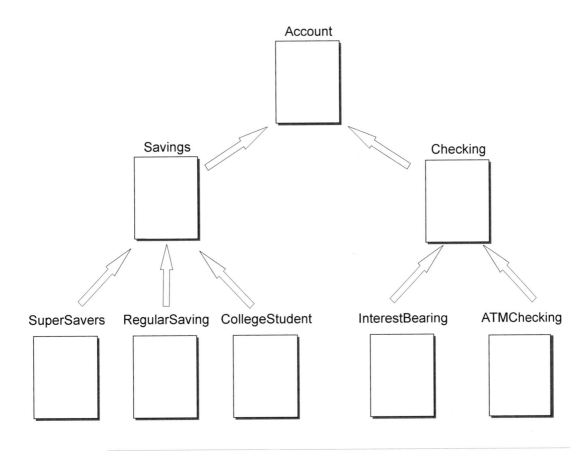

1.5   Software Engineering and Software Life Cycle

When we say *computer programming*, we are referring not only to writing Java commands, but to a whole process of software development. Knowing a programming language alone is not enough to become a proficient software developer. You must know how to design a program. This book will teach you how to design programs in an object-oriented manner.

    We construct a house in well-defined stages and apply the engineering principles in all stages. Similarly, we build a program in stages and apply disciplined methodology in all stages of program development. The sequence of stages from conception to operation of a program is called the *software life cycle*,

software life cycle

**software
engineering**

analysis

design

coding

testing

debugging

operation

**software
maintenance**

and *software engineering* is the application of a systematic and disciplined approach to the development, testing, and maintenance of a program.

There are five major phases in the software life cycle: analysis, design, coding, testing, and operation. Software starts its life from the needs of a customer. A person wants an online address book, for example. In the *analysis* phase, we perform a feasibility study. We analyze the problem and determine whether a solution is possible. Provided that a solution is possible, the result of this phase is a *requirements specification* that describes the features of a program. The features must be stated in a manner that are testable. One of the features for the address book program may be the capability to search for a person by giving his/her first name. We can test this feature by running the program and actually searching for a person. We verify that the program behaves as specified when the first name of a person in the address book and the first name of a person not in the address book are entered as a search condition. We do this testing in the testing phase, which we will explain shortly.

In the *design* phase, we turn a requirements specification into a detailed design of the program. For an object-oriented design, the output from this phase will be a set of classes/objects that fulfill the requirements. The classes/objects must be fully defined, showing how they behave and how they communicate among themselves. For the address book program, we may design objects such as Person, Phone, and others.

In the *coding* phase, we implement the design into an actual program, in our case, a Java program. Once we have a well-constructed design, implementing it into actual code is really not that difficult. The difficult part is the creation of the design, and in this book, we place more emphasis on the design aspect of the software construction.

When the implementation is completed, we move to the *testing* phase. In this phase, we run the program using different sets of data to verify that the program runs according to the specification. Two types of testing are possible for object-oriented programs: *unit testing* and *integration testing*. With unit testing, we test classes individually. With integration testing, we test that the classes work together correctly. Activity to eliminate programming error is called *debugging*. An error could be a result of faulty implementation or design. When there's an error, we need to backtrack to earlier phases to eliminate the error.

Finally, after the testing is successfully concluded, we enter the *operation* phase, in which the program will be put into actual use. The most important and time-consuming activity during the operation phase is *software maintenance*. After the software is put into use, we almost always have to make changes to it. For example, the customer may request additional features or previously undetected errors may be found. Software maintenance means making changes to software. It is estimated that close to 70 percent of the cost of software is related to software maintenance. So naturally, when we develop software, we should aim for software that is easy to maintain. We must not develop a piece of software hastily to reduce the software development cost. We should take time and care to design and code software correctly even if it takes longer and costs more to develop initially. In the long run, carefully crafted software will have a lower total cost because of the reduced maintenance cost. Here's an important point to remember:

> **Well-designed and -constructed software is easy to maintain.**

In this book, we will focus on the design, coding, and testing phases. We will present a requirements specification in the form of a problem statement for the sample programs we will develop in this book. You will see the first sample program developed by following the design, coding, and testing phases in Chapter 2. We will come back to the discussion of software engineering and the software life cycle throughout the book and provide more details.

Quick Check

1. Name the stages of the software life cycle.
2. How does the quality of design affect the software maintenance cost?
3. What is debugging?

1.6 Having Fun with Java

Before we get into the details of computer programming, let's have some fun with Java. The following Java application allows you to draw a picture by dragging the mouse (i.e., moving the mouse while holding down the left mouse button). You can erase the drawing by clicking the right mouse button. (Note to Mac users: Please click the mouse button when the text refers to the left mouse button and command-click the mouse button when the text refers to the right mouse button.) You also can erase the drawing by minimizing the window and opening it again. You don't have to understand the details of the program yet, just run the program and have fun.[1] We will explain the program code in the

---

1. For instructions on running the program, please consult your instructor or visit our website. We will discuss the general steps you take to run a Java program in the next chapter, but you will need instructions specific to the computers and software you will be using to write your own Java programs.

next chapter. Here we describe only the general ideas and classes used in the program.

```
/*
   Program FunTime

   The program will allow you to draw a picture by
   dragging a mouse (move the mouse while holding the left mouse
   button down; hold the button on Mac). To erase the picture and
   start over, click the right mouse button (command-click on Mac).
*/

import javabook.*;

class FunTime
{

   public static void main(String[ ] args)
   {
      SketchPad    doodleBoard;
      doodleBoard = new SketchPad();
      doodleBoard.setVisible( true );
   }

}
```

This statement creates a new **SketchPad** object **doodleBoard**.

This statement makes **doodleBoard** visible on the screen.

When the program is executed, the window shown in Figure 1.15 appears on the screen. Figure 1.16 is the same window after a picture is drawn on it. The

FIGURE 1.15   The window that appears on the screen when the program starts running.

FIGURE 1.16   The same window after a picture is drawn.

program consists of two classes: FunTime and SketchPad. The FunTime class is defined in the above program. The SketchPad class is predefined outside of this program (in a place called the javabook package). This program opens a Sketch-Pad window named doodleBoard and makes it appear on the screen by sending

object diagram   the message setVisible to it. An *object diagram* identifies the classes and objects used in a program, and the object diagram for this program is shown in Figure 1.17. Since we have not yet explained the details of the program, the correspondence between the object diagram and the program may not be obvious at this point. That is fine. It should become clear when we start explaining the program details in the next chapter.

FIGURE 1.17   The object diagram for the **FunTime** program.

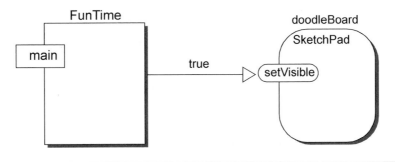

1.7   Exercises

1. Draw an object diagram of a Vehicle class and three Vehicle objects named car1, car2, and car3.

2. Identify all errors in the following object diagram:

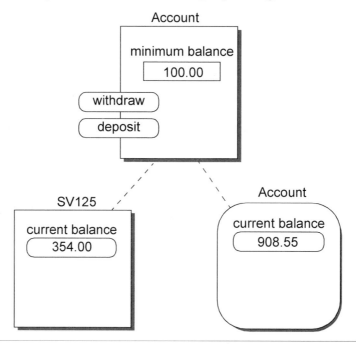

3. Draw an object diagram of a Person class with the following components:
   - Instance variables name, age, and gender.
   - Instance methods setName, getName, and getAge.
   - Class methods new and getAverageAge.

4. Design a CD class where a CD object represents a single music CD. What kinds of information (artist, genre, total playing time, etc.) do you want to know about a CD? Among the information about which you are interested, which are instance variables? Are there any class variables or class constants?

5. Suppose the Vehicle class in exercise 1 is used in a program that keeps track of vehicle registration for the Department of Motor Vehicles. What kinds of instance variables would you define for such Vehicle objects. Can you think of any useful class variables for the Vehicle class?

6. Suppose the following formulas are used to compute the annual vehicle registration fee for the vehicle registration program of exercise 5:

   - For cars, the annual fee is 2 percent of the value of the car.
   - For trucks, the annual fee is 5 percent of the loading capacity (in lbs) of the truck.

   Define two new classes Car and Truck as subclasses of Vehicle. Hint: Associate class and instance variables common to both Car and Truck to Vehicle.

7. Consider a student registration program used by the registrar's office. The program keeps track of students who are registered for a given semester. For each student registered, the program maintains the student's name, address, and phone number; the number of classes in which the student is enrolled; and the student's total credit hours. The program also keeps track of the total number of registered students. Define instance and class variables of a Student class that is suitable for this program.

8. Suppose the minimum and maximum number of courses for which a student can register is different depending on whether the student is a graduate, undergraduate, or work/study student. Redo exercise 7 by defining classes for different types of students. Relate the classes using inheritance.

9. Imagine you are given a task of designing an airline reservation system that keeps track of flights for a commuter airline. List the classes you think would be necessary for designing such a system. Describe the data values and methods you would associate with each class you identify. Note: For this and the next four exercises, we are not expecting you to design the system in complete detail. The objective of these exercises is to give a taste of thinking about a program at a very high level. Try to identify about a half dozen or so classes, and for each class, describe several methods and data values.

10. Repeat exercise 9 designing a university course scheduling system. The system keeps track of classes offered in a given quarter, the number of sections offered, and the number of students enrolled in each section.

11. Repeat exercise 9 designing the state Department of Motor Vehicles registration system. The system keeps track of all licensed vehicles and drivers. How would you design objects representing different types of vehicles (e.g., motorcycles and trucks) and drivers (e.g., class A for commercial licenses and class B for towing vehicles)?

12. Repeat exercise 9 designing a sales tracking system for a fast-food restaurant. The system keeps track of all menu items offered by the restaurant and the number of daily sales per menu item.

13. When you write a term paper, you have to consult many references: books, journal articles, newspaper articles, and so forth. Repeat exercise 9 designing a bibliography organizer that keeps track of all references you used in writing a term paper.

14. Consider the inheritance hierarchy given in Figure 1.13. List the features common to all classes and the features unique to individual classes. Propose a new inheritance hierarchy based on the types of accounts your bank offers.

15. Consider a program that maintains an address book. Design an inheritance hierarchy for the classes such as Person, ProfessionalContact, Friend, and Student that can be used in implementing such a program.

16. Do you think the design phase is more important than the coding phase? Why or why not?

17. How does the quality of design affect the total cost of developing and maintaining software?

Java Programming Basics

OBJECTIVES

After you have read and studied this chapter, you should be able to

- Identify the basic components of Java programs.
- Distinguish two types of Java programs—applications and applets.
- Write simple Java applications and applets.
- Describe the difference between object declaration and object creation.
- Describe the process of creating and running Java programs.
- Use MainWindow and MessageBox classes from the javabook package to write Java applications.
- Use the Graphics class from the standard Java package.

Introduction

We will introduce both Java applications and applets in this chapter and describe the basic structure of simple Java programs. We will also describe the steps you follow to run programs. We expect you to actually run these sample programs to verify that your computer (either your own or the one at the school's computer center) is set up properly to run the sample programs presented in the book. It is important to verify this now. Otherwise, if you encounter a problem later, you won't be able to determine whether the problem is the result of a bad program or a bad setup.

We will develop a sample application program in Section 2.4 following the design, coding, and testing phases of the software life cycle. We will develop all of our sample programs in this manner. We stress here again that our objective in this book is to teach object-oriented programming and how to apply object-oriented thinking in program development. The Java language is merely a means to implement a design into an executable program. We chose Java for this book because Java is a much easier language than other object-oriented programming languages to translate a design into an actual code. Beginning students often get lost in the language details and forget the main objective of learning how to design, but the use of Java should minimize this from happening.

To help you concentrate on program design and programming fundamentals instead of language details, we provide predefined classes for you to use in writing Java programs. We will introduce two of these predefined classes in this chapter. As nice and logical as Java can be, beginners still must learn quite a few details before becoming proficient in Java. We provide these predefined classes so that you can start writing meaningful programs immediately without knowing too much about Java language specifics. Please read the Preface for more reasons for using predefined classes in this book.

2.1   The First Java Application

Our first Java application program displays a window on the screen, as shown in Figure 2.1. The size of the window is slightly smaller than the screen, and the window is positioned at the center of the screen. Also, the window has a title Sample Java Application. Although this program is very simple, it still illustrates the fundamental structure of an object-oriented program, which is

An object-oriented program uses objects.

FIGURE 2.1   Result of running the **MyFirstApplication** program. The window has a default title
Sample Java Application. (We'll show you how to change the default title later.)

It may sound too obvious, but let's begin our study of object-oriented programming with this obvious notion. Here's the program code:

```
/*
    Program MyFirstApplication

    This program displays a window on the screen. The window is
    positioned at the center of the screen, and the size of the
    window is almost as big as the screen.
*/

import javabook.*;

class MyFirstApplication
{
    public static void main(String[] args)
    {
        MainWindow  mainWindow;
        mainWindow = new MainWindow();
        mainWindow.setVisible( true );
    }
}
```

This program declares one class called MyFirstApplication, and the class includes one method called main. From this main method, the MyFirstApplication
class creates and uses a MainWindow object named mainWindow by sending a

message **setVisible** to the object. Expressing this program as an object diagram results in the one shown in Figure 2.2.

FIGURE 2.2   The object diagram for the **MyFirstApplication** program.

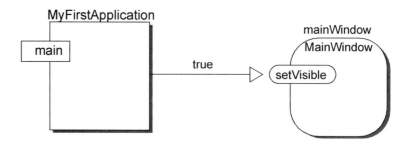

Instead of going through the program line by line from the top, we will start examining this program by concentrating on the following three lines of code:

```
MainWindow    mainWindow;
mainWindow = new MainWindow();
mainWindow.setVisible( true );
```

We will explain the rest of the program in the next section.These three lines of code represent the crux of the program, namely, an object-oriented program uses objects. The rule to remember in using objects is as follows:

> *To use an object in a program, we first declare and create an object, and then we send messages to it.*

In the remainder of this section, we will describe how to declare an object, create an object, and use an object by sending messages to the object.

Object Declaration

Every object we use in a program must be declared. An object declaration designates the name of an object and the class to which the object belongs. Its syntax is

object declaration
syntax

```
<class name>  <object names>  ;
```

where <object names> is a sequence of object names separated by commas and <class name> is the name of a class to which these objects belong. Here's how the general syntax is matched to the object declaration of the program:

Class Name
This class must be defined elsewhere.

Object Names
One object is declared here.

```
MainWindow    mainWindow;
```

Here are more examples:

```
Account    checking;
Customer   john, jack, jill;
```

The first declaration declares an Account object named checking, and the second declaration declares three Customer objects.

To declare an object as an instance of some class, the class must be defined already. We will first study how to use objects from predefined classes. Later in the book, we will show you how to define your own classes, from which you can create instances.

identifier

When we declare an object, we must give it a name. Any valid identifier that is not reserved for other uses can be used as an object name. An *identifier* is a sequence of letters and digits with the first one being a letter. We use an identifier to name a class, object, method, and others. The following words are all valid identifiers:

```
MyFirstApplication
FunTime
ComputeArea
```

Upper- and lowercase letters are distinguished, so the following four identifiers are distinct:

```
mainwindow      mAinWindow
MAINWindow      mainWINDOW
```

No spaces are allowed in an identifier, and therefore, the following three lines

```
Sample Program
My First Application
Program FunTime
```

are all invalid identifiers.

Since upper- and lowercase letters are distinguished, you can use mainWindow as the name for an object of the class MainWindow. We name objects in this manner whenever possible in this book so we can easily tell to which class the object belongs. We follow the Java naming convention of using an uppercase letter for the first letter of the class names and a lowercase letter for the first letter of the object names in this book. It is important to follow the standard naming convention so others who read your program can easily distinguish the purposes of identifiers. Programs that follow the standard naming convention are easier to read than those that do not follow the standard. And remember that software maintenance is easier with easy-to-understand programs.

naming convention

When an identifier consists of multiple words, the first letter from every word, except the first word, will be capitalized, e.g., myMainWindow, not mymainwindow.

Follow the standard naming convention in writing your Java programs to make them easier to read.

Object Creation

No objects are actually created by the declaration. An object declaration simply declares the name (identifier) that we use to refer to an object. For example, the declaration

```
Account    account;
```

designates that the name account is used to refer to an Account object, but the actual Account object is not yet created. We create an object by invoking the new operation. The syntax for new is

object creation syntax

```
<object name> = new <class name> ( <arguments> ) ;
```

where <object name> is the name of a declared object, <class name> is the name of the class to which the object belongs, and <arguments> is a sequence of values passed to the new operation. Let's match the syntax to the actual statement in the sample program:

Although this example does not pass any argument, it is possible to do so in creating a new instance of MainWindow. If we replace the preceding statement with

```
mainWindow = new MainWindow( "This is my first window" );
```

and run the program, the window shown in Figure 2.3 will appear on the screen. Notice the change in the window title. The double quotes (") are used to specify a string data value. If you don't use double quotes, then the system will treat them as five identifiers, and this will result in an error.

FIGURE 2.3   Result of running the program **MyFirstApplication** when the argument to the **new** operation is the string argument **"This is my first window"**.

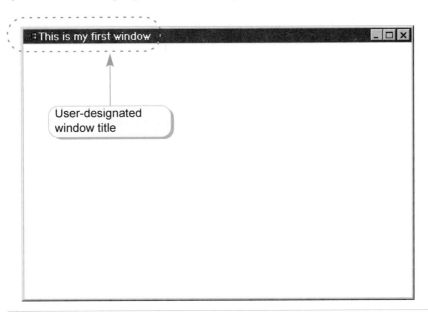

Figure 2.4 shows the distinction between object declaration and creation. The object diagram notation we introduced in Chapter 1 is a simplified version of the state-of-memory diagram, as shown in Figure 2.5.

FIGURE 2.4   Distinction between object declaration and object creation.

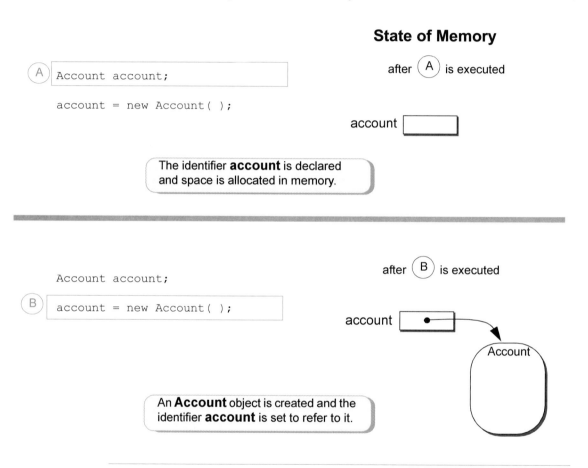

Now, consider the following object declaration and two statements of object creation:

```
Customer   customer;
customer = new Customer( );
customer = new Customer( );
```

What do you think will happen? An error? No. It is permissible to use the same name to refer to different objects of the same class. Figure 2.6 shows the state-

FIGURE 2.5   Relationship between the state-of-memory diagram and the object diagram notation.

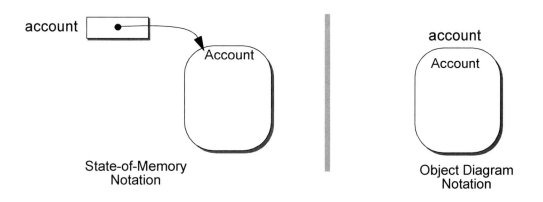

The notation we use in object diagrams is a simplified version of the one used in state-of-memory diagrams.

of-memory diagram after the second new is executed. Since there is no reference to the first Customer object anymore, it will eventually be erased and returned to the system. Remember that when an object is created, a certain amount of memory space is allocated for storing this object. If this allocated but unused space is not returned to the system for other uses, the space gets wasted. This returning of space to the system is called *deallocation*, and the mechanism to deallocate unused space is called *garbage collection*.

garbage
collection

Message Sending

After the object is created, we can start sending messages to it. The syntax for sending a message to an object is

message sending
syntax

```
<object name> . <method name> ( <arguments> ) ;
```

where <object name> is an object name, <method name> is the name of a method of the object, and <arguments> is a sequence of values passed to the method. In the sample program, we send the setVisible message with the argument true

Chapter 2

FIGURE 2.6   The state after two **new** commands are executed.

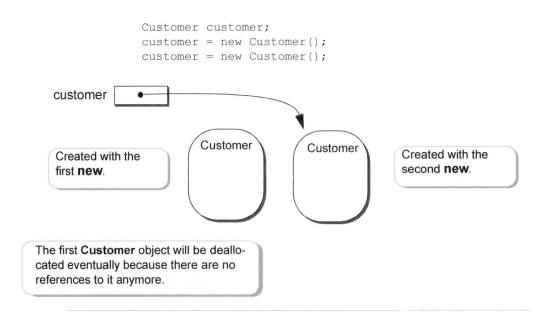

```
Customer customer;
customer = new Customer();
customer = new Customer();
```

customer

Created with the
first **new**.

Customer

Customer

Created with the
second **new**.

The first **Customer** object will be deallocated eventually because there are no
references to it anymore.

to the mainWindow object to make it appear on the screen. Once again, let's
match the components in the general syntax to the actual statement:

Object Name	**Method Name**	**Argument**
Name of the object to which	The name of the message	The argument we are
we are sending a message.	we are sending.	passing with the message.

```
mainWindow . setVisible  (  true   )  ;
```

Figure 2.7 shows the correspondence between message sending as represented in the object diagram and in the Java statement. Because the object that
receives a message must possess a corresponding method, we often substitute
the expression "sending a message" with "calling a method." We will use these
expressions interchangably.

*The expression "calling object O's method M " is synonymous
to "sending message M to object O."*

FIGURE 2.7   Correspondence between message sending as represented in the object diagram and in the actual Java statement.

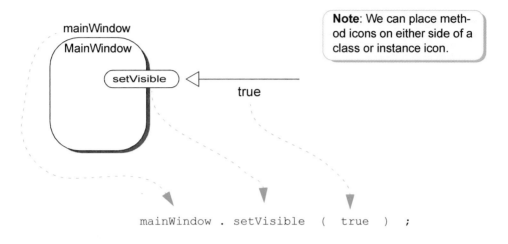

Notice the argument for the setVisible message does not include double quotes as the one for the new operation in the example shown on page 43. The argument true is one of the two possible logical values (the other is false) used in Java programs. We will study more about the use of logical values later in the book, starting from Chapter 6. For now, it suffices to remember that there are two logical values—true and false—used for certain specific purposes.

Passing true in the setVisible message makes the receiving object appear on the screen. Passing false makes the object disappear from the screen. So, for example, if we write

```
mainWindow.setVisible( true );
mainWindow.setVisible( false );
mainWindow.setVisible( true );
```

then mainWindow will appear once, disappear, and then appear on the screen again. (Note: Because the computer will execute these statements so quickly, you may not notice any difference from the original program. See exercise 26 on page 81.)

reserved word   The word true (and false) is called a *reserved word*. It is an identifier that is used for a specific purpose and cannot be used for any other purpose such as for the name of an object.

Chapter 2

1. Which of the following are invalid identifiers?

    a. one   e. hello
    b. my Window   f. JAVA
    c. 1234   g. hello,there
    d. acct122   h. DecafeLattePlease

2. What's wrong with the following code?

    ```
    MainWindow mainWindow();
    mainWindow.show();
    ```

3. Is there anything wrong with the following declarations?

    ```
    mainWindow          MainWindow;
    Account, Customer   account, customer;
    ```

4. Which of the following statements is valid?

    ```
    a.    mainWindow.setVisible( "true" );
    b.    mainWindow.setVisible( true );
    ```

2.2   Program Components

Now that we have covered the crux of the first sample program, let's examine the rest of the program. The first sample application program MyFirstApplication is composed of three parts: comment, import statement, and class declaration. These three parts are included universally in Java programs.

> *A Java program is composed of comments,* import *state-ments, and class declarations.*

You can write a Java program that includes only a single class declaration, but that is not a norm. In any nontrivial program, you will see these three components. We will explain the three components and their subparts in this section.

Comments

In addition to the instructions for computers to follow, programs contain comments in which we state the purpose of the program, explain the meaning of code, and provide any other descriptions to help programmers understand the program. Here's the comment in the sample MyFirstApplication program:

```
/*
    Program MyFirstApplication

    This program displays a window on the screen. The window is
    positioned at the center of the screen, and the size of the
    window is almost as big as the screen.
*/

import javabook.*;

class MyFirstApplication
{
    public static void main(String[] args)
    {
        MainWindow   mainWindow;
        mainWindow = new MainWindow();
        mainWindow.setVisible( true );
    }
}
```

Comment

comment
markers

A comment is any sequence of text that begins with the marker /* and terminates with another marker */. The beginning and ending markers are matched in
pairs; that is, every beginning marker must have a matching ending marker. A
beginning marker is matched with the next ending marker that appears. Any beginning markers that appear between the beginning marker and its matching
ending marker are treated as part of the comment. In other words, you cannot
put a comment inside another comment. The examples in Figure 2.8 illustrate
how the matching is done.

single-line
comment marker

Another marker for a comment is double slashes //. This marker is used for a
single-line comment. Any text between the double-slash marker and the end of a
line is a comment. The following example shows the difference between multi-
line and single-line comments:

```
/*
    This is a comment with
    three lines of
    text.
*/

// This is a comment
// This is another comment
// This is a third comment
```

FIGURE 2.8   How the beginning and ending comment markers are matched.

javadoc
comment

Although not required to run the program, comments are indispensable in writing easy-to-understand code.

The third type of comment is called a *javadoc* comment. It is a specialized comment that can appear before the class declaration and other program elements yet to be described in the book. Javadoc comments begin with the /** marker and end with the */ marker. Here's an example of a javadoc comment:

```
/**
 * This class provides basic clock functions. In addition
 * to reading the current time and today's date, you can
 * use this class for stopwatch functions.
 */
```

The asterisks on the second, third, and fourth lines are not necessary, but useful in marking the comments clearly. It is an accepted convention to place asterisks in this manner. Although not required, aligning the end marker as shown in the example is also an accepted convention. In this book, we will be using this convention for non-javadoc comments also.

One major benefit of using javadoc comments is the availability of a tool that generates a web page automatically from the javadoc comments. Javadoc comments are the standard way of documenting Java programs, and we will be using them extensively in documenting the sample programs in this book. However, the use of javadoc comments is more restricted and difficult than the other two types of comments, so we will have to introduce elements of javadoc comments gradually. We will start using javadoc comments from Chapter 4.

Information on javadoc and sample web documentation pages that are generated from javadoc comments can be found at www.drcaffeine.com/supportinfo/javadoc.html. *You can get a full documentation of the standard Java classes generated from javadoc comments at* www.java.sun.com/j2ee/j2sdkee/techdocs/api/.

Comments are intended for the programmers only and are ignored by the computer. Therefore, comments are really not necessary in making a program executable, but they are an important aspect of documenting the program. It is not enough to write a program that executes correctly. We need to document the program, and commenting the program is an important part of program documentation. Other parts of program documentation include object diagrams, programmers' work log, design documents, and user manuals. If you can write a program once and use it forever without ever modifying it, then writing a program with no comments may be tolerable. However, in the real world, using programs without ever making any changes almost never happens. For example, you may decide to add new features and capabilities or modify the way the user interacts with the program. Even if you don't improve the program, you still have to modify the program when you detect some errors in it. Also, for commercial programs, those who change the programs are most often not the ones who developed them. When the time comes for a programmer to modify his or someone else's program, he must first understand the program, and program documentation is an indispensable aid to understanding the program.

There are several different uses of comments. The first is the header comment. At the beginning of a program, we place a comment to describe the program. We characterize such a comment as a *header comment*. We also may include header comments at the beginning of methods to describe their purposes. Depending on the length and complexity of programs, the description may range from short and simple to long and very detailed. A typical header comment for a beginning programming class may look something like this:

header comment

typical header
comment for
a beginning
programming
class

```
/*
 *  Program:       TextEditor
 *
 *  Author:        C. Thomas Wu
 *                 ctwu@cs.nps.navy.mil
 *
 *  Written:       January 1, 2000
 *
 *  Course:        Comp Sci 101
 *                 Spring 2000
 *                 Program Assignment No. 7
 *
 *  Compiler:      JDK 1.2.2
 *  Platform:      Windows 98
 *
 *  Description:
 *     This is a simple text editor. The editor allows the user
 *     to save text to a file and read text from a file. The
 *     editor displays text using Courier font only and does not
 *     allow formatting (e.g., bold, italic, etc.). The editor
 *     supports standard editing functions Cut, Copy, and
 *     Paste, but does not support Undo. For more details,
 *     please refer to the TxEditReadme file.
 */
```

Note: The use of the asterisks is in the style of javadoc, but this is not a javadoc comment.

For your own programs, you should write header comments following the guideline provided by your instructor. For listing the sample programs in the book, we will include only the program name and a short description in the header comment, mainly for reference purposes. The header comment in the actual programs, available from our website, includes additional information such as compiler used, copyright notices, and others. The header comment is written in the javadoc format.

Another use of comments is to explain code whose purpose may not be obvious. Your aim is always to write easily understandable, self-explanatory program code. But there are times this is not possible, and you should attach comment to code that is not so easy to understand. There also are times when the original code may not work as intended, and as a temporary measure, you modify the code slightly so the program will continue to work. You should clearly mark such modification with a comment, so you remember what you have done. If you did not put in an appropriate comment and later read your code without remembering about the modification, you would have no idea why you wrote such code. If you cannot understand your own code, imagine the frustration of other programmers (or your T.A. or instructor) trying to understand your modified code.

Yet another use of comments is to identify or summarize a block of code. Suppose a program is divided into three major parts: getting input values from the user, performing computation using the input values, and displaying the computation results. You can place comments at the top of each part to delineate the three major parts clearly.

Remember that adding comments to a poorly designed program will not make it a better program. Your foremost goal is to develop a well-designed program that runs efficiently and is easy to understand. Commenting a program is only a means toward that goal, not a goal itself. In fact, excessive use of comments makes it harder to follow and understand a program.

> **Dr. Caffeine**
>
> *Comment markers are useful in disabling a portion of a program. Let's say you find a portion that may be causing the program to crash and you want to try out different code for the problem portion. Instead of replacing the whole problem portion with new code, you can leave the questionable code in the program by converting it into a "comment" with comment markers. You can remove the comment markers if you need this code later.*

Import Statement

We develop object-oriented programs by using predefined classes whenever possible and defining our own classes when no suitable predefined classes are available. In Java, classes are grouped into *packages*. The Java compiler comes with many packages, and we supply one package called javabook with this textbook. We will explain the motivation behind using the javabook package in the next section. You also can put your own classes into a package so they can be used in other programs. Here's the import statement in the same MyFirstApplication program:

package
javabook

```
/*
    Program MyFirstApplication

    This program displays a window on the screen. The window is
    positioned at the center of the screen, and the size of the
    window is almost as big as the screen.
.*/

import javabook.*;

class MyFirstApplication
{
    public static void main(String[] args)
    {
        MainWindow        mainWindow;
        mainWindow = new MainWindow();
        mainWindow.setVisible( true );
    }
}
```

Import Statement
The **import** statement allows the program to use classes (and their instances) defined in the designated package.

To use a class from a package, you may refer to the class in your program using the following format:

```
<package name> . <class name>
```

For example, to use the MainWindow class in the javabook package, we refer to it as

```
javabook.MainWindow
```

dot notation

which we read as "javabook dot MainWindow." This notation is called *dot notation*.

A package can include subpackages, forming a hierarchy of packages. In referring to a class in a deeply nested package, we use multiple dots. For example, we write

```
java.awt.image.ColorModel
```

fully qualified
name

to refer to the class ColorModel in the java.awt.image package; that is, the image package is inside the awt package, which in turn is inside the java package. Dot notation with the names of all packages to which a class belongs is called the class's *fully qualified name*. Using the fully qualified name of a class is frequently too cumbersome, especially when you have to refer to the same class many times in a program. You can use the import statement to avoid this problem.

An import statement at the beginning of your program eliminates the need for fully qualified names. Instead of using the expression java.awt.image.ColorModel to refer to the class, you can refer to it simply as

```
ColorModel
```

by including the import statement

```
import java.awt.image.ColorModel;
```

at the beginning of the program. Notice that the import statement is terminated by a semicolon. If you need to import more than one class from the same package, then instead of using an import statement for every class, you can import them all using asterisk notation:

```
import <package name> . * ;
```

For example, if we state

```
import java.awt.image.*;
```

then we are importing all classes from the java.awt.image package. We use this asterisk notation in our sample program, although we use only one of the many classes available in the javabook package. We could have used

```
import javabook.MainWindow;
```

but it is more conventional to use asterisk notation.

Notice that the package names are all in lowercase letters. This is another standard Java naming convention. When you create your own packages, which you will in Chapter 11, make sure to follow this naming convention.

Class Declaration

A Java program is composed of one or more classes, some of them are pre-defined classes, while others are defined by ourselves. In this sample program, there are two classes—MainWindow and MyFirstApplication. The MainWindow class is from the javabook package and the MyFirstApplication class is the class we define ourselves. To define a new class, we must *declare* it in the program. The syntax for declaring the class is

```
class <class name>
{

    <class member declarations>

}
```

where <class name> is the name of the class and <class member declarations> is a sequence of class member declarations. The word class is a reserved word used to mark the beginning of a class declaration. A class member is either a data value or a method. We can use any valid identifier to name the class. Here's the class declaration in the sample MyFirstApplication program:

```
/*
    Program MyFirstApplication

    This program displays a window on the screen. The window is
    positioned at the center of the screen, and the size of the
    window is almost as big as the screen.
*/

import javabook.*;

class MyFirstApplication
{
    public static void main(String[] args)
    {
        MainWindow    mainWindow;
        mainWindow = new MainWindow();
        mainWindow.setVisible( true );
    }
}
```

> **Class Declaration**
> Every program must include at least one class.

main class

One of the classes in a program must be designated as the *main class*. The main class of the sample program is MyFirstApplication. Exactly how you designate a class as the main class of the program depends on which Java program development tool you use. We will use the name of a main class to refer to a whole application. For example, we say the MyFirstApplication class when we refer to the class itself and say the MyFirstApplication application when we refer to the whole application.

If we designate a class as the main class, then we must define a method called main, because when a Java program is executed, the main method of a main class is executed first. We will explain how to define a method in the next section.

Method Declaration

The syntax for method declaration is

```
<modifiers> <return type> <method name> ( <parameters> )
{
    <method body>
}
```

where <modifiers> is a sequence of terms designating different kinds of methods, <return type> is the type of data value returned by a method, <method name> is the name of a method, <parameters> is a sequence of values passed to a method, and <method body> is a sequence of instructions. Here's the method declaration for the main method:

```
/*
        Program MyFirstApplication

        This program displays a window on the screen. The window is
        positioned at the center of the screen, and the size of the
        window is almost as big as the screen.
*/

import javabook.*;

class MyFirstApplication
{
    public static void main(String[] args)
    {
        MainWindow    mainWindow;
        mainWindow = new MainWindow();
        mainWindow.setVisible( true );
    }
}
```

Method Declaration
This declaration declares the **main** method.

Class member declarations appear between the left and right braces of the class declaration.

Chapter 2

Let's match these components to the actual method declaration of the sample program:

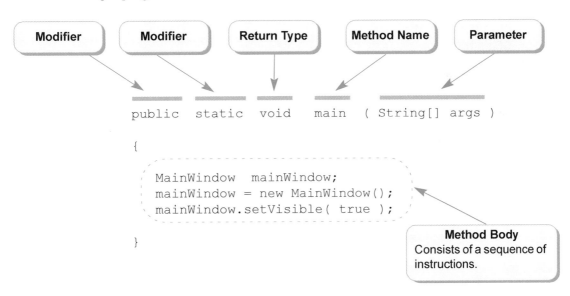

| Modifier | Modifier | Return Type | Method Name | Parameter |

```
public    static    void    main    ( String[] args )

{

    MainWindow    mainWindow;
    mainWindow = new MainWindow();
    mainWindow.setVisible( true );

}
```

Method Body
Consists of a sequence of instructions.

We will not explain the meanings of modifiers, return types, and parameters here. We will explain them in detail gradually as we progress through the book. For now, we ask you to follow a program template that we will present next.

A Program Template for Simple Java Applications

The diagram in Figure 2.9 shows a program template for simple Java applications. You can follow this program template to write very simple Java applications. The structure of the sample program MyFirstApplication follows this template.

FIGURE 2.9   A program template for simple Java applications.

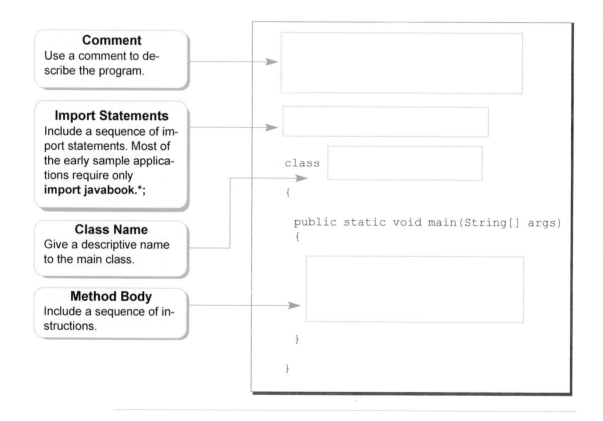

Comment
Use a comment to describe the program.

Import Statements
Include a sequence of import statements. Most of the early sample applications require only
import javabook.*;

Class Name
Give a descriptive name to the main class.

Method Body
Include a sequence of instructions.

```
class

{
    public static void main(String[] args)
    {

    }

}
```

Quick Check

1.   Name three components of a Java program.

2. Locate three program components in the FunTime program from Chapter 1.

3. Compare FunTime and MyFirstApplication and list the similarities and differences.

2.3 Edit–Compile–Run Cycle

We will walk through the steps involved in executing the first sample program. What we outline here are the overall steps common to any Java development tool you use. You need to get detailed instructions on how to use your chosen development tool to actually run programs. The steps we present in this section should serve as a guideline for more detailed instructions specific to your program development tool.

Step 1

Type in the program using an editor and save the program to a file. Use the name of the main class and the suffix .java for the filename. This file, in which *source file*   the program is in a human-readable form, is called a *source file*.

MyFirstApplication.java

```
/*
    Program MyFirstApplication

    The first sample Java application
*/

import javabook.*;

class MyFirstApplication
{
  public static void main (String[] args)
  {
    MainWindow mainWindow;
    mainWindow = new MainWindow();
    mainWindow.setVisible(true);
  }
}
```

Editor

(source file)

It is critical that you configure the development tool properly so the compiler knows where to locate the javabook package. Each development tool requires you to set the configuration differently, so please consult the relevant materials for more information.

Chapter 2

Step 2

project file

Compile the source file. Many compilers require you to create a *project file* and then place the source file in the project file in order to compile the source file. When the compilation is successful, the compiled version of the source file is created. This compiled version is called *bytecode*, and the file that contains bytecode is called a *bytecode file*. The compiler-generated bytecode file will have the same name as the source file with the suffix .class.

bytecode

bytecode file

MyFirstApplication.class

MyFirstApplication.java

Editor   Compiler

(source file)

(bytecode file)

When any error occurs in a program, an error message will be displayed. If the sample program contains no errors in syntax, then instead of an error message, you will get a message stating something like "Compiled successfully." To see what kind of error messages are displayed, try compiling the following program. We purposely introduced three errors—can you find them? Make sure to compile the correct MyFirstApplication again before proceeding to the next step.

```
class MyFirstApplication //BAD version
{
    public static main(String[] args)
    {
        mainWindow = new MainWindow();
        mainWindow.setVisible( true )
    }
}
```

compilation error

Errors detected by the compiler are called *compilation errors*. Compilation errors are actually the easiest type of errors to correct. Most compilation errors are due to the violation of syntax rules.

Step 3

Execute the bytecode file. An interpreter will go through the bytecode file and execute the instructions in it. If your program is error free, a window will appear on the screen.

If an error occurs while running the program, the interpreter will catch it and stop its execution. Errors detected by the interpreter are called *execution errors.* If you did not see the expected results, go back to the previous steps and verify that your program is entered correctly. If you still do not see the expected results, then most likely your development environment is not set up correctly. Please refer to other sources of information for further help.

execution error

2.4   The javabook Package

We have used the MainWindow and SketchPad classes from the javabook package in our sample programs. There are many useful classes in the javabook package, and in the next section, we will show you the third class from the package. We decided to provide the javabook package with this book because

To become a good object-oriented programmer, one must first learn how to use predefined classes.

Eventually, you must learn how to define your own classes, the classes you will reuse in writing programs. But before you can become adept in defining your own classes, you must first learn how to use existing classes. For this purpose, we provide the javabook classes in this book. Learning first to use the predefined javabook classes has the following advantages:

1.   It gives you a taste of how real-world programs are developed. In real-world object-oriented programming, you develop programs by reusing existing classes whenever possible. You will get hands-on experience of code reuse by using classes from the javabook package.

2.   It minimizes the impact of programming language syntax and semantics. The use of javabook classes lets students concentrate on learning concepts instead of Java language features. Using predefined classes minimizes the impact of programming language because these predefined classes hide the complexity of the underlying programming language. Remember that our objective is to teach object-oriented thinking, not Java language.

3.   It allows you to write practical programs without learning too many details of the Java language. Java comes with a number of standard packages, but using the standard classes such as java.awt from the beginning is not practical because these classes require programming sophistication that beginning students do not possess. Easy-to-use classes such as the javabook classes are most appropriate for beginning programmers.

4.   It serves as a good example of how to design classes. When the time comes for you to design your own classes, intuitive and easy to use classes from javabook should serve as your model.

Although we begin teaching object-oriented programming by using the javabook classes, you will not be dependent on them. You will become an object-oriented programmer, not a javabook programmer. We use javabook because it is pedagogically sound to do so. Complete documentation of the javabook classes are provided in Appendix A.

2.5   Sample Program: Displaying Messages

Now that you have acquired a basic understanding of Java application programs, let's write a new application. We will go through the design, coding, and testing phases of the software life cycle to illustrate the development process. Since the program we develop here is very simple, we can write it without really going through the phases. However, it is extremely important for you to get into a habit of developing a program following the software life cycle stages. Small programs can be developed in a haphazard manner, but not large programs. We will teach you the development process with small programs first, so you will be ready to use it to develop large programs later.

Mr. Espresso: If I learn programming using javabook *classes, will I be able to program only by using* javabook *classes? Will I still be able to program without using them?*

Dr. Caffeine: Keep in mind that javabook *classes are not the only predefined classes we use in this book. You will learn many classes from the standard Java packages such as* java.awt *and* java.io. *By the time you finish Chapter 12, you can program with or without the* java-book *package.*

Mr. Espresso: Another concern I have is what happens after I complete your course? Can I continue to use javabook?

Dr. Caffeine: Yes, you are free to use the javabook *classes. There are no restrictions on using them. You may use the* javabook *classes as is, or better yet, you can modify the classes to suit your needs. You can take* javabook *as the starting point of your own package. Source code for all the classes in the* javabook *package is available to you.*

Problem Statement

We start our development with a problem statement. The problem statement for our sample programs will be short, ranging from a sentence to a paragraph, but the problem statement for complex and advanced applications may contain many pages. Here's the problem statement for this sample program:

Write an application that displays the message I Love Java.

Design

In the design stage, we translate the given problem statement into a design document that can be implemented. For object-oriented programs, a design document will include a list of classes. The classes in the design document are either predefined or custom-made. For each class in the list, we identify its purpose, the methods and data values that will be defined, assumptions made in its use, and so forth. We will begin with a very simplistic design document and gradually build more detailed design documents as our sample programs become more complex later in the book.

The problem states that the program is to display a message. It does not specify how, so in the design stage, we will decide how to do this. From what we know so far, we can do this by setting the title of the MainWindow object like this:

Alternative Design **1**

```
MainWindow mainWindow;
mainWindow = new MainWindow("I Love Java");
mainWindow.setVisible( true );
```

Is this a good design? This is the best we could do from our limited knowledge, but most likely, this is not what the user wants. When the design does not meet the user's needs, we go back to the drawing board and redesign.

The first thing we do in redesign is to search for a class or classes that will perform the task we want to implement. We may start searching from the standard Java classes. If we can find suitable classes, we will use them. We may have to build a new class from these existing classes. If no suitable classes are found or building one from the existing classes seems too difficult, we will search other packages. We could search for free packages available on the Internet or packages supplied by your school's computer center. Some software companies may sell a package that contains the classes we want. If the package is within our budget, we may buy it. If no such package can be found, then we will develop the necessary classes ourselves.

In our case, we will search the javabook package first. As you become more proficient in Java language, you may want to search the Java standard libraries first. If you go through the package documentation in Appendix A, you will notice a class called **MessageBox**. This is the class we are looking for.

We will describe **MessageBox** very briefly here. More information on **MessageBox** will be given later as we use more of its features. A **MessageBox** object is used to display a single line of text. Figure 2.11 shows the **MessageBox** object with the message I Love Java. When you click the OK button, the object disappears from the screen. The sequence of declaring, creating, and sending the message is

Alternative
Design **2**

```
MessageBox messageBox;
messageBox = new MessageBox( mainWindow );
messageBox.show("I Love Java");
```

dialog box

frame

subordinate

A **MessageBox** object is a special kind of window called a *dialog box*, or more simply, *dialog*. Every dialog box requires another kind of window called a *frame* as its *owner*. A **MainWindow** object is a frame window. We will elaborate on their differences later. For now, it suffices to know that a frame is a general-purpose window and a dialog is a limited-purpose window used primarily for displaying simple information such as error messages or getting a simple response such as yes or no.

We call a dialog box a *subordinate* of the owner frame. One characteristic of this relationship is that a subordinate dialog always appears in front of its owner frame. The owner–subordinate relationship is established when a dialog box is created by passing the owner frame window as an argument in new, as in

```
messageBox = new MessageBox( mainWindow );
```

And we display the text by passing it as an argument in the show message to a Messagebox object:

```
messageBox.show( "I Love Java" );
```

The object diagram of the program is shown in Figure 2.10 and here's the design document of the program:

Design Document:	DisplayMessage
Class	**Purpose**
DisplayMessage	The main class of the program.
MainWindow	The main frame window of the program. The title is set to Display Message. This class is from java-book.
MessageBox	The dialog for displaying the required message. This class is from javabook.

Chapter 2

FIGURE 2.10   The object diagram for the DisplayMessage program.

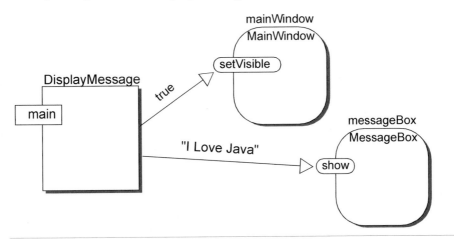

Coding

After the design is completed, we translate it into an actual code. We will implement this program using the program template of Figure 2.9.

Here's the source code for the program DisplayMessage:

```
/*
    Program DisplayMessage

    The program displays the text "I Love Java". The program uses a
    MessageBox object from the javabook package to display the text.
*/

import javabook.*;

class DisplayMessage
{
    public static void main(String[] args)
    {
        //declare two objects
        MainWindow mainWindow;
        MessageBox messageBox;

        //create two objects
        mainWindow = new MainWindow("Display Message");
        messageBox = new MessageBox(mainWindow);

        //display two objects: first the frame and then the dialog
        mainWindow.setVisible( true );
        messageBox.show("I Love Java");
    }
}
```

Testing

After the program is written, we test the program to verify that the program runs as intended. Since this program is very simple, there's not much testing strategy we can employ here. We just run the program and make sure that the main window and the dialog appear on the screen as shown in Figure 2.11. For subsequent sample programs, the testing strategy will be more involved.

2.6   The First Java Applet

Now let's move on to the second type of Java program—an applet. Here's a Java applet that displays the message I Love Java and draws a rectangle around the text:

```
/*
    Program MyFirstApplet

    An applet that displays the text "I Love Java"
    and a rectangle around the text.
*/
```

```
import java.applet.*;
import java.awt.*;

public class MyFirstApplet extends Applet
{
    public void paint( Graphics graphic)
    {
        graphic.drawString("I Love Java",70,70);
        graphic.drawRect(50,50,100,30);
    }

}
```

Notice a resemblance in the program structure between this applet and the applications we wrote earlier. Applications and applets are both programs, and, therefore, they share the same program structure, composed of three parts: a comment, an import statement, and a class declaration. Figure 2.12 identifies the three components in the applet. We include the header comment to describe the applet and two import statements to import the required java.applet and java.awt packages. The classes Applet and Graphics used in the applet are defined in java.applet and java.awt. The object diagram of MyFirstApplet is shown in Figure 2.13.

Notice that MyFirstApplet does not have a main method, because the Applet-Viewer class is the main class of the program. For applications, we define our own main class, but for applets, we use the predefined main class AppletViewer.

FIGURE 2.11   Result of running the DisplayMessage program.

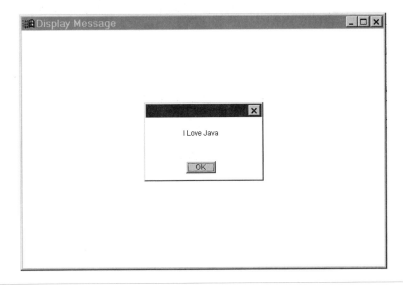

FIGURE 2.12 The applet **MyFirstApplet** with the three program components identified.

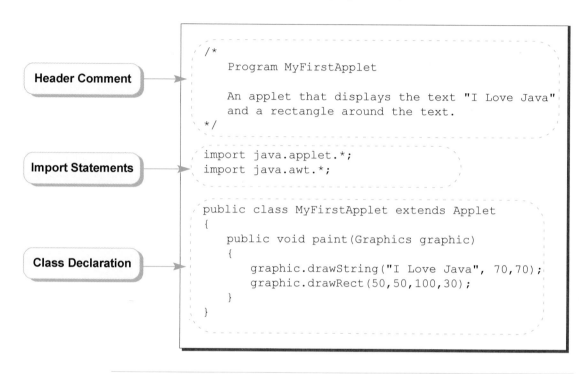

Header Comment

Import Statements

Class Declaration

```
/*
    Program MyFirstApplet

    An applet that displays the text "I Love Java"
    and a rectangle around the text.
*/

import java.applet.*;
import java.awt.*;

public class MyFirstApplet extends Applet
{
    public void paint(Graphics graphic)
    {
        graphic.drawString("I Love Java", 70,70);
        graphic.drawRect(50,50,100,30);
    }
}
```

FIGURE 2.13 The object diagram for the **MyFirstApplet** program.

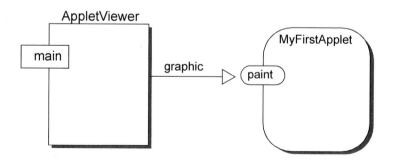

For applets, we define a subclass of Applet that the AppletViewer uses when executed. A subclass of Applet is declared as

applet declaration
syntax

```
public class <applet subclass> extends Applet
{
    <class member declarations>
}
```

public class

Notice the modifier public before class, which designates the class as a *public class*. We will discuss the significance of this modifier in Chapter 4. For now, just remember that an applet viewer requires classes to be declared as public. The Java interpreter that runs application programs does not impose this requirement, and therefore, we do not use this modifier in declaring the main class of an application (although it won't hurt if we do). The reserved word extends designates an inheritance (superclass/subclass) relationship. So by declaring

extends

```
public class MyFirstApplet extends Applet
```

we are using inheritance and establishing MyFirstApplet as a subclass of Applet. In a diagram, we represent the relationship as

We declared one method in the MyFirstApplet class:

paint method

```
public void paint(Graphics graphic)
{
    graphic.drawString("I Love Java", 70, 70);
    graphic.drawRect(50, 50, 100, 30);
}
```

The AppletViewer class automatically sends the paint message with a Graphics object as an argument to an applet. We use Graphics objects to display text, lines, and other graphics. In the sample applet, we send two messages to the object graphic. The first message

```
graphic.drawString("I Love Java", 70, 70);
```

displays the text I Love Java at the specified position (70, 70). The position is determined in the manner illustrated in Figure 2.14.

FIGURE 2.14   The diagram illustrates how the position of text is determined by the **drawString** method.

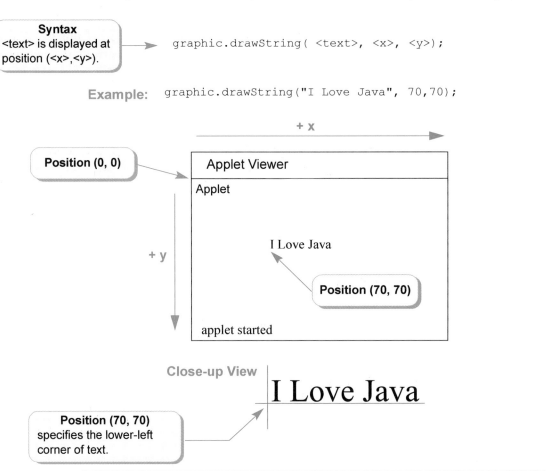

The second message

```
graphic.drawRect(50, 50, 100, 30);
```

displays a rectangle 100 pixels wide and 30 pixels high at the specified position (50, 50). The position is determined as illustrated in Figure 2.15.

A program template for simple Java applets is shown in Figure 2.16.

FIGURE 2.15   The diagram illustrates how the position of a rectangle is determined by the **drawRect** method.

Syntax
A rectangle <width> wide and <height> high is displayed at position (<x>,<y>).

```
graphic.drawRect( <x>, <y>, <width>, <height>);
```

Example:

```
graphic.drawRect(50,50,100,30);
```

Position (50, 50)

30

100

FIGURE 2.16   A program template for simple Java applets.

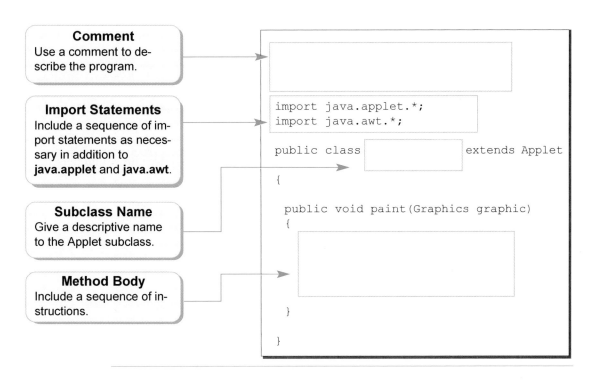

Comment
Use a comment to describe the program.

Import Statements
Include a sequence of import statements as necessary in addition to **java.applet** and **java.awt**.

Subclass Name
Give a descriptive name to the Applet subclass.

Method Body
Include a sequence of instructions.

```
import java.applet.*;
import java.awt.*;

public class              extends Applet
{

  public void paint(Graphics graphic)
  {



  }

}
```

Table 2.1 lists some of the available graphic-drawing methods.

TABLE 2.1   A partial list of drawing methods defined for the **Graphics** class.

Method	Meaning
drawLine(x1,y1,x2,y2)	Draws a line between (x1,y1) and (x2,y2).
drawRect(x,y,w,h)	Draws a rectangle with width w and height h at (x,y).
drawRoundRect(x,y,w,h,aw,ah)	Draws a rounded-corner rectangle with width w and height h at (x,y). Parameters aw and ah determine the angle for the rounded corners.
drawOval(x,y,w,h)	Draws an oval with width w and height h at (x,y).
drawString("text",x,y)	Draws the string text at (x,y).

The steps you take to run the applet are essentially the same as those you take to run the application. The only difference is the creation of an html file and the use of an applet viewer (or a web browser) to run the applet. The next diagram illustrates the steps you take to run the applet:

Running Program

applet viewer

Executing the applet MyFirstApplet displays a window called an *applet viewer* on the screen as shown in Figure 2.17. The AppletViewer class is responsible for displaying an applet viewer window and running the applet within the applet viewer window. The applet viewer provides a quick and easy way to run and test applets without using any web browser. When you use a web browser to run applets, then the browser assumes the role of the main class.

We mentioned that an applet is a mini-application that is intended to be executed within a web browser. A web browser reads a formatted document called a *Web document* or *Web page*. A web document written in *HyperText Markup*

HTML

Language (HTML) is called an *HTML document*, and a file that contains an HTML document is an *HTML file*. We use the suffix .html or .htm to name an HTML file. HTML is the standard language used for writing web documents

markup
elements

and consists of text and formatting tags called *markup elements* that specify the

FIGURE 2.17   Result of running the applet **MyFirstApplet**.

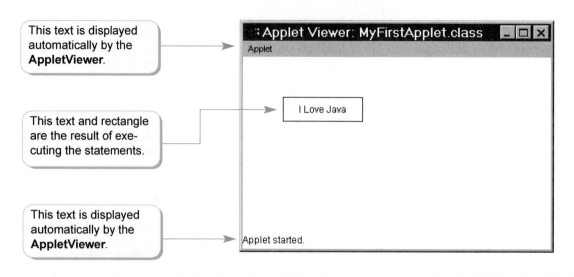

This text is displayed automatically by the **AppletViewer**.

This text and rectangle are the result of executing the statements.

This text is displayed automatically by the **AppletViewer**.

format for headers, paragraphs, hyperlinks, and other components of a document. One of the markup elements specifies the execution of an applet, giving the name of an applet to be executed, the area in the browser in which the applet is executed, and so forth.

We need an HTML file that refers to an applet's bytecode file to run the applet. We use the html file MyFirstApplet.html to run the MyFirstApplet applet.

MyFirstApplet.html

```
<HTML>
<BODY>
<APPLET CODE="MyFirstApplet.class" WIDTH=300 HEIGHT=190>
</APPLET>
</BODY>
</HTML>
```

The details of HTML are beyond the scope of this book. However, we will describe the portion necessary to run our sample applets. You can use this HTML file as a template to use with other applets by changing the APPLET tag (the third line in the MyFirstApplet.html file). This tag indicates the applet's bytecode filename and the size of the rectangular area reserved for the applet:

The bytecode file of an applet to execute. The name goes inside double quotes.

Width and height of an area in which the applet is running.

```
<APPLET CODE="MyFirstApplet.class" WIDTH=300 HEIGHT=190>
```

For example, to run MyFirstApplet in a smaller area, we can change the tag to

```
<APPLET CODE="MyFirstApplet.class" WIDTH=200 HEIGHT=100>
```

Although the AppletViewer class can read any web page, it processes only the APPLET tag and ignores other tags. So if you want to run an applet in a web page that processes all tags, you need to use a Java-aware web browser.[1] Figure 2.18 shows MyFirstApplet executed in a popular web browser, Netscape Navigator (version 3.0). Notice that Navigator is running on the Macintosh. The applet was written on the Windows 95 platform but executed in a browser on a different platform. We use the HTML file JavaBook.html that contains more tags (such as specifying the title Intro to Programming with Java and the background spiral notebook image).

Quick Check

1. How are an applet viewer and a web browser different?
2. Which class is the main class of an applet?
3. Which method of the Graphics class do you use to draw a rectangle?
4. What is the purpose of the APPLET tag in an HTML file?

---

1. Some web browsers do not understand the APPLET tag. You need Java-aware web browsers, such as Netscape Navigator 4.0 or later and MS Internet Explorer 3.0 or later that understand the APPLET tag to run Java applets.

FIGURE 2.18   Result of running the applet **MyFirstApplet** in Netscape Navigator.

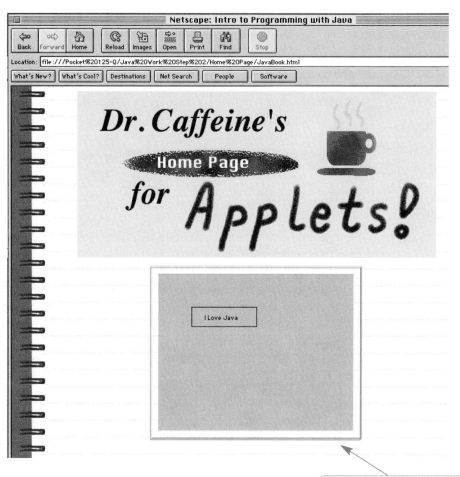

MyFirstApplet is set to run in this boxed area.

2.7   Exercises

1.   Identify all errors in the following program:

```
/*
    Program Exercise1

    A program with many errors.
//
import javabook.mainwindow;

class Exercise 1
{
    public void Main()
    {
        MainWindow mainWindow;
        mainWindow.show()
    }
}
```

2.   Identify all errors in the following program:

```
//
    Program Exercise2

    A program with many errors.
//

import    JavaBook.*;

class TWO
{
    public static void main method()
    {
        mainWindow    mainWindow;
        MessageBox    mybox1, mybox2;

        mainWindow = new MainWindow();
        messageBox.show();
        mybox2 = new MessageBox();
        mybox2.show;
    }
}
```

3.   Identify all of the errors in the following program:

```
/*
    Program Exercise3

    A program with many errors.
//
import java.applet;

class Exercise1 extends applet
{
    static public void paint()
    {
        graphic.drawString("Internet is fun and useful"));
    }
}
```

4. Describe the purpose of comments. Name the types of comments available. Can you include comment markers inside a comment?

5. What is the purpose of the import statement? Does a Java program always have to include an import statement?

6. Show the syntax for importing one class and all classes in a package.

7. Describe the class that must be included in any Java application.

8. What is a reserved word? List all the Java reserved words mentioned in this chapter.

9. Which of the following are invalid identifiers?

    a. R2D2   g. 3CPO
    b. Whatchamacallit   h. This is okay.
    c. HowAboutThis?   i. thisIsReallyOkay
    d. Java   j. aPPlet
    e. GoodChoice   k. Bad-Choice
    f. 12345   l. A12345

10. Describe the steps you take to run a Java application and the tools you use in each step. What are source files and bytecode files? What different types of errors are detected at each step?

11. Describe the difference between object declaration and object creation. Use a state-of-memory diagram to illustrate the difference.

12. Show a state-of-memory diagram after each of the following statements is executed:

```
MainWindow    window1;
MessageBox     mbox1, mbox2;

window1    = new MainWindow();
mbox1      = new MessageBox( window1 );
mbox2      = new MessageBox( window1 );
```

13. Show a state-of-memory diagram after each of the following statements is executed:

```
Person    person1, person2;

person1    = new Person();
person2    = new Person();
person2    = new Person();
```

14. Which of the following identifiers violate the naming convention for class names?

a. r2D2   e. CPO

b. whatchamacallit   f. ThisIsReallyOkay

c. Java   g. java

d. GoodName   h. aPPlet

15. Which of the following identifiers violate the naming convention for object names?

a. R2D2   e. 3CPO

b. isthisokay?   f. ThisIsReallyOkay

c. Java   g. java

d. goodName   h. anotherbadone

16. How are Java applets different from Java applications?

17. What is a web page? What tag is required to run an applet in a web browser?

18. Write a Java application that displays a MainWindow window 300 pixels wide and 200 pixels high with the title This is My first application. You

change the size of a window by sending the **setSize** message to the window. The syntax for **setSize** is

```
setSize( <width>, <height> )
```

19. In exercise 18, you used the **setSize** method to set the dimension of a Main-Window window. This method will let you set the size of a window, but not the location where this window appears on the screen. To position a window at a specified location, you use the **setLocation** method as in

```
//assume mainWindow is declared and created

mainWindow.setLocation( 50, 50 );
mainWindow.setVisible( true );
```

Through experimentation, determine how the two arguments in the **setLo**cation method affect the positioning of the window.

20. Write a Java application that displays two separate messages I Can Design and And I Can Program.

21. Write a Java application that displays a very long message. Try a message that is wider than the display of your computer screen and see what happens.

22. Write a Java applet that displays the text Hello in an applet viewer as illustrated below:

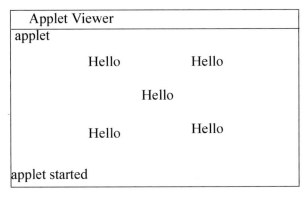

23. Write a Java applet that draws a house in an applet viewer. You might want to draw a house that is much more interesting than the one shown here. Use the methods listed in Table 2.1 as needed.

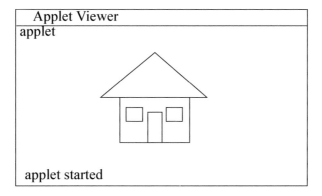

24. Add the moon and a tree to the house you drew in exercise 23.

25. If you know how to open an HTML file from a Web browser, run the Java applets from exercises 22 through 24 in a web browser.

26. Because today's computers are very fast, you will probably not notice any discernible difference on the screen between the code

```
MainWindow myWindow;
myWindow = new MainWindow( );
myWindow.setVisible( true );
```

and

```
MainWindow myWindow;
myWindow = new MainWindow( );
myWindow.setVisible( true  );
myWindow.setVisible( false );
myWindow.setVisible( true  );
```

One way to see the disappearance and reappearance of the window is to put a delay between the successive setVisible messages. To put a delay, you can use a Clock object from the javabook package. Here's a simple usage of the Clock class:

```
Clock myClock;
myClock = new Clock( );

//put statement X here
```

```
myClock.pause( 2 );          ←

//put statement Y here
```

> **Delay**
> The computer will pause for 2 seconds before executing statement Y.

The unit for the argument you pass in the pause message is seconds. If you want a half-second delay, for example, then you pass 0.5 as an argument. Using the Clock class, write a program that makes a MainWindow object appear, disappear, and appear again. The window remains visible for 5 seconds when it appears for the first time, and once it disappears, it won't reappear for 3 seconds.

27. At the Dr. Caffeine's website, you will find a Java package called galapagos (www.drcaffeine.com/packages). The galapagos package includes a Turtle class that is modeled after Seymour Papert's Logo. This Turtle has a pen, and when you move the Turtle, its pen will trace the movement. So by moving a Turtle object, you can draw many different kinds of geometrical shapes. For example, the following program commands a Turtle to draw a square:

```
import galapagos.*;

class Square
{
    public static void main( String[] arg )
    {
        Turtle turtle;
        turtle = new Turtle( );

        turtle.move( 50 );
        turtle.turn( 90 ); //make it turn 90 degrees
                           //counterclockwise
        turtle.move( 50 );
        turtle.turn( 90 );

        turtle.move( 50 );
        turtle.turn( 90 );

        turtle.move( 50 );
    }
}
```

Write a program to draw a triangle. Read the documentation and see if you can find a way to draw the square in a different color and line thickness.

28. Write another program to draw a star using a Turtle from exercise 27.

Numerical Data

OBJECTIVES

After you have read and studied this chapter, you should be able to

- Select proper types for numerical data.

- Write arithmetic expressions in Java.

- Evaluate arithmetic expressions using the precedence rules.

- Describe how the memory allocation works for objects and primitive data values.

- Write mathematical expressions using methods in the Math class.

- Write programs that input and output data using the InputBox and OutputBox classes from the javabook package.

- Apply the incremental development technique in writing programs.

- (Optional) Describe how the integers and real numbers are represented in memory.

Introduction

In writing computer programs, it is helpful for beginners to visualize three tasks: input, computation, and output. We view computer programs as getting input, performing computation on the input data, and outputting the results of the computations. For example, consider a metric converter program that accepts measurements in U.S. units (input), converts the measurements (computation), and displays their metric equivalents (output). The three tasks are not limited to numerical values, though. An input could be a mouse movement. A drawing program may accept mouse dragging (input), remember the points of mouse positions (computation), and draw lines connecting the points (output). Selecting a menu item is yet another form of input. For beginners, however, it is easiest to start writing programs that read numerical values as input and display the result of numerical computation as output.

In this chapter, we will study how to manipulate numerical data in computer programs. We also will introduce two classes—InputBox and OutputBox—from the javabook package. We use an InputBox object to get input data from the user and an OutputBox object to output data. Lastly, we will present a technique for writing programs called *incremental development*. With this technique we implement programs in small incremental steps, an approach indispensable in developing large programs. We will implement a sample program using the incremental development technique.

incremental
development

3.1   Variables

Suppose we want to compute the sum and difference of two numbers. Let's call the two numbers x and y. In mathematics, we say

$$x + y$$

and

$$x - y$$

To compute the sum and the difference of x and y in a program, we must first declare what kind of data will be assigned to them. After we assign values to them, we finally can compute their sum and difference.

Let's say x and y are integers. To declare that the type of data assigned to them is an integer, we write

```
int    x, y;
```

variable

When this declaration is made, memory locations to store data values for x and y are allocated. These memory locations are called *variables*, and x and y are the names we associate with the memory locations. Any valid identifier can be used as a variable name. After the declaration is made, we can assign only integers to x and y. We cannot, for example, assign real numbers to them.

A variable has three properties: a memory location to store the value, the type of data stored in the memory location, and the name used to refer to the memory location.

Although we must say "x and y are variable names" to be precise, we will use abbreviated forms "x and y are variables" or "x and y are integer variables" whenever appropriate.

The general syntax for declaring variables is

variable declaration
syntax

```
<data type>      <variables> ;
```

where <variables> is a sequence of identifiers separated by commas. Every variable you use in a program must be declared. We may have as many declarations as we wish. For example, we can declare x and y separately as

```
int    x;
int    y;
```

However, you cannot declare the same variable more than once; therefore, the second declaration below is invalid because y is declared twice:

```
int    x, y, z;
int    y;
```

six numerical
data types

There are six numerical data types in Java: byte, short, int, long, float, and double. The data types byte, short, int, and long are for integers, and the data types float and double are for real numbers. The data type names byte, short, and others are all reserved words. The difference among these six numerical data types is in the range of values they can represent, as shown in Table 3.1.

Chapter 3

TABLE 3.1   Java numerical data types and their precisions.

Data Type	Content	Default Value[†]	Minimum Value	Maximum Value
byte	Integer	0	−128	127
short	Integer	0	−32768	32767
int	Integer	0	−2147483648	2147483647
long	Integer	0	−9223372036854775808	9223372036854775807
float	Real	0.0	−3.40282347E+38[††]	3.40282347E+38
double	Real	0.0	−1.79769313486231570E+308	1.79769313486231570E+308

†. No default value is assigned to a local variable. A local variable is explained on page 162.
††. The character E indicates a number is expressed in scientific notation. This notation is explained on page 99.

A data type with a larger range of values is said to have a *higher precision*. For example, the data type double has a higher precision than the data type float. The trade-off for higher precision is memory space—to store a number with higher precision, you need more space. A variable of type short requires 2 bytes and a variable of type int requires 4 bytes, for example. If your program does not use many integers, then whether you declare them as short or int is really not that critical. The difference in memory usage is very small and not a deciding factor in the program design. The storage difference becomes significant only when your program uses thousands of integers. Therefore, we will almost always use the data type int for integers. We use long when we need to process very large integers that are outside the range of values int can represent. For real numbers, it is more common to use double. Although it requires more memory space than float, we prefer double because of its higher precision in representing real numbers. We will describe how the numbers are stored in memory in Section 3.8.

Here is an example of declaring variables of different data types:

```
int        i, j, k;
float      numberOne, numberTwo;
long       bigInteger;
double     bigNumber;
```

At the time a variable is declared, it also can be initialized. For example, we may initialize the integer variables count and height to 10 and 34 as

```
int count = 10, height = 34;
```

Chapter 3

> *In the same way that you can initialize variables at the time you declare them, you can declare and create an object at the same time. For example, the declaration*
>
> ```
> MainWindow mainWindow = new MainWindow();
> ```
>
> *is equivalent to*
>
> ```
> MainWindow mainWindow;
> mainWindow = new MainWindow();
> ```

Dr. Caffeine

assignment
statement

We assign a value to a variable using an *assignment statement*. To assign the value 234 to the variable named firstNumber, for example, we write

```
firstNumber = 234;
```

Be careful not to confuse mathematical equality and assignment. For example, the following are not valid Java code:

```
4 + 5 = x;
x + y = y + x;
```

The syntax for the assignment statement is

assignment
statement syntax

```
<variable> = <expression> ;
```

where <expression> is an arithmetic expression, and the value of <expression> is assigned to the <variable>. The following are sample assignment statements:

```
sum       = firstNumber + secondNumber;
solution  = x * x - 2 * x + 1;
average   = (x + y + z) / 3.0;
```

We will present a detailed discussion of arithmetic expressions in Section 3.2. One key point you need to remember about variables is

> **Before using a variable, you must first declare and assign a value to it.**

The diagram in Figure 3.1 illustrates the effect of variable declaration and assignment. Notice the similarity with this and memory allocation for object declaration and creation illustrated in Figure 2.4 on page 44. Figure 3.2 compares the two. What we have been calling object names are really variables. The only difference between a variable for numbers and a variable for objects is the contents in the memory locations. For numbers, a variable contains the numerical value itself, and for objects, a variable contains an address where the object is stored. We use an arrow in the diagram to indicate that the content is an address, not the value itself.

FIGURE 3.1   A diagram showing how two memory locations (variables) with names **firstNumber** and **secondNumber** are declared, and values are assigned to them.

State of Memory

after (A) is executed

(A)   `int firstNumber, secondNumber;`

```
firstNumber   = 234;
secondNumber = 87;
```

firstNumber [   ]

secondNumber [   ]

The variables **firstNumber** and **secondNumber** are declared and set in memory.

---

after (B) is executed

`int firstNumber, secondNumber;`

(B)
```
firstNumber   = 234;
secondNumber = 87;
```

firstNumber [234   ]

secondNumber [87   ]

Values are assigned to the variables **firstNumber** and **secondNumber**.

Figure 3.3 contrasts the effect of assigning the content of one variable to another variable for numerical data values and for objects. Because the content of a variable for objects is an address, assigning the content of a variable to another makes two variables that refer to the same object. Assignment does not create a

FIGURE 3.2   A difference between object declaration and numerical data declaration.

Numerical Data   ## Object

```
int number;
number = 237;
number = 35;
```

```
Customer customer;
customer = new Customer();
customer = new Customer();
```

number [   ]   customer [   ]

```
int number;
number = 237;
number = 35;
```

```
Customer customer;
customer = new Customer();
customer = new Customer();
```

number [237   ]

```
int number;
number = 237;
number = 35;
```

```
Customer customer;
customer = new Customer();
customer = new Customer();
```

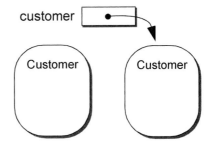

number [35   ]

FIGURE 3.3   An effect of assigning the content of one variable to another.

Numerical Data

```
int number1, number2;
number1 = 237;
number2 = number1;
```

number1 [   ]

number2 [   ]

Object

```
Customer profWu, drCafe;
profWu = new Customer();
drCafe = profWu;
```

profWu [   ]

drCafe [   ]

```
int number1, number2;
number1 = 237;
number2 = number1;
```

number1 [237   ]

number2 [   ]

```
Customer profWu, drCafe;
profWu = new Customer();
drCafe = profWu;
```

profWu [•   ] ⟶

drCafe [   ]

(Customer)

```
int number1, number2;
number1 = 237;
number2 = number1;
```

number1 [237   ]

number2 [237   ]

```
Customer profWu, drCafe;
profWu = new Customer();
drCafe = profWu;
```

profWu [•   ]

drCafe [•   ]

(Customer)

new object. Without executing the new command, no new object is created. You can view the situation where two variables refer to the same object as the object having two distinct names.

For numbers, the amount of memory space required is fixed. The values for data type int require 4 bytes, for example, and this won't change. However, with objects, the amount of memory space required is not constant. One instance of the Account class may require 120 bytes, while another instance of the same class may require 140 bytes, for example. The difference in space usage for the account objects would occur if we have to keep track of checks written against the accounts. If one account has 15 checks written and the second account has 25 checks written, then we need more memory space for the second account than the first account.

We use the new command to actually create an object. Remember that declaring an object only allocates the variable whose content will be an address. On the other hand, we don't "create" an integer because the space to store the value is already allocated at the time the integer variable is declared. Because the contents are addresses that refer to memory locations where the objects are actually stored, objects are called *reference data types*. In contrast, numerical data types are called *primitive data types*.

reference vs. primitive data types

Quick Check

1. Why are the following declarations all invalid?

```
int       a, b, a;
float     x, int;
float     w, int x;
bigNumber double;
```

2. Assuming the following declarations are executed in sequence, why are the second and third declarations invalid?

```
int       a, b;
int       a;
float     b;
```

3. Name six data types for numerical values.

4. Which of the following are valid assignment statements (assuming the variables are properly declared)?

```
x    =  12;
12   =  x;
```

Chapter 3

```
y + y  =   x;
y      =   x + 12;
```

5. Draw the state-of-memory diagram for the following code:

```
Account latteAcct, espressoAcct;

latteAcct    = new Account();
espressoAcct = new Account();
latteAcct    = espressoAcct;
```

3.2   Arithmetic Expressions

An expression involving numerical values such as

```
23 + 45
```

operator

is called an *arithmetic expression*, because it consists of arithmetic operators and operands. An *arithmetic operator*, such as + in the example, designates numerical computation. Table 3.2 summarizes the arithmetic operators available in Java.

TABLE 3.2   Arithmetic operators.

Operation	Java Operator	Example	Value (x=10, y=7, z =2.5)
Addition	+	x + y	17
Subtraction	−	x − y	3
Multiplication	*	x * y	70
Division	/	x / y	1
		x / z	4.0
Modulo division (remainder)	%	x % y	3

integer division

Notice how the division operator works in Java. When both numbers are integers, the result is an integer quotient. That is, any fractional part is truncated. Division between two integers is called *integer division*. When either or both numbers are float or double, the result is a real number. Here are some division examples:

Division Operation	Result
23 / 5	4
23 / 5.0	4.6
25.0 / 5.0	5.0

The modulo operator returns the remainder of a division. Although real numbers can be used with the modulo operator, the most common use of the modulo operator involves only integers. Here are some examples:

Modulo Operation	Result
23 % 5	3
23 % 25	23
16 % 2	0

operand

An *operand* in arithmetic expressions can be a constant, a variable, a method call, or another arithmetic expression, possibly surrounded by parentheses. Let's look at examples. In the expression

```
x + 4
```

we have one addition operator and two operands, a variable x and a constant 4.

binary operator

The addition operator is called a *binary operator* because it operates on two operands. All other arithmetic operators, except the minus, are also binary. The minus and plus operators can be both binary and unary. A unary operator operates on one operand as in

```
- x
```

In the expression

```
x + 3 * y
```

the addition operator acts on operands x and 3 * y. The right operand for the addition operator is itself an expression. Often a nested expression is called a *sub-*

subexpression

expression. The subexpression 3 * y has operands 3 and y. The following diagram illustrates this relationship:

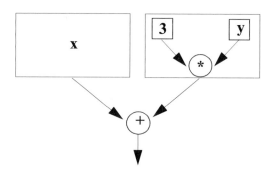

precedence
rules

When two or more operators are present in an expression, we determine the order of evaluation by following the *precedence rules.* For example, multiplication has a higher precedence than addition. Therefore, in the expression x + 3 * y, the multiplication operation is evaluated first, and the addition operation is evaluated next. Table 3.3 summarizes the precedence rules for arithmetic operators.

TABLE 3.3   Precedence rules for arithmetic operators and parentheses.

Order	Group	Operator	Rule
High	subexpression	( )	Subexpressions are evaluated first. If parentheses are nested, the innermost subexpression is evaluated first. If two or more pairs of parentheses are on the same level, then they are evaluated from left to right.
	unary operator	-, +	Unary minuses and pluses are evaluated second.
	multiplicative operator	*, /, %	Multiplicative operators are evaluated third. If two or more multiplicative operators are in an expression, then they are evaluated from left to right.
Low	additive operator	+, -	Additive operators are evaluated last. If two or more additive operators are in an expression, then they are evaluated from left to right.

The following example illustrates the precedence rules applied to a complex arithmetic expression:

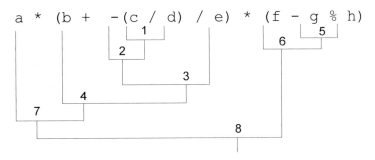

When an arithmetic expression consists of variables and constants of the same data type, then the result of the expression will be that data type also. For example, if the data type of a and b is int, then the result of the expression

```
a * b + 23
```

is also an int. When the data types of variables and constants in an arithmetic expression are of different data types, then a casting conversion will take place. A *casting conversion*, or *type casting*, is a process that converts a value of one data type to another data type. Two types of casting conversions in Java are *implicit* and *explicit*. An implicit conversion called *numeric promotion* is applied to the operands of an arithmetic operator. The promotion is based on the rules stated in Table 3.4. This conversion is called promotion because the operand is converted from a lower to a higher precision.

type casting

numeric
promotion

TABLE 3.4   Rules for arithmetic promotion.

Operator Type	Promotion Rule
Unary	**1.** If the operand is of type **byte** or **short**, then it is converted to **int**.
	2. Otherwise, the operand remains the same type.
Binary	**1.** If either operand is of type **double**, then the other operand is converted to **double**.
	2. Otherwise, if either operand is of type **float**, then the other operand is converted to **float**.
	3. Otherwise, if either operand is of type **long**, then the other operand is converted to **long**.
	4. Otherwise, both operands are converted to **int**.

Chapter 3

Instead of relying on implicit conversion, we can use explicit conversion to convert an operand from one data type to another. Explicit conversion is applied to an operand by using a *type cast operator*. For example, to convert the int variable x in the expression

type cast operator

```
x / 3
```

to float so the result will not be truncated, we apply the type cast operator (float) as

```
(float) x / 3
```

The syntax is

type casting syntax

```
( <data type> ) <expression>
```

The type cast operator is a unary operator and has a precedence higher than any binary operator. You must use parentheses to type cast a subexpression; for example, the expression

```
a + (double) (x + y * z)
```

will result in the subexpression x + y * z type casted to double.

Assuming the variable x is an int, then the assignment statement

```
x = 2 * (14343 / 2344);
```

will assign the integer result of the expression to the variable x. However, if the data type of x is other than int, then an implicit conversion will occur so the data type of the expression becomes the same as the data type of the variable. An *assignment conversion* is another implicit conversion that occurs when the variable and the value of an expression in an assignment statement are not of the same data type. An assignment conversion occurs only if the data type of the variable has a higher precision than the data type of the expression's value. For example,

assignment conversion

```
double number;
number = 25;
```

is valid, but

```
int number;
number = 234.56;
```

is not.

If we wish to assign a value to multiple variables, we can cascade the assignment operations as

```
x = y = 1;
```

which is equivalent to saying

```
y = 1;
x = 1;
```

The assignment symbol = is actually an operator and its precedence order is lower than any other operators. Assignment operators are evaluated right to left.

Quick Check

1. Evaluate the following expressions:

   ```
   a.  3 + 5 / 7
   b.  3 * 3 + 3 % 2
   c.  3 + 2 / 5 + -2 * 4
   d.  2 * (1 + -(3/4) / 2) * (2 - 6 % 3)
   ```

2. What is the data type of the result of the following expressions?

   ```
   a.  (3 + 5) / 7
   b.  (3 + 5) / (float) 7
   c.  (float) ( (3 + 5) / 7 )
   ```

3. Which of the following expressions is equivalent to $\dfrac{-b(c + 34)}{2a}$?

   ```
   a.  -b * (c + 34) /  2 * a
   b.  -b * (c + 34) / (2 * a)
   c.  -b *  c + 34  / (2 * a)
   ```

3.3   Constants

While running a program, different values may be assigned to a variable at different times (thus the name *variable*, since the values it contains can *vary*), but in some cases we do not want this to happen. In other words, we want to "lock" the assigned value so that no changes can take place. If we want a value to remain fixed, then we use a *constant*. A constant is declared in a manner similar to a variable but with the additional reserved word final. A constant must be assigned a value at the time of its declaration. Here's an example declaring four constants:

```
final double  PI = 3.14159;
final short   FARADAY_CONSTANT = 23060; // unit is cal/volt
final double  CM_PER_INCH = 2.54;
final int     MONTHS_IN_YEAR = 12;
```

constant

We use the standard Java convention to name a constant using only capital letters and underscores. Judicious use of constants makes programs more readable. You will be seeing many uses of constants later in the book, beginning with the sample program in this chapter.

named constant

The constant PI is called a *named* or *symbolic constant*. We refer to symbolic constants with identifiers such as PI and FARADAY_CONSTANT. The second type of constant is called a *literal constant*, and we refer to it using an actual value. For example, the following statements contain three literal constants:

literal constant

```
final double  PI    =  3.14159  ;
double area;
area = 2 * PI * 345.79 ;
```

Literal Constants

When we use the literal constant 2, the data type of the constant is set to int by default. Then how can we specify a literal constant of type long?[1] We append the constant with an I (a lowercase letter *L*) or L as

```
2L * PI * 345.79
```

---

1. In most cases, it is not significant to distinguish the two because of automatic type conversion; see Section 3.2.

How about the literal constant 345.79? Since the literal constant contains a decimal point, its data type can only be float or double. But which one? The answer is double. If a literal constant contains a decimal point, then it is of type double by default. To designate a literal constant of type float, we must append the letter f or F. For example:

```
2 * PI * 345.79F
```

To represent a double literal constant, we may optionally append a d or D. So, the following two constants are equivalent:

```
2 * PI * 345.79       is equivalent to    2 * PI * 345.79D
```

Since a numerical constant such as 345.79 represents a double *value, the following statements*

```
float number;
number = 345.79;
```

*for example, would result in a compilation error. The data types do not match, and the variable (*float*) has lower precision than the constant (*double*). To correct this error, we have to write the assignment statement as*

```
number = 345.79f;
```

or

```
number = (float) 345.79;
```

This is one of the common errors people make in writing Java programs, especially those with prior programming experience.

Dr. Caffeine

We also can express float and double literal constants in scientific notation

$$number \times 10^{exponent}$$

which in Java is expressed as

exponential
notation in Java

```
<number> E <exponent>
```

where <number> is a literal constant that may or may not contain a decimal point and <exponent> is a signed or unsigned integer. Lowercase e may be substituted for the exponent symbol E. The whole expression may be suffixed by f, F, d, or D. The <number> itself cannot be suffixed with symbols f, F, d, or D. Here are some examples:

```
12.40e+209
23E33
29.0098e-102
234e+5D
4.45e2
```

Here are some additional examples of constant declarations:

```
final double SPEED_OF_LIGHT = 3.0E+10D; // unit is cm/sec
final short  MAX_WGT_ALLOWED = 400;
```

3.4   The Math Class

Using only the arithmetic operators to express numerical computations is very limiting. Many computations require the use of mathematical functions. For example, to express the mathematical formula

$$\frac{1}{2}\sin\left(x - \frac{\pi}{\sqrt{y}}\right)$$

we need the trigonometric sine and square root functions. The Math class in the java.lang package contains class methods for commonly used mathematical functions. Table 3.5 is a partial list of class methods available in the Math class. The class also has two class constants PI and E for π and the natural number e, respectively. Using the Math class constant and methods, we can express the preceding formula as

```
(1.0 /2.0) * Math.sin( x - Math.PI / Math.sqrt(y) )
```

Notice how the class methods and class constants are referred to in the expression. The syntax is

```
<class name> . <method name> (  <arguments> )
```

or

```
<class name> . <class constant>
```

TABLE 3.5 **Math** class methods for commonly used mathematical functions.

Class Method	Argument Type	Result Type	Description	Example
abs(a)	int	int	Returns the absolute int value of **a**.	abs(10) → 10 abs(−5) → 5
	long	long	Returns the absolute long value of **a**.	
	float	float	Returns the absolute float value of **a**.	
acos(a)[†]	double	double	Returns the arc cosine of **a**.	acos(−1) → 3.14159
asin(a)[†]	double	double	Returns the arc sine of **a**.	asin(1) → 1.57079
atan(a)[†]	double	double	Returns the arc tangent of **a**.	atan(1) → 0.785398
ceil(a)	double	double	Returns the smallest whole number greater than or equal to **a**.	ceil(5.6)→ 6.0 ceil(5.0) → 5.0 ceil(−5.6) → −5.0
cos(a)[†]	double	double	Returns the trigono-metric cosine of **a**.	cos(π/2) → 0.0
exp(a)	double	double	Returns the natural number e (2.718...) raised to the power of **a**.	exp(2) → 7.389056099
floor(a)	double	double	Returns the largest whole number less than or equal to **a**.	floor(5.6) → 5.0 floor(5.0) → 5.0 floor(−5.6) → −6.0
log(a)	double	double	Returns the natural log-arithm (base e) of **a**.	log(2.7183) → 1.0
max(a, b)	int	int	Returns the larger of **a** and **b**.	max(10, 20) → 20
	long	long	Same as above.	
	float	float	Same as above.	
min(a, b)	int	int	Returns the smaller of **a** and **b**.	min(10, 20) → 10
	long	long	Same as above.	
	float	float	Same as above.	

Chapter 3

TABLE 3.5   **Math** class methods for commonly used mathematical functions. (Continued)

Class Method	Argument Type	Result Type	Description	Example
pow(a, b)	double	double	Returns the number **a** raised to the power of **b**.	pow(2.0, 3.0) → 8.0
random( )	<none>	double	Generates a random number greater than or equal to 0.0 and less than 1.0	Examples given in Chapter 6.
round(a)	float	int	Returns the int value of **a** rounded to the near-est whole number.	round(5.6) → 6 round(5.4) → 5 round(−5.6) → −6
	double	long	Returns the float value of **a** rounded to the nearest whole number.	
sin(a)†	double	double	Returns the trigono-metric sine of **a**.	sin(π/2) → 1.0
sqrt(a)	double	double	Returns the square root of **a**.	sqrt(9.0) → 3.0
tan(a)†	double	double	Returns the trigono-metric tangent of **a**.	tan(π/4) → 1.0

†. All trigonometric functions are computed in radians.

Quick Check

1.   What's wrong with the following?

```
a.  y = (1/2) * Math.sqrt( X ) ;

b.  y = sqrt(38.0);

c.  y = Math.exp(2, 3);

d.  y = math.sqrt( b*b - 4*a*c) / ( 2 * a );
```

2. If another programmer writes the following statements, do you suspect any misunderstanding on the part of this programmer? What will be the value of y?

```
a.  y = Math.sin( 360 ) ;
```

```
b.  y = Math.cos( 45 );
```

3.5 InputBox

We mentioned at the beginning of the chapter that computer programs include the three tasks of input, computation, and output. We explained how to implement numerical computation in Java using arithmetic expressions and assignment statements. We will now introduce two new dialog classes from the javabook package in this chapter: InputBox, which is used for input in this section, and OutputBox, which is used for output in the next section.

Like MessageBox, an InputBox object is a dialog, which means we must specify an owner frame when we create the object. As before, we will use main-Window as its owner. Here's how we declare and create an InputBox object:

InputBox declaration and creation

```
InputBox inputBox;
inputBox = new InputBox( mainWindow );
```

getInteger

To input an integer, we send the getInteger message to an InputBox object as

```
inputBox.getInteger( );
```

Executing the getInteger method will display the input dialog box shown in Figure 3.4.

FIGURE 3.4   The **InputBox** dialog after its method **getInteger** is executed.

Chapter 3

The getInteger method will only accept an integer. When the user enters a value other than an integer (e.g., a number with a decimal point or nondigit characters), an error message is displayed, as shown in Figure 3.5. Also, the input dialog box cannot be closed until a valid integer is entered.

FIGURE 3.5   The **InputBox** dialog after a noninteger value is entered by the user.

A better interface would include a meaningful prompt to inform the user what is expected. We can optionally pass text as a prompt. For example, executing the message

```
inputBox.getInteger("Enter your age:");
```

will result in the InputBox shown in Figure 3.6.

FIGURE 3.6   An **InputBox** object with a programmer-specified prompt.

getFloat
getDouble

To input real numbers, we use either the getFloat or the getDouble method. This method works just like getInteger. If we call the getFloat method, then the InputBox object will not close until the user enters a valid float number (a number with or without a decimal point). The getDouble method works in a similar way for the double number.

To use an input value in a program, we will save it to a variable first as in

```
int    birthYear;

birthYear = inputBox.getInteger("You were born in (eg 1980):");
```

The following code inputs the width and the length of a rectangle and computes the area:

```
float  width, length;
double area;

width  = inputBox.getFloat("Enter the width of a rectangle");
length = inputBox.getFloat("Enter the length of a rectangle");

area   = width * length;
```

Table 3.6 is a partial list of available InputBox methods.

TABLE 3.6   A partial list of **InputBox** methods.

CLASS:		InputBox
Method	**Argument**	**Description**
getDouble	\<none\> or text	Allows the user to enter a **double** number. The **Input-Box** dialog object will not close until the user enters a valid **double** number. If there is no argument, then the default prompt **Enter a Double** is displayed in the dialog. If a text value is passed as the argument, then it is used as a prompt in the dialog.
getFloat	\<none\> or text	Allows the user to enter a **float** number. The **Input-Box** dialog object will not close until the user enters a valid **float** number. If there is no argument, then the default prompt **Enter a Float** is displayed in the dialog. If a text value is passed as the argument, then it is used as a prompt in the dialog.
getInteger	\<none\> or text	Allows the user to enter an integer, a number without a decimal point. The **InputBox** dialog object will not close until the user enters a valid integer. If there is no argument, then the default prompt **Enter an Integer** is displayed in the dialog. If a text value is passed as the argument, then it is used as a prompt in the dialog.

Chapter 3

There is another class in the javabook package that handles the input routines. The SimpleInput class has the same functionality as the InputBox class, but works in a non-GUI environment. For more information on the SimpleInput class, please check Appendix A and our websites.

For input routines in a non-GUI environment (console input), the javabook *package includes* SimpleInput. *Information on* SimpleInput *can be found at our websites. A brief description is included in Appendix A.*

Quick Check

1. What is wrong with the following?

    ```
    final double x = 123.444;
    x = inputBox.getDouble( );
    ```

2. Which of the following code is valid?

    ```
    a.  double number;
        number = inputBox.getFloat(  );

    b.  float number;
        number = inputBox.getDouble( );
    ```

3.6   OutputBox

In this section, we will explain the third dialog class from the javabook package called OutputBox. We already know one dialog class that is used for output. To output a value, we can use a MessageBox object. We used a MessageBox object to display a text as in

```
messageBox.show("Java is fun");
```

We can use it to display an integer or real number also, as in

```
birthYear = inputBox.getInteger("You were born in (eg 1980):");
messageBox.show( birthYear );
```

> *In object-oriented programming, efficient and effective program development hinges on the appropriate use of classes. You must use a class for its intended purpose just as you use the most appropriate tool for a given task. When you want to build a deck, you would use a circular saw for cutting, but when you want to build a birdhouse, you would probably use a more precision-cutting jigsaw. A key to successful object-oriented programming is to learn how to select the most appropriate class for a given task. Later, you will learn how to design a new class if no suitable class is available.*

However, the purpose of MessageBox is to display a short message, such as an error or warning message. It is never intended to display the whole output of a program. For example, a single MessageBox is not capable of displaying more than one line of text, such as

```
You are born in 1980.
In the year 2020, you will be 40 years old.
```

An OutputBox object is intended for displaying such output that contains textual data (i.e., no drawings). Like the other dialogs MessageBox and Input-Box, we must specify the owner frame at the time we create an instance of Out-putBox. Here's how we declare and create an OutputBox object whose owner is a MainWindow object:

OutputBox declaration and creation

```
OutputBox outputBox;
outputBox = new OutputBox(mainWindow);
```

For the following examples, we assume the objects mainWindow, inputBox, and outputBox are properly created. We also assume that both mainWindow and outputBox are made visible by executing

```
mainWindow.show();
outputBox.show();
```

The method print displays an argument in an OutputBox object. For example, executing the code

```
outputBox.print("Hello, Dr. Caffeine.");
```

will result in the OutputBox object shown in Figure 3.7.

FIGURE 3.7   Result of executing **outputBox.print("Hello, Dr. Caffeine.")**.

```
OutputBox
Hello, Dr. Caffeine.
```

The print method will continue printing from the end of the currently displayed output. Executing the following statements after the preceding print message will result in the OutputBox object shown in Figure 3.8.

```
int x, y;
x = 123;
y = x + x;
outputBox.print(" x = ");
outputBox.print( x );
outputBox.print(" x + x = ");
outputBox.print( y );
outputBox.print(" THE END");
```

> Notice that we have a space here so there will be a blank space between the equal sign and the number in the output.

FIGURE 3.8   Result of sending five **print** messages to **outputBox** of Figure 3.7.

```
OutputBox
Hello, Dr. Caffeine. x = 123 x + x = 246 THE END
```

We can print an argument and skip to the next line so that subsequent output will start on the next line by sending printLine instead of print. The OutputBox object of Figure 3.9 will result if we use printLine instead of print in the preceding example; that is,

```
int x, y;
x = 123;
y = x + x;
outputBox.printLine("Hello, Dr. Caffeine.");
outputBox.print(" x = ");          ←——   print here,
outputBox.printLine( x );                  not printLine.
outputBox.print(" x + x = ");  ←——
outputBox.printLine( y );
outputBox.printLine(" THE END");
```

FIGURE 3.9   Result of sending four **printLine** messages to **outputBox**.

```
OutputBox
Hello, Dr. Caffeine.
 x = 123
 x + x = 246
 THE END
```

You also can print a specified number of blank lines with the skipLine message. For example:

```
outputBox.printLine("one");
outputBox.skipLine(2);
outputBox.printLine("two");
```

will leave two blank lines between the output lines displaying one and two. Notice that if you execute

```
outputBox.print("one");
outputBox.skipLine(2);
outputBox.printLine("two");
```

there will be only one blank line in the output.

Now suppose we want to let the user enter his/her age and display

```
You are <age> years old.
```

where <age> is replaced by the actual value entered by the user. Instead of executing

```
int age;
age = inputBox.getInteger();
outputBox.print("You are ");
outputBox.print( age );
outputBox.print(" years old.");
```

we can execute

```
int age;
age = inputBox.getInteger();
outputBox.print("You are " + age + " years old.");
```

In Java and many other programming languages, the same symbols are sometimes used for different purposes. The two plus symbols that appear in the show message are not arithmetic additions, but concatenation of values. The variable age contains an integer and this integer value is concatenated with the text "You are " and " years old" to its left and right. Notice the blank spaces after *are* and before *years*. If you don't put in these blank spaces, you would see an output like

```
You are20years old.
```

instead of

```
You are 20 years old.
```

the + symbol means addition or concatenation

operator overloading

The plus symbol in Java can signify either an arithmetic addition or a concatenation of values. A symbol that is used to represent more than one operation is called an *overloaded operator*. When the Java compiler encounters an overloaded operator, how does it know which operation the symbol represents? The Java compiler determines the meaning of a symbol by its context. If the left and the right operand of the plus symbol are numerical values, then the compiler will treat the symbol as addition. Otherwise, it will treat the symbol as concatenation. The plus symbol operator is evaluated from left to right, and the result of concatenation is a text, so the code

```
x = 1;
y = 2;
outputBox.print( "test" + x + y );
```

will result in the output

test12

while the code

```
outputBox.print( x + y + "test" );
```

will result in the output

3test

You can store the text displayed in an OutputBox object to a file by specifying the filename as an argument to the saveToFile message. For example, to save the contents to a file called prog1out.txt, you execute

saving output to a file

```
outputBox.saveToFile( "prog1out.txt" );
```

You can pass any valid filename, surrounded by double quotes, as an argument to the method. If the designated file already exists, then its current contents will be erased with the contents of outputBox. If you want to keep the current contents of the file and add the contents of outputBox to the end of the file, you use the appendToFile method

```
outputBox.appendToFile( "prog1out.txt" );
```

Once the text data are stored in the file, you can open the file using any text editor and print them. This is one way for you to get a hardcopy of the program output so you can submit it as a part of the program assignment. The second way to get a hardcopy is by taking a screen capture. (Note: Please consult our website or your instructor for more information on how to take a screen capture.)

Chapter 3

Table 3.7 is a partial list of OutputBox methods.

TABLE 3.7   A partial list of **OutputBox** methods.

CLASS:	OutputBox	
Method	**Argument**	**Description**
print	number or text	Prints out the number or text passed as an argument in the dialog. Printing will continue from the end of currently displayed output.
printLine	number or text	Same as the **print** method, but the line is skipped after the output so the next output will continue from the next line.
skipLine	integer	Skips N lines where N is an integer passed as an argument.
saveToFile	filename	Saves the contents of an **OutputBox** to a file whose name is passed as an argument. If the designated file already exists, then the current contents of the file are erased and replaced by the contents of the **OutputBox**.
appendToFile	filename	Appends the contents of an **OutputBox** to a file whose name is passed as an argument. If the designated file does not exist, then this method works like the **saveToFile** method.

Quick Check

1.   What's wrong with the following?

```
a.  int age = 10;
    outputBox.show( age );

b.  int age = 20;
    outputBox.print( "Your age is age" );
```

2.   Will the following code work?

```
age = 20;
messageBox.show( "Your age is " + age );
```

3.   Write a code (not a full program) to input the year of birth and output

```
You are born in 1980.
In the year 2120, you will be 140 years old.
```

3.7   Sample Program: Loan Calculator

In this section, we will develop a simple loan calculator program. We will develop this program using an incremental development technique, which will develop the program in small incremental steps. We start out with a barebones program and gradually build up the program by adding more and more code to it. At each incremental step, we design, code, and test the program before moving on to the next step. This methodical development of a program allows us to focus our attention on a single task at each step, and this reduces the chance of introducing errors into the program.

Problem Statement

Next time you buy a new TV or a stereo, watch out for those "0% down, 0% interest till next July" deals. Read the fine print, and you'll notice that if you don't make the full payment by the end of a certain date, a hefty interest will start accruing. You may be better off to get an ordinary loan from the beginning with a cheaper interest rate. What matters most is the total payment (loan amount + total interest) you'll have to make. To compare different loan deals, let's develop a loan calculator. Here's the problem statement:

> *Write a loan calculator program that computes both monthly and total payments for a given loan amount, annual interest rate, and loan period.*

Overall Plan

Our first task is to map out the overall plan for development. We will identify classes necessary for the program and the steps we will follow to implement the program. We begin with the outline of program logic. For a simple program such as this one, it is kind of obvious, but to practice the incremental development, let's put down the outline of program flow explicitly. We can express the program flow as having three tasks:

program tasks

1.   Get three input values: loanAmount, interestRate, and loanPeriod.
2.   Compute the monthly and total payments.
3.   Output the results.

Having identified the three major tasks of the program, we will now identify the classes we can use to implement the three tasks. First, we need an object to handle the input of three values. At this point, we have only learned about the InputBox class, so we will use it here. Second, we need an object to display the monthly and total payments. We can use either MessageBox or OutputBox. Since a MessageBox object is capable of only displaying one line of text, we will use an OutputBox object so we can display both results along with the input values for a better output. Finally, we need to consider how we are going to compute the monthly and total payments. There are no objects in standard packages or javabook that will do the computation, so we have to write our own code to do the computation.

The formula for computing the monthly payment can be found in any mathematics book that covers geometric sequences. Its formula is

$$\text{Monthly Payment} = \frac{L \times R}{\left[1 - \left(\frac{1}{1 + R} \right)^N \right]}$$

where L is the loan amount, R is the monthly interest rate, and N is the number of payments. The monthly rate R is expressed in a fractional value, e.g., 0.01 for 1 percent monthly rate. Once the monthly payment is derived, the total payment can be determined by multiplying the monthly payment and the number of months the payment is made. Since the formula includes exponentiation, we will have to use the pow method of the Math class.

Finally, we need a top-level window for the application, so we will use the only top-level window we have learned so far—a MainWindow object. We will use these objects from the main class, which we will call LoanCalculator. Let's summarize these in a design document:

program classes

Design Document:	LoanCalculator
Class	**Purpose**
LoanCalculator	The main class of the program.
MainWindow	The main frame window of the program. The title is set to Loan Calculator. This class is from javabook.
InputBox	An InputBox object is used to get three input values: loan amount, annual interest rate, and loan period. This class is from javabook.
OutputBox	An OutputBox object is used to display the input values and two computed results: monthly payment and total payment. This class is from javabook.
Math	The pow method is used to evaluate exponentiation in the formula for computing the monthly payment. This class is from java.lang. Note: You don't have to import java.lang. The classes in java.lang are available to a program without importing.

The object diagram of the program based on the classes listed in the design document is shown in Figure 3.10. Keep in mind that this is only a preliminary design. Although we are not going to see any changes made to this design document because this sample application is very simple, changes to the design document are expected as the programs we develop become larger and more complex. The preliminary document is really a working document that we will modify and expand as we progress through the development steps.

FIGURE 3.10   The object diagram for the program **LoanCalculator**.

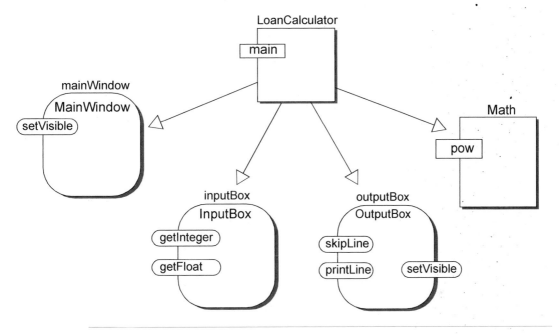

Before we can actually start our development, we must sketch the steps we will follow to implement the program. There are more than one possible sequence of steps to implement a program, and the number of possible sequences will increase as the program becomes more complex. For this program, we will implement the program in the following four steps:

development steps

1. Start with a program skeleton. In this step, we write a program skeleton that includes only object/variable declaration and object creation.

2. Add code to accept three input values.

3. Add code to output the results.

4. Add code to compute the monthly and total payments.

Notice how the four steps are defined. The first step is used to verify that the objects we need to use in the program are declared and created properly. The remaining three steps deal with the input, output, and computation aspects of the program.

The first step is almost the same for all programs. For the last three steps, any order is feasible. So why did we choose this particular order? The main reason is our desire to defer the most difficult task till the end. It's possible, but if we implement the computation part in the second incremental step, then we need to code some temporary output routines to verify that the computation is done correctly. However, if we implement the real output routines before implementing the computation routines, then there is no need for us to worry about temporary output routines. As for Step 2 and Step 3, their relative order does not matter much. We simply chose to implement the input routine before the output routine because input comes before output in the program.

Step 1 Development: Program Skeleton

Step 1 Design The design aspect of Step 1 is almost always trivial, especially for the sample programs from early chapters. All we need to do is to design the skeleton for the main class of the program.

Step 1 Code We begin with a program skeleton. Here's the skeleton:

```
/*
    Program LoanCalculator (Step 1)

    A program to compute the monthly and total payments for a given loan
    amount, annual interest rate, and number of years.

    Input:      loan amount
                annual interest rate
                loan period - number of years

    Compute:    monthly payment
                total payment
*/

import javabook.*;

class LoanCalculator
{
    public static void main (String[] args)
    {
        MainWindow   mainWindow = new MainWindow("Program LoanCalculator");
        InputBox     inputBox   = new InputBox(mainWindow);
        OutputBox    outputBox  = new OutputBox(mainWindow);

        mainWindow.setVisible( true );
        outputBox.setVisible( true );
    }
}
```

No **import** statement is necessary for the **java.lang** package. It is available to every program by default.

Step 1 Test

The skeleton program may seem so trivial and not so useful, but it does serve a very useful purpose. Successful execution of this skeleton verifies that the program setup is okay, the necessary packages are imported, and the objects are declared correctly. After the Step 1 program is compiled and executed correctly, we move on to Step 2.

Step 2 Development: Accept Input Values

Step 2 Design

The next task is to determine how we will accept the input values. We will use the InputBox class we learned in this chapter. A single InputBox object is used to accept three input values: loan amount, annual interest rate, and loan period. The problem statement does not specify the exact format of input, so we will decide that now. Based on how people normally refer to loans, the input values will be accepted in the following format:

Input	Format	Data Type
Loan amount	In dollars and cents (e.g., 15000.00)	float
Annual interest rate	In percent (e.g., 12.5)	float
Loan period	In years (e.g., 30)	int

Notice that we need to convert the annual interest rate to the monthly interest rate and the input value loan period to the number of monthly payments to use the given formula. In this case, the conversion is very simple, but even if the conversion routines were more complicated, we must do the conversion. It is not acceptable to ask users to enter an input value that is unnatural to them. For example, people do not think of interest rates in fractional values such as 0.07. They think of interest in terms of percentages such as 7%. Computer programs work for humans, not the other way around. Programs we develop should not support an interface that is difficult and awkward for humans to use.

When the user inputs an invalid value, for example, a negative loan amount, the program should respond accordingly, such as by printing an error message. We do not possess enough skills to implement such a robust program yet, so we will make the following assumptions: (1) the input values are nonnegative and (2) the loan period is a whole number.

One important objective of this step is to verify that the input values are read in correctly by the program. To verify this, we will use an OutputBox to print out the values accepted by the InputBox object. This method of printing out echo printing the values just entered is called *echo printing*. Since we are going to use an OutputBox in the final program, we will use it for echo printing in this step. In the next chatper, we will explain another technique for echo printing that uses an object from a standard Java package.

Chapter 3

Step 2 Code   Here's our Step 2 program with the added portion surrounded by a rectangle:

```
/*
    Program LoanCalculator (Step 2)

    A program to compute the monthly and total payments for a given loan
    amount, annual interest rate, and number of years.

    Input:     loan amount
               annual interest rate
               loan period - number of years

    Compute:   monthly payment
               total payment
*/

import javabook.*;

class LoanCalculator
{
    public static void main (String[] args)
    {
        MainWindow mainWindow   = new MainWindow("Program LoanCalculator");
        InputBox   inputBox     = new InputBox(mainWindow);
        OutputBox outputBox     = new OutputBox(mainWindow);

        mainWindow.setVisible( true );
        outputBox.setVisible( true );
```

```
        float loanAmount, annualInterestRate;
        int   loanPeriod;

        //get input
        loanAmount    = inputBox.getFloat("Loan Amount (Dollars&Cents):");
        annualInterestRate

                  = inputBox.getFloat("Annual Interest Rate (e.g. 9.5):");
        loanPeriod    = inputBox.getInteger("Loan Period - # of years:");

        //echo print the input values
        outputBox.printLine("Loan Amount:        $" + loanAmount);
        outputBox.printLine("Annual Interest Rate: " + annualInterestRate
                                                        + "%");
        outputBox.printLine("Loan Period (years):    " + loanPeriod);
```

```
    }
}
```

Step 2 Test   To verify the input routine is working correctly, we run the program multiple times and enter different sets of data. We enter invalid data and make sure the InputBox object accepts only the values of the correct data type. We make sure the values are displayed in the outputBox as entered.

Step 3 Development: Output Values

Step 3 Design

The third step is to add code to display the output values. We will use the OutputBox class we learned in this chapter for displaying output values. We need to display the result in a layout that is meaningful and easy to read. Just displaying numbers such as the following is totally unacceptable.

```
132.151  15858.1
```

We must label the output values so the user can tell what the numbers represent. In addition, we must display the input values with the computed result so it will not be meaningless. Imagine the user did many different loan calculations and saved the results. When he refers back to the loan figures some time later, which one of the two shown in Figure 3.11 do you think is more meaningful to him?

FIGURE 3.11   Two different display formats: One with input values displayed, and the other with only the computed values displayed.

The output format of this program will be

```
For
Loan Amount:            $ <amount>
Annual Interest Rate:     <annual interest rate> %
Loan Period (years):      <year>

Monthly payment is $ <monthly payment>
  TOTAL payment is $ <total payment>
```

Chapter 3

with \<amount\>, \<annual interest rate\>, and others replaced by the actual figures.

Since the computations for the monthly and the total payments are not yet implemented, we will use the following dummy assignment statements:

```
monthlyPayment   = 135.15;
totalPayment     = 15858.10;
```

We will replace these statements with the real ones in the next step.

Step 3 Code   Here's our Step 3 program:

```
/*
    Program LoanCalculator (Step 3)

    A program to compute the monthly and total payments for a given loan
    amount, annual interest rate, and number of years.

    Input:      loan amount
                annual interest rate
                loan period - number of years

    Compute:    monthly payment
                total payment
*/

import javabook.*;

class LoanCalculator
{
    public static void main (String[] args)
    {
        MainWindow mainWindow   = new MainWindow("Program LoanCalculator");
        InputBox   inputBox     = new InputBox(mainWindow);
        OutputBox outputBox     = new OutputBox(mainWindow);

        mainWindow.setVisible( true );
        outputBox.setVisible( true);

        float  loanAmount, annualInterestRate;
        int    loanPeriod;

        double monthlyPayment,
               totalPayment;

        //describe the program
        outputBox.printLine("This program computes the monthly and total");
        outputBox.printLine("payments for a given loan amount, annual ");
        outputBox.printLine("interest rate, and loan period.");
        outputBox.printLine("Loan Amount in dollars and cents, e.g. 12350.50");
        outputBox.printLine("Annual interest rate in percentage, e.g. 12.75");
        outputBox.printLine("Loan period in number of years, e.g. 15");
        outputBox.skipLine(2);
```

```
         //get input
         loanAmount    = inputBox.getFloat("Loan Amount (Dollars&Cents):");
         annualInterestRate
                    = inputBox.getFloat("Annual Interest Rate (e.g. 9.5):");
         loanPeriod    = inputBox.getInteger("Loan Period - # of years:");
```

```
         //compute the monthly payment
         monthlyPayment   = 132.15;     //Temporary code
         totalPayment     = 15858.10 ;  //Temporary code

         //display the result
         outputBox.printLine("For");
         outputBox.printLine("Loan Amount:          $" + loanAmount);
         outputBox.printLine("Annual Interest Rate:   " + annualInterestRate
                                                              + "%");

         outputBox.printLine("Loan Period (years):   " + loanPeriod);
         outputBox.skipLine(1);

         outputBox.printLine("Monthly payment is $ " + monthlyPayment);
         outputBox.printLine("  TOTAL payment is $ "   + totalPayment);
```

```
      }
   }
```

Step 3 Test   To verify the output routine is working correctly, we run the program and verify the layout. Most likely, we have to run the program several times to fine-tune the arguments for the printLine methods until we get the layout that looks clean and nice on the screen.

Step 4 Development: Compute Loan Amount

Step 4 Design   To verify the input routine is working correctly, we run the program multiple times and enter different sets of data. We enter invalid data and make sure the InputBox object accepts only the values of the correct data type. We make sure the values are displayed in the outputBox as entered. We are now ready to complete the program by implementing the formula derived in the design phase. The formula requires the monthly interest rate and the number of monthly payments. The input values to the program, however, are the annual interest rate and the loan period in number of years. So we need to convert the annual interest rate to a monthly interest rate and the loan period to the number of monthly payments. The two input values are converted as

```
monthlyInterestRate = annualInterestRate / 100.0 / MONTHS_IN_YEAR;

numberOfPayments    = loanPeriod  * MONTHS_IN_YEAR;
```

where MONTHS_IN_YEAR is a symbolic constant with value 12. Notice that we need to divide the input annual interest rate by 100 first because the formula for loan computation requires that the interest rate is a fractional value, for example, 0.01, but the input annual interest rate is entered as a percentage point, for example, 12.0. Please read exercise 23 on page 137 for information on how the monthly interest rate is derived from a given annual interest rate.

The formula for computing the monthly and total payments can be expressed as

```
monthlyPayment = (loanAmount * monthlyInterestRate)
                 /
                 (1 - Math.pow( 1/(1 + monthlyInterestRate),
                                numberOfPayments) );

totalPayment = monthlyPayment * numberOfPayments;
```

Let's put in the necessary code for the computations and complete the program. Here's our final program:

Step 4 Code

```
/*
    Program LoanCalculator

    A program to compute the monthly and total payments for a given loan
    amount, annual interest rate, and number of years.

    Input:     loan amount
               annual interest rate
               loan period - number of years

    Compute:   monthly payment
               total payment
*/

import javabook.*;

class LoanCalculator
{

    public static void main (String[] args)
    {

        final int MONTHS_IN_YEAR = 12;

        MainWindow mainWindow  = new MainWindow("Program LoanCalculator");
        InputBox   inputBox    = new InputBox(mainWindow);
        OutputBox  outputBox   = new OutputBox(mainWindow);

        mainWindow.setVisible( true );
        outputBox.setVisible( true );
```

```
        float  loanAmount, annualInterestRate;
        int    loanPeriod;

        double monthlyPayment,
               totalPayment;
```

```
        double monthlyInterestRate;

        int    numberOfPayments;
```

```
        //describe the program
        outputBox.printLine("This program computes the monthly and total");
        outputBox.printLine("payments for a given loan amount, annual ");
        outputBox.printLine("interest rate, and loan period.");
        outputBox.printLine("Loan Amount in dollars and cents, e.g. 12350.50");
        outputBox.printLine("Annual interest rate in percentage, e.g. 12.75");
        outputBox.printLine("Loan period in number of years, e.g. 15");
        outputBox.skipLine(2);

        //get input
        loanAmount    = inputBox.getFloat("Loan Amount (Dollars&Cents):");
        annualInterestRate
                  = inputBox.getFloat("Annual Interest Rate (e.g. 9.5):");
        loanPeriod    = inputBox.getInteger("Loan Period - # of years:");

        //compute the monthly payment
```

```
        monthlyInterestRate = annualInterestRate / 100.0 / MONTHS_IN_YEAR;

        numberOfPayments    = loanPeriod    * MONTHS_IN_YEAR;

        monthlyPayment = (loanAmount * monthlyInterestRate)
                         /
                         (1 - Math.pow(1/(1 + monthlyInterestRate),
                                   numberOfPayments ) );

        totalPayment   = monthlyPayment * numberOfPayments;
```

```
        //display the result
        outputBox.printLine("For");
        outputBox.printLine("Loan Amount:              $" + loanAmount);
        outputBox.printLine("Annual Interest Rate:     " + annualInterestRate
                                                         + "%");
        outputBox.printLine("Loan Period (years):   " + loanPeriod);
        outputBox.skipLine(1);

        outputBox.printLine("Monthly payment is $ " + monthlyPayment);
        outputBox.printLine("  TOTAL payment is $ "   + totalPayment);
    }
}
```

Chapter 3

Step 4 Test   After the program is coded, we need to run the program through a number of tests. Since we made the assumption that the input values must be valid, we will only test the program for valid input values. If we don't make that assumption, then we need to test that the program will respond correctly when invalid values are entered. We will perform such testing beginning in Chapter 6. To check that this program produces correct results, we can run the program with the following input values. The right two columns show the correct results. Try other input values as well.

Input			Output	
Loan Amount	Annual Interest Rate	Loan Period (in years)	Monthly Payment	Total Payment
10000	10	10	132.151	15858.1
15000	7	15	134.824	24268.4
10000	12	10	143.471	17216.5

Ms. Latte: *I don't like the output of the program* LoanCalculator. *The output values have varying number of decimal places. I want to show only two decimal places for the monthly and total payments. Isn't there a way to do that?*

Dr. Caffeine: *Yes, of course. You can format a* double *value X to two decimal places by the expression*

```
Math.round(X * 100) / 100.0
```

Can you tell how it works? By the way, this solution is not perfect. It will display two decimal places only if the second decimal place (i.e., the digit at the 1/100th position) is nonzero. You will learn more about output formatting in Chapter 7.

3.8   Numerical Representation (Optional)

In this section we explain how integers and real numbers are stored in memory. Although computer manufacturers have used various formats for storing numerical values, today's standard is to use the *twos-complement* format for storing integers and the *floating-point* format for real numbers. We describe these formats in this section.

twos-complement

An integer can occupy 1, 2, 4, or 8 bytes depending on which data type (i.e., byte, short, int, or long) is declared. To make the examples easy to follow, we will use 1 byte (= 8 bits) to explain twos-complement form. The same principle applies to 2, 4, and 8 bytes. (They just utilize more bits.)

The following table shows the first five and the last four of the 256 positive binary numbers using 8 bits. The right column lists their decimal equivalents.

8-Bit Binary Number	Decimal Equivalent
00000000	0
00000001	1
00000010	2
00000011	3
00000100	4
. . .	
11111100	252
11111101	253
11111110	254
11111111	255

sign bit

Using 8 bits, we can represent positive integers from 0 to 255. Now let's see the possible range of negative and positive numbers that we can represent using 8 bits. We can designate the leftmost bit as a *sign bit*: 0 means positive and 1 means negative. Using this scheme, we can represent integers from −127 to +127 as shown in the following table:

8-Bit Binary Number (with a sign bit)	Decimal Equivalent
0 0000000	+0
0 0000001	+1
0 0000010	+2
. . .	
0 1111111	+127
1 0000000	−0
1 0000001	−1
. . .	
1 1111110	−126
1 1111111	−127

Notice that zero has two distinct representations (+0 = 00000000 and −0 = 10000000), which adds complexity in hardware design. Twos-complement format avoids this problem of duplicate representations for zero. In twos-complement format all positive numbers have zero in their left-most bit. The representation of a negative number is derived by first inverting all the bits (changing 1s to 0s and 0s to 1s) in the representation of the positive number and then adding 1. The following diagram illustrates the process:

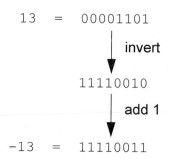

```
13   =   00001101
                      invert
         11110010
                      add 1
-13  =   11110011
```

The following table shows the decimal equivalents of 8-bit binary numbers using twos-complement representation. Notice that zero has only one representation.

8-Bit Binary Number (twos-complement)	Decimal Equivalent
00000000	+0
00000001	+1
00000010	+2
. . .	
01111111	+127
10000000	−128
10000001	−127
. . .	
11111110	−2
11111111	−1

Now let's see how real numbers are stored in memory in floating-point format. We will present only the basic ideas of storing real numbers in computer memory here. We will omit the precise details of the IEEE (Institute of Electronics and Electrical Engineers) Standard 754 that Java uses to store real numbers.

Real numbers are represented in the computer using scientific notation. In base 10 scientific notation, a real number is expressed as

$$A \times 10^N$$

where A is a real number and N an integral exponent. For example, the mass of a hydrogen atom (in grams) is expressed in decimal scientific notation as 1.67339×10^{-24}, which is equal to 0.00000000000000000000000167339.

We use base 2 scientific notation to store real numbers in computer memory. Base 2 scientific notation represents a real number as

$$A \times 2^N$$

The float and double data types use 32 bits and 64 bits, respectively, with the number A and exponent N stored as

The value A is a *normalized fraction*, where the fraction begins with a binary point, followed by a 1 bit, and the rest of the fraction. (Note: A decimal number has a decimal point; a binary number has a binary point.) The following numbers are sample normalized and unnormalized binary fractions:

normalized
fraction

Normalized	Unnormalized
.1010100	1.100111
.100011	.0000000001
.101110011	.0001010110

Since a normalized number always start with a 1, this bit does not actually have to be stored. The following diagram illustrates how the A value is stored.

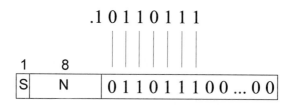

excess format

The sign bit S indicates the sign of a number, so A is stored in memory as an unsigned number. The integral exponent N can be negative or positive. Instead of using twos-complement for storing N, we use a format called *excess format*. The 8-bit exponent uses the excess-127 format, and the 11-bit exponent uses the excess-1023 format. We will explain the excess-127 format here. The excess-1023 works similarly. With the excess-127 format, the actual exponent is computed as

$$N - 127$$

Therefore, the number 127 represents an exponent of zero. Numbers less than 127 represent negative exponents, and numbers greater than 127 represent positive exponents. The following diagram illustrates that the number 125 in the exponent field represents $2^{125-127} = 2^{-2}$.

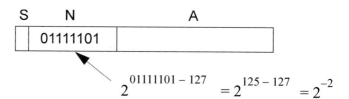

3.9   Exercises

1.   Suppose we have the following declarations:

```
int i = 3, j = 4, k = 5;
float x = 34.5f, y = 12.25f;
```

Determine the value for each of the following expressions or explain why it is not a valid expression.

```
a. (x + 1.5) / (250.0 * (i/j))      f. Math.exp(3, 2)
b. x + 1.5 / 250.0 * i / j          g. y % x
c. -x * -y * (i + j) / k            h. Math.pow(3, 2)
d. (i / 5) * y                      i. (int)y % k
e.  Math.min(i, Math.min(j,k))      j. i / 5 * y
```

2. Suppose we have the following declarations:

```
int m, n, i = 3, j = 4, k = 5;
float v, w, x = 34.5f, y = 12.25f;
```

Determine the value assigned to the variable in each of the following as-signment statements or explain why it is not a valid assignment.

```
a. w = Math.pow(3,Math.pow(i,j)); f. m = n + i * j;
b. v = x / i;                      g. n = k /(j * i) * x + y;
c. w = Math.ceil(y) % k;           h. i = i + 1;
d. n = (int) x / y * i / 2;        i. w = float(x + i);
e. x = Math.sqrt(i*i - 4*j*k);     j. x = x / i / y / j;
```

3. Suppose we have the following declarations:

```
int    i, j;
float  x, y;
double u, v;
```

Which of the following assignments are valid?

```
a. i = x;
b. x = u + y;
c. x = 23.4 + j * y;
d. v = (int) x;
e. y = j / i * x;
```

4. Write Java expressions to compute the following:

   a. The square root of $B^2 + 4AC$ (A and C are distinct variables).

   b. The square root of $X + 4Y^3$.

   c. The cube root of the product of X and Y.

   d. The area πR^2 of a circle.

   e. a sin C / sin A.

5.   Determine the output of the following program without running it:

```
/*
    Program TestOutputBox

*/

import javabook.*;

class TestOutputBox
{
    public static void main (String args[])
    {
        MainWindow mainWindow;
        OutputBox outputBox;

        mainWindow = new MainWindow("Program TestOutputBox");
        outputBox = new OutputBox(mainWindow);

        mainWindow.setVisible( true );
        outputBox.setVisible( true );

        outputBox.printLine("One");
        outputBox.print("Two");
        outputBox.skipLine(1);

        outputBox.print("Three");
        outputBox.printLine("Four");
        outputBox.skipLine(1);

        outputBox.print("Five");
        outputBox.printLine("Six");
    }
}
```

6.   Determine the output of the following code:

```
int x, y;
x = 1;
y = 2;
messageBox.show("The output is " + x + y );
messageBox.show("The output is " + (x + y) );
```

7. Write an application that displays the following pattern in an OutputBox dialog:

```
┌─────────────────────────────────────────────────────┐
│ OutputBox                                            │
├─────────────────────────────────────────────────────┤
│      OXOXOXOXOXOXOXOXOXOXOX                           │
│    X                       O                          │
│    O                       X                          │
│    X                       O                          │
│    O                       X                          │
│    X                       O                          │
│    OXOXOXOXOXOXOXOXOXOXOX                             │
│                                                      │
└─────────────────────────────────────────────────────┘
```

Starts from the second line with five leading blank spaces.

Note: The OutputBox is not drawn to scale.

8. Write an application to convert centimeters (input) to feet and inches (output). Use InputBox for input and OutputBox for output. 1 inch = 2.54 centimeters.

9. Write an application that inputs temperature in Celsius and prints out the temperature in Fahrenheit. Use InputBox for input and OutputBox for output. The formula to convert Celsius to the equivalent Fahrenheit is

$$fahrenheit = 1.8 \times celsius + 32$$

10. Write an application that accepts a person's weight and displays the number of calories the person needs in one day. A person needs 19 calories per pound of body weight, so the formula expressed in Java would be

```
calories = bodyWeight * 19;
```

Use an OutputBox dialog for display. Draw the object diagram of the program. (Note: We are not distinguishing between genders.)

11. A quantity known as *body mass index* (BMI) is used to calculate the risk of weight-related health problems. BMI is computed by the formula

$$BMI = \frac{w}{h^2}$$

Chapter 3

where w is weight in kilograms and h is height in meters. A BMI of about 20 to 25 is considered "normal." Write an application that accepts weight and height (both integers) and outputs the BMI.

12. Your weight is actually the amount of gravitational attraction exerted on you by the earth. Since the moon's gravity is only 1/6 of the earth's gravity, on the moon you would weigh only 1/6 of what you weigh on the earth. Write an application that inputs the user's earth weight and outputs his/her weight on Mercury, Venus, Jupiter, and Saturn. Use the values in the table below:

Planet	Multiply the Earth Weight by
Mercury	0.4
Venus	0.9
Jupiter	2.5
Saturn	1.1

13. When you say you are 18 years old, you are really saying that the earth has circled the sun eighteen times. Since other planets take less or more days than the earth to travel around the sun, your age would be different on other planets. You can compute how old you are on other planets by the formula

$$y = \frac{x \times 365}{d}$$

where x is the age on the earth, y is the age on planet Y, and d is the number of earth days the planet Y takes to travel around the sun. Write an application that inputs the user's earth age and print outs his/her age on Mercury, Venus, Jupiter, and Saturn. The values for d are listed in the table below:

Planet	d = Approximate Number of Earth Days for This Planet to Travel around the Sun
Mercury	88
Venus	225
Jupiter	4380
Saturn	10767

14. Write an application to solve quadratic equations of the form

$$Ax^2 + Bx + C = 0$$

where the coefficients A, B, and C are real numbers. The two real number solutions are derived by the formula

$$x = \frac{-B \pm \sqrt{B^2 - 4AC}}{2A}$$

For this exercise, you may assume that $A \neq 0$ and the relationship

$$B^2 \geq 4AC$$

holds, so there will be real-number solutions for x.

15. Write an application that reads a purchase price and an amount tendered and then displays the change in dollars, quarters, dimes, nickels, and pennies. Two input values are entered in cents, for example, 3450 for $34.50 and 70 for $0.70. Use InputBox for input and OutputBox for output. Display the output in the following format:

```
 Purchase Price:   $ 34.50
Amount Tendered:   $ 40.00

 Your change is:   $ 5.50

                   5 one-dollar bill(s)
                   2 quarter(s)

Thank you for your business. Come back soon.
```

Notice the input values are to be entered in cents (int data type), but the echo printed values must be displayed with decimal points (float data type).

16. Write an application that accepts the unit weight of a bag of coffee in pounds and the number of bags sold and displays the total price of the sale, computed as

```
totalPrice        = unitWeight * numberOfUnits * 5.99f;
totalPriceWithTax = totalPrice + totalPrice * 0.0725f;
```

where 5.99 is the cost per pound and 0.0725 is the sales tax. The letter f after 5.99 and 0.0725 designates that these two numbers are of type float. Display the result in the following manner:

```
Number of bags sold:   32
    Weight per bag:   5 lbs
  Price per pound:   $5.99
       Sales tax:   7.25%

    Total price: $ 1027.884
```

Draw the object diagram of the program.

17. If you invest P dollars at R% interest rate compounded annually, in N years, your investment will grow to

$$\frac{P\left(1 - \left(\dfrac{R}{100}\right)^{N+1}\right)}{1 - \left(\dfrac{R}{100}\right)}$$

dollars. Write an application that accepts P, R, and N and computes the amount of money earned after the N years.

18. Leonardo Fibonacci of Pisa was one of the greatest mathematicians of the Middle Ages. He is perhaps most famous for the Fibonacci sequence that can be applied to many diverse problems. One amusing application of the Fibonacci sequence is finding the growth rate of rabbits. Suppose a pair of rabbits matures in two months and is capable of reproducing another pair every month after maturity. If every new pair has the same capability, how many pairs will there be after one year? (We assume here that no pairs die.) The table below shows the sequence for the first seven months. Notice that at the end of the second month, the first pair matures and bears its first offspring in the third month, making the total two pairs.

Month #	# of pairs
1	1
2	1
3	2
4	3
5	5
6	8
7	13

The Nth Fibonacci number in the sequence can be evaluated with the formula

$$F_N = \frac{1}{\sqrt{5}}\left[\left(\frac{1+\sqrt{5}}{2}\right)^N - \left(\frac{1-\sqrt{5}}{2}\right)^N\right]$$

Write an application that accepts N and displays F_N. Note that the result of computation using the Math class is double. You need to display it as an integer.

19. Java[2] Coffee Outlet runs a catalog business. It sells only one type of coffee beans harvested exclusively in the remote area of Irian Jaya. The company sells the coffee in 2-lb bags only, and the price of a single 2-lb bag is $5.50. When a customer places an order, the company ships the order in boxes. The boxes come in three sizes: the large box holds 20 2-lb bags, the medium 10 bags, and the small 5 bags. The cost of a large box is $2.00, a medium box $1.00, and a small box $0.50. The order is shipped using the least number of boxes with the cheapest cost. For example, the order of 25 bags will be shipped in two boxes, one large and one small. Write an application that computes the total cost of an order. Use InputBox to accept the number of bags for an order and OutputBox to display the total cost including the cost of boxes. Display the output in the following format:

```
Number of Bags Ordered:   52 - $ 286.00

          Boxes Used:
                     2 Large    - $4.00
                     1 Medium   - $1.00
                     1 Small    - $0.50

     Your total cost is:   $ 291.50
```

Remember that you can format a double value X to two decimal places by the expression

```
Math.round( X * 100) / 100.0
```

Chapter 3

20. According to Newton's universal law of gravitation, the force F between two bodies with masses M_1 and M_2 is computed as

$$F = k\left(\frac{M_1 M_2}{d^2}\right)$$

where d is the distance between the two bodies and k is a positive real number called the *gravitational constant*. The gravitational constant k is approximately equal to 6.67E-8 dyne cm^2/gm^2. Write an application that accepts the mass for two bodies in grams and the distance between the two bodies in centimeters, and compute the force F. Use the appropriate format for the output. For your information, the force between the earth and the moon is 1.984E25 dynes. The mass of the earth is 5.983E27 grams, the mass of the moon is 7.347E25 grams, and the distance between the two is 3.844E10 centimeters.

21. Dr. Caffeine's Law of Program Readability states that the degree of program readability R (whose unit is *mocha*) is determined as

$$R = k \cdot \frac{CT^2}{V^3}$$

where k is Ms. Latte's constant, C is the number of lines in the program that contain comments, T is the time spent (in minutes) by the programmer developing the program, and V is the number of lines in the program that contain nondescriptive variable names. Write an application to compute the program readability R. Ms. Latte's constant is 2.5E2 mocha lines^2/min^2. (Note: This is just for fun. Develop your own law using various functions from the Math class.)

22. If the population of a country grows according to the formula

$$y = ce^{kx}$$

where y is the population after x years from the reference year, then we can determine the population of a country for a given year from two census figures. For example, given that a country with a population of 1,000,000 in 1970 grows to 2,000,000 by 1990, we can predict the country's population in the year 2000. Here's how we do the computation. Letting x be the number of years after 1970, we obtain the constant c is 1,000,000 because

$$1,000,000 = ce^{k0} = c$$

Then we determine the value of k as

$$y = 1,000,000\, e^{kx}$$

$$\frac{2,000,000}{1,000,000} = e^{20k}$$

$$k = \frac{1}{20}\ln\!\left(\frac{2,000,000}{1,000,000}\right) \approx 0.03466$$

Finally we can predict the population in the year 2000 by substituting 0.03466 for k and 30 for x (2000 − 1970 = 30). Thus, we predict

$$y = 1,000,000\, e^{0.03466(30)} \approx 2,828,651$$

as the population of the country for the year 2000. Write an application that accepts five input values—year A, population in year A, year B, population in year B, and year C—and predict the population for year C.

23. In Section 3.7, we use the formula

$$mr = \frac{ar}{12}$$

to derive the monthly interest rate from a given annual interest rate, where *mr* is the monthly interest rate and *ar* is the annual interest rate (expressed in a fractional value such as 0.083). This annual interest rate *ar* is called the *stated annual interest rate* to distinguish it from the *effective annual interest rate*, which is the true cost of a loan. If the stated annual interest rate is 9%, for example, then the effective annual interest rate is actually 9.38%. Naturally, the rate the financial institutions advertise more prominently is the stated interest rate. The loan calculator program in Section 3.7 treats the an-

Chapter 3

nual interest rate the user enters as the stated annual interest rate. If the input is the effective annual interest rate, then we compute the monthly rate as

$$mr = (1 + ear)^{\frac{1}{12}} - 1$$

where *ear* is the effective annual interest rate. The difference between the stated and effective annual interest rates is negligible only when the loan amount is small or the loan period is short. Modify the loan calculator program so that the interest rate the user enters is treated as the effective annual interest rate. Run the original and modified loan calculator programs and compare the differences in the monthly and total payments. Use the loan amount of 1, 10, and 50 million dollars with the loan period of 10, 20, and 30 years and the annual interest rate of 0.07, 0.10, and 0.18, respectively. Try other combinations also.

Visit several websites that provide a loan calculator for computing a monthly mortgage payment (one such site is the financial page at www.cnn.com). Compare your results to the values computed by the websites you visited. Determine whether the websites treat the input annual interest rate as stated or effective.

24. Using a Turtle object from the galapagos package (see exercise 27 on page 82), draw three rectangles. Use an InputBox to accept the width and the length of the smallest rectangle from the user. The middle and the largest rectangles are 40 and 80 percent larger than the smallest rectangle. The galapagos package and its documentation are available at www.drcaffeine.com/packages.

25. Write a program that draws a bar chart using a Turtle object (see exercise 27 on page 82). Input five int values and draw the vertical bars that represent the entered values in the following manner:

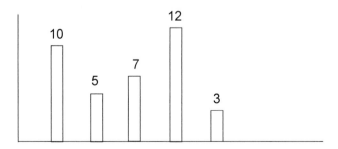

Your Turtle must draw everything shown in the diagram, including the axes and numbers.

4

Defining Instantiable Classes

OBJECTIVES

After you have read and studied this chapter, you should be able to

- Define an instantiable class with multiple methods and a constructor.
- Differentiate the local and instance variables.
- Define and use value-returning methods.
- Distinguish private and public methods.
- Distinguish private and public data members.
- Describe how the arguments are passed to the parameters in method definitions.
- Use System.out for temporary output to verify the program code.

Introduction

The sample application programs we have written so far included only one class, the main class of the program. And the main class contained only one method, the main method. From this main method, we used only predefined classes from javabook and other standard packages such as java.lang. For small programs, this arrangement may be acceptable. But for large programs, it is not. We cannot develop large application programs in a similar manner for the following two reasons:

1. Placing all programming code for a large application in a single method main makes the method very huge and impossible to manage.

2. Predefined classes alone cannot satisfy all of our programming needs in writing a large application.

Even for the simple LoanCalculator program in the previous chapter the size of its main method is approaching the limit that can be considered acceptable. We don't write a program whose main method is 10 pages long. A large program that is properly built will include many classes—some predefined and others we defined—and each of these classes will include many methods.

Learning how to define instantiable classes is the first step toward mastering the skills necessary in building large programs. A class is *instantiable* if we can create instances of the class. The MainWindow, InputBox, and OutputBox classes are all instantiable classes while the Math class is not. In this chapter you will learn how to define instantiable classes and different types of methods included in the instantiable classes.

instantiable class

4.1   Defining Instantiable Classes

Suppose we want to write a program that converts Japanese yen to U.S. dollars and vice versa. What kinds of objects do you think are necessary? Well, we can do a simple input and output with InputBox and OutputBox. But what about the conversion process? Is there any class in javabook or standard Java packages that does currency conversion? No, so we will have to define one ourselves. As an illustration for defining instantiable classes, we will define a class called CurrencyConverter. Through this example, we will provide you the basics of defining instantiable classes. We will cover only the very basics in this section. We will provide in the remainder of the chapter a more detailed explanation of the basic features introduced here.

When we design our own class, we start with the specification for the class. We must decide how we want to interact with the class and its instances. We must decide what kinds of instance and class methods the class should support. We will design the class so that we can use it in a way that is natural and logical for us to use. Let's start with one possible design. After we design the class, we will discuss an alternative way to design the class.

How should a CurrencyConverter object behave? What would be a natural and logical way for us to interact with it? Since we want the object to be able to do the conversion between a foreign currency and the U.S. dollar, let's define two methods, one for converting U.S. dollars to the equivalent amount in the foreign currency and another for the reverse transaction. Let's call these methods fromDollar and toDollar. To convert $200 U.S. to Japanese yen, for example, we will have to write something like this:

```
CurrencyConverter    yenConverter;
double               amountInYen, amountInDollar;

yenConverter = new CurrencyConverter();
...
amountInYen   = yenConverter.fromDollar( 200 );
                                              //from dollar
                                              //to yen
```

And to convert ¥15,000 to U.S. dollars, we will write

```
amountInDollar = yenConverter.toDollar( 15000 );
                                 //from yen to dollar
```

Since the exchange rate fluctuates, we need a method, say, setExchangeRate, to set the exchange rate before doing the conversion. Assuming the exchange rate is ¥130.77 for $1.00 U.S., we will do the conversion as

```
CurrencyConverter    yenConverter;
double               amountInYen, amountInDollar;

yenConverter     = new CurrencyConverter();
yenConverter.setExchangeRate(130.77);

amountInYen      = yenConverter.fromDollar( 200 );
amountInDollar   = yenConverter.toDollar( 15000 );
```

Once the class is defined, we can easily create additional CurrencyConverter objects for other currencies. For example, if we want to convert U.S. dollars into German marks and Japanese yen, then we can do the following:

```
CurrencyConverter    yenConverter, markConverter;
double               amountInYen, amountInMark;

yenConverter     = new CurrencyConverter();
yenConverter.setExchangeRate(130.77);

markConverter    =  new CurrencyConverter( );
markConverter.setExchangeRate(1.792);

amountInYen      =   yenConverter.fromDollar( 200 );
amountInMark     =   markConverter.fromDollar( 200 );
```

Because any currency can be converted to a dollar equivalent and vice versa, we can do the conversion between two currencies other than the U.S. dollar, for example, between Japanese yen and German marks. For example, to convert ¥10,000 to the equivalent German marks, we first convert the yen to dollars and then the dollars to marks as in

```
amountInDollar= yenConverter.toDollar( 10000 );
amountInMark  = markConverter.fromDollar(amountInDollar);
```

Being able to do a conversion easily between any two currencies is a direct benefit of defining a separate class for currency conversion.

A CurrencyConverter object has three methods: setExchangeRate, toDollar, and fromDollar. Its object diagram (at this point) is

Alternative Design for CurrencyConverter

We gave one possible design for the CurrencyConverter class. Is there any alternative design? The way the class is implemented, we must create a new instance of each foreign currency for which we want to do a conversion. Another possibility is to design the class so that one instance of the class can handle conversions for more than one foreign currency. We won't get into any more detail here because we do not yet have the necessary programming skills to implement this alternative design.

Suppose we know how to implement the alternative design of Currency-Converter. Which design alternative is better? When we design a class, we must always consider alternative designs to select the one most appropriate for a given program. Whether one design is better than the other depends on how the class is used in programs. Unlike the engineering disciplines, we do not have a formula to measure the effectiveness of a software. Instead of mathematical formulae, we have design guidelines we can follow in designing classes. One such guideline is keep the class simple. Whenever appropriate in the remainder of the book, we will mention the design alternatives for the classes used in the sample programs and discuss their pros and cons.

The CurrencyConverter Class

Let's implement the class using the first design. Figure 4.1 is a template for defining a class. In this class, we need to define three methods—setExchange-Rate, toDollar, and fromDollar—and any data values used by these methods. We call the data values for the class *data members*, which include variables and

data members

Chapter 4

FIGURE 4.1   A program template for a class definition.

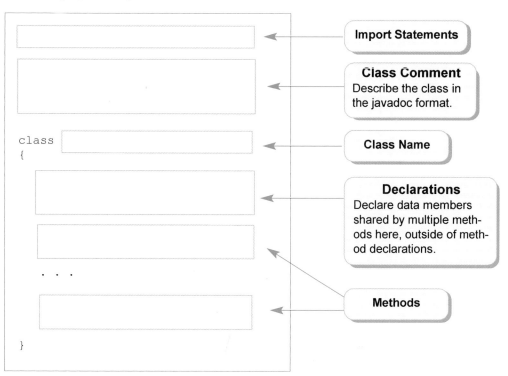

constants. We will first identify the data members of the class and then define the three methods. We will explain the rules for defining the data members and methods along the way.

What kind of data members does a CurrencyConverter object need in order for the object to carry out the conversion task? To do the conversion, the object must keep track of the exchange rate. This exchange rate is used by the two methods toDollar and fromDollar. What will be the data type for the exchange rate? The data type int is not acceptable because we expect the rate will include decimal places. So the data type should be either float or double. But which? Since the magnitude of the number is small, float seems adequate. However, to maintain the higher accuracy for conversion where the exchange rate may include more than five or six decimal places, we will use the data type double for the exchange rate.

> There were times when computer memory was very expensive. In those days, the main memory size was something like 64K (note: 64Mb memory, which is common for today's desktop PC, is 1000 times larger than 64K memory), so the memory was a precious commodity. To run a program in such an environment, we would use data type float to save space, unless data type double is really necessary. In today's computing environment, with an abundance of memory, there isn't much to gain by using float instead of double. For example, representing 25 real numbers as float requires 100 bytes while doing the same using double requires 200 bytes. Saving of 100 bytes is insignificant and negligible today. Using double is more of a standard in Java, and in this book, double will be a preferred data type for representing real numbers.

Here's the partial class declaration with the variable exchangeRate declared as data type double:

```
/**
 * This class is used to do the currency conversion
 * between a foreign currency and the U.S. dollar.
 *
 * @author Dr. Caffeine
 */
class CurrencyConverter
{
    /**
     * how much $1.00 U.S. is worth in the foreign currency
     */
    private double exchangeRate;

    //method declarations come here

}
```

Notice that we are using here the javadoc style comment introduced in Chapter 2 to describe the class and its one data member exchangeRate. Starting from this chapter, we will gradually introduce the elements of javadoc comments. The javadoc comments begin with the marker /** and end with the marker */. The asterisks on the lines between the first and the last markers have no significance; they are there to provide a visual aid to highlight the comments in the program. It is an accepted standard to use the asterisks in this manner for the javadoc comments.

javadoc tags

@author tag

Inside the javadoc comments, we can use a number of *javadoc tags*, special markers that begin with the @ mark. In this example, we see one javadoc tag @author, which we use to list the authors of the class. We will introduce other javadoc tags later in the chapter.

For more information on javadoc, please visit www.drcaffeine.com/additionaltopics.

instance
variable

The variable exchangeRate is declared within the class declaration, but outside of any method of the class. The variable exchangeRate is an *instance variable*, which is equivalent to the term *instance data value* we used in Chapter 1. Every object of the class will have its own copy of an instance variable.

Mr. Espresso: *Is it really important to use javadoc comments? Can I stick to regular comments?*

Dr. Caffeine: *It's true that you have to learn a few extra items to use javadoc comments, but the benefits warrant a little extra effort.*

Mr. Espresso: *Benefits like online documentation?*

Dr. Caffeine: *Yes, the online documents for the Java standard library classes, for example, are produced by commenting the classes in javadoc. The online documents for the javabook package are also produced by using javadoc.*

Mr. Espresso: *But what if I don't want to produce any online documents?*

Dr. Caffeine: *Using javadoc does not mean you have to generate online documents. By using javadoc, which is really no different from other styles of commenting, you leave an option open. You don't have to redo all of your comments in the javadoc format if you decide later to publish online documents. Moreover, since javadoc is a standard, other programmers will have an easier time reading your code with javadoc comments than reading code with a nonstandard style of comments.*

Dr. & Mr.

Figure 4.2 shows that three CurrencyConverter objects have their own copy of exchangeRate.

FIGURE 4.2

Every object of a class has its own copy of instance variables. **CurrencyConverter** objects have their own copy of the **exchangeRate** instance variable.

```
CurrencyConverter    markConverter, yenConverter, poundConverter;

markConverter = new CurrencyConverter();
markConverter.setExchangeRate( 1.792 );

yenConverter = new CurrencyConverter();
yenConverter.setExchangeRate( 130.77 );

poundConverter = new CurrencyConverter( );
poundConverter.setExchangeRate( 1.66 );
```

markConverter   yenConverter   poundConverter

Notice the use of the reserved word private in declaring exchangeRate. This modifier is called a *visibility modifier*, and it specifies the visibility, or accessibility, of the data members and methods. Another visibility modifier is public. The full explanation of the visibility modifier will require a whole section, so we will defer its discussion until the next section. For now, it suffices to know that the data type for exchangeRate is double.

visibility modifier

Now let's study how the methods are defined. We will start with the setExchangeRate method. Its purpose is to set the instance variable exchangeRate to the value passed to the method. The method is declared as

```
public void setExchangeRate( double rate )
{
    exchangeRate = rate;
}
```

Chapter 4

The syntax for defining a method, as given in Chapter 2, is

```
<modifiers> <return type> <method name> ( <parameters> )
{

    <statements>
}
```

The following diagram shows how the components in the general syntax correspond to the actual elements in the exchangeRate method:

Since the method returns no value, it is declared as void. Notice that the method has no static modifier. If the method declaration includes the static modifier, then it is a class method. If the method declaration does not include the static modifier, then it is an instance method.

> *Instance methods are declared **WITHOUT** the static modifier. Class methods are declared **WITH** the static modifier.*

We must declare the setExchangeRate method as an instance method because class methods cannot access instance variables, but this method needs to access the instance variable exchangeRate. Class methods can access only the class variables and constants, while the instance methods can also access them in addition to the instance variables.

> *Class methods can access class variables and constants but not instance variables. Instance methods can access all of them.*

When we define an instantiable class, we are in essence defining how the instances of the class will behave. So it makes sense that the methods we define for the class are instance methods. There are times when a class method is useful and necessary, but for the most part, when we define an instantiable class, we will define the instance methods almost exclusively. We will describe the use of class methods for the instantiable classes later in the book.

The visibility modifier public designates the setExchangeRate method as accessible from outside methods. If two methods belong to different classes, then they are *outside methods* relative to each other. If this method is declared private, then we will not be able to call the method from outside as in

outside method

```
class TestProgram
{
    public static void main (String args[] )
    {
        CurrencyConverter yenConverter;
        yenConverter = new CurrencyConverter();

        yenConverter.setExchangeRate( 130.77 );
        . . .
    }
}
```

This call is valid if the method is declared **public** and invalid if the method is declared **private**.

Since all three methods are intended to be called from the outside methods, the three methods are all declared public.

method header comment

As a part of class documentation, we include a *method header comment* to every method to describe the method. A typical method header comment in javadoc looks something like this:

```
/**
 * Converts a given amount in dollars into
 * an equivalent amount in a foreign currency.
 *
 * @param dollar the amount in dollars to be converted
 *
 * @return amount in foreign currency
 */
```

In the method header comment, we record the method's purpose, list of parameters passed to the method, and the value returned from the method. For the list of parameters, we attach a short description of each parameter in addition to the parameter's name. Each parameter is marked by the @param javadoc tag. Its syntax is

@param tag

```
@param <parameter name> <description>
```

The <description> portion can go beyond one line. If the method returns a value,
then we add the @return javadoc tag. Its syntax is

@return tag

```
@return <description>
```

To save space, we will show the javadoc method comments only in the final listing of the class.

Now let's move on to the second method. The toDollar method accepts an
amount in a foreign currency and returns the equivalent amount in U.S. dollars.
The amount in the foreign currency, which is a double value, is passed to the
method as an argument, so the corresponding parameter is declared as double.
Since the method returns a double value, we must declare its return type as double. The method is therefore declared as

```
public double toDollar( double foreignMoney )
{
    //method body comes here
}
```

value-returning
method

We call a method that returns a value a *value-returning method*, or *non*-void
method. A value-returning method must include a return statement of the format

return statement
syntax

```
return <expression> ;
```

The void method, on the other hand, must not include any return statement.

We can convert a given value foreignMoney into the equivalent dollar
amount by the expression

```
foreignMoney / exchangeRate
```

so the complete method is defined as

```
public double toDollar( double foreignMoney )
{
    return (foreignMoney / exchangeRate) ;
}
```

We use the parentheses in the return statement to delineate the expression part of
the statement clearly.

Chapter 4

The method to convert a given amount in dollars to the equivalent amount in a foreign currency is similarly defined as

```
public double fromDollar( double dollar )
{
    return (dollar * exchangeRate) ;
}
```

We are now ready to provide the complete listing of the CurrencyConverter class. In listing the data members and methods of a class, we will use the following convention:

class listing convention

```
class <class name>
{
    // data members

    // public methods

    // private methods
}
```

We first list the data members, then the public methods in alphabetical order, and finally the private methods in alphabetical order. For the public and private method groups, we will include a block comment that provides a quick reference to the methods in the group. For example, we will include the following comment for the public method group of the CurrencyConverter class:

```
//-------------------------------------------------
//   Public Methods:
//
//      double   fromDollar          ( double   )
//      void     setExchangeRate     (          )
//      double   toDollar            ( double   )
//
//-------------------------------------------------
```

Such a list in the source code, of course, is not needed by the javadoc generator to produce similar indexes to methods and data members when creating online documentation from the source code. However, we still include such quick reference list of methods in the source code so that programmers reading the program will have a handy reference to the list of methods without referring to any online documentation. Notice that we don't use the javadoc style for a quick reference list because javadoc comments are used only for describing the class and its data members and methods.

The Java compiler does not care how we order the methods and data members in the class declaration. We adopt the listing convention to make the class declaration easier for us to follow.

Here's the class declaration:

```
/**
 * This class is used to do the currency conversion
 * between a foreign currency and the U.S. dollar.
 *
 * @author Dr. Caffeine
 */

class CurrencyConverter
{
//-----------------------------------------------------------------
//      Data Members
//-----------------------------------------------------------------

    /**
     * how much $1.00 U.S. is worth in the foreign currency
     */
    private double exchangeRate;

//-----------------------------------------------------------------
//      Public Methods:
//
//          double      fromDollar          (   double      )
//          void        setExchangeRate     (               )
//          double      toDollar            (   double      )
//
//-----------------------------------------------------------------

    /**
     * Converts a given amount in dollars into
     * an equivalent amount in a foreign currency.
     *
     * @param dollar the amount in dollars to be converted
     *
     * @return amount in foreign currency
     */
    public double fromDollar( double dollar )
    {
        return (dollar * exchangeRate) ;
    }


    /**
     * Sets the exchange rate to the value passed
     * to this method.
     *
     * @param rate the exchange rate
     *
     */
```

```
public void setExchangeRate( double rate )
{
    exchangeRate = rate;
}

/**
 * Converts a given amount in a foreign currency into
 * an equivalent dollar amount.
 *
 * @param   foreignMoney the amount in dollars to be converted
 *
 * @return amount in dollar
 */
public double toDollar( double foreignMoney )
{
    return (foreignMoney / exchangeRate) ;
}

}
```

Quick Check

1. The following is invalid. Why?

```
public void myMethod( int one )
{
    return   (one + one) ;
}
```

2. Which of the following methods are class methods?

```
public  static void    one( ) { ... }
private        int     two( ) { ... }
private static int     three( ) { ... }
public         float   four( ) { ... }
```

4.2   Instantiable Classes and Constructors

When we design a class, we try to make the class as robust as we can. We do not want the class to be so fragile that a simple misstep by the programmer will cause the class to stop working properly. Consider the following sequence of statements that use a CurrencyConverter object to convert $200 to the equivalent in yen:

```
CurrencyConverter     yenConverter;
double                amountInYen;

yenConverter     = new CurrencyConverter();
amountInYen      = yenConverter.fromDollar( 200 );
```

Does the code work? No, it does not, because the method setExchangeRate is not called to set the exchange rate. The programmer must call the setExchange-Rate method before calling the fromDollar method in order to perform the currency conversion correctly.

The way the class is currently defined, the correct value for exchangeRate is not set when an instance of the CurrencyConverter class is created. This means that we must rely on the programmer to call the setExchangeRate method before calling the fromDollar method. But there's no way for us to ensure that the programmer will call the setExchangeRate method. When we design a class, we must define the class as robust as it can be so the class will not "break" easily under the programmer's misuse of the class. One possible solution is to define a special method called a constructor so that an instance of the Currency-Converter class cannot be created without setting the value for exchangeRate.

constructor   A *constructor* is a special method that is executed when the new message is sent to the class, that is, when a new instance of the class is created. The name of a constructor must be the same as the name of the class. For the Currency-Converter class, we can define its constructor as

```
public CurrencyConverter( double rate )
{
    exchangeRate = rate;
}
```

To call this constructor, we create a new CurrencyConverter object

```
CurrencyConverter    moneyChanger;
moneyChanger = new CurrencyConverter( 130.45 );
```

The syntax of a constructor is

```
public <class name> ( <parameters> )
{
    <statements>
}
```

where <class name> is the name of the class to which this constructor belongs. The following diagram shows how the components in the general syntax correspond to the actual elements in the constructor of the CurrencyConverter class:

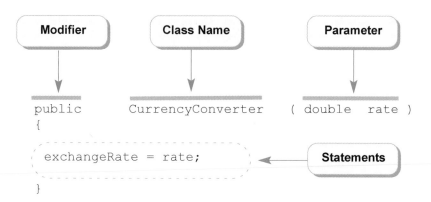

```
public       CurrencyConverter  ( double   rate )
{
    exchangeRate = rate;
}
```

Notice that a constructor does not have a return type. Although there is no static modifier in the declaration, the constructor is a class method. The modifier of a constructor does not have to be public, but non-public constructors are rarely used, so we will not discuss non-public constructors.

If no constructor is defined for a class, then the Java compiler will include a default constructor. Since we did not define any constructor for the Currency-Converter class before, the default constructor

```
public CurrencyConverter()
{
}
```

was added to the class by the compiler. A default constructor has no parameters. Once we define our own constructor, no default constructor is added. This means once the constructor

```
public CurrencyConverter( double   rate )
{
    exchangeRate = rate;
}
```

is defined, we will not be allowed to create a CurrencyConverter object as

```
CurrencyConverter    moneyChanger;
moneyChanger  =  new CurrencyConverter( );
```

because no matching constructor is defined for the class. However, it is possible to define multiple constructors for a class, so the programmer can create a new instance of the class in different ways. For example, if we want the programmers to create a new instance either as

```
moneyChanger = new CurrencyConverter( );
```

or

```
moneyChanger = new CurrencyConverter( 142.00 );
```

we simply define two constructors for the class.

There will be no problems defining multiple constructors as long as the constructors defined for a class have either

1. A different number of parameters.

2. Different data types for the parameters if the number of parameters is the same.

For example, the following three constructors

```
public ClassA( int X )
{
    . . .
}

public ClassA(        ) //different number of parameters
{
    . . .
}

public ClassA( double X )  //same number of parameters as
{                          //the first one, but a different
    . . .                  //data type
}
```

are valid, but the following two constructors

```
public ClassB( int X , double Y )
{
    . . .
}
```

```
public ClassB( int A, double B  )
{                 //invalid: same number and same data types
   ...
}
```

are not. Notice that parameter names are irrelevant in deciding whether the constructor is valid or not. Only the number of parameters and their data types are relevant.

The purpose of the constructor is to initialize an object to a valid state. For example, when the CurrencyConverter class has the default constructor only, then a newly created CurrencyConverter object is not in a valid state since the object does not have a valid exchange rate at the time of its creation. Whenever an object is created, we must ensure that it is created in a valid state by properly initializing all data members in a constructor. We can guarantee this by always defining a constructor to a class and initializing data members in the constructor's method body.

Always define a constructor and initialize data members fully in the constructor so an object will be created in a valid state.

Remember that even after we add constructors to the CurrencyConverter class, the setExchangeRate method is still necessary for the class because we want the programmer to be able to change the exchange rate to different rates after the object is created.

Quick Check

1. Which of the following constructors are invalid?

    ```
    public int ClassA( int one )
    {
        ...
    }

    public ClassB( int one, int two )
    {
        ...
    }

    void ClassC( )
    {
        ...
    }
    ```

2. Are there any conflicts in the following three constructors for ClassX to be valid?

```
public ClassX( int X )
{
    . . .
}

public ClassX( float X )
{
    . . .
}

public ClassX( int Y )
{
    . . .
}
```

4.3 Visibility Modifiers: public and private

The modifiers public and private designate the accessibility of data members and methods. Although valid in Java, we do not recommend that programmers, especially beginners, leave out the visibility modifier in declaring data members and methods. From the object-oriented design standpoint, we recommend you always designate the data members and methods as private or public. We will explain how to use these modifiers in this section.

The instance variable exchangeRate of CurrencyConverter is declared private. No outside methods—the methods that belong to classes other than CurrencyConverter—can therefore directly access exchangeRate. To explain why we declare the instance variable private, let's see what happens if we declare exchangeRate as public. Suppose we change the declaration to

```
class CurrencyConverter
{
    public double exchangeRate;
    . . .
}
```

If a data member is declared public, then any outside method can access it using dot notation. For example, we can set the exchange rate without using the setExchangeRate method as

```
CurrencyConverter yenConverter;
yenConverter = new CurrencyConverter( );

yenConverter.exchangeRate = 130.77;
```

Direct access to the public instance variable using dot notation.

You can read the value of **exchangeRate** just as well by using dot notation as in the following code:

```
double yenRate = yenConverter.exchangeRate;
outputBox.printLine("One U.S. dollar is worth "
                    + yenRate + " yen." );
```

On the surface, it seems better to declare the data members public. Why bother hiding **exchangeRate** by declaring it private and defining the method **setExchangeRate** to set the value if you can read and write the value of **exchangeRate** directly by declaring it public? To explain why declaring data members public is considered a bad design, let's modify the class so that a fee is automatically charged and deducted from the converted amount. Let's say the rate of charge is 5 percent of the exchange rate. We add the second instance variable **feeRate** to store this fee rate. We will declare **feeRate** as public to illustrate the point. The fee rate is based on the exchange rate, so we will set it inside the **setExchangeRate** method as

```
public void setExchangeRate( double rate )
{
    exchangeRate = rate;
    feeRate = rate * 0.05;
}
```

The conversion routines are now defined as

```
public double toDollar( double foreignMoney )
{
    return foreignMoney / (exchangeRate + feeRate);
}


public double fromDollar( double dollar )
{
    return dollar * (exchangeRate - feeRate) ;
}
```

Because the instance variable feeRate is public, we cannot prevent programmers from writing code such as

```
CurrencyConverter   yenConverter;
yenConverter =  new CurrencyConverter( );
yenConverter.setExchangeRate( 130.77 );

yenConverter.feeRate = 0.0;
...
```

thereby breaking the CurrencyConverter class. If the instance variable feeRate is private, then programmers using the CurrencyConverter class cannot modify its value directly. They can modify the value only through the setExchangeRate method. So by declaring the data members private, we can maintain the integrity of the class and enforce the rule, because the values of the data members are changed only via the methods we define. The programmers cannot access or modify the data member values through the back door.

Declaring the data members private ***ensures the integrity of the class.***

Consider another scenario. Imagine what would happen had we designed the CurrencyConverter class without the setExchangeRate method. We declare the instance variable exchangeRate as public and let the programmers modify its value directly. Now, suppose we need to modify the class to keep track of two exchange rates that automatically include charge, one for converting a dollar amount to the equivalent amount in a foreign currency and another for converting an amount in a foreign currency to the equivalent dollar amount. We will call these rates fromDollarRate and toDollarRate, respectively. The methods for conversion become something like

```
public double toDollar( double foreignMoney )
{
    return ( foreignMoney / toDollarRate );
}

public double fromDollar( double dollar )
{
    return ( dollar * fromDollarRate );
}
```

Chapter 4

When the public instance variable exchangeRate is replaced by two rates fromDollarRate and toDollarRate, then all the statements in the programmer's code that refer to exchangeRate, such as

```
yenConverter.exchangeRate = 130.77;
```

must be replaced by something like

```
yenConverter.toDollarRate = 130.77 * 1.05;
yenConverter.fromDollarRate = 130.77 * 0.95;
```

assuming the rate of charge is 5 percent of the exchange rate. Forcing the programmers to make such changes is not good. We can avoid changing the programmer's code if the exchangeRate is declared private and we define the method setExchangeRate. We only need to replace the private instance variable exchangeRate by two private instance variables toDollarRate and fromDollarRate. They are set in the new setExchangeRate method as

```
public void setExchangeRate( double rate )
{
    exchangeRate   = rate;
    toDollarRate   = rate * 1.05;
    fromDollarRate = rate * 0.95;
}
```

The programmer's code that includes the statement

```
yenConverter.setExchangeRate( 130.77 );
```

will continue to work without modification.

When we design an instantiable class, we are designing the behavior of the instances. Behavior of the instances is determined by the set of public methods we define for the class. We use data members to keep track of data values necessary to support the public methods. We consider the data members as an internal detail of the class. As such, we should declare them private. Similarly, we may need to define a set of methods that are used only by the methods of the same class. Since the methods are used internally, we should declare these methods private also. Any components that are only for internal use should be declared private.

The only data members we may want to declare as public are the class constants. Since a class constant is "read only" by its nature, it won't have a negative impact if we declare it as public. For example, we may include a class constant FEE_RATE, which is declared as

```
public static final double FEE_RATE = 0.05; //5% fee rate
```

and define the setExchangeRate method as

```
public void setExchangeRate( double rate )
{
    exchangeRate   = rate;
    toDollarRate   = rate * (1.00 + FEE_RATE);
    fromDollarRate = rate * (1.00 - FEE_RATE);
}
```

With this modification in place, the programmer can write code such as

```
double dollarAmount;

yenConverter.setExchangeRate( 130.77 );

dollarAmount = yenConverter.toDollar( 15000.0 );

outputBox.printLine("Y15,000.00 is equal to");
outputBox.printLine("$ " + dollarAmount);
outputBox.printLine("with the fee rate: "
                        + CurrencyConverter.FEE_RATE);
```

Notice that the class data members and the class methods are accessed by the syntax

```
<class name> . <class data members | class methods>
```

where the vertical bar (|) represents OR. This is how we used the methods and constants from the Math class. Keep in mind that a class constant may or may not be public. That depends on its usage.

Here are some guidelines for you to follow.

Guidelines in determining the visibility of data members and methods:

1. Declare the class and instance variables *private.*

2. *Declare the class and instance methods* private *if they are used only by the other methods in the same class.*

3. *Declare the class constants* public *if you want to make their values directly readable by outside methods. If the class constants are used for internal purposes only, then declare them* private.

Quick Check

1. If the data member feeRate is private, is the following statement valid?

```
feeCharge = currencyChanger.feeRate;
```

2. Suppose you wrote down important information such as your bank account number, student registration ID, and so forth, on a single sheet of paper. Will this sheet be declared private, and kept in your desk drawer, or public, and placed next to the dorm's public telephone?

4.4   Local Variables, Return Values, and Parameter Passing

We will provide more detailed coverage on methods in this section. Specifically, we will discuss how local variables are declared, how arguments are passed to a method, and how values are returned from a method.

local variable   A variable declared within the method declaration is called a *local variable*. Local variables are used for temporary purposes, such as storing intermediate results of a computation. For example, we can rewrite the method

```
public double fromDollar( double dollar )
{
    return dollar * (exchangeRate - feeRate);
}
```

using local variables as

```
public double fromDollar( double dollar )
{
    double amount, fee;

    fee    = exchangeRate - feeRate;
    amount = dollar * fee;

    return amount;
}
```

These are **local variables**.

While instance variables are accessible from all instance methods of the class, local variables and parameters are accessible only from the method in which they are declared, and they are available only while the method is being executed. Memory space for local variables and parameters is allocated upon declaration and at the beginning of the method, respectively, and erased upon exiting from the method. Figure 4.3 shows how memory space is allocated and deallocated for the two local variables and the one parameter when the modified fromDollar method is executed.

FIGURE 4.3   How memory space for a local variable and a parameter is allocated and deallocated.

Chapter 4

Local variables and parameters are erased when the execution of a method is completed.

The next topic is the mapping of arguments to the corresponding parameters. In the example shown in Figure 4.3, the constant argument 200 was passed to the parameter of the fromDollar method. The passed value was used in the method and erased upon exiting from the method. In this example the argument was a constant. What would happen if the argument is a variable, and the value of the corresponding parameter was changed during the method execution? Let's study how the values are passed between the argument and the corresponding parameter.

When a method is called, the value of the argument is passed to the matching parameter, and separate memory space is allocated to store this value. This way of passing the value of arguments is called a *pass-by-value scheme*. Since separate memory space is allocated for each parameter during the execution of the method, the parameter is local to the method, and, therefore, changes made to the parameter will not affect the value of the corresponding argument.

pass-by-value

Consider the following myMethod method of the Tester class. The method does not do anything meaningful. We use it here to illustrate how the pass-by-value scheme works.

```
class Tester
{
    public void myMethod(int one,  float two )
    {
        one = 25;
        two = 35.4f;
    }
}
```

What will be the output from the following code?

```
Tester tester;
int    x, y;

tester = new Tester();
x = 10;
y = 20;

tester.myMethod( x, y );

outputBox.printLine( x + "     " + y );
```

The output will be

```
10      20
```

because with the pass-by-value scheme, the values of arguments are passed to the parameters, but changes made to the parameters are not passed back to the arguments. Figure 4.4 shows how the pass-by-value scheme works.

Notice that the arguments are matched against the parameters in the left-to-right order, that is, the value of the leftmost argument is passed to the leftmost

FIGURE 4.4   How memory space for the parameters is allocated and deallocated.

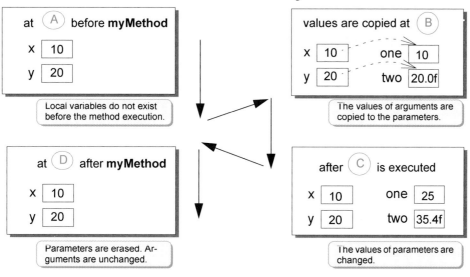

parameter, the value of the second leftmost argument is passed to the second leftmost parameter, and so forth. The number of arguments in the method call must match the number of parameters in the method definition. For example, the following calls to myMethod of the Tester class are all invalid because the number of arguments and parameters does not match.

```
tester.myMethod( 12 );
tester.myMethod( x, y, 24.5);
```

Since we are assigning the value of an argument to the matching parameter, the data type of an argument must be assignment compatible with the data type of the matching parameter. For example, we can pass an integer argument to a float parameter, but not vice versa. In the following, the first call is valid, but the second one is invalid:

```
tester.myMethod( 12, 25 );
tester.myMethod( 23.0, 34.5 );
```

The name of the parameter and the argument can be the same. Keep in mind, however, that the values of arguments are still passed to a method by the pass-by-value scheme, that is, local copies are made whether the argument and the parameter share the same name or not.

The key points to remember about arguments and parameters:

1. *Arguments are passed to a method using the pass-by-value scheme.*

2. *Arguments are matched to the parameters from left to right. The data type of an argument must be assignment compatible to the data type of the matching parameter.*

3. *The number of arguments in the method call must match the number of parameters in the method definition.*

4. *Parameters and arguments do not have to have the same name.*

5. *Local copies, which are distinct from arguments, are created even if the parameters and arguments share the same name.*

6. *Parameters are input to a method, and they are local to the method. Changes made to the parameters will not affect the value of corresponding arguments.*

Finally, let's study how values are returned from methods. Consider the following toDollar method:

> The data type of the value returned from a method must match the declared return type of the method.

```
public  double  toDollar( double foreignMoney )
{

    return  foreignMoney / (exchangeRate + feeRate) ;

}
```

Because a value is returned from the method, we can place the call to the method anywhere an expression can appear. For example, the following statement is valid:

```
double totalAmount;

totalAmount = yenConverter.toDollar( 100 )
                    + yenConverter.toDollar( 50 ) ;
```

Similarly, we can pass the returned value as an argument to another method call, such as

```
double yenAmount;

yenAmount
  = yenConverter.fromDollar( markConverter.toDollar(100) );
```

to convert 100 German marks to the equivalent yen. Note: Fees are charged twice here because there are two conversions. See Exercise 12 on page 187.

4.5 Loan Calculator Program with an Instantiable Class

In the previous chapter, we wrote a loan calculator program that computes the monthly and total payments for a given loan amount, loan period, and interest rate. We wrote the program using the simplified program structure where we had one main class with one method (main). We will implement the program

Chapter 4

again, but this time we will use an instantiable class called LoanCalculator. The problem statement is given in Section 3.7 on page 113. We will go through the incremental development process to derive the instantiable LoanCalculator class. We will also introduce the syntax for calling a method from another method that belongs to the same class.

Problem Statement

The problem statement is the same as before from Chapter 3. We will repeat the statement to refresh your memory:

> *Write a loan calculator program that computes both monthly and total payments for a given loan amount, annual interest rate, and loan period.*

Overall Plan

The tasks we identified in the previous chapter for the program are still the same. They are

program
tasks

1. Get three input values: loanAmount, interestRate, and loanPeriod.
2. Compute the monthly and total payments.
3. Output the results.

The main difference in this implementation is the use of an instantiable LoanCalculator class. Instead of building the program using only the main class and performing all the tasks in one big main method, we will define an instantiable class LoanCalculator. An instance of the LoanCalculator class will manage other objects such as MainWindow, InputBox, and OutputBox. The LoanCalculator class is organized logically with multiple methods. Figure 4.5 shows the structural difference between the two programs.

An instance of the LoanCalculator class acts like a top-level agent that manages all other objects in the program. The purpose of the main class is to create a LoanCalculator object and give it a command to carry out the loan calculation. The LoanCalculator object is built from a number of methods with each method doing a single function. What kinds of methods will the object need?

Since the LoanCalculator object is the top-level agent of the program that manages other objects, we need a method to create these objects. We will do this in the constructor. We will define separate methods for input, computation, and output to organize the class more logically. Designing a set of single-task methods is more manageable and easier to understand than having one method that performs all three tasks of input, computation, and output. We will call the

FIGURE 4.5   The object diagrams for the Chapter 3 **LoanCalculator** program and the one we are designing here. Not all methods are shown here to simplify the diagrams.

Chapter 3 Program

Chapter 4 Program

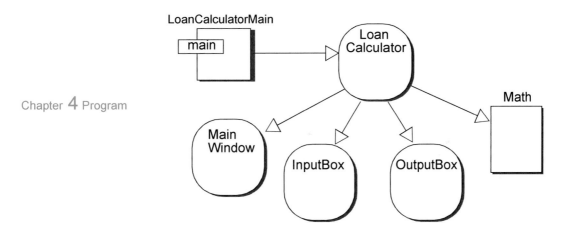

methods getInput, computePayment, and displayOutput. We will also include one method called describeProgram that describes the purpose of the program to the user.

We need the main class for the program, and we need to define its main method. In this main method, we have to create an instance of the LoanCalculator class. How should the main method interact with the LoanCalculator object? One possibility is to call the methods getInput, computePayment, and so forth individually as in

Alternative Design 1

```
public static void main ( String[ ] args )
{
    LoanCalculator loanCalculator;
    loanCalculator = new LoanCalculator( );

    loanCalculator.describeProgram();
    loanCalculator.getInput();
    loanCalculator.computePayment();
    loanCalculator.displayOutput();
}
```

The methods are all public methods and are called individually from the main method. The object diagram for this design is shown in Figure 4.6.

FIGURE 4.6   The object diagram for design alternative 1. **MainWindow**, **OutputBox**, and **InputBox** objects are not shown.

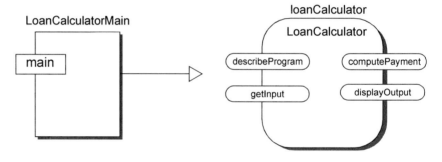

Notice that these four methods must be called in the correct sequence. For example, the program will not work if the main method calls displayOutput before calling computePayment. Except for the describeProgram method, these methods are not independent of each other. They must be called in the right se-

> One of our goals in developing programs is to design them so that they are easy to understand, which is critical in program maintenance. Program maintenance includes correcting errors undetected during development, making minor adjustments, and performing other tasks related to the upkeep of the program. Those who maintain programs are not normally the people who developed them, and maintenance personnel must understand the programs they maintain. A class with a number of cleanly written short methods is more understandable than a class with one gigantic method even if it is cleanly written. Even if the developers themselves perform maintenance, the same argument applies. You may not easily understand code you wrote a week earlier.

quence. The reason we divide the class into several methods is to make the class understandable for those who will implement and maintain the class.

Alternative Design 2

We should provide a lot simpler interface to the user of the LoanCalculator class. Since an instance of the class is the top-level agent, much like a general contractor, we will provide one method the programmer can call to initiate the whole task. We will name the method start. All other methods will be private and called from the start method. The object diagram for this design is shown in Figure 4.7. We will adopt this design for our implementation.

FIGURE 4.7   The object diagram for alternative design 2. **MainWindow**, **OutputBox**, and **InputBox** objects are not shown.

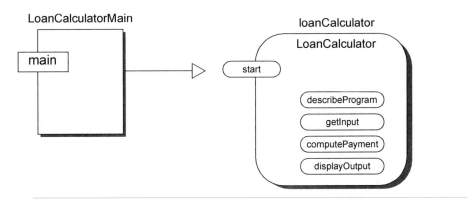

Chapter 4

Let's summarize alternative design 2 for the LoanCalculator class:

Design Document: The LoanCalculator Class		
Method	**Visibility**	**Purpose**
start	public	Starts the loan calculation by calling the other private methods.
computePayment	private	Given three parameters—loan amount, loan period, and interest rate—it computes monthly and total payments.
describeProgram	private	Displays a short description of the program in Output-Box.
displayOutput	private	Displays the result—monthly and total payments—in OutputBox.
getInput	private	Uses InputBox to get three input values—loan amount, loan period, and interest rate.

Chapter 4

We will implement the program in five steps:

development
steps

1. Start with the main class and a skeleton of the LoanCalculator class. The skeleton LoanCalculator class will include only an object/variable declaration and a constructor to create objects.

2. Implement the getInput method of LoanCalculator to accept three input values.

3. Implement the displayOutput method of LoanCalculator to display the results.

4. Implement the computePayment method of LoanCalculator to compute the monthly and total payments.

5. Implement the describeProgram method of LoanCalculator to display a brief description of the program.

Step 1 Development: Program Skeleton

Step 1 Design

There are two classes we have to define for the program: LoanCalculatorMain and LoanCalculator. The main class is now called LoanCalculatorMain. Its main method will declare and create an instance of LoanCalculator and send a message start to it to carry out the loan computation. So the method body of the main method will look like this:

```
LoanCalculator   loanCalculator;
loanCalculator = new LoanCalculator();
loanCalculator.start();
```

This is all we have to design for the main class because the real workhorse of this program is a LoanCalculator object. For the LoanCalculator class, we will begin with the skeleton and develop it incrementally. The purpose of the skeleton LoanCalculator class is to declare and create all the necessary data members. Since these data members will be shared among the methods, we will declare them as instance variables. We will include one class constant MONTHS_IN_YEAR. Their declaration will be as follows:

```
class LoanCalculator
{
    private final int   MONTHS_IN_YEAR = 12;

    private MainWindow  mainWindow;
    private InputBox    inputBox;
    private OutputBox   outputBox;
```

```
    private float        loanAmount,
                         annualInterestRate,
                         monthlyInterestRate;

    private double       monthlyPayment,
                         totalPayment;

    private int          loanPeriod,//loan period in years
                         numberOfPayments;
    ...
}
```

We will not repeat the design for the data members here because their role is the same as in the Chapter 3 program. Some of these data members have to be initialized correctly when a new LoanCalculator object is created, so we will define a constructor to do the necessary initialization. The constructor will be defined as

```
public LoanCalculator()
{
    mainWindow = new MainWindow("L O A N  C A L C U L A T O R");
    inputBox   = new InputBox(mainWindow);
    outputBox  = new OutputBox(mainWindow);
}
```

Since the main method calls the start method of LoanCalculator, we need to implement this method before we can compile the program. The start method will call the other private methods. It is written as

```
public void start ( )
{
    mainWindow.show();
    outputBox.show();

    describeProgram();
    getInput();
    computePayment();
    displayOutput();
}
```

> No dot notation is used here.

Notice that dot notation is not used in calling the four private methods. When a call is made from a method to another method that belongs to the same class, dot notation is not used. This rule applies equally to both data members and methods. Figure 4.8 illustrates the difference between calling another method of the same class and a method of a different class.

Chapter 4

FIGURE 4.8   The difference between calling a method belonging to the same class and a method
                  belonging to a different class.

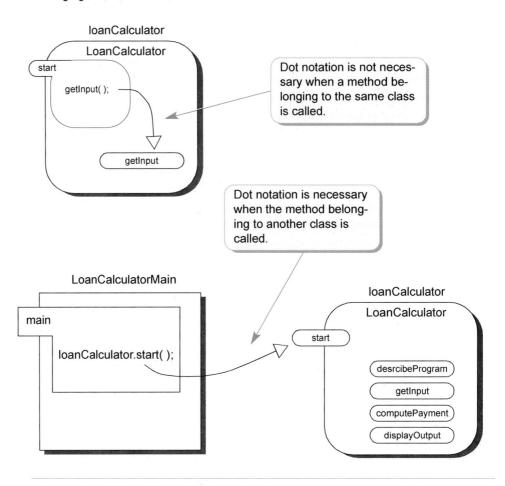

Dot notation is not necessary when you call a method from another method if the two methods belong to the same class.

We will define the four private methods with only a temporary output statement inside their method body to verify that the methods are called correctly. A method that has no "real" statements inside the method body is called a *stub*. The four methods are defined as

stub

```
private void describeProgram()
{
    outputBox.printLine("inside describeProgram"); //TEMP
}

private void getInput()
{
    outputBox.printLine("inside getInput");    //TEMP
}

private void computePayment()
{
    outputBox.printLine("inside computePayment");//TEMP
}

private void displayOutput()
{
    outputBox.printLine("inside displayOutput");//TEMP
}
```

Notice the comment marker //TEMP after the output statements. It is our convention to attach this comment marker so we can easily and quickly locate temporary statements.

For the temporary output statements, we use an OutputBox object because we will be using an OutputBox object in the class anyway. However, we can use a system object to do this type of temporary output for code verification purposes. This system object is available in the System class, and we refer to the output object as System.out. We can use this object just like an OutputBox object, with the only difference being the method name println instead of the more meaningful printLine. For example, you can include the statement

System.out

```
System.out.println("inside setup");
```

instead of

```
outputBox.printLine("inside setup");
```

When you call the println method of System.out, the text is displayed in the default standard output window. The exact appearance of this output window depends on the system you are using. You may want to experiment with System.out and see how it works on your system.

Step 1 Code

Let's put our design in an actual code. The class declaration for the main class is as follows:

File: LoanCalculatorMain.java

```java
/**
 * The LoanCalculator main program to compute the monthly and total
 * payments for a given loan amount, annual interest rate, and number
 * of years. This class uses a LoanCalculator object for the actual
 * task of loan payment computation.
 *
 * @author Dr. Caffeine
 *
 */
class LoanCalculatorMain
{
    public static void main (String[] args)
    {
        LoanCalculator loanCalculator;
        loanCalculator = new LoanCalculator( );
        loanCalculator.start();
    }
}
```

And the skeleton **LoanCalculator** class is defined as follows.

File: LoanCalculator.java

```java
import javabook.*;

/**
 * This class handles the input, computation, and output of loan
 * calculation.
 *
 * @author Dr. Caffeine
 */
class LoanCalculator
{

//----------------------------------
// Data Members
//----------------------------------

    private final int    MONTHS_IN_YEAR = 12;

    private MainWindow   mainWindow;
    private InputBox     inputBox;
    private OutputBox    outputBox;

    private float        loanAmount,
                         annualInterestRate,
                         monthlyInterestRate;

    private double       monthlyPayment,
                         totalPayment;

    private int          loanPeriod,            //loan period in years
                         numberOfPayments;
```

> For the sake of brevity, we will not 'javadoc' the data members here. The actual source file will include javadoc comments for data members also.

```
//-------------------------------
// Constructors
//-------------------------------

    /**
     * Default constructor. The default window title is "LOAN CALCUALTOR".
     */
    public LoanCalculator()
    {
        mainWindow = new MainWindow("L O A N   C A L C U L A T O R");
        inputBox  = new InputBox(mainWindow);
        outputBox = new OutputBox(mainWindow);
    }


//---------------------------------------------------
//      Public Methods:
//
//          void    start   (       )
//
//---------------------------------------------------

    /**
     * Top level method that calls other private methods
     * to compute the monthly and total loan payments.
     */
    public void start ( )
    {
        mainWindow.show();
        outputBox.show();

        describeProgram();    //tell what the program does
        getInput();           //get three input values
        computePayment();     //compute the monthly payment and total
        displayOutput();      //display the results
    }


//---------------------------------------------------
//      Private Methods:
//
//          void    computePayment   (       )
//          void    describeProgram  (       )
//          void    displayOutput    (       )
//          void    getInput         (       )
//
//---------------------------------------------------

    /**
     * Computes the monthly and total loan payments.
     *
     */
    private void computePayment()
    {
        outputBox.printLine("inside computePayment");  //TEMP
    }

    /**
     * Provides a brief explanation of the program to the user.
     *
     */
```

```
    private void describeProgram()
    {
        outputBox.printLine("inside describeProgram"); //TEMP
    }

    /**
     * Displays the input values and monthly and total payments.
     *
     */
    private void displayOutput()
    {
        outputBox.printLine("inside displayOutput");   //TEMP
    }

    /**
     * Gets three input values--loan amount, interest rate, and
     * loan period--using an InputBox object.
     *
     */
    private void getInput()
    {
        outputBox.printLine("inside getInput");        //TEMP
    }

}
```

Step 1 Test   We run the Step 1 program and verify that both mainWindow and outputBox appear on the screen and the following text appears in outputBox:

```
inside describeProgram
inside getInput
inside computePayment
inside displayOutput
```

After the Step 1 program is compiled and executed correctly, we move on to Step 2.

Step 2 Development: Accept Input Values

Step 2 Design   In the second step of coding, we implement the getInput method. We will reuse the pattern we derived in Chapter 3, namely, using an inputBox for accepting input values and an outputBox for echo printing.

Step 2 Code   Here's the method:

```
    private void getInput()
    {
        loanAmount
          = inputBox.getFloat("Loan Amount (Dollars&Cents):");
        annualInterestRate
          = inputBox.getFloat("Annual Interest Rate(e.g. 9.5):");
        loanPeriod
          = inputBox.getInteger("Loan Period - # of years:");
```

```
//TEMP
outputBox.printLine("Loan Amount: $" + loanAmount);
outputBox.printLine("Annual Interest Rate:"
        + annualInterestRate + "%");
outputBox.printLine("Loan Period (years):" + loanPeriod);
//TEMP
}
```

Step 2 Test   As before, to verify the input routine is working correctly, we run the program multiple times. For each run, we enter a different set of data to verify that the InputBox object will not accept any invalid input. We also make sure the values entered are displayed correctly in outputBox.

Step 3 Development: Output Values

Step 3 Design   In the third step of development, we implement the displayOutput method. We use outputBox to display the three input values and monthly and total payments. We will again reuse the design of output layout from Chapter 3. Since the computePayment method is not yet implemented, we will include the temporary assignment statements for monthly and total payments in the computePayment method. The real computePayment will be implemented in the next step.

Step 3 Code   Here are the two methods:

```
private void displayOutput()
{
    outputBox.printLine("For");
    outputBox.printLine("Loan Amount: " + loanAmount);
    outputBox.printLine("Annual Interest Rate: "
                    + annualInterestRate + "%");
    outputBox.printLine("Loan Period (years): " + loanPeriod);
    outputBox.skipLine(1);

    outputBox.printLine("Monthly payment is $ "+ monthlyPayment);
    outputBox.printLine("  TOTAL payment is $ "   + totalPayment);
}

private void computePayment()
{
    monthlyPayment = 132.15;//TEMP
    totalPayment   = 15858.10 ;//TEMP
}
```

Step 3 Test   To verify the output routine is working correctly, we run the program multiple times and verify that the layout looks okay for different values. It is common for a programmer to run the program several times before the layout looks clean on the screen.

Step 4 Development: Compute Loan Amount

Step 4 Design   In the fourth step of development, we replace the temporary computePayment method with the final one. We have already used the necessary formula in Chapter 3. We will reuse the formula here.

Step 4 Code   Here's the method:

```java
private void computePayment()
{
    monthlyInterestRate
            = annualInterestRate / 100.0/ MONTHS_IN_YEAR;

    numberOfPayments = loanPeriod  * MONTHS_IN_YEAR;

    monthlyPayment
            =   (loanAmount * monthlyInterestRate)
                /
                (1 - Math.pow(1/(1 + monthlyInterestRate),
                                numberOfPayments ) );

    totalPayment   =  monthlyPayment * numberOfPayments;
}
```

Step 4 Test   After the method is added to the class, we need to run the program through a number of test data. As in Chapter 3, we made the assumption that the input values must be valid, so we will only test the program for valid input values. For sample test data, we repeat the table from Chapter 3. The right two columns show the correct results. Remember that these three values are only suggestions, not a complete list of test data. You must try other input values as well.

Input			Output	
Loan Amount	Annual Interest Rate	Loan Period (in years)	Monthly Payment	Total Payment
10000	10	10	132.151	15858.1
15000	7	15	134.824	24268.4
10000	12	10	143.471	17216.5

Step 5 Development: Finalize

Step 5 Design   Now in the last step of development, we finalize the class declaration by completing the describeProgram method, the only method still undefined. We may give a very long description or a very terse one. An ideal program will let the

Step 5 Code

user decide. We do not know how to write such code yet, so we will display a
short description of the program to outputBox.

Here's the method.

```
private void describeProgram()
{
    outputBox.printLine
        ("This program computes the monthly and total");
    outputBox.printLine
        ("payments for a given loan amount, annual ");
    outputBox.printLine
        ("interest rate, and loan period (# of years).");
    outputBox.skipLine(2);
}
```

Step 5 Test

You may feel that there's not much testing we can do in this step. After all, we
add only a single method that carries out a simple output routine. However,
many things can go wrong between Step 4 and Step 5. You may have deleted
some lines of code inadvertently. You may have deleted a necessary file by mistake. Anything could happen. The point is to test after every step of development to make sure everything is in order.

4.6 Exercises

1. Consider the following instantiable class.

```
class QuestionOne
{
    public    final int   A = 345;
    public    int         b;
    private   float       c;

    private void methodOne( int a)
    {
        b = a;
    }

    public float methodTwo( )
    {
        return 23;
    }
}
```

Identify invalid statements in the following main class. For each invalid
statement, state why it is invalid.

```
class Q1Main
{
    public static void main( String[] args )
    {
        QuestionOne q1;
        q1 = new QuestionOne( );

        q1.A = 12;
        q1.b = 12;
        q1.c = 12;

        q1.methodOne( 12 );
        q1.methodOne( );
        System.out.println( q1.methodTwo( 12 ) );
        q1.c = q1.methodTwo( );
    }
}
```

2.   What will be the output from the following code?

```
class Q2Main
{
    public static void main( String[] args )
    {
        QuestionTwo q2;
        q2 = new QuestionTwo( );
        q2.init();

        q2.increment();
        q2.increment();

        System.out.println( q2.getCount() );
    }
}

class QuestionTwo
{
    private  int count;

    public void init( )
    {
        count = 1;
    }

    public void increment( )
    {
        count = count + 1;
    }
```

```
        public int getCount( )
        {
            return count;
        }
    }
```

3. What will be the output from the following code? Q3Main and Question-Three classes are the slightly modified version of Q2Main and Question-Two.

```
class Q3Main
{
    public static void main( String[] args )
    {
        QuestionThree q3;
        q3 = new QuestionThree( );
        q3.init();

        q3.count = q3.increment() + q3.increment();

        System.out.println( q3.increment() );
    }
}

class QuestionThree
{
    public  int   count;

    public void init( )
    {
        count = 1;
    }

    public int increment( )
    {
        count = count + 1;
        return count;
    }
}
```

4. Determine the output of the following program.

```
/*
    Program Question4
*/

import javabook.*;

class Question4
{
```

```
    private int x, y, z;
    private MainWindow mainWindow;
    private OutputBox  outputBox;

    public void start ( )
    {
        int    x, y;

        setup();

        x = y = 10;
        modify(x, y);

        printout();
    }


    private void setup( )
    {
        mainWindow = new MainWindow( );
        outputBox = new OutputBox(mainWindow);
        mainWindow.setVisible( true );
        outputBox.setVisible( true );

        x = 100;
        y = 200;
        z = 300;
    }

    private void modify( int x, int y)
    {
        z = x + y;
        x = z;
        y = 2 * z;
    }

    private void printout( )
    {
        outputBox.printLine("x = " + x);
        outputBox.printLine("y = " + y);
        outputBox.printLine("z = " + z);
    }

}


/* Main Class */
class Q4Main
{
    public static void main( String[ ] args )
    {
        Question4 q4;
        q4 = new Question4( );
        q4.start( );
    }
}
```

5. Improve the following program Question5 by converting the class into two classes: the main Q5Main class and the instantiable Question5 class. Avoid duplicating the same code for computing the circumference of two circles. Define a private method in Question5 that accepts the radius of a circle as its parameter and returns the circumference of the circle.

```
/*
    Program Question5

*/
class Question5
{

    public static void main (String[ ] args )
    {
        double          radius ;
        double          circumference;

        MainWindow      mainWindow;
        OutputBox       outputBox;
        InputBox        inputBox;

        int             smallRadius, largeRadius;
        double          smallCircum, largeCircum;

        mainWindow      = new MainWindow( );
        outputBox       = new OutputBox(mainWindow);
        inputBox        = new InputBox(mainWindow);

        //compute circumference of a smaller circle
        smallRadius = inputBox.getDouble("Radius of smaller circle:");
        radius = smallRadius;
        smallCircum = 2 * Math.PI * radius;

        //compute circumference of a larger circle
        largeRadius = inputBox.getDouble("Radius of larger circle:");
        radius = largeRadius;
        largeCircum = 2 * Math.PI * radius;

        //Display the difference
        outputBox.printLine("Difference in circumference of two circles");
        outputBox.printLine("Circumference of smaller circle: " + smallCircum);
        outputBox.skipLine(2);
        outputBox.printLine("Circumference of larger circle: " + largeCircum);
        ouputBox.skipLine(2);
        outputBox.printLine("Difference: " + (largeCircum - smallCircum));
    }


}
```

6. Write an application that converts centimeters (input) to feet and inches (output). Use InputBox for input and OutputBox for output. 1 inch = 2.54 centimeters. Implement this application by defining and using an instantiable class whose instance is capable of converting metric measurements to U.S. units and vice versa. Some of the possible public methods are

```
public double toFeet      ( double centimeter ) { ... }
public double toInches    ( double centimeter ) { ... }
public double toCentimeter( int     feet,
                            int     inches    ) { ... }
public double toCentimeter( double yard       ) { ... }
```

7. Write an application that displays the recommended weight given the user's age and height. The formula for calculating the recommended weight is

```
recommendedWeight = (height - 100 + age % 10) * 0.90
```

8. Write an application that computes the total ticket sales of a concert. There are three types of seatings: A, B, and C. The program accepts the number of tickets sold and the price of a ticket for each of the three types of seats. The total sales are computed as

```
totalSales = numberOfA_Seats * pricePerA_Seat +
             numberOfB_Seats * pricePerB_Seat +
             numberOfC_Seats * pricePerC_Seat;
```

Write this application using only one class, the main class of the program.

9. Redo exercise 8 by using an instantiable SeatType class. An instance of the SeatType class keeps track of the ticket price for a given type of seat (A, B, or C).

10. Write an application that accepts the unit weight of a bag of coffee in pounds and the number of bags sold and displays the total price of the sale, computed as

```
totalPrice         = unitWeight * numberOfUnits * 5.99;
totalPriceWithTax = totalPrice + totalPrice * 0.0725;
```

where 5.99 is the cost per pound and 0.0725 the sales tax. Display the result in the following manner:

```
Number of bags sold:  32
   Weight per bag:  5 lbs
  Price per pound:  $5.99
       Sales tax:  7.25%

    Total price: $ 1027.884
```

You don't have to worry about formatting.

11. Write an application that computes the area of a circular region (the shaded area in the diagram) given the radius of the inner and the outer circles, r_i and r_o, respectively.

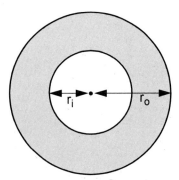

We compute the area of the circular region by subtracting the area of the inner circle from the area of the outer circle. Define an instantiable Circle class that has methods to compute the area and circumference. You set the circle's radius with the setRadius method.

12. In Section 4.3, we modified the conversion methods of the CurrencyConverter class to include the fee deduction. With the modified methods, the sequence of calls such as

```
yenAmount
    = yenConverter.fromDollar( markConverter.toDollar(100) );
```

will result in charging the fee twice. Modify the class to eliminate this double-charging problem.

13. Write an instantiable WeightConverter class. An instance of this class is created by passing the gravity of an object relative to the earth's gravity (see exercise 12 on page 132). For example, the moon's gravity is approximately 0.167 of the earth's gravity, so we create a WeightConverter instance for the moon as

```
WeightConverter  moonWeight;
moonWeight = new WeightConverter( 0.167 );
```

To compute how much you weigh on the moon, you pass your weight on earth to the convert method as

```
yourMoonWeight = moonWeight.convert( 160 );
```

Chapter 4

Define the WeightConverter class. Use this class and redo exercise 12 on page 132.

14. Write an application that teaches children how to read a clock. Use two InputBox objects to enter the hour and minute. The application program draws a clock that looks something like

To draw a clock hand, you use the drawLine method of the Graphics class. The endpoints of the line are determined as

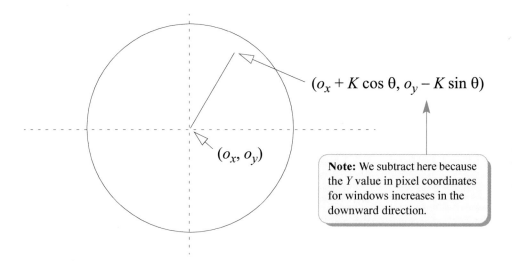

$(o_x + K \cos \theta, o_y - K \sin \theta)$

Note: We subtract here because the Y value in pixel coordinates for windows increases in the downward direction.

The value for constant K determines the length of the clock hand. Make the K larger for the minute hand than for the hour hand. The angle θ is expressed in radians. The angle θ_{min} of the minute hand is computed as

$$(90 - Minute \times 6.0)\frac{\pi}{180}$$

Chapter 4

and the angle θ_{hr} of the hour hand is computed as

$$\left(90 - \left(\text{Hour} + \frac{\text{Minute}}{60.0}\right) \times 30.0\right)\frac{\pi}{180}$$

where Hour and Minute are input values. The values 6.0 and 30.0 designate the degrees for one minute and one hour (i.e., the minute hand moves 6 degrees in one minute and the hour hand moves 30.0 degrees in one hour). The factor $\frac{\pi}{180}$ converts a degree into the radian equivalent.

You can draw the clock on the main window by getting the window's Graphic object as

```
MainWindow mainWindow = new MainWindow();
mainWindow.setVisible( true );
Graphics graphic = mainWindow.getGraphics();
        //make sure mainWindow is visible on the screen
        //before calling its getGraphics method
. . .
graphic.drawOval(100, 100, 200, 200);
. . .
```

15. Extend the application in exercise 14 by drawing a more realistic, better looking clock. For example,

Visit Dr. Caffeine's homepage at http://www.drcaffeine.com and see the applet version of the clock.

16. In the Turtle exercises from the earlier chapters, we dealt with only one Turtle (e.g., see exercise 27 on page 82). It is possible, however, to let multiple turtles draw on a single drawing window. To associate multiple turtles to a

single drawing, we create an instance of TurtleDrawingWindow and add turtles to it as in

```
TurtleDrawingWindow canvas = new TurtleDrawingWindow( );
Turtle winky, pinky, tinky;

winky = new Turtle( ); //create turtles
pinky = new Turtle( );
tinky = new Turtle( );

//now add turtles to the drawing window
canvas.add( winky );
canvas.add( pinky );
canvas.add( tinky );
```

Ordinarily, when you start sending messages such as turn and move to a Turtle, it will begin moving immediately. When you have only one Turtle, this is fine. However, if you have multiple turtles and want them to start moving at the same time, you first have to pause them, give instructions, and then command them to start moving. Here's the basic idea:

```
winky.pause( );
pinky.pause( );
tinky.pause( );

//give instructions to turtles here,
//e.g. pinky.move(50); etc.

//now let the turtles start moving
winky.start( );
pinky.start( );
tinky.start( );
```

Using these Turtle objects, draw the following three triangles:

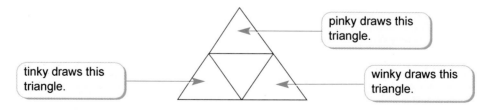

Use a different pen color for each triangle. Run the same program without pausing and describe what happens.

5

Processing Input with Applets

OBJECTIVES

After you have read and studied this chapter, you should be able to

- Define an applet with multiple methods.
- Incorporate a simple event-handling routine to an applet to process input.
- Construct input-processing applets using Label, TextField, and Button objects from the java.awt package.
- Convert string data to numerical data.
- Use the reserved word this in your programs.
- Run applets without using an applet viewer or browser.

Introduction

In this chapter, we will teach you how to write applets that can process input data. To write an input processing applet, you need to know how to define a class with multiple methods, the topic you learned in the previous chapter, because an input processing applet will necessarily require multiple methods. To understand how an applet processes input data, you must learn what events are and how events are handled in Java programs. We will cover the basics of events and event handling in this chapter.

event

Actions such as moving a mouse, selecting a menu item, entering data, and pressing the ENTER key are all events. When the user makes one of these actions, we say an *event is generated*. We program applets so that a designated method will be executed in response to the generated events. We will cover only a rudimentary event-handling technique in this chapter and defer a more detailed discussion on event handling until Chapter 13.

The standard applet classes we discuss in this chapter are from the java.awt and java.applet packages. For the discussion on the Swing version of applets, please visit Dr. Caffeine's website. Please notice that an understanding of this chapter is required before studying the Swing version.

> ***Discussion on the Swing version of applets can be found at***
> www.drcaffeine.com/additionaltopics.

5.1   Placing GUI Objects on Applets

To write an applet that is capable of processing input data, you must first master a number of new concepts. Not to overwhelm you with too many new concepts, we will keep the number of new concepts introduced in this chapter to a bare minimum, just enough for you to be able to write simple input-processing applets. To explain and illustrate the new concepts introduced here, we will build a sample applet called GreetingApplet. This applet accepts a name entered by the user and replies back with a personalized greeting. For example, when the user enters her name Mireille and presses the ENTER key (the RETURN key on the Mac), the applet displays the greeting Nice to meet you, Mireille. Figure 5.1 shows the applet viewer window when the applet starts.

Figure 5.2 shows the same applet viewer window after the user enters her name and presses the ENTER key.

We will develop this applet in two steps. In this section, we describe how to place objects—one for displaying text and another for accepting the user input—on the applet. In the next section, we will show you how to add code that will be executed when the ENTER key is pressed.

FIGURE 5.1   The applet viewer window when the applet **GreetingApplet** is started.

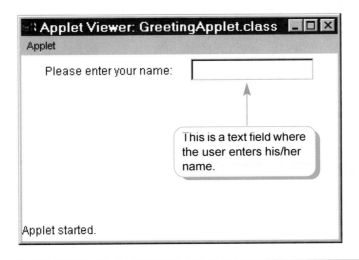

FIGURE 5.2   The applet viewer window after the user enters her name and presses the ENTER key.

We begin with a new template for an applet. This new template, shown in Figure 5.3, is a more general version of the one we introduced in Chapter 2. Using this template our GreetingApplet is declared as

```
import java.applet.*;
import java.awt.*;

/**
 * This applet reads the user's name and
 * displays a personalized greeting.
 */
public class GreetingApplet extends Applet
{
    //Object declarations come here

    //Method declarations come here
}
```

Now, let's identify the objects we need for this applet. To process the user input and display a message on an applet, we will use objects from the standard Java class library. Specifically, we use a Label object to display a text and a TextField object to accept the user input. The Label and TextField classes are from

Label and
TextField

FIGURE 5.3   A template for an applet that is more general than the one we introduced in Chapter 2.

GUI

the standard java.awt package. Objects from these classes are called *GUI* (graphical user interface) objects because they are used for the graphical, windows-based user interface. The word awt in the java.awt stands for *abstract windowing toolkit*, and the java.awt package contains classes for supporting GUI.

For this applet, we use two Label objects, which we will name prompt and greeting, and one TextField object, which we will name inputLine. These three objects are data members of the class that are shared by multiple methods. As such we will declare them within the class declaration but outside of any method. We declare them as

```
public class GreetingApplet extends Applet
{
    private Label       prompt;
    private Label       greeting;
    private TextField   inputLine;

    //Method declarations come here
}
```

Now that the declaration is done, we need a place to create them. Following the guideline of always declaring a constructor and creating data members in it, we will define a constructor to create them.

To create a Label object, we either pass the text that will be displayed on an applet, as in

```
prompt = new Label("Please enter your name:");
```

or pass no argument, as in

```
greeting = new Label( );
```

To create a TextField object, we specify its size by providing the number of characters visible. For example, the statement

```
inputLine = new TextField( 15 );
```

creates a TextField object wide enough to show 15 characters. Notice that this is the maximum number of characters that are visible, not the number of characters you can enter. If you enter more than 15 characters, you will see the text is scrolled to the left as you enter more characters, always showing the maximum of 15 characters.

The constructor for the GreetingApplet is declared as

Chapter 5

```
public GreetingApplet( )
{
    prompt   = new Label("Please enter your name:");
    greeting = new Label( );
    inputLine = new TextField( 15 );
}
```

To make these three GUI objects visible on the applet, creating them inside the constructor is not enough. We are required to associate these objects with the applet by "adding" them to the applet as in

```
add( prompt    );
add( greeting );
add( inputLine );
```

in order to make these objects visible. Note: Since we did not assign any text to greeting, it won't be visible yet. We will introduce the code later to assign the greeting message to greeting.

The add method is inherited from its superclass Applet, and therefore, no dot notation is necessary. We will put these three statements inside the constructor. Here's the full definition of the Step 1 GreetingApplet class:

```
//------------ Program GreetingApplet (Step 1) --------------------//

import java.applet.*;
import java.awt.*;

/**
 * An applet that reads the user's name and
 * displays a personalized greeting.
 */
public class GreetingApplet extends Applet
{
//--------------------------------
//      Data Members
//--------------------------------
    private Label       prompt;     //to prompt user for input
    private Label       greeting;   //to display the personalized greeting
    private TextField   inputLine;  //to accept user input


//--------------------------------
//      Constructor
//--------------------------------

    /**
     * Default constructor that creates one TextField and
     * two Label objects.
     */
    public GreetingApplet( )
    {
        //create the data members
        prompt   = new Label("Please enter your name:");
        greeting = new Label( );
```

```
        inputLine = new TextField( 15 );

        //now attach them to an applet, so they become
        //visible on the applet.
        add( prompt   );
        add( greeting );
        add( inputLine );
    }
}
```

Executing the class (with a corresponding HTML file) will produce the applet viewer window shown in Figure 5.1. You might want to comment out the three add statements in the constructor and verify that no GUI objects will be visible.

The order of adding GUI objects is significant. Change the order of the three add statements and see what happens. For example, if you switch the order of the add statements in the constructor to

```
        add( inputLine );
        add( prompt   );
        add( greeting  );
```

then the applet viewer window shown in Figure 5.4 will appear on the screen. The placement of GUI objects on an applet is dictated by the layout manager associated with the applet. A *layout manager* is an object that controls the placement and size of GUI objects laid out on a container. A *container* object is an object that can contain other GUI objects, for example, frame windows, dialogs, and applets are all containers. There are several layout manager classes in the java.awt package. Three of the more common ones are FlowLayout, CardLayout, and GridLayout. The default layout manager for an applet is a FlowLayout object. With this layout manager, the GUI objects are placed in the left-to-right, top-to-bottom order. If the next GUI object to be placed does not fit in the current row, then it will be placed on the next row. For example, if we change the text of prompt to Would you kindly enter your name?, the applet viewer window shown in Figure 5.5 will appear on the screen. The second object inputLine does not fit on the first row, so it is placed on the second row. Notice that the GUI objects on each row are center aligned.

Although layout managers are interesting and useful in writing more advanced programs, learning different ones is not essential to understanding the fundamentals of object-oriented programming. We also would like to keep our discussion of input-processing applets simple, so we will not cover the layout managers any further. However, we do cover in Section 5.3 a technique called *absolute positioning* to place GUI objects without using a layout manager.

layout manager
container

Chapter 5

FIGURE 5.4   The applet viewer window with the order of the **add** statements switched.

FIGURE 5.5   The applet viewer window with a longer message for the label. Notice that objects in a single row are center-aligned. Alignment becomes more evident if there's only one object in a single row.

Quick Check

1. What is a layout manager?
2. Which method of an applet do you use to make GUI objects visible on the applet?
3. What is the purpose of the numerical argument in the following statement?

```
myTextField = new TextField( 20 );
```

Ms. Latte: *Instead of using* Label *and* TextField, *why can't we simply use an* InputBox *for input?*

Dr. Caffeine: *Because* InputBox *and other dialog windows we used in sample applications require a* Frame *object as their owner. An* Applet *object cannot be an owner of dialog windows. Even though it is possible to use dialog boxes in applets, it is strongly recommended that you don't mix the two.*

Ms. Latte: *Why?*

Dr. Caffeine: *Because applets and dialog boxes are not compatible. Remember that an applet is intended to be executed within a browser. Imagine a situation where an applet opens a dialog box, but instead of interacting with this dialog box, the user moves on to a next web page. This dialog box remains on the screen, but the applet itself is gone from the screen because the browser is now showing a different page.*

Dr. & Ms.

Chapter 5

5.2   Adding ActionListener to an Event Source

When you run the Step 1 GreetingApplet program, you will notice that you can enter text into the TextField object inputLine. You can press the backspace key to delete a character, highlight the text, and perform other editing functions. The functionality that allows the user to enter and edit text is coded in the TextField class, so we don't have to do anything about it. However, when you press the ENTER key, nothing happens. We will now add code to process the pressing of the ENTER key. We will refer to the pressing of the ENTER key as the *ENTER key event*.

event source
and
event listener

To process an event, we need two types of objects: event source and event listener objects. An *event source* is an object that generates an event, and an *event listener* is an object that listens to the generated events. An event listener must register itself to an event source in order to "listen" to the events generated by the event source. When an event source generates an event, it calls a certain method of the registered event listeners.

Many GUI objects such as text fields, buttons, scroll bars, and others are primary event sources. A single event source can generate different types of events. For example, when a TextField object is active and the ENTER key is pressed, the object generates an *action event*. Not all GUI objects generate action events. In fact, among the GUI objects discussed in this chapter, only Text-Field and Button generate action events.

action event

TextField *objects (and* Button *objects covered in Section 5.4) generate action events.* Label *objects do not generate action events.*

mouse movement
event

You know a TextField object is *active* when the vertical line is blinking in it. When the mouse cursor is moved over the TextField object, it generates a *mouse movement event* (even if it is not active). A TextField object can generate other types of events. Here we will discuss the action events only. We will cover other types of events in Chapter 13.

mouse motion
and action event
listeners

Any object can be an event listener. A type of event listener that listens to mouse movement events is called a *mouse motion event listener*. A type of event listener that listens to action events is called an *action event listener*. To process an action event generated by a TextField object, we need an action event listener. For the GreetingApplet program, we will set the applet to be an action event listener to the action events that inputLine generates.

To set a GreetingApplet object be an action event listener, we must do four things:

1. Import the Java event-handling classes with

   ```
   import java.awt.event.*;
   ```

2. Modify the class declaration to include the clause implements Action-Listener

   ```
   public class GreetingApplet extends Applet
                       implements ActionListener
   {
       . . .
   }
   ```

3. Add the actionPerformed method to the GreetingApplet class declaration.

4. Register the GreetingApplet object to the event source inputLine as its action event listener.

interface

abstract method

ActionListener is called an *interface*. Although technically they are different, we can view an interface as a special kind of a class that includes only a set of constants and a set of abstract methods. An *abstract method* is a method that has no method body. We say a class *implements* the interface if the class provides the method body for the abstract methods defined in the interface.

> The purpose of interfaces in Java is to dictate common behavior among objects from diverse classes. Suppose we want objects from different classes such as Truck, BankAccount, Appliance, Stock, *and so on, to share one common behavior of computing their market value. We can define an interface, say,* Asset, *with one abstract method* computeCurrentWorth. *We will make all these classes implement the* Asset *interface by providing the method body for the* computeCurrentWorth *method. Notice that they share the common behavior of evaluating their worth, but the individual implementation, the formulas they use to evaluate the market value, will be very different. A similar effect can be achieved if the language allows a class to inherit from more than one superclass, but Java does not allow it. Instead, Java provides interfaces. We will not get into any more details here. You will see more examples of interfaces in Chapters 13 and later.*

The ActionListener interface includes one abstract method called actionPerformed, and for the GreetingApplet to implement the ActionListener interface, its class declaration must include the definition for the actionPerformed method. This actionPerformed method is the method the event source object calls when it generates an action event. Inside the method body, we place the code we want to be executed in response to the generated event. The outline of the GreetingApplet class looks like this:

```
public class GreetingApplet extends Applet
                        implements ActionListener
{
    //Object declarations come here

    public GreetingApplet( )
    {
        . . .
    }
```

Chapter 5

```
public void actionPerformed( ActionEvent event )
{
    //response code comes here
}

}
```

This applet follows the template for input-processing applets. This template, shown in Figure 5.6, is an extension of the one shown earlier in Figure 5.3.

FIGURE 5.6   A template for an input-processing applet. This template is an extension of the one shown in Figure 5.3.

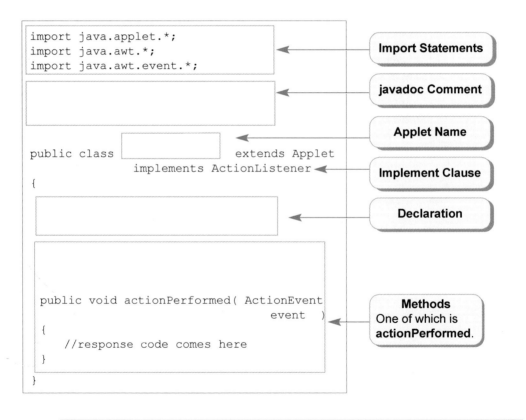

The actionPerformed method takes one parameter of type ActionEvent. For each type of events, Java defines a separate class. Other event classes include WindowEvent, MouseEvent, and TextEvent. These event objects contain information relevant to the generated event, which is useful in the method that processes the event.

We will add the code to register the applet to the event source as its action event listener in the constructor. The event source is inputLine, and to add an action listener to it, we call its addActionListener method with the action listener object as the argument, as in

```
inputLine.addActionListener( <action listener> );
```

with <action listener> replaced by the reference to the actual listener. We will make this call inside the constructor of the GreetingApplet, and to refer to an object itself within the method of the object, we use the reserved word this. In an object diagram, we can represent the reserved word this as

reserved word
this

Here's the modified constructor:

```
public GreetingApplet( )
{
    //create GUI objects
    prompt    = new Label("Please enter your name:");
    greeting  = new Label( );
    inputLine = new TextField( );

    //add GUI objects to the applet
    add( prompt   );
    add( greeting );
    add( inputLine );

    //add this applet as an action listener
    inputLine.addActionListener( this );
}
```

Inside the actionPerformed method, we include the code to process the ENTER key event. Inside the method body, we

1. Fetch the name entered in inputLine by calling its getText method.

Chapter 5

2. Concatenate the name returned by the getText method with the message Nice to meet you and the period as

```
"Nice to meet you, " + inputLine.getText() + "."
```

3. Assign the resulting string from Step 2 to the Label object greeting by calling its setText method.

4. Call the add method to place greeting and call the doLayout method.

We call the add method again because a new text was assigned to greeting and this could change its dimension. Since the dimension of greeting has possibly changed, we ask the layout manager to adjust the placement of GUI objects based on their new sizes by calling the doLayout method. The actionPerformed method is defined as follows:

```java
public void actionPerformed( ActionEvent event )
{
    greeting.setText( "Nice to meet you,"
                         + inputLine.getText( ) + "." );
    add( greeting );
    doLayout();
}
```

Notice that the ActionEvent parameter is not used in the method.

Here's the final, complete listing of GreetingApplet. Its object diagram is shown in Figure 5.7.

```java
//------------ Program GreetingApplet (Final Version) ------------------//

import java.awt.*;
import java.applet.*;              ActionListener and
import java.awt.event.*;  ◄------  ActionEvent are de-
                                   fined in this package.
/**
 * This applet accepts the user's name via a TextField object.
 * When the user presses the ENTER key, the applet displays
 * a personalized greeting "Nice to meet you, <user name>."
 * with <user name> replaced by the actual name entered by the user.
 */

public class GreetingApplet extends Applet implements ActionListener
{

//-------------------------------
//      Data Members
//-------------------------------

    private    Label     prompt;    //to prompt user for input
    private    Label     greeting;  //to display the personalized greeting
    private    TextField inputLine;  //to accept user input
```

```java
//--------------------------------
//     Constructor
//--------------------------------
    /**
     * Default constructor that creates one TextField and
     * two Label objects. This GreetingApplet is set to be
     * an ActionListener of itself.
     */
    public GreetingApplet( )
    {
        //create GUI objects
        prompt    = new Label("Please enter your name:");
        greeting  = new Label( );
        inputLine = new TextField( );

        //add GUI objects to the applet
        add( prompt   );
        add( greeting );
        add( inputLine );

        //add this applet as an action listener
        inputLine.addActionListener( this );
    }

//-----------------------------------------------------
//     Public Methods:
//
//         void   actionPerformed  (  ActionEvent  )
//
//-----------------------------------------------------
    /**
     * Implements the abstract method defined in the interface
     * ActionListener. The method retrieves the text from the
     * TextField object 'inputLine' and displays the personalized
     * greeting using the Label object 'greeting'.
     */
    public void actionPerformed( ActionEvent event )
    {
        greeting.setText( "Nice to meet you,"
                        + inputLine.getText( ) + "." );
        add( greeting );
        doLayout();
    }
}
```

Chapter 5

Quick Check

1. What is the purpose of the addActionListener method?

2. In the GreetingApplet program, which object can be an event source and which object is an action event listener?

3. When does the class need to implement the actionPerformed method?

FIGURE 5.7   The object diagram for the **GreetingApplet** program.

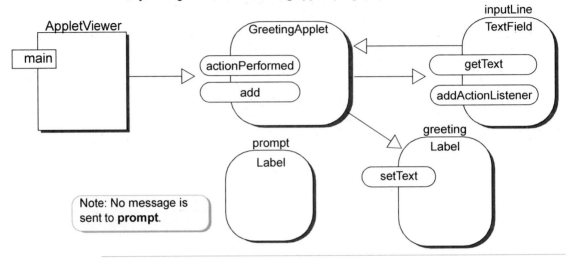

5.3   Absolute Positioning of GUI Objects

We used the default FlowLayout manager in the previous section. It is also possible to place GUI objects without any layout manager by using the technique

absolute
positioning

called *absolute positioning*. With this technique, we specify the size and the location of GUI objects to place on an applet. To use absolute positioning, we

reserved word
null

need to set the layout manager of an applet to null by passing the argument null
to the setLayout method as in

setLayout
method

```
setLayout( null );
```

The reserved word null means nothing or no object. Thus, assigning null to a layout manager means the applet has no layout manager.

We designate the location and size of GUI objects placed in the applet by

setBounds
method

calling the GUI objects' setBounds method. Its general syntax is

```
<object name> . setBounds( <x> , <y> , <width> , <height> );
```

where <x> and <y> specify the top, left corner and <width> and <height> specify
the dimensions of the object. The order of adding GUI objects is irrelevant in
the case of absolute positioning.

If we change the constructor of the GreetingApplet to

```
public GreetingApplet()
{
    prompt    = new Label("Please enter your name:");
    inputLine = new TextField( ); //no argument here

    setLayout( null );   //no layout manager

    add( prompt    );    //attach the GUI
    add( inputLine );    //objects to this applet

    //set the position and size of GUI objects
       prompt.setBounds( 65, 20, 150, 25 );
    inputLine.setBounds( 65, 55, 150, 25 );
}
```

> The applet will have no layout manager

> Set the position and size of GUI objects. Make sure the size of the **Label** object is big enough to make all of its text visible.

then you will see the applet viewer window shown in Figure 5.8. Figure 5.9 shows how the setBounds method works.

FIGURE 5.8   The applet with no layout manager and with absolute positioning of GUI objects.

If an applet is using the default FlowLayout manager, then the GUI objects in the applet will move when you resize the applet viewer window. However, with no layout manager and absolute positioning, the GUI objects on the applet will not move when you resize the applet viewer window. This is one effect of setting the layout manager to null and using absolute positioning. Remember that you can use absolute positioning only when you set the layout manager to null.

FIGURE 5.9   The **setBounds** method takes four arguments: x, y, width, and height in pixel values .

```
inputLine.setBounds( 65, 55, 150, 25);
```

If you want to use the absolute positioning approach to place GUI objects on an applet, then you must set the layout manager to **null**.

5.4   The Button Class

In the GreetingApplet program, the user informs the program that she has finished entering her name by pressing the ENTER key, and the applet is programmed to respond to this ENTER key event. Let's modify the applet by adding another GUI object. Instead of the user pressing the ENTER key, she will now click a button.

A type of button called a *pushbutton* is one of the most common GUI objects used in today's window-based programs. Figure 5.10 shows a modified GreetingApplet named GreetingAppletWithButton, which now includes a button.

To add a pushbutton to an applet, we create an instance of the Button class from the java.awt package. The way we interact with a Button object is very similar to the way we interact with other GUI objects. To create a Button object, we pass the label of a button (the text that appears inside a button). For example, the button in GreetingAppletWithButton is declared and created as

```
Button    helloButton;
helloButton = new Button( "Say Hello" );
```

FIGURE 5.10   An applet viewer window running **GreetingAppletWithButton** after the user clicked on the button. This applet uses absolute positioning for laying out the GUI objects.

A button is another kind of GUI object that generates action events. A button generates an action event when we click on it. So, if we want to process the button click event, then we add an action listener to a button. For the GreetingAppletWithButton, we add the applet as its action event listener in the constructor as

```
public GreetingAppletWithButton( )
{
    //code for creating GUI objects and
    //adding them to the applet

    helloButton.addActionListener( this );
}
```

> The applet is the action event listener of **helloButton**.

When helloButton generates an action event, it calls the action listener's actionPerformed method. This actionPerformed method is the same as in GreetingApplet because the response the applet makes is still the same.

It is possible to register different action listeners to a single event source and to register a single action listener to different event sources. For example, we can register the applet as an action listener to both inputLine and helloButton. This means that the user can either click on a button or press the ENTER key (when inputLine is active) when she's done entering her name. To register the applet to both inputLine and helloButton, we simply include the following two statements in the constructor:

```
inputLine.addActionListener( this );

helloButton.addActionListener( this );
```

Both inputLine and helloButton will call the actionPerformed method of GreetingAppletWithButton when they generate an action event.

You can register multiple event listeners to a single event source and register a single event listener to multiple event sources.

5.5   Converting Text to a Numerical Value

Suppose we want to write an applet that accepts the user's year of birth and prints out the message You will be <N> years old in the year 2020, with <N> replaced with the actual age of the user. This applet will be very similar to GreetingApplet of the previous section. We need to learn only one new concept to write this applet, namely, the data conversion from text to a numerical value.

A TextField object we use to input data from the user will accept data as text value. To perform a numerical computation on this input text data, we must first convert it to a number. Let's see how we can perform the data conversion. First, text data in Java is called a *string*, and we can use a variable of type String. We will only show a very simple use of String variables in this section. A full discussion of string manipulation will be presented in Chapter 8.

Using String variables, we can rewrite the actionPerformed method of GreetingApplet as

string

```
public void actionPerformed( ActionEvent event )
{
    String name, message;

    name      = inputLine.getText();
    message   = "Nice to meet you, " + name + ".";

    greeting.setText( message );
}
```

Because the getText method of TextField returns a String value, it is not valid to write

```
int age;
age = inputLine.getText();
```

because the data type does not match. We were able to do something like

```
int age;
InputBox inputBox = new InputBox(...);

age = inputBox.getInteger( );
```

because the getInteger method does the conversion for us. The InputBox class also uses a TextField object to get the user input, but the text input data are converted to an appropriate data type (int for getInteger, float for getFloat, and so forth) before returning the value to the caller.

Since we are using TextField objects directly in our applets, we must do our own data conversion. To convert string data to a numerical value of type double, float, int, and others, we can use a Double object. Do not confuse this Double with the numerical data type double. An instance of the Double class is an object that contains a double value as its value. The following diagram illustrates a Double object containing a double value 23.56789.

Double

To convert a string to a double, we first create a Double object with the string as its argument. For example,

```
Double doubleObject;
doubleObject = new Double( "234.5" );
```

An error will result if the passed string cannot be converted to a double value, for example, "12ABC". Once the Double object is created, we can get a double value by calling the object's doubleValue method

```
double x;
x = doubleObject.doubleValue();
```

The double variable x will hold the numerical value 234.5. It is also possible to get an int or a float value from doubleObject. If we execute

```
int i;
i = doubleObject.intValue();
```

then the int variable i will hold the integer value 235. Notice the value is rounded.

We can convert a double value to a string value using a Double object also. The following code converts the float value 45.88 to the string value "45.88":

```
Double doubleObject;
String str;

doubleObject = new Double( 45.88 ); //pass a double value
str = doubleObject.toString();
```

Notice that we pass a float value as an argument in creating a new Float object. We can create a Double object by passing either a string or a double value.

The Double class is called a *wrapper* class because it "wraps" a double value with a set of methods useful in manipulating it. Other wrapper classes whose instances contain a numerical value are Integer, Long, and Float. Their respective conversion methods are intValue, longValue, and floatValue.

We will use these data conversion routines in the next section's sample program.

Quick Check

1. What will be the state of memory after the following code is executed? Draw the state of memory diagram.

    ```
    Double    myDoubleObj;
    myDoubleObj = new Double( "12.345" );
    ```

2. What is the value of x?

    ```
    Double    myDoubleObj1, myDoubleObj2;
    double    x;

    myDoubleObj1 = new Double( "12.0" );
    myDoubleObj2 = new Double( "12.6" );

    x = myDoubleObj1.doubleValue()
            + myDoubleObj2.intValue();
    ```

3. What is the output?

```
Float      myFloatObj;

myFloatObj = new Float( "22.66" );

outputBox.printLine(
    (int) Math.round( myFloatObj.floatValue() ) );
```

5.6   Sample Program: Finding Body Mass Index (BMI)

As a summary of the topics covered in this chapter, we will develop an applet that computes your body mass index. A *body mass index* (BMI) is defined by the formula

$$BMI = \frac{w}{h^2}$$

where w is weight in kilogram and h is height in meters. A person with a BMI of 20 to 26 is generally considered healthy, although there's no agreed-upon BMI at which health risks become significant. But most experts agree that you need to be concerned if your BMI is 27 or above. If you are interested in BMI and healthy living in general, you can start by exploring the website http://www.healthyweight.com.

Problem Statement

Write an applet that displays a BMI of a person given his or her weight (in kilograms) and height (in meters).

Overall Plan

As always, our initial task is to map out the overall plan for development. Let's begin with the visual appearance of the applet and identify GUI objects necessary for the program. First, we need two TextField objects to input height and weight. For these two TextField objects, we need to attach labels so the user knows which is for weight and which is for height. We will use two Label objects for this purpose. We also need a third Label object to display the user's BMI.

Now, how should the user let the program know she's done entering the weight and height? We can let both TextField objects be an event source so the user can press the ENTER key when either one of the TextField objects is active. This approach will work but does not support a good user interface, because it's not obvious to the user just by looking at the applet that she must press the ENTER key to tell the applet to compute the BMI. It is a much better user interface

Chapter 5

if we use a pushbutton. When the user sees a pushbutton on an applet, it immediately becomes obvious that she needs to click on the button to initiate some action. So let's add a Button to the applet. Here's our initial design document:

Design Document:	BMIApplet Program
Class	**Purpose**
BMIApplet	The main applet class. The applet viewer will create an instance of this class.
TextField	Two TextField objects are used: one for inputting weight and another for inputting height.
Label	Three Label objects are used: two for labeling the TextField objects and the third one for displaying the BMI.
Button	One Button object with label Compute BMI is used. When this button is clicked, the applet displays the computed BMI.

Figure 5.11 is the object diagram for the applet at this point. Notice the arrow from computeButton to the BMIApplet because computeButton is the one calling the applet's actionPerformed method.

We will develop the applet in the following four steps:

1. Start with a skeleton BMIApplet class. The skeleton class will include data member declarations and a partially defined constructor that creates and places GUI objects.

2. Add code to the constructor to create and place all GUI objects on the applet.

3. Define the actionPerformed method to process the button click action event. We will include a dummy output statement to verify the button click event is properly detected.

4. Add code to compute and display the BMI and finalize the code.

Step 1 Development: Applet Skeleton

We will start with a skeleton for the BMIApplet. The structure we learned in this chapter is to make an applet an action event listener, so the class declaration will look like this:

```
public class BMIApplet extends Applet implements ActionListener
{
    . . .
}
```

FIGURE 5.11   The object diagram for the program **BMIApplet**.

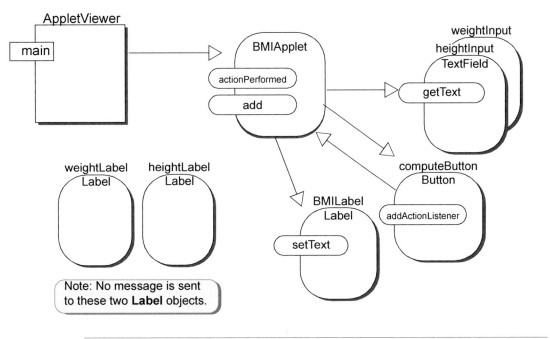

We have identified seven GUI objects in the overall planning stage, and these GUI objects will be the data members of the class. Their declaration will be as follows:

```
private    Label      heightLabel,
                      weightLabel,
                      BMILabel;

private    TextField  heightInput,
                      weightInput;

private    Button     computeButton;
```

Since the applet implements the ActionListener interface, we must include the actionPerformed method. We also need a constructor to create and place GUI objects on the applet. The class design document at this point is therefore as follows:

Design Document:	The BMIApplet Class	
Method	**Visibility**	**Purpose**
`<Constructor>`	`public`	Create and place GUI objects on the applet.
`actionPerformed`	`public`	Includes response code for the button click action event. The method computes and displays the BMI for a given height and weight.

Step 1 Code

Let's put our design in an actual code. We will begin with a shell constructor that includes only a code to create and place a button. The **actionPerformed** method will include no statements in the method body. We will complete the method in Step 3. The class declaration for the Step 1 applet is as follows

```
//------------ Program BMIApplet (Step 1) ------------------//

import java.awt.*;
import java.applet.*;
import java.awt.event.*;

/**
 * This applet computes the body mass index (BMI).
 * It accepts the user's height and weight and displays
 * his/her BMI according to the formula
 * BMI = weight / (height * height)
 */
public class BMIApplet extends Applet implements ActionListener
{

//---------------------------------
//      Data Members
//---------------------------------

private   Label      heightLabel,  //label for heightInput
                     weightLabel,  //label for weightInput
                     BMILabel;     //label for displaying a BMI

private   TextField  heightInput,  //to accept the user's height
                     weightInput;  //to accept the user's weight

private   Button     computeButton;//the user clicks this button
                                   //to compute the BMI

//---------------------------------
//      Constructor
//---------------------------------

/**
 * Default constructor for creating and placing GUI objects
 * on this applet.
 */
```

```
public BMIApplet( )
{
   //TEMP: Just add a button
   computeButton = new Button("Compute BMI");

   add( computeButton );
}

//-------------------------------------------------------
//     Public Methods:
//
//         void   actionPerformed  (   ActionEvent   )
//
//-------------------------------------------------------
   /**
    * Implements the abstract method defined in the interface
    * ActionListener.
    */
   public void actionPerformed( ActionEvent event )
   {
      //code comes here
   }
}
```

Since this is an applet, we need an HTML file to run it. We will use our default HTML file whose content is shown below. The file is saved as BMIApplet.html.

```
<HTML>
<BODY>
<APPLET CODE="BMIApplet.class" WIDTH=300 HEIGHT=190></APPLET>
</BODY>
</HTML>
```

Step 1 Test

We run the Step 1 applet and verify that an applet appears with a button labeled Compute BMI on it. After the Step 1 program is compiled and executed correctly, we move on to Step 2.

Step 2 Development: Layout of GUI Objects

Step 2 Design

In this step, we will complete the constructor by creating all GUI objects and placing them on the applet. We have two choices: use the default layout manager FlowLayout or set the layout manager to null and use absolute positioning.

Alternative Design 1

If we use the default layout manager, then we have to place the GUI objects in the right order. To realize the layout we designed in the overall planning stage, we must execute the following statements in order:

```
add( heightLabel );
add( heightInput );
```

Chapter 5

```
add( weightLabel );
add( weightInput );

add( computeButton );

add( BMILabel );
```

Using the FlowLayout manager, the actual appearance is also affected by the length of the text assigned to the labels and the values assigned to WIDTH and HEIGHT in the BMIApplet.html. We have to try out different combinations before settling on the one that looks best.

Alternative Design **2**   If we use absolute positioning, then we must set the layout manager to null and call the setBounds method for all GUI objects to set their position and size. If we call the setBounds method, then the order of adding the GUI objects is irrelevant. The sequence of calls may look something like this:

```
heightLabel.setBounds(  60,   20, 150, 25 );
heightInput.setBounds(  70,   50, 180, 25 );
weightLabel.setBounds(  60,   80, 150, 25 );
weightInput.setBounds(  70,  110, 180, 25 );
computeButton.setBounds( 70,  140, 120, 25 );
    BMILabel.setBounds(  60,  170, 150, 25 );
```

We will adopt the first alternative design and leave the second alternative as an exercise.

Step 2 Code   Here's the code to create and place the GUI objects on the applet:

```
public BMIApplet( )
{
   //create the GUI objects
   heightLabel
      = new Label("Your height (in meters, e.g. 1.88):");
   heightInput = new TextField( 15 );

   weightLabel
      = new Label("Your weight (in kilograms, e.g. 180.5):");
   weightInput  = new TextField( 15 );

   computeButton = new Button("    Compute BMI    ");

   BMILabel    = new Label( "This is your BMI Computer.");

   //place the GUI objects on the applet
   //order of adding is significant
   add( heightLabel );
```

```
        add( heightInput );

        add( weightLabel );
        add( weightInput );

        add( computeButton );

        add( BMILabel );
    }
```

Step 2 Test

We run the Step 2 program and experiment with different combinations of the text for labels and the values for the WIDTH and HEIGHT attributes in BMI-Applet.html. After we get the right combinations that make the applet's visual appearance to our liking, we move on to Step 3.

Step 3 Development: Process the Button Click Event

Step 3 Design

In this step, we implement the actionPerformed method. The task of the action-Performed method is to accept two input values and compute the BMI. The input values are retrieved from the two TextField objects. Since the values returned by the getText method are string data, we need to convert them to numerical values. We discussed the conversion from string to numerical value in Section 5.5. Since the input values will include a decimal point, we will use the double data type for the numerical values. Once we have two numerical values, we use the given formula to compute the BMI. Given double values for height and weight, the resulting BMI also will be float. Since it is more common among health experts to use a whole number for BMI, we will round off the result to get an integer, that is, 25 instead of 24.6345.

Here's the outline of the actionPerformed method:

```
    Task 1. Get input from heightInput and weightInput.

    Task 2. Convert textual input values to equivalent numeri-
            cal values.

    Task 3. Compute BMI from the given two numbers. Round off
            the result to integer.

    Task 4. Display the result.
```

In order to make computeButton call the actionPerformed method of the applet, we must add the statement to register this applet as an action event listener to computeButton in the constructor as

Chapter 5

```
computeButton.addActionListener( this );
```

Step 3 Code   We are now ready to put our design into an actual code. The actionPerformed method is defined as

```
public void actionPerformed( )
{
    String heightString, weightString, result;
    double height, weight;
    int    BMI;

    //Get input values
    heightString = heightInput.getText( );
    weightString = weightInput.getText( );

    //Convert input to numbers
    height = convertToDouble( heightString );
    weight = convertToDouble( weightString );

    //Compute the BMI
    BMI = computeBMI( height, weight );

    //Display the result
    result = "Your BMI is " + BMI;
    BMILabel.setText( result );

    add( BMILabel );
    doLayout( );
}
```

Notice the use of the two methods convertToFloat and computeBMI. We use
these two private methods to keep the actionPerformed method concise and,
therefore, easy to comprehend. For the two private methods, we use the temporary method body, defined as

```
private double convertToDouble( String str )
{
    return 123.5; //TEMP
}

private int computeBMI( double height, double weight )
{
    return 24; //TEMP
}
```

We modify the constructor to include the statement to add the applet as an action listener:

```
public BMIApplet
{
    //same as before

    computeButton.addActionListener( this );
}
```

Step 3 Test

Run the Step 3 applet and verify that the message

```
Your BMI is 24.
```

appears on the applet when you click the button.

Step 4 Development: Compute the BMI

Step 4 Design

The design document for the BMIApplet class now includes two private methods, that were defined in Step 3. Here's the design document:

Design Document:	The BMIApplet Class	
Method	Visibility	Purpose
. . .	. . .	. . .
computeBMI	private	The method computes the BMI for given height and weight passed as parameters. The method returns the BMI as int.
convertToDouble	private	The method converts a given String value to a double value.

The final task is to complete these two private methods. The computeBMI method implements the formula that computes the BMI given values for height and weight in double. The statement will be

```
BMI = weight / (height * height);
```

Be careful not to express the formula erroneously as

```
BMI = weight / height * height;
```

Chapter 5

This statement is wrong because it is equivalent to the mathematical expression

$$\frac{w}{h} \times h$$

Remember that the precedence rule causes the division to be evaluated before the multiplication.

We decided in the previous step that the value of BMI will be represented as an integer so we need to round off the value to the nearest integer value and typecast the result to type int. So the final form will be as

```java
BMI = (int) Math.round( weight / (height * height) );
```

The conversion of input text to a double value is done by using the technique explained in Section 5.5. We use a Double object and its doubleValue method as

```java
Double doubleObj = new Double( str ); //str is a String
double number    = doubleObj.doubleValue();
```

For this routine to work correctly, we must assume that the input values are valid. If the user enters an input that contains a character other than 0 through 9 or a decimal point, the conversion will not work. We have to make this assumption because we do not know yet how to test for the validity of input. We will learn this in the next chapter.

Step 4 Code

The computeBMI method is defined as

```java
private int computeBMI( double height, double weight )
{
    int BMI;

    BMI = (int) Math.round( weight / (height * height) );

    return BMI;
}
```

The convertToDouble method is defined as

```java
private double convertToDouble( String str )
{
    Double doubleObj = new Double( str );
    return doubleObj.doubleValue();
}
```

Step 4 Test

Now we are ready to input different values and verify that the applet produces the correct results. Run the applet by entering many different input values. Here are some of the possible input values:

Input		Output
height	weight	BMI
1.82	70	21
1.82	90	27
1.65	55	20
1.79	80	25
1.70	65	22

5.7   Running an Applet as an Application

We used an applet viewer to run applets. To run simple applets like the ones we developed in this chapter, we actually do not need an applet viewer. We can use any frame window to run applets. The MainWindow class in javabook is one such frame window. Just as we place GUI objects on an applet, we can place an applet on a frame window because a frame window is a container and an applet is itself a GUI component.

We will show you how to run the GreetingApplet as an application. It is actually very simple. Assuming the GreetingApplet class is already defined, we just have to define the main class. In the main method, we create an instance of MainWindow and place a GreetingApplet object on this MainWindow object. Here's the main class:

```
import javabook.*;

/**
 * This program executes an applet as an application
 */
class GreetingApplication
{
    public static void main( String args[] )
    {
        MainWindow       mainWindow;
        GreetingApplet   greetingApplet;

        mainWindow     = new MainWindow("My Applet Runner");
        greetingApplet = new GreetingApplet();

        greetingApplet.init(); //make sure you initialize it
```

Chapter 5

```
            //add greetingApplet to mainWindow and
            //show the window
            mainWindow.add( greetingApplet );
            mainWindow.setVisible( true );
        }
    }
```

That's it. There are situations where you have to do more, but for simple applets, you can run them as an application using the technique explained here. Remember we mentioned earlier that an applet viewer is the main class of the applet programs. We are simply defining our own main class, just as we do with any other application programs. Notice that when we run an applet as an application, an HTML file is no longer necessary. Being able to run an applet as an application gives programmers a lot of opportunities and flexibility. Using this technique, we can develop one applet and run the same applet as a regular applet on a browser or as a stand-alone application.

Since a MainWindow object by default is almost as big as the screen size, you may want to resize and position the window. You can do it by calling the window's **setSize** and **move** methods. You can put the following two statements before you show the window:

```
    mainWindow.setSize( 400, 300 );     //pass the width
                                        //and height
    mainWindow.setLocation( 250, 200 ); //set the top left
                                        //corner to (250, 200)
```

5.8   Exercises

1. Identify the problems with the following constructor of an applet. Assume the GUI objects are all properly declared in the data member declaration section.

```
    public MyApplet( )
    {
        //create objects
        textField = new TextField( );
        label    = new Label( );

        label.addActionListener( this );
    }
```

2. What is the difference between Double and double?

3. If an applet is declared as

```
public class MyApplet extends Applet implements ActionListener
{
    ...
}
```

which public method must be added to this applet?

4. Identify which of the following statements are invalid:

```
Float     floatObj1 = new Float("123");
Integer   intObj    = new Integer("123.0");
Float     floatObj2 = new Float(12.3);
int sum = floatObj.floatValue( ) + floatObj.intValue();
```

5. (Challenge) Consider the last statement of the constructor from the Greet-ingApplet program in Section 5.2 on page 203:

```
public GreetingApplet( )
{
    ...

    //add this applet as an action listener
    inputLine.addActionListener( this );
}
```

What will be the problem if we rewrite the constructor to

```
public void init( )
{
    ...

    //add a GreetingApplet object as an action listener
    inputLine.addActionListener( new GreetingApplet() );
}
```

Note: The code does not have any syntax error.

6. Identify all errors in the following applet.

```
/*
    Class QuestionApplet

*/

import java.awt.*;
import java.applet.*;
```

```
private class QuestionApplet extends Applet
{

    private    Button    button;
    private    Label     greeting;

    public Applet( )
    {
        greeting    = new Label("Hello, how are you?");
        button      = new Button("Good Bye" );

        add( greeting  );
        add( button );

    }

    public void actionPerformed( Event event )
    {
        greeting.setText( "Well, good-bye.");
    }
}
```

7. Write an applet that converts a given Celsius temperature to the equivalent Fahrenheit temperature. The formula for conversion is

    ```
    fahrenheit = (9.0/5.0) * celsius + 32.0;
    ```

8. Rewrite the LoanCalculator application in Chapter 4 as an applet. Use three TextField objects for getting the loan amount, interest rate, and loan period. Every time the user presses the ENTER key, the applet displays the monthly and total payments. Include appropriate labels for input and output.

9. Write an applet that converts centimeters (input) to feet and inches (output). Use TextField for input and two Label objects for output. 1 inch = 2.54 centimeters.

10. Write an applet that converts feet and inches (input) to centimeters.

11. Modify the BMIApplet so the applet computes the BMI when the user clicks on the button or presses the ENTER key. The ENTER key event is valid only when the weightInput object is active. The ENTER key event acts like a shortcut for clicking on the button, where the user enters her height, presses the TAB key to move to weightInput, enters her weight, and then presses the ENTER key. This sequence works faster than the user removing her hand from the keyboard and clicking on the button with a mouse after entering two values.

12. Modify the BMIApplet so the user can enter his/her weight in pounds (float) and height in feet (int) and inches (int). Use absolute position for the layout of the GUI objects as shown below:

13. Write an applet called RecommendedWeightApplet that computes the user's recommended weight given his/her height. For this applet use the following formula for calculating the recommended weight:

```
recommendedWeight = (height - 100 + age % 10) * 0.90;
```

The height is entered in centimeters.

14. Modify the RecommendedWeightApplet of exercise 13 so the user can enter his or her height in feet and inches. Use separate TextField objects for feet and inches input.

15. Write an applet that acts like an adding machine. The user enters numbers one number at a time. When the user presses the ENTER key or clicks on the Add button after each entry, the applet adds the number to the running sum. Display the running sum using a Label object.

16. Rewrite the clock application from Chapter 4, exercise 14, on page 188, as an applet. Use two TextField objects to enter the hour and the minute. Define a private method drawClock that draws a clock given the hour and the minute. The actionPerformed method gets the two values from TextField objects, converts them to float, and passes them as arguments to the drawClock method. The drawClock method should call other private methods such as drawFace, drawHourHand, and drawMinuteHand.

17. An earned run average (ERA) of a baseball pitcher is computed by multiplying the total earned runs by 9 and dividing the result by the total number of innings pitched. Write an applet that computes the ERA.

Chapter 5

18. A slugging percentage of a baseball player is computed by dividing the total bases of all hits by the total times at bat (single = 1 base, double = 2 bases, triple = 3 bases, and home run = 4 bases). Write an applet that computes the slugging percentage. The applet accepts five input values: number of singles, number of doubles, number of triples, number of home runs, and number of times at bat.

19. Select one applet from the earlier exercises and run it without using an applet viewer or browser by defining your own main class.

6

Selection Statements

OBJECTIVES

After you have read and studied this chapter, you should be able to

- Implement selection control in a program using if statements.
- Implement selection control in a program using switch statements.
- Write boolean expressions using relational and boolean operators.
- Evaluate given boolean expressions correctly.
- Nest an if statement inside another if statement's then or else part correctly.
- Choose the appropriate selection control statement for a given task.
- Write applications using the ListBox class from javabook and the Color class from the standard java.awt package.

Introduction

Decisions, decisions, decisions. From the moment we are awake until the time we go to sleep, we are making decisions. Should I eat cereal or toast? What should I wear to school today? Should I eat at the cafeteria today? And so forth. We make many of these decisions by evaluating some criteria. If the number of students in line for registration seems long, then come back tomorrow for another try. If today is Monday, Wednesday, or Friday, then eat lunch at the cafeteria.

Computer programs are no different. Any practical computer program contains many statements that make decisions. Often a course of action is determined by evaluating some kind of a test (e.g., Is the input value negative?). Statements in programs are executed in sequence, which is called *sequential execution* or *sequential control flow*. However, we can add decision-making statements to a program to alter this control flow. For example, we can add a statement that causes a portion of a program to be skipped if an input value is greater than 100. The statement that alters the control flow is called a *control statement*. In this chapter we describe some important control statements, called *selection statements*. In the next chapter we will describe other control statements, called *repetition statements*.

sequential execution

control statement

6.1   The if Statement

Suppose we wish to enter a student's test score and print out the message You did not pass if the score is less than 70 and You did pass if the score is 70 or higher. Here's how we express this logic in Java:

```
//Assume messageBox and inputBox are declared and created
//Assume testScore is declared

testScore = inputBox.getInteger("Enter test score:");

if (testScore < 70)

    messageBox.show("You did not pass");    ← This statement is executed if the testScore is less than 70.

else

    messageBox.show("You did pass");    ← This statement is executed if the testScore is 70 or higher.
```

We use an if statement to specify which block of code to execute. A block of code may contain zero or more statements. Which block is executed depends on the result of evaluating a test condition called a *boolean expression*. The if statement in the program follows this general format:

if statement
syntax

```
if ( <boolean expression> )
    <then block>

else
    <else block>
```

Figure 6.1 illustrates the correspondence between the if statement we wrote and the general format.

FIGURE 6.1   Mapping of the sample **if** statement to the general format.

The <boolean expression> is a conditional expression that is evaluated to either true or false. For example, the following three expressions are all conditional:

```
testScore < 80
testScore * 2 > 350
30 < w / (h * h)
```

relational
operators

The six *relational operators* we can use in conditional expressions are

```
<       // less than
<=      // less than or equal to
==      // equal to
!=      // not equal to
>       // greater than
>=      // greater than or equal to
```

Here are some more examples:

Chapter 6

```
a * a <= c    //true if a * a is less than or equal to c
x + y != z    //true if x + y is not equal to z
a == b        //true if a is equal to b
```

If the boolean expression evaluates to true, then the statements in the <then block> are executed. Otherwise, the statements in the <else block> are executed. We will cover more complex boolean expressions in the next section. Notice that we can reverse the relational operator and switch the then and else blocks to derive the equivalent code, e.g.,

```
if (testScore >= 70)
    messageBox.show("You did pass");

else
    messageBox.show("You did not pass");
```

Notice that the reverse of < is >=, not >.

selection statement

The if statement is called a *selection* or *branching statement* because it selects (or branches to) one of the alternative blocks for execution. In our example, either

```
messageBox.show("You did not pass");
```

or

```
messageBox.show("You did pass");
```

is executed depending on the value of the boolean expression. We can illustrate a branching path of execution with the diagram shown in Figure 6.2.

In the preceding if statement, both blocks contain only one statement. The then or else block can contain more than one statement. The general format for both the <then block> and the <else block> is either a

```
<single statement>
```

or a

```
<compound statement>
```

FIGURE 6.2   The diagram showing the control flow of the sample **if** statement.

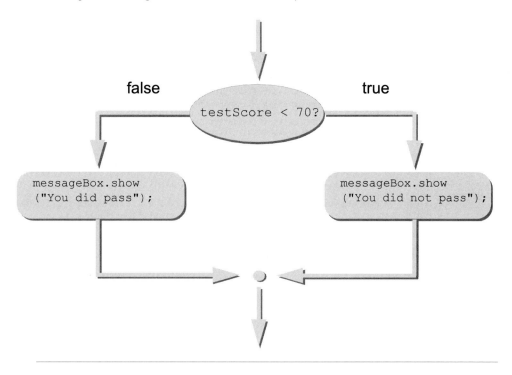

where <single statement> is a Java statement and <compound statement> is a sequence of Java statements surrounded by braces as shown below with $n \geq 0$ statements:

```
{
    <statement 1>
    <statement 2>
    ...
    <statement n>
}
```

If multiple statements are needed in the <then block> or the <else block>, they must be surrounded by braces { and }. For example, suppose we want to print out additional messages for each case. Let's say we also want to print Keep up the good work when the student passes and print Try harder next time when the student fails. Here's how:

Chapter 6

```
if (testScore < 70)
{
    messageBox.show("You did not pass");
    messageBox.show("Try harder next time");
}
else
{
    messageBox.show("You did pass");
    messageBox.show("Keep up the good work");
}
```

Compound Statements

The braces are necessary to delineate the statements inside the block. Without the braces, the compiler will not be able to tell whether a statement is a part of the block or the statement that follows the if statement.

Notice the absence of semicolons after the right braces. A semicolon is never necessary immediately after a right brace. A compound statement may contain zero or more statements, so it is perfectly valid for a compound statement to include only one statement. Indeed, we can write the sample if statement as

```
if (testScore < 70)
{
    messageBox.show("You did not pass");
}
else
{
    messageBox.show("You did pass");
}
```

Although not required, many programmers prefer to use the syntax for the compound statement even if the then or else block includes only one statement. In this textbook, we will use the syntax for the compound statement regardless of the number of statements inside the then and else blocks. Following this policy is beneficial for a number of reasons. One of them is the ease of adding temporary output statements inside the blocks. Frequently, we want to include a temporary output statement to verify the boolean expression is written correctly. Suppose we add output statements such as

```
if (testScore < 70)
{
    System.out.println("inside then: " + testScore);
    messageBox.show("You did not pass");
}
```

```
else
{
    System.out.println("inside else: " + testScore);
    messageBox.show("You did pass");
}
```

If we always use the syntax for the compound statement, we just add and delete the temporary output statements. However, if we use the syntax of the single statement, then we have to remember to add the braces when we want to include a temporary output statement. Another reason for using the compound statement syntax exclusively is to avoid the dangling else problem. We will discuss this problem in Section 6.3.

The placement of left and right braces does not matter to the compiler. The compiler will not complain if you write the preceding if statement as

```
if (testScore < 70)
{   messageBox.show("You did not pass");
    messageBox.show("Try harder next time"); } else {
    messageBox.show("You did pass");
    messageBox.show("Keep up the good work");
}
```

However, to keep your code readable and easy to follow, you should format your if statements using one of the two most common styles:

Style 1

```
if ( <boolean expression> ) {
    . . .
}
else {
    . . .
}
```

Style 2

```
if ( <boolean expression> )
{
    . . .
}
else
{
    . . .
}
```

In this book, we will use Style 1, mainly because this style is more common among programmers. If you prefer Style 2, then go ahead and use it. Whichever

Chapter 6

style you choose, be consistent, because consistent look and feel are very important to make your code readable. Let's summarize the key points to remember:

Rules for writing the then and else blocks:

1. *Left and right braces are necessary to surround the statements if the then or else block contains multiple statements.*
2. *Braces are not necessary if the then or else block contains only one statement.*
3. *A semicolon is not necessary after a right brace.*

Now let's study a second version of the if statement. Suppose we want to print out the message You are an honor student if the test score is 95 or above and print out nothing otherwise. For this type of testing, we use the second version of the if statement, whose general format is

if-then statement syntax

```
if ( <boolean expression> )
    <then block>
```

The second version contains only the <then block>. Using this version and the compound statement syntax, we express the selection control as

```
if (testScore >= 95) {
    messageBox.show("You are an honor student");
}
```

Figure 6.3 shows the diagram that illustrates the control flow for this if statement. To distinguish the two, we call the first version *if–then–else* and the second version *if–then*.

Notice that the if–then statement is not necessary, because we can write any if–then statement using if–then–else by including no statement in the else block. For instance, the sample if–then statement can be written as

```
if (testScore >= 95) {
    messageBox.show("You are an honor student");
}
else { }
```

In this book, we use if-then statements whenever appropriate.

FIGURE 6.3   The diagram showing the control flow of the second version of the **if** statement.

Quick Check

1. Identify the invalid if statements:

   a.   ```
         if (a < b) then
             x = y;
         else
             x = z;
         ```

   b.    ```
         if ( a < b )
             else x = y;
         ```

   c.   ```
         if (a < b)
             x = y;
         else {
             x = z;
         };
         ```

   d.    ```
         if ( a < b ) {
             x = y; } else
             x = z;
         ```

2. Express the following if–then statements using if–then–else.

   a.   ```
         if (a < b) x = y;
         ```

   b.    ```
         if ( a < b ) { }
         ```

   c.   ```
         if (a < b) x = y;
         if (a >= b) x = z;
         ```
         ```

6.2   Boolean Expressions and Variables

In addition to the arithmetic operators introduced in Chapter 3 and relational operators introduced in the previous section, boolean expressions can contain conditional and boolean operators. A *boolean operator*, also called a *logical operator*, takes boolean values as its operands and returns a boolean value. Three boolean operators are *AND*, *OR*, and *NOT*. In Java, symbols &&, ||, and ! represent the AND, OR, and NOT operators, respectively. Table 6.1 explains how these operators work.

boolean operator

TABLE 6.1   Boolean operators and their meanings.

A	B	A && B	A || B	!A
false	false	false	false	true
false	true	false	true	true
true	false	false	true	false
true	true	true	true	false

The AND operation results in true only if both A and B are true. The OR operation results in true if either A or B is true. The NOT operation is true if A is false and false if A is true. Combining boolean operators with relational and arithmetic operators, we can come up with a long boolean expression such as

```
(x + 150) == y || x < y && !(y < z && z < x)
```

Now consider the following expression:

```
x / y > z || y == 0
```

What will be the result if y is equal to 0? Easy, the result is true, many of you might say. Actually a runtime error called *arithmetic exception* will result, because the expression

arithmetic exception

```
x / y
```

causes a problem known as a *divide-by-zero* error. Remember that you cannot divide a number by zero.

divide-by-zero error

However, if we reverse the order to

```
y == 0 || x / y > z
```

then no arithmetic exception will occur because the test x / y > z will not be evaluated. For the OR operator ||, if the left operand is evaluated to true, then the right operand will not be evaluated, because the whole expression is true, whether the value of the right operand is true or false. We call such evaluation method a *short-circuit evaluation*. For the AND operator &&, the right operand need not be evaluated if the left operand is evaluated to false, because the result will then be false whether the value of the right operand is true or false.

short-circuit
evaluation

Just as the operator precedence rules are necessary to evaluate arithmetic expressions unambiguously, they are required for evaluating boolean expressions. Table 6.2 expands Table 3.3 by including all operators introduced so far.

TABLE 6.2   Operator precedence rules. Groups are listed in descending order of precedence. An operator with a higher precedence will be evaluated first. If two operators have the same precedence, then their associativity rule is applied.

Group	Operator	Precedence	Associativity
subexpression	( )	9 (If parentheses are nested, then innermost subexpression is evaluated first.)	left to right
unary operators	– !	8	right to left
multiplicative operators	* / %	7	left to right
additive operators	+ –	6	left to right
relational operators	< <= > >=	5	left to right
equality operators	== !=	4	left to right
boolean AND	&&	3	left to right
boolean OR	||	2	left to right
assignment	=	1	right to left

Chapter 6

In mathematics, we specify the range of values for a variable as

```
80 ≤ x < 90
```

In Java, to test that the value for x is within the specified lower and upper bounds, we express it in Java as

```
80 <= x && x < 90
```

You cannot specify it as

```
80 <= x < 90
```

 Wrong!

which is a syntax error because the relational operators (<, <=, etc.) are binary operators whose operands must be numerical values. Notice that the result of the subexpression

```
80 <= x
```

is a boolean value, which cannot be compared to the numerical value 90. Their data types are not compatible.

The result of a boolean expression is either true or false, which are the two values of data type boolean. As is the case with other data types, a value of a data type can be assigned to a variable of the same data type. In other words, we can declare a variable of data type boolean and assign a boolean value to it. Here are examples:

```
boolean pass, done;

pass = 70 < x;
done = true;
```

One possible usage of boolean variables is to keep track of the program settings or user preferences. A variable (of any data type, not only boolean) used for this purpose is called a *flag*. Suppose we want to allow the user to display either short or long messages. Many people, when using a new program, prefer to see long messages such as Enter a person's age and press the Enter key to continue. But once they are familiar with the program, many users prefer to see short messages such as Enter age. We can use a boolean flag to remember the user's preference. We can set the flag longMessageFormat at the beginning of

boolean flag

Chapter 6

the program to true or false depending on the user's choice. Once this boolean flag is set, we can refer to the flag at different points in the program as

```
if (longMessageFormat) {

    //display the message in long format
}
else {
    //display the message in short format
}
```

One very common error in writing programs is mixing up the assignment and equality operators. We frequently make a mistake of writing

```
if (x = 5) ...
```

when we actually wanted to say

```
if (x == 5) ...
```

Quick Check

Chapter 6

1. Evaluate the following boolean expressions. Assume x, y, and z have some numerical values.

    a. `4 < 5 || 6 == 6`
    b. `2 < 4 && (false || 5 <= 4)`
    c. `x <= y && !(z != z) || x > y`
    d. `x < y || z < y && y <= z`

2. Identify errors in the following boolean expressions and assignments.

    a. `boolean done;`
        `done = x = y;`

    b. `2 < 4 && (3 < 5) + 1 == 3`

    c. `boolean quit;`
        `quit = true;`
        `quit == ( 34 == 20 ) && quit;`

> **Mr. Espresso:** *Dr. Caffeine, I realized, after executing the program, that my* if *statement was wrong. I wrote it as*
>
> ```
> if ( 70 <= x & x < 90 )
> ```
>
> *but it compiled and ran correctly. I thought the boolean AND is a double ampersand.*
>
> **Dr. Caffeine:** *The single ampersand is also a boolean operator for AND. Unlike double ampersand, the single ampersand will not do a short-circuit evaluation. It will evaluated both left and right operands. We also have a single vertical bar OR.*
>
> **Mr. Espresso:** *Well then, which one should I use?*
>
> **Dr. Caffeine:** *Use double ampersand for AND and double vertical bar for OR. You most likely will never encounter a situation where you cannot use the double ampersand or the double vertical bar.*

Dr. & Mr.

6.3   Nested-if Statements

nested-if statement

The then and else clauses of an if statement can contain any statement including another if statement. An if statement that contains another if statement either in its then or else block is called a *nested-if* statement. Let's look at an example. In the earlier example, we printed out the messages You did pass or You did not pass depending on the test score. Let's modify the code to print out three possible messages. If the test score is lower than 70, then we print You did not pass as before. If the test score is 70 or higher, then we will check the student's age. If the age is less than 10, we will print You did a great job. Otherwise, we will print You did pass as before. Figure 6.4 is a diagram showing the logic of this nested test. The code is written as follows:

```
if (testScore >= 70) {
    if (studentAge < 10) {
        messageBox.show("You did a great job");
    }
    else {
        messageBox.show("You did pass"); //test score >= 70
    }                                    //and age >= 10
}
else { //test score < 70

    messageBox.show("You did not pass");
}
```

Chapter 6

FIGURE 6.4   A diagram showing the control flow of the example nested-**if** statement.

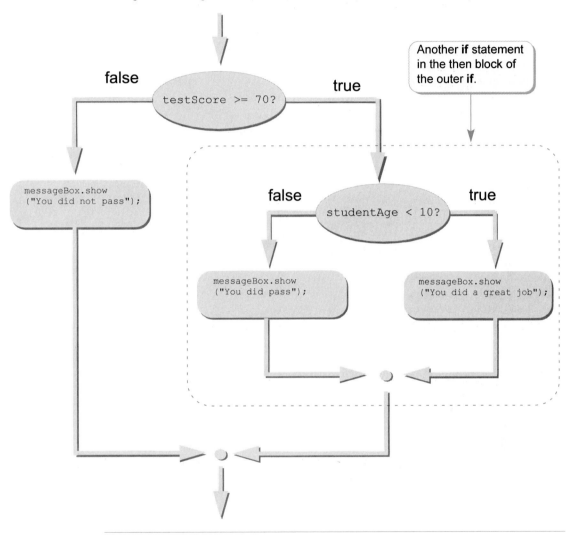

Since the then clause of the outer if contains another if statement, the outer if is called a nested-if statement. It is possible to write if tests in different ways to achieve the same result. For example, the preceding code can also be expressed as

```
if (testScore >= 70 && studentAge < 10) {

    messageBox.show("You did a great job");
}
```

```
        else {
            //either testScore < 70 OR studentAge >= 10

            if (testScore >= 70) {
                messageBox.show("You did pass");
            }
            else {
                messageBox.show("You did not pass");
            }
        }
```

Several other variations can also achieve the same result. As a general rule, we strive to select the one that is most readable (i.e., most easily understood) and most efficient. Often no one variation stands out, and the one you choose depends on your preferred style of programming.

Here's an example in which one variation is clearly a better choice. Suppose we input three integers and determine how many of them are negative. Here's the first variation. To show the structure more clearly, we purposely do not use the braces in the then and else blocks.

> In this and the following examples, we purposely do not use the braces so we can provide a better illustration of the topics we are presenting.

```
if (num1 < 0)
    if (num2 < 0)
        if (num3 < 0)
            negativeCount = 3; //all three are negative
        else
            negativeCount = 2; //num1 and num2 are negative
    else
        if (num3 < 0)
            negativeCount = 2; //num1 and num3 are negative
        else
            negativeCount = 1; //num1 is negative
else
    if (num2 < 0)
        if (num3 < 0)
            negativeCount = 2; //num2 and num3 are negative
        else
            negativeCount = 1; //num2 is negative
    else
        if (num3 < 0)
            negativeCount = 1; //num3 is negative
        else
            negativeCount = 0; //no negative numbers
```

It certainly did the job. But elegantly? Here's the second variation:

```
negativeCount = 0;

if (num1 < 0)
        negativeCount++;
if (num2 < 0)
        negativeCount++;
if (num3 < 0)
        negativeCount++;
```

The statement

```
negativeCount++;
```

increments the variable by one and, therefore, is equivalent to

```
negativeCount = negativeCount + 1;
```

increment and decrement operators

The double plus operator (++) is called the *increment operator*, and the double minus operator (−−) is the *decrement operator* (which decrements the variable by one).

Which version do you like better? The second variation is the only reasonable way to go. The first variation is not even an option because it is very inefficient and very difficult to read. You apply the nested-if structure if you have to test conditions in some required order. In this example these three tests are independent of each other, so they can be executed in any order. In other words, it doesn't matter whether you test num1 first or last.

Notice that we indent the then and else clauses to show the nested structure clearly. Indentation is used as a visual guide for the readers. It makes no difference to a Java compiler. For example, we make our intent clear by writing the statement as

```
if (x < y)
    if (z != w)
        a = b + 1;
    else
        a = c + 1;
else
    a = b * c;
```

But to the Java compiler, it does not matter if we write the same code as

```
if (x < y)if (z != w)a = b + 1;else a = c + 1; else a = b * c;
```

> **Mr. Espresso:** *Dr. Caffeine, in finding the count of negative integers, I can see the second variation is much better than the first one. But for the first example, it's not clear to me which one is better. How do you tell?*
>
> **Dr. Caffeine:** *Well, it takes blood, sweat, and tears. When you become an accomplished programmer, you can instinctively tell which style is better.*
>
> **Mr. Espresso:** *I don't mind bloodletting, sweating, and crying, but there must be some kind of guideline I can use before I can tell the difference "instinctively."*
>
> **Dr. Caffeine:** ***Rule 1:*** *Minimize the number of nestings.* ***Rule 2:*** *Avoid complex boolean expressions. Make them as simple as possible. Don't include many ANDs and ORs.* ***Rule 3:*** *Eliminate any unnecessary comparisons.* ***Rule 4:*** *Don't be satisfied with the first correct statement. Always look for improvement.* ***Rule 5:*** *Read your code again. Can you follow the statement easily? If not, try to improve it.*

Although indentation is not required to run the program, using proper indentation is an important aspect of good programming style. Since the goal is to make your code readable, not to follow any one style of indentation, you are free to choose your own style. We recommend Style 1 or Style 2 shown on page 235.

The next example shows a style of indentation accepted as standard for a nested-if statement in which nesting occurs only in the else clause. Instead of determining whether a student passes or not, we will now display a letter grade based on the following formula:

Test Score	Grade
$90 \leq score$	A
$80 \leq score < 90$	B
$70 \leq score < 80$	C
$60 \leq score < 70$	D
$score < 60$	F

The statement can be written as

```
if (score >= 90)
    messageBox.show("Your grade is A");
else
    if (score >= 80)
        messageBox.show("Your grade is B");
    else
        if (score >= 70)
            messageBox.show("Your grade is C");
        else
            if (score >= 60)
                messageBox.show("Your grade is D");
            else
                messageBox.show("Your grade is F");
```

However, the standard way to indent the statement is

```
if (score >= 90)
    messageBox.show("Your grade is A");

else if (score >= 80)
    messageBox.show("Your grade is B");

else if (score >= 70)
    messageBox.show("Your grade is C");

else if (score >= 60)
    messageBox.show("Your grade is D");

else
    messageBox.show("Your grade is F");
```

We mentioned that indentation is meant for human eyes only. For example, we can clearly see the intent of a programmer just by looking at the indentation when we read

```
if (x < y)
    if (x < z)
        messageBox.show("Hello");
else
    messageBox.show("Good bye");
```

Indentation style A

A Java compiler, however, will interpret the above as

```
if (x < y)
    if (x < z)
        messageBox.show("Hello");
    else
        messageBox.show("Good bye");
```

Indentation style B

Chapter 6

dangling else
problem

This example has a *dangling else* problem. The Java compiler matches an **else** with the previous unmatched if, so the compiler will interpret the statement by matching the **else** with the inner if (if (x < z)), whether you use indentation style A or B. If you want to express the logic of indentation style A, you have to express it as

```
if (x < y) {
    if (x < z)
        messageBox.show("Hello");
}
else
    messageBox.show("Good bye");
```

This dangling else problem is another reason why we recommend that beginners use the syntax for <compound **statement**> in the then and else blocks. In other words, always use the braces in the then and else blocks.

Quick Check

1. Rewrite the following nested-if statements without using any nesting:

    a.
    ```
    if ( a < c )
        if ( b < c )
            x = y;
        else
            x = z;
    else
        x = z;
    ```

    c.
    ```
    if ( a < b  )
        if ( a >= b )
            x = z;
        else
            x = y;
    else
        x = z;
    ```

    b.
    ```
    if ( a == b )
        x = y;
    else
        if ( a > b )
            x = y;
        else
            x = z;
    ```

2. Format the following if statements with indentation.

    a.
    ```
    if ( a < b  ) if ( c > d ) x = y;
    else x = z;
    ```

    b.
    ```
    if ( a < b  ) { if ( c > d ) x = y; }
    else x = z;
    ```

    c.
    ```
    if ( a < b ) x = y; if ( a < c ) x = z;
    else if ( c < d ) z = y;
    ```

6.4   ListBox

In many situations we want to give users an option of selecting one out of many choices. For example, in a drawing program we may provide users with a choice of colors. We can use the InputBox class to let users enter the name of the color, but they might misspell the color. For example, one user may enter "Maganta" instead of "Magenta." Therefore, we need to verify that the entry is a valid color. By providing a list of choices, we force users to make a valid choice, and we can simplify input processing.

> *It is considered a better interface to allow the user to enter only values that are valid instead of detecting errors after the user has entered an invalid value.*

A ListBox object in the javabook package provides a list of items the user can select. Here's an example that lists the names of five colors. A ListBox object is a dialog and requires an owner frame window. We create a ListBox instance as in

```
MainWindow mainWindow  = new MainWindow();
ListBox    colorList    = new ListBox(mainWindow);
```

The default ListBox is modal. (Note: A modal dialog box disables all other windows of the program once it appears on the screen.) We will discuss how to use a modal ListBox in this chapter and how to use a modeless ListBox later in the book. The default ListBox has the title Select One. If you wish to specify your own title, pass the title as the second argument when you create an object, as in

```
colorList = new ListBox(mainWindow, "Select Color");
```

We add the names of the colors using the addItem message

```
colorList.addItem("Magenta");
colorList.addItem("Cyan");
colorList.addItem("Red");
colorList.addItem("Blue");
colorList.addItem("Green");
```

and execute

```
selection = colorList.getSelectedIndex();
```

to make the colorList appear on the screen as shown in Figure 6.5.

Chapter 6

FIGURE 6.5   The **ListBox** object **colorList**. The figure on the right shows the index values of the items in the list.

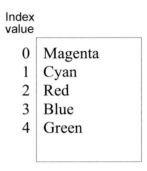

Index value	
0	Magenta
1	Cyan
2	Red
3	Blue
4	Green

The variable selection is an int. When the user makes a selection by clicking on the choice and then clicking on the OK button, the getSelectedIndex method returns the index value of the selected choice. The choice at the top has the index value 0, the second from the top is 1, and so forth. Notice that the index of the first item in the list is zero, not one. Assigning zero to the first position is called *zero-based indexing*, which is used very frequently in computer programming.

zero-based indexing

> ***Zero-based indexing assigns the value of zero to the first item in a list of items.***

The getSelectedIndex method returns NO_SELECTION if the user clicks the OK button without selecting a choice, and it returns CANCEL if the user clicks the Cancel button or the close box. After the value is returned by the getSelectedIndex method, the ListBox disappears from the screen. NO_SELECTION and CANCEL are public class constants of type int, and we refer to them as

```
ListBox.NO_SELECTION
```

and

```
ListBox.CANCEL
```

The following code displays the name of the selected color:

```
selection = colorList.getSelectedIndex();

if (selection == ListBox.NO_SELECTION)
    messageBox.show("You made no selection");

else if (selection == ListBox.CANCEL)
    messageBox.show("You canceled the ListBox");

else if (selection == 0)
    messageBox.show("You selected Magenta");

else if (selection == 1)
    messageBox.show("You selected Cyan");

else if (selection == 2)
    messageBox.show("You selected Red");

else if (selection == 3)
    messageBox.show("You selected Blue");

else if (selection == 4)
    messageBox.show("You selected Green");
```

The value of **NO_SELECTION** is set to -1 and **CANCEL** to -2, so we could write the above code as

```
selection = colorList.getSelectedIndex();

if (selection == -1)
    messageBox.show("You made no selection");

else if (selection == -2)
    messageBox.show("You canceled the ListBox");

    . . .
```

but doing so would defeat the purpose of having public class constants defined in ListBox. Why? Because the use of a symbolic constant makes the code more readable and its modification easier. Suppose we wish to modify the ListBox to return distinct values for different events. By having a symbolic constant defined for each event, the code would look something like

```
selection = colorList.getSelectedIndex();

if (selection == ListBox.NO_SELECTION)
    . . .

else if (selection == ListBox.CANCEL)
    . . .
```

instead of the more cryptic

```
selection = colorList.getSelectedIndex();

if (selection == -1)
    . . .

else if (selection == -2)
    . . .
```

Also, without the use of a symbolic constant, modifying the code is more difficult. Suppose the value –1 becomes necessary for a different purpose. If a class constant is used, all we have to do is assign a different value to this constant and compile the class again. Code such as

```
if (selection == ListBox.NO_SELECTION)
```

would continue to work. However, code such as

```
if (selection == -1)
```

would have to be modified. If hundreds of programs used ListBox, you would have to modify all of them in this fashion. With the use of a constant, none of these programs would require modification. Every program would continue to work.

Table 6.3 is a partial list of ListBox methods and class constants.

6.5   The switch Statement

Another Java statement that implements a selection control flow is the switch statement. Suppose we want to direct the students to the designated location for them to register for classes. The location where they register is determined by their grade level. The user enters 1 for freshman, 2 for sophomore, 3 for junior, and 4 for senior. Using the switch statement, we can write the code as

TABLE 6.3   A partial list of **ListBox** methods.

CLASS:	ListBox	
Method	**Argument**	**Description**
`<constructor>`	`MainWindow`	Creates a ListBox object.
`addItem`	`String`	Adds the argument String value to the list. Items are added to the list from top to bottom. The top-most item has the index value of zero, the next item's value is one, and so forth.
`getSelectedIndex`	`<none>`	Returns the index value of the selected item in the list. See the explanation of class constants.
Class Constant		**Description**
`NO_SELECTION`		This value is returned by the getSelectedIndex method when the user clicks the OK button without selecting a choice.
`CANCEL`		This value is returned by the getSelectedIndex method when the user clicks the CANCEL button or the dialog's close box.

```
int gradeLevel;

gradeLevel
    = inputBox.getInteger("Grade (Frosh-1,Soph-2,...):" );

switch (gradeLevel) {

    case 1: outputBox.printLine("Go to the Gymnasium");
            break;

    case 2: outputBox.printLine("Go to the Science Auditorium");
            break;

    case 3: outputBox.printLine("Go to Harris Hall Rm A3");
            break;

    case 4: outputBox.printLine("Go to Bolt Hall Rm 101");
            break;
}
```

Chapter 6

The syntax for the switch statement is

switch statement
syntax

```
switch ( <arithmetic expression> ) {

    <case label 1> : <case body 1>
    ...
    <case label n> : <case body n>
}
```

Figure 6.6 illustrates the correspondence between the switch statement we wrote and the general format.

FIGURE 6.6   Mapping of the sample **switch** statement to the general format.

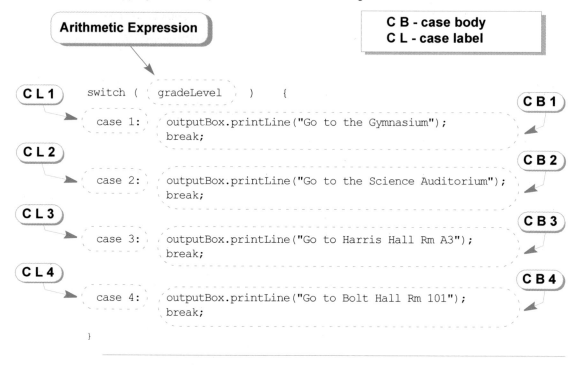

The <case label i> has the form

default
reserved word

```
case <constant>      or      default
```

and <case body i> is a sequence of zero or more statements. Notice that <case body i> is not surrounded by left and right braces. The <constant> can be either a named or literal constant.

The data type of <arithmetic expression> must be char, byte, short, or int. (Note: We will cover the data type char in Chapter 8.) The value of <arithmetic expression> is compared against the constant value i of <case label i>. If there is a matching case, then its case body is executed. If there is no matching case, then the execution continues to the statement that follows the switch statement. No two cases are allowed to have the same value for <constant>, and the cases can be listed in any order.

Notice that each case in the sample switch statement is terminated with the break statement. The break statement causes execution to continue from the statement following this switch statement, skipping the remaining portion of the switch statement. The following example illustrates how the break statement works:

```
//Assume necessary declaration and object creation are done

selection = 1;

switch (selection) {
    case 0: outputBox.printLine(0);
    case 1: outputBox.printLine(1);
    case 2: outputBox.printLine(2);
    case 3: outputBox.printLine(3);
}
```

When this code is executed the following output is produced:

```
1
2
3
```

because after the statement in case 1 is executed, statements in the remaining cases will be executed also. To execute statements in one and only one case, we need to include the break statement at the end of each case, as we have done in the first example. Figure 6.7 shows the effect of the break statement.

The break statement is not necessary in the last case, but for consistency we place it in every case. Also, by doing so we don't have to remember to include the break statement in the last case when we add more cases to the end of the switch statement.

Individual cases do not have to include a statement, so we can write something like

FIGURE 6.7   A diagram showing the control flow of the **switch** statement with and without the **break** statements.

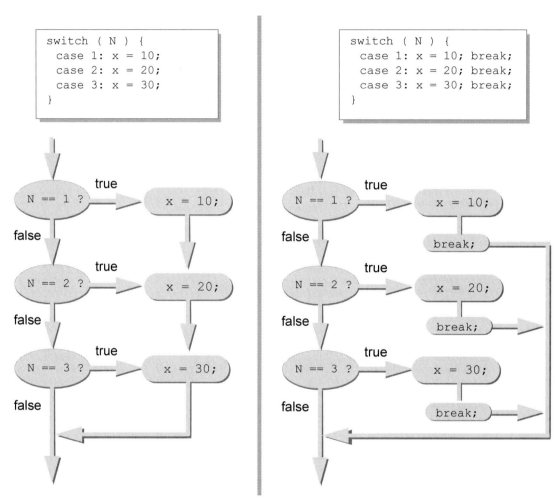

```
int ranking;
ranking = inputBox.getInteger();

switch (ranking) {
    case 10:
    case  9:
    case  8: messageBox.show("Master");
             break;
```

```
case    7:
case    6: messageBox.show("Journeyman");
           break;

case    5:
case    4: messageBox.show("Apprentice");
           break;
}
```

The code will print **Master** if the value of ranking is either 10, 9, or 8; Journey-man if the value of ranking is either 7 or 6; or Apprentice if the value of ranking is either 5 or 4.

We may include a default case that will always be executed if there is no matching case. For example, we can add a default case to print out an error message if any invalid value for ranking is entered.

```
switch (ranking) {

    case 10:
    case  9:
    case  8: messageBox.show("Master");
             break;

    case  7:
    case  6: messageBox.show("Journeyman");
             break;

    case  5:
    case  4: messageBox.show("Apprentice");
             break;

    default: messageBox.show("Input error: Invalid Data");
             break;
}
```

There can be at most one default case. Since the execution continues to the next statement if there is no matching case (and no default case is specified), it is safer to always include a default case. By placing some kind of output statement in the default case, we can detect an unexpected switch value. Such style of programming is characterized as *defensive programming*. Although the default case does not have to be placed as the last case, we recommend you do so, in order to make the switch statement more readable.

defensive programming

Quick Check

1. What's wrong with the following switch statement?

```java
switch ( N ) {
    case  0:
    case  1:   x = 11;
               break;
    default:   System.out.println("Switch Error");
               break;
    case  2:   x = 22;
               break;
    case  1:   x = 33;
               break;
}
```

2. What's wrong with the following switch statement?

```java
switch ( ranking ) {
    case  >4.55:  pay = pay * 0.20;
                  break;

    case  =4.55:  pay = pay * 0.15;
                  break;

    default:      pay = pay * 0.05;
                  break;
}
```

6.6   Sample Program: Drawing Shapes

Let's write a program that will draw a geometric shape, such as a rectangle, in a size and color specified by the user. This program illustrates the use of ListBox and control statements. The program uses the class Color from the standard java.awt package for specifying the color of the drawing. As always, we will develop this program following incremental development steps.

Problem Statement

Write an application that will draw a geometric shape specified by the user. The user can specify the shape's position, size, and color.

*The program can draw lines, rectangles, and circles in the colors
magenta, cyan, red, blue, or green.*

Overall Plan

We will begin with our overall plan for the development. Let's begin with the
outline of program logic. We want the user to select the shape, its position, and
its color, and then draw the shape as specified. We express the program flow as
having four tasks:

program
tasks

1. Get the shape the user wants to draw.
2. Get the color the user wants to use.
3. Get the position and size of the selected shape.
4. Draw the selected shape as specified.

Let's look at each task and determine an object that will be responsible for
handling the task. For the first two tasks, we can use either an InputBox object or
a ListBox object. Which one is the better one for this task? If we use an InputBox
object, the user must remember the valid shapes and colors that can be entered.
When the user enters an invalid shape, for example, the program needs to display an error message. Instead of doing it this way, we will use a ListBox object
to list the selections of valid shapes. By using this ListBox object, the user cannot specify an invalid shape, he or she can only select one from the available
shapes in the list. For the same reason, we will use a ListBox object to list the
valid colors. Since we have to provide two separate lists—one for shapes and
another for colors—we will use two separate ListBox objects.

We will use an InputBox for the third task. Since the user needs to enter
three or four values depending on the shape selected, an InputBox object will be
the simplest and most flexible to use for the purpose.

Finally, for the task of actually drawing the selected shape, we need to define our own class. The task is too specific to the program and there is no suitable object in the standard or javabook package that does the job. We will call
the new class DrawingBoard. We will design the details of DrawingBoard in the
later step.

In addition to the tasks identified, we need an object to display the program
description. We will use an OutputBox for this purpose. This OutputBox also
will be used for printing out temporary messages while developing the program.

We will define a top-level control object that manages all these objects. We
will call this class DrawShape. Our main class will be DrawShapeMain, whose

Chapter 6

task is to create an instance of DrawShape and start the instance. Here's our working design document:

Design Document:	DrawShape
Class	**Purpose**
DrawShapeMain	The main class of the program.
DrawShape	The top-level control object that manages other objects in the program.
ListBox	One ListBox object is used for listing the available shapes: rectangle, circle, and line. Another ListBox object is used for listing the available colors: magenta, cyan, red, blue, and green. This class is from javabook.
InputBox	An InputBox object is used to get values for the position and size of the shape to be drawn. This class is from javabook.
OutputBox	An OutputBox object is used to display the program description. The object is used also for printing out temporary messages during the program development. This class is from javabook.
DrawingBoard	A core object that does the actual drawing.
MainWindow	The main window of the application.

Figure 6.8 is the object diagram for this program.

We will implement this program in the following six major steps:

1. Start with a program skeleton. Define the DrawShapeMain and the DrawShape classes.

2. Add code to allow the user to select a shape.

3. Add code to allow the user to select a color.

4. Add code to allow the user to specify the size and location of the selected shape.

5. Add code to draw the selected shape.

6. Finalize the code by tying up loose ends.

Notice that the steps we outline here follow the general pattern of implementing the input routines first, then the output routines, and finally the computation tasks. In this sample program, the drawing functionality includes the features of both output and computation tasks.

FIGURE 6.8   The object diagram for the **DrawShape** program.

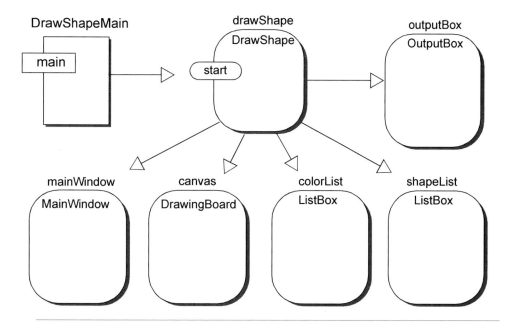

Step 1 Development: Program Skeleton

Step 1 Design   We begin the development with the main class and the skeleton DrawShape class. The purpose of the main class is to create an instance of DrawShape and let the object carry out the program tasks. So the code in the main method will look like

```
DrawShape drawShape = new DrawShape( );
drawShape.start();
```

We will call the public method of the DrawShape class start. The purpose of this method is to carry out the program tasks, so we will declare it as

```
public void start( )
{
    describeProgram();   //tell what the program does
    selectShape();       //let the user select the shape,
    selectColor();       //color,
    selectDimension();   //position & size
    draw();              //draw the selected shape
}
```

Chapter 6

By looking at this method, we can tell the responsibility assigned to a Draw-Shape object. The five methods called from the start method are all private, so the object diagram for the class at this point is

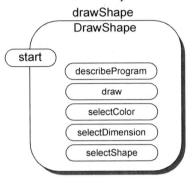

We will declare all these private methods in this step, but their method body does not contain any statement (except the temporary output statement). We will complete the method body in the subsequent development steps.

Since the DrawShape class is an instantiable class, we will define its constructor. Inside the constructor, we will create and initialize objects DrawShape manages. Since we are defining only a skeleton in this step, we will create and initialize only a MainWindow object and an OutputBox object inside the constructor. We use an OutputBox to display temporary messages to verify the methods we define here are called correctly. In the subsequent steps, we will add more code to create and initialize other objects.

Our working design document for the DrawShape class is as follows:

Design Document:	The DrawShape Class	
Method	**Visibility**	**Purpose**
`<constructor>`	`public`	Creates and initializes the objects used by a DrawShape object.
`start`	`public`	Starts the shape drawing task by calling the other private methods.
`describeProgram`	`private`	Displays a short description of the program in an OutputBox object from javabook.
`draw`	`private`	Draws the selected shape in the color and dimension set by the user.
`selectColor`	`private`	Lets the user select the color of the shape. Selection is made by using a ListBox object from javabook.

Design Document:	The DrawShape Class	
Method	**Visibility**	**Purpose**
`selectDimension`	`private`	Lets the user specify the dimension of the shape to be drawn.
`selectShape`	`private`	Lets the user select the shape to draw. Selection is made by using a ListBox object from javabook. Possible choices are line, circle, and rectangle.

Step 1 Code   As mentioned already, we include temporary output statements in the five private methods to verify that they are called correctly in the right order. The main class DrawShapeMain will not change. The class given here is the final version. Here's the code:

File: DrawShapeMain.java

```java
/**
 * The DrawShape main program to draw the shape (rectangle, circle,
 * or line) selected by the user. The selected shape is drawn in the
 * position, size, and color the user specifies.
 *
 * @author Dr. Caffeine
 *
 */
class DrawShapeMain
{
    public static void main (String[] args)
    {
        DrawShape drawShape = new DrawShape( );
        drawShape.start();
    }
}
```

File: DrawShape.java

```java
import javabook.*;

/**
 * This class is the top-level controller object for managing
 * all other objects in the program.
 *
 * @author Dr. Caffeine
 *
 */
class DrawShape
{

//-------------------------------
// Data Members
//-------------------------------

    private MainWindow mainWindow;
    private OutputBox  outputBox;
```

```
//-------------------------------
// Constructors
//-------------------------------

    /**
     * Default constructor. The default window title is "Drawing Shape".
     */
    public DrawShape( )
    {
        mainWindow = new MainWindow("Drawing Shape");
        outputBox  = new OutputBox(mainWindow);

        mainWindow.setVisible( true );
        outputBox.setVisible( true );
    }

//-------------------------------------------------
//     Public Methods:
//
//         void   start  (       )
//
//-------------------------------------------------
    /**
     * Top-level method that calls other private methods
     * to draw the selected shape in user-specified
     * position, size, and color.
     */
    public void start ( )
    {
        describeProgram();
        selectShape();
        selectColor();
        selectDimension();
        draw();
    }

//-------------------------------------------------
//     Private Methods:
//
//     void   describeProgram  (         )
//     void   draw             (         )
//     void   selectColor      (         )
//     void   selectDimension  (         )
//     void   selectShape      (         )
//
//-------------------------------------------------

    /**
     * Provides a brief explanation of the program to the user.
     *
     */
    private void describeProgram( )
    {
        outputBox.printLine("Inside describeProgram");
    }


    /**
     * Draws the selected shape in a chosen position, size,
     * and color.
```

```
     *
     */
    private void draw( )
    {
        outputBox.printLine("Inside draw");
    }

    /**
     * Lets the user select the color from a ListBox.
     */
    private void selectColor( )
    {
        outputBox.printLine("Inside selectColor");
    }


    /**
     * Lets the user select the size and position using an InputBox.
     *
     */
    private void selectDimension( )
    {
        outputBox.printLine("Inside selectDimension");
    }


    /**
     * Lets the user select the shape from a ListBox.
     *
     */
    private void selectShape( )
    {
        outputBox.printLine("Inside selectShape");
    }
}
```

Step 1 Test

We execute the main class and the skeleton DrawShape class to verify that the skeleton classes are coded correctly. When the mainWindow and outputBox appear on the screen, we know the constructor was executed properly. If the five private methods are coded correctly and called in the correct sequence, we will see the output

```
Inside describeProgram
Inside selectShape
Inside selectColor
Inside selectDimension
Inside draw
```

on an outputBox. After we verify the correct execution of the Step 1 program, we will proceed to implement the private methods of DrawShape.

Step 2 Development: Select a Shape

Step 2 Design   In the second development step, we add a routine that allows the user to select a shape. We decided in the overall planning step that we will use a ListBox object to list the available shapes. There are three choices: line, circle, and rectangle. We will define a symbolic constant for each of these shapes to make the program easier to read. We will create and initialize a ListBox object called shapeListBox in the constructor. The selection of a shape will be handled in the selectShape method. After the shape is selected by the user, the program will prompt the user for a color and dimension before drawing the selected shape. This means that we have to remember which shape was selected in the select-Shape method. Since the getSelectedIndex method returns an integer, we will use an integer variable selectedShape to remember the selected shape.

Step 2 Code   The constants, a ListBox object, and an int variable are declared in the data member section of the DrawShape class as

```
//-------------------------------
//     Data Members
//-------------------------------
private final int   LINE      = 0,
                    CIRCLE    = 1,
                    RECTANGLE = 2;

private ListBox     shapeListBox;

private int         selectedShape;
```

The constructor now will include code to create and initialize shapeListBox:

```
public DrawShape( )
{
    ...

    shapeListBox = new ListBox(mainWindow, "Select Shape:");
    shapeListBox.addItem("Line");
    shapeListBox.addItem("Circle");
    shapeListBox.addItem("Rectangle");
}
```

Finally we implement the selectShape method as

```
private void selectShape( )
{
    outputBox.printLine("Inside selectShape"); //TEMP
```

```
        selectedShape = shapeListBox.getSelectedIndex();
        outputBox.printLine("Selected Shape: " + selectedShape);
                                                        //TEMP
    }
```

Notice that we include a temporary output statement at the end of the method so we can verify the selection is made correctly.

Now we run the program several times, each time selecting a different shape, and verify that the correct message shows up in outputBox. After we verify that everything is okay, we proceed to the next step.

Step 3 Development: Select a Color

In the third development step, we add a routine that allows the user to select a color. This step is similar to Step 2. Instead of shape, we work with colors. So we will use another ListBox object to list the available colors. There are five choices: magenta, cyan, red, blue, and green. We will define a symbolic constant for each of these colors to make the program easier to read. We will create and initialize a ListBox object called colorListBox in the constructor. The selection of a color will be handled in the selectColor method. We will use an integer variable selectedColor to remember the selected color.

The constants, a ListBox object, and an int variable are declared in the data member section of the DrawShape class as

```
//----------------------------------
//      Data Members
//----------------------------------
private final int    MAGENTA   = 0,
                     CYAN      = 1,
                     RED       = 2,
                     BLUE      = 3,
                     GREEN     = 4;

private ListBox      colorListBox;

private int          selectedColor;
```

The constructor now will include code to create and initialize colorListBox:

```
public DrawShape( )
{
    ...

    colorListBox = new ListBox(mainWindow, "Select Color:");
    colorListBox.addItem("Magenta");
```

```
                              colorListBox.addItem("Cyan");
                              colorListBox.addItem("Red");
                              colorListBox.addItem("Blue");
                              colorListBox.addItem("Green");
                          }
```

Finally we implement the selectColor method as

```
        private void selectColor( )
        {
            outputBox.printLine("Inside selectColor"); //TEMP
            selectedColor = colorListBox.getSelectedIndex();
            outputBox.printLine("Selected Color: " + selectedColor);
                                                            //TEMP
        }
```

Like the selectShape method, we place a temporary output statement at the end of the method so we can verify the color selection is made correctly.

Step 3 Test
Now we run the program several times, each time selecting a different color, and verify that the correct message shows up in outputBox. After we verify that everything is okay, we proceed to the next step.

Step 4 Development: Select the Shape Dimension

Step 4 Design
In the fourth development step, we add a routine that allows the user to specify the dimension of the selected shape. The values the user must provide will be different for each of the three shapes. We will ask the user to specify a line by giving two end points. For a circle, we ask the user to enter the center point and the radius. We could have used a diameter, but we believe entering a radius is more natural. For a rectangle, we ask the user to enter the point for the top left corner and the width and height of the rectangle.

Now, how shall we code the input routines for different shapes? Since each shape requires different input values, we will define a separate method for each type of shape: getCircleDimension, getLineDimension, and getRectangleDimension. The selectDimension method will call one of these methods based on the value of selectedShape. These individual methods will get input values appropriate for the shape and retain the values entered for later processing. We add the three new methods to our working design document of the DrawShape class.

Design Document:	The DrawShape Class	
Method	**Visibility**	**Purpose**
. . .	. . .	. . .
getCircleDimension	private	Lets the user enter the circle's center point and radius.
getLineDimension	private	Lets the user enter the line's two end points.
getRectangleDimension	private	Lets the user enter the rectangle's point at the top left corner and its width and height.

We will use an InputBox object for getting input values, the only object we know at this point for the data-inputting task. The actual drawing is done by another method, so the purpose of these methods is only to input required values and validate the input. We use the variables originX, originY, endX, endY, radius, width, and height for storing values. The variables originX and originY are used by all three methods. For a line, they represent one end point. For a circle, they represent the center point. And for a rectangle, they represent the top left corner point.

We consider any negative input value as invalid. When an invalid input value is entered, the get dimension method will display an error message. We will use a MessageBox object for displaying an error message. Since the drawing will not occur until the drawShape method is called, we need to keep the record of what has happened during the get dimension method, that is, whether there was any input error. If there is any error, then the drawShape method will not draw any shape. Let's use a boolean variable canDraw for this purpose. The variable canDraw is set to false when there is an input error.

Step 4 Code   The objects and variables necessary for this step are declared in the data member section of the DrawShape class as

```
//---------------------------------
//      Data Members
//---------------------------------
private InputBox      inputBox;
private MessageBox    messageBox;

private boolean       canDraw;   //false if there's an input
                                 //error

private int           originX,
                      originY,
```

```
                                    endX,
                                    endY,
                                    radius,
                                    width,
                                    height;
```

The constructor will now include code to create and initialize inputBox and messageBox:

```
public DrawShape( )
{
    ...

    inputBox  = new InputBox(mainWindow);
    messageBox = new MessageBox(mainWindow);


    ...
}
```

We implement the selectDimension method as

```
private void selectDimension( )
{
    switch (selectedShape) {

        case ListBox.CANCEL: //user canceled, so do nothing
                canDraw = false;
                break;
        case ListBox.NO_SELECTION: //no shape selected
                canDraw = false;
                break;
        case LINE:
                getLineDimension();
                break;

        case CIRCLE:
                getCircleDimension();
                break;

        case RECTANGLE:
                getRectangleDimension();
                break;
        default:
                messageBox.show("ListBox Error");
                canDraw = false;
                break;
    }
}
```

Notice how we add code for handling the cases in which no shape is selected. It is important for you to remember that whenever you use a selection control, you have to make sure that all possible cases are handled. Also, it is a good idea to include the default case to a switch statement.

When you write a selection control statement, make sure that all possible cases are covered.

Since the variable selectedShape is set to the value returned from a ListBox object, this default case should never be called. If it were ever called, then the List-Box class was not used correctly (e.g., adding items in the wrong order or adding incorrect items), so we display the message ListBox Error.

The three methods for getting dimensions are defined as follows:

```
private void getCircleDimension()
{
    originX = inputBox.getInteger("X-coord of the center");
    originY = inputBox.getInteger("Y-coord of the center");
    radius  = inputBox.getInteger("Radius of the circle");

    //make sure everything is positive
    if (originX < 0 || originY < 0 || radius < 0) {
       messageBox.show("Negative number is entered. " +
                       "Cannot draw a circle.");
       canDraw = false;
    }
    else { //input is okay
       canDraw = true;
       outputBox.printLine("circle dimensions okay");
                                                    //TEMP
    }
}


private void getLineDimension()
{
    originX = inputBox.getInteger("X-coord of starting point");
    originY = inputBox.getInteger("Y-coord of starting point");
    endX    = inputBox.getInteger("X-coord of ending point");
    endY    = inputBox.getInteger("Y-coord of ending point");

    //make sure everything is positive
    if (originX < 0 || originY < 0 || endX < 0 || endY < 0){
       messageBox.show("Negative number is entered. " +
                       "Cannot draw a line.");
       canDraw = false;
    }
```

```
      else { //input is okay
         canDraw = true;
         outputBox.printLine("line dimensions okay"); //TEMP
      }
   }


   private void getRectangleDimension()
   {
      originX  = inputBox.getInteger("X-coord of origin");
      originY  = inputBox.getInteger("Y-coord of origin");
      width    = inputBox.getInteger("Rectangle width");
      height   = inputBox.getInteger("Rectangle height");

      //make sure everything is positive
      if (originX < 0 || originY < 0 || width < 0 || height < 0) {
         messageBox.show("Negative number is entered. " +
                         "Cannot draw a rectangle.");
         canDraw = false;
      }
      else { //input is okay
         canDraw = true;
         outputBox.printLine("rectangle dimensions okay");
                                                          //TEMP

      }

   }
```

Step 4 Test   Now we run the program several times, each time selecting a different shape, and verify that the correct get dimension method is called. We try both correct and incorrect input values and verify that the appropriate error message is displayed when invalid values are entered. After we verify the program, we move on to the most difficult step.

Step 5 Development: Draw the Shape

Step 5 Design   In the fifth development step, we add a routine that draws the selected shape in the color and dimension the user designated. The very first question we need to ask ourselves at this point is "Who will do the drawing?" Which object should be the one responsible for taking care of drawing? Should it be DrawShape? We certainly can make a DrawShape object responsible for the drawing task by adding more methods to it. But will it be a good design? Adding code for the actual drawing operations to the DrawShape class would make it bloated. One design principle of object-oriented programming is to use many objects, with each object dedicated to a single well-defined task. It is not a good design to construct a single object that does everything. In other words, we want an object that is specialized in a single well-defined task, not a jack-of-all-trades, because single-task objects are much easier to mix and match in writing different programs. We call this design principle a *single-task object (STO) principle*.

The Single-Task Object (STO) Principle: Design an object that is specialized in a single well-defined task.

Remember that the responsibility of a DrawShape object is to manage other objects in the program. It controls two ListBox objects that allow the user to select the shape and color, for example. Objects such as InputBox, ListBox, and OutputBox are called *interface objects* because they handle the user interface component of the program. A DrawShape object is called a *controller object* because it controls and instructs other objects to perform the actual work. Following the STO principle will direct us to design our own class to handle the actual drawing operations. We will call this class DrawingBoard.

interface objects

controller objects

We will design the DrawingBoard class here, but we will defer the implementation until Chapter 11. There are two reasons for doing this. First, to implement this class fully and properly requires additional knowledge not yet covered. Trying to introduce all the necessary topics here will make this section too long. Second, and more importantly, it illustrates a real-world situation where a chief programmer or a system designer designs the class and leaves the implementation to another programmer. One of the major benefits of object-oriented programming is the ease of delineating the roles of class designer and class implementor. The designer will determine how the object will interact with other objects in the program by defining the object's public methods. The class implementor will implement the class using whatever technique he decides is most appropriate. This division of labor allows the chief programmer to contract out the implementation of a class to multiple freelance programmers, for example, and choose the best implementation.

design vs. implementation

We will be a class designer of the DrawingBoard class here. We will be our own implementor for the class and implement it in Chapter 11. To complete this sample program, we will use the DrawingBoard class in the javabook package, which is implemented according to our design specification.

Now let's begin our design. What kind of public methods should a DrawingBoard object support? What would be a natural way for our DrawShape object to interact with a DrawingBoard object? Since the actual drawing is done by a DrawingBoard object, we will need three drawing methods, one for each shape:

drawLine, drawCircle, and drawRectangle. The arguments for these methods will be as follows:

Drawing Methods of DrawingBoard
`public void drawLine( int x1, int y1, int x2, int y2 )`
Draws a line from point (x1,y1) to (x2,y2)
`public void drawCircle( int centerX, int centerY, int radius)`
Draws a circle centered at (centerX,centerY) with radius radius.
`public void drawRectangle(int x, int y, int width, int height)`
Draws a rectangle whose top left corner is at (x,y) with width width and height height.

DrawingBoard Design Alternative 1

Where should this drawing take place? We need a window to draw a shape, so we will make DrawingBoard a window. The first alternative is to design the DrawingBoard class as a subclass of MainWindow using the inheritance we introduced in Chapter 2. This means a DrawingBoard object is a specialized MainWindow that has an added capability of drawing shapes, just like, say, a CheckingAccount object is a specialized Account that has additional rules for withdrawal. The SketchPad class we used in the sample program from Chapter 1 is also a subclass of MainWindow. If we make DrawingBoard a subclass of MainWindow, then the program will have only one window because an instance of DrawingBoard is also a main window.

DrawingBoard Design Alternative 2

The second alternative is to design the DrawingBoard class distinct from the MainWindow class. The DrawingBoard class will only have a drawing capability, and the program will need an instance of MainWindow for its main window. So if we take this alternative, the program will have two separate windows—one MainWindow and one DrawingBoard.

Which alternative is better? If a program supports a simple functionality, such as the FunTime program from Chapter 1 or a simple text editor that comes with a system (e.g., Notepad for Windows or SimpleText for the Mac), then it is more appropriate to use only one window. Simple functionality requires a simple interface. It is also less threatening to novice users. If a program supports an advanced functionality, then a multiple window interface is more appropriate. For example, it is more of a standard to see one main window and multiple document windows in a high-end commercial software such as a word processing or illustration program.

The program we are developing here has a very simple functionality, so we will adopt the first alternative. Since the DrawingBoard class is a subclass of MainWindow, an instance of DrawingBoard will serve the role of main window. This means the MainWindow class is not needed for the program anymore. We will therefore remove the class from the program and update the design document and the object diagram accordingly. Since the DrawingBoard object canvas is now the main window of the program, the statements to create various dialogs in the constructor are changed to

```
canvas    = new DrawingBoard( ); //subclass of MainWindow
outputBox = new OutputBox( canvas );

shapeListBox = new ListBox( canvas, "Select Shape:" );
colorListBox = new ListBox( canvas, "Select Color:" );

inputBox  = new InputBox( canvas );
messageBox = new MessageBox( canvas );
```

setColor Design Alternative 1

We now have one final design decision to make for the DrawingBoard class. Since we need to draw a shape in color, the DrawingBoard class must support a method we can use to designate the color. What would be a natural interface for such method? Since we are allowing the user to select one of the possible five colors, we define a method for each color, such as setColorToRed, setColorToCyan, and so forth. This approach is not acceptable because the class would be too limited in usage. What will happen if we want to draw in any one of 256 colors?

setColor Design Alternative 2

We can define a method by which we pass an integer. We can set an agreement that 0 means magenta, 1 means cyan, and so forth. With this approach, we will define a method like this:

`public void setColor( int colorCode )`

Sets the color to colorCode. All subsequent shapes will be drawn in the set color. Color coding is as follows: 0 for magenta, 1 for cyan, 2 for red, 3 for blue, and 4 for green.

This approach is also not acceptable. First, the class is not reusable. This class cannot be used for other programs that require 10 different colors, for example. If we want to support more colors in our DrawShape class, we will not be able to use this DrawingBoard class without modifying it. Second, the coding scheme as such is very limiting and restrictive. How can we extend this scheme to 256 colors?

java.awt.Color

To designate the color for drawing, we will use the Color class from the standard java.awt package. A Color object uses a coloring scheme called a *RGB scheme,* which specifies a color by combining three values, ranging from 0 to 255, for red, green, and blue. For example, the color black is expressed by setting red, green, and blue to zero, and the color white by setting all three values to 255. We create, for example, a Color object for the pink color by executing

Chapter 6

```
Color pinkColor;
pinkColor = new Color(255,175,175);
```

Instead of dealing with the three numerical values, we can use the public class constants defined in the Color class. The class constants for common colors are

```
Color.black          Color.magenta
Color.blue           Color.orange
Color.cyan           Color.pink
Color.darkGray       Color.red
Color.gray           Color.white
Color.green          Color.yellow
Color.lightGray
```

setColor
Design
Alternative 3

Each of the above is a Color object with its RGB values correctly set up. We will pass a Color object as an argument to the setColor method.

setColor Method of DrawingBoard
`public void setColor( Color color)`
Sets the color to color. All subsequent shapes will be drawn in the color color.

We will call the setColor method of canvas to set its drawing color at the time the user selects the color, which is inside the selectColor method. The basic idea is something like this:

```
//let the user select the color
selectedColor = colorListBox.getSelectedIndex();

switch ( selectedColor ) {

    case MAGENTA: canvas.setColor( Color.magenta );
                  break;

    case CYAN:    canvas.setColor( Color.cyan );

    //and so forth
}
```

This code works fine as long as the user selects a color, but what if he clicks the Cancel button or the OK button without making a selection? Let's decide we will draw the selected shape in black if no color is selected. We will add the following case to the switch statement:

```
case ListBox.CANCEL:
case ListBox.NO_SELECTION:
        messageBox.show("No color selected. " +
                        "Will draw in black.");
        canvas.setColor( Color.black );
```

Finally, the actual drawing is done in the draw method. The boolean variable canDraw is set by one of the get dimension methods. If this variable is true, then we call a drawing method of canvas to draw the selected shape. The logic of the code can be expressed as

```
if (canDraw) {
    switch (selectedShape) {
        case LINE:
                //draw a line
                break;

        case CIRCLE:
                //draw a circle
                break;

        case RECTANGLE:
                //draw a rectangle;
                break;
    }
}
```

Step 5 Code   We are now ready to code. The Color class is from the java.awt package, so we need to add the import statement

```
import java.awt.*;
```

The declaration for mainWindow is removed and the one for canvas is added

```
//-----------------------------------
//      Data Members
//-----------------------------------

private DrawingBoard canvas;
```

The statement

`private MainWindow mainWindow`

is removed.

We modify the selectColor method to

```
private void selectColor( )
{
    selectedColor = colorListBox.getSelectedIndex();

    switch (selectedColor) {

        case ListBox.CANCEL:
        case ListBox.NO_SELECTION:
                    messageBox.show("No color is selected. "
                                    + "Will draw in black.");
                    canvas.setColor( Color.black );
                    break;

        case MAGENTA:
                    canvas.setColor(Color.magenta);
                    break;

        case CYAN:   canvas.setColor(Color.cyan);
                     break;

        case RED:    canvas.setColor(Color.red);
                     break;

        case GREEN:  canvas.setColor(Color.blue);
                     break;

        case BLUE:   canvas.setColor(Color.green);
                     break;

        default:     messageBox.show("ListBox Error" );
                     break;
    }
}
```

The draw method will call a corresponding method of canvas to draw the selected shape, provided that the boolean flag canDraw is true:

```
private void draw( )
{
    if (canDraw) {
        switch (selectedShape) {
            case LINE:
                canvas.drawLine(originX, originY, endX, endY);
                break;

            case CIRCLE:
                canvas.drawCircle(originX, originY, radius);
                break;
```

```
            case RECTANGLE:
                canvas.drawRectangle(originX, originY,
                                        width, height);
                break;
        }
    }
}
```

Step 5 Test

Now we run the program multiple times and test that all three drawing methods work correctly. We try different colors and dimensions for each shape and verify that they are drawn correctly. When you run the program, most likely the first thing you will notice is that outputBox hides the shape drawn. And even after you moved or closed outputBox, you still do not see any shape is drawn. What happened? Is the drawing not working?

Let's say you drew a shape on a window. If you cover this shape by moving another window over it, then the shape will be erased. Similarly, if you attempt to draw a shape on a portion of a window that is hidden by another window, then the shape will not be drawn. (Note: There's a way to eliminate this problem, but that requires advanced techniques. Check the Web link listed at the end of this section.) To test this, let's run the program again, but this time without showing an OutputBox object. To hide outputBox, we comment out the statement in the constructor:

```
public DrawShape( )
{
    ...
    //outputBox.setVisible( true );
    ...
}
```

> Comment this statement so outputBox won't be displayed on the screen.

When you run the program again, you should see the shape is drawn correctly.

When you run the Step 5 program (the one that shows outputBox), you will notice that you cannot close outputBox until after you select a shape and color. But by that time it's too late to close it. What we need to do here is to allow the user to close outputBox before the selectShape method is executed. The OutputBox class has a method called waitUntilClose that will suspend the program execution until an OutputBox object is closed. We place a call to this method inside the describeProgram method as

waitUntilClose

```
private void describeProgram( )
{
    //printLine statements to describe the program
```

```
            //come here

            outputBox.printLine("Close this window to continue.");

            outputBox.waitUntilClose();
    }
```

Run the program with this describeProgram and verify that the program runs correctly.

To learn an advanced technique that eliminates the problem of dis-appearing shapes in the DrawShape program, please visit www.drcaf-feine.com/additionaltopics.

Step 6 Development: Finalize

program review

We finalize the program in the last step. We will perform a critical review of the program looking for any unfinished method, inconsistency or error in the methods, unclear or missing comments, and so forth. We should also not forget to improve the program for cleaner code and better readability.

The describeProgram method is incomplete, so we need to complete the method by adding code to describe the program. Please add whatever description you feel is appropriate. There are still temporary output statements we used for verification purposes. Either we delete them from the program or comment them out. We recommend that you leave them in the program by commenting them out so when the time comes for you to modify, debug, or update the program, you do not have to reenter them again.

6.7   Exercises

1. Indent the following if statements properly.

   a. `if (a == b) if (c == d) a = 1; else b = 1; else c = 1;`

   b. `if (a == b) a = 1; if (c == d) b = 1; else c = 1;`

   c. `if (a == b) {if (c == d) a = 1; b = 2; } else b = 1;`

   d. `if (a == b) {`
       `if (c == d) a = 1; b = 2; }`
       `else {b = 1; if (a == d) d = 3;}`
       `else c = 1;`

2. Which two of the following three if statements are equivalent?

   a. `if (a == b)`
       `    if (c == d) a = 1;`
       `        else b = 1;`

Chapter 6

b.
```
if (a == b) {
    if (c == d) a = 1; }
    else b = 1;
```
c.
```
if (a == b)
    if (c == d) a = 1;
else b = 1;
```

3. Evaluate the following boolean expressions. For each of the following expressions, assume x is 10, y is 20, and z is 30. Indicate which of the following boolean expressions are always true and which are always false, regardless of the values for x, y, or z.

a.
```
x < 10 || x > 10
```
b.
```
x > y && y > x
```
c.
```
(x < y + z) && (x + 10 <= 20)
```
d.
```
z - y == x && Math.abs(y - z) == x
```
e.
```
x < 10 && x > 10
```
f.
```
x > y || y > x
```
g
```
!(x < y + z) || !(x + 10 <= 20)
```
h.
```
!(x == y)) && (x != y) && (x < y || y < x)
```

4. Express the following switch statement using nested-if statements.

```
switch (grade) {
    case 10:
    case  9:   a = 1;
               b = 2;
               break;

    case  8:   a = 3;
               b = 4;
               break;

    default:   a = 5;
               break;
}
```

5. Write an if statement to find the smallest of three given integers without using the min method of the Math class.

6. Draw control flow diagrams for the following two **switch** statements.

```
switch (choice) {              switch (choice) {
  case 1:  a = 0;                case 1:  a = 0;
           break;
                                 case 2:  b = 1;
  case 2:  b = 1;
           break;                case 3:  c = 2;

  case 3:  c = 2;                default: d = 3;
           break;              }

  default: d = 3;
           break;
}
```

7. Write an if statement that prints out a message based on the following rules:

If the Total Points Are	Message to Print
≥ 100	You won a free cup of coffee.
≥ 200	You won a free cup of coffee and a regular-size doughnut.
≥ 300	You won a free cup of coffee and a regular-size doughnut and a 12-oz. orange juice.
≥ 400	You won a free cup of coffee and a regular-size doughnut and a 12-oz. orange juice and a combo breakfast.
≥ 500	You won a free cup of coffee and a regular-size doughnut and a 12-oz. orange juice and a combo breakfast and a reserved table for one week.

8. Rewrite the following if statement using a **switch** statement:

```
selection = colorList.getSelectedIndex();

if (selection == ListBox.NO_SELECTION)
    messageBox.show("You made no selection");

else if (selection == ListBox.CANCEL)
    messageBox.show("You canceled the ListBox");

else if (selection == 0)
    messageBox.show("You selected Magenta");

else if (selection == 1)
    messageBox.show("You selected Cyan");

else if (selection == 2)
    messageBox.show("You selected Red");

else if (selection == 3)
    messageBox.show("You selected Blue");

else if (selection == 4)
    messageBox.show("You selected Green");
```

9. Describe how the following code runs without actually executing the code.

```
MainWindow mainWindow = new MainWindow();
OutputBox  outputBox  = new OutputBox( mainWindow );

outputBox.show();
outputBox.printLine("one");
outputBox.waitUntilClose( );

outputBox.show();
outputBox.printLine("two");
outputBox.waitUntilClose( );

outputBox.show();
outputBox.printLine("three");
outputBox.waitUntilClose( );

outputBox.show();
outputBox.printLine("four");
outputBox.waitUntilClose( );
```

10. At the end of movie credits you see the year movies are produced in Roman numerals, for example, MCMXCVII for 1997. To help the production staff determine the correct Roman numeral for the production year, write an ap-

plet or application that reads a year and displays the year in Roman numerals.

Roman Numeral	Number
I	1
V	5
X	10
L	50
C	100
D	500
M	1000

Remember that certain numbers are expressed using a "subtraction," for example, IV for 4, CD for 400, and so forth.

11. Write an applet or application that replies either Leap Year or Not a Leap Year given a year. It is a leap year if the year is divisible by 4 but not by 100 (e.g., 1796 is a leap year because it is divisible by 4 but not by 100). A year that is divisible by both 4 and 100 is a leap year if it is also divisible by 400 (e.g. 2000 is a leap year, but 1800 is not).

12. A million is 10^6 and a billion is 10^9. Write an applet that reads a power of 10 (6, 9, 12, etc.) and displays how big the number is (Million, Billion, etc.). Display an appropriate message for the input value that has no corresponding word. The table below shows the correspondence between the power and the word for that number.

Power of 10	Number
6	Million
9	Billion
12	Trillion
15	Quadrillion
18	Quintillion
21	Sextillion
30	Nonillion
100	Googol

13. Extend the TestScoreEvaluator program on page 230 to print out an appropriate message if the value entered is outside the range of possible test scores, that is, less than zero or greater than 100.

14. Write an applet RecommendedWeightAppletWithTest by extending the RecommendedWeightApplet (see exercise 13 on page 227). The extended applet will include the following test:

```
if (the height is between 140cm and 230cm)

    compute the recommended weight

else

    display an error message
```

15. Extend the RecommendedWeightAppletWithTest applet in exercise 14 by allowing the user to enter his/her weight and printing out the message You should exercise more if the weight is more than 10 pounds over the ideal weight and You need more nourishment if the weight is more than 20 pounds under the recommended weight.

16. After starting a successful coffee beans outlet business, Java^2 Coffee Outlet is now venturing into the fast-food business. The first thing the management decides is to eliminate the drive-through intercom. Java^2 Lo-Fat Burgers is the only fast-food establishment in town that provides a computer screen and mouse for its drive-through customers. You are hired as a free-lance computer consultant. Write a program that lists items for three menu categories: entree, side dish, and drink. The following table lists the items available for each entry and their prices. Use three ListBox objects for listing items from the three menu categories and an OutputBox object for displaying the total price of the order.

Entree		Side Dish		Drink	
Tofu Burger	$3.49	Rice Cracker	$0.79	Cafe Mocha	$1.99
Cajun Chicken	$4.59	No-Salt Fries	$0.69	Cafe Latte	$1.99
Buffalo Wings	$3.99	Zucchini	$1.09	Espresso	$2.49
Rainbow Fillet	$2.99	Brown Rice	$0.59	Oolong Tea	$0.99

17. Improve the clock program of exercise 14 on page 188 from Chapter 4. Modify the program so you only accept numbers between 0 and 12 for hour and between 0 and 59 for minute. Print out an appropriate error message for an invalid input value.

Chapter 6

18. Java^2 Coffee Outlet (see exercise 19 from Chapter 3) decided to give discounts to volume buyers. The discount is based on the following table:

Order Volume	Discount
≥ 25 bags	5% of the total price
≥ 50 bags	10% of the total price
≥ 100 bags	15% of the total price
≥ 150 bags	20% of the total price
≥ 200 bags	25% of the total price
≥ 300 bags	30% of the total price

Each bag of beans costs $5.50. Write an application that accepts the number of bags ordered and prints out the total cost of the order in the following style using an OutputBox object.

```
Number of Bags Ordered:   173 - $ 951.50

              Discount:
                          20% - $ 190.30

    Your total charge is:   $ 761.20
```

19. Employees at Java^2 Lo-Fat Burgers earn the basic hourly wage of $7.25. They will receive time and a half of their basic rate for overtime hours. In addition to this, they will receive a commission on the sales they generate while tending the counter. The commission is based on the following formula:

Sales Volume	Commission
$1.00 to $99.99	5% of the total sales
$100.00 to $299.99	10% of the total sales
≥ $300.00	15% of the total sales

Write an application that inputs the number of hours worked and the total sales and computes the wage.

20. Combine exercise 18 and exercise 11 of Chapter 4 to compute the total charge including discount and shipping costs. The output should look like the following:

```
Number of Bags Ordered:   43 - $ 236.50

                 Discount:

                          5% - $ 11.83

              Boxes Used:

                          1 Large - $3.00
                          2 Medium - $2.00

     Your total charge is:   $ 229.67
```

Note: The discount applies to the cost of beans only.

21. You are hired by Expressimo Delivery Service to develop an application that computes the delivery charge. The company allows two types of packaging, letter and box, and three types of service, Next Day Priority, Next Day Standard, and 2-Day. The following table shows the formula for computing the charge:

Package Type	Next Day Priority	Next Day Standard	2-Day
letter	$12.00, up to 8 oz.	$10.50, up to 8 oz.	Not available
box	$15.75 for the first lb. Add $1.25 for each additional lb over the first lb.	$13.75 for the first lb. Add $1.00 for each additional lb over the first lb.	$7.00 for the first lb. Add $0.50 for each additional lb over the first lb.

The program will input three values from the user: the type of package, the type of service, and the weight of the package.

22. Write an applet version of exercise 21. You can use TextField objects or Choice objects for input. If you use Choice objects, then you need to explore the class on your own. The Choice class from the standard java.awt package works very much like the ListBox class from the javabook package.

Chapter 6

23. Ms. Latte's Mopeds 'R Us rents mopeds at Monterey Beach Boardwalk. To promote business during the slow weekdays, the store gives a huge discount. The rental charges are as follows:

Moped Type	Weekday Rental	Weekend Rental
50cc Mopette	$15.00 for the first three hours, $2.50 per hour after the first three hours.	$30.00 for the first three hours, $7.50 per hour after the first three hours.
250cc Mohawk	$25.00 for the first three hours, $3.50 per hour after the first three hours.	$35.00 for the first three hours, $8.50 per hour after the first three hours.

Write an application or an applet that computes the rental charge given the type of moped, when it is rented (either weekday or weekend), and the number of hours rented.

7

Repetition Statements

OBJECTIVES

After you have read and studied this chapter, you should be able to

- Implement repetition control in a program using while statements.

- Implement repetition control in a program using do–while statements.

- Implement repetition control in a program using for statements.

- Nest a loop repetition statement inside another repetition statement.

- Choose the appropriate repetition control statement for a given task.

- Prompt the user for a yes–no reply using the ResponseBox class from the javabook package.

- Output formatted data using the Format class from the javabook package.

- (Optional) Write simple recursive methods.

Introduction

The selection statements we covered in the previous chapter alter the control flow of a program. In this chapter we will cover another group of control statements called repetition statements. *Repetition statements* control a block of code to be executed for a fixed number of times or until a certain condition is met. We will describe Java's three repetition statements: while, do–while, and for. In addition to the repetition statements, we will introduce two classes for javabook: ResponseBox and Format. A ResponseBox object is used to get a yes or no response from the user, and it is a very convenient object to use in conjunction with a repetition statement. The Format class is helpful in displaying formatted output values. For example, we may want to output numerical values with their rightmost digit aligned to help the user see the magnitude of the numbers clearly and easily. Finally, in an optional section at the end of the chapter, we will describe recursive methods. A *recursive method* is a method that calls itself. Instead of using a repetition statement, a recursive method can be used to program the repetition control flow.

*repetition
statements*

*recursive
method*

7.1   The while Statement

Suppose we want to compute the sum of the first 100 positive integers 1, 2, . . . , 100. Here's how we compute the sum using a while statement:

```
int sum = 0, number = 1;

while (number <= 100) {
    sum    =   sum + number;
    number = number + 1;
}
```

Let's analyze the while statement. The statement follows the general format

*while statement
syntax*

```
while ( <boolean expression> )

    <statement>
```

loop body

where <statement> is either a <single statement> or a <compound statement>. The <statement> of the sample while statement is a <compound statement> and therefore has the left and right braces. Repetition statements are also called *loop statements*, and we characterize the <statement> as the *loop body*. Figure 7.1 shows how this while statement corresponds to the general format. As long as the <boolean expression> is true, the loop body is executed. Figure 7.2 is a diagram showing the control flow of the sample code.

FIGURE 7.1   Correspondence of the example **while** statement to the general format.

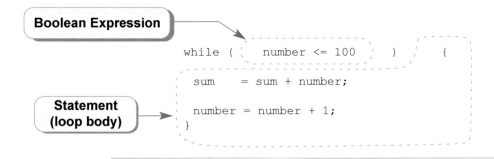

FIGURE 7.2   A diagram showing the control flow of a **while** statement.

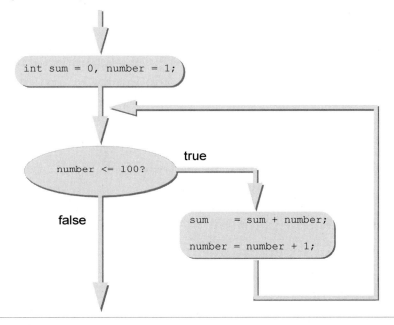

Let's modify the loop so this time we keep on adding the numbers 1, 2, 3, and so forth, until the sum becomes more than 1,000,000. Here's how we write the while statement:

```
int sum = 0, number = 1;

while ( sum <= 1000000 ) {
    sum    =  sum + number;
    number = number + 1;
}
```

Chapter 7

Notice how the <boolean expression> is modified, and it is the only part of the while statement that is modified.

Let's try another example. This time, we compute the product of the first 20 odd integers. (Note: The ith odd integer is 2 * i – 1. For example, the fourth odd integer is 2 * 4–1 = 7.)

```
int product = 1, number = 1, count = 20, lastNumber;

lastNumber = 2 * count - 1;

while (number <= lastNumber) {
    product = product * number;
    number  = number + 2;
}
```

count-controlled loop

The first and the third sample while statements are called *count-controlled loops* because the loop body is executed for a fixed number of times (as if we were counting).

Now let's study how the repetition control in the program will improve the user interface of the program. In earlier sample programs, we assumed the input data were valid. The programs we have written may produce wrong results or simply stop running if the user enters an invalid value. Assuming that the input values are valid makes the writing of programs easier because we do not have to write code to handle the invalid values. Although easier for us to write such programs, it would be an inferior interface from the user's standpoint. Requiring the user to make no mistake in entering input values is too restrictive and not user-friendly. We need to develop programs that are more user-friendly. Imagine you successfully entered 19 values, but on the 20th input value, you mistyped. A user-hostile program would stop, and you would have to run the program again. A more user-friendly program would allow you to reenter a correct 20th value.

All we could have done using a selection statement was to print out an error message if the user enters an invalid value. To allow the user to reenter the value until the correct value is entered, we need a repetition control. Let's look at an example. Suppose we want to input a person's age, and the value must be between 0 and 130. We know the age cannot be negative, so the age input must be greater than or equal to 0. We set the upper bound to 130 to take into account the possibility of some long-living human beings in a remote hamlet in Timbuktu. Let's say we will let the user enter the age until the valid age is entered. We can code this repetition control using a while statement:

```
age = inputBox.getInteger("Your Age (between 0 and 130):");

while (age < 0 || age > 130) {
    messageBox.show("An invalid age was entered. " +
                    "Please try again.");
    age = inputBox.getInteger
                    ( "Your Age (between 0 and 130):" );
}
```

Notice how we add the assignment

```
age = inputBox.getInteger("Your Age (between 0 and 130):");
```

to input the age *before* the while statement. Without this input statement, the variable age will not have a value when the boolean expression is evaluated for the very first time. This reading of a value before the testing is done is called a *priming read.*

priming read

Our next example keeps reading in integers and computes their running sum until a negative number is entered.

```
int sum = 0, number;

number = inputBox.getInteger(); //priming read

while (number >= 0) {
    sum = sum + number;
    number = inputBox.getInteger();
}
```

The previous two sample statements are called sentinel-controlled loops. With a *sentinel-controlled loop*, the loop body is executed repeatedly until any one of the designated values called a *sentinel* is encountered. The sentinel for this example is any negative number and the sentinel for the one before is any valid age between 0 and 130.

sentinel-controlled loop

Quick Check

1. Write a while statement to add numbers 11 through 20. Is this a count-controlled or sentinel-controlled loop?

2. Write a while statement to read in real numbers using InputBox and stop when a negative number is entered. Is this a count-controlled or sentinel-controlled loop?

Chapter 7

7.2   Pitfalls in Writing Repetition Statements

infinite loop

No matter what you do with the while statement (and other repetition state-ments), make sure that the loop will eventually terminate. Watch out for an *infinite loop* such as this one:

```
int product = 0;

while (product < 500000)
    product = product * 5;
```

Do you know why this is an infinite loop? The variable product is multiplied by 5 in the loop body, so the value for product should eventually become larger than 500000, right? Wrong. The variable product is initialized to 0, so product remains 0. The boolean expression product < 500000 will never be false, and, therefore, this while statement is an infinite loop. You have to make sure the loop body contains a statement that eventually makes the boolean expression false.

Here's another example of an infinite loop.

```
int count = 1;

while (count != 10) {
    count = count + 2;
}
```

overflow error

Since the variable count is initialized to 1 and the increment is 2, count will nev-er be equal to 10. Note: In theory, this while statement is an infinite loop, but in programming languages other than Java, this loop will eventually terminate be-cause of an overflow error. An *overflow error* will occur if you attempt to assign a value larger than the maximum value the variable can hold. When an overflow error occurs, the execution of the program is terminated in almost all program-ming languages. With Java, however, an overflow will not cause the program termination. When an overflow occurs in Java, a value that represents infinity (IEEE 754 infinity, to be precise) is assigned to a variable and no abnormal ter-mination of a program will happen. Also, in Java an overflow occurs only with float and double variables; no overflow will happen with int variables. When you try to assign a value larger than the maximum possible integer an int vari-able can hold, the value "wraps around" and becomes a negative value.

Whether the loop terminates or not because of an overflow error, the logic of the loop is still an infinite loop, and we must watch out for it. When you write a loop, you must make sure that the boolean expression of the loop will eventually become **false**.

Another pitfall for which you have to watch out is using real numbers for testing and increment. Consider the following two loops:

```
//Loop 1
float count = 0.0f;

while (count != 1.0f)
    count = count + 0.3333333f; //there are seven 3s


//Loop 2
float count = 0.0f;

while (count != 1.0f)
    count = count + 0.33333333f; //there are eight 3s
```

The second **while** terminates correctly, but the first **while** is an infinite loop. Why the difference? Because only an approximation of real numbers can be stored in a computer. We know in mathematics that

$$\frac{1}{3} + \frac{1}{3} + \frac{1}{3}$$

is equal to 1. However, in a computer, an expression such as

```
1.0/3.0 + 1.0/3.0 + 1.0/3.0
```

may or may not get evaluated to 1.0 depending on how precise the approximation is. In general, you want to avoid using real numbers as counter variables because of this imprecision. However, at the same time, you should not shy away from writing a loop such as

```
float count = 0.0f;

while (count <= 1.0f) {
    ...
    count = count + 0.25f;
}
```

if it helps to express the logic more clearly.

Chapter 7

Another thing for which you have to watch out in writing a loop is the so-called *off-by-one error*. Suppose we want to execute the loop body 10 times. Does the following code work?

```
count = 1;
while (count < 10 ) {
    . . .
    count++;
}
```

No, the loop body is executed nine times. How about the following code?

```
count = 0;
while (count <= 10 ) {
    . . .
    count++;
}
```

No, this time the loop body is executed 11 times. The correct while loop is

```
count = 0;
while (count < 10 ) {
    . . .
    count++;
}
```

or

```
count = 1;
while (count <= 10 ) {
    . . .
    count++;
}
```

Yes, you can write the desired loop as

```
count = 1;
while (count != 10 ) {
    . . .
    count++;
}
```

but this condition for stopping the count-controlled loop is dangerous. We already mentioned about the potential trap of an infinite loop. In summary,

Watch out for the off-by-one error (OBOE).

And here are the points for you to remember in writing a loop.

The checklist for the repetition control:

1. **Make sure the loop body contains a statement that will eventually cause the loop to terminate.**

2. **Make sure the loop repeats exactly the correct number of times.**

3. **If you want to execute the loop body N times, then initialize the counter to 0 and use the test condition counter < N or initialize the counter to 1 and use the test condition counter <= N.**

The loop body in the sample repetition statements included statements such as

```
sum = sum + number;
```

shorthand
assignment
operator

This assignment statement can be expressed succinctly without repeating the same variable sum by using the *shorthand assignment operator* +=:

```
sum += number;
```

Table 7.1 lists shorthand assignment operators available in Java.

TABLE 7.1   Shorthand assignment operators.

Operator	Usage	Meaning
+=	a += b;	a = a + b;
-=	a -= b;	a = a - b;
*=	a *= b;	a = a * b;
/=	a /= b;	a = a / b;
%=	a %= b;	a = a % b;

Chapter 7

These shorthand assignment operators have precedence lower than any other arithmetic operators, so, for example, the statement

```
sum *= a + b;
```

is equivalent to

```
sum = sum * (a + b);
```

We will be using shorthand assignment operators from now on.

Quick Check

1. Which of the following is an infinite loop?

    a.
    ```
    int sum = 0, i = 0;
    while ( i >= 0 ) {
        sum += i;
        i++;
    }
    ```

    b.
    ```
    int sum = 0, i = 100;
    while ( i != 0 ) {
        sum += i;
        i--;
    }
    ```

2. For each of the following loop statements, determine the value of sum after the loop is executed.

    a.
    ```
    int count = 0, sum = 0;
    while ( count < 10 ) {
        sum += count;
        count++;
    }
    ```

    b.
    ```
    int count = 1, sum = 0;
    while ( count <= 30 ) {
        sum    += count;
        count += 3;
    }
    ```

    c.
    ```
    int count = 0, sum = 0;
    while ( count < 20 ) {
        sum    += 3*count;
        count += 2;
    }
    ```

7.3   The do–while **Statement**

pretest loop

The while statement is characterized as a *pretest loop* because the test is done before execution of the loop body. Because it is a pretest loop, the loop body may not be executed at all. The do–while is a repetition statement that is characterized as a *posttest loop.* With a posttest loop statement, the loop body is executed at least once.

posttest loop

The general format for the do–while statement is

do–while syntax

```
do

   <statement>

while ( <boolean expression> ) ;
```

The <statement> is executed until the <boolean expression> becomes false. Remember that <statement> is either a <single statement> or a <compound statement>. We will adopt the same policy for the if statement; that is, we will use the syntax of <compound statement> even if there is only one statement in the loop body. In other words, we will use the left and right braces even if the loop body contains only one statement.

Let's look at a few examples. We begin with the second example from Section 7.1, which adds the whole numbers 1, 2, 3, . . . until the sum becomes larger than 1,000,000. Here's the equivalent code in a do–while statement:

```
int sum = 0, number = 1;
do {

    sum += number;
    number++;

} while ( sum <= 1000000 );
```

Figure 7.3 shows how this do–while statement corresponds to the general format and Figure 7.4 is a diagram showing the control flow of this do–while statement.

Let's rewrite the routine that inputs a person's age using the do–while statement. Here's our first attempt:

```
do {

    age = inputBox.getInteger("Your Age (between 0 and 130):");

} while (age < 0 || age > 130);
```

It works, but unlike the version using the while statement, the code does not display an error message. The user could be puzzled as to why the input is not ac-

FIGURE 7.3   Correspondence of the example **do–while** statement to the general format.

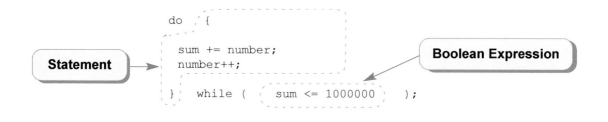

```
do    {

    sum += number;
    number++;

}     while (      sum <= 1000000      );
```

Statement

Boolean Expression

FIGURE 7.4   A diagram showing the control flow of the **do–while** statement.

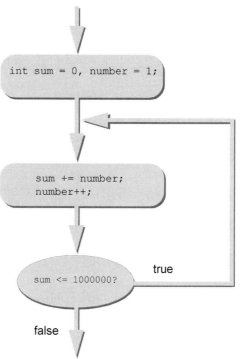

cepted. Suppose the user tries to enter 130 but actually enters 139 unintentionally. Without an error message to inform the user that the input was invalid, he or she may wonder why the program is asking again for input. A program should not be confusing to the user. We must strive for a program with a user-friendly interface.

To display an error message, we rewrite the do–while statement as

```
do {

    age = inputBox.getInteger("Your Age (between 0 and 130):");

    if (age < 0 || age > 130) {
        messageBox.show("An invalid age was entered. " +
                                "Please try again.");
    }

} while (age < 0 || age > 130);
```

This code is not as good as the version using the while statement. Do you know why? This do–while statement includes an if statement inside its loop body. Since the loop body is executed repeatedly, it is important not to include any extraneous statements. The if statement is repeating the same boolean expression of the do–while. Duplicating the testing conditions tends to make the loop statement harder to understand. For this example, we can avoid the extra test inside the loop body and implement the control flow a little more clearly by using a while statement. In general, the while statement is more frequently used than the do–while statement. However, the while statement is not universally better than the do–while statement. It depends on a given task, and our job as programmers is to use the most appropriate one. We choose the repetition statement that implements the control flow clearly, so the code is easy to understand.

boolean variable
and loop

When you have multiple conditions to stop the loop and if you need to execute different responses to each of the multiple conditions, then the use of boolean variables often clarifies the meaning of the loop statement. Consider the following example. Suppose we need to compute the sum of odd integers entered by the user. We will stop the loop when the sentinel value 0 is entered, an even integer is entered, or the sum becomes larger than 1,000. Without using any boolean variables, we can write this loop as

```
sum = 0;
do {

    num = inputBox.getInteger();

    if (num == 0)    //sentinel
        messageBox.show("Sum = " + sum);

    else if (num % 2 == 0)    //invalid data
        messageBox.show("Error: even number was entered");

    else {
        sum += num;
        if (sum > 1000)  //pass the threshold
            messageBox.show("Sum became larger than 1000");
```

```
        }

    } while ( !(num % 2 == 0 || num == 0 || sum > 1000) );
```

The ending condition is tricky. We need to stop the loop if any one of the three conditions num % 2 == 0, num == 0, or sum > 1000 is true. So we repeat the loop when none of the three conditions are true, which is expressed as

```
    !(num % 2 == 0 || num == 0 || sum > 1000)
```

We can also state the condition as

```
    do {

        . . .

    } while( num % 2 != 0 && num != 0 && sum <= 1000 );
```

> Note:
> !(a || b) is equal to (!a && !b)

which means "repeat the loop while num is odd and num is not 0 and sum is less than or equal to 1,000." Regardless of the method used, the test conditions are duplicated inside the loop body and in the boolean expression.

Now, using a boolean variable the loop becomes

```
    boolean repeat = true;

    sum = 0;
    do {

        num = inputBox.getInteger();

        if (num % 2 == 0)  {  //invalid data
            messageBox.show("Error: even number was entered");
            repeat = false;
        }
        else if (num == 0)  {  //sentinel
            messageBox.show("Sum = " + sum);
            repeat = false;
        }
        else {
            sum += num;
            if (sum > 1000) { //pass the threshold
                messageBox.show("Sum became larger than 1000");
                repeat = false;
            }
        }
    } while ( repeat );
```

> Be careful not to use the reserved word **continue** instead of **repeat**.

> Set the boolean variable to **false** so the loop terminates.

This loop eliminates duplicate tests. The use of boolean variables is helpful in making loop statements readable, especially when the loop has multiple stop conditions.

Quick Check

1. Write a do–while loop to compute the sum of the first 30 positive odd integers.

2. Rewrite the following while loops as do–while loops.

   a.
   ```
   int count = 0, sum = 0;
   while ( count < 10 ) {
       sum += count;
       count++;
   }
   ```

   b.
   ```
   int count = 1, sum = 0;
   while ( count <= 30 ) {
       sum    += count;
       count += 3;
   }
   ```

7.4   ResponseBox

We will introduce another class from the javabook package that is used for getting a yes or no response from the user. Let's begin with a simple example. Executing the code

```
MainWindow mainWindow = new MainWindow();
ResponseBox yesNoBox = new ResponseBox(mainWindow);

yesNoBox.prompt("Do you love Java?");
```

will result in the window shown in Figure 7.5. The string argument you pass to the prompt method is displayed in the dialog. The dialog by default contains two buttons labeled Yes and No. When the user clicks on a button, a value identifying the clicked button is returned.

Let's see how the buttons are identified. Consider the following example:

Chapter 7

```
int selection;

selection = yesNoBox.prompt("Click a button");

switch (selection) {

    case ResponseBox.YES:
        messageBox.show("Yes button was clicked");
        break;

    case ResponseBox.NO:
        messageBox.show("No button was clicked");
        break;
}
```

The **yesNoBox** object returns the value ResponseBox.YES when the user clicks the button labeled YES and ResponseBox.NO when the user clicks the button labeled NO. The YES and NO are the public class constants of the ResponseBox class.

All of the applications we have written so far have performed a single task (e.g., calculated a monthly payment or drew a shape) and then stopped. A ResponseBox object can be used in conjunction with a control statement to provide a very convenient way of asking the user to repeat a task or not. Here's how we write such a program:

```
do {
    //code for one computation comes here

    choice = yesNoBox.prompt("Repeat again?");

} while (choice == ResponseBox.YES);
```

FIGURE 7.5   A **ResponseBox** dialog box with the prompt "Do you love Java?"

We could also use the while statement to prompt the user before doing any work. Such a prompt is useful if the task is long and the user cannot cancel it in the middle. Here's how:

```
choice
    = yesNoBox.prompt("Do you want to start the computation?");

while (choice == ResponseBox.YES) {

    //code for computation comes here

    choice = yesNoBox.prompt("Repeat another computation?");
}
```

Notice that two statements, one before the while statement and another at the end of the loop body, prompt the user with different questions.

In some situations, instead of asking for a simple yes or no answer, we would like a user to select one of two options. For example, we can give the user a choice of Fahrenheit or Celsius for displaying the temperature of a given city. A ResponseBox object can be adapted for this purpose.

We can create an instance of the ResponseBox class with one, two, or three buttons by passing the number of buttons as the second argument in the new message. For example, to create a three-button ResponseBox, we say

```
ResponseBox threeButtonBox = new ResponseBox(mainWindow,3);
```

Buttons are identified from left to right by the class constants BUTTON1, BUTTON2, and BUTTON3. The labels for the buttons are set by the setLabel message. For example, to label the buttons left to right as OK, Cancel, and Help, we execute this code:

```
threeButtonBox.setLabel( ResponseBox.BUTTON1, "OK"     );
threeButtonBox.setLabel( ResponseBox.BUTTON2, "Cancel" );
threeButtonBox.setLabel( ResponseBox.BUTTON3, "Help"   );
```

The following code illustrates the creation of a two-button ResponseBox and how the response is tested:

```
int choice;
ResponseBox selectTemperature
            = new ResponseBox(mainWindow,2);
```

Chapter 7

```
selectTemperature.setLabel(ResponseBox.BUTTON1, "Celsius");
selectTemperature.setLabel(ResponseBox.BUTTON2, "Fahrenheit");

choice
    = selectTemperature.prompt("Celsius or Fahrenheit?");

if (choice == ResponseBox.BUTTON1) {

    // display the temperature in Celsius
}
else {

    // display the temperature in Fahrenheit
}
```

Executing the code results in the ResponseBox object shown in Figure 7.6. Notice the size of a button is adjusted to the size of its label. If you prefer to have the same size for both buttons, pad the text of the shorter label with spaces so that both labels have the same number of characters (counting the spaces, of course), for example:

```
selectTemperature.setLabel(ResponseBox.BUTTON1, "  Celsius ");
selectTemperature.setLabel(ResponseBox.BUTTON2, "Fahrenheit");
```

The yes–no ResponseBox is created by default if you don't pass a second argument to the new message. The labels Yes and No are assigned to the first and second buttons (from the left) automatically.

Chapter 7

FIGURE 7.6   The **ResponseBox** object with user-specified button labels.

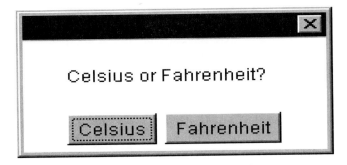

Table 7.2 is a list of ResponseBox methods and class constants.

TABLE 7.2   A list of **ResponseBox** methods.

CLASS:	ResponseBox	
Method	**Argument**	**Description**
`<constructor>`	`MainWindow`	Creates a ResponseBox object.
`<constructor>`	`MainWindow, int`	Creates a ResponseBox object with N (the second argument) buttons, 1 <= N <= 3. If an invalid N is passed, then the object will include one button.
`prompt`	`String`	Prompts the user with the text passed as an argument. Returns an integer that identifies the clicked button. See the explanation of the class constants.
`setLabel`	`int, String`	Sets the label of the designated button with the passed String. The first argument identifies the button. See the explanation of the class constants.
Class Constant		**Description**
`YES`		This value identifies the Yes button.
`NO`		This value identifies the No button.
`BUTTON1`		This value identifies the leftmost button. The value of BUTTON1 is equal to the value of YES.
`BUTTON2`		This value identifies the middle button. Note: the middle button becomes the rightmost button if there are only two buttons. The value of BUTTON2 is equal to the value of NO.
`BUTTON3`		This value identifies the rightmost button when the ResponseBox includes three buttons.

Quick Check

1. Write a code to create a ResponseBox with three buttons labeled ONE, TWO, and THREE.

2. Using the ResponseBox object created in question 1 above, write code that displays a message indicating which button was clicked.

7.5   The for Statement

The for statement is the third repetition control statement and is especially suitable for count-controlled loops. Let's begin with an example. The following code computes the sum of 20 integers entered by the user:

```
int i, sum = 0, number;
for (i = 0; i < 20; i++) {
    number = inputBox.getInteger();
    sum += number;
}
```

The general format of the for statement is

```
for ( <initialization>; <boolean expression>; <increment>  )

    <statement>
```

Figure 7.7 shows the correspondence of the sample code above to the general format. The diagram in Figure 7.8 shows how this statement is executed. The **control variable** variable i in the statement is called a *control variable*, and it keeps track of the number of repetitions. In the sample code, the control variable i is first initialized to 0, and immediately the boolean expression is evaluated. If the evaluation results in true, the loop body is executed. Otherwise, the execution of the for statement is terminated, and the control flows to the statement following this for

FIGURE 7.7   Correspondence of the example **for** statement to the general format.

FIGURE 7.8   A diagram showing the control flow of the example **for** statement.

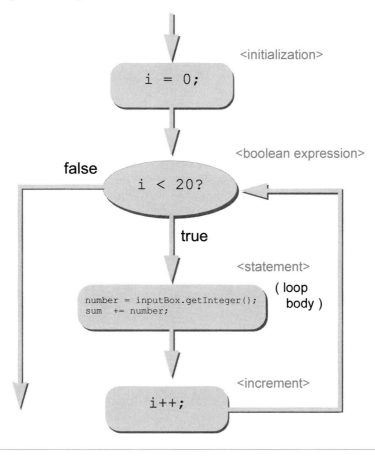

statement. Every time the loop body is executed, the increment operator (i++) is executed and then the boolean expression is evaluated.

The <initialization> component also can include a declaration of the control variable. We can do something like this:

```
for (int i = 0; i < 10; i++)
```

instead of

```
int i;
for (i = 0; i < 10; i++)
```

The control variable may be initialized to any value, although it is almost always 0 or 1.

The <increment> expression in the example increments the control variable by 1. We can increment it with values other than one, including negative values; for example,

```
for (int i = 0; i < 100; i += 5) // i = 0, 5, 10, ... , 95

for (int j = 2; j < 40; j *= 2)// j = 2, 4, 8, 16, 32

for (int k = 100; k > 0; k--) // k = 100, 99, 98, 97, ..., 1
```

Notice that the control variable appears in all three components: <initialization>, <conditional expression>, and <increment>. A control variable does not have to appear in all three components, but this is the most common style. Many other variations are allowed for these three components, but for novices, it is safer to use this style exclusively.

Let's look at an example from physics. When an object is dropped from height H, the position P of the object at time t can be determined by the formula

$$P = -16t^2 + H$$

For example, if a watermelon is dropped from the roof of a 256-foot-high building, it will drop like this:

256 ft. at **t = 0**

240 ft. at **t = 1**

192 ft. at **t = 2**

112 ft. at **t = 3**

0 ft. at **t = 4**

We can use a for statement to compute the position P at time t. We will input the initial height and compute the position every second. We repeat this computation until the watermelon touches the ground. The time the watermelon touches the ground is derived by solving for *t* when *P* = 0.

$$0 = -16t^2 + H$$

$$t = \sqrt{\frac{H}{16}}$$

```
double            initialHeight,
                  position,
                  touchTime;

MainWindow    mainWindow= new MainWindow("Drop WaterMelon");
OutputBox     outputBox = new OutputBox(mainWindow);
InputBox      inputBox  = new InputBox(mainWindow);

mainWindow.setVisible( true );
outputBox.setVisible( true );

initialHeight = inputBox.getDouble("Initial Height:");
touchTime     = Math.sqrt(initialHeight / 16.0);

outputBox.printLine("    Time t      Position at Time t ");
outputBox.skipLine(1);

for (int time = 0; time < touchTime;  time++) {
    position = -16.0 * time*time + initialHeight;
    outputBox.print("     " + time);
    outputBox.printLine("            " + position);
}

//print the last second
outputBox.printLine("     " + touchTime + "        0.00");
```

Running the above code with the input value 500.0 for the initial height will result in the **OutputBox** shown in Figure 7.9.

Quick Check

1. Write a **for** loop to compute

    a. the sum of 1, 2, . . . , 100.

    b. the sum of 2, 4, . . . , 500.

    c. the product of 5, 10, . . . , 50.

Chapter 7

2.   Rewrite the following while loops as for statements.

a.
```
int count = 0, sum = 0;
while ( count < 10 ) {
    sum += count;
    count++;
}
```

b.
```
int count = 1, sum = 0;
while ( count <= 30 ) {
    sum    += count;
    count += 3;
}
```

FIGURE 7.9   The positions of a watermelon dropped from a height of 500 feet.

```
OutputBox

    Time t          Position at Time t

     0                    500.0
     1                    484.0
     2                    436.0
     3                    356.0
     4                    244.0
     5                    100.0
     5.59017                0.0
```

7.6   Nested-for Statements

In many processing tasks, we need to place a for statement inside another for statement. In this section, we will introduce a simple nested for statement. We will be seeing more examples of nested for statements later in the book, especially in Chapter 12 on array processing.

Suppose we want to display a quick reference table for clerks at the Rugs-R-Us carpet store. The table in Figure 7.10 lists the prices of carpets ranging in size from 11×5 feet to 20×25 feet. The width of a carpet ranges from 11 feet to 20 feet with an increment of 1 foot. The length of a carpet ranges from 5 feet to 25 feet with an increment of 5 feet. The unit price of a carpet is $19 per square foot.

FIGURE 7.10   The price table for carpets ranging in size from 11 × 5 feet to 20 × 25 feet whose unit price is $19 per square foot.

Length

Carpet Price Table					
	5	10	15	20	25
11	1045	2090	3135	4180	5225
12	1140	2280	3420	4560	5700
13	1235	2470	3705	4940	6175
14	1330	2660	3990	5320	6650
15	1425	2850	4275	5700	7125
16	1520	3040	4560	6080	7600
17	1615	3230	4845	6460	8075
18	1710	3420	5130	6840	8550
19	1805	3610	5415	7220	9025
20	1900	3800	5700	7600	9500

Width

We use a nested-for statement to print out the table. Let's concentrate first on printing out prices. We'll worry about printing out length and width values later. The following nested-for statement will print out the prices:

```
int         price;
MainWindow  mainWindow  = new MainWindow();
OutputBox   outputBox   = new OutputBox(mainWindow);

mainWindow.setVisible( true );
outputBox.setTitle("Carpet Price Table");
outputBox.setVisible( true );

for (int width = 11; width <= 20; width++) {

    for (int length = 5; length <= 25; length += 5) {
        price = width * length * 19; //$19 per sq ft.
        outputBox.print("   " + price);
    }

    //finished one row; now move on to the next row
    outputBox.skipLine(1);
}
```

outer
for

inner
for

Chapter 7

The outer for statement is set to range from the first row (width = 11) to the last row (width = 20). For each repetition of the outer for, the inner for statement is executed, which ranges from the first column (length = 5) to the fifth column (length = 25). The loop body of the inner for computes the price of a single carpet size and prints out this price. So the complete execution of the inner for, which causes its loop body to be executed five times, completes the output of one row. The following shows the sequence of values for the two control variables.

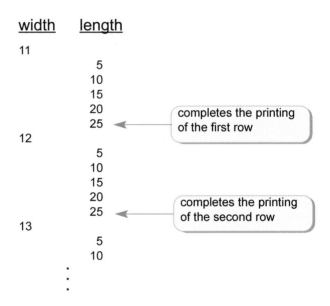

Now let's add the code to print out the row and column index values for width and length.

```
int              price;
MainWindow       mainWindow    = new MainWindow();
OutputBox        outputBox = new OutputBox(mainWindow);
mainWindow.setVisible( true );
outputBox.setTitle("Carpet Price Table");
outputBox.setVisible( true );

outputBox.printLine("      5      10      15      20      25");
outputBox.skipLine(1);

for (int width = 11; width <= 20; width++) {

      outputBox.print(width + "    ");
```

Modified Parts

```
for (int length = 5; length <= 25; length += 5) {
    price = width * length * 19; //$19 per sq ft.
    outputBox.print("    " + price);
}

//finished one row; now move on to the next row
ouputBox.skipLine(1);
}
```

The next improvement is to include the labels Width and Length in the output. This enhancement is left as exercise 16 at the end of the chapter. Also, in the example, literal constants are used for the carpet sizes and the increment value on length (11, 20, 5, 25, and 5), but in a real program, named constants should be used.

Quick Check

1. What will be the value of sum after the following nested-for loops are executed?

   a.
```
int sum = 0;
for (int i = 0; i < 5; i++) {
    sum = sum + i;
    for (int j = 0; j < 5; j++) {
        sum = sum + j;
    }
}
```

   b.
```
int sum = 0;
for (int i = 0; i < 5; i++) {
    sum = sum + i;
    for (int j = i; j < 5; j++) {
        sum = sum + j;
    }
}
```

2. What is wrong with the following nested-for loop?

```
int sum = 0;
for (int i = 0; i < 5; i++) {
    sum = sum + i;
    for (int i = 5; i > 0; i--) {
        sum = sum + j;
    }
}
```

7.7   The Format Class

In the table shown in Figure 7.10, the values are aligned very nicely. We purposely selected the unit price and the ranges of width and length so that the table output would look good. Notice that the output values are all four digit numbers. Realistically, we cannot expect output values to be so uniform. Let's change the unit price to $15 and the range of widths to 5 through 14 feet and see what happens. The result is shown in Figure 7.11, which is not as neat as the previous output. What we need is a way to format the output so the values are printed out with the proper alignment.

FIGURE 7.11   The price table for carpets with $15 per square foot and width ranging from 5 through 14.

Carpet Price Table				
5	10	15	20	25
5 375	750	1125	1500	1875
6 450	900	1350	1800	2250
7 525	1050	1575	2100	2625
8 600	1200	1800	2400	3000
9 675	1350	2025	2700	3375
10 750	1500	2250	3000	3750
11 825	1650	2475	3300	4125
12 900	1800	2700	3600	4500
13 975	1950	2925	3900	4875
14 1050	2100	3150	4200	5250

Format class from javabook

In this section we introduce the Format class from the javabook package, which we use to format output values. Let's start with an example. When we execute the following code (assuming outputBox was properly created)

```
int i = 12, j = 6789, k = 908766;
double x = 123.4, y = 2.90899, z = 900.0;

outputBox.printLine("i " + i);
outputBox.printLine("j " + j);
outputBox.printLine("k " + k);
```

```
outputBox.printLine("x " + x);
outputBox.printLine("y " + y);
outputBox.printLine("z " + z);
```

we will get the output shown in Figure 7.12. Values are printed using as many spaces as they require, no more and no less.

FIGURE 7.12   Unformatted output of integers and floats.

```
OutputBox
i 12
j 6789
k 908766
x 123.4
y 2.90899
z 900.0
```

Now let's see how we can format these six values using the Format class. The basic idea of formatted output is to allocate the same amount of space for the output values and align the values within the allocated space. We call the space occupied by an output value the *field* and the number of characters allocated to a field its *field width*.

field

Figure 7.13 shows the formatted output that is generated by executing the following code:

```
outputBox.printLine( "i " + Format.rightAlign(10, i) );
outputBox.printLine( "j " + Format.rightAlign(10, j) );
outputBox.printLine( "k " + Format.rightAlign(10, k) );

outputBox.printLine( "x " + Format.rightAlign(10, 3, x) );
outputBox.printLine( "y " + Format.rightAlign(10, 3, y) );
outputBox.printLine( "z " + Format.rightAlign(10, 3, z) );
```

To format an integer, we use

formatting integers

```
Format.leftAlign   ( <fieldWidth>, <int expression> );
Format.rightAlign  ( <fieldWidth>, <int expression> );
Format.centerAlign ( <fieldWidth>, <int expression> );
```

FIGURE 7.13   Formatted output of integers and floats.

```
OutputBox
i         12
j       6789
k     908766
x     123.400
y       2.909
z     900.000
```

where <fieldWidth> designates the field width and <int expression> is an arithmetic expression whose value is an int. The method names leftAlign, rightAlign, and centerAlign designate the alignment of an output value within a field. The following code will produce the output shown in Figure 7.14.

```
int i = 1234, j = 567, k = 89, l = 123456789;

outputBox.printLine( Format.leftAlign(6,i) + "I" );
outputBox.printLine( Format.leftAlign(6,j) + "Love" );
outputBox.printLine( Format.leftAlign(6,k) + "Java" );
outputBox.printLine( Format.leftAlign(6,l) + "Programming");
outputBox.skipLine(1);

outputBox.printLine( Format.rightAlign(6,i) );
outputBox.printLine( Format.rightAlign(6,j) );
outputBox.printLine( Format.rightAlign(6,k) );
outputBox.printLine( Format.rightAlign(6,l) );
outputBox.skipLine(1);

outputBox.printLine( Format.centerAlign(6,i) + "Yes" );
outputBox.printLine( Format.centerAlign(6,j) + "Java" );
outputBox.printLine( Format.centerAlign(6,k) + "Is" );
outputBox.printLine( Format.centerAlign(6,l) + "Hot" );
```

When the integer to be displayed has more digits than designated in <field-Width>, then the number is displayed using the minimum number of spaces necessary to display the number. For example, if the designated field width is 3, but the integer has 5 digits, then the number is displayed using 5 spaces.

FIGURE 7.14   Formatted output of integers, demonstrating various alignments.

```
OutputBox
1234    I
567     Love
89      Java
123456789Programming

  1234
   567
    89
123456789

 1234 Yes
  567 Java
  89  Is
123456789Hot
```

formatting strings

The same format statements can be used for a string value. For example, the following code will produce the output shown in Figure 7.15.

```java
for (int width = 10; width > 5; width-- )
    outputBox.printLine( Format.rightAlign(width, "Jakarta") );
```

FIGURE 7.15   Formatted output of the string "Jakarta".

```
OutputBox
   Jakarta
  Jakarta
 Jakarta
Jakarta
Jakarta
```

To format a real number (float or double), we need additional arguments to specify the decimal places:

formatting real numbers

```
Format.leftAlign  (<fieldWidth>,<decimalPlaces>,<real expr>);
Format.rightAlign (<fieldWidth>,<decimalPlaces>,<real expr>);
Format.centerAlign(<fieldWidth>,<decimalPlaces>,<real expr>);
```

where <decimalPlaces> designates the number of digits shown to the right of the decimal point and <real expr> is an arithmetic expression whose value is either float or double. The value for <fieldWidth> must be at least as large as the value of <decimalPlaces> plus two. We add two because a decimal point and a minus sign will occupy one space each. When the real number to be displayed has more digits than designated in <fieldWidth>, the number is displayed using the minimum number of spaces necessary to display the number. Here's an example:

```
double x = -123.4, y = 5.67, z = 8.911, w = 12345.6789;

outputBox.printLine( Format.leftAlign(6,2,x) + "I" );
outputBox.printLine( Format.leftAlign(6,2,y) + "Love" );
outputBox.printLine( Format.leftAlign(6,2,z) + "Java" );
outputBox.printLine( Format.leftAlign(6,2,w)
                                          + "Programming");
outputBox.skipLine(1);

outputBox.printLine( Format.rightAlign(6,3,x) );
outputBox.printLine( Format.rightAlign(6,3,y) );
outputBox.printLine( Format.rightAlign(6,3,z) );
outputBox.printLine( Format.rightAlign(6,3,w) );
outputBox.skipLine(1);

outputBox.printLine(Format.centerAlign(6,1,x) + "Yes");
outputBox.printLine(Format.centerAlign(6,1,y) + "Java");
outputBox.printLine(Format.centerAlign(6,1,z) + "Is");
outputBox.printLine(Format.centerAlign(6,1,w) + "Hot");
```

Figure 7.16 shows the results of executing the example code.

FIGURE 7.16   Formatted output of real numbers, demonstrating various alignments.

```
OutputBox
-123.40I
5.67  Love
8.91   Java
12345.68Programming

-123.400
 5.670
 8.911
12345.679

-123.4Yes
  5.7 Java
  8.9 Is
12345.7Hot
```

Table 7.3 is a list of Format methods.

TABLE 7.3   A list of **Format** methods.

CLASS:	Format	
Class Method	Argument	Description
leftAlign	int, long or int or String	The first argument designates the field width. The second argument is left aligned in the given field. The method returns the formatted value as a String.
leftAlign	int, int, double or float	The first argument designates the field width. The second argument designates the decimal places. The third argument is left aligned in the given field. The method returns the formatted value as a String.
centerAlign	int, long or int or String	Same as the first version of leftAlign, but with the center alignment.
centerAlign	int, int, double or float	Same as the second version of leftAlign, but with the center alignment.
rightAlign	int, long or int or String	Same as the first version of leftAlign, but with the right alignment.
rightAlign	int, int, double or float	Same as the second version of leftAlign, but with the right alignment.

Chapter 7

Quick Check

1.   Determine the output of the following code:

```
outputBox.printLine(Format.leftAlign(8,2,10.23)+ "X");
outputBox.printLine(Format.centerAlign(8,2,12.094)+ "X");
outputBox.printLine(Format.rightAlign(8,2,0.3333)+ "X");
outputBox.printLine(Format.leftAlign(8,2,2.1)    + "X");
```

2.   What's wrong with the following code?

```
outputBox.printLine(Format.centerAlign(2,1033.23)+ "Y");
outputBox.printLine(Format.leftAlign(12.94, 6, 2)+ "Y");
outputBox.printLine(Format.rightAlign(6,2,"Hi")  + "Y");
```

7.8   Loan Tables

The LoanCalculator program computed the monthly and total payments for a given loan amount, annual interest rate, and loan period. To see the monthly payment for the same loan amount and loan period but with a different interest rate, we would need to repeat the calculation, entering the three values again. To illustrate the use of the concepts introduced in this chapter, let's design a program that generates a loan table (similar to the carpet price table) for a given loan amount so we can compare different monthly payments easily and quickly. The columns of the table are the loan periods in number of years (5, 10, 15, 20, 25, 30), and the rows are interest rates ranging from 6 percent to 10 percent in increments of 0.25.

In this section, we will provide a discussion of the relevant methods only. Let's begin with a design of the topmost start method of the modified LoanCalculator class, which we will call LoanTable. The start method can be expressed as

```
tell the user what the program does;
prompt the user "Do you want to generate a loan table?";
while (the user says YES) {

    input the loan amount;
    generate the loan table;

    prompt the user "Do you want another loan table?";
}
```

pseudocode

The start method is expressed in pseudocode. A *pseudocode* is an informal language we often use to express an algorithm. Pseudocode is useful in expressing an algorithm without being tied down to the rigid syntactic rules of a programming language. We can express a simple algorithm in the actual programming language statements, but for a more complex algorithm, especially those involving nonsequential control flow logic, pseudocode is very helpful in expressing the algorithm concisely and clearly. Whenever appropriate, we will be using pseudocode to express more complex algorithms in the remainder of the book.

Translating the pseudocode into Java code will result in

```
public void start ( )
{
  int response;

  describeProgram();
  response = yesNoBox.prompt("Do you want to run the program?");

  while (response == ResponseBox.YES) {

      loanAmount = getLoanAmount();        //get input
      generateLoanTable(loanAmount);       //generate one table

      response = yesNoBox.prompt("Do you want another loan table?");
  }
}
```

Notice how the use of the object yesNoBox and methods describeProgram and getLoanAmount makes the actual start method almost as easy to read as the pseudocode. By using objects and well-designed (sub)methods, we can express methods that are as easy to read as pseudocode.

The describeProgram method tells the user what the program does if the user requests it. The getLoanAmount method gets the loan amount from the user. The method will allow the user to enter the loan amount between 100.0 and 500,000.0. The generateLoanTable method generates the loan table, which we will explain in detail next.

We use a nested loop to generate the table. Both the inner and outer loops are count-controlled loops. The loop for columns (years) will range from 5 to 30 with an increment of 5 and the loop for rows (rates) will range from 6.0 to 10.0 with an increment of 0.25. So the nested loop will be as follows:

```
private static final int BEGIN_YEAR = 5;
private static final int END_YEAR = 30;
private static final int YEAR_INCR= 5;

private static final float BEGIN_RATE= 6.0f;
private static final float END_RATE= 10.0f;
private static final float RATE_INCR= 0.25f;

private int   year;
private float rate;

...

for (rate = BEGIN_RATE; rate <= END_RATE; rate += RATE_INCR){

  for (year = BEGIN_YEAR; year <= END_YEAR; year += YEAR_INCR){
```

Chapter 7

```
   . . .

       //compute and display the monthly loan payment
       //for a given year and rate
   }
}
```

To compute the monthly loan payment, we define a method getMonthlyPayment that takes the arguments amount, monthlyRate, and numOfPayments for the loan amount, monthly interest rate, and the number of payments. The method is defined as follows:

```
private double getMonthlyPayment( double   amount,
                                  double   monthlyRate,
                                  int      numOfPayments )
{
    double payment;

    payment =
        (amount * monthlyRate)   /
        (1 - Math.pow( 1/(1 + monthlyRate), numOfPayments) );

    return payment;
}
```

We use the field width of 10 and two decimal places for the monthly loan payments, so we display the loanAmount as

```
outputBox.print( Format.rightAlign(10, 2, loanAmount) );
```

To output the complete table with column and row labels, we write the nested loop as

```
//print the column labels
outputBox.print(Format.rightAlign(10," ");
for (year = BEGIN_YEAR; year <= END_YEAR; year += YEAR_INCR){
    outputBox.print( Format.centerAlign(10, year) );
}

outputBox.skipLine(1);

for (rate = BEGIN_RATE; rate <= END_RATE; rate += RATE_INCR){

    //print the row label
    outputBox.print( Format.centerAlign(10, 2, rate ) );
```

```
//compute monthly rate

monthlyRate = rate / 100.0 / MONTHS_IN_YEAR;

for (year = BEGIN_YEAR; year <= END_YEAR; year+= YEAR_INCR){

    payments = year * MONTHS_IN_YEAR; //total # of payments

    loanPayment =
        getMonthlyPayment(loanAmount, monthlyRate,
                                        payments);
    outputBox.print(Format.rightAlign(10, 2, loanPayment));
}

outputBox.skipLine(1);
}
```

7.9 Sample Program: Hi-Lo Game

After the mundane task of dealing with mortgages, let's play a game. We will write a program that plays a Hi-Lo game. This program illustrates the use of repetition control, the random number generator, and the testing strategy. The objective of the game is to guess a secret number between 1 and 100. The program will respond with HI if the guess is higher than the secret number and LO if the guess is lower than the secret number. The maximum number of guesses allowed is six. If you allow up to seven, one can always guess the secret number. Do you know why?

Problem Statement

> *Write an application that will play Hi-Lo games with the user. The objective of the game is for the user to guess the computer-generated secret number in the least number of tries. The secret number is an integer between 1 and 100, inclusive. When the user makes a guess, the program replies with HI or LO depending on whether the guess is higher or lower than the secret number. The maximum number of tries allowed for each game is six. The user can play as many games as she wants.*

Overall Plan

We will begin with our overall plan for the development. Let's identify the major tasks of the program. The first task is to generate a secret number every time the game is played, and the second task is to play the game itself. We also need to add a loop to repeat these two tasks every time the user wants to play the Hi-Lo game. We can express this program logic in pseudocode as

program
tasks

```
do {

    Task 1: generate a secret number;

    Task 2: play one game;

} while ( the user wants to play );
```

Let's look at the two tasks and determine objects that will be responsible for handling the tasks. For the first task, we will use the random method of the Math class. We will examine this method in detail later to determine whether it is the one we can use in the program. If this method does not meet our needs, then we will explore further and most likely have to derive our own random number generator.

For the second task of playing the game itself, we need an object to accept the user's guess and another object to respond to the user with a HI or LO. For input, we will use an InputBox object. For output, we will use a MessageBox object. If we want the game to be slightly easier, we could use an OutputBox and display the history of guesses along with the hints:

```
GUESS          HINT
  50            LO
  60            HI
  55            LO
```

We opt to use a MessageBox so the game player has to keep track in her mind of the guesses she made and the hints. At the end of one game, we use this MessageBox object to display either You guessed it in <N> tries or You lost. Secret number was <X> with <N> or <X> replaced with the actual value.

Finally, we will define a top-level control object that manages all other objects. We will call this class HiLo. Our main class will be HiLoMain, whose task is to create an instance of HiLo and start the instance. We also need a way for the user to tell the program whether to play another game or not. We will use a ResponseBox object for this purpose. Here's our working design document:

Design Document: HiLo	
Class	**Purpose**
HiLoMain	The main class of the program.
HiLo	The top-level control object that manages other objects in the program.
MessageBox	A **MessageBox** object is used to show the hint **HI** or **LO** after each guess. This class is from **javabook**.
InputBox	An **InputBox** object is used to get a guess from the player. This class is from **javabook**.
OutputBox	An **OutputBox** object is used to display the rules of the Hi-Lo game. This class is from **javabook**.
ResponseBox	A **ResponseBox** object is used to get the user's instruction to play another game or not. This class is from **javabook**.
MainWindow	The main window of the application. This class is from **javabook**.

Figure 7.17 is the object diagram for this program.

FIGURE 7.17   The object diagram for the **HiLo** program.

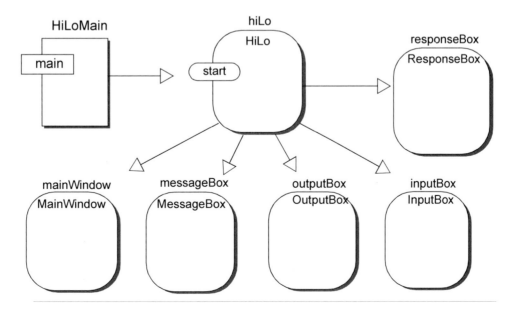

We will implement this program using the following four major steps:

development steps

1. Start with a program skeleton. Define the HiLoMain and HiLo classes.

2. Add code to the HiLo class to play a game using a dummy secret number.

3. Add code to the HiLo class to generate a random number.

4. Finalize the code by removing temporary statements and tying up loose ends.

Step 1 Development: Program Skeleton

Step 1 Design

The structure of the HiLoMain class is the same as other main classes. All we need is to declare, create, and start a HiLo object. Instead of forcing the user to play at least one game, we will implement the program so the user has an option of not playing a game at all. In pseudocode we can express this logic as

```
describe the game rules;

prompt the user to play a game or not;

while ( answer is yes ) {

    generate the secret number;

    play one game;

    prompt the user to play another game or not;
}
```

Notice that we use a while loop here, so the user can quit the program without playing a game. If we use a do–while loop instead, then the user must play at least one game before stopping the program. We opt to use the while loop because the user may not want to play the game at all after reading the game rules.

We use a private method describeRules to display the game rules. To prompt the user to play a game or not, we will use a ResponseBox, and to generate a secret number, we define another private method called generateSecret-Number. Lastly, we define a third private method playGame to play one game. We declare these three methods private because these methods are for internal use. As always, we will use the constructor to perform necessary object creation and initialization. The object diagram for the HiLo class at this point is

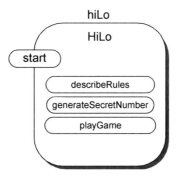

Our working design document for the HiLo class is as follows:

Design Document:	The HiLo Class	
Method	**Visibility**	**Purpose**
`<constructor>`	`public`	Creates and initializes the objects used by a HiLo object.
`start`	`public`	Starts the Hi-Lo game playing. The user has an option of playing a game or not.
`describeRules`	`private`	Displays the game rules in OutputBox.
`generate-SecretNumber`	`private`	Generates a secret number for the next Hi-Lo game.
`playGame`	`private`	Plays one Hi-Lo game.

Step 1 Code   For the skeleton program, we include temporary output statements in the private methods to verify that they are called correctly in the right order. Here's the skeleton:

File: HiLoMain.java

```java
/**
 * The HiLo main program for playing Hi-Lo games. The objective of the
 * game is to guess the secret number (any integer between 1 and 100)
 * with the least number of tries. The maximum number of tries
 * allowed is six. The program will display the hint HI if the guess
 * is higher than the secret number and LO if the guess is lower than
 * the secret number. The message "You guessed it in <N> tries" or
 * "You lost. Secret no.was <X>" appears at the end of one game.
 *
 * @author Dr. Caffeine
 *
 */
class HiLoMain
{
    public static void main (String[] args)
```

Chapter 7

```
    {
        HiLo hiLo = new HiLo( );
        hiLo.start();
    }
}
```

```
import javabook.*;

/**
 * This class is the top-level controller object for managing
 * all other objects in the HiLo program.
 *
 * @author Dr. Caffeine
 *
 */
class HiLo      // Step 1: Skeleton
{

//--------------------------------
// Data Members
//--------------------------------

    private MainWindow   mainWindow;
    private MessageBox   messageBox;
    private OutputBox    outputBox;
    private ResponseBox  responseBox;
    private InputBox     inputBox;

//--------------------------------
// Constructors
//--------------------------------
    /**
     * Default constructor. The default window title is "Drawing Shape".
     */
    public HiLo( )
    {
        mainWindow   = new MainWindow ("Let's Play HiLo");
        outputBox    = new OutputBox  ( mainWindow );
        responseBox  = new ResponseBox( mainWindow );
        messageBox   = new MessageBox ( mainWindow );
        inputBox     = new InputBox   ( mainWindow );

        mainWindow.setVisible( true );
        outputBox.setVisible( true );
    }

//---------------------------------------------------
//     Public Methods:
//
//          void   start  (      )
//
//---------------------------------------------------

    /**
     * Top level method that calls other private methods
     * to play the Hi-Lo games.
     */
```

```java
    public void start ( )
    {
        int answer;

        describeRules();

        answer = responseBox.prompt("Do you want to play a Hi-Lo game?);

        while ( answer == ResponseBox.YES ) {

            generateSecretNumber( );

            playGame();

            answer = responseBox.prompt
                            ("Do you want to play another Hi-Lo game?");
        }
    }

//---------------------------------------------------
//      Private Methods:
//
//      void    describeRules         (           )
//      void    generateSecretNumber(           )
//      void    playGame             (           )
//
//---------------------------------------------------

    /**
     * Provides a brief explanation of the program to the user.
     *
     */
    private void describeRules( )
    {
        outputBox.printLine("Inside describeRules");        //TEMP
    }

    /**
     * Generates a random number between 1 and 100.
     *
     */
    private void generateSecretNumber( )
    {
        outputBox.printLine("Inside generateSecretNumber");//TEMP
    }

    /**
     * Plays one Hi-Lo game.
     *
     */
    private void playGame( )
    {
        outputBox.printLine("Inside playGame");             //TEMP
    }

}
```

Step 1 Test

The main class HiLoMain will not change. The class given here is the final version. We execute the main class and the skeleton HiLo class to verify that the classes are coded correctly. To verify the correct execution of Step 1 we attempt to play the game

1. Zero times.

2. One time.

3. One or more times.

For the first run, we select No to the prompt Do you want to play a Hi-Lo game? and make sure the program stops without playing a game. For the second run, we select Yes to the first prompt and verify that the messages Inside generateSecretNumber and Inside playGame are shown in outputBox. We select No to the prompt Do you want to play another Hi-Lo game? and make sure the program stops. For the third run, we make sure we can play more than one game. After we verify all the scenarios work correctly, we proceed to the next step.

Step 2 Development: Play a Game with a Dummy Secret Number

Step 2 Design

In the second development step, we add a routine that plays a Hi-Lo game. We decided in the overall planning step that we will use an InputBox object to accept the user guess and a MessageBox object to display a hint. Let's begin with the control flow of the playGame method.

There are two cases to end a Hi-Lo game: either the user guesses the number in less than six tries or uses up all six tries without guessing the number. So we need a counter to keep track of the number of guesses made. Let's call this counter guessCount. We stop the game when guessCount becomes larger than six or the user's guess is equal to the secret number. At the end of the game, we output an appropriate message. Expressing this in pseudocode, we have

```
//Method: playGame

set guessCount to 0;

do {
    get next guess;

    increment guessCount;

    if (guess < secretNumber) {
        print the hint LO;
    }
    else if (guess > secretNumber) {
        print the hint HI;
```

```
        }

    } while (guessCount < number of guesses allowed &&
              guess != secretNumber );

    if (guess  == secretNumber) {

        print the winning message;
    }
    else {
        print the losing message;
    }
```

All variables used in this method will be local except secretNumber, which will be an instance variable. The value for secretNumber is set inside the generateSecretNumber method.

To support a better user interface, we will include an input error handling that allows the user to enter only values between 1 and 100. We will do this input-error-checking routine in a new private method getNextGuess because we do want to keep the playGame method clean and simple. If we include the code for input error handling directly inside the playGame method, the method would become too cluttered and lose the overall clarity of what the method is doing. Pseudocode for the getNextGuess method is

```
//Method: getNextGuess

get input value;

while ( input < 1 || input > 100 ) {
    print an error message;
    get input value;
}
```

The working design document of the class now includes this new private method:

Design Document:	The HiLo Class	
Method	**Visibility**	**Purpose**
. . .	. . .	. . .
getNextGuess	private	Returns the next guess from the user. Only accepts a guess between 1 and 100. Prints an appropriate error message when an invalid guess is entered.

Step 2 Code

In the Step 2 coding, we need to implement three methods. In addition to the playGame and getNextGuess methods, we need to define a temporary generateSecretNumber method so we can test the playGame method. The temporary generateSecretNumber method assigns a dummy secret number to the instance variable secretNumber. The temporary method is coded as

```
private void generateSecretNumber( )
{
    secretNumber = 45;       //TEMP
}
```

Any number will do; we simply picked the number 45. Knowing that the secret number is 45, we will be able to test whether the playGame method is implemented correctly or not.

We implement the playGame method as

```
private void playGame( )
{
    int guessCount = 0;
    int guess;

    do {
        //get the next guess
        guess = getNextGuess();

        guessCount++;

        //check the guess
        if (guess < secretNumber) {
            messageBox.show("Your guess is LO");
        }
        else if (guess > secretNumber) {
            messageBox.show("Your guess is HI");
        }

    } while ( guessCount < MAX_GUESS_ALLOWED &&
              guess != secretNumber );

    //output appropriate message
    if ( guess == secretNumber ) {
        messageBox.show("You guessed it in "
                            + guessCount  + " tries.");
    }
    else {
        messageBox.show("You lost. Secret No. was "
                            + secretNumber);
    }
}
```

> getNextGuess is a new private method.

> Repeat the loop if the number of tries is not used up and the correct guess is not yet made.

> This is a class constant whose value is set to 6.

The getNextGuess method will accept an integer between 1 and 100. The method uses a while loop to accomplish this:

```
private int getNextGuess( )
{
    int nextGuess;

    nextGuess
      = inputBox.getInteger("Enter Guess between 1 and 100");

    while (nextGuess < 1 || nextGuess > 100) {
       messageBox.show("Guess must be between 1 and 100");
       nextGuess = inputBox.getInteger("Your Guess:");
    }

    System.out.println("Guess: " + nextGuess); //TEMP

    return nextGuess;
}
```

The necessary constant and instance variable are declared in the data member section of the HiLo class as

```
//-----------------------------------
// Data Members
//-----------------------------------
private final int    MAX_GUESS_ALLOWED = 6;

private int          secretNumber;
```

Step 2 Test   We need to test two methods in this step. To verify the getNextGuess method, we input both invalid and valid guesses. Notice that we place a temporary output statement in the method to verify the input value. We verify the method by running the following tests:

1. Enter a number less than 1.

2. Enter a number greater 100.

3. Enter a number between 2 and 99.

4. Enter 1.

5. Enter 100.

test cases

The first two tests are called *error cases*, the third is called the *normal case*, and the last two are called *end cases*. One of the common errors beginners make is the loop statement that does not process the end cases correctly. When our code handles all three types of cases correctly, we will proceed to test the play-Game method.

To verify the playGame method, we need to perform a more elaborate testing. Knowing that the dummy secret number is 45, we verify the playGame method by running the following tests:

1. Enter a number less than 45 and check that the correct hint LO is displayed.

2. Enter a number greater than 45 and check that the correct hint Hi is displayed.

3. Enter the correct guess and check that the game terminates after displaying the appropriate message.

4. Enter six wrong guesses and check that the game terminates after displaying the appropriate message.

When all four tests are successfully completed, we proceed to the next step.

Step 3 Development: Generate a Random Number

Step 3 Design

In the third development step, we add a routine that generates a random number between 1 and 100. We search for any existing class that will do the job, and luckily we found the method random from the Math package. If we were not successful in finding any existing class, then we would have to define our own random number generator by consulting any relevant mathematics references (or searching the Internet).

pseudorandom number generator

The method random is called a *pseudorandom number generator* and returns a number (type double) that is greater than or equal to 0.0 but less than 1.0, that is, $0.0 \leq X < 1.0$. The generated number is called a *pseudorandom number* because the number is not truly random. When we call this method repeatedly, eventually the numbers generated will repeat themselves. Therefore, theoretically the generated numbers are not random, but for all practical purposes, they are random enough. Since the number returned from the random method ranges from 0.0 up to but not including 1.0, we need to convert it to a number between 1 and 100. If an X is a number returned by random, then the following property holds:

$$0 \leq X \times 100 < 100$$

Since the expression $X \times 100$ is a real number, we truncate it to get an integer value:

$$0 \le \lfloor X \times 100 \rfloor \le 99$$

Since we need a value between 1 and 100, the secret number is computed as

$$secretNumber = \lfloor X \times 100 \rfloor + 1$$

Step 3 Code

The generateSecretNumber method is defined as

```
private void generateSecretNumber( )
{
    double X = Math.random();

    secretNumber = (int) Math.floor( X * 100 ) + 1;

    System.out.println("Secret Number: " + secretNumber);
                                                    // TEMP
}
```

The method includes a temporary statement to output the secret number so we can stop the game anytime we want by entering the correct guess.

Step 3 Test

To verify that the method generates correct random numbers, we will write a separate test program. If we don't use such a test program and instead include the method immediately in the HiLo class, we have to play the game, say, 100 times to verify that the first 100 generated numbers are valid. The test program generates N random numbers and stops whenever an invalid number is generated. We will set N to 1000. Here's the test program:

TestRandom
class for testing

```
class TestRandom
{
    public static void main ( String args[] )
    {
        int    N = 1000, count = 0, number;
        double X;

        do {

            count++;

            X      = Math.random();
            number = (int) Math.floor( X * 100 ) + 1;

        } while ( count < N &&
```

Chapter 7

```
                               1 <= number && number <= 100 );

              if ( number < 1 || number > 100 ) {
                  System.out.println("Error: " + number);
              }
              else {
                  System.out.println("Okay");
              }
          }
      }
```

Keep in mind that successfully generating 1,000 valid random numbers does not guarantee that the 1,001st number is also valid. We did not make any formal mathematical proof that the routine for the random number generator works correctly. What we are doing here is making an assumption that no user wants to play more than 1,000 Hi-Lo games in one session, which we believe is a practical assumption. After the TestRandom class is executed correctly, we make the necessary changes to the HiLo class and run it. When we verify that the program runs as expected, we proceed to the final step.

Step 4 Development: Finalize

program
review

We finalize the program in the last step. We will perform a critical review of the program looking for any unfinished method, inconsistency, or error in the methods, unclear or missing comments, and so forth. We should also not forget to keep an eye on any improvement we can make to the existing code.

We still have a temporary code inside the describeRules method, so we will complete the method by adding code to describe the game rules. This method is left as an exercise. Use responseBox and display the game rules only if the user wants to see them.

There are still temporary output statements that we used for verification purposes. Either we can delete them from the program or comment them out. We will leave them in the program by commenting them out so when the time comes for us to modify, debug, or update the program, we do not have to reenter them.

7.10   (Optional) Recursive Methods

In addition to the three repetition control statements we introduced in this chapter, there is a fourth way to control the repetition flow of a program by using recursive methods. A *recursive method* is a method that contains a statement (or statements) that makes a call to itself. We will explain recursive methods briefly in this section. Realistic examples of recursive methods will be given in Chapter 15.

So far, we have seen only methods that call other methods, something like

```
methodOne(...)
{
    ...
    methodTwo(...);  //methodOne called methodTwo
    ...
}


methodTwo(...)
{
    ...
}
```

A recursive method calls itself, and it looks something like

```
methodOne(...)
{
    ...
    methodOne(...);  //calls the method itself
    ...
}
```

At first glance, it seems like a recursive call will never end since the call is made to the same method. Indeed, if you do not follow the rules, you could end up with infinite recursive calls. In this section we will explain how to write recursive methods correctly.

Suppose we want to compute the factorial of N. The *factorial* of N is the product of the first N positive integers, denoted mathematically as

```
N! = N * (N-1) * (N-2) * ... * 2 * 1
```

We will write a recursive method to compute the factorial of N. Mathematically, we can define the factorial of N recursively as

$$
factorial(N) = \begin{cases} 1 & \text{if } N = 1 \\ N * factorial(N-1) & \text{otherwise} \end{cases}
$$

The definition states that if N is 1, then the function factorial(N) has the value 1. Otherwise, the function factorial(N) is the product of N and factorial(N–1). For example, the function factorial(4) is evaluated as

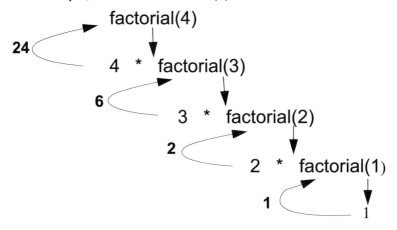

The recursive factorial method parallels the preceding mathematical definition. The method is defined as

```
public int factorial(int N)
{
    if (N == 1)              ←——————  Test to stop or continue

        return 1;           ←——————  End case: recursion stops

    else                                 Recursive case: re-
                                         cursion continues
        return N * factorial(N-1);       with a recursive call.
}
```

The diagram in Figure 7.18 illustrates the sequence of calls for the recursive factorial method. Recursive methods will contain three necessary components.

The three necessary components in a recursive method are

1. A test to stop or continue the recursion.

2. An end case that terminates the recursion.

3. A recursive call(s) that continues the recursion.

To ensure that the recursion will stop eventually, we must pass arguments different from the incoming parameters. In the factorial method, the incoming param-

FIGURE 7.18 The sequence of calls for the recursive **factorial** method.

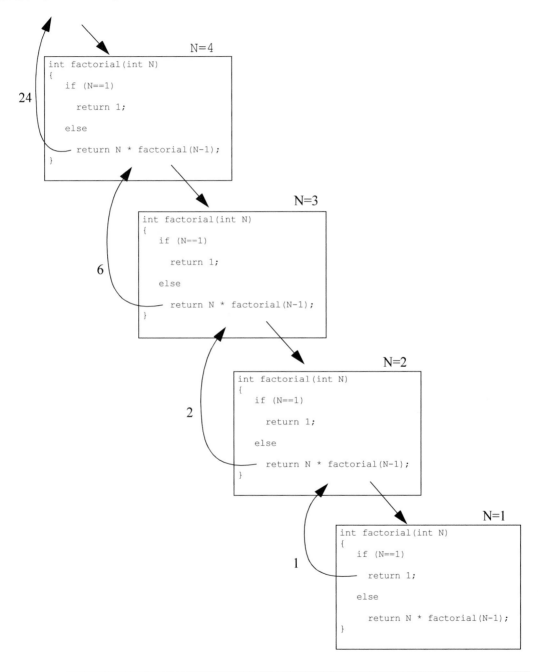

eter was N, while the argument passed in the recursive call was N–1. This difference of 1 between the incoming parameter and the argument will eventually make the argument in a recursive call be 1, and the recursion will stop.

Let's implement two more mathematical functions using recursion. The next method computes the sum of the first *N* positive integers 1, 2, . . . , *N*. Notice how this method includes the three necessary components of a recursive method.

```
public int sum ( int N )
{
    if (N == 1)
        return 1;
    else
        return N + sum( N-1 );
}
```

The last method computes the exponentiation A^N where A is a real number and N is a positive integer. This time, we have to pass two arguments: A and N. The value of A will not change in the calls, but the value of N is decremented after each recursive call.

```
public float exponent ( float A, int N )
{
    if (N == 1)
        return A;

    else
        return A * exponent( A, N-1 );
}
```

Although we use only mathematical functions to illustrate recursive methods, recursion is not limited to mathematical functions. More examples of recursive methods that implement nonnumerical operations appear in Chapter 16.

We used factorial, sum, and exponentiation as examples to introduce some of the basic concepts of recursion, but we should never write these methods using recursion. The methods can be written more efficiently with an iterative (i.e., nonrecursive) manner using a simple for loop. In practice, we use recursion if certain conditions are met.

Use recursion if

1. A recursive solution is natural and easy to understand.

2. A recursive solution does not result in excessive duplicate computation.

3. The equivalent iterative solution is too complex.

7.11 Exercises

1. Identify all the errors in the following repetition statements. Some errors are syntactical while others are logical (e.g., infinite loops).

```
a.  for (int i = 10; i > 0; i++) {
        x = y;
        a = b;
    }
b.  sum = 0;
    do {
        num = inputBox.getInteger();
        sum += num;
    } until (sum > 10000);

c.  while (x < 1 && x > 10) {
        a = b;
    }

d.  while (a == b) ;
    {
        a = b;
        x = y;
    }

e.  for (int i = 1.0; i <= 2.0; i += 0.1) {
        x = y;
        a = b;
    }
```

2. Write for, do–while, and while statements to compute the following sums and products.

a. $1 + 2 + 3 + \cdots + 100$

b. $5 + 10 + 15 + \cdots + 50$

c. $1 + 3 + 7 + 15 + 31 + \cdots + (2^{20}-1)$

d. $1 + \dfrac{1}{2} + \dfrac{1}{3} + \dfrac{1}{4} + \cdots + \dfrac{1}{15}$

e. $1 \times 2 \times 3 \times \cdots \times 20$

f. $1 \times 2 \times 4 \times 8 \times \cdots \times 2^{20}$

3. What will be the value of sum after each of the following nested loops is executed?

    a.
    ```
    sum = 0;
    for (int i = 0; i <= 10; i++)
        for (int j = 0; j <= 10; j++)
            sum += i ;
    ```

    b.
    ```
    sum = 0;
    j = 0;
    do {
        j++;
        for (int i = 5; i > j; i--)
            sum = sum + (i+j);
    } while (j < 11);
    ```

    c.
    ```
    sum = 0;
    i = 0;
    while (i < 5) {
        j = 5;
        while (i != j) {
            sum += j;
            j--;
        }
        i++;
    }
    ```

    d.
    ```
    sum = 0;
    for (int i = 0; i <= 10; i++)
        for (int j = 10; j > 2*i; j--)
            sum = sum + (j - i);
    ```

4. Determine the output from the following code.

    ```
    num = 123;
    for (int i = 0; i <= 5; i++) {
        display.printLine( Format.centerAlign(5 + 2*i, num) );
        display.skipLine( (int) Math.ceil(i/2) );
    }
    for (int j = 0; j <= 6; j += 2) {
        display.printLine( Format.rightAlign(15-j,num) );
        display.skipLine( (int) Math.ceil(j % 2) );
    }
    ```

5. Rewrite the following nested-for statements using nested do–while and while statements.

```
a.  sum = 0;
    number = 0;
    for (int i = 0; i <= 10; i++)
        for (int j = 10; j >= i; j--) {
            number++;
            sum = sum + (j - i);
        }

b.  product = 1;
    number = 0;
    for (int i = 1; i < 5; i++)
        for (int j = 1; j < 5; j++) {
            number++;
            product *= number;
        }
```

6. You can compute sin x and cos x using the following power series:

$$\sin x = x - \frac{x^3}{3!} + \frac{x^5}{5!} - \frac{x^7}{7!} + \cdots$$

$$\cos x = 1 - \frac{x^2}{2!} + \frac{x^4}{4!} - \frac{x^6}{6!} + \cdots$$

Write a program that evaluates sin x and cos x using the power series. Use the double data type and increase the number of terms in the series until the overflow occurs. You can check if the overflow occurs by comparing the value against Double.POSITIVE_INFINITY. Compare the results you obtained to the values returned by the sin and cos methods of the Math class.

7. Write an application to print out the numbers 10 through 49 in the following manner:

```
10 11 12 13 14 15 16 17 18 19
20 21 22 23 24 25 26 27 28 29
30 31 32 33 34 35 36 37 38 39
40 41 42 43 44 45 46 47 48 49
```

How would you do it? Here is an example of poorly written code:

```
MainWindow mainWindow = new MainWindow( );
OutputBox outputBox   = new OutputBox(mainWindow);
```

```
for (int i = 10; i < 50; i++) {
   switch (i) {
      case 19:
      case 29:
      case 39: outputBox.printLine(" " + i); //move to the
               break;                        //next line

      default: outputBox.print(" " + i);
   }
}
```

This code is not good because it works only for printing 10 through 49. Try to develop the code so that it can be extended easily to handle any range of values. You can do this coding in two ways: with a nested-for statement or with modulo arithmetic. (If you divide a number by 10 and the remainder is 9 then the number is either 9, 19, 29, or 39, and so forth.)

8. A *prime number* is an integer greater than one and divisible only by itself and one. The first seven prime numbers are 2, 3, 5, 7, 11, 13, and 17. Write a method that returns true if its argument is a prime number. Write another method that prints out all factors of the argument.

9. A *perfect number* is a positive integer that is equal to the sum of its proper divisors. A proper divisor is a positive integer other than the number itself that divides the number evenly (i.e., no remainder). For example, six is a perfect number because the sum of its proper divisors 1, 2, and 3 is equal to 6. Eight is not a perfect number because $1 + 2 + 4 \neq 8$. Write an application that accepts a positive integer and determines whether the number is perfect. Also, display all proper divisors of the number. Try a number between 20 and 30 and another number between 490 and 500.

10. Write an application that lists all perfect numbers between six and *N*, an upper limit entered by the user. After verifying the program with a small number for *N*, gradually increase the value for *N* and see how long the program takes to generate the perfect numbers. Since there are only a few perfect numbers, you might want to display the numbers that are not perfect so you can easily tell that the program is still running.

11. Write a method that returns the number of digits in an integer argument; for example, 23,498 has five digits.

12. Your freelance work with Java[2] Lo-Fat Burgers was a success (see exercise 16 of Chapter 6). The management loved your new drive-through ordering system because the customer had to order an item from each of the three menu categories. As part of a public relations campaign, however, management decided to allow a customer to skip a menu category. Modify

the program to handle this option. Before listing items from each category, use a ResponseBox object to ask the customer whether he or she wants to order an item from that category.

13. Extend the program in exercise 12 so that customers can order more than one item from each menu category. For example, the customer can buy two orders of Tofu Burgers and three orders of Buffalo Wings from the Entree menu category.

14. Complete the loan table application discussed in Section 7.8.

15. Implement the describeRules method of the HiLo class from Section 7.9. Use a ResponseBox object to ask the user whether or not to display the game rules.

16. The price table for carpet we printed out in Section 7.6 contains index values for width and length, but not labels to identify them. Write an application to generate the table below:

Carpet Price Table

		LENGTH				
		5	10	15	20	25
	11	1045	2090	3135	4180	5225
	12	1140	2280	3420	4560	5700
	13	1235	2470	3705	4940	6175
	14	1330	2660	3990	5320	6650
WIDTH	15	1425	2850	4275	5700	7125
	16	1520	3040	4560	6080	7600
	17	1615	3230	4845	6460	8075
	18	1710	3420	5130	6840	8550
	19	1805	3610	5415	7220	9025
	20	1900	3800	5700	7600	9500

17. Extend the HiLo class to allow the user to designate the lower and upper bounds of the secret number. In the original HiLo class, the bounds are set to 1 and 100, respectively.

Chapter 7

18. Using a DrawingBoard object, write an application that draws the following pattern of seven rectangles whose sides are 10, 20, 30, . . . , and 70 pixels wide.

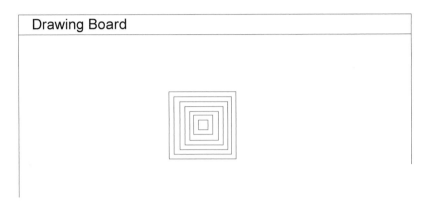

19. A formula to compute the Nth Fibonacci number was given in exercise 18 in Chapter 3. The formula is useful in finding a number in the sequence, but a more efficient way to output a series of numbers in the sequence is to use the recurrence relation $F_N = F_{N-1} + F_{N-2}$, with the first two numbers in the sequence F_1 and F_2 both defined as 1. Using this recurrence relation, we can compute the first 10 Fibonacci numbers as follows:

```
F1  = 1
F2  = 1
F3  = F2 + F1 =  1 +  1 =  2
F4  = F3 + F2 =  2 +  1 =  3
F5  = F4 + F3 =  3 +  2 =  5
F6  = F5 + F4 =  5 +  3 =  8
F7  = F6 + F5 =  8 +  5 = 13
F8  = F7 + F6 = 13 +  8 = 21
F9  = F8 + F7 = 21 + 13 = 34
F10 = F9 + F8 = 34 + 21 = 55
```

Write an application that accepts N, $N \geq 1$, from the user and displays the first N numbers in the Fibonacci sequence. Use OutputBox and Format for display.

20. Modify the application of exercise 19 to generate and display all the numbers in the sequence until a number becomes larger than the value maxNumber entered by the user.

21. Improve the LoanCalculator class from Chapter 4 to accept only the valid input values for loan amount, interest rate, and loan period. The original

LoanCalculator class assumed the input values are valid. For the exercise, let the loan amount between $100.00 and $1,000,000.00, the interest rate between 5% and 20%, and the loan period between 1 year and 30 years be valid.

22. The monthly payments for a given loan are divided into amounts that apply to the principal and to the interest. For example, if you make a monthly payment of $500, only a portion of the $500 goes to the principal and the remainder is the interest payment. The monthly interest is computed by multiplying the monthly interest rate and the unpaid balance. The monthly payment minus the monthly interest is the amount applied to the principal. The following table is the sample loan payment schedule for a one-year loan of $5,000 with a 12 percent annual interest rate.

Payment #	Interest	Principal	Unpaid Balance	Total Interest to Date
1	50.00	394.24	4605.76	50.00
2	46.06	398.19	4207.57	96.06
3	42.08	402.17	3805.40	138.13
4	38.05	406.19	3399.21	176.19
5	33.99	410.25	2988.96	210.18
6	29.89	414.35	2574.61	240.07
7	25.75	418.50	2156.11	265.82
8	21.56	422.68	1733.42	287.38
9	17.33	426.91	1306.51	304.71
10	13.07	431.18	875.34	317.78
11	8.75	435.49	439.85	326.53
12	4.40	435.45	0.00	330.93

Write an application that accepts a loan amount, annual interest rate, and loan period (in number of years) and displays a table with five columns: payment number, the interest and principal paid for that month, the remaining balance after the payment, and the total interest paid to date. Note: The last payment is generally different from the monthly payment, and your application should print out the correct amount for the last payment. Use the Format class to align the output values neatly.

Chapter 7

23. Instead of dropping a watermelon from a building, let's shoot it from a cannon and compute its projectile. The (x, y) coordinates of a watermelon at time t are

$$x = V \cdot \cos(\text{Alpha}) \cdot t$$

$$y = V \cdot \sin(\text{Alpha}) \cdot t - \frac{g \cdot t^2}{2}$$

where g is the acceleration of gravity, V is the initial velocity, and Alpha is the initial angle. The acceleration of gravity on earth is 9.8 m/sec^2.

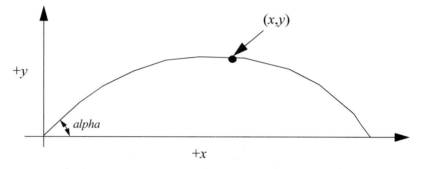

Write an application that inputs an initial velocity V (m/sec) and an initial angle alpha (in degrees) and computes the projectile of a watermelon cannon ball. The program should repeat the computation until the user wants to quit. The program outputs the (x,y) coordinate value for every second, that is, t = 0, 1, 2, and so forth. The program stops the output when the y value becomes zero or less. To use the cos and sin methods of the Math class, don't forget that you have to convert the input angle given in degrees to radians. You can convert using the following formula:

$$\text{Radian} = \frac{\text{Degree} \times \pi}{180}$$

Note: Air resistance is not considered in the formula. Also, we assumed the watermelon will not get smashed at firing.

24. Extend exercise 16 on page 227 by drawing a more realistic clock. Instead of drawing a clock like draw a circle at five-minute intervals as

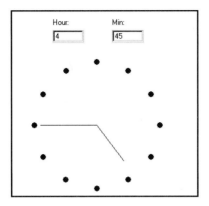

Use a for loop to draw 12 circles.

25. Write an applet that draws a multiplication table as shown below:

Applet Viewer									
applet									
	1	2	3	4	5	6	7	8	9
1	1	2	3	4	5	6	7	8	9
2	2	4	6	8	10	12	14	16	18
3	3	6	9	12	15	18	21	24	27
4	4	8	12	16	20	24	28	32	36
5	5	10	15	20	25	30	35	40	45
6	6	12	18	24	30	36	42	48	54
7	7	14	21	28	35	42	49	56	63
8	8	16	24	32	40	48	56	64	72
9	9	18	27	36	45	54	63	72	81

applet started

Use the drawString and drawLine methods to draw the multiplication table.

26. Extend the applet from exercise 25 to allow the user to enter two single-digit numbers. When the user presses the ENTER key, draw a rectangle around the product of the two numbers. The applet should look something like this:

Applet Viewer									
applet									

applet

9 X 7

	1	2	3	4	5	6	7	8	9
1	1	2	3	4	5	6	7	8	9
2	2	4	6	8	10	12	14	16	18
3	3	6	9	12	15	18	21	24	27
4	4	8	12	16	20	24	28	32	36
5	5	10	15	20	25	30	35	40	45
6	6	12	18	24	30	36	42	48	54
7	7	14	21	28	35	42	49	56	63
8	8	16	24	32	40	48	56	64	72
9	9	18	27	36	45	54	63	72	81

applet started

Surround the product of two given numbers with a rectangle.

Use two TextField objects for entering single-digit numbers. Every time the user enters new numbers and presses the ENTER key, draw a new rectangle around the product. When you draw a new rectangle, you need to erase the previous rectangle. No erase method is available, but you can "erase" by drawing the same rectangle again in white (assuming that the background color is white). To change the color of a drawing to white, you send the message setColor to a Graphics object. The sequence for erasing the old rectangle and drawing a new rectangle is

```
graphic.setColor(Color.white);
graphic.drawRect(...);          //erase the old rectangle

graphic.setColor(Color.black);  //reset color to black or
                                //any other color you prefer
graphic.drawRect(...);          //draw a new rectangle
```

Don't forget to resize the applet viewer in the HTML file to make the window wide enough for the entire multiplication table.

27. Repeat exercise 18 on page 348 using a Turtle object. See exercise 27 on page 82 for information on the Turtle class.

28. Using a Turtle object, draw a circle. The input to the program is the radius of the circle. See exercise 27 on page 82 for information on the Turtle class.

29. (Optional) Write a recursive method to compute the sum of the first N positive integers. Note: This is strictly for exercise. You should not write the real method recursively.

30. (Optional) Write a recursive method to compute the sum of the first N positive odd integers. Note: This is strictly for exercise. You should not write the real method recursively.

8

Characters and Strings

OBJECTIVES

After you have read and studied this chapter, you should be able to

- Declare and manipulate data of the char data type.

- Write string processing programs using String and StringBuffer objects.

- Differentiate the String and StringBuffer classes and use the correct class in solving a given task.

- Distinguish the primitive and reference data types and show how the memory allocation between the two is different.

- Tell the difference between equality and equivalence testings for String objects.

- Show, by using the state-of-memory diagrams, how objects are passed to methods and returned from methods.

Introduction

Early computers in the 1940s and 50s were more like gigantic calculators because they were used primarily for numerical computation. However, as computers have evolved to possess more computational power, our use of computers is no longer limited to numerical computation. Today we use computers for processing information of diverse types. In fact, most application software today such as word processors, database management systems, presentation software, and graphics design software is not intended specifically for number crunching. These programs still perform numerical computation, but their primary data are text, graphics, video, and other nonnumerical data. In this chapter you will learn about two nonnumerical data types in Java: char and String. The third nonnumerical data type boolean was already covered in Chapters 6 and 7.

8.1   Characters

In Java single characters are represented using the data type char. Character constants are written as symbols enclosed in single quotes, for example, 'a', 'X', and '5'. Just as we use different formats to represent integers and real numbers using 0s and 1s in computer memory, we use special codes of 0s and 1s to represent single characters. For example, we may assign 1 to represent 'A' and 2 to represent 'B'. We can assign codes similarly to lowercase letters, punctuation marks, digits, and other special symbols. In the early days of computing, different computers not only used different coding schemes but also different character sets. For example, one computer could represent the symbol ¼, while other computers could not. Individualized coding schemes did not allow computers to share information. Imagine sending electronic mail to your friend who uses a computer with a different coding scheme. You write, "Thank you for helping me with my programming assignment," and your friend reads, "τhiσ ισ φυστ an εξαmple." To avoid this problem, U.S. computer manufacturers devised several

ASCII

coding schemes. One of the coding schemes widely used today is *ASCII* (American Standard Code for Information Interchange). We pronounce ASCII "askey." Table 8.1 shows the 128 standard ASCII codes.

Adding the row and column indexes gives you the ASCII code for a given character. For example, the value 87 is the ASCII code for the character 'W'. Not all characters in the table are printable. ASCII codes 0 through 31 and 127 are nonprintable control characters. For example, ASCII code 7 is the bell (the computer beeps when you send this character to output), and code 9 is the tab.

To represent all 128 ASCII codes, we need seven bits ranging from 000 0000 (0) to 111 1111 (127). Although seven bits are enough, ASCII codes occupy a byte (eight bits) because the byte is the smallest unit of memory you can access. Computer manufacturers use the extra bit for other nonstandard symbols (e.g., lines and boxes). Using 8 bits, we can represent 256 symbols in total, 128 standard ASCII codes and 128 nonstandard symbols.

TABLE 8.1   ASCII codes.

	0	1	2	3	4	5	6	7	8	9
0	nul	soh	stx	etx	eot	enq	ack	bel	bs	ht
10	lf	vt	ff	cr	so	si	dle	dc1	dc2	dc3
20	cd4	nak	syn	etb	can	em	sub	esc	fs	gs
30	rs	us	sp	!	"	#	$	%	&	'
40	(	)	*	+	,	-	.	/	0	1
50	2	3	4	5	6	7	8	9	:	;
60	<	=	>	?	@	A	B	C	D	E
70	F	G	H	I	J	K	L	M	N	O
80	P	Q	R	S	T	U	V	W	X	Y
90	Z	[	\	]	^	_	`	a	b	c
100	d	e	f	g	h	i	j	k	l	m
110	n	o	p	q	r	s	t	u	v	w
120	x	y	z	{	}	|	~	del		

The standard ASCII codes work just fine as long as we are dealing with the English language because all letters and punctuation marks used in English are included in the ASCII codes. We cannot say the same for other languages. For languages such as French and German, the additional 128 codes may be used to represent character symbols not available in standard ASCII. But what about different currency symbols? What about non-European languages? Chinese, Japanese, and Korean all use different coding schemes to represent Kanji (ideograph) characters. Eight bytes are not enough to represent thousands of ideographs. If we try to read Japanese characters using ASCII codes, we will see gibberish. See for yourself by visiting foreign Web sites, such as the home pages of foreign newspapers presented in their native languages.

Unicode

To accommodate the character symbols of non-English languages, the Unicode Consortium established the *Unicode Worldwide Character Standard*, commonly known simply as *Unicode*, to support the interchange, processing, and display of the written texts of diverse languages. The standard currently contains 34,168 distinct characters, which cover the major languages of the Americas, Europe, the Middle East, Africa, India, Asia, and Pacifica. To accommodate

Chapter 8

such a large number of distinct character symbols, Unicode characters occupy two bytes. Unicode codes for the character set shown in Table 8.1 are the same as ASCII codes.

Java, being a language for the Internet, uses the Unicode standard for representing char constants. Although Java uses the Unicode standard internally to store characters, many platforms cannot display non-ASCII characters. For example, you need a Japanese version of Windows 95 or special add-on software to read Japanese characters displayed on a computer screen. The same is true for the Chinese and Korean languages.

Characters are declared and used in a manner similar to data of other types. The declaration

```
char ch1, ch2 = 'X';
```

declares two char variables ch1 and ch2 with ch2 initialized to 'X'. We can display the ASCII code of a character by converting it to an integer. For example, we can execute

```
messageBox.show("ASCII code of character X is " + (int)'X' );
```

Conversely, we can see a character by converting its ASCII code to the char data type, for example,

```
message.show("Character with ASCII code 88 is " + (char)88 );
```

Because the characters have numerical ASCII values, we can compare characters just as we compare integers and real numbers. For example, the comparison

```
'A' < 'c'
```

returns true because the ASCII value of 'A' is 65 while that of 'c' is 99.

Quick Check

1.   Determine the output of the following statements:

   a.   `System.out.println( (char) 65 );`

```
b.        System.out.println( (int) 'C' );

c.        System.out.println( 'Y' );

d.        if ( 'A' < '?' )
              System.out.println( 'A' );
          else
              System.out.println( '?' );
```

2. How many distinct characters can you represent by using eight bits?

8.2   Strings

String class

A *string* is a sequence of characters that is treated as a single value. The String data type is used to represent strings in Java. We have been using strings all along. For example, the text with double quotes that we've been passing to a MessageBox object is a literal constant of type String. For example:

```
messageBox.show("Welcome to Bali");
```

Also, we used String variables to write code such as

```
String name, greeting;

name = inputLine.getText(); //inputLine is a TextField object
greeting = "Welcome to Bali, " + name;
```

In this section you will learn more about the String data type and how to manipulate strings. To input a string, you can send the getString message to an InputBox object. The following code reads in a person's name and greets the user:

```
//assume inputBox and messageBox are declared
//and initialized correctly

String name;

name = inputBox.getString("What is your name?");
messageBox.show("Hello, " + name + ". Nice to meet you.");
```

Now let's see how we can manipulate strings. Let's say we want to input a person's name and determine the number of vowels the name contains. The basic idea is very simple:

```
for each character ch in the string {
    if (ch is a vowel) then {
        increment the counter
    }
}
```

There are two details we need to know before being able to translate the above into actual code. First, we need to know how to refer to an individual character in the string. Second, we need to know how to determine the size of the string, that is, the number of characters the string contains, so we can write the boolean expression to stop the loop correctly.

charAt

We access individual characters of a string by sending the message charAt to the String object. For example, to display the individual characters of the string Sumatra one at a time, we can say

```
String name = "Sumatra";
for (int i = 0; i < 7; i++) {
    messageBox.show( name.charAt(i) );
}
```

Each character in a string has an index we use to access the character. We use zero-based indexing, that is, the first character has index 0, the second character has index 1, the third character has index 2, and so forth. To refer to the first character of name, for example, we say

```
name.charAt(0)
```

Figure 8.1 illustrates how the charAt message works. Notice that we are sending a message to name; String is, in fact, a class in the java.lang package and name is an instance. Note: Strictly speaking, we must say "name is a variable of type String whose value is a reference to an instance of String." However, when the value of a variable X is a reference to an instance of class Y, we usually say "X is an instance of Y" or "X is a Y object." For example, we say canvas is a Drawing-Board object

> *If the value of a variable* X *is a reference to an object of class* Y, *then we say "* X *is a* Y *object" or "* X *is an instance of* Y.*"*

Since String is a class, just like MainWindow, InputBox, and others, we need to create an instance of a class using the new method. The statements

FIGURE 8.1   An indexed expression is used to refer to individual characters in a string.

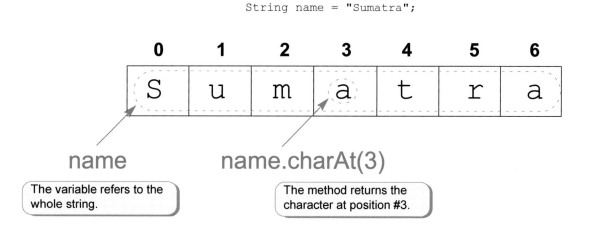

We will use shorthand notation in this book whenever appropriate. Remember that this shorthand works for the String class only. In the next section, we will discuss more about differences between objects such as String and the data types such as int, char, float, and others that are not objects (i.e., we cannot send messages to them).

In the sample code, we know exactly how many characters are in the string Sumatra, so there's no problem in expressing the condition to stop the execution of the for statement. But how can we write code that works on a string of any length? To find out the number of characters in any given string, we send the message length to the string. In order to print out individual characters of name, we would say

```
String name;
int numberOfCharacters;

name = inputBox.getString();
numberOfCharacters = name.length();

for (int i = 0; i < numberOfCharacters; i++) {
    messageBox.show( "" + name.charAt(i) );
}
```

Notice that if the string's length is N, then the characters are indexed from 0 to N-1, so we could express the preceding for loop as

```
for (int i = 0; i <= numberOfCharacters - 1; i++)
```

We will use the first style almost exclusively to be consistent.

Now that we know how to determine the size of a given string and refer to individual characters of a string, we can implement the code for counting the number of vowels. Here is the code:

```
String     name;

int        numberOfCharacters,
           vowelCount = 0;

char       letter;

name = inputBox.getString("What is your name?");
numberOfCharacters = name.length();

for (int i = 0; i < numberOfCharacters; i++) {

    letter = name.charAt(i);

    if (   letter == 'a' || letter == 'A' ||
           letter == 'e' || letter == 'E' ||
           letter == 'i' || letter == 'I' ||
           letter == 'o' || letter == 'O' ||
           letter == 'u' || letter == 'U'  ) {

        vowelCount++;
    }
```

```
    }

    messageBox.show(name + ", your name has " +
                        vowelCount + " vowels");
```

We can shorten the boolean expression in the if statement by using the toUpperCase method of the String class. This method converts every character in a string to uppercase. Here's the rewritten code:

```
String      name, nameUpper;

int         numberOfCharacters,
            vowelCount = 0;

char        letter;

name = inputBox.getString("What is your name?");

numberOfCharacters = name.length();
nameUpper = name.toUpperCase();

for (int i = 0; i < numberOfCharacters; i++) {

    letter = nameUpper.charAt(i);

    if (   letter == 'A' ||
           letter == 'E' ||
           letter == 'I' ||
           letter == 'O' ||
           letter == 'U'   ) {

        vowelCount++;
    }
}

messageBox.show(name + ", your name has " +
                    vowelCount + " vowels");
```

Notice that the original string name is unchanged. A new, converted string is returned from the method and assigned to the second String variable nameUpper.

Let's try another example. This time we read in a string and count how many words the string contains. For this example we consider a word as a sequence of characters separated, or delimited, by blank spaces. We treat punctuation marks and other symbols as part of a word. Expressing the task in pseudocode, we have the following:

```
read in a sentence;

while (there are more characters in the sentence) {

    look for the beginning of the next word;

    now look for the end of this word;

    increment the word counter;

}
```

We use a while loop here instead of do–while to handle the case when the input sentence contains no characters, that is, it is an empty string. Let's implement the routine. Here's our first attempt:

```
//Attempt No. 1

int    index, wordCount, numberOfCharacters;
String sentence = inputBox.getString("Enter a sentence:");

numberOfCharacters  = sentence.length();
index               = 0;
wordCount           = 0;

while (index < numberOfCharacters ) {
```

Skip blank spaces until a character that is not a blank space is encountered. This is the beginning of a word.

```
    //ignore blank spaces
    while (sentence.charAt(index) == ' ') {
        index++;
    }
```

Once the beginning of a word is detected, we skip nonblank characters until a blank space is encountered. This is the end of the word.

```
    //now locate the end of the word
    while (sentence.charAt(index) != ' ') {
        index++;
    }

    //another word has been found, so increment the counter
    wordCount++;
}
```

This implementation has a problem. The counter variable index is incremented inside the two while loops, and this index could become equal to numberOfCharacters, which is an error, because the position of the last character is numberOfCharacters – 1. We need to modify the two while loops so that index will not become larger than numberOfCharacters –1. Here's the modified code:

```
//Attempt No. 2

int    index, wordCount, numberOfCharacters;
String sentence = inputBox.getString("Enter a sentence:");

numberOfCharacters  = sentence.length( );
index               = 0;
wordCount           = 0;

while ( index < numberOfCharacters ) {

    //ignore blank spaces
    while (index < numberOfCharacters &&
            sentence.charAt(index) == ' ') {
        index++;
    }

    //now locate the end of the word
    while (index < numberOfCharacters &&
            sentence.charAt(index) != ' ') {
        index++;
    }

    //another word is found, so increment the counter
    wordCount++;

}
```

Notice that the order of comparisons in the boolean expression

```
index < numberOfCharacters && sentence.charAt(index) == ' '
```

is critical. If we switch the order to

```
sentence.charAt(index) == ' ' && index < numberOfCharacters
```

out-of-bound
error

and if the last character in the string is a space, then an *out-of-bound error* will occur because the value of index is a position that does not exist in the string sentence. By putting the expression correctly as

```
index < numberOfCharacters && sentence.charAt(index) != ' '
```

we will not get an out-of-bound error because the boolean operator && is a short circuit operator. If the relation index < numberOfCharacters is false, then the second half of the expression sentence.charAT(index) != ' ' will not get evaluated.

There is still a problem with the Attempt No. 2 code. If the sentence ends with one or more blank spaces, then the value for wordCount will be one more than the actual number of words in the sentence. It is left as an exercise to correct this bug (see exercise 17 on page 408).

Our third example counts the number of times the word Java occurs in the input. The repetition stops when the word STOP is read. Lowercase and uppercase letters are not distinguished when comparing an input word to Java, but the word STOP for terminating the loop must be in all uppercase letters. Here's the pseudocode:

```
javaCount = 0;
repeat    = true;
while (repeat) {
    read in next word;

    if (word is "STOP") {
        repeat = false;
    }
    else if (word is "Java" ignoring cases) {
        javaCount++;
    }

}
```

And here's the actual code. Pay close attention to how the strings are compared.

```
int       javaCount = 0;
boolean   repeat    = true;
String    word;

while ( repeat ) {

    word = inputBox.getString("Next word:");

    if ( word.equals("STOP") ) {
        repeat = false;
    }
    else if ( word.equalsIgnoreCase("Java") ) {
        javaCount++;
    }

}
```

String comparison is done by two methods—equals and equalsIgnore-
Case—whose meanings should be clear from the example. Another comparison
method is compareTo. This method compares two String objects str1 and str2 as
in

compareTo

```
str1.compareTo( str2 );
```

and returns 0 if they are equal, a negative integer if str1 is less than str2, and a
positive integer if str1 is greater than str2. The comparison is based on the lexi-
cographical order of Unicode. For example, caffeine is less than latte. Also, the
string jaVa is less than the string java because the Unicode value of V is smaller
than the Unicode value of v. (See the ASCII table, Table 8.1.)

Some of you may be wondering why we don't say

```
if ( word == "STOP" )
```

We can, in fact, use the equality comparison symbol == to compare two String
objects, but the result is very different from the result of the method equals. We
will explain the difference in the next section.

substring

Another useful string method is substring. This method returns a new string
from a given string. If str is a String object, then the expression

```
str.substring ( beginIndex, endIndex )
```

returns a new string that is a substring of str from position beginIndex to endIndex – 1. The value of beginIndex must be between 0 and str.length() – 1 and the
value of endIndex must be between 0 and str.length(). In addition, the value of
beginIndex must be less than or equal to the value of endIndex. Passing invalid
values for beginIndex or endIndex will result in a runtime error.

The following code creates a new string Javanist from Alpinist using the
substring method.

```
String oldWord = "Alpinist";
String newWord = "Java" + oldWord.substring(4,8);
```

> This method returns the substring of **old-
> word** from index **4** to **7**, that is, **"nist"**.

Our next example prints out the words from a given sentence using one line
per word. For example, given an input sentence

```
I want to be a Java programmer
```

the code will print out

```
I
want
to
be
a
Java
programmer
```

This code is a modification of the previous sample code that counts the number of words in a given sentence. Instead of just counting the words, we need to extract the word from the sentence and print it out. Here's how we write the code:

```
int        index,    numberOfCharacters,
           beginIdx, endIdx;

String     word, sentence = inputBox.getString();

numberOfCharacters = sentence.length();
index = 0;

while ( index < numberOfCharacters ) {

    //ignore leading blank spaces
    while (index < numberOfCharacters &&
            sentence.charAt(index) == ' ') {
        index++;
    }

    beginIdx = index;

    //now locate the end of the word
    while (index < numberOfCharacters &&
            sentence.charAt(index) != ' ') {
        index++;
    }

    endIdx = index;

    if (beginIdx != endIdx) {
        //another word is found, extract it from the
        //sentence and print it out
        word = sentence.substring( beginIdx, endIdx );
        outputBox.printLine( word );
    }
}
```

Can you tell the purpose of the test

```
if (beginIdx != endIdx)
```

in the code? For what kinds of input sentences will the variables beginIdx and endIdx be equal? We'll leave this as an exercise: see exercise 18 on page 408.

Quick Check

1. Determine the output of the following code:

   a.
   ```
   String str = "Programming";
   for (int i = 0; i < 9; i+=2) {
       System.out.print( str.charAt( i ) );
   }
   ```

   b.
   ```
   String str = "World Wide Web";
   for (int i = 0; i < 10; i ++ ) }
       if ( str.charAt(i) == 'W') {
           System.out.println( 'M' );
       }
       else {
           System.out.print( str.charAt(i) );
       }
   }
   ```

2. Write a loop that prints out a string in reverse. If the string is Hello then the code outputs olleH. Use System.out.

3. Assuming two String objects str1 and str2 are initialized as follows:

   ```
   String str1 = "programming";
   String str2 = "language";
   ```

   Determine the value of each of the following expressions if they are valid. If they are not valid, state the reason why.

   a.   `str1.compareTo( str2 )`

   b.   `str2.compareTo( str2 )`

   c.   `str2.substring( 1, 1 )`

   d.   `str2.substring( 0, 7 );`

```
e.        str2.charAt( 11 );

f.        str1.length( ) + str2.length( )
```

4. What is the difference between the two String methods equals and
    equalsIgnoreCase?

8.3   Primitive versus Reference Types

We discussed numerical data types in Chapter 5 and nonnumerical data types in
this chapter. In addition, we have been using various javabook classes and their
objects since Chapter 2. Let's study how these data types, classes, and objects
are related. The taxonomy of data types is shown in Figure 8.2.

FIGURE 8.2   The taxonomy of data types.

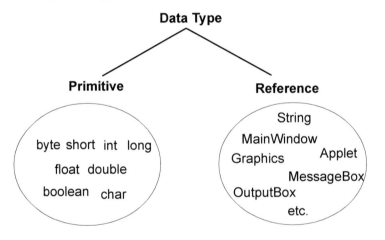

---

primitive vs.
reference

Data types are classified into two groups: *primitive* and *reference*. Nonnumerical data types char and boolean and all of the numerical data types are
primitive. All of the objects you have learned so far are reference data types.

Let's first review the use of the primitive data types. If w is a variable of the
primitive data type X, then it means we can assign a value of type X to w, for example:

```
int num1;
num1 = 14;
```

Assigning the value 14 to
the variable number of
type **int**.

We stated in Chapter 3 that a variable has three attributes: name, data type, and value. A memory location is allocated to a variable where we can store a value of the declared data type and access the stored value using the given name. In Chapter 3, we explained the difference between object declaration and primitive (numerical) data declaration (see Figure 3.2 on page 89) and showed the effect of assigning the content of one variable to another (Figure 3.3 on page 90). Since knowing the difference between the primitive and the object data values clearly is very important, let's go over this topic again, this time using a String and an int. We will include here some new concepts not covered in Chapter 3.

By stating

```
int num1;
```

we are allocating a memory location to store a value of type int and naming this location num1. To store an integer value in this memory location, that is, to assign an integer value to the variable num1, we write

```
num1 = 14;
```

The diagram in Figure 8.3 illustrates the state of memory after this assignment is executed.

FIGURE 8.3   Effect of assigning an integer value to a variable.

Now let's see what happens when we assign the value of a variable to another variable. Consider the following assignment statements using integers:

```
int num1, num2;

num1 = 14;
num2 = num1;
num1 += 5;
```

Figure 8.4 shows the effect of these assignment statements on memory. When two integer variables are declared, two memory locations are reserved to store integer values. For all primitive data types, the Java compiler knows exactly how many bytes of memory to allocate. An int variable, for instance, requires four bytes or 32 bits. The statements at points A and B in Figure 8.4 illustrate the effect of having two separate memory locations; that is, adding 5 to num1 affects only num1.

FIGURE 8.4   Effect of assigning values to integer variables.

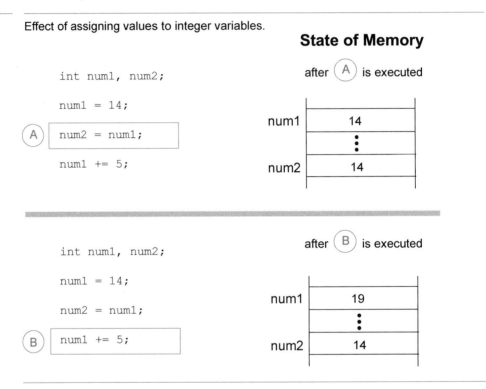

Let's study how memory allocation works when reference data types are used. Consider the following declaration:

```
String str;
str = "Jakarta";
```

Figure 8.5 shows the state of memory after this assignment is executed. When a variable is of the reference data type, the memory location of the variable contains the address of another memory location where the data value is actually stored. Since the content of the variable is not a value but the address of

FIGURE 8.5   Effect of assigning a **String** value to a variable.

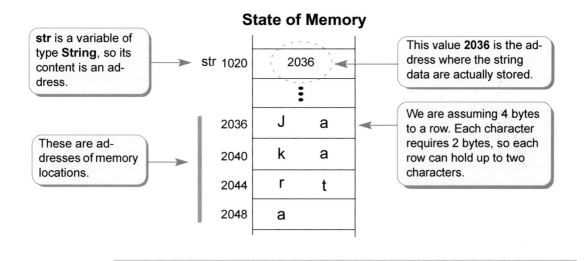

State of Memory

str is a variable of type **String**, so its content is an address.

str 1020   2036

This value **2036** is the address where the string data are actually stored.

These are addresses of memory locations.

2036	J	a
2040	k	a
2044	r	t
2048	a	

We are assuming 4 bytes to a row. Each character requires 2 bytes, so each row can hold up to two characters.

another location where the data value is stored, this data type is called a reference data type. But why use such a roundabout way of storing data? Why can't we just store the value in the manner shown in Figure 8.6?

FIGURE 8.6   Hypothetical memory management scheme for storing a String value.

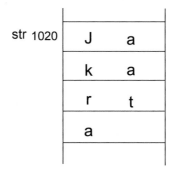

str 1020

J	a
k	a
r	t
a	

With primitive data types, the number of bytes required to store a value is always the same. For example, once we allocate four bytes of memory for an int variable, we will always have enough space to store any integer of type int in this location because all integers require only four bytes. What about String data?

What do you think would happen if we store the string values directly at the memory location 1020 and execute the following code?

```
String str;
str = "Jakarta";
...
str = "Irian Jaya";
```

Assuming the memory location 1036 already contains an integer, the effect of executing the second assignment statement is shown in Figure 8.7. We ran out of space to store the last two characters. We cannot just store the last two characters in the next available memory locations beyond location 1040 because such noncontiguous allocation of memory for a single data value is cumbersome to manage and inefficient.

FIGURE 8.7   Memory shortage problem with the hypothetical memory management scheme.

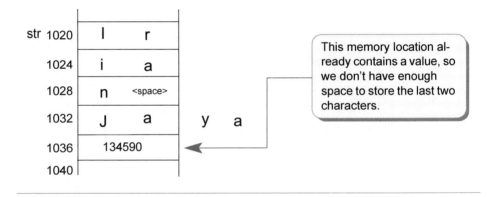

We see that a primitive data type requires a fixed amount of memory space, but a reference data type requires a varying amount of memory depending on the actual values assigned. In order to accommodate this varying size requirement, the memory location of a variable of reference data type will contain the address of another location where the actual value is stored. This allocation scheme is illustrated in Figure 8.5.

Because the values of reference data types are objects, we prefer the diagram in Figure 8.8 to the one shown in Figure 8.5. The arrow in Figure 8.8 clearly indicates that the content of variable str is an address and refers to another memory location. We will use this simplified diagram style in the rest of the chapter, whenever appropriate.

Chapter 8

FIGURE 8.8   A preferred style of diagram for representing memory allocation for a reference data type.

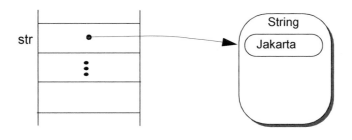

In object diagrams we simplify the diagram even further to

Figure 8.9 shows how memory allocation and assignment statements work with a reference data type. Because the contents of memory locations word1 and word2 are references, the assignment statement makes both variables refer to the same object. There's one object, and it makes no difference whether we access the object using word1 or word2. If you need to make word2 refer to another String object containing the string Java, then you must create another object as in

```
word2 = "Java" ; //or word2 = new String("Java");
```

which will result in the state of memory shown as case B in Figure 8.10.

Notice how declaration and object creation are different. No String objects are created by the declaration

```
String word1, word2;
```

Chapter 8

FIGURE 8.9   Effect of assignment statements on reference data type **String**.

State of Memory

Both **word1** and **word2** are allocated
memory, but no actual objects are
created yet, so both are **null**.

after Ⓐ is executed

Ⓐ   `String word1, word2;`

word1

word2

Both **word1** and
word2 are allocated
memory, but no ac-
tual objects are cre-
ated yet, so both
are **null**.

`word1 = new String("Java");`

`word2 = word1;`

One **String** object is created and assigned to **word1**; that is, **word1**
points to the object.

after Ⓑ is executed

`String word1, word2;`

Ⓑ   `word1 = new String("Java");`

`word2 = word1;`

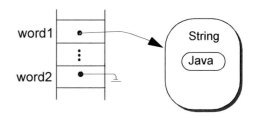

word1

word2

String

Java

Content of **word1** (which is a reference to the **String** object) is assigned to **word2**, making **word2**
also point to the same **String** object.

after Ⓒ is executed

`String word1, word2;`

`word1 = new String("Java");`

Ⓒ   `word2 = word1;`

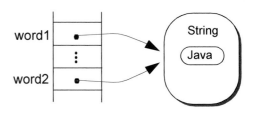

word1

word2

String

Java

Only the memory locations to store the addresses are allocated, as shown in the first diagram of Figure 8.9. We need to call the new method (either explicitly or implicitly) to create an object. We use the symbol ●————➥ when the content of a variable is not referring to any address. We call such reference a *null reference* or *null pointer*. When a variable contains the address of a location where an object is stored, we say "a variable points to an object" or "a variable refers to an object." We can test whether a variable points to an object or not by using the reserved word null:

```
if ( word1 == null )
```

And we can reset a variable back to null as in

```
word1 = null;
```

As stated earlier, when the content of variable X is a reference to an instance of the class Y, the expression we commonly use is "X is a Y object" or "X is an instance of the Y class." For example, given the code

```
MessageBox display;
display = new MessageBox();
```

we commonly say "display is a MessageBox object" or "display is an instance of the MessageBox class" instead of saying "display is a variable that refers or points to a MessageBox object" or "display is a variable that refers or points to an instance of the MessageBox class."

We are now ready to explain the difference, which we mentioned at the end of Section 8.2, between the tests

```
if ( word1 == word2 ) ...
```

and

```
if ( word1.equals(word2) ) ...
```

We can explain the difference very easily using Figure 8.10. The equality test == is true if the contents of memory locations allocated to variables are the same. For a primitive data type, the contents are values themselves, but for a reference data type, the contents are addresses. So for a reference data type, the

FIGURE 8.10   The difference between the equality test and the equals method.

Case A: Referring to the same object.

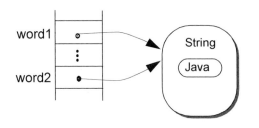

```
word1 == word2          is true

word1.equals( word2 )   is true
```

Note: If **x == y** is **true**, then **x.equals(y)** is also **true**. The reverse is not always true.

Case B: Referring to different objects having identical string values.

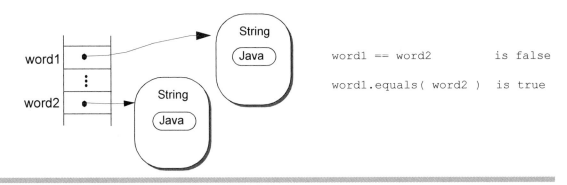

```
word1 == word2          is false

word1.equals( word2 )   is true
```

Case C: Referring to different objects having different string values.

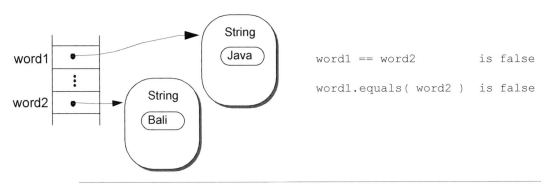

```
word1 == word2          is false

word1.equals( word2 )   is false
```

equality test is true if both variables refer to the same object, because they both contain the same address. The equals method, on the other hand, is true if the String objects to which the two variables refer contain the same string value. To distinguish the two types of comparisons, we will use the term *equivalence test* for the equals method.

Quick Check

1. Show the state of memory after the following statements are executed:

```
String str1, str2, str3;
str1 = "Jasmine";
str2 = "Oolong";
str3 = str2;
str2 = str1;
```

8.4 StringBuffer

A String object is immutable, which means that once a String object is created, we cannot change it. In other words, we can read individual characters in a string, but we cannot add, delete, or modify characters of a String object. Remember that the methods of the String class, such as toUpperCase and substring, do not modify the original string; they return a new string. Java adopts this immutability restriction to implement an efficient memory allocation scheme for managing String objects.

Creating a new string from the old one will work for most cases, but sometimes manipulating the content of a string directly is more convenient. When we need to compose a long string from a number of words, for example, being able to manipulate the content of a string directly is much more convenient than creating a new copy of a string. *Manipulation* here means operations such as replacing a character, appending a string with another string, deleting a portion of a string, and so forth. If we need to manipulate the content of a string directly, we must use the StringBuffer class. For example, the code

```
StringBuffer word = new StringBuffer( "Java" );
word.setCharAt(0, 'D');
word.setCharAt(1, 'i');
```

will modify the string Java to Diva. No new string is created, the original string Java is modified. Also, you must use the new method to create a StringBuffer object.

Chapter 8

Mr. Espresso: *I understand Figure 8.10, but what if one of the operands is a literal string constant, such as*

```
word = inputBox.getString();
if (word == "STOP")
      repeat = false;
```

Dr. Caffeine: *An unnamed* String *object is created automatically when a literal
string constant appears in Java code. Executing your sample code
will result in a situation like this:*

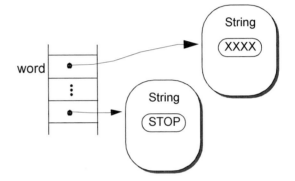

The equality testing and the equals *method work just fine.*

Mr. Espresso: *But how can the Java interpreter access unnamed objects?*

Dr. Caffeine: *"Unnamed" simply means that no explicit name is given by the programmer. The Java interpreter keeps track of the memory loca-
tion where the reference to this literal string constant is stored.*

StringBuffer

Let's look at some examples using StringBuffer objects. The first example
reads a sentence and replaces all vowels in the sentence with the character X.

```
StringBuffer  tempStringBuffer;
String        inSentence;
int           numberOfCharacters;
char          letter;
```

> Create **temp-
> StringBuffer**
> for string ma-
> nipulation.

```
inSentence        = inputBox.getString("Enter a sentence:");
tempStringBuffer  = new StringBuffer(inSentence);

numberOfCharacters = tempStringBuffer.length();
```

```
for (int index = 0; index < numberOfCharacters; index++) {

    letter = tempStringBuffer.charAt(index);

    if (   letter == 'a' || letter == 'A' ||
           letter == 'e' || letter == 'E' ||
           letter == 'i' || letter == 'I' ||
           letter == 'o' || letter == 'O' ||
           letter == 'u' || letter == 'U'  ) {

        tempStringBuffer.setCharAt(index,'X');
    }
}

messageBox.show( tempStringBuffer );
```

Notice how the input routine is done. We are reading in a String object and converting it to a StringBuffer object, because we cannot simply assign a String object to a StringBuffer variable. For example, the following code is invalid:

```
StringBuffer strBuffer = inputBox.getString( );
```

We are required to create a StringBuffer object from a String object as in

```
String       str  = "Hello";
StringBuffer strBuf = new StringBuffer( str );
```

You cannot input* StringBuffer *objects. You have to input* String *objects and convert them to* StringBuffer *objects.

Our next example constructs a new sentence from input words that have an even number of letters. The program stops when the word STOP is read. Let's begin with the pseudocode:

```
set tempStringBuffer to empty string;

repeat = true;

while ( repeat ) {

    read in next word;

    if (word is "STOP")
```

```
                    repeat = false;

            else if (word has even number of letters)

                append word to tempStringBuffer;
        }
```

And here's the actual code:

> Create **StringBuffer** with the empty string for its value.

```
        boolean   repeat = true;
        String    word;

        StringBuffer tempStringBuffer = new StringBuffer("");

        while ( repeat ) {
            word = inputBox.getString("Next word:");

            if ( word.equals("STOP") )
                repeat = false;
            else if ( word.length() % 2 == 0 )
                tempStringBuffer.append(word + " ");

        }
```

> Append word and a space to **tempStringBuffer**.

We use the append method to append a String or a StringBuffer object to the end of a StringBuffer object. The method append also can take an argument of the primitive data type. For example, all the following statements are valid:

```
        int    i   = 12;
        float  x   = 12.4f;
        char   ch  = 'W';

        StringBuffer str = new StringBuffer("");

        str.append(i);
        str.append(x);
        str.append(ch);
```

Any primitive data type argument is converted to a string before it is appended to a StringBuffer object.

Notice that we can write the second example using only String objects. Here's how:

```
        boolean repeat = true;
        String word, newSentence;
```

```
newSentence = ""; //empty string
while ( repeat ) {
    word = inputBox.getString("Next word:");

    if ( word.equals("STOP") )
        repeat = false;
    else if ( word.length() % 2 == 0 )
        newSentence = newSentence + word;
                                    //string concatenation
}
```

Although this code does not explicitly use any StringBuffer object, the Java compiler may use StringBuffer when compiling the string concatenation operator. For example, the expression

```
newSentence + word
```

can be compiled as if the expression were

```
new StringBuffer().append(word).toString()
```

Using the append method of StringBuffer is preferable to using the string concatenation operator + because we can avoid creating temporary string objects by using StringBuffer.

In addition to appending a string at the end of StringBuffer, we can insert a string at a specified position using the insert method. The syntax for this method is

```
<StringBuffer> . insert ( <insertIndex>, <value> ) ;
```

where the <insertIndex> must be greater than or equal to 0 and less than or equal to the length of <StringBuffer> and the <value> is an object or a value of the primitive data type. For example, to change the string

```
Java is great
```

to

```
Java is really great
```

we can execute the following code:

```
StringBuffer str = new StringBuffer("Java is great");
str.insert(8, "really ");
```

Quick Check

1. Determine the value of **str** after the following statements are executed:

    a. ```
        StringBuffer str
                = new StringBuffer("Caffeine");
        str.insert(0, "Dr. ");
        ```

    b.  ```
        String      str  = "Caffeine";
        StringBuffer str1 =
            new StringBuffer( str.substring(1, 3) );
        str1.append('e');
        str = "De" + str1;
        ```

    c. ```
        String   str = "Caffeine";
        StringBuffer str1 =
            new StringBuffer(str.substring(4, 8));
        str1.insert(3,'f');
        str = "De" + str1;
        ```

2.  Assume a **String** object **str** is assigned as

    ```
    String str = inputBox.getString();
    ```

    Write a code segment to replace all occurrences of lowercase vowels in a given string to the letter **C** by using **String** and **StringBuffer** objects.

3. Find the errors in the following code:

    ```
    String      str  = "Caffeine";
    StringBuffer str1 = str.substring(1, 3);
    str1.append('e');
    System.out(str1);
    str1 = str1 + str;
    ```

8.5   Passing Objects as Parameters

We explained in Section 4.4 that the value of the argument is passed to the matching parameter of a method, and separate memory space is allocated to store this value. This way of passing the value of arguments is called a *pass-by-value scheme*. We described in Section 4.4 how the pass-by-value scheme works using the primitive data type, specifically the numerical data type. We
    ```

will go over the scheme in this section using the reference data type. We will use String and StringBuffer objects for examples.

Consider the following myMethod method of the Tester class. The method replaces the first character of strBuf with the character Y. The method is not doing anything useful. We use it here for an illustrative purpose only. To keep the example simple, we do not include any testing in the method to make sure that strBuf has one or more characters. Here's the class:

```
class Tester
{
    public void myMethod(StringBuffer strBuf)
    {
        strBuf.setCharAt(0, 'Y');
    }
}
```

What will be the output from the following code?

```
Tester          tester;
StringBuffer  word = new StringBuffer( "Java" );

tester = new Tester();
tester.myMethod( word );
outputBox.printLine( "Word is " + word );
```

The output is

```
Word is Yava
```

not

```
Word is Java
```

as some of you might have expected because the key rule of the pass-by-value scheme states

Changes made to the parameters will not affect the value of corresponding arguments.

This is true, but remember that the value of a variable of the reference data type is an address. In other words, "passing an object to a method" really means "passing the address of an object to a method."

When you "pass an object to a method," you are actually passing the address of an object to the method.

Figure 8.11 shows how the pass-by-value scheme works with the reference data type. We use arrows to represent that the contents of the variables are memory addresses. Notice how the value of the variable word did not change after the method myMethod was executed. It still points to the same object. However, the object itself was changed via the access from the local variable strBuf.

In many cases, we do not want the original object to change when a method is executed. In these cases, we need to create a local copy of the object inside the method and manipulate this local copy. Consider the following modified version of myMethod:

```
public void myMethod(StringBuffer strBuf)
{
    StringBuffer localCopy
        = new StringBuffer( strBuf.toString() );
    localCopy.setCharAt(0, 'Y');
}
```

> Note: You need to pass a **String** object to create a new **StringBuffer** object.

Figure 8.12 shows the state-of-memory diagram for the modified myMethod. Notice how the local StringBuffer object is created. Since this is a separate copy, changing it won't affect the original StringBuffer object word.

Be careful not to confuse a simple assignment and an object creation. For example, if you simply assign the parameter to a local variable, such as

```
public void myMethod(StringBuffer strBuf)
{
    StringBuffer localCopy = strBuf;
    localCopy.setCharAt(0, 'Y');
}
```

> This is an assignment, not an object creation.

then all you are doing is adding one more reference to the object. In the state-of-memory diagram, this is what you have:

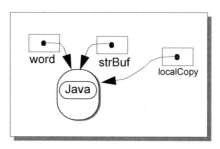

FIGURE 8.11   How the memory space for parameters is allocated and deallocated.

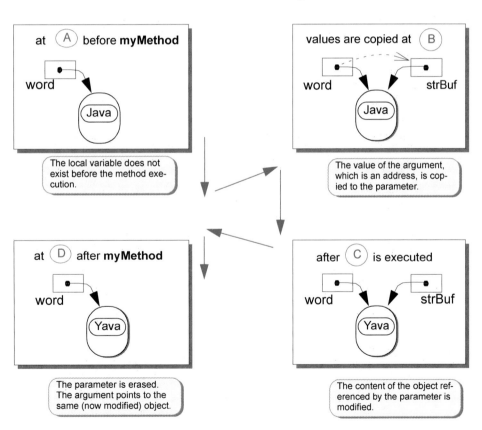

FIGURE 8.12   How a local copy of the passed object is created and manipulated. The original object will not change.

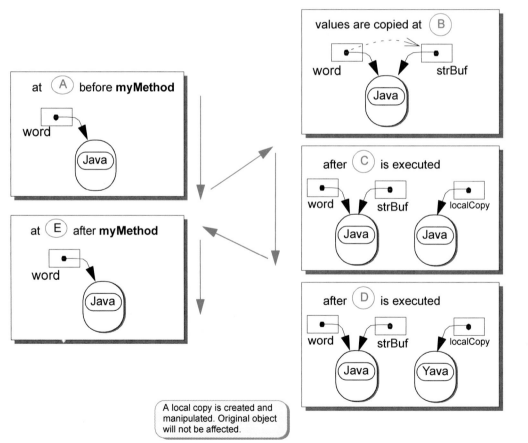

A local copy is created and manipulated. Original object will not be affected.

If you do not want the original object to be modified when a method is executed, make a local copy of the object inside the method. Remember that a simple assignment of the reference data type will not create a new object.

Quick Check

1. Draw the state-of-memory diagram for the following code:

```
String    str1 = "Daisy",
          str2 = "Iris";
Tester    tester = new Tester( );

tester.exchange( str1, str2);
...
class Tester
{
    public void exchange( String one, String two )
    {
        String temp;
        temp    = one;
        one     = two;
        two     = temp;
    }
}
```

8.6 Returning an Object from Methods

Now let's study how an object is returned from a method. In the previous section, we explained that "passing an object as an argument to a method" really means passing the address of the object to the method. The same rule applies when we "return an object from a method." In other words, we are really passing the address of the object back from the method.

To illustrate an object-returning method, let's define a method that accepts a name (String) and returns a personalized Hi greeting. For example, if the argument to the method is

```
Bill
```

then the method will return

```
Hi, Bill
```

Chapter 8

The method is defined as

```
public String sayHi( String name )
{
    String greeting;
    greeting = "Hi, " + name;
    return greeting;
}
```

We use a local variable **greeting** for a new String. At the end of the method, the content of **greeting**, which is the address to the newly created String, is returned from the method.

Assuming the method is defined in the **Tester** class, we can call the **sayHi** method as

```
String      name,
            hiMsg;
Tester      tester;
tester      = new Tester();

name        = inputBox.getString( );
hiMsg       = tester.sayHi( name );
```

Figure 8.13 shows how the method returns a String object. Remember that we use the expression "return an object" to mean "return the address of an object."

It is not necessary to create an object for every variable you declare. Many novice programmers often make this mistake. For example, if all you want is two references to the same object, you write something like this:

```
                Person drCafe, profWu;
                profWu = new Person();
                drCafe = profWu;
```

You don't write

```
                Person drCafe, profWu;
                profWu = new Person();
                drCafe = new Person();  //not necessary
                drCafe = profWu;
```

FIGURE 8.13   How the reference data type is returned from the **sayHI** method.

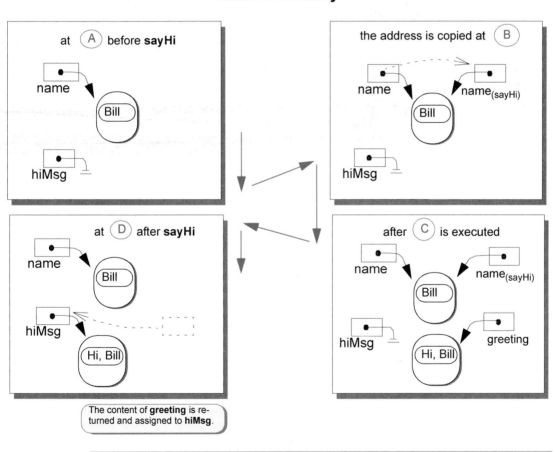

The content of **greeting** is returned and assigned to **hiMsg**.

1. Draw the state-of-memory diagram for the following code:

```
String    str, name = "Iris";
Tester    tester = new Tester( );
str       = tester.toUpper( name );
...
class Tester
{
    public String toUpper( String str )
    {
        String allUpper;
        allUpper = str.toUpperCase();
        return allUpper;
    }
}
```

2. The following code uses the Tester class from question 1. Determine the output.

```
String    str = "Internet";
Tester    tester = new Tester( );

System.out.println( str + " is " +
                        tester.toUpper( str ) );
```

8.7   Sample Program: Word Play

Let's review the String and StringBuffer objects by writing a sample program. We will write an application program that plays a word game called Eggy-Peggy. The program will convert a given string by placing the word **egg** in front of every vowel. For example:

```
Twinkle twinkle little star
```

becomes

```
Twegginklegge twegginklegge leggittlegge steggar
```

Problem Statement

Write an application that will play the Eggy-Peggy word play with the user. The program will convert a string given by the user to a new string by placing the word "egg" in front of all vowels in the given string.

Overall Plan

As usual, let's begin the program development by first identifying the major tasks of the program. The first task is to get an input string from the user, and the second task is to generate a new eggy-peggy string from the given string. So the user can play many times, we will add a loop to repeat these two tasks every time the user wants to play Eggy-Peggy. We can express this program logic in pseudocode as

program
tasks

```
while ( the user wants to play ) {

    Task 1: get a string from the user;

    Task 2: generate a new eggy-peggy string;

    Task 3: display the result;
}
```

Let's look at the three tasks and determine objects that will be responsible for handling the tasks. For the first task, we will use an InputBox. Although the width of an inputBox may not be wide enough to see the full string, the user can still enter a long string. We will use the getString method of InputBox to read the input string.

For the second task of generating an eggy-peggy string, we anticipate the use of a StringBuffer object. The task of placing the word egg in front of all vowels calls for a direct string manipulation, so a StringBuffer object seems to be the right object for the task. We will get into a more detailed design in a later step.

For the last task of printing out the eggy-peggy string, we will use an OutputBox. Although MessageBox is adequate if we want to show the eggy-peggy string only, we think it is more fun for the user to see both the input string and the eggy-peggy string, so we will use an OutputBox.

Finally, we will define a top-level control object that manages all other objects. We will call this class EggyPeggy. Our main class will be EggyPeggy-Main, whose task is to create an instance of EggyPeggy and start the instance. We also need a way for the player to tell the program whether to play another

Chapter 8

game or not. We will use a ResponseBox object for this purpose. Here's our working design document:

program classes

Design Document:	EggyPeggy
Class	**Purpose**
EggyPeggyMain	The main class of the program.
EggyPeggy	The top-level control object that manages other objects in the program.
InputBox	An InputBox object is used to get a string from the player. This class is from javabook.
OutputBox	An OutputBox object is used for the input string and the eggy-peggy string.
ResponseBox	A ResponseBox object is used to get the player's instruction to play another game or not.
String	String objects are used for storing strings.
StringBuffer	A StringBuffer object is used during the conversion process.
MainWindow	The main window of the application.

Figure 8.14 is the object diagram for this program.

We will implement this program using the following four major steps:

development steps

1. Start with a program skeleton. Define the EggyPeggyMain and EggyPeggy classes.

2. Add code to do the input and output routines.

3. Add code to play an Eggy-Peggy game.

4. Finalize the code by removing temporary statements and tying up loose ends.

Step 1 Development: Skeleton

Step 1 Design

The design of EggyPeggyMain is trivial. Its structure is the same as other main classes. All we need is to declare, create, and start an EggyPeggy object. In pseudocode we can express the main logic for an EggyPeggy object as

```
prompt the user to play Eggy-Peggy or not;

while ( answer is yes ) {

    get an input string;
```

FIGURE 8.14   The object diagram for the **EggyPeggy** program. Note: **String** and **StringBuffer** objects
are not shown here.

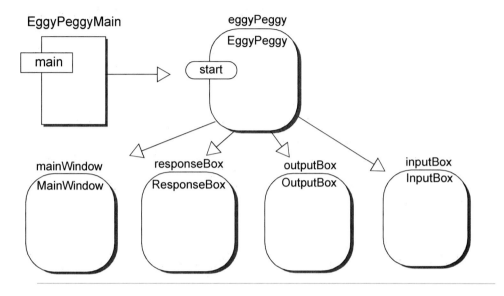

```
        generate an eggy-peggy string from the input string;

        display the input and eggy-peggy strings;

        prompt the user to play another Eggy-Peggy or not;
    }
```

We will use the constructor to perform the necessary initialization and the
method describeGame to provide a brief explanation of the Eggy-Peggy game.
We will use a ResponseBox for prompting the user to play a game or not. We
will define private methods for handling input and output. The object diagram
for the EggyPeggy class at this point is

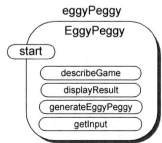

Our working design document for the EggyPeggy class is as follows:

Design Document:	The EggyPeggy Class	
Method	**Visibility**	**Purpose**
`<constructor>`	`public`	Creates the objects used by an **EggyPeggy** object.
`start`	`public`	Starts the Eggy-Peggy game playing. The player has an option of playing a game or not.
`describeGame`	`private`	Displays the game rules in **OutputBox**.
`displayResult`	`private`	Shows the input string and the eggy-peggy string in an **OutputBox**.
`generateEggyPeggy`	`private`	Plays one EggyPeggy game.
`getInput`	`private`	Gets the input string using **InputBox**.

Step 1 Code For the skeleton, we include temporary output statements in the private methods to verify that they are called correctly in the right order. Here's the skeleton:

File: EggyPeggyMain.java

```java
/**
 * The EggyPeggy main program for word game Eggy-Peggy.
 * The program reads in a string from the user and generates a new
 * converted string that includes the word "egg" in front of all
 * vowels in the input string.
 *
 * @author Dr. Caffeine
 *
 */
class EggyPeggyMain
{
    public static void main (String[] args)
    {
        EggyPeggy eggyPeggy = new EggyPeggy( );
        eggyPeggy.start();
    }
}
```

File: EggyPeggy.java

```java
import javabook.*;

/**
 * This class is the top-level controller object for managing
 * all other objects in the EggyPeggy program.
 *
 * @author Dr. Caffeine
 *
 */
class EggyPeggy     // Step1: Skeleton
```

```
{
    //-------------------------------
    // Data Members
    //-------------------------------

    private MainWindow   mainWindow;
    private InputBox     inputBox;
    private OutputBox    outputBox;
    private ResponseBox  responseBox;

    //-------------------------------
    // Constructors
    //-------------------------------

    /**
     * Default constructor.
     * The default window title is "Let's Play EggyPeggy".
     */
    public EggyPeggy( )
    {
        mainWindow    = new MainWindow ("Let's Play EggyPeggy");
        outputBox     = new OutputBox  ( mainWindow );
        responseBox   = new ResponseBox( mainWindow );
        inputBox      = new InputBox   ( mainWindow );

        mainWindow.show();
        outputBox.show();
    }


    //----------------------------------------------------
    //      Public Methods:
    //
    //          void    start  (        )
    //
    //----------------------------------------------------

    /**
     * Top-level method that calls other private methods
     * to play the Eggy-Peggy games.
     */
    public void start ( )
    {
        int answer;

        describeGame();

        answer = responseBox.prompt("Do you want to play Eggy-Peggy?");

        while ( answer == ResponseBox.YES ) {

            getInput( );
            generateEggyPeggy( );
            displayResult( );

            answer
            = responseBox.prompt("Do you want to play another Eggy-Peggy?");
        }
    }
```

Chapter 8

```
//-----------------------------------------------------
//      Private Methods:
//
//      void    describeGame         (          )
//      void    displayResult        (          )
//      void    generateEggyPeggy    (          )
//      void    getInput             (          )
//
//-----------------------------------------------------

    /**
     * Provides a brief explanation of the program to the user.
     *
     */
    private void describeGame( )
    {
        outputBox.printLine("Inside describeGame");       //TEMP
    }


    /**
     * Show the input string and the eggy-peggy string generated
     * from the input string.
     *
     */
    private void displayResult( )
    {
        outputBox.printLine("Inside displayResult");       //TEMP
    }


    /**
     * Generate a new string from the input string by putting the
     * word "egg" in front of all vowels in the input string.
     *
     */
    private void generateEggyPeggy( )
    {
        outputBox.printLine("Inside generateEggyPeggy");   //TEMP
    }


    /**
     * Read in the input string using InputBox.
     *
     */
    private void getInput( )
    {
        outputBox.printLine("Inside getInput");            //TEMP
    }

}
```

Step 1 Test   As before, EggyPeggyMain, the main class, will not change. The class given here is the final version. We execute the main class and the skeleton EggyPeggy class to verify that the classes are coded correctly. To verify the correct execution of Step 1, we attempt to play the game

1. Zero times.

2. One time.

3. One or more times.

For the first run, we select No to the prompt Do you want to play Eggy-Peggy? and make sure the program stops without playing a game. For the second run, we select Yes to the first prompt and verify that the messages Inside getInput and others are shown in outputBox. We next select No to the prompt Do you want to play another Eggy-Peggy? and make sure the program stops. For the third run, we verify that we can play more than one game. If everything works correctly and as expected, we move on to the next step.

Step 2 Development: Input and Output Routines

Step 2 Design   In the second development step, we add routines to handle input and output. We decided in the overall planning step that we will use an InputBox object to accept a string and an OutputBox object to display both the input string and the eggy-peggy string. Let's begin with the design of the input routine.

To fully design the input routine, we need to decide which strings are valid and which are not. The problem statement did not specify any condition on the input string, so let's define some validity rules ourselves. What types of strings should be considered invalid? Should we place the maximum number of characters a valid string can contain? Should a string with all spaces be considered invalid? What about a string with no characters, an empty string? For this program, we will consider any string to be valid, so the user does not have to worry about whether an input is valid or not.

Since we accept any string as a valid input, the statement using the getString method of inputBox is all that suffices for the input routine. So the getInput method will contain a single statement. We will use an instance variable inputString to store the input string. If we need to do some error checking or some form of input validation later, we can do it in this method.

The output routine in the displayResult method will print out the input string and the generated eggy-peggy string. We will use a second instance variable eggyPeggyString to store the eggy-peggy string. To verify the output routine, we will add a temporary assignment statement in the generateEggyPeggy method to assign a dummy string to eggyPeggyString.

Step 2 Code   To code the Step 2 design, we first add two new instance variables:

```
//------------------------------
// Data Members
//------------------------------

private String    inputString,
                  eggyPeggyString;
```

We then define the getInput method as

```
private void getInput( )
{
    inputString
    = inputBox.getString("Enter the original sentence:");
}
```

and temporarily define the generateEggyPeggy method as

```
private void generateEggyPeggy( )
{
    eggyPeggyString = "Dummy Eggy Peggy String";
    outputBox.printLine("Inside generateEggyPeggy");
}
```

Finally, we define the displayResult method as

```
private void displayResult( )
{
    outputBox.skipLine(3);
    outputBox.printLine("Input String:");
    outputBox.printLine("              " + inputString);

    outputBox.skipLine(1);
    outputBox.printLine("Eggy Peggy:");
    outputBox.printLine("              " + eggyPeggyString);
}
```

Step 2 Test   For testing, we play many games, and for each game we play, we will enter a string different from the previous strings. We will enter very long strings, very short strings, no strings, and so forth. Even though the actual processing is not yet implemented, we can still test and verify that different strings can be entered into the program. It is important to test whatever is testable at the earliest possible time.

Test a program routine at the earliest possible time.

Remember that testing an input routine will require us to enter both valid and invalid input values. For this program, we decided that all strings are valid. For the valid input values, we enter both types of values: those that are commonly expected and those that are not. For this program, we expect strings will contain several to up to 50 or so characters. We do not expect strings with less than several characters, including those with zero characters, to occur frequently. We should also test other strings that are not normally expected, such as the one with all blank spaces. The test data are as follows:

Step 2 Test Data	
Data Value	**Purpose**
`Empty string.`	Test the end case.
`String whose length is less than 3.`	Test the cases not expected to happen frequently.
`String with nonletter characters, e.g., all blank spaces, all symbols, etc.`	Test the cases not expected to happen frequently.
`Strings whose length ranges from about 5 to 50.`	Test the normal cases.

Before proceeding to the next step, we make sure that the program accepts various types of input strings without crashing. After we verify this, we will move on to the next step.

Step 3 Development: Generate an Eggy-Peggy String

Step 3 Design

In the third development step, we add a routine that generates an eggy-peggy string from a given input string. The key idea is to check every character in the input string. If the character is a vowel, then we will append the word egg and the vowel to the output string. If the character is not a vowel, then we will append the character only to the output string. We will use a StringBuffer object while creating the output string. At the end of the routine, we will convert this StringBuffer object to a String object. Expressing this in pseudocode, we have

Alternative Design **1**

```
for the first to the last character in inputString {
    if (character is a vowel) {
        append "egg" and character to output StringBuffer;
    }
    else {
        append character only to output StringBuffer;
    }
}
convert output StringBuffer to String;
```

Chapter 8

An alternative approach is to use String objects only and string concatenation operations to implement the routine. Expressing this approach in pseudocode, we have

```
for the first to the last character in inputString {
    if (character is a vowel) {
        outString = outString + "egg" + character;
    }
    else {
        outString = outString + character;
    }
}
```

This alternative is less efficient than the first one, because a new String object is created for every concatenation, and the routine will perform $N + 2 * M$ concatenations, where N is the number of nonvowels and M is the number of vowels. If you do a lot of string manipulation operations, StringBuffer objects are generally preferred over String objects because no new objects are created if you use a StringBuffer object for string manipulation. We will implement the first design alternative.

The generateEggyPeggy method is defined as

```
private void generateEggyPeggy( )
{
    StringBuffer  outputStrBuf  = new StringBuffer("");
    int           length        = inputString.length();
    char          ch;

    for (int i = 0; i < length; i++ ) {
        ch = inputString.charAt(i);

        if ( isVowel(ch) ) {
            outputStrBuf.append( EGG ); //if vowel, append
        }                               //"egg" first

        outputStrBuf.append( ch );
    }

    eggyPeggyString = outputStrBuf.toString();
}
```

Notice that we must append the character whether it is a vowel or not, so we changed the if–then–else statement in the pseudocode to an if–then statement.

The word EGG is a string constant defined in the data member declaration section as

```
private final StringEGG = "egg";
```

The method isVowel is a new private method that returns true if the argument character is a vowel and returns false otherwise. We are defining this method ourselves here because there is no such method in the standard library. If there was one, then we would have used it. We could have done the testing right inside the generateEggyPeggy method, but that would tend to lengthen the code, so we decided to add a separate method. The working design document now includes this method:

Design Document:	The EggyPeggy Class	
Method	**Visibility**	**Purpose**
. . .	. . .	. . .
isVowel	private	Returns true if the argument character is a vowel and false otherwise.

The method is defined as

```
private boolean isVowel(char letter)
{
    boolean result = false;

    if (   letter == 'a' || letter == 'A' ||
           letter == 'e' || letter == 'E' ||
           letter == 'i' || letter == 'I' ||
           letter == 'o' || letter == 'O' ||
           letter == 'u' || letter == 'U'   ) {

        result = true;
    }

    return result;
}
```

Step 3 Test   We basically repeat the testing procedures we performed in Step 2. We enter many different types of strings including empty strings and strings with only spaces and verify that the program works correctly.

Step 4 Development: Finalize

program
review

As always, we finalize the program in the last step. We perform a critical review to find any inconsistency or error in the methods, any incomplete methods, places to add more comments, and so forth.

We still have a temporary code inside the describeGame method, so we will complete the method by adding code to describe the Eggy-Peggy game. For the several previous sample programs also, we did not complete the method that explains the program to the user until the very last development step. We could have implemented such method at the very first step, but there are two reasons why we don't do that. The first one is pedagogic. The program-explaining methods follow the same pattern, and, basically, if you've seen one, you've seen them all. There is not much pedagogic value in discussing such methods. The second one is pragmatic. If you define a program description method at the beginning, it is very likely that you have to change it in a later step. Why? Because as you go through the development steps, the program design may change, and this change would require a new description of the program.

final test

Any changes we make, no matter how trivial they may seem, could affect the program. So it is mandatory to test the program again after any changes are made. We will complete the final testing by repeating the testing procedures of the previous steps.

8.8   Exercises

1. Use boolean variables to improve the readability of the following loop statements:

a.
```
numberOfCharacters = sentence.length();
index = 0;
wLocation = 0;
jCount = 0;
nonJCount = 0;

do {
    if (index < numberOfCharacters) {
        letter = sentence.charAt(index);
        if (letter == 'J' || letter == 'j')
            jcount++;
        else if (letter == 'W')
            wLocation = index;
        else
            nonJCount++;
    }
    index++;
while (index < numberOfCharacters && letter != 'W' );
```

b.
```
product = 1.0f;
number = 0;
while ( number == 10 || !(product > 10000.0f && number < 0)
)
    if (number == 10)
        tenCount++;
    else if (product <= 10000.0f)
        if (number > 0)
            product *= number;
        else if (number == 0)
            product = 1;
```

2. What is the difference between 'a' and "a"?

3. Discuss the difference between

```
str = str + word; //string concatenation
```

and

```
tempStringBuffer.append(word)
```

where str is a String object and tempStringBuffer is a StringBuffer object.

4. Show that if x and y are String objects and x == y is true, then x.equals(y) is also true, but the reverse is not necessarily true.

5. What will be the output from the following code?

```
StringBuffer word1, word2;
word1 = new StringBuffer("Lisa");
word2 = word1;
word2.insert(0, "Mona ");
outputBox.printLine(word1);
```

6. Show the state of memory as shown in Figure 8.10 after the execution of each statement in the following code:

```
String word1, word2;
word1 = "Hello";
word2 = word1;
word1 = "Java";
```

7. Using a state-of-memory diagram like the one shown in Figure 8.10, illustrate the difference between a null string and an empty string, a string that

Chapter 8

has no characters in it. Show the state-of-memory diagram for the following code. Variable word1 is a null string, while word2 is an empty string.

```
String word1, word2;
word1 = null;
word2 = "";
```

8. Using a state-of-memory diagram like the one shown in Figure 8.10, show how the following two groups of statements differ.

```
String word1, word2;              String word1, word2;

word1 = "French Roast";           word1 = "French Roast";
word2 = word1;                    word2 = "French Roast";
```

9. Write an applet that reads in a character and displays the character's ASCII code. The getText method of the TextField class returns a String object, so you need to use a char value as in

```
inputString   = inputField.getText();
character      = inputString.charAt(0);
```

Display an error message if more than one character is entered.

10. Write a method that returns the number of uppercase letters in a String object passed to the method as a parameter. Use the class method isUpperCase of the Character class, which returns true if the passed parameter of type char is an uppercase letter. You need to explore the Character class from the java.lang package on your own.

11. Redo exercise 10 without using the Character class. Hint: The ASCII code of any uppercase letter will fall between 65 (code for 'A') and 90 (code for 'Z').

12. Write a method that reads a sentence and prints out the sentence with all uppercase letters changed to lowercase and all lowercase letters changed to uppercase.

13. Write a method that reads a sentence and prints out the sentence in reverse order. For example, the method will display

```
?uoy era woH
```

for the input

```
How are you?
```

14. Write a method that transposes words in a given sentence. For example, given an input sentence

```
The gate to Java nirvana is near
```

the method outputs

```
ehT etag ot avaJ anavrin si raen
```

To simplify the problem, you may assume the input sentence contains no punctuation marks. You may also assume that the input sentence starts with a nonblank character and there is exactly one blank space between the words.

15. Improve the method in exercise 14 by removing the assumptions. For example, an input sentence could be

```
Hello, how are you? I   use JDK 1.2.2.   Bye-bye.
```

An input sentence may contain punctuation marks and more than one blank space between two words. Transposing the above will result in

```
olleH, woh era uoy? I esu KDJ 1.2.2. eyB-eyb.
```

Notice the position of punctuation marks does not change and only one blank space is inserted between the transposed words.

16. Write a variation of the Eggy-Peggy program. Implement the following four variations:

- Sha   Add sha to the beginning of every word.
- Na   Add na to the end of every word.
- Sha Na Na   Add sha to the beginning and na na to the end of every word.
- Ava   Move the first letter to the end of the word and add ava to it.

Use a ListBox object to list the four variations, from which the user can select one. Use InputBox for reading in a sentence. You may want to widen the InputBox object using its resize method.

17. The sample code on page 365 that counts the number of words in a given sentence has a bug. If the input sentence has one or more blank spaces at the end, the value for wordCount will be one more than the actual number of words in the sentence. Correct this bug.

18. The sample code on page 368 for counting the number of words in a given string includes the test

```
if (beginIdx != endIdx) ...
```

Describe the type of input sentences that will result in the variables beginIdx and endIdx becoming equal.

19. Write an application that reads in a sentence and displays the count of individual vowels in the sentence. Use OutputBox to display the result in the following format. Count only the lowercase vowels.

```
Vowel counts for the sentence

        Mary had a little lamb.

# of 'a' : 4
# of 'e' : 1
# of 'i' : 1
# of 'o' : 0
# of 'u' : 0
```

20. The word game Eggy-Peggy is an example of encryption. Encryption has been used since ancient times to communicate messages secretly. One of the many techniques used for encryption is called a *Caesar cipher*. With this technique, each character in the original message is shifted N positions. For example, if $N = 1$, then the message

I drink only decaf

becomes

J!esjol!pomz!efdbg

The encrypted message is decrypted to the original message by shifting back every character N positions. Shifting N positions forward and backward is achieved by converting the character to ASCII code and adding or subtracting N. Write an application that reads in the original text and the value for N and displays the encrypted text. Make sure the ASCII value resulting from encryption falls between 32 and 126. For example, if you add 8 (value of N) to 122 (ASCII code for 'z'), you should "wrap around" and get 35.

21. Write an application that reads the encrypted text and the value for N and displays the original text using the Caesar cipher technique.

22. Another encryption technique is called a *Vignere cipher*. This technique is similar to a Caesar cipher in that a key is applied cyclically to the original message. For this exercise a key is composed of uppercase letters only. Encryption is done by adding the code values of the key's characters to the code values of the characters in the original message. Code values for the key characters are assigned as follows: 0 for A, 1 for B, 2 for C, . . . , and 25 for Z. Let's say the key is COFFEE and the original message is I drink only decaf. Encryption works as follows:

Decryption reverses the process to generate the original message. Write an application that reads in a text and displays the encrypted text. Make sure the ASCII value resulting from encryption or decryption falls between 32 and 126. You can get the code for key characters by (int) keyChar - 65.

23. Write an application that reads the encrypted text and displays the original text using the Vignere cipher technique.

24. A public-key cryptography allows anyone to encode messages while only people with a secret key can decipher them. In 1977, Ronald Rivest, Adi

Shamir, and Leonard Adleman developed a form of public-key cryptography called the *RSA system*.

To encode a message using the RSA system, one needs *n* and *e*. The value *n* is a product of any two prime numbers *p* and *q*. The value *e* is any number less than *n* that cannot be evenly divided into *y* (i.e., y ÷ e would have a remainder), where $y = (p-1) \times (q-1)$. The values *n* and *e* can be published in a newspaper or posted on the Internet, so anybody can encrypt messages. The original character is encoded to a numerical value *c* using the formula

$$c = m^e \bmod n$$

where *m* is a numerical representation of the original character (e.g., 1 for A, 2 for B, and so forth).

Now, to decode a message, one needs *d*. The value d is a number that satisfies the formula

$$(e \cdot d) \bmod y = 1$$

where *e* and *y* are the values defined in the encoding step. The original character *m* can be derived from the encrypted character *c* by using the formula

$$m = c^d \bmod n$$

Write a program that encodes and decodes messages using the RSA system. Use large prime numbers for *p* and *q* in computing the value for *n*, because when *p* and *q* are small, it is not that difficult to find out the value of *d*. When *p* and *q* are very large, however, it becomes practically impossible to determine the value of *d*. Use the ASCII codes as appropriate for the numerical representation of characters. Visit http://www.rsasecurity.com for more information on how the RSA system is applied in the real world.

25. Write an applet that determines if an input word is a palindrome. A palindrome is a string that reads the same forward and backward, for example, *noon* and *madam*. Ignore the case of the letter, so, for example, *maDaM*, *MadAm*, and *mAdaM* are all palindromes.

26. Write an applet that determines if an input sentence is a palindrome, for example, *A man, a plan, a canal, Panama!* You ignore the punctuation marks, blanks, and the case of the letters.

9

Arrays

OBJECTIVES

After you have read and studied this chapter, you should be able to

- Manipulate a collection of data values using an array.

- Declare and use an array of primitive data types in writing a program.

- Declare and use an array of objects in writing a program.

- Describe how a two-dimensional array is implemented as an array of arrays.

- Manipulate a collection of objects using a vector.

- Use a MultiInputBox object from the javabook package to input an array of strings.

- Define a method that accepts an array as its parameter and a method that returns an array.

- Describe how the self-reference pointer works and use it in methods.

Introduction

Suppose you want to write a program that maintains up to 100 accounts. Would you use 100 variables without hesitation? Or would you be doubtful? If you think there must be a better way than using 100 distinct variables, you are correct. In this chapter you will learn about arrays. An *array* is a collection of data values of the same type. If your program needs to deal with a certain number of similar data values, such as 10 integers, 15 Student objects, 20 real numbers, 100 Account objects, and so forth, then you will use an array. In this chapter we will explain different types of arrays and how to use them properly in a program.

9.1   Array Basics

Suppose we want to compute the annual average rainfall from 12 monthly averages. We can use three variables and compute the annual average as

```
double sum, rainfall, annualAverage;

sum = 0.0;

for (int i = 0; i < 12; i++) {
    rainfall = inputBox.getDouble("Rainfall for month "
                                          + (i+1));
    sum += rainfall;
}

annualAverage = sum / 12.0;
```

Now suppose we want to compute the difference between the annual and monthly averages for every month and display a table with three columns as shown in Figure 9.1.

To compute the difference between the annual and monthly averages, we need to remember the 12 monthly rainfall averages. Without remembering the 12 monthly averages, we won't be able to derive the monthly variations after the annual average is computed. Instead of using 12 variables januaryRainfall, februaryRainfall, and so forth to solve this problem, we use an array.

array

We mentioned that an *array* is a collection of data values of the same type. For example, we may declare an array consisting of double, but not an array consisting of both int and double. The following declares an array of double:

array declaration

```
double[] rainfall;
```

FIGURE 9.1 Monthly rainfall figures and their variation from the annual average.

Annual Average Rainfall: 15.03 mm

Month	Monthly Average	Variation from Annual Average
1	13.3	1.73
2	14.9	0.13
3	14.7	0.33
4	23.0	7.97
5	25.8	10.77
6	27.7	12.67
7	12.3	2.73
8	10.0	5.03
9	9.8	5.23
10	8.7	6.33
11	8.0	7.03
12	12.2	2.83

The square brackets indicate the array declaration. The brackets may be attached to a variable instead of the data type. For example, the declaration

```
double rainfall[];
```

is equivalent to the previous declaration. In Java, an array is an object, so we need to use the method new to actually create an array.

In Java, an array is an object.

The following statement creates an array of 12 double values and associates the identifier rainfall to the newly created array.

```
rainfall = new double[12]; //create an array of size 12
```

Figure 9.2 shows the created array.

Like any other objects, we can declare and create an array in one statement as in

FIGURE 9.2   An array of 12 **double** values.

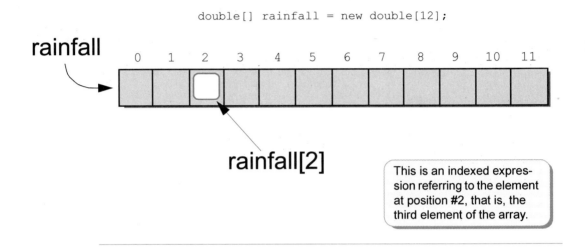

This is an indexed expression referring to the element at position #2, that is, the third element of the array.

```
double[] rainfall = new double[12];
```

indexed
expression

array element

The number 12 designates the size of the array—the number of values the array contains. We use a single identifier to refer to the whole collection and use an *indexed expression* to refer to the individual values of the collection. An individual value in an array is called an *element* of the array. Zero-based indexing is used to indicate the position of an element in the array. They are numbered 0, 1, 2, . . . , and size − 1, where size is the size of an array. For example, to refer to the third element of the rainfall array, we use the indexed expression

```
rainfall[2]
```

Instead of a literal constant like 2, we can use an expression such as

```
rainfall[i+3]
```

Notice that the index for the first position in an array is zero. Like a String object, Java uses zero-based indexing for an array.

The index of the first position in an array is 0.

Using the rainfall array, we can input 12 monthly averages and compute the annual average

```
double[] rainfall = new double[12];
double  annualAverage,
        sum = 0.0;

for (int i = 0; i < 12; i++) {

    rainfall[i] = inputBox.getDouble("Rainfall for month "
                                      + (i+1));
    sum += rainfall[i];
}

annualAverage = sum / 12.0;
```

Can also be declared as

```
double rainfall[] = new double[12];
```

Figure 9.3 shows how the array would appear after all 12 values are entered.

FIGURE 9.3   An array of 12 **double** values after all 12 are assigned values.

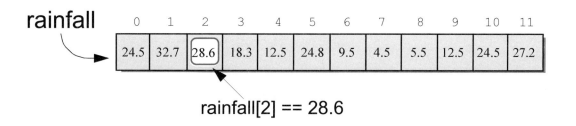

rainfall

rainfall[2] == 28.6

After the 12 monthly averages are stored in the array, we can print out the table as

```
double difference;

for (i = 0; i < 12; i++) {
    outputBox.print( Format.rightAlign(3,i+1) ); //month #

    //average rainfall for the month
    outputBox.print( Format.rightAlign(17,1,rainfall[i]) );

    //difference between the monthly and annual averages
    difference = Math.abs( rainfall[i] - annualAverage );
    outputBox.printLine( Format.rightAlign(17,2,difference) );
}
```

Chapter 9

length

An array has a public constant length for the size of an array. Using this constant, we can rewrite the for loop as

```
for (i = 0; i < rainfall.length; i++) {
    . . .
}
```

This for loop is more general since we do not have to modify the loop statement when the size of an array is changed. Also, the use of length is necessary when the size of an array is not known in advance. This happens, for example, when we write a method with an array as its parameter. We need to write the method so it can handle an array of any size. We will provide an example of such a method in Section 9.3.

> *It is very easy to mix up the* length *constant of an array and the* length *method of a* String *object. It is a public constant for an array, so we use it as*
>
> ```
>                 int size = rainfall.length;
> ```
>
> *It is a method for a* String *object, so we use it as*
>
> ```
>                 String str  = "This is a string";
>                 int     size = str.length();
> ```

Dr. Caffeine

Notice the prompts for the inputBox in the previous example are "Rainfall for month 1", "Rainfall for month 2", and so forth. A better prompt will spell out the month name, for example, "Rainfall for January", "Rainfall for February", and so forth. We can easily achieve a better prompt by using an array of strings. Here's how:

```
double[]   rainfall  = new double[12];//an array of double
String[]   monthName = new String[12];//an array of String
double     annualAverage,
           sum = 0.0;

monthName[0]  = "January";
monthName[1]  = "February";
monthName[2]  = "March";
monthName[3]  = "April";
monthName[4]  = "May";
monthName[5]  = "June";
monthName[6]  = "July";
monthName[7]  = "August";
```

> Remember these are shorthand for **String** object creation, e.g.,
>
> ```
> ... = new String("May");
> ```

```
monthName[8]   = "September";
monthName[9]   = "October";
monthName[10]  = "November";
monthName[11]  = "December";

for (int i = 0; i < rainfall.length; i++) {
    rainfall[i] = inputBox.getDouble("Rainfall for "
                                     + monthName[i]);
    sum += rainfall[i];
}

annualAverage = sum / 12.0;
```

Instead of assigning array elements individually, we can initialize the array at the time of declaration. We can, for example, initialize the monthName array by

```
String[] monthName = { "January", "February", "March",
                       "April", "May", "June", "July",
                       "August", "September", "October",
                       "November", "December"  };
```

No size is specified.

Notice that we do not specify the size of an array if the array elements are initialized at the time of declaration. The size of an array is determined by the number of values in the list. In the above example, there are 12 values in the list, so the size of the array monthName is set to 12.

Let's try some more examples. We assume the rainfall array is declared, and all 12 values are read in. The following code computes the average rainfall for the odd months (January, March, . . .) and the even months (February, April, . . .).

```
double   oddMonthSum, oddMonthAverage,
         evenMonthSum, evenMonthAverage;

oddMonthSum  = 0.0;
evenMonthSum = 0.0;

//compute the average for the odd months
for (int i = 0; i < rainfall.length; i += 2)
    oddMonthSum += rainfall[i];
oddMonthAverage = oddMonthSum / 6.0;

//compute the average for the even months
for (int i = 1; i < rainfall.length; i += 2)
    evenMonthSum += rainfall[i];
evenMonthAverage = evenMonthSum / 6.0;
```

Chapter 9

We can compute the same result using one for loop as

```
for (int i = 0; i < rainfall.length; i += 2 ) {
    oddMonthSum += rainfall[i];
    evenMonthSum += rainfall[i+1];
}

oddMonthAverage  = oddMonthSum / 6.0;
evenMonthAverage = evenMonthSum / 6.0;
```

To compute the average for each quarter (Quarter 1 has January, February, and March, Quarter 2 has April, May, and June, and so forth), we can write

```
for (int i = 0; i < 3; i++ ) {
    quarter1Sum += rainfall[i];
    quarter2Sum += rainfall[i+3];
    quarter3Sum += rainfall[i+6];
    quarter4Sum += rainfall[i+9];
}

quarter1Average = quarter1Sum / 3.0;
quarter2Average = quarter2Sum / 3.0;
quarter3Average = quarter3Sum / 3.0;
quarter4Average = quarter4Sum / 3.0;
```

We can use another array to store the quarter averages instead of using four variables:

```
double[] quarterAverage = new double[4];

for (int i = 0; i < 4; i++) {

    sum = 0;

    for (int j = 0; j < 3; j++) { //compute the sum of
        sum += rainfall[3*i + j];  //one quarter
    }

    quarterAverage[i] = sum / 3.0;//average for Quarter i+1

}
```

Notice how the inner for loop is used to compute the sum of one quarter. The following table illustrates how the values for the variables i and j and the expression 3*i + j change.

i	j	3*i + j
0	0	0
	1	1
	2	2
1	0	3
	1	4
	2	5
2	0	6
	1	7
	2	8
3	0	9
	1	10
	2	11

In the previous examples, we used a constant to specify the size of an array, such as the literal constant 12 in the following declaration:

```
double[] rainfall = new double[12];
```

Using constants to declare the array sizes does not always lead to an efficient space usage. Suppose, for example, we declare an integer array of size 100:

```
int[] number = new int[100];
```

fixed-size array declaration

We call the declaration of arrays with constants a *fixed-size array declaration*. There are two potential problems with fixed-size array declarations. The first problem is that the program only can process up to 100 numbers. What if we need to process 101 numbers? We have to modify the program and compile it again. The second problem is a possible underutilization of space. The above declaration allocates 100 spaces whether they are used or not. Suppose the program on the average processes 20 numbers. Then, the program's average space usage is only 20 percent of the allocated space. With Java, we are not limited to fixed-size array declaration. We can declare an array of different size every time we run the program. The following code prompts the user for the size of an array and declares an array of designated size:

Chapter 9

```
int    size;
int[]  number;

size   = inputBox.getInteger("Size of an array:");
number = new int[size];
```

With this approach, every time the program is executed, only the needed amount of space is allocated for the array. Any valid integer arithmetic expression is allowed for size specification; for example,

```
size = inputBox.getInteger();
number = new int[size*size + 2* size + 5];
```

variable-size array declaration

We call the declaration of arrays with nonconstant values a *variable-size array declaration*. You will be seeing an example of a variable-size array in the next section.

Ms. Latte: *Can I use an index other than an integer?*

Dr. Caffeine: *No, not with Java. You must use an integer. Also, the array index must always start with 0.*

Ms. Latte: *Why? It seems more natural to start with 1.*

Dr. Caffeine: *Java adopted this feature from the programming language C. Using the zero-based indexing, the index value of an element indicates the number of elements in front of the element. For example, an index value of zero for the first element indicates that there are zero elements in front of it; an index value of four for the fifth element indicates that there are four elements in front of it. Zero-based indexing allows a simpler formula to compute the actual memory address of array elements.*

Quick Check

1.   Which of the following statements are invalid?

```
a.  float  number[23];

b.  float  number = { 1.0f, 2.0f, 3.0f };

c.  int    number;
    number = new Array[23];
```

```
d. int[] number = [ 1, 2, 3, 4 ];
```

2. Write a code fragment to compute the sum of all positive real numbers stored in the following array.

```
double[] number = new double[25];
```

3. Describe the difference between the following two code fragments.

```
//code fragment 1
for (int i = 0; i < number.length; i++) {
    if ( i % 2 == 0 ) {
        outputBox.printLine( number[i] );
    }
}

//code fragment 2
for (int i = 0; i < number.length; i++) {
    if ( number[i] % 2 == 0 ) {
        outputBox.printLine( number[i] );
    }
}
```

9.2   Arrays of Objects

Array elements are not limited to primitive data types. Indeed, since a String is an object, we actually have seen an example of an array of objects already in Section 9.1. In this section we will explore further arrays of objects. To illustrate the processing of an array of objects, we will use the Person class in the following examples. We will define this Person class later in the chapter to introduce additional object-oriented concepts. Here's the portion of the Person class definition we will use in this section:

Public Methods of the Person Class
`public int        getAge      (            )`
Returns the age of a person. Default age of a person is set to 0.
`public char       getGender(              )`
Returns the gender of a person. The character F stands for female and M for male. Default gender of a person is set to the character U for unknown.
`public String    getName    (            )`
Returns the name of a person. Default name of a person is set to Not Given.

Public Methods of the Person Class
`public   void      setAge     ( int age    )`
Sets the age of a person.
`public   void      setGender( char gender )`
Sets the gender of a person to the argument **gender**. The character **F** stands for female and **M** for male. The character **U** designates unknown gender.
`public   void      setName   ( String name)`
Sets the name of a person to the argument **name**.

The following code creates a **Person** object:

```
Person latte;

latte = new Person( );
latte.setName("Ms. Latte");
latte.setAge(20);
latte.setGender('F');

outputBox.printLine( "Name: " + latte.getName()   );
outputBox.printLine( "Age : " + latte.getAge()    );
outputBox.printLine( "Sex : " + latte.getGender() );
```

Now let's study how we can create and manipulate an array of **Person** objects. An array of objects is declared and created just like an array of primitive data types. The following are a declaration and a creation of an array of **Person** objects.

```
Person[]  person;       //declare the person array
person = new Person[20];  //and then create it
```

Execution of the above code will result in a state shown in Figure 9.4.

Notice that the elements, that is, **Person** objects, are not yet created; only the array is created. Array elements are initially null. Since each individual element is an object, it also must be created. The following code creates a **Person** object and sets it as the array's first element.

```
person[0] = new Person( );
```

Figure 9.5 shows the state after the first **Person** object is added to the array.

FIGURE 9.4   An array of **Person** objects after the array is created.

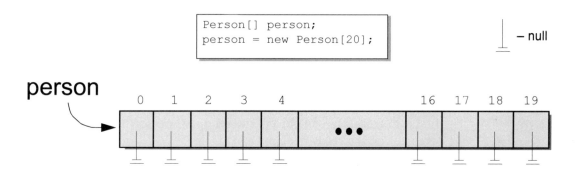

FIGURE 9.5   The person array with one **Person** object added to it.

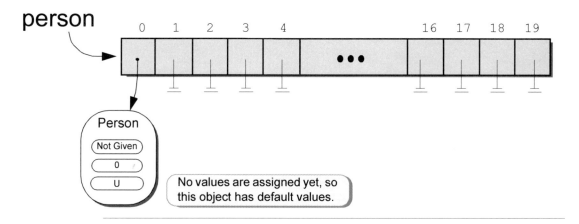

Notice that no data values are assigned to the object yet. The object has default values at this point. To assign data values to this object, we can execute

```
person[0].setName  ( "Ms. Latte" );
person[0].setAge   ( 20 );
person[0].setGender( 'F' );
```

The indexed expression

```
person[0]
```

is used to refer to the first object in the **person** array. Since this expression refers to an object, we write

```
person[0].setAge( 20 );
```

to call this **Person** object's **setAge** method, for example. This is the syntax we use to call an object's method. We are just using an indexed expression to refer to an object instead of a simple variable.

Let's go through typical array processing to illustrate the basic operations. The first is to create **Person** objects and set up the **person** array. We assume that the **person** array is already declared and created.

```
String    name, inpStr;
int       age;
char      gender;

for (int i = 0; i < person.length; i++) {

    //read in data values
    name   = inputBox.getString("Enter name:");
    age    = inputBox.getInteger("Enter age:");
    inpStr = inputBox.getString("Enter gender:");
    gender = inpStr.charAt(0);

    //create a new Person and assign values
    person[i] = new Person( );

    person[i].setName  ( name   );
    person[i].setAge   (  age   );
    person[i].setGender( gender );
}
```

Note: To focus on array processing, we used the most simplistic input routine. For instance, we did not perform any input error checking, but this is not to say that input error checking is unimportant. We simply want to focus on array processing.

To find the average age, we execute

find the average age

```
float sum = 0, averageAge;

for (int i = 0; i < person.length; i++) {
    sum += person[i].getAge();
}
averageAge = sum / (float) person.length;
```

To print out the name and age of the youngest and the oldest persons, we can execute

find the youngest
and the oldest
person

```
String    nameOfYoungest, nameOfOldest;
int       min, max, age;

nameOfYoungest = nameOfOldest = person[0].getName();
min = max = person[0].getAge();

for (int i = 1; i < person.length; i++) {
    age = person[i].getAge();

    if ( age < min ) {        //found a younger person
        min           = age;
        nameOfYoungest= person[i].getName();
    }
    else if ( age > max ) { //found an older person
        max           = age;
        nameOfOldest  = person[i].getName();
    }
}
outputBox.printLine("Oldest  : " + nameOfOldest + " is "
                                  + max + " years old.");

outputBox.printLine("Youngest: " + nameOfYoungest + " is "
                                  + min + " years old.");
```

Instead of using separate String and int variables, we can use the index to the youngest and the oldest persons. Here's the code:

```
int    minIdx,       //index to the youngest person
       maxIdx;       //index to the oldest person

minIdx = maxIdx = 0;

for (int i = 1; i < person.length; i++) {

    if ( person[i].getAge() < person[minIdx].getAge() ) {
        //found a younger person
        minIdx     = i;
    }
    else if (person[i].getAge() > person[maxIdx.getAge() ) {
        //found an older person
        maxIdx     = i;
    }
}

outputBox.printLine("Oldest: " + person[maxIdx].getName()
```

```
                                  + " is "
                                  + person[maxIdx].getAge()
                                  + " years old.");

        outputBox.printLine("Youngest: "
                                  + person[minIdx].getName()
                                  + " is "
                                  + person[minIdx].getAge()
                                  + " years old.");
```

Yet another approach is to use variables for Person objects. Figure 9.6 shows how the Person variables oldest and youngest point to objects in the person array. Here's the code using Person variables:

```
Person    youngest,     //points to the youngest person
          oldest;       //points to the oldest person

youngest = oldest = person[0];

for (int i = 1; i < person.length; i++) {

    if ( person[i].getAge() < youngest.getAge() ) {
        //found a younger person
        youngest  = person[i];
    }
    else if ( person[i].getAge() > oldest.getAge() ) {
        //found an older person
        oldest    = person[i];
    }
}

outputBox.printLine("Oldest  : " + oldest.getName()
        + " is " +   oldest.getAge() + " years old.");

outputBox.printLine("Youngest: " + youngest.getName()
        + " is " + youngest.getAge() + " years old.");
```

find a particular person

Our next example is to search for a particular person. We can scan through the array until the desired person is found. Suppose we want to search for a person whose name is Latte. If we assume the person is in the array, then we can write

```
int i = 0;

while ( !person[i].getName().equals("Latte") ) {
    i++;
}

outputBox.printLine("Found Ms. Latte at position " + i);
```

FIGURE 9.6   An array of **Person** objects with two **Person** variables.

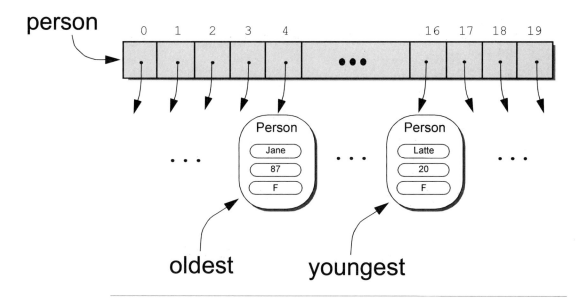

The expression

```
person[i].getName().equals("Latte")
```

is evaluated left to right and is equivalent to

```
Person p  =  person[i];
String str=  p.getName();

str.equals("Latte");
```

In this example, we assume that the person for whom we are searching is in the array. If we cannot assume this, then we need to rewrite the terminating condition to take care of the case when the person is not in the array. Here's how:

```
int i = 0;

while ( i < person.length &&//still more persons to search
        !person[i].getName().equals("Latte") ) {
    i++;
}
```

Chapter 9

```
if (i == person.length) {
   //not found - unsuccessful search
   outputBox.printLine("Ms. Latte was not in the array");
}
else {
   //found - successful search
   outputBox.printLine("Found Ms. Latte at position " + i);
}
```

delete a particular person

Now let's consider the deletion operation. The deletion operation requires some kind of a search routine to locate the Person object to be removed. To concentrate on the deletion operation, we will assume there's a search method that returns the index of the Person object in the array to be removed. There are two possible ways to remove an object from the array. The first approach is to reset the array element to null. Remember that each element in an array of objects is a reference to an object, so removing an object from an array could be accomplished by setting the reference to null. Figure 9.7 illustrates how the object at position 1 is deleted using Approach 1.

FIGURE 9.7   Approach 1 deletion: Setting a reference to **null**. The array length is 4.

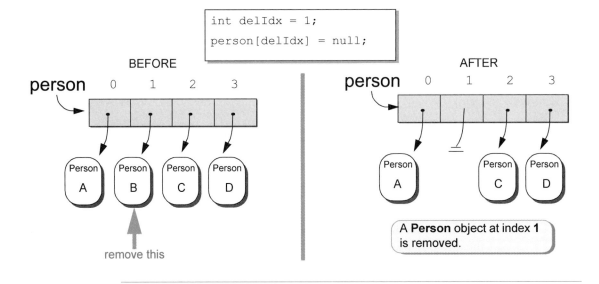

Since any index position can be set to null, there can be "holes," that is, null references, anywhere in the array. Instead of intermixing real and null references, the second approach will pack the elements so the real references occur at the beginning, and the null references at the end:

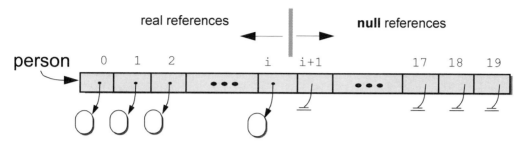

With Approach 2, we must fill the hole. There are two possible solutions. The first solution is to pack the elements. If an object at position J is removed (i.e., this position is set to null), then elements from position J+1 till the last non-null reference are shifted one position lower. And, finally, the last non-null reference is set to null. The second solution is to replace the removed element by the last element in the array. The first solution is necessary if the Person objects are arranged in some order (e.g., in ascending order of age). The second solution is a better one if the Person objects are not arranged in any order. Since we are not arranging them in any order, we will use the second solution. Figure 9.8 illustrates how the object at position 1 is replaced by the last element.

The search routine we presented earlier in this section assumes the full array; that is, all elements are non-null references. With the deletion routine, either Approach 1 or 2, given above, an array element could be a null. The search routine must therefore be modified to handle the null references correctly. The modified search routine is left as an exercise.

In both Figures 9.7 and 9.8, we removed the icon for Person B in the diagrams when the array element was set to null as though the object was erased from the memory. Eventually, the object will indeed get erased, but the operation of assigning null to the array element will not erase the object by itself. The operation simply initiates a chain reaction that will eventually erase the object from the memory.

As we have shown you several times already, a single object can have multiple references pointing to it. For example, the following code will result in two references pointing to a single Person object:

```
Person p1, p2;

p1 = new Person();
p2 = p1;
```

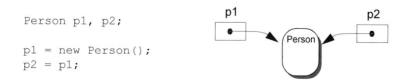

FIGURE 9.8   Approach 2 deletion: Replace the removed element with the last element in the array. The array length is 4.

```
int delIdx  = 1;
int last    = 3;

person[delIdx] = person[last];

person[last]   = null;
```

BEFORE

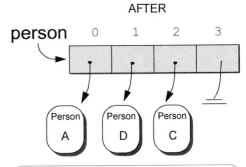

AFTER

A **Person** object at index **1** is removed and the last object at index **3** replaces the removed object.

When an object has no references pointing to it, then the system will erase the object and make the memory space available for other uses. We call the erasing of an object *deallocation* of memory, and the process of deallocating memory is called *garbage collection*. Unlike other programming languages, garbage collection is automatically done in Java, so we do not have to be conscious about it when developing Java programs.

garbage
collection

Quick Check

1.   Which of the following statements are invalid?

    a.   `Person[25] person;`

    b.   `Person[ ] person;`

    c.   `Person person[] = new Person[25];`

    d.   `Person person[25] = new Person[25];`

2. Write a code fragment to print out the name of those who are older than 20. Assume the following declaration and that the array is already set up correctly.

```
Person[ ]  friend = new Person[100];
```

9.3   Passing Arrays to Methods

We discussed the passing of an object to a method using String objects as illustrations in Chapter 8. Since an array is also an object, the rules for passing an object to a method and returning an object from the method apply to arrays also. However, there are some additional rules we need to remember in passing an array to a method and returning it from a method. We will cover these topics in this section.

Let's define a method that returns the index of the smallest element in an array of real numbers. The array to search for the smallest element is passed to the method. Here's the method:

```
public int searchMinimum(float[] number)
{
    int indexOfMinimum = 0;

    for (int i = 1; i < number.length; i++) {
        if (number[i] < number[indexOfMinimum]) { //found a
            indexOfMinimum = i;                    //smaller element
        }
    }
    return indexOfMinimum;
}
```

Notice that we use the square brackets to designate that number is an array. The square brackets may also be attached to the parameter as in

```
public int searchMinimum(float number[])
```

To call this method (from a method of the same class), we write something like

```
float[] arrayOne, arrayTwo;

//create and assign values to arrayOne and arrayTwo
...
```

```
//get the index of the smallest element of arrayOne
int minOne = searchMinimum( arrayOne );

//get the index of the smallest element of arrayTwo
int minTwo = searchMinimum( arrayTwo );

//output the result
outputBox.print("Mimimum value in Array One is ");
outputBox.print(arrayOne[minOne] + " at position " + minOne);

outputBox.skipLine(2);

outputBox.print("Mimimum value in Array Two is ");
outputBox.print(arrayTwo[minTwo] + " at position " + minTwo);
```

Just like other objects, an array is a reference data type, so we are passing the reference to an array, not the whole array, when we call the searchMinimum method. For example, when the method is called with arrayOne as its argument, the state of memory shown in Figure 9.9 will result. There are two references to the same array object. The method does not create a separate copy of the array.

> **When an array is passed to a method, only its reference is passed. A copy of the array is NOT created in the method.**

Now let's try another example in which we return an array (actually the reference to the array) from a method. Suppose we want to define a method that inputs float values and returns the values as an array of float. We can define the method as

```
public float[] readFloats()
{
    float[] number;
    int N = inputBox.getInteger("How many input values?");

    number = new float[N];

    for (int i = 0; i < N; i++) {
        number[i] = inputBox.getFloat("Number " + i);
    }
    return number;
}
```

The square brackets beside the method return type float indicate that the method returns an array of float. Because an array is a reference data type, when we say "returns an array of float," we are really saying "returns the reference to

FIGURE 9.9   Passing an array to a method means we are passing a reference to an array. We are not passing the whole array.

Execution Flow

an array of float." We will use the shorter expression in general and use the longer expression only when we need to be precise.

The readFloats method is called in the following manner:

```
float[] arrayOne, arrayTwo;

//assign values to arrayOne and arrayTwo
arrayOne = readFloats();

arrayTwo = readFloats();
```

Since a new array is created by the method, we do not have to create an array from the calling side. In other words, we don't have to do the following:

```
float[] arrayOne, arrayTwo;

arrayOne = new float[30]; //this statement is NOT necessary

arrayOne = readFloats();
```

It won't cause an error if you create an array from the calling side, but you are doing a very wasteful operation. First, it takes up extra memory space. And second, it slows down the whole operation because the computer must garbage collect the extra memory space that is not being used.

Let's try an alternative approach. This time, instead of creating an array inside the method and returning the array, the calling side creates an array and passes this array to the method:

```
int[] myIntArray = new int[50];

readIntegers(myIntArray);
```

The method **readIntegers** fills the passed array with integers. The method is defined as

```
public void readIntegers(int[] number)
{
    for (int i = 0; i < number.length; i++) {
        number[i] = inputBox.getInteger("Number " + i);
    }
}
```

Notice the return type of **readIntegers** is void because we are not returning an array. The method modifies the array that is passed to it.

Be careful not to mix the two alternative approaches. The following method will not work:

```
public void badMethod( float[] number )
{
    int N = inputBox.getInteger("How many input values?");

    number = new float[N];
```

```
        for (int i = 0; i < N; i++) {
            number[i] = inputbox.getFloat("Number " + i);
        }
    }
```

The code such as

```
    float[] arrayOne = new float[30];

    badMethod( arrayOne );
```

will leave **arrayOne** unchanged. Figure 9.10 shows the effect of creating a local array in **badMethod** and not returning it (note: the return type of **badMethod** is void).

Quick Check

1. What will be an output from the following code?

    ```
    int[] list = {10, 20, 30, 40 };
    myMethod( list );
    outputBox.printLine( list[1] );
    outputBox.printLine( list[3] );
    ...
    public void myMethod(int[] intArray)
    {
        for (int i = 0; i < intArray.length; i+=2) {
            intArray[i] = i;
        }
    }
    ```

2. If we replace **myMethod** of question 1 with the following, what will be an output?

    ```
    public void myMethod(int[] intArray)
    {
        int[] local = intArray;
        for (int i = 0; i < local.length; i+=2) {
            local[i] = i;
        }
    }
    ```

Chapter 9

FIGURE 9.10   Effect of creating a local array and not returning it.

Execution Flow

This is a newly created array completely separate and different from the argument array. Changes made to this array will not affect the original array.

9.4   MultiInputBox

While an InputBox object is capable of accepting only a single input value, a MultiInputBox object from the javabook package can accept multiple input values. A MultiInputBox object allows the user to input N string values using N TextField objects. The programmer can specify N labels. Figure 9.11 shows a MultiInputBox with three labels and three text fields for entering bank information.

FIGURE 9.11   A **MultiInputBox** object (from the **javabook** package) to enter three values.

In general, designing a customized input dialog for Bank, Account, Student, and so forth is preferable, but there are times a generic dialog, such as MultiInputBox, with labels on one column and text fields on another is sufficient. Using the MultiInputBox class is a quick and easy way to handle input routines of a program if the program does not require a fancy user interface. The MultiInputBox class is useful in building prototypes also. Instead of spending time designing customized input dialogs, you can start building a program prototype by using MultiInputBox objects. When the prototype is functioning properly, you can then improve the user interface of the program with customized input dialogs.

There are two ways to create a MultiInputBox object. The first is by passing an owner frame and the integer argument that specifies the number of labels and text fields the MultiInputBox object will contain, for example:

```
MultiInputBox multiBox = new MultiInputBox(mainWindow, 3);
```

We use the **setLabels** method to assign the labels. The argument to the method is an array of strings. The following code creates the dialog shown in Figure 9.11.

```
String[] label = { "Name", "Address", "Phone Number"};
multiBox.setLabels(label);
```

If the **setLabels** method is not called, then the dialog will contain no labels.

The second way to create a MultiInputBox object is to pass an array of strings as its second parameter, for example:

```
String[] label = { "Name", "Address", "Phone Number"};
MultiInputBox multiBox
                = new MultiInputBox(mainWindow, label);
```

The MultiInputBox class is a descendant of Dialog, so the methods applicable to Dialog are applicable to MultiInputBox also (the title of MultiInputBox shown in Figure 9.11 is set by calling its setTitle method). We will discuss only the method unique to the MultiInputBox class.

We retrieve input values from a MultiInputBox by calling the method get-Inputs. The method returns an array of strings. For example,

```
String[] answer;

answer = multiBox.getInputs();
```

The array answer is null if either the Cancel button is clicked or no input value is entered. Notice that the getInputs method returns an array of strings. If we execute

```
MultiInputBox multiBox = new MultiInputBox(mainWindow, 3);
String[]      labels = { "Name", "Address", "Age"};
String[]      answer;

multiBox.setLabels(labels);

answer = multiBox.getInputs();
```

then the answer array like the one shown in Figure 9.12 will result.

FIGURE 9.12   The **answer** array returned from **multiBox**.

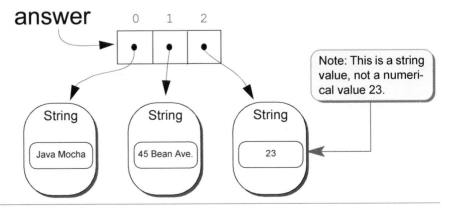

Since we want the third input as an int, we need to do a String to int conversion. You can convert using the Convert class from the javabook package as

```
int age = Convert.toInt(answer[2]);
```

or convert using the Integer class from java.lang as

```
Integer intObj = new Integer(answer[2]);
int age = intObj.intValue();
```

Table 9.1 is a list of MultiInputBox methods.

TABLE 9.1   A list of **MultiInputBox** methods.

CLASS:	**MultiInputBox**	
Method	**Argument**	**Description**
`<constructor>`	`MainWindow, int`	Creates a MultiInputBox object. The second argument specifies the number of labels.
`<constructor>`	`MainWindow, array of String`	Creates a MultiInputBox object. The second argument is an array of String for labels.
`setLabels`	`array of String`	Sets the labels of a MultiInputBox object to the passed array of String.
`getInputs`	`<none>`	Returns an array of String entered by the user.

9.5   Self-Referencing Pointer

In this section, we will describe an object-oriented programming concept called a *self-referencing pointer*. In Java, the reserved word this is used as a self-referencing pointer. We used the self-referencing pointer in Chapter 5 but provided only a brief explanation. We will provide a more complete explanation in this section. We will define a Person class to illustrate the use of a self-referencing pointer. The list of public methods of the Person class was given earlier in Section 9.2.

Let's begin with the data members of the Person class. For each person we maintain the name, gender, and age information. To keep track of this information, we will use instance variables. We declare the class as

Chapter 9

```
class Person
{
//--------------------------
// Data Members
//--------------------------

    private   String    name;
    private   int       age;
    private   char      gender;

    //the rest of the class definition comes here

}
```

In the list given in Section 9.2, we see three "read" methods that return the value of instance variables—getAge, getGender, and getName—and three "write" methods that assign the values to instance variables—setAge, setGender, and setName. The "read" methods that return the values are called *accessors* or *access methods*, and the "write" methods that assign values to the object are called *mutators* or *mutator methods* because they change the value of instance variables.

accessors

mutators

The access methods are easy. Since we have included an instance variable for each of the three items of information, all we need to do is to return the value of the respective instance variable. They are defined as

```
public int getAge( )
{
    return age;
}

public char getGender( )
{
    return gender;
}

public String getName( )
{
    return name;
}
```

Now let's see how we can define the mutator methods. Basically, we need to do the inverse of what we did with the access methods; that is, we need to assign a value to the respective instance variable. For example, we may define the set-Age method as

```
public void setAge( int anAge )
{
    age = anAge;
}
```

Notice how we named the parameter. We use the identifier anAge, because we cannot use the identifier age as the parameter. Doing so would conflict with the instance variable age in the method body. To avoid the naming conflict, we use a different identifier for the parameter.

A second way to avoid the naming conflict is by using the self-referencing pointer this. In order to explain the use of the self-referencing pointer, let's review how an identifier in a method is associated to a variable. If there's a matching local declaration or a matching parameter, then the identifier is associated to the local variable or the parameter. Note: The parameter is a local declaration, so you cannot have a method declaration with the local variable and the parameter sharing the same identifier, such as

```
public void bad( int local )
{
    int local;
    ...
}
```
Cannot be the same name.

Otherwise, if there's a matching instance or class variable, then the identifier is associated to the instance or class variable. Figure 9.13 illustrates these points.

FIGURE 9.13 How identifiers used in a method are associated to a local variable, parameter, or instance/class variable.

```
class Person
{
    int age;
    ...
    public void setAge(int age)
    {
        ...  age  ...

    }
}
```
There's a matching parameter, so 'age' refers to this parameter.

```
class Person
{
    int age;
    ...
    public void setAge(int pAge)
    {
        ...  age  ...

    }
}
```
There's no matching parameter or local declaration, so 'age' refers to the instance variable.

Chapter 9

Rules for associating an identifier to a local variable, a parameter, and an instance/class variable:

1. *If there's a matching local variable declaration or a parameter, then the identifier refers to the local variable or the parameter.*
2. *Otherwise, if there's a matching instance or class variable, then the identifier refers to the instance or class variable.*
3. *Otherwise, it is an error because there's no matching declaration.*

Using the self-referencing pointer this, we can avoid the naming conflict even if we use the same identifier for an instance variable and the parameter. We can define the setAge method as

```
public void setAge( int age )
{
    this.age = age;
}
```

Because of the matching parameter declaration, the identifier age in the method refers to this parameter. To refer to the instance variable age from this method, we use the expression this.age. Figure 9.14 shows how the associations are made. We read the expression this.age as "this object's age instance variable." By using the dot notation with the reserved word this, we are able to refer to the object's instance variable.

FIGURE 9.14   Using the self-referencing pointer to avoid the naming conflict.

```
class Person
{
    int age;◄
    . . .
    public void setAge(int age)
    {

        this.age   =   age  ;

    }
}
```

You can always use the reserved word this in referring to the object's data members and methods. In many cases, its use is optional, so we don't use it explicitly. In the case of the setAge method, because the identifier age is used as the parameter, we must use the expression this.age to avoid the naming conflict. When there are no naming conflicts, the use is optional. For example, when we write the setAge method as

```
public void setAge( int anAge )
{
    age = anAge;
}
```

then we don't have to use the self-referencing pointer, because there's no ambiguity. However, we could also write the method using the this pointer explicitly as

```
public void setAge( int age )
{
    this.age = age;
}
```

This rule applies also to calling a method that belongs to the same class. We explained earlier in Chapter 4 (see Figure 4.8 on page 174) that when we call a method from another method that belongs to the same class, no dot notation is used. Consider the following example:

```
class Tester
{
    public void methodOne( )
    {
    }

    public void methodTwo( )
    {
        methodOne();
    }
}
```

You don't need dot notation to call a method that belongs to the same class

The methodTwo method also can be written by explicitly using the dot notation with the self-referencing pointer this:

```
public void methodTwo( )
{
    this.methodOne();
}
```

Chapter 9

The setAge method shows only one example of using the self-referencing pointer this. There are other usages that we will describe later in this section and also in the later chapters.

The self-referencing pointer refers to an instance of a class, and therefore, the use of the this pointer is valid only inside the instance methods. The this pointer inside the class methods does not make sense, and it is not allowed.

The constructor of the Person class is defined as

```
public Person ( )
{
    age = 0;
    name = "Not Given";
    gender = 'U';
}
```

Up till now, we managed to define a class using only one constructor. However, a class is not limited to one constructor. It is possible to define multiple constructors to a class. For the Person class, we can define a second constructor that accepts three values so the three attributes of a Person object can be initialized at the time the object is created. The second constructor is defined as

```
public Person(String name, int age, char gender)
{
    this.name    = name;
    this.age     = age;
    this.gender  = gender;
}
```

and it is called as in

```
Person p = new Person( "Ms. Latte", 20, 'F' );
```

Using the self-referencing pointer this, it is possible, and preferable, to define the first constructor as

```
public Person ( )
{
    this( "Not Given", 0,'U' );
}
```

The first constructor calls the second constructor for the actual initialization, instead of performing the actual initialization. By defining the first constructor in this manner, we can guarantee consistent initialization, because the second constructor is the only method that carries out the actual initialization procedure. Since there's only one place where the initialization procedure is defined, it is also easier to manage any changes made to the initialization procedure. You may want to see how the multiple constructors for javabook classes such as InputBox and ResponseBox are defined.

Quick Check

1. What will be an output from the following code?

```
Tester testOne = new Tester();
testOne.methodOne(15);
...
class Tester
{
    private int x;

    public void methodTwo( )
    {
        System.out.println(x);
    }

    public void methodOne(int x)
    {
        this.x = x + 1;
        methodTwo();
    }
}
```

2. What's wrong with the following code?

```
public void setAge( int anAge )
{
    age = this.anAge;
}
```

9.6   Sample Development: The Address Book

In this section, we will design a class called an AddressBook to maintain a collection of Person objects. The AddressBook class is implemented by using an array. We will use the Person class defined in the previous section. Through the design of the AddressBook class, we will reiterate the key principles of object-oriented design.

Notice that we are not developing a complete program here. We are designing only one of the many classes we need for a complete address book program. For the complete program, we need a main window, objects for doing input and output, and so forth. In this section, we will concentrate on one class that is only responsible for maintaining a collection of Person objects. This class will not perform, for example, input and output of Person objects, following the single-task object (STO) principle described in Chapter 6. We will discuss the importance of the STO principle while we develop the AddressBook class. One objective we have in designing the AddressBook class is to make the class reusable in many different programs. Many of the design decisions we will make during the development are based on implementing a reusable class.

Problem Statement

> Write an AddressBook *class that manages a collection of* Person *objects. An* AddressBook *object will allow the programmer to add, delete, or search for a* Person *object in the address book.*

Overall Plan

Our first task is to come up with an overall design of the class. Let's begin by first identifying the core operations that an address book object must support. The problem statement indicated three major operations: add, delete, and search. These three operations are pretty much a standard in any collection of data values. For any kind of collections, you will always want to be able to add a new item, delete an old item, and search for an item or items. An address book is no exception as it is a collection of information about people for which you would want to add, delete, and search data.

Our task here is to design a class that will maintain an address book by supporting these three operations. We will define three methods for the class: add, delete, and search.

Our working design document for the AddressBook class is therefore as follows:

Design Document: The Public Methods of the AddressBook Class	
Method	Purpose
AddressBook	A constructor to initialize the object. We will include multiple constructors as necessary.
add	Adds a new **Person** object to the address book.
delete	Deletes a specified **Person** object from the address book.
search	Searches a specified **Person** object in the address book and returns this person if found.

The object diagram for the AddressBook class at this point is

We will implement the class in the following order:

development steps

1. Implement the constructor(s).

2. Implement the add method.

3. Implement the search method.

4. Implement the delete method.

5. Finalize the class.

This order of development follows a natural sequence. To implement any instance method of a class, we need to be able to create a properly initialized object, so we will begin the class implementation by defining a constructor. As a part of defining a constructor, we will identify necessary data members. We will add more data members as we progress through the development steps. The second step is to implement the add routine, because without being able to add a new **Person** object, we won't be able to test other operations. For the third step, we will implement the search routine. And for the fourth step, we will implement the last routine. Although we could implement the delete routine before the search routine, we need some form of searching to test the correctness of the delete routine. In other words, we delete a person and attempt to search for this person, verifying that the search will not find the deleted person. So we will implement the search routine before the delete routine.

Step 1 Development: Skeleton with Constructors

Step 1 Design

In Step 1, we will identify the data members and define a constructor(s) to initialize them. The main data member for the class is a structure we will use to keep track of a collection of Person objects. We will use an array, the only data structure we have learned so far for this purpose. We will create this array in the constructor. At the time we create an array, we must declare its size. Remember that the size of an array is the maximum number of elements this array can hold. The actual number of Person objects stored in the array will be anywhere from zero to the size of the array.

We have two possible alternatives for specifying the size of an array. First, we can let the programmer pass the size as an argument to the constructor. Second, we can set the size to a default value. Both alternatives are useful. If the programmer has a good estimate of the number of Person objects to manage, she can specify the size in the constructor. Otherwise, she can use the default size by not specifying the size in the constructor. We will define two constructors to support both alternatives. This will give programmers a flexibility in creating an AddressBook object.

If we are going to provide a constructor in which the programmer can pass the size of an array, then we need to write the constructor so it won't crash when an invalid value is passed as an argument. What would be an invalid argument value? Since we are dealing with a collection of objects, and the size of a collection cannot be negative, an argument value of less than zero is invalid. Also, even though a collection whose size is zero may make sense in theory, such a collection makes no sense in practice. Therefore, we will consider zero also as an invalid argument value. We will require an argument to a constructor to be a positive integer.

How should the constructor behave if the programmer passes an invalid argument value? The constructor does not have a return type, so we can't return a boolean value to report the status back (e.g., true for successful creation of an object, false otherwise). We want to define a constructor to be reliable so that an instance of the class is created and initialized to a consistent state. If there's a possibility that a constructor could fail (e.g., trying to create an array of negative size inside the constructor) and not create an instance, then we must add code to verify that an instance is indeed created every time the constructor is called. To guarantee that the constructor will create an instance, the constructor will create an array of the default size when an invalid value is passed to it as an argument.

Increase the reliability of a class by defining a constructor that will not fail to create an instance and initialize an instance to a valid state.

Step 1 Code

At this point, we have only one data member—an array of objects. We will call it entry because a Person object is a single entry in an address book. We will set the default size of entry to 25. There is no particular reason for selecting this size. We simply picked a number that is not too small or too big. We can change this value later if we need to.

We will define two constructors. The first constructor will call the second constructor with the value 25 (default size) as its argument. The second constructor creates an array of Person objects of the size passed as its parameter. Inside the second constructor, we include a temporary test output statement. The class is defined as follows:

File: AddressBook.java

```java
/**
 * This class is designed to manage an address book that contains
 * Person objects. The user can specify the size of the address book
 * when it is created. If no size is specified, then the default size
 * is set to 25 Person objects.
 *
 * @author Dr. Caffeine
 *
 */
class AddressBook
{

//----------------------------------
// Data Members
//----------------------------------
    private static final int   DEFAULT_SIZE = 25;
    private Person[]           entry;

//----------------------------------
// Constructors
//----------------------------------
    /**
     * Default constructor.
     * Creates an address book of size 25.
     */
    public AddressBook( )
    {
        this( DEFAULT_SIZE );
    }
    /**
     * Creates an address book with the designated size.
     *
     * @param size the size of this address book.
     */
    public AddressBook( int size )
    {
        if (size <= 0 ) { //invalid data value, use default
            size = DEFAULT_SIZE;
        }
```

Chapter 9

```
        entry = new Person[size];

        System.out.println("array of "+ size + " is created."); //TEMP
    }
}
```

To test this class, we have included a temporary output statement inside the second constructor. We will write a test program to verify that we can create an AddressBook object correctly. The test data are as follows:

Step 1 Test Data	
Data Value	**Purpose**
Negative numbers	Test the invalid data.
0	Test the end case of invalid data.
1	Test the end case of valid data.
>= 1	Test the normal cases.

We will use a very simple test program:

```
class TestAddressBook
{
    public static void main ( String[] args )
    {
        AddressBook myBook;

        myBook = new AddressBook( -10 ); //Error
        myBook = new AddressBook(   0 ); //Error
        myBook = new AddressBook(   4 );
    }
}
```

Run the program several times with a different set of test data and verify that you get the correct results.

Step 2 Development: Implement the add Method

In the second development step, we will implement the add method. We mentioned in the overall design step that this class will not do any input or output of person data. This decision is based on the STO principle. A single object doing both the input/output routines and maintaining the array will reduce its usability. For example, had the AddressBook class used InputBox and OutputBox to handle the input and output of person data, the use of this class would dictate or impose the style of input and output routines on the programmers. The programmer will not have an option of using the input and output objects appropriate for his or her uses.

Following the STO principle, we will let the programmer decide how she will input and output person data. The task of the add method is to accept a Person object as its parameter and add the passed Person object to the array. Since the array is limited in size, what should we do if there is no more space to add another Person object? There are two alternatives. The first alternative is to return false if a new Person object cannot be added to the array; that is, the array is full. The method will return true otherwise. The second alternative is to increase the array size. Since the size of an array object cannot be changed once the object is created, we need to create another array with a larger size than the original if we choose to implement the second alternative.

Alternative Design 1

Alternative Design 2

Since the second alternative is more accommodating and less restrictive to the programmer, we will implement this alternative. When the array is full, we will create a new array, copy the objects from the original array to this new array, and finally set the variable entry to point to this new array. We will set the size of the new array to one and a half times larger than the original array. This size increment is just an estimate. Any value between 125 and 200 percent of the old array is reasonable. You don't want to make it too small, say, 105 percent, since that will cause the enlarge method to be called too frequently. You don't want to make it too large either, since that will likely result in wasted space. Figure 9.15 illustrates the process of creating a larger array.

Now let's think about how to add a Person object to the array. To add a new object, we need to locate a position at which to insert the object. Since we are not maintaining Person objects in any particular order, we will add a new person at the first available position. If we fill the positions from the low to high indices (0, 1, 2, ...), we can use a variable to remember the index of the next available position. Since we are using an array, the index of the next available position is also the number of Person objects currently in the array, so we will call this variable count. Figure 9.16 illustrates the add operation.

Step 2 Code

First we add a new instance variable count to the class:

```
//----------------------------
// Data Members
//----------------------------

private int     count; //number of elements in the array,
                       //which is also the position to add
                       //the next Person object
```

We modify the constructor to initialize this data member:

```
public AddressBook( int size )
{
    count = 0;

    //same as before
}
```

(Note: Because we defined the first constructor to call the second constructor, we can implement this change by rewriting only one constructor instead of two.) The add method is defined as

FIGURE 9.15   How a new array that is 150 percent larger than the original array is created. The size of the original array is 4.

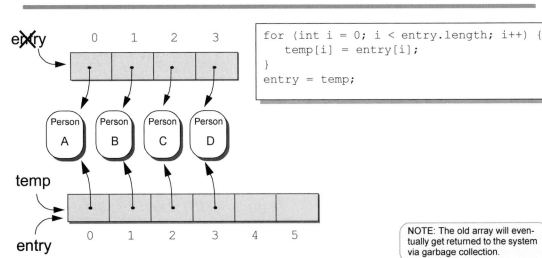

NOTE: The old array will eventually get returned to the system via garbage collection.

```
public void add( Person newPerson )
{
    if (count == entry.length) { //no more space left,
        enlarge( );                 //create a new larger array
    }

    //at this point, entry refers to a new larger array
    entry[count] = newPerson;
    count++;
}
```

The enlarge method is a new private method that creates a new, larger array.

Design Document:	The AddressBook Class	
Method	**Visibility**	**Purpose**
. . .	. . .	. . .
enlarge	private	Creates a new array that is 150 percent larger than the old array.

FIGURE 9.16   Adding a new **Person** object to the next available location. The array length is **4**.

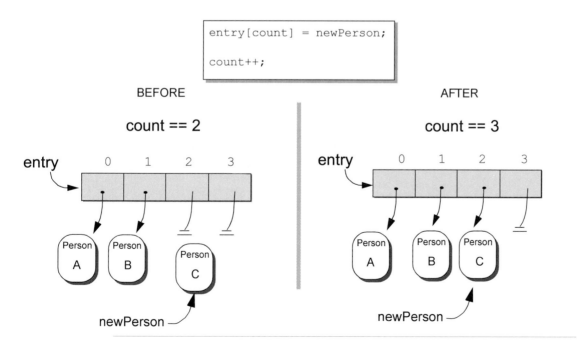

```
private void enlarge( )
{
    //create a new array whose size is 150% larger
    //than the current array
    int newLength = (int) (1.5 * entry.length);
    Person[] temp = new Person[newLength];

    //now copy the data to the new array
    for (int i = 0; i < entry.length; i++) {
        temp[i] = entry[i];
    }

    //finally set the variable entry to point to the new array
    entry = temp;

    System.out.println("Inside the method enlarge"); //TEMP
    System.out.println("Size of a new array: "
                            + entry.length); //TEMP
}
```

Step 2 Test

We will write a test program to verify that a new **Person** object is added to the array correctly. In addition, we need to test that a new array 150 percent larger than the old one is created when there are no more spaces left in the array. The test data are as follows:

Step 2 Test Data	
Test Sequence	**Purpose**
Create the array of size 4	Test that the array is created correctly.
Add four Person objects	Test that the **Person** objects are added correctly.
Add the fifth Person object	Test that the new array is created and the **Person** object is added correctly (to the new array).

The Step 2 test program is as follows:

```
class TestAddressBook
{
    public static void main ( String[] args )
    {
        AddressBook   myBook;
        Person        person;

        myBook = new AddressBook( 4 );

        //add four Person objects
```

Chapter 9

```
for (int i = 0; i < 4; i++) {
    person = new Person("Ms. X"+i, 10, 'F');
    myBook.add( person );
}

//add the fifth person and see if
//a new array is created
person = new Person("fifth one", 10, 'F');
myBook.add( person );
    }
}
```

Run the program several times with different sizes for the address book and verify that you get the correct results.

Step 3 Development: Implement the search Method

Step 3 Design   In the third development step, we implement the search method. The method can return one or more Person objects that meet the search criteria. We have several options for the search criteria. Since we keep track of name, age, and gender for each person, we can use any one of them as the search criterion. In this implementation, we will use the person's name. The search routine for the other two criteria will be left as an exercise.

To implement the search method, we will make an assumption that the name is unique so that there will be at most one matching Person object. If the name is not unique, then there are two possibilities. The search method can return one Person object (among many) that matches the given name or return all Person objects that match the given name. We will leave the case when the name is not unique as an exercise. Notice that the add method we implemented in Step 2 does not check the person data. In other words, there is no mechanism to disallow the addition of a Person object with a duplicate name. We will leave the implementation of the modified add method as an exercise also.

There are two possible outcomes with the search method—a successful or an unsuccessful search. The method has to return a value by which the programmer can verify the result of the search. We will define the search method so that it will return a matching Person object if it is found and null otherwise. The search routine will start scanning the array from the first position until the desired Person object is found (successful search) or no more Person objects are left in the array (unsuccessful search). Expressing the search routine in pseudocode, we have

```
set loc to 0;
while ( loc < count &&
        name of Person at entry[loc] != searchName ) {
    loc++;
}
```

Chapter 9

```
if (loc == count) {
    foundPerson = null;
}
else {
    foundPerson = entry[loc];
}

return foundPerson;
```

Step 3 Code   Translating the pseudocode into an actual code will result in the following
method:

```
public Person search( String searchName )
{
    Person foundPerson;
    int    loc = 0;

    while ( loc < count &&
            !searchName.equals( entry[loc].getName() ) ) {
        loc++;
    }

    if (loc == count) {
        foundPerson = null;
    }
    else {
        foundPerson = entry[loc];
    }

    return foundPerson;
}
```

Step 3 Test   To test the search method, we will build an address book that contains five
Person objects. We will give names Ms. X0, Ms. X1, . . . , and Ms. X4 to them.
After the address book is set up, we test various cases of the search. We test for
successful and unsuccessful searches. For the successful searches, we test for
the end cases and normal cases. The end cases involve searching for persons
stored at the first and last positions of the array. Off-by-one error (OBOE) is
very common in processing an array, so it is very important to test these end cases.

After a successful execution, we will test the class again by changing the
size of the array. One test size we should not forget to test is the end case for the
array size, which is one. Also, we need to test the cases where the array is not
fully filled, such as an array of size 5 containing only two Person objects.

The test data are as follows:

Step 3 Test Data	
Test Sequence	**Purpose**
Create the array of size 5 and add five **Person** objects with unique names.	Test that the array is created and set up correctly. Here, we will test the case where the array is 100 percent filled.
Search for the person in the first position of the array	Test that the successful search works correctly for the end case.
Search for the person in the last position of the array	Test another version of the end case.
Search for a person somewhere in the middle of the array.	Test the normal case.
Search for a person not in the array.	Test for the unsuccessful search.
Repeat the above steps with an array of varying sizes, especially the array of size 1.	Test that the routine works correctly for arrays of different sizes.
Repeat the testing with the cases where the array is not fully filled, say, array length is 5 and the number of objects in the array is 0 or 3.	Test that the routine works correctly for other cases.

The Step 3 test program is written as follows:

```
class Tester
{
    public static void main ( String[] args )
    {
        TestAddressBook tester = new TestAddressBook();
        tester.setupArray( 5 );
        tester.testSearch();
    }
}

class TestAddressBook
{
    AddressBook    myBook;
    Person         person;
```

```
private void setupArray( int N )
{
    myBook = new AddressBook( N );

    //add N Person objects
    for (int i = 0; i < N; i++) {
        person = new Person("Ms. X"+i, 10, 'F');
        myBook.add( person );
    }
}

private void testSearch( )
{
    //test for the end case
    person = myBook.search("Ms. X0");

    if ( person == null ) {
        System.out.println
            ("Error: Didn't find the person it should");
    }
    else {
        System.out.println
            (person.getName() + " is found okay.");
    }
}
}
```

Notice the TestAddressBook class is now an instantiable class. Since the code for testing is getting longer, it is not practical any more to do everything in a single main method. For testing, we will modify the method body of setupArray and testSearch as necessary to test all other cases described in the test data table.

Step 4 Development: Implement the delete Method

Step 4 Design

In the fourth development step, we implement the delete method. To delete a Person object, the programmer must somehow specify which Person object to remove from the address book. Similar to the search method, we will use the name of a person to specify which person to delete. Since we assume the name is unique, the delete method will remove at most one Person object. There are two possible outcomes: the specified person is removed from the address book (successful operation) and the specified person is not removed because he/she is not in the address book (unsuccessful operation). We will define the delete method so that it will return true if the operation is successful and false otherwise.

The removal of an element in an array of objects is done by setting the element to null. This will leave a "hole." We will fill this hole by replacing the removed element with the last element, as explained earlier (see Figure 9.8). This filling operation is necessary for other methods, specifically the add method, to work correctly.

To fill the hole, we need to know the location of the hole. To find this location, we write a private search method called findIndex. The method is very similar to the search method. The only difference is that the return value of findIndex is an index of an element in the array, whereas the return value of search is a Person object. Using this findIndex method, the delete method can be expressed as

```
boolean status;
int     loc;

loc = findIndex( searchName );

if ( loc is not valid) {
    status = false;
}
else { //found, pack the hole
    replace the element at index loc+1 by the last element
    at index count;

    status = true;

    count--;   //decrement count,
               //since we now have one less element
}
return status;
```

Step 4 Code

The private findIndex method will look like this:

```
private int findIndex( String searchName )
{
    int loc = 0;

    while ( loc < count &&
            !searchName.equals( entry[loc].getName() ) ) {
        loc++;
    }

    if (loc == count) {
        loc = NOT_FOUND;
    }

    return loc;
}
```

Chapter 9

The constant NOT_FOUND is set in the data member section as

```
//--------------------------
// Data Members
//--------------------------

private static final int   NOT_FOUND = -1;
```

Using this findIndex method, the delete method is defined as

```
public boolean delete( String searchName )
{
    boolean    status;
    int        loc;

    loc = findIndex( searchName );

    if (loc == NOT_FOUND) {
        status = false;
    }
    else { //found, pack the hole

        entry[loc] = entry[count-1];

        status = true;
        count--;        //decrement count,
                        //since we now have one less element
    }
    return status;
}
```

Step 4 Test   To test the delete method, we will build an address book that contains five Person objects as before. Test cases are: delete the first person in the array, delete the last person in the array, delete someone in the middle (normal case), try to delete a nonexisting person.

After a successful execution, we will test the class again by changing the size of an array. One test size we should not forget to test is the end case for the array size, which is one. Also, we need to test the cases where the array is not fully filled, such as an array of size 5 containing only two Person objects.

The test data are as follows:

Step 4 Test Data	
Test Sequence	**Purpose**
Create the array of size 5 and add five **Person** objects with unique names.	Test the array is created and set up correctly. Here, we will test the case where the array is 100 percent filled.
Search for a person to be deleted next.	Verify that the person is in the array before deletion.
Delete the person in the array	Test that the **delete** method works correctly.
Search for the deleted person.	Test that the **delete** method works correctly by checking the value **null** is returned by the search.
Attempt to delete a nonexisting person.	Test that the unsuccessful operation works correctly.
Repeat the above steps by deleting persons at the first and last positions.	Test that the routine works correctly for arrays of different sizes.
Repeat testing where the array is not fully filled, say, an array length is 5 and the number of objects in the array is 0 or 3.	Test that the routine works correctly for other cases.

The Step 4 test program is written as follows:

```
class Tester
{
    public static void main ( String[] args )
    {
        TestAddressBook tester = new TestAddressBook();
        tester.setupArray( 5 );
        tester.testDelete();
    }
}

class TestAddressBook
{
    AddressBook    myBook;
    Person         person;

    private void setupArray( int N )
    {
        myBook = new AddressBook( N );
```

```
        //add N Person objects
        for (int i = 0; i < N; i++) {
            person = new Person("Ms. X"+i, 10, 'F');
            myBook.add( person );
        }
    }


    private static void testDelete( )
    {
        //first make sure the person is in the array
        person = myBook.search("Ms. X2");

        if ( person == null ) {
            System.out.println
                ("Error: Didn't find the person it should");
        }
        else {
            System.out.println
                    (person.getName() + " is found okay.");

            boolean success = myBook.delete("Ms. X2");

            if ( success ) {
                person = myBook.search("Ms. X2");

                if (person == null) {
                    System.out.println("Okay: Deletion works");
                }
                else {
                    System.out.println
                            ("Error: Person is still there");
                }
            }
            else {
                System.out.println
                        ("Error: Deletion has a problem");
            }
        }
    }
```

Modify the method body of setupArray and testDelete as necessary to test all other cases described in the Step 4 test data table.

Step 5 Development: Finalize

program
review

As always, we finalize the program in the last step. We perform a critical review to find any inconsistency or error in the methods, incomplete methods, places to add more comments, and so forth.

final test

Since the three operations of add, delete, and search are interrelated, it is critical to test these operations together. The test program should try out various combinations of add, delete, and search operations to verify that they work together correctly.

After we complete the class implementation and testing, we may consider improvement or extension. In addition to the several alternative designs, it is possible to add other operations. For example, we may want to add an operation to modify a Person object. Another common operation that is useful in manipulating a collection of objects is scanning. *Scanning* is an operation to visit all elements in the collection. Scanning is useful in listing all Person objects in the address book. These extended operations are left as an exercise.

scanning

9.7 Two-Dimensional Arrays

A table organized in rows and columns is a very effective means for communicating many different types of information. Figure 9.17 shows sample data displayed in a tabular format. In Java, we represent tables as *two-dimensional arrays*. The arrays we have discussed so far are *one-dimensional arrays* because they have only one index. In this section, we describe how two-dimensional arrays are used in Java.

two-dimensional
array

Let's begin with an example. Consider the following table with four rows and five columns. The table contains the hourly rate of programmers based on their skill level. The rows represent the grade levels and the columns represent the steps within a grade level. Reading the table, we know a programmer with skill grade level 2, step 1 earns $36.50 an hour.

<table>
<tr><th></th><th colspan="5">Step</th></tr>
<tr><th></th><th>0</th><th>1</th><th>2</th><th>3</th><th>4</th></tr>
<tr><td>0</td><td>10.50</td><td>12.00</td><td>14.50</td><td>16.75</td><td>18.00</td></tr>
<tr><td>1</td><td>20.50</td><td>22.25</td><td>24.00</td><td>26.25</td><td>28.00</td></tr>
<tr><td>2</td><td>34.00</td><td>36.50</td><td>38.00</td><td>40.35</td><td>43.00</td></tr>
<tr><td>3</td><td>50.00</td><td>60.00</td><td>70.00</td><td>80.00</td><td>99.99</td></tr>
</table>

Grade (row label)

We declare the pay scale table as

```
double[][] payScaleTable;
```

Chapter 9

FIGURE 9.17   Examples of information represented as tables.

Distance Table (in miles)

	Los Angeles	San Francisco	San Jose	San Diego	Monterey
Los Angeles	—	600	500	150	450
San Francisco	600	—	100	750	150
San Jose	500	100	—	650	50
San Diego	150	750	650	—	600
Monterey	450	150	50	600	—

Multiplication Table

	1	2	3	4	5	6	7	8	9
1	1	2	3	4	5	6	7	8	9
2	2	4	6	8	10	12	14	16	18
3	3	6	9	12	15	18	21	24	27
4	4	8	12	16	20	24	28	32	36
5	5	10	15	20	25	30	35	40	45
6	6	12	18	24	30	36	42	48	54
7	7	14	21	28	35	42	49	56	63
8	8	16	24	32	40	48	56	64	72
9	9	18	27	36	45	54	63	72	81

Tuition Table

	Day Students	Boarding Students
Grades 1 – 6	$ 6,000.00	$ 18,000.00
Grades 7 – 8	$ 9,000.00	$ 21,000.00
Grades 9 – 12	$ 12,500.00	$ 24,500.00

or

```
double payScaleTable[][];
```

and create the array as

```
payScaleTable = new double[4][5];
```

The payScaleTable array is a *two-dimensional array* because two indices—one for the row and another for the column—are used to refer to an array element. For example, to refer to the element at the second column (column #1) of the third row (row #2), we say

```
payScaleTable[2][1]
```

Figure 9.18 illustrates how the two indices are used to access an array element of a two-dimensional array.

FIGURE 9.18   Accessing an element of a two-dimensional array.

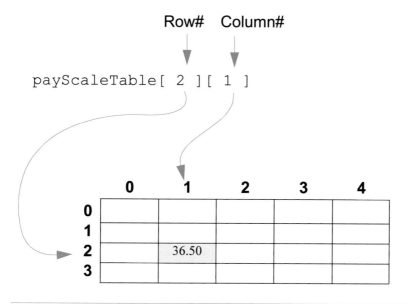

Let's go over some examples to see how the elements of two-dimensional arrays are manipulated. The code below finds the average pay of the Grade 2 programmers.

Chapter 9

```
double average, sum = 0.0;

for (int j = 0; j < 5; j++) {
    sum += payScaleTable[2][j];
}

average = sum / 5;
```

The next example prints out the pay difference between the lowest and highest steps for each grade level.

```
double difference;

for (int i = 0; i < 4; i++) {
    difference = payScaleTable[i][4] - payScaleTable[i][0];
    outputBox.printLine("Pay difference at Grade Level " +
                        i + " is " + difference);
}
```

The following code adds $1.50 to every skill level.

```
for (int i = 0; i < 4; i++) {
    for (int j = 0; j < 5; j++) {
        payScaleTable[i][j] += 1.50;
    }
}
```

In the previous examples, we used literal constants such as 5 and 4 to keep them simple. For real programs, we need to write a loop that will work for two-dimensional arrays of any size, not just with the one with four rows and five columns. We can use the length field of an array to write such a loop. Using the length field, we can rewrite the third example as

```
for (int i = 0; i < payScaleTable.length; i++) {
    for (int j = 0; j < payScaleTable[i].length; j++) {
        payScaleTable[i][j] += 1.50;
    }
}
```

Do you notice a subtle difference in the code? Let's examine the difference between the expressions

```
payScaleTable.length
```

and

```
payScaleTable[i].length
```

First, there is actually no explicit structure called "two-dimensional array" in Java. We only have one-dimensional arrays in Java. However, we can have an array of arrays, and this is how the conceptual two-dimensional array is implemented in Java. The sample array creation

```
payScaleTable = new double[4][5];
```

is really a shorthand for

```
payScaleTable = new double[4][ ];

payScaleTable[0] = new double[5];
payScaleTable[1] = new double[5];
payScaleTable[2] = new double[5];
payScaleTable[3] = new double[5];
```

which is equivalent to

```
payScaleTable = new double[4][ ];

for (int i = 0; i < 4; i++) {
    payScaleTable[i] = new double[5];
}
```

Figure 9.19 shows the effect of executing the five statements. The expression

```
payScaleTable.length
```

refers to the length of the payScaleTable array itself

FIGURE 9.19   Executing the statements on the left in sequence will create the array of arrays shown on the right.

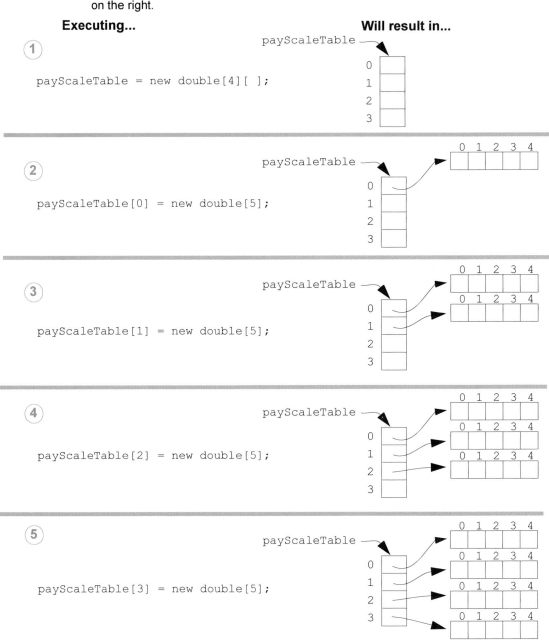

and the expression

```
payScaleTable[1].length
```

refers to the length of an array stored at row 1 of payScaleTable.

payScaleTable

payScaleTable[1].length == 5

We call an array that is part of another a *subarray*. The payScaleTable has four subarrays of the same length. Since we allocate the subarrays individually, we can create subarrays of different length. The following code creates a triangular array whose subarray triangularArray[i] has length i.

```
triangularArray = new double[4][ ];

for (int i = 0; i < 4; i++)
    triangularArray[i] = new double[i+1];
```

The resulting triangularArray looks like

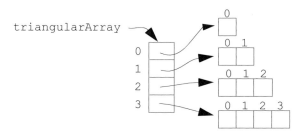

triangularArray

An array of arrays can be initialized at the time of declaration. The following declaration initializes the payScaleTable array:

```
double[][] payScaleTable
      = { {10.50, 12.00, 14.50, 16.75, 18.00},
          {20.50, 22.25, 24.00, 26.25, 28.00},
          {34.00, 36.50, 38.00, 40.35, 43.00},
          {50.00, 60.00, 70.00, 80.00, 99.99}  };
```

There is no limit to the number of dimensions an array can have. We can declare three-dimensional, four-dimensional, and higher-dimensional arrays. However, arrays with dimension higher than two are not frequently used in object-oriented languages. For example, data that were represented as a three-dimensional array in a non-object-oriented language can be represented more naturally as a one-dimensional array of objects with each object containing an array or some other form of data structure (see exercise 13 on page 478).

Quick Check

1. Write a code fragment to compute the average pay of the pays stored in the payScaleTable array.

2. Write a code fragment that finds the largest integer in the following two-dimensional array.

    ```
    int[][] table = new int[10][10];
    ```

3. What is an output from the following code.

    ```
    int[][] table = new int[10][5];

    outputBox.printLine(table.length);
    outputBox.printLine(table[4].length);
    ```

9.8   Vectors

In Section 9.6, we defined a method called enlarge that handles the overflow condition. When the original array runs out of space to store additional Person objects, the enlarge method is used to create a new array whose capacity is 150 percent of the original array. If we have to develop many applications that require overflow handling, we can define a class that handles the overflow condition so we don't have to implement the same enlarge method repeatedly in the applications we develop. We might call the new class ExpandableArray. By using this class, we can keep adding a new element without worrying about the overflow condition because the class handles the overflow condition automatically.

It turns out there's no need for us to write such ExpandableArray class because the Java standard library java.util already includes a class called Vector. The Vector class implements an expandable array of objects. Internally, the Vector class maintains an array of objects, and when the overflow condition occurs,

java.util

its array is replaced with a bigger array. In this section, we describe the basics of the Vector class.

Here's a code that creates a vector named friends and adds four Person objects to the vector:

```
import java.util.*;                    The Vector class is
...                                    defined in this package.
Vector friends;
Person person;
                                       This creates a vector whose
                                       internal data array has the
friends = new Vector( );               default capacity of 10.

person = new Person("jane", 10, 'F');
friends.add( person );

person = new Person("jack",  6, 'M');  Adds a new person to
friends.add( person );                 the end of the vector.

person = new Person("jill",  8, 'F');
friends.add( person );

person = new Person("john", 14, 'M');
friends.add( person );
```

When we create a new Vector object friends with the default constructor as

```
friends = new Vector( );
```

the friends vector is created with the default initial capacity of 10. When we add the eleventh element to this vector, the capacity is doubled, that is, its internal data array is replaced with a new array that is double in capacity. In this example, the new capacity of friends will be 20. The second time the overflow occurs, the capacity will be increased to 40, and so on.

Although the increase in capacity is handled automatically by the Vector class, it does not mean the operation is free. It costs time to replace the existing internal data array with the one bigger in capacity. So if we know beforehand that we will use, say, a minimum of 500 Person objects, then we should create a vector with 500 as its initial capacity. We can create such a vector by passing the initial capacity in the constructor as

```
friends = new Vector( 500 );
```

Chapter 9

This way we do not have to worry about the costly operation of doubling the internal data array until we add the 501st **Person** object. Now, since the default increment is to double the capacity, the new capacity of friends will be 1000 **Person** objects when the 501st person is added to the vector. If the default increment of doubling the capacity is too much, we can designate the capacity increment when we create a vector. The following statement will create a vector with the initial capacity of 250 and the capacity increment of 20:

```
friends = new Vector( 250, 20 );
```

Instead of doubling in capacity, the capacity will increase in the sequence of 250, 270, 290, 310, and so forth. We must be careful here not to make the capacity increment too small, since that will increase the frequency of overflow occurrence.

To find out the current capacity of a vector, we use its capacity method. To find out the number of objects contained in a vector, we use its size method. The following code will print out 10 and 3:

```
Vector sample = new Vector( );

sample.add( "one java" );
sample.add( "two java" );
sample.add( "three"    );

System.out.println( sample.capacity( ) + "     " +
                    sample.size( )                     );
```

Objects we store in a vector can be accessed by giving their index position in the vector, much like the way we did with the array. We use the elementAt method to access an object at index i as

> Type casting is required.

```
Person p = (Person) friends.elementAt( i );
```

Notice that we need to type cast the element to a **Person** object because the elements inside a vector can be an instance of any class. A compile-time error will occur if we forget to type cast the returned element.

Here's a code to display the name of all **Person** objects in the friends vector:

```
Person p;

int limit = friends.size( );
```

```
for (int i = 0; i < limit; i++ ) {

    p = (Person) friends.elementAt( i );

    System.out.println( p.getName( ) );
}
```

Another approach to scan the elements inside a vector is to use the elements method. When we call the elements method of a vector, an Enumeration object that supports two methods hasMoreElements and nextElement is returned. Here's how we print out the name of all Person objects using the second approach:

```
Person p;
Enumeration enum = friends.elements( );            Check if there are
                                                    more elements to
while ( enum.hasMoreElements( ) ) {                 access.

    p = (Person) enum.nextElement( );              Access the next
                                                    element.
    System.out.println( p.getName( ) );
}
```

The nextElement method returns the next element in the enumeration. When the method is called for the first time, the first element is returned if the enumeration is not empty. The second element is returned when the method is called for the second time; and so on. It will be an error to call the nextElement method when there are no more elements to access in the enumeration. To check wheter the enumeration has more elements, we use the hasMoreElements method. It returns true if there are more elements in the enumeration to access.

Using the second approach is restrictive because you can access the elements only in one direction, starting from the first element. With the first approach, you can visit the elements in any order by changing the parameter you pass in the elementAt method. So what is the advantage of the second approach? First, accessing the elements from the first to the last element in a simple linear order is a very commonly used operation for a collection of objects, and the use of enumeration is a handy way to do this. Second, although we limit our discussion to the Vector class in this section, the Java standard library java.util includes other classes that handle a collection of objects (these classes are called *Collection* classes). All of these Collection classes support the elements method, but only some of them support the elementsAt method. So the second approach can be used without change even if we implement friends using a Collection class different from Vector, while the first appproach can be used only when friends is implemented with a Collection class that supports the elementsAt method.

To remove an element from a vector, we can use the remove method with the index of an element to be removed as its parameter. The following code removes the third Person object from friends:

```
friends.remove( 2 ); //the third Person is at index 2
```

All elements after the removed element are moved one position to fill the hole created by the removal of the second element. So the third, fourth, fifth, and other elements before the removal become the second, third, fourth, and so forth, elements after the removal. The size of the vector is reduced by one after the removal.

Unlike an array, a vector cannot include primitive data such as int and double values as its elements. A vector element must be an instance of some class. The following code, therefore, will result in a compile-time error:

```
Vector sample = new Vector( );

sample.add( 15 );
sample.add( 30 );
```

If we need to add primitive data values to a vector, then we must use wrapper classes such as Integer, Float, and Double. Wrapper classes are explained in Section 5.5. To add integers, we have to do something like this:

```
Vector intVector = new Vector( );

intVector.add( new Integer( 15 ) );
intVector.add( new Integer( 30 ) );
...
```

When we access the elements of intVector, they are Integer objects, so we need to use the intValue method of the Integer class to get the integer value. The following code displays the integer values stored in intVector:

```
Integer intObject;
Enumeration enum = intVector.elements( );

while ( enum.hasMoreElements( ) ) {

    intObject = (Integer) enum.nextElement( );

    System.out.println( intObject.intValue( ) );
}
```

This covers the basics of using the Vector class. For additional methods not covered in this section, please refer the Java 2 API reference for the Vector class. A sample program that uses the Vector class can be found at the book's web site.

For additional discussion on vectors and a sample program using the Vector ***class, please visit*** www.drcaffeine.com/additionaltopics*.*

Quick Check

1. What is the output from the following code?

   ```
   Vector vector = new Vector( 3, 2 );

   for (int i = 0; i < 6; i++ ) {
      vector.add( "element " + i );
      System.out.println( vector.capacity( ) + "    " +
                          vector.size( ) );
   }
   ```

2. What is the output from the following code?

   ```
   Vector vector = new Vector( );

   for (int i = 0; i < 6; i++ ) {
      vector.add( "element " + i );
   }

   vector.remove( 1 );
   vector.remove( 3 );

   System.out.println( vector.elementAt( 2 ) );
   ```

9.9   Exercises

1. Identify problems with the following code:

```
public int searchAccount ( int[25] number )
{
    number = new int[15];

    for (int i = 0; i < number.length; i++)
        number[i] = number[i-1] + number[i+1];

    return number;
}
```

2. Identify problems with the following code:

```
class Q2
{
    private int alpha;
    private int beta;

    public static void classMethod()
    {
        this.beta = this.alpha * 2;
    }

    public Q2( )
    {
        Q2( 0, 0 );
    }

    public Q2( int x, int y )
    {
        alpha = this.x;
        beta = this.y;
    }
}
```

3. Declare an array of float of size 365 to store daily temperatures for one year. Using this data structure, write the code to find

    • The hottest and coldest days of the year.

    • The average temperature of each month.

    • The difference between the hottest and coldest days of every month.

- The temperature of any given day. The day is specified by two input values: month (1 . . . 12) and day (1 . . . 31). Reject invalid input values (e.g., 13 for month and 32 for day).

4. Repeat exercise 3 using a two-dimensional array of float with 12 rows and each row having either 28, 30, or 31 columns.

5. Repeat exercise 3 using an array of Month objects with each Month object having an array of float of size 28, 30, or 31.

6. For exercises 3 to 5, the following three data structures are used:
   - 1-D array of float of size 365.
   - 2-D array of float with 12 rows. Each row has either 28, 30, or 31 columns.
   - An array of Month objects with each Month object having an array of float of size 28, 30, or 31.

   Discuss the pros and cons of each approach.

7. Suppose you want to maintain the highest and lowest temperatures for every day of the year. What kind of data structure would you use? Describe the alternatives and list their pros and cons.

8. If a car dealer's service department wants a program to keep track of customer appointments, which data structure would you choose, an array or a vector? If the number of appointments they accept is fixed on any given day, which data structure is appropriate? What are the criteria you use to decide which data structure to use? Explain.

9. In Figure 9.8 on page 430, the last statement

   ```
   person[last] = null;
   ```

   is significant. Show the state-of-memory diagram when the last statement is not executed.

10. Write an application that computes the standard deviation of N real numbers. The standard deviation s is computed according to the following formula:

$$s = \sqrt{\frac{(x_1 - \bar{x})^2 + (x_2 - \bar{x})^2 + \cdots + (x_N - \bar{x})^2}{N}}$$

The variable $\bar{x}$ is the average of N input values x_1 through x_N. The program first prompts the user for N and then declares any array of size N.

11. Using the payScaleTable 2-D array from Section 9.7, write the code to find
  - the average pay for every grade level
  - the average pay for every step (i.e., average of every column)

12. Declare a 2-D array for the tuition table shown in Figure 9.17.

13. Suppose you want to maintain information on the location where a product is stored in a warehouse. Would you use a three-dimensional array such as location[i][j][k] where i is the warehouse number, j is the aisle number, and k is the bin number? Or would you define three classes Warehouse, Aisle, and Bin? Describe the alternatives and list their pros and cons.

14. The search method of the AddressBook class returns only one Person object. Modify the method so that it will return all Person objects that match the search criteria. You can use an array to return multiple Person objects.

15. Write new search routines for the AddressBook class. The search method given in the chapter finds a person with a given name. Add second and third search methods that find all persons given an age and a gender, respectively.

16. Modify the add method of the AddressBook class. The method given in the chapter does not check for any duplicate names. Modify the method so that no Person object with a duplicate name is added to the address book.

17. Modify the AddressBook class to allow the programmer to access all Person objects in the address book. Make this modification by adding two methods: getFirstPerson and getNextPerson. The getFirstPerson method returns the first Person object in the book. The getNextPerson method returns the next Person object if there is one. If there is no next person in the book, getNextPerson returns null. The getFirstPerson method must be called before calling the getNextPerson method.

18. Write a complete address book maintenance application. The user of the program has four options: add a new person, delete a person, modify the data of a person, and search for a person by giving the name. Use the AddressBook class, either the original one from the chapter or the modified one from the previous exercises. You have to decide how to allow the user to enter the values for a new person, display person information, and so forth.

19. Design a currency converter class whose instance will handle conversion of all currencies. In Chapter 4 we designed a currency converter class where we created one instance for each currency. A single instance of the new currency converter class you design here will handle all currencies. Instead of having specific conversion methods such as toDollar, toYen, and so forth, the new currency converter class supports one generic conversion method called **exchange**. The method has three arguments: fromCurrency, toCurrency, and amount. The first two arguments are String and give the names of currencies. The third argument is float. To convert 250 dollars to yen, we write

```
yen = converter.exchange( "dollar", "yen", 250.0 );
```

To set the exchange rate for a currency, we use the **setRate** method. This method takes two arguments: the first argument is the currency name and the second argument is the rate. For example, if the exchange rate for yen is 140 yen to a dollar, then we write

```
converter.setRate( "yen", 140.0 );
```

Use an array to keep track of exhange rates.

20. Extend the Java^2 Lo-Fat Burgers drive-through ordering system of exercise 16 on page 285 so the program can output sales figures. For each item on the menu, the program keeps track of the sales. At closing time, the program will output the sales figure in a format similar to the following:

```
    Item           Sales Count              Total
Tofu Burger            25              $   87.25
Cajun Chicken          30              $  137.70
   ...


    Today's Total Sales:   $ 2761.20
```

21. Extend the watermelon projectile computing program of exercise 23 on page 350 to output the average distance covered between each time interval. Use the formula

$$\sqrt{(x_2 - x_1) + (y_2 - y_1)}$$

to compute the distance between two coordinate points (x_1, y_1) and (x_2, y_2).

10

Sorting and Searching

OBJECTIVES

After you have read and studied this chapter, you should be able to

- Perform linear and binary search algorithms on small arrays.
- Determine whether a linear or binary search is more effective for a given situation.
- Perform selection and bubble sort algorithms.
- Describe the heapsort algorithm and show how its performance is superior to the other two algorithms.
- Apply basic sorting algorithms to sort an array of objects.

Introduction

In this chapter, we cover searching and sorting. In the previous chapter, we presented a case study of maintaining an address book and described a basic searching method to locate a student given his/her name. In this chapter, we will present a better searching algorithm called *binary search*. Another fundamental operation we study in computer science is sorting—a technique to arrange elements in some order. We will explain basic sorting algorithms in this chapter. To keep our examples simple, we will use an array of integers to illustrate searching and sorting algorithms, but all the techniques we present here are equally applicable to any array of objects as well as primitive data types.

10.1 Searching

Let's start with the problem statement for searching:

> *Given a value* X, *return the index of* X *in the array, if such* X *exists. Otherwise, return* NOT_FOUND *(–1). We assume there are no duplicate entries in the array.*

successful and
unsuccessful
searches

There are two possible outcomes in searching: either we locate an *X* or we don't. We will call the first a *successful search* and the latter an *unsuccessful search*. Figure 10.1 illustrates the successful and unsuccessful searches. As obvious as this may sound, it is critical to differentiate the two because it is possible for one searching algorithm to perform superbly for successful searches, but very poorly for unsuccessful searches. When we analyze the performance of a searching

FIGURE 10.1   Successful and unsuccessful searches.

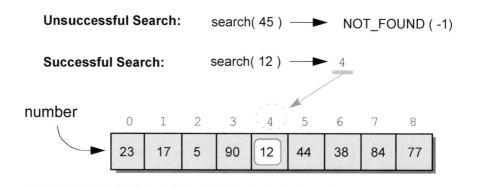

algorithm, we normally derive two separate performances, one for a successful search and another for an unsuccessful search.

Linear Search

linear search

The search technique we used earlier in the book is called a *linear search* because we search the array from the first to the last position in a linear progression. The linear search is also called a *sequential search*. The linear search algorithm can be expressed as

```
public int linearSearch ( int[] number, int searchValue )
{
    int       loc   = 0;

    while ( loc < number.length &&
            number[loc] != searchValue ) {

        loc++;
    }

    if ( loc == number.length) { //Not found
        return NOT_FOUND;
    }
    else {
        return loc;                //Found, return the position
    }
}
```

> There are still more elements to search.

> And **searchValue** is not found yet.

If the number of entries in the array is N, then there will be N comparisons for an unsuccessful search (i.e., you search for a value not in the array). In the case of a successful search, there will be a minimum of one comparison and a maximum of N comparisons. On the average, there will be approximately $N/2$ comparisons.

Is there a way to improve the linear search? If the array is sorted, then we can improve the search routine using the binary search technique.

Binary Search

binary search

If the values in the array are arranged in ascending or descending order, then we call the array *sorted*. In the following explanation of the binary search, we assume the array is sorted in ascending order. The crux of binary search is the winning strategy you apply for the Hi-Lo game. When you try to guess a secret number, say, between 1 and 100, your first guess would be 50. If your guess is HI, then you know the secret number is between 1 and 49. If your guess is LO, then you know the secret number is between 51 and 100. By guessing once, you eliminated half of the possible range of values from further consideration. This is the core idea of binary search.

Consider the following sorted array:

Let's suppose we are searching for 77. We first search the middle position of the array. Since this array has 9 elements, the index of the middle position is 4, so we search number[4]. The value 77 is not in this position. Since 77 is larger than 38 and because the array is sorted, we know that if 77 is in the array, it must be in the right half of the array. So next, we search the middle position of the right half of the array, which is position 6. Figure 10.2 illustrates the effect of making one comparison in the binary search.

The search value 77 was found after two comparisons. In contrast, the linear search would take seven comparisons to locate 77. So there is a net reduction of five comparisons. How good is the binary search in general? Let's study the worst-case situation. In the binary search, after we make one comparison, we can eliminate one-half of the array from further consideration. So the number of comparisons in the worst case is the number of times you can divide the array into halves. Suppose the original size of an array is N and the value we search is not in the array. Then after one comparison, we have to search the remaining $N/2$ elements. After two comparisons, we have to search $N/4$ elements, and so on. The following table shows this relationship. The left column is the number of comparisons and the right column is the number of elements we still need to search after making K comparisons.

Number of Comparisons	Number of Elements
0	N
1	$N/2 = N/2^1$
2	$N/4 = N/2^2$
. . .	. . .
K	$N/2^K$

FIGURE 10.2   Effect of one comparison in binary search.

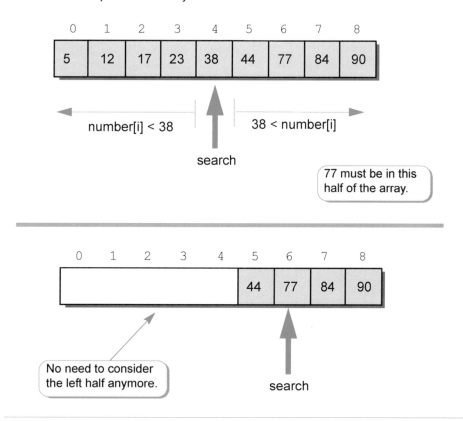

The maximum number of comparisons K is derived by solving the following equation:

$$N = 2^K$$

$$\log_2 N = K$$

This is a remarkable improvement. If the size of the original array is 2048, for example, then the unsuccessful binary search takes at most $\log_2 2048 = 10$ comparisons, while the unsuccessful linear search takes 2048 comparisons. The difference between the two algorithms gets larger and larger as the size of an array gets larger.

Now let's write a binary search method. The key point in the method is how to stop the search. If the search value is in the array, we will eventually locate it, so the stopping condition for the successful search is easy. What about the case for an unsuccessful search? How can we detect that there are no more elements in the array to search for? Should we use some kind of a counter? We certainly can use a counter, but we can implement the method without using any counter. To compute the middle location for the next comparison, we need two indexes— low and high. The low and high indexes are initialized to 0 and N−1. The middle location is computed as

```
mid = (low + high) / 2; //the result is truncated
```

If number[mid] is less than the search value, then low is reset to mid+1. If number[mid] is greater than the search value, then high is reset to mid−1. And the search continues. Eventually, we will locate the search value or we will run out of elements to compare. We know that there are no more elements to compare when low becomes larger than high. Figure 10.3 shows how this works.

Here's the binarySearch method:

```java
public int binarySearch ( int[] number, int searchValue )
{
    int      low   = 0,
             high  = number.length - 1,
             mid   = (low + high) / 2;

    while ( low <= high && number[mid] != searchValue ) {

        if (number[mid] < searchValue) {
            low = mid + 1;
        }
        else  { //number[mid] > searchValue
            high = mid - 1;
        }

        mid   = (low + high) / 2;
    }

    if ( low > high) {
        mid = NOT_FOUND;
    }

    return mid;
}
```

FIGURE 10.3   How the unsuccessful search is terminated in the binary search routine.

Quick Check

1. Suppose an array contains 2048 elements. What are the least and the most numbers of comparisons for a successful search using linear search?

2. Repeat the previous question with binary search.

10.2 Sorting

In this section we will describe two basic sorting algorithms. A more advanced sorting algorithm will be presented in Section 10.3. Let's start with the problem statement for sorting:

Given an array of N values, arrange the values into ascending order.

Selection Sort

Given a list of integers, how would you sort them? The most natural sorting algorithm for a human looks something like this:

1. Find the smallest integer in the list.

2. Cross out the number from further consideration and copy it to a new (sorted) list.

3. Repeat Steps 1 and 2 until all numbers are crossed out in the list.

Figure 10.4 shows this human sorting algorithm with the first three numbers being copied to the new list.

FIGURE 10.4 Human sorting algorithm after three numbers are moved to the sorted list.

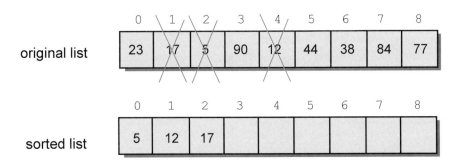

We can write a real computer program based on this sorting algorithm, but the resulting program will not be a good one. There are two problems. First, we need an extra array to keep the sorted list. This may not sound like much, but when you consider an array of, say, 10,000 elements, using a second array is very wasteful. Second, crossing out numbers is effective for humans only. We humans can see the cross marks and will not consider the numbers once they are crossed out, but in computer programs, we still have to write code to check every element whether it is crossed out or not. We can "cross out" an element by replacing it with a negative number, say, −1, if the numbers are all positive. If not, then we have to use other means to "cross out" an element. So crossing out the numbers does not reduce the number of comparisons in the program.

Although we do not want to implement this human sorting algorithm as is, we can derive an algorithm based on the idea of finding the smallest number in a given list and moving it to the correct position in the list. This sorting algorithm is called *selection sort*.

The selection sort is comprised of *passes*. Figure 10.5 shows the effect of the first pass on a sample array of *N* (= 9) elements. First we locate the smallest element in the array and set the index min to point to this element. Then we exchange number[start] and number[min]. After the first pass, the smallest element is moved to the correct position. We increment the value of start by one and then execute the second pass. We start the first pass with start = 0 and end the last pass with start = N-2. Figure 10.6 shows the sequence of eight passes made to the sample array.

selection sort

sorting passes

FIGURE 10.5   Effect of executing the first pass in the selection sort.

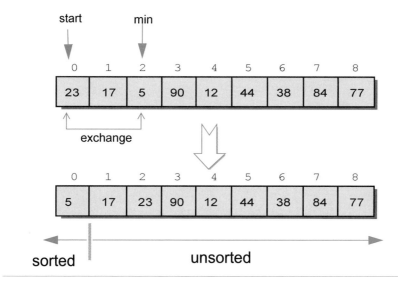

Here's the selectionSort method:

```
public void selectionSort( int[] number )
{
    int startIndex, minIndex, length, temp;
    length = number.length;

    for (startIndex = 0; startIndex <= length-2; startIndex++){
        //each iteration of the for loop is one pass
```

FIGURE 10.6   Eight passes to sort the sample array of nine elements.

```
            minIndex = startIndex;

            //find the smallest in this pass at
            //position minIndex
            for (i = startIndex+1; i <= length-1; i++) {
                if (number[i] < number[minIndex]) minIndex = i;
            }
            //exchange number[startIndex] and number[minIndex]
            temp                = number[startIndex];
            number[startIndex]  = number[minIndex];
            number[minIndex]    = temp;
        }
    }
```

Let's analyze the selection sort algorithm. In analyzing different sorting algorithms, we normally count two things: the number of comparisons and the number of data movements (exchanges). We will show you how to count the number of comparisons here. Counting the number of data movements is left as an exercise. Keep in mind that the analysis we provide in this chapter is an informal one. A detailed analysis is beyond the scope of this book, so we will give only a taste of the formal analysis.

The selection sort has one comparison (the if statement inside the nested-for loop), so we can easily count the total number of comparisons by counting the number of times the inner loop is executed. For each execution of the outer loop, the inner loop is executed length – start times. The variable start ranges from 0 to length-2. So the total number of comparisons is computed by finding the sum of the right column in the following table:

Start	Number of Comparisons (Length – Start)
0	length
1	length – 1
2	length – 2
. . .	. . .
length – 2	2

The variable length is the size of the array. Replacing length with N, the size of the array, the sum of the right column is

$$N + (N - 1) + (N - 2) + \cdots + 2$$

$$= \sum_{i = 2}^{N} i = \left(\sum_{i = 1}^{N} i \right) - 1 = \frac{N(N + 1)}{2} - 1$$

$$= \frac{N^2 + N - 2}{2} \cong N^2$$

The total number of comparisons is approximately the square of the size of an array. This is a quadratic function, so the number of comparisons grows very fast as the size of an array gets larger. Is there a better sorting algorithm? The answer is yes.

Bubble Sort

The effect of one pass of the selection sort is the movement of the smallest element to its correct position. Since an array gets sorted only by moving the elements to their correct position, the whole sorting routine will complete sooner if we increase the number of data movements. In the selection sort, we make one exchange per pass. If we could move more elements toward their correct positions in one pass, we would be able to complete the sorting sooner than with the selection sort. The bubble sort is one such algorithm that increases the number of data movements for the same number of comparisons as the selection sort makes.

The key point of the bubble sort is to make pairwise comparisons and exchange the positions of the pair if they are out of order. Figure 10.7 shows the effect of pairwise comparisons in the first past of the bubble sort. After the first pass, the largest element 90 has moved to its correct position in the array. This is the guaranteed effect of one pass. In addition, we notice that many other elements also have moved toward their correct position, like bubbles move toward the water's surface.

In the worst case, the bubble sort will make $N-1$ passes, so the worst case performance is the same as for the selection sort. However, in the average case, we can expect a better performance from the bubble sort. The bubble sort exhibits the following two properties:

- After one pass through the array, the largest element will be at the end of the array.

- During one pass, if no pair of consecutive entries is out of order, then the array is sorted.

Using these properties, we can express the bubbleSort method in pseudocode as

```
bottom    = number.length - 2;
exchanged = true;

while ( exchanged ) { //continue if the exchange is made

    //do one pass of sorting
    exchanged = false; //reset the variable

    for (i = 0; i <= bottom; i++) { //pairwise comparison
        if ( number[i] > number[i+1] ) {
            //the pair is out of order
            exchange them;

            exchanged = true; //an exchange is made
        }
    }
    //one pass is done, decrement the bottom index by one
    bottom--;
}
```

This **while** loop performs at most $N-1$ passes for an array with N elements. The loop will terminate when there are no exchanges in one pass.

One pass of bubble sort.

FIGURE 10.7 Effect of executing the first pass in the bubble sort.

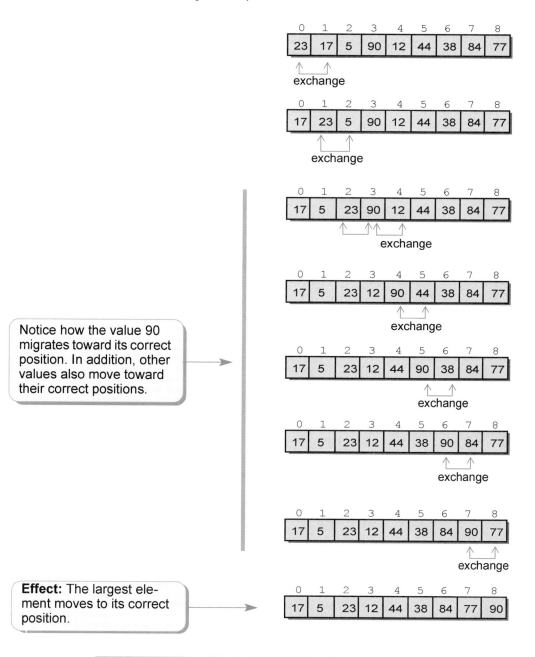

Notice how the value 90 migrates toward its correct position. In addition, other values also move toward their correct positions.

Effect: The largest element moves to its correct position.

Translating the pseudocode into an actual method, we have

```
public void bubbleSort( int[] number )
{
    int       temp, bottom, i;
    boolean   exchanged = true;

    bottom = number.length - 2;

    while ( exchanged )  {

        exchanged = false;

        for (i = 0; i <= bottom; i++) {
            if (number[i] > number[i+1]) {

                temp        = number[i];      //exchange
                number[i]   = number[i+1];
                number[i+1] = temp;

                exchanged   = true; //exchange is made

            }
        }

        bottom--;
    }
}
```

On average, we expect the bubble sort to finish sorting sooner than the selection sort, because there will be more data movements for the same number of
comparisons and there is a test to exit the method when the array gets sorted.
The worst case of the bubble sort happens when the original array is in descending order. Notice that if the original array is already sorted, the bubble sort will
perform only one pass whereas the selection sort will perform $N - 1$ passes.

Quick Check

1. Show the result of the second pass of bubble sort applied to the array
    at the bottom of Figure 10.7.

2. For an array with N elements, what is the least number of compari-
    sons the bubble sort will execute?

10.3 Heapsort

Selection and bubble sorts are two fundamental sorting algorithms that take approximately N^2 comparisons to sort an array of N elements. One interesting sorting algorithm that improves this performance to approximately $1.5N \log_2 N$ is *heapsort*. We will describe the heapsort algorithm and analyze its performance in this section.

heapsort

The heapsort algorithm uses a special data structure called a *heap*. A heap consists of nodes, which contain data values, and edges, which link the nodes. Figure 10.8 shows a sample heap. We use integers as data values for the examples in this section. The topmost node is called the *root* of a heap. Nodes in a heap are indexed 0, 1, 2, and so forth in the top-to-bottom, left-to-right order starting from the root. A node in a heap has either zero, one, or two *children*. The children of a node are distinguished as the node's *left* and *right children*. If a node has only one child, then it is the left child of the node.

root node

left and right children

FIGURE 10.8   A sample heap that includes nine nodes.

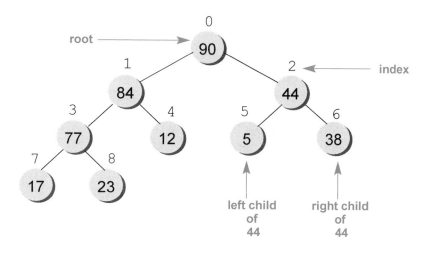

heap constraints

A heap must satisfy the following two constraints:

1. **Structural Constraint**: Nodes in a heap with N nodes must occupy the positions numbered 0, 1, ..., $N–1$. Figure 10.9 shows examples of nonheaps that violate the structural constraint.

2. **Value Relationship Constraint**: A value stored in a node must be larger than the maximum of the values stored in its left and right children. Figure 10.10 shows examples of nonheaps that violate the value relationship constraint.

FIGURE 10.9   Sample heaps and nonheaps that violate the structural constraint.

FIGURE 10.10   Sample heaps and nonheaps that violate the value relationship constraint. Violations are indicated by blue ellipses.

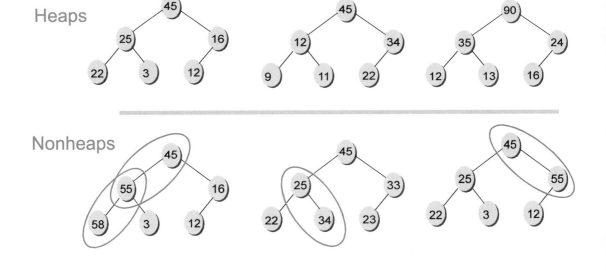

heapsort
phases

How can we use the heap structure to sort N elements? Heapsort is carried out in two phases:

1. **Construction Phase**: Construct a heap given N elements.

2. **Extraction Phase**: Pull out the value in the root successively, creating a new heap with one less element after each extraction step.

We will begin the description of heapsort from the extraction phase. Consider the heap shown in Figure 10.8. Since every node in the heap satisfies the value relationship constraint, we can conclude that the value in the root node is the largest among the values stored in the heap. Now, after we remove the value 90 from the heap, we must create a new heap that has one less element. We can build such a heap by first moving the last element (value 23 in the figure) to the root position. With the value 23 in the root position, we have met the structural constraint for the heap with 8 elements. However, the value relationship constraint is not met. The violation occurs because 23 is smaller than the larger of its two children. By swapping 84 and 23, the violation is eliminated. Since the value 23 is now at a new location, we must check again if the violation occurs at this position. It does, because 77 is larger than 23, so we swap again. We repeat the process until there are no more children to consider or the value moved into a new position meets the value relationship constraint. We will call this process

rebuild step

a *rebuild step*. One rebuild step is illustrated in Figure 10.11.

Using a heap with N elements, we can sort the given N elements by performing the rebuild steps $N-1$ times. Figure 10.12 illustrates the rebuild steps for the sample heap. Notice how the array for the sorted list is filled from the end. All we have to do now is to figure out how to build a heap from a given unsorted list of N elements. Let's study the construction phase of the algorithm.

We will illustrate the construction phase with the following unsorted nine elements:

```
23, 17, 5, 90, 12, 44, 38, 84, 77
```

If we assign the given numbers to a heap structure in the ascending index order, we have the heap structure shown in Figure 10.13. This heap structure is not truly a heap because it violates the value relationship constraint. The construction phase will eliminate any violations of the value relationship contraint. The key concept for the construction phase is the rebuild step we used in the extraction phase. We will bulid a complete heap in a bottom-up fashion. We start out with a small heap and gradually build bigger and bigger heaps until the heap contains all N elements. Figure 10.14 shows the sequence of rebuild steps. The triangles indicate where the rebuild steps are applied. In the extraction step, the rebuild step is always applied to the root node. In the construction step, each rebuild

FIGURE 10.11 One rebuild step after the value 90 is pulled out from the heap. Net result of a single rebuild step is a new heap that contains one less element.

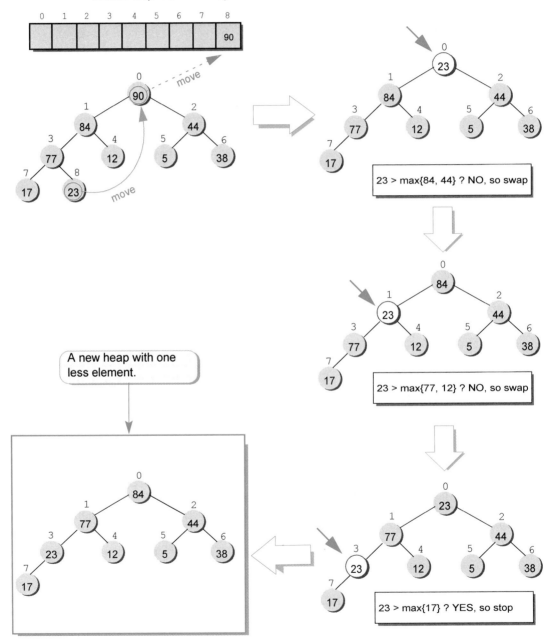

FIGURE 10.12   Eight rebuild steps to sort a heap with 9 elements.

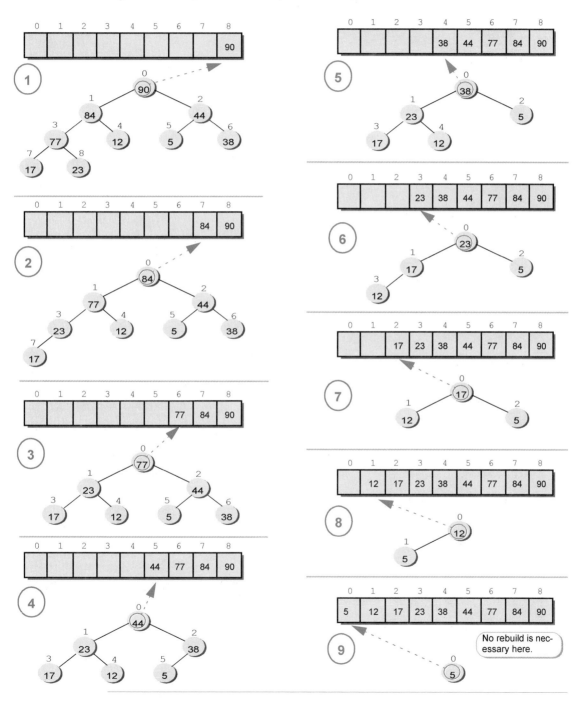

FIGURE 10.13   A heap structure with given numbers assigned in the ascending index order.

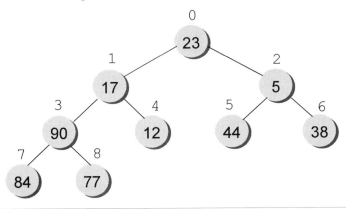

step is applied successively, beginning with the node at index $\lfloor (N-2)/2 \rfloor$ and ending with the node at index 0 (i.e., the root node).

Now let's consider how we can implement this algorithm in Java. We must first decide how to represent a heap. Among the possible alternatives, the data structure we learned in this book that can be used here very effectively is an array. Figure 10.15 shows the correspondence between the heap and the array representation. An important aspect in deciding which data structure to use is the ease of locating a given node's left and right child. With an array implementation, we can locate any node's left and right child easily. A node with index I has its left child at index $2 \cdot I + 1$ and right child at index $2 \cdot I + 2$.

Since the heapsort algoithm is more involved than the insertion or bubble sort algorithm, we will put all the necessary code in a single class called Heap to provide a complete picture. To simplify our implementation so we can focus on the algorithm, we will allow only integers. You can modify the class to allow any objects to be sorted; see exercise 9 on page 517. The following code illustrates how to use the Heap class:

```
int[ ] number = { 90, 44, 84, 12, 77, 23, 38, 5, 17 };
int[ ] sortedList;

Heap heap = new Heap( );

heap.setData( number );   //assign the original list

sortedList = heap.sort( );//sort the list

for (int i = 0; i < sortedList.length; i++ ) { //print out
    System.out.print("   " + sortedList[i]);   //the sorted
}                                              //list
```

FIGURE 10.14   Sequence of rebuild steps applied in the construction phase. Rebuild steps are carried out at index positions 3, 2, 1, and 0.

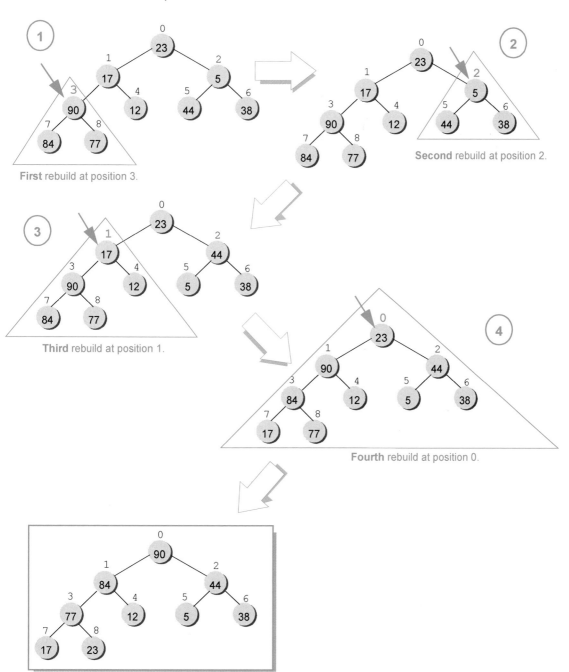

FIGURE 10.15   A sample heap and the corresponding array implementation.

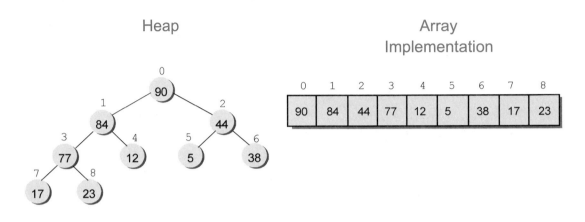

The Heap class will include two arrays as its data members: one to implement a heap and another to store the sorted list.

```
/**
 * This class implements the heapsort algorithm. This class
 * can sort only integers.
 */
class Heap
{
    /**
     * Implements the heap
     */
    private int[ ] heap;

    /**
     * Stores the sorted list
     */
    private int[ ] sortedList;

    // methods come here
    . . .
}
```

Now let's look at the methods. The setData method initializes the two data members as follows:

```
public void setData( int[ ] data )
{
    heap        = new int[ data.length ];
    sortedList = new int[ data.length ];

    for (int i = 0; i < data.length; i++ ) {
        heap[i] = data[i];
    }
}
```

Notice that we copy the contents of the data array to the heap array. If we simply assign the parameter to the data member heap as

```
heap = data;
```

then all we are doing is setting two names referring to the same object, see Figure 9.9 on page 433. Since we do not want to change the original data array, we make a separate copy.

The sort method calls two private methods that implement the two phases of the heapsort alorithm:

```
public int[ ] sort( )
{
    construct( );   //perform the construction phase

    extract( );    //perform the extraction phase

    return sortedList;
}
```

Here's the construct method:

```
private void construct( )
{
    int      current, maxChildIndex;
    boolean done;

    for (int i = (heap.length-2) / 2; i >= 0; i--) {

        current = i;
        done    = false;

        while ( !done ) {//perform one rebuild step
                         //with the node at index i
```

```
                          if ( 2*current+1 > heap.length-1 ) {
                              //current node has no children, so stop
                              done = true;
                          }
                          else {
                              //current node has at least one child,
                              //get the index of larger child
                              maxChildIndex
                                      = maxChild( current, heap.length-1 );

                              if ( heap[current] < heap[maxChildIndex] ) {

                                  //a child is larger, so swap and continue
                                  swap( current, maxChildIndex );
                                  current = maxChildIndex;
                              }
                              else { //the value relationship constraint
                                      //is satisfied, so stop
                                  done = true;
                              }
                          }
                      }
                  }

              testPrint( heap.length );   //TEMP
          }
```

And here's the **extract** method:

```
          private void extract( )
          {
              int     current, maxChildIndex;
              boolean done;

              for (int size = heap.length-1; size >= 0; size--) {

                  //remove the root node data
                  sortedList[size] = heap[ 0 ];

                  //move the last node to the root
                  heap[ 0 ] = heap[size];

                  //rebuild the heap with one less element
                  current = 0;
                  done    = false;

                  while ( !done ) {
```

```
            if ( 2*current+1 > size ) {
                //current node has no children, so stop
                done = true;
            }
            else {
                //current node has at least one child,
                //get the index of larger child
                maxChildIndex = maxChild( current, size );

                if ( heap[current] < heap[maxChildIndex] ) {

                    //a child is larger, so swap and continue
                    swap( current, maxChildIndex );
                    current = maxChildIndex;
                }
                else { //value relationship constraint
                       //is satisfied, so stop
                    done = true;
                }
            }
        }

        testPrint( size );   //TEMP
    }
}
```

A number of methods are shared by both methods. The maxChild method
returns the index of a node's left or right child, whichever is the larger. This
method is called only if a node has at least one child. The first parameter is the
index of a node and the second parameter is the index of the last node in a heap.
The second parameter is necessary to determine whether a node has a right child
or not. The method is defined as follows:

```
private int maxChild( int location, int end )
{
    //Precondition: node at location has at least one child

    int result, leftChildIndex, rightChildIndex;

    rightChildIndex = 2*location + 2;
    leftChildIndex  = 2*location + 1;

    if ( rightChildIndex <= end &&
            heap[leftChildIndex] < heap[rightChildIndex]) {

        result = rightChildIndex;
    }
```

```
        else {
            result = leftChildIndex;
        }

        return result;
    }
```

The other two methods shared by the **construct** and **extract** methods are swap and testPrint. The **swap** method interchanges the contents of two array elements and the **testPrint** method outputs the heap array for verification and debugging purposes. You can comment out the calls to **testPrint** from the **construct** and **extract** methods after you verify that the algorithm is implemented correctly. Here are the two methods:

```
    private void swap ( int loc1, int loc2 )
    {                                               \
        int temp;

        temp = heap[loc1];
        heap[loc1] = heap[loc2];
        heap[loc2] = temp;
    }


    private void testPrint( int limit )
    {
        for (int i = 0; i < limit; i++) {
            System.out.print ( " " + heap[i] );
        }

        System.out.println ( "    " );
    }
```

There are several improvements we can make to the simple Heap class we provided here. These improvements are left as exercises.

Performance

How good is the heapsort? We mentioned in the previous section that the performances of both selection and bubble sort algorithms are approximately N^2 comparisons for sorting N elements. The heapsort algorithm is substantially more complex in design and implementation than the other two basic sorting algorithms. Is the extra complexity worth our effort? The answer is yes. The performance of the heapsort algorithm is approximately $1.5N\log_2 N$ comparisons for sorting N elements. This is a remarkable improvement. Consider the difference between the two performances for a large N. For example, to sort 100,000 elements, the selection or bubble sort requires 10,000,000,000 comparisons, while the heapsort requires only $1.5 \cdot 100{,}000 \log_2 100{,}000 \approx 2{,}491{,}695$ comparisons. If a single comparison takes one microsecond (one millionth of a second), then the selection or bubble sort takes about 2.8 hours while the heapsort takes only about 2.492 seconds. (Note: The sorting operation itself may complete in a few seconds, but printing out the sorted 100,000 elements would take an enormous amount of time .)

Let's study how the performance of $1.5 N \log_2 N$ comparisons is derived. What we need to count is the number of comparisons made during the rebuild steps in both the construction and extraction phases. During the extraction phase, the rebuild process is carried for $N-1$ times. If we let K be the maximum number of comparisons required in one rebuild step, then the total number of comparisons will be $(N-1) \cdot K$. In one rebuild step, we start comparing the value in the root node with the larger of its two children. If the value relationship constraint is not violated, the rebuild step terminates immediately. If there is a violation, we make a swap and continue. This compare-and-swap operation is carried out until either the value relationship constraint is met or there are no more nodes to compare. This means that the maximum number of comparisons K is derived by finding out how many times the value relationship constraint violation can occur before the nodes to compare are exhausted.

level

depth

Consider the heap shown in Figure 10.16. We define the *level* of a node in a heap to be the number of nodes in the path from the root to this node. For example, the level of a node 44 in the sample heap is three. The *depth* of a heap is defined to be the largest level of the nodes in the heap. The depth of the sample heap is therefore four. Since the compare-and-swap operation starting from the root can never continue comparing beyond the largest level of the nodes, the depth of a heap is the value we seek for K. Thus, the value for K is derived by finding the depth of a heap with N elements.

At level 1, there is one node. At level 2, there are two nodes. Since a node at level i can have at most 2 children, the maximum number of nodes are level $i+1$ is double the number of nodes at level i. Assuming the maximum number of nodes at all levels, the number of elements at level i is 2^{i-1}, so the maximum total number of nodes in a heap of depth K is

$$\sum_{i=1}^{K} 2^{i-1} = 2^K - 1$$

Because a heap must satisfy the structural constraint, we know the relationships

$$2^{K-1} - 1 \ < \ N \ \le \ 2^K - 1$$

$$2^{K-1} < \ N + 1 \ \le \ 2^K$$

FIGURE 10.16   A sample heap with depth = 4, which is defined to be the largest level of all nodes in a heap.

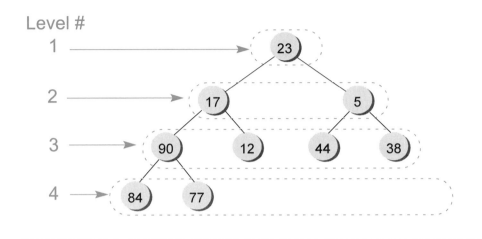

will hold. By applying $\log_2$ to all terms, we have

$$K - 1 < \log_2(N + 1) \le K$$

so

$$K = \lceil \log_2(N + 1) \rceil$$

Finally, the total number of comparisons for the extraction phase is

$$N \cdot K = N \cdot \lceil \log_2(N + 1) \rceil \approx N\log_2 N$$

The construction phase will perform approximately $N/2$ rebuild steps. Each rebuild step will take no more than K comparisons, so the total number of comparisons for the construction phase is

$$\frac{N}{2}\log_2 N$$

The total number of comparisons for both phases is therefore

$$1.5N\log_2 N$$

Quick Check

1. The following structure violates the value relationship constraints. Use the contruction phase routine of the heapsort to eliminate the violations.

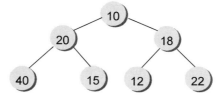

2. Identify all violations on structural and value relationship constraints in the following structure:

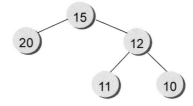

10.4 Sample Program: Sorting an AddressBook

Let's put the our basic knowledge of sorting algorithms into practice. In the previous chapter we presented the AddressBook class that maintains a collection of Person objects. We will extend the AddressBook class by incorporating a sorting routine. The new AddressBook class will include a method that sorts the Person objects in alphabetical order of their names or in descending order of their ages.

In describing the basic sorting algorithms, we limit the data values to integers. This makes the comparison test easy. We write something like this:

```
if ( number[i] < number[i+1] ) {
    //do something...
}
else {
    //do something else...
}
```

But how do we compare Person objects? We cannot say

```
Person p1 = new Person( "Jack", 18, 'M' );
Person p2 = new Person( "Jill", 19, 'F' );

if ( p1 < p2 ) {
    ...
}
```

Cannot compare **Person** objects like this, because it does not make sense. Comparison operators other than equal (==) do not apply for objects.

because the comparison operators such as $<$, $>$, and others except the equal operator are meaningful only for comparing primitive data values. To be able to compare Person objects, we need to modify the class. Let's suppose that we want to compare two Person objects based on either their names or ages. We first add the following two constants to the Person class of Chapter 9:

```
class Person
{
    ...
    public static final int NAME = 0;
    public static final int AGE  = 1;
    ...
}
```

Next, we add a variable to the Person class to set which attribute to use in comparing two objects:

```
private static int compareAttribute = NAME;
```

Notice that the variable is a class variable because this information is not specific to any individual Person objects, but applies to the whole class. We initialize it to NAME so the Person objects will be compared on the name attribute as a default. We define a class method to let the programmer set the comparison attribute. The class method is defined as

```
public static void setCompareAttribute( int attribute )
{
    compareAttribute = attribute;
}
```

Although it is not a syntax error to initialize a class variable inside a constructor, it is a logical error to do so. You cannot define a constructor that includes an initialization of the compareAttribute variable as in

```
public Person( )
{
    ...
    compareAttribute = NAME;
}
```

This definition is valid because the class variables can be accessed from the instance methods, but it is wrong to do so here. This constructor will set the class variable compareAttribute that is shared by all instances of the Person class every time a new Person object is created. This is not what we want. We need to initialize it exactly once when the class is loaded into the memory. One way to do this is to initialize at the point the class variable is declared as shown, or to use the static block as

static block

```
class Person
{
    ...

    static {
        compareAttribute = NAME;
    }
    ...
}
```

Use the static
block to initialize
class variables.

The rule to remember is never to initialize the class variables in the constructor.

**Do not initialize class variables in the constructor. Initialize
the class variables in the** static **block.**

Now we are ready to add a method compareTo that will compare the designated Person objects' names or ages and return the comparison result. The method is used in the following manner:

```
//Persons p1 and p2 are defined and created already

//First set the comparison attibute to NAME
Person.setCompareAttribute( Person.NAME );

int comparisonResult = p1.compare( p2 );

if ( comparisonResult < 0 ) {
    //p1's name is lexicographically less than p2's name
}
else if ( comparisonResult == 0 ) {
    //p1's name is equal to p2's name
}
else { //comparisonResult > 0
    //p1's name is lexicographically larger than p2's name
}
```

To compare two Person objects on their ages, we write

```
//Persons p1 and p2 are defined and created already

//First set the comparison attribute to AGE
Person.setCompareAttribute( Person.AGE );

int comparisonResult = p1.compare( p2 );

if ( comparisonResult < 0 ) {
   //p1 is younger than p2
}
else if ( comparisonResult == 0 ) {
   //p1's age is the same as p2's age
}
else { //comparisonResult > 0
   //p1 is older than p2
}
```

Here's the compareTo method:

```
public int compareTo( Person person )
{
   int comparisonResult;

   if ( compareAttribute == AGE ) {
      int p2age = person.getAge( );

      if (this.age < p2age) {
         comparisonResult = LESS;
      }
      else if (this.age == p2age) {
         comparisonResult = EQUAL;
      }
      else { //this.age > p2age
         comparisonResult = MORE;
      }
   }
   else { //compare names with String's compareTo
      String    p2name = person.getName( );
      comparisonResult = this.name.compareTo( p2name );
   }

   return comparisonResult;
}
```

Compare this **Person's** age to p2's age.

Compare this **Person's** name to p2's name.

The constants LESS, EQUAL, and MORE are defined in the Person class as

```
private static int LESS  = -1;
private static int EQUAL =  0;
private static int MORE  =  1;
```

The compareTo method of the String class behaves just like our compareTo method. Indeed, our compareTo method is modeled after the String class's compareTo method. The wrapper classes Integer, Float, Double, and others also define the analogous compareTo method. Having consistent naming and behavior for comparing two objects of the same class allows the implementation of a more general code. See exercise 9 on page 517.

Now we are ready to add a sorting routine to the AddressBook class. The sort method accepts one integer parameter that specifies the attribute to compare in sorting the Person objects. The method returns an array of Person objects sorted on the designated attribute. We use the bubble sort algorithm for the method. Using the heapsort algorithm is left as an exercise. Here's the sort method.

```
public Person[ ] sort ( int attribute )
{
    Person[ ] sortedList = new Person[ count ];
    Person p1, p2, temp;

    //copy references to sortedList; see Figure 10.17
    for (int i = 0; i < count; i++) {
        sortedList[i] = entry[i];
    }

    //Set the comparison attribute
    Person.setCompareAttribute( attribute );

    //begin the bubble sort on sortedList
    int        bottom, i, comparisonResult;
    boolean    exchanged = true;

    bottom = sortedList.length - 2;

    while ( exchanged )   {

        exchanged = false;

        for (i = 0; i <= bottom; i++) {
            p1 = sortedList[i];
            p2 = sortedList[i+1];

            comparisonResult = p1.compareTo(p2, attribute);

            if ( comparisonResult > 0 ) { //p1 is 'larger'
                sortedList[i]   = p2;     //than p2,so
                sortedList[i+1] = p1;     //exchange

                exchanged   = true;       //exchange is made
            }
```

```
            }
            bottom--;
        }
        return sortedList;
    }
```

The sort method first creates a temporary array called sortedList and copies the references from the entry array into this sortedList. We do this so we can sort the objects on a specified attribute without affecting the order maintained in the entry array. Figure 10.17 illustrates how this sortedList array is used in sorting the Person objects on the age attribute.

FIGURE 10.17   The diagram illustrates how the separate array is used in sorting. Notice that the original array is unaffected by the sorting.

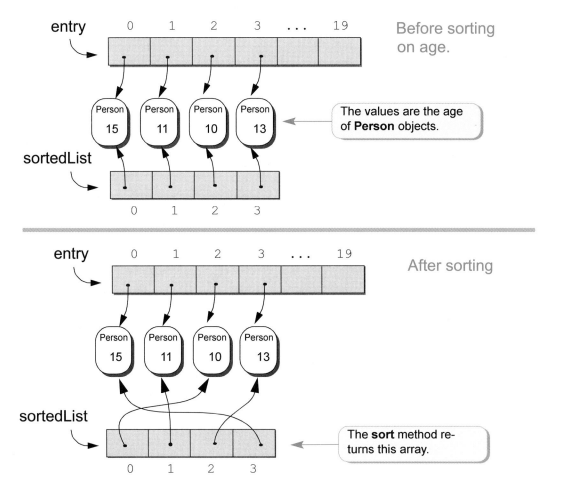

10.5 Exercises

1. Consider the following array of sorted integers:

0	1	2	3	4	5	6	7	8	9	10	11
10	15	25	30	33	34	46	55	78	84	96	99

Using the binary search algorithm, search for 23. Show the sequence of array elements that are compared, and for each comparison, indicate the values for low and high.

2. We assumed all elements in an array are distinct, that is, there are no duplicate values in the array. What will be an effect to the linear search algorithm
if an array contains duplicate values?

3. Will the sorting algorithms presented in this chapter work if the unsorted array contains any duplicate values?

4. In this chapter we analyzed sorting algorithms by counting the number of
comparisons. Another possible method for analyzing the algorithms is
counting the number of data exchanges. How many data exchanges do the
selection and bubble sort make in the worst case? Regardless of the original
list, the selection sort will make the same number of data exchanges. However, the number of data exchanges the bubble sort makes depends on the
arrangement of elements in the original list.

5. Another simple sorting algorithm is called an *insertion sort*. Suppose we
have a sorted list of N elements and we need to insert a new element X into
this list to create a sorted list of $N+1$ elements. We can insert X at the correct
position in the list by comparing it with elements list[$N-1$], list[$N-2$],
list[$N-3$], and so forth. Every time we compare X and list[i], we shift list[i]
one position to list[i+1] if X is smaller than list[i]. When we find list[i] that
is smaller than X, we put X at position $i+1$ and stop. We can apply this logic
to sort an unordered list of N elements. We start with a sorted list of one element and insert the second element to create a sorted list of two elements.
Then we add the third element to create a sorted list of three elements.
Figure 10.18 illustrates the steps in the insertion sort.

Write a method that implements the insertion sort algorithm. You may simplify the method by sorting only integers.

6. Analyze the insertion sort algorithm of exercise 5 by counting the number
of comparisons and data exchanges. Provide the analysis for the worst case.

FIGURE 10.18   Steps in an insertion sort.

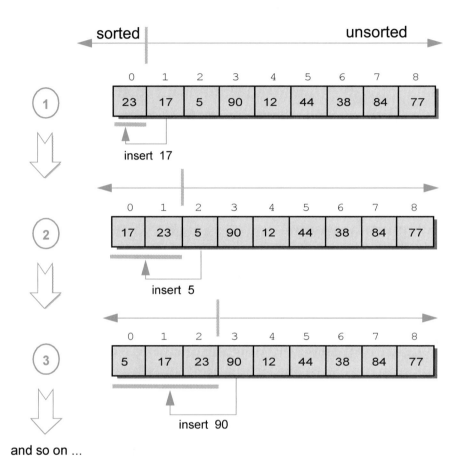

and so on ...

7. Write a test program to compare the performances of selection sort, bubble sort, and heapsort algorithms experimentally. Use the random method from the Math class to generate 1000 integers and sort the generated integers using the three sorting algorithms. For each execution, record the time it took to sort the numbers. You can use the Clock class from the javabook package to record the execution time. For example,

```
Clock myClock = new Clock( );

myClock.start( );  //starts the clock
```

```
//sort the integers

myClock.stop( );    //stops the clock

//record the elaspsed time
double elaspedTime = myClock.getElapsedTime( );
```

8. Consider the following property about the bubble sort:

    • *If the last exchange made in some pass occurs at the Jth and*
      (J+1)st positions, then all elements from the (J+1)st to the Nth
      positions are in their correct location.

    Rewrite the bubble sort algorithm using this property.

9. The Heap class given in Section 10.3 sorts only the integers. Improve the
    class by making it possible to sort any objects that recognize the compareTo
    method, which is described in Section 10.4, so the new Heap class will be
    able to sort Person, Integer, Double, and String objects among others. Since
    the elements in the internal array can be any object, declare an array of Ob-
    ject objects. All Java classes are automatically a subclass of Object, unless
    they are declared explicitly as a subclass of another class. The declaration of
    heap will be like

```
private Object[ ] heap;
```

    and the setData method will be like

```
public void setData( Object[ ] data )
{
    heap        = new Object[ data.length ];
    sortedList = new Object[ data.length ];

    for (int i = 0; i < data.length; i++ ) {
        heap[i] = data[i];
      }
    }
```

10. In the Heap class, we used two separate arrays: one for the heap and another
    for the sorted list. It turns out we can do everything with just one array. No-
    tice that the heap will decrease in size by one element after every rebuild
    step. The unused space at the end of the heap array can be used to store the
    sorted list. Modify the Heap class so it will use only one array.

11. Modify the Heap class by defining a separate method called rebuild, which will be used by both the construct and extract methods.

12. In Section 10.4, we implemented the sorting routine for the AddressBook class with the bubble sort algorithm. Modify the sorting routine by using the Heap class of exercise 9.

13. Instead of maintaining an unsorted list and returning the sorted list when the sort method is called, modify the AddressBook class so that it maintains the sorted list of Person in alphabetical order. Modify the seach routine by using the binary search algorithm.

11

File Input and Output

OBJECTIVES

After you have read and studied this chapter, you should be able to

- Include a FileDialog object in your program to let the user specify a file.

- Write bytes to a file and read them back from the file using FileOutputStream and FileInputStream.

- Write values of primitive data types to a file and read them back from the file using DataOutputStream and DataInputStream.

- Write text data to a file and read them back from the file using PrintWriter and BufferedReader.

- Write objects to a file and read them back from the file using ObjectOutputStream and ObjectInputStream.

- Write exception-handling routines using the try–catch block.

Introduction

Suppose we write a program that maintains an array of **Person** objects. The user can add to, delete from, or modify **Person** objects in the array. To make this program practical, we must save the data to a file. If we don't, then the user must reenter the same data every time he or she runs the program because any data used by the program will be erased from the main memory at program termination. If the data were saved, then the program can read them back from the file and rebuild the array so the user can work on the data without reentering them. In this chapter you will learn how to save data to and read data from a file. We call the action of saving data to a file *file output* and the action of reading data from a file *file input*. We will introduce several classes from the java.io package for performing file input and output. We used the techniques described in this chapter to implement the saveToFile and appendToFile methods of the Output-Box class.

file output and input

11.1   File **and** FileDialog **Objects**

In this section we introduce two key objects for reading data from or writing data to a file. We use the term "file access" to refer to both read and write operations. If we need to be precise, we write "read access" or "write access." Let's study the read access first. Suppose we want to read the contents of a file sample.data. Before we begin the actual operation of reading data from this file, we must first create a File object (from the java.io package) and associate it to the file. We do so by calling a File constructor:

File

```
File inFile = new File("sample.data");
```

The argument to the constructor designates the name of the file to access. The system assumes the file is located in the *current directory*. For the following examples, we assume the directory structure shown in Figure 11.1, with Ch11 being the current directory. When you run a program whose source file is located in directory X, then the current directory is X. Please refer to your Java compiler manuals for other options for designating the current directory.

current directory

It is also possible to open a file that is stored in a directory other than the current directory by providing a path name and a file name. Assuming there's a file xyz.data in the JavaProjects directory, we can open it by executing

```
File inFile = new File("C:\\JavaProjects", "xyz.data");
```

This style of designating the path name is for the Windows platform. For the UNIX platform, we use the slash for a delimiter, for example,

Chapter 11

FIGURE 11.1   Directory structure used for the examples in this section. We assume the Windows 98 environment.

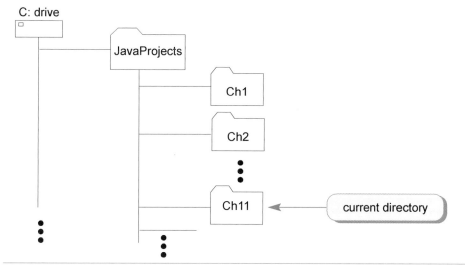

```
"/JavaProjects"
```

For the Mac platform, we also use a slash. If the name of a hard disk is MacHD, then we write

```
"/MacHD/JavaProjects"
```

We will assume the Windows platform for all of the examples in this chapter. The actual path name specified by the string "C:\\JavaProjects" is

```
C:\JavaProjects
```

because the backslash is the delimiter used in the Windows platform. However, the backslash symbol has a special purpose when used inside the double quotes. The backslash is called an *escape character*. It is used to specify a nonprintable, control character. For example, we indicate a control character for a new line (ASCII code 10) as '\n' and a control character for a tab (ASCII code 9) as '\t'. Using a new line control character, we can express the statement such as

escape character

```
outputBox.printLine("Hello");
```

as

```
outputBox.print("Hello\n");
```

Since the backslash symbol has this special purpose, if we designate the string as

```
"C:\JavaProjects"
```

then the compiler will try to interpret J as a control character. So, to include the backslash character itself in the string, we use double slashes.

Now let's get back to the path name discussion. The path name could be absolute or relative to the current directory. The absolute path name is the full path name beginning with the disk drive name, for example,

```
"C:\\JavaProjects\\Ch11"
```

The relative path name is relative to the current directory. For example, if the current directory is Ch11, then the relative path name

```
"..\\Ch2"
```

is equivalent to the full path name

```
"C:\\JavaProjects\\Ch2"
```

where the two dots (..) in the string means "one directory above."

We can check if a File object is associated correctly to an existing file by calling its exists method:

```
if ( inFile.exists( ) ) {
    // inFile is associated correctly to an existing file
}
else {
    // inFile is not associated to any existing file
}
```

When a valid association is established, we say *the file is opened*; a file must be opened before doing any input and output to the file.

A file must be opened before performing any file access operation.

A File object also can be associated to a directory. For example, suppose we are interested in listing the content of directory Ch11. We can first create a File object and associate it to the directory. After the association is made, we can list the contents of the directory by calling the object's list method:

```
File    directory  = new File("C:\\JavaProjects\\Ch11");
String filename[] = directory.list();

for (int i = 0; i < filename.length; i++) {
    outputBox.printLine(filename[i]);
}
```

We check whether a File object is associated to a file or a directory by calling its boolean method isFile. The following code will print out I am a directory:

```
File file = new File("C:\\JavaProjects\\Ch11");

if (file.isFile()) {
    outputBox.printLine("I am a file");
}
else {
    outputBox.printLine("I am a directory);
}
```

FileDialog

We can use a FileDialog object from the java.awt package to let the user select a file or a directory. The object has two modes: LOAD and SAVE. You open the object in the LOAD mode if you want to read data from the selected file and in the SAVE mode if you want to write data to the selected file. When the statements

```
FileDialog fileBox = new FileDialog( mainWindow, "Open",
                                     FileDialog.LOAD  );
fileBox.setVisible( true );
```

are executed, a FileDialog shown in Figure 11.2 appears on the screen.

The user can browse (navigate) the directories and select the desired file by clicking on the filename in the list or typing in the filename in the File name: text field. To retrieve the name of the file the user has selected, we use the get-File method (provided that the dialog is already visible):

```
String filename = fileBox.getFile();
```

The code assigns the name of the selected file to filename. If the Cancel button of FileDialog is clicked, then the getFile method returns null. Also, if the Open button is clicked without any file being selected, then null is returned.

We also can get the path name to the directory where the selected file is located. Executing the statement

FIGURE 11.2   A **FileDialog** object appearing on the screen in the **LOAD** mode.

```
String directoryPath = fileBox.getDirectory();
```

will assign the path name C:\JavaProjects\Ch11\ to directoryPath if the user selects a file in the Ch11 directory. Since the user can select a file from a directory different from the current directory, we should use directoryPath in creating a File object:

```
File inFile = new File( directoryPath, filename );
```

To select a file for saving data, we create and open the FileDialog in the SAVE mode:

```
FileDialog fileBox = new FileDialog( mainWindow, "Save As",
                                     FileDialog.SAVE );
fileBox.setVisible( true );
```

The resulting dialog is shown in Figure 11.3.

FIGURE 11.3   A **FileBox** object opened in the **SAVE** mode.

Notice that the button is now labeled Save instead of Open. When the user selects an existing file in the SAVE mode of FileDialog, a warning message is displayed, as shown in Figure 11.4. This reduces the chance the user will erroneously overwrite any existing file. If the No button is clicked in the warning message box, then the FileDialog remains on the screen.

FIGURE 11.4   A message dialog warning of a file overwrite.

Quick Check

1. This question is specific to the Windows platform. Suppose you want to open a file prog1.java inside the directory C:\JavaProjects\ Ch11\Step4. What is the actual String value you pass in the constructor for the File class?

2. What is wrong with the following statement?

```
FileDialog fD = new FileDialog( "Open" );
```

3. Which method of the FileDialog object do you use to get the filename of the selected file? What is returned from the method if the Cancel button of the FileDialog object is clicked?

11.2 Low-Level File I/O

Once a file is opened by properly associating a File object to it, the actual file access can commence. In this section, we will introduce basic objects for file operations. In order to actually read data from or write data to a file, we must

stream

source
destination

create one of the Java stream objects and attach it to the file. A *stream* is simply a sequence of data items, usually eight-bit bytes. Java has two types of streams: an input stream and an output stream. An input stream has a *source* from where the data items come, and an output stream has a *destination* to where the data items are going. To read data items from a file, we attach one of the Java input stream objects to the file. Similarly, to write data items to a file, we attach one of the Java output stream objects to the file.

Java comes with a large number of stream objects for file access operations. We will cover only those that are straightforward and easy to learn for beginners. We will study two of them in this section—FileOutputStream and FileInputStream. These two objects provide low-level file access operations. In the next section, we will study other stream objects.

FileOutput-
Stream

Let's first study how to write data values to a file using FileOutputStream. Using a FileOutputStream object, we can output only a sequence of bytes, that is, values of data type byte. In this example, we will output an array of bytes to a file named sample1.data. First, we create a File object:

```
File outFile = new File( "sample1.data" );
```

Then we associate a new FileOutputStream object to outFile:

```
FileOutputStream outStream
                    = new FileOutputStream( outFile );
```

Now we are ready for output. Consider the following byte array:

```
byte[] byteArray = {10, 20, 30, 40, 50, 60, 70, 80};
```

We write the whole byte array at once to the file by executing

```
outStream.write(byteArray);
```

Notice that we are not dealing with the File object directly, but with outStream. It is also possible to write array elements individually, for example,

```
//output the first and fifth bytes
outStream.write(byteArray[0]);
outStream.write(byteArray[4]);
```

After the values are written to the file, we must close the stream:

```
outStream.close();
```

If the stream object is not closed, then some data may get lost due to data caching. Because of the physical characteristics of secondary memory such as hard disks, the actual process of saving data to a file is a very time-consuming operation, whether you are saving one byte or 100 bytes. So instead of saving bytes individually, we save them in a block of, say, 500 bytes to reduce the overall time it takes to save the whole data. The operation of saving data as a block is called *data caching*. To carry out data caching, a part of memory is reserved as a *data buffer* or *cache,* which is used as a temporary holding place. A typical size for a data buffer is anywhere from 1K to 2K. Data are first witten to a buffer, and when the buffer becomes full, the data in the buffer are actually written to a file. If there are any remaining data in the buffer and the file is not closed, then those data will be lost. Therefore, to avoid losing any data, it is important to close the file at the end of the operations.

data caching
and buffer

To ensure that all data are saved to a file, close the file at the end of file access operations.

Here's the complete program:

File: TestFileOutputStream.java

```java
import java.io.*;

/**
 * Program TestFileOutputStream
 *
 * A test program to save data to a file using FileOutputStream
 */

class TestFileOutputStream
{
    public static void main (String[] args) throws IOException
    {
        //set up file and stream
        File             outFile   = new File("sample1.data");
        FileOutputStream outStream = new FileOutputStream(outFile);

        //data to output
        byte[] byteArray = {10, 20, 30, 40, 50, 60, 70, 80};

        //write data to the stream
        outStream.write(byteArray);

        //output done, so close the stream
        outStream.close();
    }
}
```

Notice the last two words in the method declaration

Mr. Espresso: I don't understand why you have to create both File *and* FileIn-putStream *objects. Why not just use one object?*

Dr. Caffeine: File *represents the physical file that is a source of data.* Stream *objects represent the mechanism we associate to a file to perform input and output routines.* Stream *objects can be associated to a nonfile data source such as a serial port.*

Now it's true that you can make a shortcut statement like

```
fileOutputStream outStream
    = new FileOutputStream("input.txt");
```

where you avoid the explicit creation of a File *object. But this shortcut does not eliminate the fact that the* Stream *object is associated to a file.*

```
public static void main (String[] args) throws IOException
```

exception

They indicate the method may possibly throw an I/O exception. An *exception* is an error condition that violates the semantic rules of Java programs. For example, when you try to read data from a nonexisting file or attempt to read beyond the end of the file, an I/O exception will be thrown. An I/O exception is only one of the many different types of Java exceptions. If an exception occurs while executing a method, we say that *the method raises or throws an exception.* Not all methods will throw an exception; we call those that do *exception-throwing methods.*

When we use an exception-throwing method in our program, we can do one of two things. One is to *catch* a thrown exception and provide exception-handling code to process the thrown exception. We will describe how to do this in Section 11.4. Another, which we will use here, is to propagate a thrown exception to the caller of the method. To propagate an exception, we append the words throws IOException (or whatever the type of the thrown exception) to the method declaration as illustrated below:

```
public static void main (String[ ] args) throws IOException
{
   ... = new FileOutputStream(outFile);
   ...
   outStream.write(byteArray);
   ...
   outStream.close();
}
```

These statements all throw an **IOException**, and therefore, we add **throws IOException** to the method we define.

When an IOException is thrown by the method close, for example, then the method main propagates this thrown exception to its caller. The method that called our main method can either handle the exception or propagate it further. If a thrown exception is not handled by any method in the propagation chain, the Java interpreter will eventually handle it. We will discuss more on exception handling in Section 11.4. For the next two sections, we will use the propagation approach in dealing with exceptions.

FileInput-
Stream

To read the data into a program, we reverse the steps in the output routine. We use the read method of FileInputStream to read in an array of bytes. First we create a FileInputStream object:

```
File             inFile    = new File( "sample1.data" );
FileInputStream  inStream  = new FileInputStream( inFile );
```

Then we read the data into an array of bytes:

```
inStream.read(byteArray);
```

Before we call the read method, we must declare and create byteArray:

```
int    filesize  = (int) inFile.length();
byte[] byteArray = new byte[filesize];
```

We use the length method of the File class to determine the size of the file, which in this case is the number of bytes in the file. We create an array of bytes whose size is the size of the file.

The following program uses FileInputStream to read in the byte array from the file sample1.data.

File: TestFileInputStream.java

```
import javabook.*;
import java.io.*;

/**
 *    Program TestFileInputStream
 *
 *    A test program to read data from a file using FileInputStream
 */

class TestFileInputStream
{
    public static void main (String[] args) throws IOException
    {
        MainWindow mainWindow   = new MainWindow();
        OutputBox outputBox     = new OutputBox(mainWindow);

        mainWindow.setVisible( true );
```

```
outputBox.setVisible( true );

//set up file and stream
File            inFile    = new File("sample1.data");
FileInputStream inStream  = new FileInputStream(inFile);

//set up an array to read data in
int fileSize = (int)inFile.length();
byte[] byteArray = new byte[fileSize];

//read data in and display them
inStream.read(byteArray);
for (int i = 0; i < fileSize; i++) {
    outputBox.printLine(byteArray[i]);
}

//input done, so close the stream
inStream.close();
    }
}
```

It is possible to output data other than bytes if we can convert (i.e., type cast) them into bytes. For example, we can output character data by type casting them to bytes.

```
File             outFile  = new File("sample1.data");
FileOutputStream outStream= new FileOutputStream(outFile);


//data to output
byte[] byteArray = { (byte) 'J',
                     (byte) 'a',         ← Type cast charac-
                     (byte) 'v',           ters to bytes.
                     (byte) 'a' };

//write data to the stream
outStream.write(byteArray);

//output done, so close the stream
outStream.close();
```

To read the data back, we use the read method again. If we need to display the bytes in the original character values, we need to type cast byte to char. Without the type casting, numerical values would be displayed. The following code illustrates the type casting of byte to char for display.

```
MainWindow mainWindow = new MainWindow();
OutputBox outputBox   = new OutputBox(mainWindow);
```

```
File              inFile    = new File("sample1.data");
FileInputStream  inStream  = new FileInputStream(inFile);

//set up an array to read data in
int     fileSize  = inFile.length();
byte[] byteArray = new byte[fileSize];

//read data in and display them
inStream.read(byteArray);

for (int i = 0; i < fileSize; i++) {

    outputBox.printLine( (char) byteArray[i] );
}

//input done, so close the stream
inStream.close();
```

> Type cast byte array back to characters for display.

Type casting char to byte or byte to char is simple because ASCII uses eight bits. But what if we want to perform file I/O on numerical values such as integers and real numbers? It takes more than simple type casting to output these numerical values to FileOutputStream and read them back from FileInput-Stream. An integer takes four bytes, so we need to break a single integer into four bytes and perform file I/O on these four bytes. Such conversion would be too low level and tedious. Java provides stream objects that allow us to read from or write numerical values to a file without doing any conversions ourselves. We will discuss two of them in the next section.

Quick Check

1. What is the method you call at the end of all file I/O operations?
2. What is wrong with the following statements? Assume that out-Stream is a properly declared and created FileOutputStream object.

    ```
    byte[ ]  byteArray = { (byte) 'H', (byte) 'i' };
    ...
    outStream.print( byteArray );
    ...
    outStream.close( );
    ```

3. When do you need to add the terms

    ```
    throws IOException
    ```

    to a method definition?

11.3   High-Level File I/O

By using DataOutputStream, we can output Java primitive data type values. A DataOutputStream object will take care of the details of converting the primitive data type values to a sequence of bytes. Let's look at the complete program first. The following program writes out values of various Java primitive data types to a file. The names of the output methods (those preceded with write) should be self-explanatory.

File: TestDataOutputStream.java

```java
import java.io.*;


/**
 *  Program TestDataOutputStream
 *
 *  A test program to save data to a file using DataOutputStream for
 *  high-level I/O.
 */


class TestDataOutputStream
{
    public static void main (String[] args) throws IOException
    {
        //set up the streams
        File            outFile        = new File("sample2.data");
        FileOutputStream outFileStream = new FileOutputStream(outFile);
        DataOutputStream outDataStream= new DataOutputStream(outFileStream);

        //write values of primitive data types to the stream
        outDataStream.writeInt(987654321);
        outDataStream.writeLong(11111111L);
        outDataStream.writeFloat(22222222F);
        outDataStream.writeDouble(3333333D);
        outDataStream.writeChar('A');
        outDataStream.writeBoolean(true);

        //output done, so close the stream
        outDataStream.close();
    }

}
```

> Notice the argument to the constructor for the **DataOutputStream**.

Notice the sequence of statements for creating a DataOutputStream object:

```java
File            outFile        = new File("sample2.data");
FileOutputStream outFileStream= new FileOutputStream(outFile);
DataOutputStream outDataStream
                    = new DataOutputStream(outFileStream);
```

DataOutput-Stream

The argument to the DataOutputStream constructor is a FileOutputStream object. A DataOutputStream object does not get connected to a file directly. The diagram in Figure 11.5 illustrates the relationships established among the three objects. The role of the DataOutputStream object is to provide high-level access to a file by converting a primitive data value into a sequence of bytes, which are then written to a file via a FileOutputStream object.

FIGURE 11.5 A diagram showing how the three objects **outFile**, **outFileStream**, and **outDataStream** are related.

```
File            outFile       = new File("sample2.data");
FileOutputStream outFileStream = new FileOutputStream(outFile);
DataOutputStream outDataStream = new DataOutputStream(outFileStream);
```

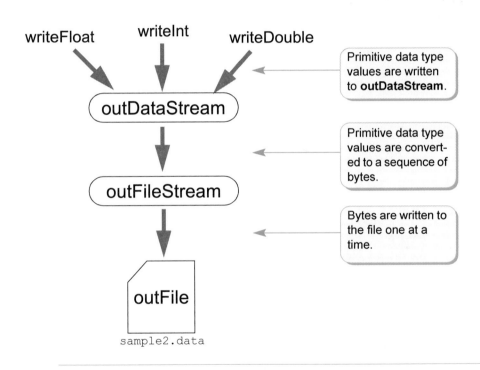

To read the data back from the file, we reverse the operation. We use three objects: File, FileInputStream and DataInputStream. The following program reads the data saved by the program TestDataOutputStream.

DataInput-
Stream

File: TestDataInputStream.java

```
import java.io.*;
import javabook.*;

/**
```

```
 *    Program TestDataInputStream
 *
 *    A test program to load data from a file using DataInputStream for
 *    high-level I/O.
 */

class TestDataInputStream
{
    public static void main (String[] args) throws IOException
    {
        MainWindow mainWindow = new MainWindow();
        OutputBox outputBox = new OutputBox(mainWindow);
        mainWindow.setVisible( true );
        outputBox.setVisible( true );

        //set up file and stream
        File inFile = new File("sample2.data");
        FileInputStream inFileStream = new FileInputStream(inFile);
        DataInputStream inDataStream = new DataInputStream(inFileStream);

        //read values back from the stream and display them
        outputBox.printLine(inDataStream.readInt());
        outputBox.printLine(inDataStream.readLong());
        outputBox.printLine(inDataStream.readFloat());
        outputBox.printLine(inDataStream.readDouble());
        outputBox.printLine(inDataStream.readChar());
        outputBox.printLine(inDataStream.readBoolean());

        //input done, so close the stream
        inDataStream.close();
    }
}
```

Figure 11.6 shows the relationship among the three objects. Notice that we must read the data back in the precise order. In other words, if we write data in the order of integer, float, and character, then we must read the data back in that order, as illustrated in Figure 11.7. If we don't read them back in the correct order, the results will be unpredictable.

binary file

Both FileOutputStream and DataOutputStream objects produce a *binary file* in which the contents are stored in the format (called *binary format*) in which they are stored in the main memory. Instead of storing data in binary format, we can store them in ASCII format. With the ASCII format, all data are converted to string data. A file whose contents are stored in ASCII format is called a *textfile*. One major benefit of a textfile is that we can easily read and modify the contents of a textfile using any text editor or word processor.

textfile

PrintWriter

PrintWriter is an object we use to generate a textfile. Unlike DataOutputStream, where we have a separate write method for each individual data type, PrintWriter supports only two output methods: print and println (for print line). An argument to the methods can be any primitive data type. The methods convert the parameter to string and output this string value. The constructor of PrintWriter, similar to the one for DataOutputStream, requires an output stream

FIGURE 11.6   A diagram showing how the three objects **inFile**, **inFileStream**, and **inDataStream** are related.

```
File              inFile       = new File("sample2.data");
FileInputStream inFileStream = new FileInputStream(inFile);
DataInputStream inDataStream = new DataInputStream(inFileStream);
```

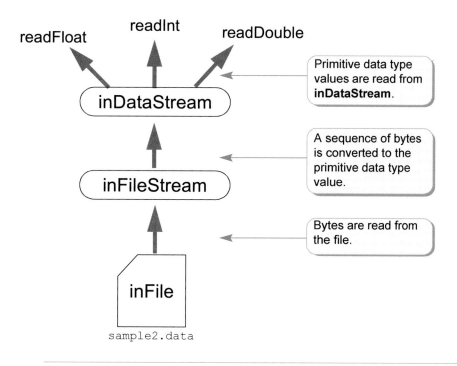

sample2.data

as its argument. In the following program, the parameter is again an instance of FileOutputStream.

File: TestPrintWriter.java

```java
import java.io.*;


/**
 *   Program TestPrintWriter
 *
 *   A test program to save data to a file using PrintWriter for
 *   high-level I/O.
 */
```

Chapter 11

```
class TestPrintStream

{
    public static void main (String[] args) throws IOException
    {
        //set up file and stream
        File                outFile         = new File("sample3.data");
        FileOutputStream outFileStream   = new FileOutputStream(outFile);
        PrintWriter         outStream       = new PrintWriter(outFileStream);

        //write values of primitive data types to the stream
        outStream.println(987654321);
        outStream.println(11111111L);
        outStream.println(22222222F);
        outStream.println(33333333D);
        outStream.println('A');
        outStream.println(true);

        //output done, so close the stream
        outStream.close();
    }
}
```

> We use **print** and **println** with **Print-Writer**. The **print** and **println** methods convert primitive data types to strings before writing to a file.

FIGURE 11.7   The order of write and read operations must match to read the stored data back correctly.

```
outStream.writeInteger(...);
outStream.writeLong(...);
outStream.writeChar(...);
outStream.writeBoolean(...);
```

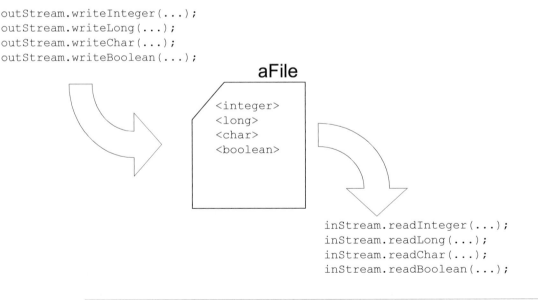

aFile

```
<integer>
<long>
<char>
<boolean>
```

```
inStream.readInteger(...);
inStream.readLong(...);
inStream.readChar(...);
inStream.readBoolean(...);
```

To read the data from a textfile we use the FileReader and BufferedReader objects. The relationship between FileReader and BufferedReader is similar to the one between FileInputStream and DataInputStream. To read data back from a textfile, we first need to associate a BufferedReader object to a file. The following sequence of statements associates a BufferedReader object to a file sample3.data:

```
File             inFile      = new File("sample3.data");
FileReader       fileReader  = new FileReader(inFile);
BufferedReader bufReader
                             = new BufferedReader(fileReader);
```

Then we read data using the readLine method of BufferedReader

```
String str = bufReader.readLine( );
```

and convert the String to a primitive data type as necessary.

Here's the program to read back from sample3.data, which was created by the program TestPrintWriter:

File: TestBufferedReader.java

```java
import java.io.*;
import javabook.*; //to use the Convert class

/**
 *    Program TestBufferedReader
 *
 *    A test program to load data from a file using the readLine method of
 *    BufferedReader for high-level String input.
 */

class TestBufferedReader
{
    public static void main (String[] args) throws IOException
    {
        MainWindow mainWindow = new MainWindow();
        OutputBox outputBox = new OutputBox(mainWindow);
        mainWindow.setVisible( true );
        outputBox.setVisible( true );

        //set up file and stream
        File             inFile      = new File("sample3.data");
        FileReader       fileReader  = new FileReader(inFile);
        BufferedReader   bufReader   = new BufferedReader(fileReader);
        String str;

        //get integer
        str = bufReader.readLine();
        int i = Convert.toInt(str);

        //get long
        str = bufReader.readLine();
        long l = Convert.toLong(str);

        //get float
        str = bufReader.readLine();
```

Notice we are reading in strings. Numbers are stored in ASCII format, so we can't use **readInt**, **readFloat**, and so on. We need to convert strings to primitive data types.

```
        float f = Convert.toFloat(str);

        //get double
        str = bufReader.readLine();
        double d = Convert.toDouble(str);

        //get char
        str = bufReader.readLine();
        char c = Convert.toChar(str);

        //get boolean
        str = bufReader.readLine();
        boolean b = Convert.toBoolean(str);


        outputBox.printLine(i);
        outputBox.printLine(l);
        outputBox.printLine(f);
        outputBox.printLine(d);
        outputBox.printLine(c);
        outputBox.printLine(b);

        //input done, so close the stream
        bufReader.close();
    }
}
```

> Note: Here we only output so there's no real need to perform data conversion, but in general you need to convert String data to primitive data types before being able to use them.

Since the data stored in the file are strings, we need to convert them into primitive data types. For data conversion, the program uses the Convert class from the javabook package. If you do not use the Convert class, the code for conversion may look something like this:

> Could replace these with
> **int i**
> **= Integer.parseInt(str);**

```
        str = inStream.readLine();
        Integer intObj = new Integer(str);
        int i = intObj.intValue();

        //get long
        str = outStream.readLine();
        Long longObj = new Long(str);
        long l = longObj.longValue();
```

> Could replace these with
> **long l =**
> **Long.parseLong(str);**

```
        //get float
        str = outStream.readLine();
        Float floatObj = new Float(str);
        float f = floatObj.floatValue();

        //get double
        str = outStream.readLine();
        Double doubleObj = new Double(str);
        double d = doubleObj.doubleValue();
```

```
//get char
str = outStream.readLine();
char c = str.charAt(0);

//get boolean
str = outStream.readLine();
Boolean booleanObj = Boolean(str);
boolean b = booleanObj.booleanValue();
```

Quick Check

1. Which type of files can be opened and viewed by a text editor?
2. Which class is used to generate a textfile?
3. Assume bufReader is properly declared and created. What is wrong with the following?

    ```
    double d = bufReader.readDouble( );
    ```

11.4 Handling Exceptions

In Section 11.2 we mentioned that many of the file I/O methods throw exceptions. In earlier examples, we used one of the two ways to handle exceptions. We will now describe the second way of handling exceptions by catching a thrown exception and providing exception-handling code to process the thrown exception.

checked and
unchecked
exceptions

There are two types of exceptions: checked and unchecked exceptions: A *checked exception* is an exception that is checked at compile time. All other exceptions are *unchecked exceptions*, also called *runtime exceptions,* because they are unchecked at compile time and detected only at runtime. Runtime exceptions are thrown when you try to divide a number by 0 or try to access a nonexisting object, for example. Runtime exceptions are considered unrecoverable, and, therefore, we do not handle these exceptions. We only need to handle the checked exceptions. We mentioned one approach for handling checked exceptions, the IOException, in Section 11.2. We will explain another approach to handling checked exceptions in this section.

For the remainder of the section, we use the term *exception* to refer to a checked exception. We have two ways to take care of thrown exceptions. The first way, which we have already explained in Section 11.2, is to add a throw clause to the method header. Consider the following simplified sample object that computes the sum of three integers read from a specified file.

```
class FindSum
{
    private int sum;

    public int getSum()
    {
        return sum;
    }

    void computeSum (String fileName ) throws IOException
    {
        File inFile  = new File(fileName);

        FileInputStream inFileStream
                    = new FileInputStream(inFile);
        DataInputStream inDataStream
                    = new DataInputStream(inFileStream);

        //read three integers
        int i = inDataStream.readInt();
        int j = inDataStream.readInt();
        int k = inDataStream.readInt();

        sum = i + j + k;

        inDataStream.close();
    }
}
```

We used the propagation approach in declaring the computeSum method. The method that calls computeSum can propagate the exception thrown by computeSum. And the exception propagation can continue until the Java interpreter handles the exception. For simple programs, this may be acceptable, but in general, you should use the second approach, in which you write a response code to process a thrown exception.

Let's see how we can use the second approach in the FindSum class. To specify a response code to a thrown exception, we need to declare a catch block. Here's one way to rewrite the FindSum class:

```
class FindSum
{
    private int     sum;
    private boolean  success;

    public int getSum()
    {
        return sum;
    }
```

```
public boolean isSuccess()
{
    return success;
}

void computeSum (String fileName )
{
    success = true;

    try {
        File inFile   = new File(fileName);
        FileInputStream inFileStream
                    = new FileInputStream(inFile);
        DataInputStream inDataStream
                  = new DataInputStream(inFileStream);

        //read three integers
        int i = inDataStream.readInt();
        int j = inDataStream.readInt();
        int k = inDataStream.readInt();

        sum = i + j + k;

        inDataStream.close();
    }
    catch (IOException e) {
        success = false;
    }
}
}
```

The declaration of the computeSum method does not include the throws
clause anymore, which means that the method will not propagate an exception.
Instead, it is modified to catch a thrown IOException. The syntax for catching an
exception is

Try Block →

```
try {

    <statements>

}
```

Catch Block →

```
catch ( <ExceptionType> <identifier> ) {

    <statements>
}
```

where <ExceptionType> is the class of thrown exception and <identifier> refers to an instance of the class <ExceptionType>. At the top of the exception class hierarchy is the Exception class. There are nine immediate subclasses of the Exception class, of which the IOException class is one. The IOException class is also a superclass of the classes FileNotFoundException, EOFException, InterruptedIOException, and others. When an exception occurs, an instance of the appropriate class is created and passed to a relevant catch block. An instance of Exception and its subclasses contains information regarding the thrown exception.

The idea is to place statements that call exception-throwing methods in the try block and catch a thrown exception. For the computeSum method, we placed all of the exception-throwing methods in the try block and added one catch block. Inside the catch block, we set the instance variable success to false to signal that there was an error in performing file I/O. The code for using a FindSum object can be written as

```
FindSum findSum = new FindSum();

findSum.computeSum("sampleint.dat");

if (findSum.isSuccess()) {
    int total = findSum.getSum();
    outputBox.printLine("Sum = " + total);
}
else {
    outputBox.printLine("Error in File I/O");
}
```

If an exception is thrown during the execution of the try block, then the catch block is executed and the variable success is set to false. A call to the method isSuccess returns false and the message Error in File I/O is displayed.

We can modify the catch block of the computeSum method to print out an error message to System.out, in addition to setting the instance variable success to false:

```
try {
    ...
}
catch (IOException e) {
    success = false;
    System.out.println(e);
}
```

System.out, which you may have been using already, is a PrintWriter object you use for debugging and testing purposes. Output values written to System.out are displayed in the DOS window for the Windows platform and in a similar type of window for other platforms. We can print out the sequence of method calls up to the point the exception occurs by calling the printStackTrace method of the IOException object e as

```
try {
    ...
}
catch (IOException e) {
    success = false;
    e.printStackTrace();
}
```

We can attach multiple catch blocks to a single try block, each catching a specific exception. For the computeSum method, statements that throw exceptions all throw exceptions of type IOException, but some of them are throwing more detailed exceptions. For instance, the constructor

```
new FileInputStream(inFile);
```

will throw a FileNotFoundException if the file inFile does not exist. Also, the method

```
readInt()
```

will throw an EOFException if you attempt to read beyond the end of the file. If we want to process these exceptions differently, then we can add multiple catch blocks as

```
try {
    ...
}
catch (FileNotFoundException e) {
    success = false;
    System.out.println("File " + fileName
                              + " does not exist.");
}
catch (EOFException e) {
    success = false;
    System.out.println("Error: " +
                  "Cannot read beyond end of file");
}
```

```
catch (IOException e) {
    success = false;
    System.out.println("General I/O exception is thrown");
}
```

When an exception is thrown by a statement inside the try block, control is immediately passed to the matching catch block and statements following the exception-throwing statement will not get executed. If you want to include statements that will always get executed whether there is an exception or not, place these statements in the finally block. The finally block comes at the end:

```
try {
    ...
}
catch (IOException e) {
    ...
}
finally {
    //statements placed here
    //will always get executed
}
```

You will be seeing more examples of exception handling in the following chapters.

Quick Check

1. What is the purpose of the try–catch block?
2. True or false. If your method calls another method that can throw an exception, then your method must include a try–catch block.

11.5   Object I/O

With Java 1.1, you can store objects just as easily as you can store primitive data values. Java 1.0 and many other object-oriented programming languages won't allow programmers to store objects directly. In those programming languages, we must write code to store individual data members of an object separately. For example, if a Person object has data members name (String), age (int), and gender (char), then we have to store the three values individually using the file I/O techniques explained earlier in the chapter. (Note: String is an object, but it can be treated much like any other primitive data types because of its immutability.) Now, if the data members of an object are all primitive data types (or a String), then storing the data members individually is a chore but not that difficult. However, if a data member is a reference to another object or to an array of objects, then storing data can become very tricky. Fortunately with Java 1.1 and 1.2, we don't have to worry about them; we can store objects directly to a file.

In this section, we will describe various approaches for storing objects. To write objects to a file, we use ObjectOutputStream, and to read objects from a file, we use ObjectInputStream. Let's see how we write Person objects to a file. First we need to modify the definition of the Person class in order for ObjectOutputStream and ObjectInputStream to perform object I/O. We modify the definition by adding the phrase implements Serializable to it as

ObjectOutput-Stream

ObjectInput-Stream

> **Serializable is defined in java.io.**

```
import java.io.*;
class Person implements Serializable
{
    //the rest is the same
}
```

We will defer the explanation of the keyword implements until Chapter 13. For now, just remember that whenever you want to store an object to a file, modify its class definition by adding the phrase implements Serializable to it.

> ***If you want to perform an object I/O, then the class definition must include the phrase*** implements Serializable.

If the class is a subclass, then the class definition will be something like

```
class Student extends Person implements Serializable
```

To write a Person object to a file, we first create an ObjectOutputStream object:

```
File               outFile
                        = new File("objects.data");
FileOutputStream   outFileStream
                        = new FileOutputStream(outFile);
ObjectOutputStream outObjectStream
                        = new ObjectOutputStream
                                        (outFileStream);
```

To save a Person object, we write

```
Person person = new Person("Mr. Espresso", 20, 'M');

outObjectStream.writeObject( person );
```

It is possible to save different types of objects to a single file. Assuming the Account and Bank classes are defined properly, we can save both types of objects to a single file:

```
Account    account1, account2;
Bank       bank1, bank2;

account1  = new Account(); //create objects
account2  = new Account();
bank1     = new Bank();
bank2     = new Bank();

outObjectStream.writeObject( account1 );
outObjectStream.writeObject( account2 );
outObjectStream.writeObject( bank1    );
outObjectStream.writeObject( bank2    );
```

We can even mix objects and primitive data type values, for example,

```
outObjectStream.writeInt    ( 15       );
outObjectStream.writeObject( account1 );
outObjectStream.writeChar  ( 'X'      );
```

To read objects from a file, we use FileInputStream and ObjectInputStream. We use the method readObject to read an object. Since we can store any types of objects to a single file, we need to type cast the object read from the file. Here's an example of reading a Person object we saved in the file objects.data.

```
File              inFile
                     = new File("objects.data");

FileInputStream   inFileStream
                     = new FileInputStream(inFile);

ObjectInputStream inObjectStream
                     = new ObjectInputStream(inFileStream);

Person person = (Person) inObjectStream.readObject();
```

Need to type cast to the object type we are reading

Because there is a possibility of wrong type casting, the readObject method can throw a ClassNotFoundException, in addition to an IOException. You can catch or propagate either or both exceptions. If you propagate both exceptions, then the declaration of a method that contains the call to readObject will look like this:

```
public void myMethod( ) throws IOException, ClassNotFoundException
{
   . . .
}
```

If the file contains two Account and two Bank objects, then we must read them in the correct order:

```
account1  = (Account) inObjectStream.readObject();
account2  = (Account) inObjectStream.readObject();
bank1     = (Bank)    inObjectStream.readObject();
bank2     = (Bank)    inObjectStream.readObject();
```

Consider the following array of Person objects where N represents some integer value:

```
Person[] people = new Person[N];
```

Assuming that all N Person objects are in the array, we can store them to file as

```
//save the size of an array first
outObjectStream.writeInt( people.length );

//save Person objects next
for (int i = 0; i < people.length; i++ ) {
   outObjectStream.writeObject( people[i] );
}
```

We store the size of an array at the beginning of the file so we know exactly how many Person objects to read back:

```
int N = inObjectStream.readInt();

for (int i = 0; i < N; i++) {
   people[i] = (Person) inObjectStream.readObject();
}
```

Since an array itself is an object, we can actually store the whole array at once instead of storing individual elements one at a time. The whole people array can be stored at once by

```
outObjectStream.writeObject( people );
```

and the whole array is read back at once by

```
people = (Person[]) inObjectStream.readObject( );
```

Notice how the type casting is done. We are reading an array of Person objects, so the type casting is (Person[ ]).

Quick Check

1. When do you have to include the clause implements Serializable to a class definition?
2. True or false. You cannot save the whole array at once. You must save the array elements individually.

11.6 Sample Class: Saving an AddressBook Object

As an illustration of object I/O, we will write a class that handles the storage of an AddressBook object. The class will provide methods to write an Address-Book object to a file and to read the object back from the file.

Problem Statement

Write a class that manages file I/O of an AddressBook object.

Overall Plan

Before we begin designing the class, we must modify the definition of the AddressBook class by adding the phrase implements Serializable:

```
import java.io.*;
class AddressBook implements Serializable
{
    //same as before
}
```

This modification allows us to store an AddressBook object to a file.

Since the class handles the file I/O operations, we will call the class AddressBookStorage. Following the STO (single-task object) principle, this class will be responsible solely for file I/O of an AddressBook object. The class will not perform, for instance, any operations that deal with a user interface.

What kinds of core operations should this class support? Since the class handles the file I/O, the class should support two public methods to write and read an AddressBook object. Let's call the methods write and read. The argument will be an AddressBook object we want to write or read. If fileManager is an AddressBookStorage object, then the calls should be something like

```
fileManager.write( addressBook );
```

and

```
addressBook = fileManager.read( );
```

For an AddressBookStorage to actually store an AddressBook object, it must know the file to which an address book is written or from which it is read. How should we let the programmer specify this file? One possibility is to let the programmer pass the filename to a constructor, such as

```
AddressBookStorage fileManager
        = new AddressBookStorage("book.data");
```

Another possibility is to define a method to set the file, say, setFile, which is called as

```
fileManager.setFile( "book.data" );
```

Instead of choosing one over the other, we will support both. If we don't provide the setFile method, fileManager can input and output to a single file only. By using the setFile method, the programmer can change the file if he needs to. As for the constructor, we do not want to define a constructor with no argument because we do not want the programmer to create an AddressBookStorage object without specifying a filename. Yes, he can call the setFile method later, but as the AddressBookStorage class designer, we cannot ensure he will call the setFile method. If the programmer doesn't call the method, then the subsequent calls to the write or read method will fail. You might suggest that we set a default filename in a no-argument constructor. But what will be the default filename? No matter which filename we choose, there's a possibility that a file with this filename already exists, which will result in the file being erased. To make our class reliable, we will not provide a no-argument constructor.

The object diagram for the AddressBookStorage class at this point is

We will implement the class in the following order:

development
steps

1. Implement the constructor and the setFile method.

2. Implement the write method.

3. Implement the read method.

4. Finalize the class.

This order of development follows a natural sequence. We begin with the constructor as usual. Since the constructor and the setFile method carry out similar operations, we will implement them together. We will identify necessary data members in this step. The second step is to implement the file output routine, because without being able to write an AddressBook object, we won't be able to test the file input routine. For the third step, we will implement the file input routine.

Step 1 Development: Constructor and setFile

Step 1 Design In Step 1, we will identify the data members and define a constructor to initialize them. We will also implement the setFile method, which should be very similar to the constructor.

We need File, FileInputStream, FileOutputStream, ObjectInputStream, and ObjectOutputStream objects to do object I/O. Should we define a data member for each type of object? This is certainly a possibility, but we should not use any unnecessary data members. We need ObjectInputStream and ObjectOutput-Stream objects only at the time the actual read and write operations take place. We can create these objects in the read and write methods, only when they are needed. Had we used data members for all those objects, we would need to create and assign objects every time the setFile method is called. But calling the setFile method does not necessarily mean the actual file I/O will take place. Consider the case where the user changes the filename before actually saving an address book to a file. This will result in calling the setFile method twice before doing the actual file I/O. To avoid this type of unnecessary repetition, we will use one data member only, a String variable filename to keep the filename. The setFile method simply assigns the parameter to this variable. The constructor can do the same by calling this setFile method.

Step 1 Code   At this point, we have only one data member:

```
//-------------------------
// Data Members
//-------------------------

private  String  filename; //name of the file to store
                           //an AddressBook object
```

The setFile method assigns the parameter to the data member as

```
public void setFile( String filename )
{
    this.filename = filename;
}
```

and the constructor will simply call this method as

```
public AddressBookStorage( String filename )
{
    setFile( filename );
}
```

The class is defined as follows:

File: AddressBookStorage.java

```
class AddressBookStorage
{

//-------------------------------
// Data Members
//-------------------------------

    private String   filename;

//-------------------------------
// Constructors
//-------------------------------

    public AddressBookStorage( String filename )
    {
        setFile( filename );
    }
```

```
//----------------------------
//  Public Methods
//
//      void    setFile          ( String        )
//
//----------------------------

    public void setFile( String filename )
    {
        this.filename = filename;
        System.out.println("Inside setFile. Filename is " + filename );
                                                                //TEMP

    }
}
```

Step 1 Test

To test this class, we have included a temporary output statement inside the setFile method. We will write a test program to verify that we can create an AddressBookStorage object and use the setFile method correctly:

```
class TestAddressBookStorage
{
    public static void main ( String[] arg )
    {
        AddressBookStorage fileManager;

        fileManager = new AddressBookStorage( "one.data" );
        fileManager.setFile("two.data");
        fileManager.setFile("three.data");
    }
}
```

Step 2 Development: Implement the write Method

Step 2 Design

In the second development step, we will implement the write method. From the data member filename, we will create an ObjectOutputStream object and write the parameter AddressBook object to it. A sequence of method calls to create an ObjectOutputStream object can throw an IOException, so we must either propagate it or handle it. Following the STO principle, the method will propagate the thrown exception. The responsibility of an AddressBookStorage object is taking care of file I/O for others. When there's an exception, the object will inform the caller about the exception and let the caller decide what to do about it.

Step 2 Code

The write method is written as

```
public void write( AddressBook book ) throws IOException
{
    //first create an ObjectOutputStream
    File   outFile  = new File( filename );
```

```
FileOutputStream    outFileStream
                = new FileOutputStream(outFile);
ObjectOutputStream outObjectStream
                = new ObjectOutputStream(outFileStream);

//save the data to it
outObjectStream.writeObject( book );

//and close it
outObjectStream.close();
}
```

Step 2 Test   We will write a test program to verify that the data are saved to a file. Since we do not have a method to read the file contents yet, we can only verify at this point that the file is created and this file has something in it. To do so, we run the following Step 2 test program first. Then, we use whatever tool that is available (e.g., Windows Explorer, DOS command dir, UNIX command ls, etc.) and check that the specified file exists and the file size is greater than zero.

The Step 2 test program is as follows (**TestAddressBookStorage** is now an instantiable class):

```
class Tester
{
    public static void main (String[] args) throws IOException
    {
        TestAddressBookWrite tester
                        = new TestAddressBookWrite( 15 );

        tester.testWrite( "book.data" );
    }
}

class TestAddressBookWrite
{
    AddressBook         myBook;
    AddressBookStorage  fileManager;

    public TestAddressBookWrite( int N )
    {
        myBook = new AddressBook( N );

        Person person;
        for (int i = 0; i < N; i++) { //add N Person objects
            person = new Person("Ms. X"+i, 10, 'F');
            myBook.add( person );
        }
    }
```

```
public void testWrite( String filename )
{
    fileManager = new AddressBookStorage( filename );

    try {
        fileManager.write( myBook );
    }
    catch ( IOException e ) {
        System.out.println("Error: " +
                        "IOException is thrown.");
    }
}
}
```

Run the program several times with different sizes for the address book and verify that the resulting files have different sizes.

Step 3 Development: Implement the read Method

Step 3 Design

In the third development step, we will implement the read method. The method reads the AddressBook object saved in the file and returns this object to the caller. Like the write method, if there's an exception, this method will propagate it back to the caller and let the caller decide what to do to the thrown exception.

Step 3 Code

The read method is written as

```
public AddressBook read( ) throws IOException,
                            ClassNotFoundException
{
    AddressBook book;

    //first create an ObjectInputStream
    File    inFile    = new File( filename );
    FileInputStream   inFileStream
                    = new FileInputStream(inFile);
    ObjectInputStream inObjectStream
                    = new ObjectInputStream(inFileStream);

    //read the data from it
    book = (AddressBook) inObjectStream.readObject(  );

    //close it
    inObjectStream.close();

    //and read the object
    return book;
}
```

Step 3 Test   We will write a test program to verify that the data can be read back from a file. This test program also verifies that the write method in Step 2 is saving the data correctly. Before you run this test program, don't forget to run the Step 2 test program to make sure that the file is available. The Step 3 test program is as follows:

```java
class Tester
{
    public static void main ( String[] args )
            throws IOException, ClassNotFoundException
    {
        TestAddressBookRead tester
                        = new TestAddressBookRead(  );

        tester.testRead( "book.data" );
    }
}


class TestAddressBookRead
{
    AddressBook         myBook;
    AddressBookStorage  fileManager;

    public void testRead( )
    {
        fileManager = new AddressBookStorage( filename );

        try {
            myBook = fileManager.read( );
            printout();
        }
        catch ( IOException e ) {
            System.out.println
                        ("Error: IOException is thrown.");
        }
        catch ( ClassNotFoundException e ) {
            System.out.println
                ("Error: ClassNotFoundException is thrown.");
        }
    }

    private void printout()
    {
        Person person;

        person = myBook.search( "Ms. X5" );
```

```
                    if (person != null) {
                        System.out.println( person.getName()   );
                        System.out.println( person.getAge()    );
                        System.out.println( person.getGender() );
                    }
                    else {
                        System.out.println("Error: Object not found");
                    }
                }
            }
```

Run the program several times changing the method body of printout to access different Person objects in the address book as necessary and verify that you can read the Person object in the file correctly. If you did exercise 17 on page 478, then use the getFirstPerson and getNextPerson methods to access all Person objects in the address book.

Step 4 Development: Finalize

program
review

final test

We finalize the program in the last step. We perform a critical review for finding any inconsistency or error in the methods, incomplete methods, places to add more comments, and so forth. And, as always, we will carry out the final test. As the result of the critical review and final testing, we may identify and wish to implement any additional features.

11.7   Exercises

1. What will happen if you forget to close a file?

2. What is the difference between binary files and textfiles?

3. Using the try–catch block, write code that opens a file default.dat when an attempt to open a user-designated file raises an exception.

4. Using a File object, write code to display files in a user-specified directory and its subdirectories. (Note: For those who studied the optional section on recursion in Chapter 7, this problem can be implemented using recursion.)

5. Write code to store and read the contents of the payScaleTable 2-D array from Section 9.7 in the following two file formats:

    • a file of float values.
    • a file of 2-D array.

6. Write an application that reads a textfile and converts its content to an Eggy-Peggy text. Save the converted text to another textfile. Use FileDialog to let the user specify the input and output files. Create the input file using a text editor.

7. Write an application that randomly generates N integers and stores them in a binary file integers.dat. The value for N is input by the user. Open the file with a text editor and see what the contents of a binary file look like.

8. Write an application that reads the data from the file integers.dat generated in exercise 7. After the data are read, display the smallest, the largest, and the average.

9. Repeat exercise 7, but this time, store the numbers in a textfile integers.txt. Open this file with a text editor and verify that you can read the contents.

10. Repeat exercise 8 with the textfile integers.txt generated in exercise 9.

11. Write a currency converter application. Allow the user to specify the from and to currencies and the amount to exchange. Use whatever interface methods are appropriate to input these three values. When the application starts, read the exchange rates from a textfile rate.txt. Use a text editor to create this textfile. By using a textfile, you can easily update the exchange rates. The format for the textfile is as follows:

```
<name of currency> <units per dollar>
```

For example, the following shows how much a dollar is worth in five foreign currencies:

```
French franc              5.95
Indonesian rupiah     12900.0
Japanese yen            145.91
Mexican peso              9.18
Papua New Guinea kina     2.381
```

You can get the exchange rates from various websites, one of which is http://www.oanda.com.

12. Extend the AddressBookStorage class by adding import and export capabilities. Add a method export that stores the contents of AddressBook to a textfile. Add a second method import that reads the textfile back and constructs an AddressBook. This type of import/export feature is a convenient means to move data from one application to another.

13. Extend the encryption application of exercise 22 on page 409 so that the original text is read from a user-specified textfile and the encrypted text is stored to another user-specified textfile.

14. Extend the watermelon projectile computation program of exercise 23 page 350 so the output is saved to a file. Which file format would you use

for the program: a binary file or a textfile? Or would you consider using an array to keep the (x,y) coordinates and save this array using an object I/O?

15. Extend any application you have written before by adding a quote-of-the-day dialog. When the user starts the application, a quote of the day is displayed (either a MessageBox or an OutputBox). The quotes are saved in a textfile. Use a random number generator to select the quote to display.

16. Write an application that removes extra spaces from a textfile. In the days of the typewriter, it was a common practice to leave two spaces after the periods. We shouldn't be doing that anymore with the computer, but many people still do. Read an original textfile and output an edited version to another textfile. The edited version should replace two or more consecutive spaces with one space.

17. Write a mail merge application. You use two files for this program. The first is a textfile that contains a template letter in the following style:

```
Dear <<N>>,

Because you are <<A>> years old and <<G>>, we have a
free gift for you. You have absolutely nothing to buy;
just pay the shipping and handling charge of $9.99. To
claim your gift, call us now immediately.

Thank you,
Office of Claims Department
```

The tags <<N>>, <<A>>, and <<G>> are placeholders for the person's name, age, and gender. The second file contains the name, age, and gender information of people to whom you want to send a letter. Use whatever format you wish for the second file. Read two files and print out the letter with the placeholders replaced by the actual values from the second file. Run the program multiple times, each time using a different template file. For this program, output the personalized letter to an OutputBox. You can also use saveToFile of the OutputBox class to save the personalized letters.

12

Reusable Classes and Packages

OBJECTIVES

After you have read and studied this chapter, you should be able to

- Describe four different object categories and use them effectively in designing classes.

- Define a package and place reusable classes in it.

- Write a method that calls the superclass's method explicitly by using the reserved word super.

- Define overloaded methods.

Introduction

reusable
classes

One of the key benefits of using object-oriented technology is reusability. We say a class is *reusable* if it can be used in different programs. For example, pre-defined classes in the javabook and the standard Java packages are all highly re-usable. Although reusability of classes is very important, it does not mean that every class we design should be reusable. There are classes that we need to de-sign specifically for a particular program, and these classes are not reusable at all. What is important here is to design the classes accordingly. If a class is in-tended to be reusable, then we must design it carefully so that it is indeed reus-able. In this chapter we will cover the topics related to defining reusable classes.

12.1 Object Categories

We have already mentioned on several occasions the importance of the STO principle. For a class to be reusable, we must implement it following the STO principle:

Design a class that implements a single well-defined task. Do not overburden the class with multiple tasks.

How do we know whether a class is overburdened or not? There is no mathe-matical formula to answer this question, but there are guidelines we can follow. One helpful design guideline is the categorization of objects. We classify the roles objects play into four categories. We know that an object is overburdened if the object is doing two different categories of tasks, for example.

We divide object tasks into four categories: user interface, controller, appli-cation logic, and storage.

user interface
object

- A *user interface object* handles the interaction between the user and the program. InputBox, OutputBox, ResponseBox, and others from the javabook package are all user interface objects.

controller
object

- A *controller object* supervises other objects in the program. Objects such as EggyPeggy from Section 8.7 on page 392 and HiLo from Section 7.9 on page 325 are controller objects.

application logic
object

- An *application logic object* captures the logic of the real world for which the program is written. An AddressBook object from Chapter 9 that models the functionality of an address book in the real world is an example of an application logic object. An application logic object does not have to model a real-world concept. It could be an intangible or imaginary object that does not have any real-world counterpart.

storage
object

- A *storage object* takes care of file input and output. An Address-BookStorage object from Chapter 11 is a storage object.

Keep in mind that these categories are informal guidelines. It is possible to design a single object that implements more than one category of tasks. It does not necessarily imply that this object is overburdened and poorly designed. However, when you end up in an object that performs multiple categories of tasks, then you should be extra careful to make sure that the object is designed properly. If an object, for example, does both storage and user interface of the program, it is very likely that this object is not designed properly. However, just because it does two different types of tasks does not mean the object is poorly designed. Whether an object is designed properly or not depends mainly on how the object is intended to be used. For example, if an object that implements both storage and user interface tasks is very easy to reuse in many different programs, then the object meets its purpose and we can say that it is designed properly.

Normally, controller objects are specific to a particular program, so their degree of reusability is very low, almost none. Application logic objects have a good chance of being highly reusable, and to make them highly reusable, we must design them correctly. We will illustrate this point in the next section. The reusability of the user interface objects may be high or low depending on how closely the objects are tied to specific application objects. For example, an InputBox object is a generic object that can input any primitive data, so its reusability is quite high. On the other hand, a dialog object specifically designed to input three data values of a Person is less reusable. It is reusable only when the Person object is reused. A storage object's reusability depends on the degree of reusability of the application object it stores. If the storage object is designed to store any classes of objects, then its reusability is high. On the other hand, if it is designed to store one specific class of objects, then its reusability is low.

Quick Check

1. Name four categories of object roles?
2. Quickly go over the objects in the Chapters 8 and 9 sample programs, and for each object, tell its category.
3. Suppose we design an airline reservation system and include a Fare-Calculator class. Is an instance of this class an application logic object? Does a FareCalculator object model a real-world counterpart? Or is it an intangible object that exists in the cyberspace of programming?

12.2 Method Overriding and Overloaded Methods

One application logic object we used earlier is the DrawingBoard class that we used in Chapter 6 to implement the DrawShape program. In this section, we will define the DrawingBoard class as promised in Chapter 6. While defining the class, we will introduce two new concepts in object-oriented programming.

The following is the table of public methods of the DrawingBoard class we used in Chapter 6. We will implement these and the second version of the drawRectangle method here.

Public Methods of DrawingBoard
`public void drawLine( int x1, int y1, int x2, int y2 )`
Draws a line from point (x1,y1) to (x2,y2)
`public void drawCircle( int centerX, int centerY, int radius)`
Draws a circle centered at (centerX,centerY) with radius radius.
`public void drawRectangle(int x, int y, int width, int height)`
Draws a rectangle whose top left corner is at (x,y) with width width and height height.
`public void setColor( Color color)`
Sets the color to color. All subsequent shapes will be drawn in the color color.

The class diagram for DrawingBoard is shown in Figure 12.1. The class has one private instance variable graphic of type Graphics. We need this Graphics object to draw lines, rectangles, and other geometric figures on a window. We have seen the Graphics class back in Chapter 2. You might want to look at the first sample applet in Chapter 2 to review the Graphics class. The variable graphic is initialized inside the setVisible method as

```
public void setVisible( boolean state )
{
    super.setVisible( state );        This statement calls the
    graphic = getGraphics();          ancestor's setVisible
}                                     method.
```

The method calls the ancestor's show method and initializes the variable graphic using the inherited method getGraphics. The syntax for calling an ancestor's method is

```
super . <method name> ( <parameters> ) ;
```

FIGURE 12.1   The diagram for the **DrawingBoard** class.

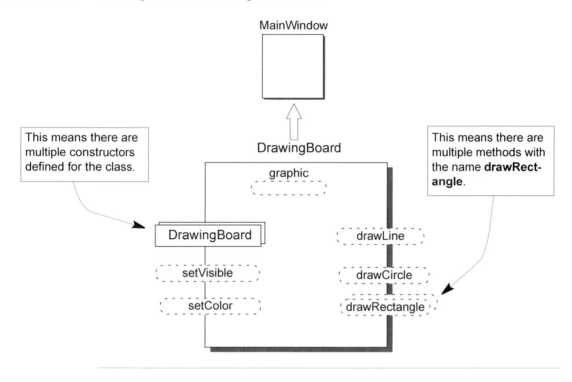

method
overriding

We say the setVisible method of the DrawingBoard class *overrides* the inherited setVisible method of the ancestor class. The subclass's method can completely rewrite the inherited method or add code to it. The setVisible method here is the latter case. It calls the ancestor's setVisible method and adds one line of code for initializing the variable graphic. By writing the setVisible method this way, we made sure that the instance variable graphic refers to a valid Graphics object when the window appears on the screen.

Some of you may be wondering why we do not call the getGraphics method inside the constructor. We do not because the method is meaningful only after the window appears on the screen. In other words, if we call the method inside the constructor, before the window actually appears on the screen, then the getGraphics method does not return a valid Graphics object. You might want to experiment with this by placing a call to the getGraphics method in the constructor instead.

The diagram in Figure 12.1 shows that the class has more than one method called drawRectangle. We used only one of them in Chapter 6. A class can have multiple methods with the same name, provided that they have different signa-

method
signature

tures. The *signature* of a method is determined by the method name and the number and data types of parameters. The following three methods have different signatures:

```
public void myMethod( int one, float two)
public void myMethod( int one, double two)
public void myMethod( int one, float two, long three)
```

overloaded
methods

If multiple methods have the same name but different signatures, we say the method name is *overloaded* and call these methods *overloaded methods*. We have been using overloaded methods all along. For example, we can pass a numerical value or a string to the show method of MessageBox because the methods are overloaded. There are numerous overloaded methods in the javabook and the standard Java packages.

The drawRectangle methods are overloaded methods. They are defined as

```
public void drawRectangle(int x, int y, int width, int height)
{
    graphic.drawRect(x, y, width, height);
}
```

```
public void drawRectangle(Rectangle rect)
{
    graphic.drawRect(rect.x, rect.y, rect.width, rect.height);
}
```

The Rectangle class is from java.awt. A Rectangle object represents a rectangle using four public instance variables: x and y define the top left corner of the rectangle and width and height define the size of the rectangle. The class provides methods you can use to manipulate rectangles (moving, resizing, etc.). Please refer to a reference manual for more details on Rectangle.

The signature of a method does not include its modifier (public, private, static, etc.) and return type. For example, the declarations

```
public void one ( int x )
private void one ( int x )

public int two ( float y )
public float two ( float y )

public static void three ( )
public void three ( )
```

method
prototype

will result in errors because the methods with the same name do not have different signatures. We use the term *method prototype* to include the access modifier and the return type with the method signature. The sample declarations above have the same signatures but different prototypes.

> **Method signatures do not include the access modifier and return type. Method prototypes are signatures plus the modifier and the return type.**

A class can have multiple constructors. In other words, we can overload constructors. There are two constructors defined for the DrawingBoard class. The first constructor is defined as

```
public DrawingBoard(String title)
{
    super(title);
    setResizable(false);
    setBackground(Color.white);    //white background
}
```

The constructor first calls the superclass's constructor and sets the window title. Then, it sets the window as nonresizable and the background to white. The window title is passed to the constructor by the user as in

```
DrawingBoard doodleBoard;
doodleBoard = new DrawingBoard( "My Etch-A-Sketch" );
```

The second constructor is defined as

```
public DrawingBoard( )
{
    this( "D R A W I N G    B O A R D" ); //calls the other
                                          //constructor
}
```

When the user creates a DrawingBoard object by calling the second constructor as in

```
DrawingBoard doodleBoard;
doodleBoard = new DrawingBoard( );
```

then the window title will be DRAWING BOARD (with spaces between the letters).

The second constructor simply calls the first constructor by using the reserved word this and passing a title. The reserved word this refers to "this object." So the second constructor is indicating something like "call this object's constructor." The compiler knows which constructor to invoke by matching its signature against the arguments in the call. We will discuss a further use of the reserved word this in the next chapter. We could have defined the second constructor as

```
public DrawingBoard( )
{
   super( "D R A W I N G    B O A R D" );
   setResizable(false);
   setBackground(Color.white);    //white background
}
```

but this would duplicate the code. Suppose we want to change the background color to gray. We have to change both constructors. It is not uncommon to have four or five constructors defined for a class, and duplicating the code as such would make it harder to modify the code later because you have to make changes to every constructor, instead of changing just one constructor.

It is very common to find classes in the standard Java packages that support multiple constructors because they increase the usability of the class. If your class supports only one constructor, then the programmer using your class has only one way to create an instance. If, however, your class supports multiple constructors, then the programmer has an option of choosing the constructor that works best for her or him.

Try to define multiple constructors to your class to increase its usability.

The method for drawing a circle is defined as

```
public void drawCircle(int x, int y, radius)
{
   graphic.drawOval( x - radius, y - radius,
                  2 * radius, 2 * radius );
}
```

This method calls the drawOval method of the Graphics class. The drawCircle method is a more meaningful and intuitive function than the drawOval method to draw a circle. Instead of passing four parameters to the drawOval method, the user can draw a circle with the drawCircle method by passing three parameters—the circle's center point (x, y) and its radius.

Here's the complete class definition:

```
package javabook;

import java.awt.*;

/**
 * DrawingBoard Class
 *
 * This class provides a simple window for drawing lines,
 * circles, and rectangles in color.
 *
 * @author Dr. Caffeine
 *
 */

public class DrawingBoard extends MainWindow
{

//--------------------------------
// Data Members
//--------------------------------

    private Graphics graphic;

//--------------------------------
// Constructors
//--------------------------------

    /**
     * Default constructor.
     * The default window title is "D R A W I N G   B O A R D".
     */
    public DrawingBoard( )
    {
        this ( "D R A W I N G    B O A R D" );
    }

    /**
     * Constructs a Drawingboard object with the given title and sets
     * the background color to white.
     *
     * @param title the title of this object
     */
    public DrawingBoard( String title )
    {
        setTitle( title );
        setResizable(false);
        setBackground(Color.white);    //white background
    }

//----------------------------------------------------
//      Public Methods:
//
//         void   drawCircle    ( int, int, int     )
//         void   drawLine      ( int, int, int, int)
//         void   drawRectangle ( Rectangle         )
//         void   drawRectangle ( int, int, int, int )
//
```

```
//        void    setColor      ( Color                    )
//        void    setVisible     ( boolean                  )
//
//-------------------------------------------------

    /**
     * Draws a circle with center point (x, y) and radius.
     *
     * @param x      the x coordinate of the center point
     * @param y      the y coordinate of the center point
     * @param radius the radius of the circle
     */
    public void drawCircle(int x, int y, int radius)
    {
        graphic.drawOval(x - radius, y - radius, 2*radius, 2*radius);
    }


    /**
     * Draws a line from (x1,y1) to (x2,y2)
     *
     * @param x1    the x coordinate of the first point
     * @param y1    the y coordinate of the first point
     * @param x2    the x coordinate of the second point
     * @param y2    the y coordinate of the second point
     */
    public void drawLine(int x1, int y1, int x2, int y2)
    {
        graphic.drawLine(x1, y1, x2, y2);
    }


    /**
     * Draws a rectangle rect.
     *
     * @param rect the Rectangle object to draw
     */
    public void drawRectangle( Rectangle rect )
    {
        graphic.drawRect( rect.x, rect.y, rect.width, rect.height );
    }


    /**
     * Draws a rectangle at (x,y) with width and height
     *
     * @param x        the x coordinate of the rectangle's top left corner
     * @param y        the y coordinate of the rectangle's top left corner
     * @param width    the width of the rectangle
     * @param height   the height of the rectangle
     */
    public void drawRectangle(int x, int y, int width, int height)
    {
        graphic.drawRect(x, y, width, height);
    }


    /**
     * Sets the color. Subsequent drawings will be in this color
     * until changed again.
     *
     * @param color  the color to use in the subsequent drawings
     */
    public void setColor(Color color)
    {
```

```
        graphic.setColor(color);
    }

    /**
     * Makes the window visible and sets the Graphics object.
     *
     * @param state true to make this window visible
     */
    public void setVisible( boolean state )
    {
        super.setVisible( state );
        graphic = getGraphics();
    }

}
```

Quick Check

1. Which two of the following declarations have the same method signature?

```
public     int    quizMethod( int one, float two )
public     void   quizMethod( int one, float two )
private    void   quizMethod( int one, int   two )
```

2. What is the difference between method signature and method prototype?

12.3 Sample Classes: Reusable EggyPeggy and HiLo

In Chapters 7 and 8, we wrote two sample game programs: Hi-Lo and Eggy-Peggy. In those two sample programs, we used user interface objects from the javabook package. The HiLo and EggyPeggy classes in those programs were both controller objects managing other objects. In addition, they handled the logic of the program. So they were overburdened, but this was not critical because these two classes were written specifically for those programs and never intended to be reused in other programs.

In this section, we will define them as application logic objects and show you how they can be made reusable. By defining them as application logic objects, the programmer will be able to reuse them in many different ways. Since the instances of the redesigned classes are now strictly application logic objects, the programmer must supply the code for the user interface, storage, and other tasks of the program. But this gives the programmer flexibility in building different kinds of programs. For example, it is possible for the programmer to write both application-based and applet-based Hi-Lo programs using the same

HiLo application logic object. For the program's user interface and other tasks, the programmer can build the classes herself or himself or reuse existing classes.

Through the implementation of these two reusable classes, we will highlight key points of designing reusable classes. As always, we will develop the two classes incrementally. Let's begin with the EggyPeggy class.

EggyPeggy

We will design a reusable EggyPeggy class whose instance can play Eggy-Peggy games. The class implements an application logic object, and as such, an instance of the class will not handle tasks such as input/output, data storage, or control of other objects. The class is strictly geared toward playing an Eggy-Peggy game. One criterion of reusability is how general the class is. When a class is too limited in capability, then its reusability is low. For example, an EggyPeggy object that can add any user-designated word in front of every vowel is more general, and thus, more reusable, than an EggyPeggy object that can only add the fixed word egg in front of every vowel. Since our objective is to make the class reusable, we will implement a more general EggyPeggy class.

Design a class as general as possible to increase its reusability.

Problem Statement

Write a class that converts a given string to an Eggy-Peggy string by placing the programmer-specified word in front of all vowels in the given string. If the programmer does not specify the word, then the default prefix "egg" will be used.

Overall Plan

When we design a reusable class whose instance methods are called by other classes and objects, we start thinking about the public instance methods of the class. What kinds of methods should the class support so the programmer can use the class easily and effortlessly? What kinds of methods are natural and logical from the programmer's standpoint? These are the types of questions we ask ourselves in designing a reusable class.

What kinds of methods should the EggyPeggy class support? The problem statement indicated a conversion process of generating a new string from a given string. So let's define a method called convert. The programmer will use this method in the following manner:

```
String          newString, inputString;
EggyPeggy       eggyPeggyMaker;
```

```
...
eggyPeggyMaker     = new EggyPeggy();

inputString        = inputBox.getString();
newString          = eggyPeggyMaker.convert( inputString );
```

Since an EggyPeggy object is required to allow the programmer to set any word as a prefix attached in front of vowels, let's define a method to set the prefix. We will call the method setPrefixWord, and this method is used in the following manner:

```
...
eggyPeggyMaker.setPrefixWord("roll");//set the prefix
...                                  //first
newString = eggyPeggyMaker.convert( inputString );
                                     //and then convert
```

Our working design document for the EggyPeggy class at this point is as follows:

Design Document: The EggyPeggy Class		
Method	**Visibility**	**Purpose**
<constructor>	public	Creates and initializes the objects used by an EggyPeggy object.
convert	public	Returns a new String by converting a given String passed as an argument.
setPrefixWord	public	Sets the prefix word to a String passed as an argument.

And its object diagram at this point is

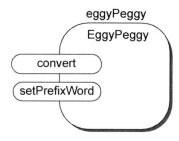

We will implement the class in the following two steps:

development
steps

1. Start with a class skeleton. Define the necessary data members and constructors.

2. Implement the setPrefixWord and convert methods. Add any private methods as necessary.

Step 1 Development: Skeleton with Constructors

Step 1 Design

Let's start with data members of the class. An EggyPeggy object allows a programmer-specified prefix word, so we need a data member of type String to remember this word. If no prefix word is set by the programmer, the object will use the default prefix word egg. We can use a constant to keep this default prefix word. The declaration for the data members should look like

```
//--------------------------------
// Data Members
//--------------------------------

private static final String DEFAULT_PREFIX = "egg";

private String prefix;
```

What kinds of constructors should the class support? We will define one constructor with which the programmer can set the prefix word at the time an instance is created. Here's the constructor:

```
public EggyPeggy( String prefix )
{
    this.prefix = prefix;
}
```

Let's define a second constructor that will allow the programmer to create an instance with a default prefix word. Since we use a default prefix word, this constructor accepts no arguments:

```
public EggyPeggy()
{
    this( DEFAULT_PREFIX );
}
```

Step 1 Code

Here's the skeleton for the class with stub public methods:

```
/**
 * EggyPeggy Class
 *
 * This class plays the word game Eggy-Peggy. Pass the original string to
 * the convert method, and it will return an Eggy-Peggy string, a string
 * where all vowels are preceded by the word 'egg'. You can change the
 * default prefix
 * word 'egg' to any word you like by calling the setPrefixWord method.
 *
 * @author Dr. Caffeine
 */

class EggyPeggy
{
//-------------------------------
// Data Members
//-------------------------------

    private static final String DEFAULT_PREFIX = "egg";

    private String prefix;

//-------------------------------
// Constructors
//-------------------------------
    /**
     * Default constructor. Uses the default prefix "egg".
     */
    public EggyPeggy()
    {
        this( DEFAULT_PREFIX );
    }

    /**
     * Constructs an EggyPeggy object with the given prefix.
     *
     * @param prefix the text to be added as a prefix
     */
    public EggyPeggy( String prefix )
    {
        this.prefix = prefix;
    }

//-------------------------------------------------
//      Public Methods:
//
//          String    convert         ( String  )
//          void      setPrefixWord   ( String  )
//
//-------------------------------------------------
    /**
     * Converts an argument string to an Eggy-Peggy string.
     * Data member prefix is the word placed in front of
     * all vowels in the original string.
     *
     * @param  originalSentence the original text before conversion
     * @return the newly created Eggy-Peggy text
     */
```

```
public String convert( String originalSentence )
{
    String newString;

    System.out.println("Inside convert: prefix is " + prefix);//TEMP

    newString = "temp new string";
    return newString;
}

/**
 * Sets the prefix word to the passed argument.
 *
 * @param  prefix the prefix text to be used for the conversion
 */
public void setPrefixWord( String prefix )
{
    System.out.println("Inside setPrefixWord");    //TEMP
}
}
```

Step 1 Test   In order to test the skeleton **EggyPeggy** class, we need to write a test main class. The test main class will create an instance of the **EggyPeggy** class and call the **convert** and **setPrefixWord** methods several times. One possible test main class is the following:

```
class TestEggyPeggy
{
    public static void main (String args[])
    {
        EggyPeggy eggyPeggy1, eggyPeggy2;
        String      str1, str2;

        eggyPeggy1 = new EggyPeggy( );
        eggyPeggy2 = new EggyPeggy("bacon");

        eggyPeggy1.setPrefixWord("avocado");

        str1 = eggyPeggy1.convert("testing one");
        str2 = eggyPeggy2.convert("testing two");
    }
}
```

When you execute the test main class, you should see the following printout in the standard output window **System.out**:

```
Inside setPrefixWord
Inside convert: prefix is egg
Inside convert: prefix is bacon
```

Notice that the **setPrefixWord** method has no effect on the data member **prefix** at this point. We call the method in the test main class basically to verify the method is declared correctly.

Step 2 Development: Implement setPrefixWord **and** convert

Step 2 Design   In the second step of development, we complete the two public methods and add whatever private methods we design to support the public methods. The task of the **setPrefixWord** method is to set the prefix word, which can be accomplished by including the same statement we have in the second constructor:

```
this.prefix = prefix;
```

The overall idea of converting a given string to an Eggy-Peggy string was already designed in Chapter 8. Since we are now writing a method that accepts an original string as an argument and returns the converted string, we modify the pseudocode in Chapter 8 to the following:

```
for the first to the last character in argument string {

    if (character is a vowel) {
        append "egg" and character to a StringBuffer object;
    }
    else {
        append character only to a StringBuffer object;
    }

}

convert the StringBuffer to a String;

return the String;
```

We will add a private method **isVowel** that checks whether a given character is a vowel or not. The method returns **true** if the argument character is a vowel. This method was already designed and implemented in Chapter 8, and we will use it here. The EggyPeggy class document now includes one private method **isVowel**. The working design document now includes this method:

Design Document:	The EggyPeggy Class	
Method	**Visibility**	**Purpose**
. . .	. . .	. . .
isVowel	private	Returns true if the argument character is a vowel and false otherwise.

The setPrefixWord method is defined as follows:

```
public void setPrefixWord( String prefix )
{
    this.prefix = prefix;
}
```

And to avoid code duplication, we will modify the second constructor to

```
public EggyPeggy( String prefix )
{
    setPrefixWord( prefix );
}
```

The convert method is defined as follows:

```
public String convert( String originalSentence )
{
    int             numberOfCharacters;
    char            letter;
    StringBuffer    encryptedSentence;

    encryptedSentence    = new StringBuffer("");
    numberOfCharacters   = originalSentence.length();

    for (int index = 0; index < numberOfCharacters; index++) {
        //get the next letter
        letter = originalSentence.charAt(index);

        if ( isVowel(letter) ) {
            //add the prefix string and then the vowel
            //to encryptedSentence
            encryptedSentence.append(prefix + letter);
        }
        else {
            //add the letter to encryptedSentence
            encryptedSentence.append(letter);
        }
    }

    return encryptedSentence.toString();
}
```

The isVowel method is the same as in Chapter 8, but we will list it again here for easy reference. The method is implemented as follows:

```
private boolean isVowel(char letter)
{
    boolean result = false;

    if (   letter == 'a' || letter == 'A' ||
           letter == 'e' || letter == 'E' ||
           letter == 'i' || letter == 'I' ||
           letter == 'o' || letter == 'O' ||
           letter == 'u' || letter == 'U'    )  {

        result = true;
    }
    return result;
}
```

Step 2 Test

We modify the **TestEggyPeggy** main class from Step 1 to test the Step 2 program. Expressed in pseudocode, the test routine will look something like this:

```
eggyPeggy1 = new EggyPeggy( );
eggyPeggy2 = new EggyPeggy( "bacon" );

str1 = eggyPeggy1.convert( <testString1> );
output str1;

eggyPeggy1.setPrefixWord( "avocado" );
str1 = eggyPeggy1.convert( <testString1> );
output str1;

str2 = eggyPeggy2.convert( <testString2> );
output str2;

eggyPeggy2.setPrefixWord( "tomato" );
str2 = eggyPeggy2.convert( <testString2> );
output str2;
```

You should try various strings (e.g., empty string, string with one character, string with no vowels, string with only vowels, etc.) for <testString1> and <testString2>.

HiLo

Now let's move on to redesign the HiLo class so its instance becomes an application logic object. The HiLo class we developed in Chapter 7 illustrated the use of repetition control and predefined objects. A HiLo object in that program controls other objects from the javabook package. It was a controller object and not intended to be reusable. Here, we will design a new HiLo class as an application logic class that captures the functionality of game playing only. By making this class implement the logic of the Hi-Lo game, the class becomes reusable in different types of programs. For example, the programmer can use it in writing a program that supports either a GUI or a CUI (*character-based user interface*).

As we did with the application logic EggyPeggy class, we will design the new HiLo class as general as possible to increase its reusability. In the original class, the game is limited to guessing a secret number between 1 and 100. Also, the number of guesses allowed was fixed. We will remove these restrictions. Here is the new problem statement.

Problem Statement

> *Write an application logic class that will play Hi-Lo games. The objective of the game is for the user to guess the computer-generated secret number in the least number of tries. The programmer can set the low and high bounds of a secret number and the number of guesses the user is allowed. If the number of guesses allowed is not set by the programmer, then it is set by the* HiLo *object based on the designated low and high bounds. The default low and high bounds are 1 and 100. The default number of guesses for the default low and high bounds is 7.*

Overall Plan

As we did with the EggyPeggy class, let's begin our design of the new HiLo class with its public instance methods. What kinds of public methods should a HiLo object support? From the given problem statement and thinking from the programmer's viewpoint, we envision our program will use a HiLo object in the following manner:

```
hiLo = new HiLo( );

while (the user wants to play game) {

    hiLo.newGame( );
    do {
        get next userGuess;

        answer = hiLo.nextGuess( userGuess );

        if (answer is LO)
            output LO message;

        else if (answer is HI)
            output HI message;
```

```
        } while ( answer != BINGO && game is not over );

        if ( answer == BINGO )
            output YOU WIN message;
        else
            output YOU LOSE message;
    }
```

The three statements surrounded by the dotted ellipse are the calls to the methods of the HiLo class. The three methods are

1. Constructor.

2. newGame to start a new game.

3. nextGuess to pass a new guess and get a result back.

Let's begin the design of the HiLo class from these methods. The constructor we included in the pseudocode passes no arguments:

```
    hiLo  =  new HiLo( );
```

When this constructor is called, we will initialize a HiLo object with default values for the low and high bounds of a secret number and the number of guesses allowed. We will perform this assignment of default values so the created object is initialized properly, that is, we do not leave any attributes (data members) of an object undefined.

In addition to this constructor, we can define constructors in which the programmer can pass the values for an object's data members. The class will allow the programmer to set the low and high bounds of a secret number and the number of guesses allowed. We can define different constructors to accept any combinations of these three values, but to do so would result in far too many constructors (some of which may not be natural, e.g., passing the low bound and the number of guesses). Defining too many constructors would make them more difficult to use. We will define two additional constructors. A second constructor will accept two arguments—the low and high bounds. The number of guesses allowed will be computed from the given low and high bounds. To create a HiLo object with 100 and 300 as the low and high bounds, for example, we call the second constructor as

```
    hiLo  = new HiLo( 100, 300 );
```

A third constructor will allow the programmer to pass all three values—the low and high bounds and the number of guesses allowed. For example, the statement

```
hiLo  = new HiLo( 1, 100, 3 );
```

will create a HiLo object with low and high bounds of 1 and 100 and the number of guesses allowed of 3.

After a HiLo object is created, we will call its newGame method every time we play a new game. The newGame method will reset an object to play another game. One of the key functions of the method is to generate a new secret number. We will use a pseudorandom number generator to generate a secret number as before. The method will also initialize whatever data members that need to be initialized at the beginning of a new game.

When the programmer calls the newGame method, should we allow him or her to change the low and high bounds and the number of guesses? If we allow this option, then a single HiLo object can play different types of Hi-Lo games. If we don't allow this option, then a single instance can play many games but the values for the low and high bounds and the number of allowed guesses remain the same for every game it plays. To write a program that plays different types of Hi-Lo games, the programmer must create many instances of the HiLo class.

We will adopt the scenario that a single instance can play many games of the same type. The newGame method we define here therefore has no parameters. We will leave the alternative design of newGame as an exercise for you to think about the pros and cons of the two approaches.

Every time the user enters a new guess, we will call the nextGuess method, passing the user guess as its argument. The nextGuess method will reply back with a result. There are basically three possible results: LO, HI, or BINGO. What should be the data type for this result? One possibility is a String. The method can return a String such as "LO", "HI", and "BINGO". Although the use of a String is a very general way of passing information back, it is also error-prone. It is very easy for the programmer to make a mistake and compare the String HI against Hi, for example. When the number of values to return from a method is only a handful or less, then a simple integer is better. By declaring public class constants for each of the possible return values, we can reduce programmer errors. We will declare the constants as

```
public static final int HI = 1;
public static final int LO = 2;
//and so forth
```

Using these constants, the portion of pseudocode can be stated as

```
...
if ( answer == HiLo.LO )
   ...
else if ( answer == HiLo.HI )
   ...
```

Are there any portions in the pseudocode that we need to translate into a public method of HiLo? Notice the condition for stopping the do–while loop. The loop is continued if the secret number was not yet guessed and not all of the allowed number of guesses were used up. We use the expression

```
answer != HiLo.BINGO
```

to test that the correct guess was not yet made. How should we express that the game is not over, that is, the number of allowed guesses is not used up yet? Whose responsibility is it to check this condition? Should it be the responsibility of a programmer who is using a HiLo object? The programmer can use a counter for this purpose. Or should it be the responsibility of a HiLo object?

We indicated that the role of HiLo objects is to play Hi-Lo games. All tasks involved in playing a Hi-Lo game should be carried out by the HiLo object, including keeping track of the number of guesses made. Since this object is the one that keeps track of the number of allowed guesses, it is logical for this object to let the programmer know whether the game is over or not. In other words, the programmer should not be bothered with the task of keeping a counter for the number of guesses made. We will let a HiLo object tell the programmer when the number of allowed guesses is used up.

Alternative Design 1 One way is to define a method such as isGameNotOver, which returns true if the game is not over and false otherwise. However, we usually do not include the negation in a query method, because if we indeed define such method, we have to state something like

```
!isGameNotOver()
```

to check that the game is over. Double negation is very difficult and awkward to read, so a better way is to define a method isGameOver and negate it as !hiLo.is-GameOver() in the do–while loop:

```
do {

    //process one guess

} while ( answer != HiLo.BINGO && //guess not correct and
          !hiLo.isGameOver( ) ); //game is not yet over
```

Alternative
Design **2**

Since a HiLo object keeps track of the number of guesses the user has made, it is possible to code the nextGuess method to return a fourth value, say, GAMEOVER in addition to LO, HI, and BINGO. With this approach, the do–while loop is expressed as

```
do {

    //process one guess

} while ( answer != HiLo.BINGO && //guess not correct and
          answer != HiLo.GAMEOVER ); //game is not yet over
```

We will adopt the second design because it is more consistent and logical; that is, the nextGuess method will return one of the four possible outcomes of making a guess.

Our working design document for the HiLo class at this point is as follows:

Design Document: The HiLo Class		
Method	**Visibility**	**Purpose**
<constructors>	public	Creates and initializes a HiLo object.
newGame	public	Resets an object for a new game.
nextGuess	public	Checks the next guess and returns the result. The return type int is used to indicate the result.

And its object diagram at this point is

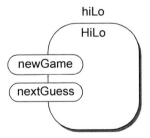

We will implement the class in the following four logical steps:

development
steps

1. Start with a class skeleton. Define the necessary data members and constructors. Add any other methods necessary to implement the constructors.

2. Implement the newGame method. Add any other methods necessary to implement this method.

3. Implement the nextGuess method. Add any other methods necessary to implement this method.

4. Finalize the class implementation with final review and code modification/extension.

Step 1 Development: Skeleton with Constructors

Step 1 Design   Let's start with data members of the class. Using the first constructor, a HiLo object is created with default values for the low and high bounds of a secret number and the number of guesses allowed. Let's define constants for these default values:

```
private static final int DEFAULT_MAX_GUESSES =   7;
private static final int DEFAULT_LOW         =   1;
private static final int DEFAULT_HIGH        = 100;
```

We also need to define constants for values returned by the nextGuess method:

```
public  static final int HI      = 1;
public  static final int LO      = 2;
public  static final int BINGO   = 3;
public  static final int GAMEOVER= 4;
```

Since the low and high bounds of a secret number and the number of guesses allowed are different for each HiLo object, we need a variable for each of these values. Also, we have to keep track of the number of the guesses made and the secret number for each game. The variable declarations are as follows:

```
private int numberOfGuessesAllowed;
private int guessLowBound;
private int guessHighBound;

private int guessCount;
private int secretNumber;
```

Now, let's think about the constructors. We will use the technique of defining one constructor that initializes the object and having all other constructors directly or indirectly call this constructor. We will add code to initialize the object to the constructor to accept three arguments: low bound, high bound, and number of guesses. Is the following an acceptable way to define this?

```
public HiLo( int low, int high, int numberOfGuesses )
{
    guessLowBound = low;
    guessHighBound = high;
    numberOfGuessesAllowed = numberOfGuesses;
}
```

If the programmer makes no mistakes in calling the constructor, it is acceptable, but it is not wise to assume that the programmer will make no mistakes. We must aim to design the class that is as robust as possible. What would happen if the programmer gets confused and switches the low and high by mistake? What would happen if the programmer passes a nonpositive number as the third argument?

When an invalid value is passed to the constructor, we will initialize the data members using the following rule:

```
if ( low > high ) {
    switch the low and high;
}

if ( numberOfGuesses <= 0 ) {
    //if the given numberOfGuesses is invalid
    //derive the value from the given low and high
    numberOfGuessesAllowed = maxGuess( low, high );
}

//assign arguments to data members

//set to play a new game
newGame();
```

The maxGuess method determines the number of guesses allowed based on the low and the high bounds. The idea is to derive a formula to compute the maximum number of allowed guesses based on the range of a secret number so that we allow more guesses when a range is bigger and fewer guesses when a range is smaller. What kind of formula should it be?

If you always use the middle value of low and high as the next guess, you can make a correct guess in N tries where N is derived as

$$N = \lceil \log_2(high - low + 1) \rceil$$

For example, if the low is 1 and high is 100, then N is 7. Your first guess is 50. If this guess is, say, low, then your next guess is 75. You continue in this manner, and the maximum times you need to guess the number is 7. Try it. The basic idea behind this formula is that you cannot divide 100 more than 7 times until the range of values where the secret number is located becomes empty.

Since the Math class does not support the logarithm of base 2, we need to convert the formula to the logarithm of base 10:

$$N = \left\lceil \log_2(\text{high} - \text{low} + 1) \right\rceil$$

$$= \left\lceil \frac{\log_{10}(\text{high} - \text{low} + 1)}{\log_{10}(2)} \right\rceil$$

Note:
$$\log_a b = \frac{\log_c b}{\log_c a}$$

Expressing the formula in a Java statement, we have the following:

```
Math.ceil( Math.log( high - low + 1 ) / Math.log( 2 ) )
```

Now, notice the call to the method newGame at the end of the constructor. Whenever a new instance is created, it should be in a state ready to play a game, instead of relying on the programmer to always call the newGame method before starting a new game. We will work on this method in the next step.

Finally, we will define two additional constructors. These two constructors will call the three-argument constructor in the following manner. The constructor with two arguments will call the three-argument constructor as

```
this( low, high, maxGuess(low, high) );
```

In order for this call to work correctly, the maxGuess method must be a class method (i.e., with the static modifier). An instance of a class is created inside a constructor, and we can call an instance method from a constructor without a problem. However, this constructor with two arguments is calling another constructor, so no instance is actually created in this contructor. The three-argument constructor is the only constructor where an instance is actually created. For this reason, we must declare the maxGuess method as a class method.

The constructor with no argument will call the three-argument constructor as

```
this( DEFAULT_LOW, DEFAULT_HIGH, DEFAULT_MAX_GUESSES );
```

Note that it is also possible for this constructor to call the two-argument constructor instead as

```
this( DEFAULT_LOW, DEFAULT_HIGH );
```

and get rid of the constant DEFAULT_MAX_GUESS. The two-argument constructor will compute the value of 7 given DEFAULT_LOW and
DEFAULT_HIGH. We will retain the constant DEFAULT_MAX_GUESS, so we
can set other values for a default maximum number of guesses allowed.

Step 1 Code   Here's the Step 1 implementation of the HiLo class:

File: HiLo.java

```java
/**
 *  HiLo Class
 *
 * This class plays the Hi-Lo games. The objective of the game is for the
 * user to guess the computer-generated secret number in the least number
 * of tries. The low and high bounds of a secret number and the number of
 * guesses can be set by the programmer. If the number of guesses allowed
 * is not set by the programmer, then the default value is determined
 * based on the low and high bounds. The default low and high bounds, if
 * not set by the programmer, are 1 and 100. The default number of guesses
 * for the default low and high bounds is 7.
 *
 * @author Dr. Caffeine
 *
 */
class HiLo
{
//---------------------------------
// Data Members
//---------------------------------

    public  static final int HI      = 1;
    public  static final int LO      = 2;
    public  static final int BINGO   = 3;
    public  static final int GAMEOVER = 4;

    private static final int DEFAULT_MAX_GUESSES =   7;
    private static final int DEFAULT_LOW         =   1;
    private static final int DEFAULT_HIGH        = 100;

    private int numberOfGuessesAllowed;
    private int guessLowBound;
    private int guessHighBound;

    private int guessCount;
    private int secretNumber;

//---------------------------------
// Constructors
//---------------------------------

    /**
     * Default constructor.
     * Uses the default values for low, high, and the number of guesses.
     */
    public HiLo( )
    {
        this(DEFAULT_LOW, DEFAULT_HIGH, DEFAULT_MAX_GUESSES);
    }
```

```
/**
 * Constructs a HiLo object with the given low and high values.
 * The number of guesses is computed from the values of low and high.
 *
 * @param low   the low bound for the secret number
 * @param high  the high bound for the secret number
 */
public HiLo(int low, int high)
{
    this( low, high, maxGuess(low,high));
}


/**
 * Constructs a HiLo object with the given values for low,
 * high, and the number of guesses.
 *
 * @param low       the low bound for the secret number
 * @param high      the high bound for the secret number
 * @param numGuess  the number of guesses allowed
 */
public HiLo(int low, int high, int numGuess)
{
    if (low > high) {
        int temp = low;
        low = high;
        high = temp;
    }

    if ( numGuess <=0  ) {
        numGuess = maxGuess(low, high);
    }

    guessLowBound = low;
    guessHighBound = high;
    numberOfGuessesAllowed = numGuess;

    newGame();

    System.out.println("low bound:      " + guessLowBound);          //TEMP
    System.out.println("high bound:     " + guessHighBound);         //TEMP
    System.out.println("max guesses:    " + numberOfGuessesAllowed);
    System.out.println("secret number:  " + secretNumber);           //TEMP
    System.out.println("   ");                                       //TEMP
}

//-------------------------------------------------
//    Public Methods:
//
//        void       newGame        (           )
//        int        nextGuess      ( int       )
//
//-------------------------------------------------

/**
 * Sets this HiLo object for a new game.
 */
public void newGame()
{
    System.out.println("Inside newGame");    //TEMP
}
```

```
/**
 * Determines whether or not the guess is the secret number.
 *
 * @param  guess \ the next guess to evaluate
 * @return the answer HI, LO, BINGO, or GAME_OVER
 */
public int nextGuess( int guess )
{

    System.out.println("Inside nextGuess"); //TEMP

    return 0;           //Dummy return statement
}

//-------------------------------------------------
//     Private Methods:
//
//         static int maxGuess      ( int, int    )
//
//-------------------------------------------------

/**
 * Computes the maximum number of allowed guesses.
 *
 * @param  low   the low bound of the secret number
 * @param  high  the high bound of the secret number
 * @return       the maximum number of guesses allowed
 */
private static int maxGuess( int low, int high )
{
    return (int) Math.ceil( Math.log(high-low+1) / Math.log( 2 ) );
}

}
```

Step 1 Test

In order to test the skeleton HiLo class, we need to write a test main class. The purpose of this test program is to verify that the constructors are executed correctly, that is, values for the data members are set correctly. To verify this, we included the temporary output statements in the third constructor. One possible test main class is the following:

```
class TestHiLo
{
    public static void main (String args[])
    {
        //create a HiLo object
        HiLo hiLo1, hiLo2, hiLo3, hiLo4;

        hiLo1 = new HiLo( );
        hiLo2 = new HiLo( 200, 500 );
        hiLo3 = new HiLo( 101, 150, 3 );
        hiLo4 = new HiLo( 500, 250 );
    }
}
```

When you execute this test program, you should see something like the following printout in the standard output window System.out. Notice the secret numbers in the actual printout would be different.

```
low bound:      1
high bound:     100
max guess:      7
secret number:  34

low bound:      200
high bound:     500
max guess:      9
secret number:  344

low bound:      101
high bound:     150
max guess:      3
secret number:  129

low bound:      250
high bound:     500
max guess:      8
secret number:  417
```

Make sure you run the test program with other argument values for the constructors, such as the following:

Test Input for the Constructors	
low	high
10	10
100	32000
−35	−150
0	1

Step 2 Development: Implement the newGame **Method**

Step 2 Design   In the second step of development, we complete the newGame method and add whatever methods are necessary to fully implement the newGame method. The task of the newGame method is to reset the object for a new game. To start a new game, we need to generate a new secret number. For every game, we need a counter to track the number of guesses made, so we will reset this counter in the newGame method also.

We use a pseudorandom number generator from the Math class to generate a new secret number. The code we used in the previous HiLo class in Chapter 7 is

```
double X = Math.random();
secretNumber = (int) Math.floor( X * 100 ) + 1;
```

This code is based on the fixed low and high bounds of 1 and 100. We need to generalize the code for any low and high bounds. The code is now modified to

```
double X = Math.random();
secretNumber = (int) Math.floor( X * (high-low+1) ) + low;
```

Try out different values for the low and high bounds and verify that this formula works. The value (high–low+1) gives the number of distinct values in a given range. For example, with low = 201 and high = 500, there are 300 distinct values. If you multiply this number by the pseudorandom number X, where 0 <= X < 1.0, you get a value between 0 and 299, inclusive. Finally, if you add this value to low, then you get a number anywhere between 201 and 500.

The working design document now includes the getRandomNumber method:

Design Document: The HiLo Class		
Method	**Visibility**	**Purpose**
. . .	. . .	. . .
getRandomNumber	private	Returns a pseudorandom number (int) between guessLowBound and guessHighBound. This number will be the secret number.

Step 2 Code   The newGame method is defined as follows:

```
public void newGame(  )
{
    guessCount = 0;
    secretNumber = getRandomNumber();
}
```

and the private getRandomNumber method is defined as follows:

```
private int getRandomNumber(  )
{
    double    X;
    int       number;

    X      = Math.random();
```

```
        number = (int) Math.floor( X * (guessHighBound -
                                  guessLowBound + 1 ) )
                            + guessLowBound;

        System.out.println("New secret number: " + number);
                                                    //TEMP
        return number;
    }
```

Step 2 Test

We modify the **TestHiLo** main class from Step 1 to verify that the correct secret numbers are generated. The test routine will look something like this:

```
    HiLo hiLo;

    hiLo = new HiLo( 200, 500 );
    for (int i = 0; i < 100; i++ ) {
        hiLo.newGame();
    }
```

Run the program and verify that 100 correct secret numbers are generated. Once you verify this, run the program multiple times changing the values you pass in the constructor. When everything is working correctly, move on to Step 3.

Step 3 Development: Implement the nextGuess Method

Step 3 Design

In the third step of development, we complete the **nextGuess** method and add whatever methods necessary to fully implement this method. The basic task of this method can be expressed as follows:

```
    int status;

    guessCount++;

    if (userGuess == secretNumber)
        status = BINGO;

    else if (guessCount == numberOfGuessesAllowed)
        status = GAMEOVER;

    else if (userGuess < secretNumber)
        status = LO;

    else  // userGuess > secretNumber
        status = HI;

    return status;
```

This code is acceptable if the passed userGuess is always valid and as long as the value for userGuess is inside the ranges of guessLowBound and guessHighBound. To make this method robust, we include code to handle the invalid userGuess. We extend the code to the following:

```
int status;

guessCount++;

if (userGuess == secretNumber)
    status = BINGO;

else if (guessCount == numberOfGuessesAllowed)
    status = GAMEOVER;

else if ( !isValid(userGuess) )
    status = INVALID;

else if (userGuess < secretNumber)
    status = LO;

else  // userGuess > secretNumber
    status = HI;

return status;
```

We add one constant to the data declaration section:

```
public static final int INVALID = -1;
```

The isValid method is a private method that returns true if the passed argument falls between the set low and high bounds. The working design document now includes this method:

Design Document: The HiLo Class		
Method	**Visibility**	**Purpose**
. . .	. . .	. . .
isValid	private	Returns true if the passed argument falls between guessLowBound and guessHighBound.

Step 3 Code   The nextGuess method is defined as follows:

```
public int nextGuess( int userGuess)
{
    int status;

    guessCount++;

    if (userGuess == secretNumber) {
        status = BINGO;
    }
    else if (guessCount == numberOfGuessesAllowed) {
        status = GAMEOVER;
    }
    else if (!isValid(userGuess) ) {
        status = INVALID;
    }
    else if (userGuess < secretNumber) {
        status = LO;
    }
    else { // userGuess > secretNumber
        status = HI;
    }

    return status;
}
```

and the private isValid method is defined as follows:

```
private boolean isValid( int guess )
{
    boolean status;

    if (guessLowBound <= guess && guess <= guessHighBound){
        status = true;
    }
    else {
        status = false;
    }
    return status;
}
```

Since we are returning a boolean value, we can write the method without using the if statement as

```
private boolean isValid( int guess )
{
    boolean status;
```

```
                    status = guessLowBound <= guess &&
                                    guess <= guessHighBound;

            return status;
        }
```

Step 3 Test

The testing strategy for the Step 3 HiLo class is the same as the one we employed in Chapter 7. We play multiple games testing the error cases, normal cases, and end cases. Since we still have temporary output statements in the getRandom-Number method and the third constructor, we know the secret number and other key values for each game. With this knowledge, we will be able to go through different cases to verify that the class works correctly in all cases.

Step 4 Development: Finalize

code review

We finalize the program in the last step. We will perform a critical review of the class looking for any unfinished methods, making sure all methods work cooperatively, commenting out all temporary output statements, and confirming no necessary methods are missing. We will also review the class for any possible improvements we can make to the existing methods.

Are there any methods we might want to add to the class to increase its usability? Are there any methods we can improve? Reviewing the currently defined methods, we notice that the class does not include any access methods. When a game is over, the programmer may wish to output a message such as

```
        Sorry, you lost. You used up all 9 guesses. The secret num-
        ber was 345, generated from the range between 100 and 500.
```

In order to output such a message, the programmer must know the values for the low and high bounds, the number of guesses allowed, and the secret number. These values are maintained by a HiLo object, so it is natural to provide access methods to get the values. We will add the following access methods to the class:

```
        public int getSecretNumber( )
        {
            return secretNumber;
        }

        public int getLowBound()
        {
            return guessLowBound;
        }
```

```
public int getHighBound()
{
    return guessHighBound;
}

public int getMaxGuess( )
{
    return numberOfGuessesAllowed;
}
```

12.4 Package Organization

Now that we have learned how to define reusable classes, let's study how we can manage their source files for effective reuse. The most primitive way to reuse a class is to put the source file or the bytecode file of the class in the same folder that includes the other classes of your program. This approach of reuse is, of course, unacceptable because you would end up duplicating multiple copies of the same source file in different folders. This would be a maintenance nightmare. If you have to make modifications to the class, you have to locate all copies of the source files and make changes to every copy. A proper way to reuse code is to put the source file or the bytecode file of a class in a package. We will explain how to create a package in this section.

Let's start with some basic facts about the package. First, the classes in a package must be placed in a folder whose name is the name of the package. For example, all the classes of the javabook package are placed in the javabook folder. Second, packages can be nested. For example, the standard package awt is placed in the package java. To use the classes in the package awt, we import them by using the import statement

```
import java.awt.*;
```

Third, if you want others to use the classes but not modify them, then you should place only the bytecode files in the package. If you put in the source files also, then you cannot prohibit other programmers from changing them.

To put a class in a package, we need to do a little more than just placing the bytecode (or source) file in the corresponding folder. We have to make a modification to the source file. Specifically, we need to add one declaration at the beginning of the source file and an accessibility modifier (e.g., public) to the class declaration. Let's say we want to place the HiLo and EggyPeggy classes defined in the previous section in a package called game. Here's one possible sequence of steps to achieve it:

1. Create the folder called **game** and put the source file of the two classes into it. You can place this new folder anywhere you want, but you should place the folder at the location where it is convenient for other programs to access. We place the **javabook** package under the **Projects** folder along with the other folders for the chapter sample code.

2. Include the declaration

   ```
   package game;
   ```

   before all other declarations and statements in the two source files and add the modifier public to the class declaration. For example, the source file for the **HiLo** class becomes

   ```
   /*
       HiLo Class
          . . .
   */

   package game;

   public class HiLo
   {
          . . .
   }
   ```

3. Compile the classes. The **game** folder now contains the source and bytecode files of the two classes.

To make a class in a package accessible to outside classes (classes that are not in this package), we must declare the class public. If the class has no modifier, then the class is accessible only to other classes in the same package. For example, if we declare the **HiLo** class as

```
public class HiLo
{
       . . .
}
```

then the class is accessible to an outside class via an import statement

```
import game.*;
```

If, on the other hand, we declare the HiLo class as

```
class Hilo
{
    ...
}
```

then the class is not accessible to an outside class. In other words, the following declaration will result in an error:

```
import game.*;
...
Hilo   myHiLoGame; //Error: Class HiLo is not accessible
                //          because it is not a public class
```

> **A class in a package is accessible to other classes outside of the package only if the class is declared** public.

A class in a package is always accessible to other classes in the same package without using the import statement. If we declare multiple classes for the program but do not include the package statement in these classes, then the Java compiler considers these classes to be placed in a default, unnamed package. Since they are in the same package, they are accessible to each other. This is the reason why we have never put the public access modifier in the class declaration.

12.5 Exercises

1. When do you want to declare a class in a package public?

2. What is the purpose of defining multiple constructors?

3. Which of the following method declarations have the same signature?

```
public void one ( int x, int y)   /* 1 */
{
    ...
}

private void one ( int x, int y) /* 2 */
{
    ...
}
```

```
public int one ( int x, int y)     /* 3 */
{
    . . .
}

private void one ( int x, float y) /* 4 */
{
    . . .
}
```

4. Identify problems with the following class declaration. Note: The class not doing anything meaningful is not a problem here.

```
package vehicle;
package truck;

import vehicle.*;

public class OffRoad
{
    private int      weight;
    private String   vin;

    public offroad()
    {
        weight = 5000;
    }
}
```

5. Rewrite the Java^2 Lo-Fat Burgers drive-through system using instantiable classes (see exercise 12 on page 346 in Chapter 7).

6. Rewrite the ComputeMonthlyPayment program of Chapter 4 using instantiable classes.

7. Define a LoanCalculator class whose instances are application logic objects. Define set methods (mutators) to assign values for loan amount, annual interest rate, and loan period. The methods computeMonthlyPayment, computeTotalPayment, and computeTotalInterest return the amounts for monthly payment, total payment, and total interest, respectively. Use this class and write an application-based or an applet-based loan calculator program.

8. Extend the LoanCalculator class of exercise 7 by adding a new method called getLoanTable that returns a loan payment schedule table as described in exercise 22 on page 349 in Chapter 7. You must decide on the data type for this table very carefully. Possible data types for the table are

1. A 2-D array of float.

2. A 1-D array of LoanTableEntry objects

3. A LoanTable object.

A single LoanTableEntry object includes information on one row of a loan payment schedule table, that is, payment number, interest, principal, unpaid balance, and total interest paid to date. A single LoanTable object includes information on the whole table. If you choose the second or the third option, then you need to implement the LoanTableEntry or the LoanTable class yourself. Extend the loan calculator program of exercise 7 by including a new method getPaymentScheduleTable.

9. Define a Person class whose instance is used to keep track of a person's information. The Person object maintains a first and last name, address, phone number, and age. Write a test program to verify that the Person class works correctly.

10. Define a Student class as a subclass of Person. A Student object keeps the record of three midterms and one final exam. The highest possible score for the midterms is 50 and for the final is 100. The three midterms and the final exam are respectively 60 percent and 40 percent of the course score. The final course grade is computed as

Course Score	Final Course Grade
$85 \le \text{score} \le 100$	A
$78 \le \text{score} < 85$	B
$65 \le \text{score} < 78$	C
$40 \le \text{score} < 65$	D
$0 \le \text{score} < 40$	F

Write a test program to verify that the Student class works correctly.

11. Define a RentalCar class whose instance is used to keep track of a rental car's information, such as car model, daily rental rate, tank capacity (in gallons), number of free miles per day, the charge per mile for the miles over the mileage allowance, and the status (rented or available). Define any additional instance and class variables you think are necessary.

12. Write an application logic Encrypter class that is capable of encrypting and decrypting a given text using either Ceaser or Vignere cipher (see exercise 20 on page 408 and exercise 22 on page 409).

13. Java^2 Coffee Outlet is expanding again. This time the company is getting into the rental car business. Being a good corporate citizen keen to the need for recycling, the company started a new subsidiary, Java^2 Recycled Rentals, which specializes in renting refurbished used cars. The company maintains a fleet of five cars. You are hired as a freelance developer to write an online rental system. Using the RentalCar class from exercise 11, write a program that supports two operations: rental and return. When the user selects the rental option, list the cars available for rental using a ListBox object. Display the daily rental charge, number of free miles, and the charge per mile over the mileage allowance for the car the user selected; then ask the user whether he or she wishes to rent the car. If the user says Yes, then remove the car from the available list. When a car is rented out, record the current mileage on the car. When the user selects the return option, list the cars currently rented out using a ListBox object. After the user selects a car, prompt the user for the mileage reading and the number of days rented, then display the total charge.

14. Rewrite the HiLo class so the player has an option of specifying the three levels of difficulty: Beginner, Intermediate, and Expert. The class will allow a fewer number of guesses for a higher level of difficulty. Suppose N is the number of guesses allowed that is computed automatically by the HiLo class from the given low and high bounds. If the player chooses the Beginner level, then the maximum number of guesses she is allowed to make is twice the N. If she chooses the Intermediate level, then it is N. And if she chooses the Expert level, then it is one-half of N.

15. Rewrite the HiLo class by adding a second form of newGame. The second newGame method accepts the low and high bounds of a secret number. So every time a new game is started, the programmer has the option of changing the low and high bounds. What are the advantages and disadvantages of the second newGame method?

16. Write a new class called Arithmetic that plays arithmetic games. An Arithmetic object asks N problems involving addition, subtraction, division, and multiplication, for example, 4 + 5, 5 * 3, and so forth. Each problem includes one operator, and the operands are limited to single digits. The value for N is set by the programmer. The object keeps track of the number of problems asked and the number of problems answered correctly. The programmer can prompt the Arithmetic object for the number of correct answers by calling the getCorrectCount method. Use the pseudorandom number generator from the Math class to select the operands and the operator for each problem. To select an operator, you can generate a random number between 1 and 4. If the number is 1, then use addition; if the number is 2, then use subtraction; and so forth.

17. Create a new package called game and place the EggyPeggy, HiLo, and Arithmetic classes in it. Using this package, write an application that allows the user to play three games: Eggy-Peggy, Hi-Lo, and Arithmetic. The player can choose any of them and play as many times as he or she wishes.

18. Using the game package created in exercise 17, write an applet that allows the user to play three games: Eggy-Peggy, Hi-Lo, and Arithmetic. See exercise 17.

19. Define a new class called BlackJack and add it to the game package. A BlackJack object plays the dealer for the blackjack card game. Use the pseudorandom number generator to generate numbers between 1 and 13. The numbers 11, 12, and 13 represent Jack, Queen, and King, respectively. Use an OutputBox object to display the hands of both the dealer and the player. You can use a symbol such as an asterisk to represent a card whose face is down. Use a ResponseBox object to prompt the player to hit another card or stay.

20. Extend the game-playing application from exercise 17 to include the blackjack card game created in exercise 19.

21. Write a checkbook application program. The program maintains multiple checkbooks. For each checkbook, the user can deposit, write a check, and withdraw. Since this program is for personal record-keeping use, the balance can become negative. When a new check is written, a CheckBook object will automatically assign the next available check number. The user will have the options of voiding a check and overriding the automatically assigned check number. The beginning check number is set when the object is initially created. At the beginning of the program execution, you must read in information from a file. At the end of the program execution, the data are written back to the file. Some of the classes you should include for the program are listed below:

program classes

Design Document:	CheckBook
Class	**Purpose**
CheckBookMain	The main class of the program.
CheckBookController	The top-level control object that manages other objects in the program.
CheckBook	A CheckBook object contains a collection of Check objects.
Check	A Check object is used to represent a single check.

program
classes

Design Document:	CheckBook
Class	**Purpose**
CheckBookStorage	A **CheckBookStorage** object is responsible for the file I/O of **CheckBook** objects.
<interface classes>	Standard and custom-made objects for handling the user interface of the program.

13

GUI Objects and Event-Driven Programming

OBJECTIVES

After you have read and studied this chapter, you should be able to

- Write GUI application programs using Frame, Dialog, and Button objects from the java.awt package.

- Write GUI application programs with menus using Menu, MenuItem, and MenuBar objects from the java.awt package.

- Write event-driven programs using Java's delegation-based event model.

- Write GUI application programs that process mouse events.

- Understand how the SketchPad class introduced in Chapter 1 is implemented.

- Run applets as applications.

Introduction

graphical
user interface

The objects from the standard java.awt packages are called *graphical user interface* (GUI) objects, and they are used to handle the user interface aspect of programs. Some of the GUI objects from the package are shown in Figure 13.1.

event-driven
programming

The style of programming we use with these GUI objects is called *event-driven programming*. An *event* occurs when the user interacts with a GUI object. For example, when you move the cursor, click on a button, or select a menu choice, an event occurs. In event-driven programs, we program objects to respond to these events by defining event-handling methods. In this chapter we will introduce objects from the java.awt package and show you how to write event-handling methods. Basic event-handling topics were already discussed in Chapter 5, so for those who studied Chapter 5, some of the topics in this chapter will be a review.

FIGURE 13.1   Various GUI objects from the **java.awt** package.

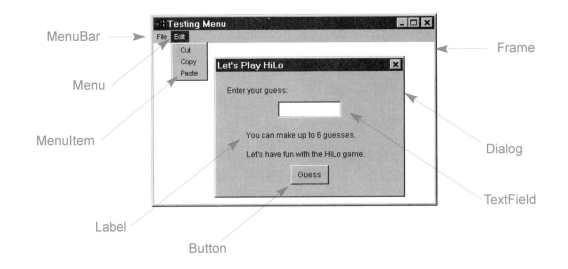

Since our objective for the chapter is to teach event-driven programming and not to teach the java.awt classes, we will cover only those that are fundamental to event-driven programming and easy to understand for beginners. We encourage you to explore other java.awt classes not covered in this chapter on your own. Since GUI objects such as ListBox in the javabook package are programmed to work in a manner similar to many of the java.awt objects, you will find many of the java.awt classes familiar. We also encourage you to study the source code of the javabook classes to see how they are implemented using the classes from java.awt.

Swing classes   A new set of GUI objects collectively called *Swing classes* are now part of the Java 2 platform (JDK 1.2 or above). The Swing classes extend the standard AWT classes (those from java.awt) by adding a new set of components and a collection of support classes. Because the Swing classes are implemented fully in Java, the use of Swing classes allows programmers to develop true cross-platform applications where applications behave exactly the same no matter on which platform they are executed. The implementation of the standard AWT classes, however, are done by using the native GUI objects. For example, an AWT Button is implemented by using the Windows button object for the Windows platform, the Macintosh button object for the Mac platform, and so forth. Because the behavior of underlying platform-specific GUI objects are not necessarily identical, an application based on the standard AWT classes may not behave the same on the different platforms. In addtion, there are other advantages in using Swing classes over the standard AWT classes.

Although the use of the Swing classes is generally preferable over the use of the standard AWT classes in writing practical programs, we do not cover the Swing classes here, because our objective, as stated earlier, is to teach the fundamentals of event-driven programming. For those who want or need to learn the Swing classes, a separate document explaining the Swing classes is available from our website. Since the basic knowledge of event-driven programming and AWT classes is helpful in understading the Swing classes, we recommend you finish this chapter before reading the Swing document from our website.

The document that explains the Swing classes is available from our website at www.drcaffeine.com/additionaltopics.

13.1 Placing Buttons on a Frame

Let's write a simple GUI program to show how to manipulate GUI objects. The program will include one window that has two buttons labeled CANCEL and OK. When you click the CANCEL button, the window's title is changed to You clicked CANCEL. Likewise, when you click the OK button, the window's title is changed to You clicked OK. Figure 13.2 shows the window when it is first opened and after the CANCEL button is clicked.

frame   There are two types of windows in GUI programs: frame and dialog. A *frame* is a general-purpose window in which the user interacts with the application. Windows in which the user writes a document, draws a picture, sends e-mail, and so on are all frames. A Java GUI application program must have at least one frame that serves as the program's main window.

FIGURE 13.2   A sample window when it is first opened and after the **CANCEL** button is clicked.

dialog

A *dialog* is a limited-purpose window used primarily for displaying simple information such as error messages or getting a simple response such as yes or no. For example, windows in which the user selects a file to open or confirms that he wants to print a document are all dialogs.

Two of the classes in the java.awt package are Frame and Dialog. The Frame class contains the most rudimentary functionalities to support features found in any frame window, such as minimizing the window, moving the window, resizing the window, and so forth. In writing applications, we do not create an instance of the Frame class because a Frame object is not capable of doing anything meaningful. For example, if we want to use a frame window for a word processor, we need a frame window capable of allowing the user to enter, cut, and paste text; change font; print text; and so forth. To design such a frame window, we would define a subclass of the Frame class and add methods and data members to implement the needed functionalities.The main window for our earlier sample programs is an instance of the MainWindow class from the javabook package, which is a subclass of the Frame class that adds four functionalities: sets the string Sample Java Application as the default window title, terminates the program when the close box is clicked,[1] adjusts the size of the

---

1. This functionality is supported by the Frame class in most platforms, but not by the Windows platform.

window to roughly the size of the screen, and displays the window at the center of the screen.

Similar to the Frame class, the Dialog class contains the most rudimentary functionalities to support features found in any dialog box. Again, we actually never create an instance of the Dialog class, but rather define a subclass of the Dialog class to support a dialog box in a program. The javabook classes Input-Box, ListBox, MessageBox, OutputBox, and ResponseBox are all subclasses of Dialog. We will explain how to define and use dialog classes in Section 13.6.

For our sample program, we need a frame to place two buttons, so we will first define a subclass of Frame called MyFirstFrame. Inside a constructor, we can set its properties. For this sample, we will set the following properties:

1. 300 pixels wide and 200 pixels high.

2. Not resizable (i.e., the user cannot drag the edge and change the window size).

3. Program MyFirstFrame as the frame title.

4. The top-left corner of the frame at the screen position (150, 250).

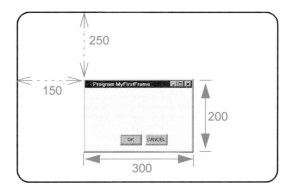

To set the frame's size, we pass its width and height to the setSize method. To designate the frame as not resizable, we pass the boolean argument false to the setResizable method. To set the frame's title, we pass the title to the setTitle method. And finally, to position the frame's top-left corner to the coordinate (*x*, *y*), we pass the values *x* and *y* to the setLocation method. The shell MyFirst-Frame class is declared as

```
import java.awt.*;

class MyFirstFrame extends Frame
{
    private static final int FRAME_WIDTH    = 300;
```

```
private static final int FRAME_HEIGHT   = 200;
private static final int FRAME_X_ORIGIN = 150;
private static final int FRAME_Y_ORIGIN = 250;

public MyFirstFrame( )
{
    setSize        ( FRAME_WIDTH,  FRAME_HEIGHT );
    setResizable ( false );
    setTitle       ( "Program MyFirstFrame" );
    setLocation    ( FRAME_X_ORIGIN, FRAME_Y_ORIGIN );
}
}
```

To open this frame in a program, we need to define the main class, such as the following:

File: TestMyFirstFrame.java

```
/**
 * Program TestMyFirstFrame
 *
 * This main class is for testing MyFirstFrame
*/
class TestMyFirstFrame
{
    public static void main (String args[] )
    {
        MyFirstFrame frame = new MyFirstFrame( );
        frame.setVisible( true );
    }
}
```

When you run TestMyFirstFrame, an instance of MyFirstFrame appears on the screen as expected. However, when you try to close the frame, you cannot. This is because the frame does not include the code to close the window. When you click the close box of the frame, an event is generated, but there's no code in the MyFirstFrame class to process this window-closing event. We will explain the event handling in the next section. But before that, let's place the buttons on this frame.

The type of button we explain here is called a *pushbutton*. Since we discuss the pushbuttons only, we will simply call them buttons. To use a button in a program, we create an instance of the Button class. We will create two buttons and place them on the frame in the constructor. Let's name the two buttons cancelButton and okButton. We add their declaration in the MyFirstFrame class as

```
class MyFirstFrame extends Frame
{
    Button cancelButton, okButton;
    ...
}
```

layout
manager

To place buttons on a frame, we can use a layout manager. We discussed the layout manager and its purpose in Chapter 5. We will repeat the discussion here for those who omitted the applet-based sample programs. The *layout manager* for a frame (and also for a dialog and an applet) controls how the GUI objects are placed on the frame. The default layout manager for a frame is a FlowLayout manager, which places GUI objects in the top-to-bottom, left-to-right order. It is also possible not to use any layout manager. If we don't use a layout manager, then we can place GUI objects precisely at the location where we want to position them. We call this approach *absolute positioning*. We will use absolute positioning for the sample programs in the remainder of the book.

absolute
positioning

Although using a layout manager can be advantageous in some situations, knowing various layout managers does not really contribute much to the learning of object-oriented and event-driven programming. For this reason, we will not cover layout managers in this book.

> *A benefit of using a layout manager is the automatic adjustment of GUI objects when their container (frame, dialog, applet, etc.) is resized. For example, if you place a* Button *at the center of the container using some layout manager, then this* Button *will still be positioned at the center when the size of the container is changed. This automatic adjustment is important also when you consider running your program on different platforms, because by using a layout manager effectively you will get a more consistent look to your frames and dialogs across different platforms. With absolute positioning, a frame that looks nice on one platform may not appear as nice on another platform.*

In order to use absolute positioning, we must set the layout manager of a frame to none in the constructor. We do this by passing null to the setLayout method:

```
setLayout(null);
```

After the layout manager is set to null , we place two buttons at the position and in the size we want by calling the button's setBounds method as in

```
okButton.setBounds( 100, 150, 60, 30 );
```

where the first two arguments specify the position of the button and the last two arguments specify the width and height of the button. Figure 13.3 illustrates how the four arguments are used. Notice that the positioning is relative to the frame's top-left corner.

FIGURE 13.3   The diagram illustrating how the **setBounds** method works.

```
frame = new Frame();
frame.setSize(300,200);
frame.setLayout( null );
okButton = new Button("OK");
okButton.setBounds(100, 150, 60, 30);
```

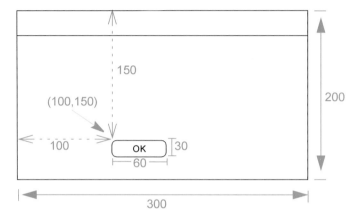

Setting the bounds of a button alone does not make it visible on the frame. To make it visible, we must attach it to the frame by calling the add method. For example, to add okButton, we call

```
add( okButton );
```

Here's the MyFirstFrame class with a modified portion that adds okButton and cancelButton:

```
class MyFirstFrame extends Frame
{
    ...

    private static final int BUTTON_WIDTH    =   60;
    private static final int BUTTON_HEIGHT   =   30;

    Button okButton, cancelButton;

    public MyFirstFrame( )
    {
```

```
    ...
okButton = new Button( "OK" );
okButton.setBounds(100, 150,  BUTTON_WIDTH,
                              BUTTON_HEIGHT);
add( okButton );

cancelButton = new Button( "CANCEL" );
cancelButton.setBounds(170, 150,  BUTTON_WIDTH,
                                 BUTTON_HEIGHT );
add( cancelButton );
    }
  }
```

If you run the TestMyFirstFrame program again, then you will see two buttons on the frame. When you click the buttons, of course, nothing happens because there's no code defined in the class that handles the button click event. We'll add the code to handle the button click events and the window close events in the next section.

Quick Check

1. What is a layout manager? How is it useful?

2. Using the setBounds method, position a button 50 pixels wide and 30 pixels high at the location (125, 85).

3. Give two ways to make a frame appear on the screen.

13.2 Handling Events

Let's complete the MyFirstFrame class by adding the event-handling code that processes the button click event and the window close event. We will write the code for processing the button clicks first.

The event-handling model of Java is based on the concept of delegation. The *delegation-based event model* classifies event-handling objects into two types: *event source objects* and *event listener objects*. An object can be an event source, event listener, or both.

delegation-based event model

event source and listener

An event source object sends events to event listeners. For example, when a button is clicked, the button sends an event called an *action event* to the listeners. The button where the event has originated is the event source. The button is said to "fire" or "generate" an event. For the button object to know to which listeners to send the action event, we must register listeners with the button. We do this by calling the addActionListener method of the button object. The action event is sent to all registered listeners. The listeners can then process the event.

action event

For our sample program, cancelButton and okButton are event sources of the button click events. But which object should be an event listener? It is common to let the object that contains event sources be their event listener. In our case, this object is an instance of MyFirstFrame. To register a MyFirstFrame object as the event listener of two buttons, we add the following two statements to the constructor of MyFirstFrame:

```
cancelButton.addActionListener( this ); //add this frame
okButton.addActionListener( this );  //as an action event
                                      //listener
```

When the two buttons fire an action event, they send the fired event to their action listener by calling the listener's actionPerformed method. This means that any class that is designated as an action listener must include the actionPerformed method. To designate the MyFirstFrame class as an action listener, we must declare that the class implements the ActionListener interface as

```
import java.awt.event.*;  ←——  Event-handling classes
                                are in this package.

class MyFirstFrame extends Frame implements ActionListener
{
    . . .
}
```

interface

abstract
method

ActionListener is not a class but an interface. You have seen a sample interface Serializable in Section 11.5. An *interface* declares a new reference data type that includes only constants and abstract methods. An *abstract method* is a method that has no method body, just the method prototype. No instances can be created from an interface. To create an instance, we need a class that *implements* the interface. For a class to implement an interface, the class must provide a method body to all of the abstract methods defined in the interface. The ActionListener interface includes only one abstract method, actionPerformed. An argument to the actionPerformed method is ActionEvent. An instance of ActionEvent represents an action event and supports methods we can use to find out properties of a generated event.

The actionPerformed method of MyFirstFrame is called by either cancelButton or okButton, so the logic of the method is something like this:

```
if (the event source is cancelButton) {
    set the frame title to "You clicked CANCEL"
}
else { //the event source is okButton because this listener
```

```
                        //is registered with only two event sources
                set the frame title to "You clicked OK";
        }
```

We can find out which object is an event source by calling the getSource meth-od of ActionEvent. Using this method, we can define the actionPerformed meth-od of MyFirstFrame as

```
        public void actionPerformed( ActionEvent event )
        {
            Button clickedButton = (Button) event.getSource();

            if (clickedButton == cancelButton) {
                setTitle( "You clicked CANCEL" );
            }
            else { //the event source is okButton
                setTitle( "You clicked OK" );
            }
        }
```

> Notice that we need to typecast the returned object to **Button**.

Because the getSource method can return an instance from different classes, we need to typecast the returned object to Button.

We can get the label of an event source button by calling the getActionCom-mand method of ActionEvent. This method returns a String object. Using this method, we can write the actionPerformed method as

```
        public void actionPerformed( ActionEvent event )
        {
            String label = event.getActionCommand();

            if (label.equals("CANCEL") {
                setTitle( "You clicked CANCEL" );
            }
            else { //the event source is okButton
                setTitle( "You clicked OK" );
            }
        }
```

Here's the MyFirstFrame class with a modified portion that handles the but-ton click events using the second version of actionPerformed:

```
        class MyFirstFrame extends Frame implements ActionListener
        {
            ...
            public MyFirstFrame( )
            {
```

```
        . . .
        okButton.addActionListener( this );
        cancelButton.addActionListener( this );
    }

    public void actionPerformed( ActionEvent event )
    {
        String label = event.getActionCommand();

        if (label.equals("CANCEL")) {
            setTitle( "You clicked CANCEL" );
        }
        else { //the event source is okButton
            setTitle( "You clicked OK" );
        }
    }
}
```

Now we are ready to add the code to close the frame (i.e., make it disappear from the screen) when its close box is clicked. Since this frame is the main window of the program, we will also terminate the program when the frame's close box is clicked. If we terminate a program, all windows of the program will be closed automatically, so we do not have to call any method explicitly to close them.

window event

Actions such as resizing, moving, and clicking on the close box you perform on a frame are called *window events*, and the class that represents a window event is WindowEvent. Only frames and dialogs can be event sources of window events. The class, whose instances are window event listeners, must implement the WindowListener interface. The WindowListener interface includes seven abstract methods: windowActivated, windowClosed, windowClosing, windowDeactivated, windowDeiconified, windowIconified, and windowOpened. So any class that implements the WindowListener interface must define all seven methods. The argument to all these methods is WindowEvent. When the window is first opened, windowOpened is called. When the close box is clicked, windowClosing is called. When the window is actually closed, windowClosed is called. When the window is minimized or restored, windowIconified and windowDeiconified are called, respectively. And when the window becomes active or inactive, windowActivated and windowDeactivated are called, respectively.

Most of the time we are not interested in handling all seven events. If you do not want to process a certain window event, then define the corresponding event-handling method with an empty method body, that is, a method body with no statements in it. For our sample program, we want to process only the window closing event, so we will define the windowClosing method with a real method body and define all the others with empty method bodies.

The window event source of our program is an instance of MyFirstFrame. But which object shall we let be a window event listener? We will define a new class whose instance will be our window event listener. Let's call this class ProgramTerminator. We will define the windowClosing method to terminate the program (and consequently, close the frame). A program is terminated by calling the exit method of the System class as

```
System.exit(0);
```

Here's the complete definition of the ProgramTerminator class:

File: ProgramTerminator.java

```java
import java.awt.event.*;

/**
 *  ProgramTerminator Class
 *
 *  A ProgramTerminator object terminates the program when its main window
 *  generates a window closing event.
 */

class ProgramTerminator implements WindowListener
{
    public void windowClosing( WindowEvent event )
    {
        System.exit(0);
    }

    public void windowActivated    ( WindowEvent event ) { }
    public void windowClosed       ( WindowEvent event ) { }
    public void windowDeactivated  ( WindowEvent event ) { }
    public void windowDeiconified  ( WindowEvent event ) { }
    public void windowIconified    ( WindowEvent event ) { }
    public void windowOpened       ( WindowEvent event ) { }
}
```

An empty method body means it contains no statement.

Need to implement all abstract methods of **WindowListener**.

Now we need to add this window event listener to the event source MyFirstFrame in the constructor:

```java
public MyFirstFrame ( )
{
    ...
    addWindowListener( new ProgramTerminator( ) );
}
```

Chapter 13

Run the TestMyFirstFrame program, and this time, when you click the frame's close box, the program will terminate. Here's the complete definition of My-FirstFrame: (Note: In addition to the usual omission of the javadoc comments for the data members, we will omit javadoc header comments for most methods for the sake of concise listing. The actual source code will include all javadoc comments.)

File: MyFirstFrame.java

```java
import java.awt.*;
import java.awt.event.*;

/**
 * MyFirstFrame class
 *
 * A sample frame to illustrate the placing of GUI objects
 * and event handling.
 *
 */

class MyFirstFrame extends Frame implements ActionListener
{
//-------------------------------
//  Data Members
//-------------------------------
    private static final int FRAME_WIDTH   = 300;
    private static final int FRAME_HEIGHT  = 200;

    private static final int FRAME_X_ORIGIN = 150;
    private static final int FRAME_Y_ORIGIN = 250;

    private static final int BUTTON_WIDTH = 60;
    private static final int BUTTON_HEIGHT= 30;

    Button okButton, cancelButton;

//-------------------------------
//  Constructors
//-------------------------------
    public MyFirstFrame( )
    {
        //set the frame properties
        setSize        ( FRAME_WIDTH, FRAME_HEIGHT );
        setResizable ( false );
        setTitle       ( "Program MyFirstFrame" );
        setLocation  ( FRAME_X_ORIGIN, FRAME_Y_ORIGIN );

        //create and place two buttons on the frame
        okButton = new Button( "OK" );
        okButton.setBounds(100, 150, BUTTON_WIDTH, BUTTON_HEIGHT);
        add( okButton );

        cancelButton = new Button( "CANCEL");
        cancelButton.setBounds(170, 150, BUTTON_WIDTH, BUTTON_HEIGHT);
        add( cancelButton );

        //register this frame as an action listener of two buttons
            okButton.addActionListener( this );
        cancelButton.addActionListener( this );
```

> For the sake of concise program listing, we will omit javadoc header comments for most methods.

```
        //register a ProgramTerminator as this frame's window listener
        addWindowListener( new ProgramTerminator() );
    }

//-----------------------------
// Constructors
//-----------------------------
    public void actionPerformed( ActionEvent event )
    {
        String label = event.getActionCommand();

        if (label.equals( "CANCEL" )) {
            setTitle( "You clicked CANCEL" );
        }
        else { //the event source is okButton
            setTitle( "You clicked OK" );
        }
    }
}
```

We mentioned earlier that a single object can be an event source and an event listener. In other words, an instance of MyFirstFrame, which is a window event source, can also be a window event listener. To make it a window event listener, the class must implement the WindowListener interface and define the abstract methods. Here's how to define MyFirstFrame as a window event listener of itself (in addition to being an action listener of two buttons):

```
class MyFirstFrame extends Frame
                implements ActionListener, WindowListener
{
    ...
    public MyFirstFrame
    {
        ...
        addWindowListener( this );
    }


    public void windowClosing( WindowEvent event )
    {
        System.exit(0);
    }

    public void windowActivated   ( WindowEvent event ) { }
    public void windowClosed      ( WindowEvent event ) { }
    public void windowDeactivated ( WindowEvent event ) { }
    public void windowDeiconified ( WindowEvent event ) { }
    public void windowIconified   ( WindowEvent event ) { }
    public void windowOpened      ( WindowEvent event ) { }
}
```

13.3 Placing TextField Objects on a Frame

Another very common GUI object in the java.awt package is TextField. A Text-Field object allows the user to enter a single line of text. The input box we use to enter a value in an InputBox is a TextField object. Like the Button class, an instance of TextField generates an action event. A TextField object generates an action event when the user presses the ENTER key while the object is active (it is active when you see the vertical blinking line in it).

The way we set its size and position and register its action listener is the same as we did for the Button class. Let's modify the MyFirstFrame class by adding a TextField object. Let's call the new class MySecondFrame. The effect of clicking the buttons CANCEL and OK is the same as before. If the user presses the ENTER key while the TextField object is active, then we will change the title to whatever text is entered in this TextField object. In the data declaration part, we add

```
TextField inputLine;
```

and in the constructor we create a TextField object and register the frame as its action listener:

```
public MySecondFrame
{
    //same as the constructor of MyFirstFrame
    ...
    inputLine = new TextField( );
    inputLine.setBounds(90, 50, 130, 25);
    add( inputLine );

    inputLine.addActionListener( this );
}
```

Now we need to modify the actionPerformed method to handle the button click events and the ENTER key events. We have three event sources (two buttons and one text field), so the first thing we must do in the actionPerformed method is determine the source. We will use the instanceof operator to determine the class to which the event source belongs. Here's the general idea:

reserved word
instanceof

```
if ( event.getSource() instanceof Button ) {
    //event source is a button, either cancelButton
    //or okButton
    ...
}
```

```
else { //event source must be inputLine
   ...
}
```

We use the getText method of TextField to retrieve the text the user has entered. The complete method is written as

```
public void actionPerformed( ActionEvent event )
{
    if ( event.getSource() instanceof Button ) {
        Button clickedButton = (Button) event.getSource();
        if (clickedButton == cancelButton) {
            setTitle( "You clicked CANCEL" );
        }
        else { //the event source is okButton
            setTitle( "You clicked OK" );
        }
    }
    else {
        TextField textField = (TextField) event.getSource();
        setTitle("You entered '" +
                            textField.getText() + "'");
    }
}
```

Notice that we wrote the else part as

```
TextField textField = (TextField) event.getSource();
setTitle("You entered '" + textField.getText() + "'");
```

so the style is parallel to the one used in the then part. Since we know that the event source is inputLine in the else part, we can write it more succinctly as

```
setTitle("You entered '" + inputLine.getText() + "'");
```

Quick Check

1. What is the purpose of the instanceof operator?
2. What user action will result in a TextField object generating an action event?

13.4 Menus

Nontrivial programs with a graphical user interface will almost always support menus. In this section we will describe how to display menus and process menu events using Menu, MenuItem, and MenuBar from the java.awt package. Figure 13.1 shows these objects. MenuBar is a bar where the menus are placed. Menu is a single menu in the MenuBar. In Figure 13.1, we have two Menu objects: File and Edit. MenuItem is an individual menu choice in the Menu. When a menu selection is made (e.g., selecting the item Cut under the Edit menu), a menu action event occurs. We process the menu selections by registering an action listener to menu items. Although it is more common to register one action listener to all menu items, we could register a different listener to individual menu items.

Let's write a sample code to illustrate the display of menus and the processing of menu item selections. We will create two menus, File and Edit, with the following menu items:

```
  File                 Edit
 ┌───────────┐
 │  New      │     ┌────────────┐
 │  Open...  │     │  Cut       │
 │  Save     │     │  Copy      │
 │  Save As..│     │  Paste     │
 ├───────────┤     └────────────┘
 │  Quit     │
 └───────────┘
```

If the menu item Quit is selected, then we terminate the program. When a menu item other than Quit is selected, we will print a message that identifies the selected menu item, for example:

```
Menu item 'New' is selected
```

Figure 13.4 shows a MenuFrame when it is first opened and after the menu choice Save is selected.

One possible sequence of steps to create and add menus is as follows:

1. Create a MenuBar object and attach it to a frame.

2. Create a Menu object.

3. Create MenuItem objects and add them to the Menu object.

4. Attach the Menu object to the MenuBar object.

Some variations to the given order are possible, but you cannot add new MenuItem objects to a Menu once it is attached to a MenuBar.

FIGURE 13.4 **MenuFrame** window when it is first opened and after the menu item **Save** is selected.

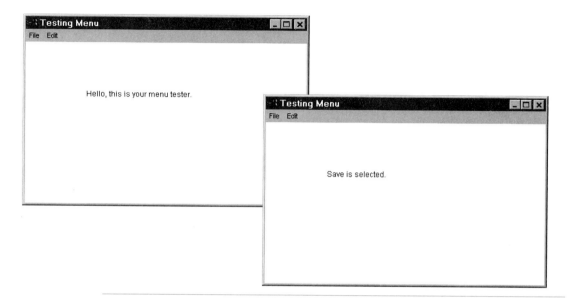

We will create two Menu objects: fileMenu and editMenu. We create a file-Menu object as

```
fileMenu = new Menu( "File" );
```

The argument to the Menu constructor is the name of the menu. After the menu is created, we add a menu item to it. A menu item is the event source of menu selection, so we need to register an action listener to every menu item we add to the menu. In this sample code, we will let a MenuFrame object be the action listener of all menu items. To create and add a menu item New to fileMenu, we execute

```
item = new MenuItem("New");        //New
item.addActionListener( this );
fileMenu.add( item );
```

We repeat this sequence for all other menu items. Menu items are placed from the top in the order they are added to the menu. We can also include a horizontal line as a separator between menu items by calling the menu's addSeparator method

```
fileMenu.addSeparator();
```

After the menus and their menu items are created, we attach them to a menu bar. In the constructor, we create a MenuBar object, attach it to the frame by calling the frame's setMenuBar method, and add these two Menu objects to the menu bar

```
MenuBar menuBar = new MenuBar();
setMenuBar(menuBar);                     //attach it to the frame
menuBar.add(fileMenu);
menuBar.add(editMenu);
```

To display which menu item was selected, we use a Label object response. We add response to the frame by

```
response = new Label("Hello, this is your menu tester.");
response.setBounds(100, 100, 250, 50);
add(response);
```

Finally, in the constructor, we register a ProgramTerminator object as the frame's window event listener.

When a menu item is selected, the registered action listener's actionPerformed method is called. The actionPerformed method of the MenuFrame is defined as follows: If an event source is a menu item, the getActionCommand method of ActionEvent returns the menu's text. We test if the returned text is Quit. If it is, we terminate the program. Otherwise, we set the text of response to indicate which menu item was selected. Here's the method body of Action-Performed:

```
String     menuName;

menuName = event.getActionCommand();

if ( menuName.equals("Quit") ) {
   System.exit(0);
}
else {
   response.setText("Menu item '" + menuName +
                     "' is selected");
}
```

Here's the complete program:

```java
import java.awt.*;
import java.awt.event.*;

/**
 * Class MenuFrame
 *
 * This frame includes one MenuBar, two Menu objects File and Edit,
 * and eight MenuItem objects. When a menu item is selected, a string
 * showing which menu choice is selected will appear on the frame.
 */

class MenuFrame extends Frame implements ActionListener
{
//-------------------------------
// Data Members
//-------------------------------
    private static final int FRAME_WIDTH    = 450;
    private static final int FRAME_HEIGHT   = 300;
    private static final int FRAME_X_ORIGIN = 150;
    private static final int FRAME_Y_ORIGIN = 250;

    private Label    response;
    private Menu     fileMenu;
    private Menu     editMenu;

//-------------------------------
// Constructor
//-------------------------------
    public MenuFrame( )
    {
        //set frame properties
        setTitle      ( "Testing Menu" );
        setSize       ( FRAME_WIDTH, FRAME_HEIGHT );
        setResizable  ( false  );
        setLocation   ( FRAME_X_ORIGIN, FRAME_Y_ORIGIN );
        setLayout     ( null   );

        //create two menus and their menu items
        createFileMenu();
        createEditMenu();

        //add the two menus to the menubar
        MenuBar menuBar = new MenuBar();
        setMenuBar(menuBar);
        menuBar.add(fileMenu);
        menuBar.add(editMenu);

        //create and position the response label
        response = new Label("Hello, this is your menu tester.");
        response.setBounds(100, 100, 250, 50);
        add(response);

        addWindowListener( new ProgramTerminator() );
    }
```

```
//-------------------------------
//  Menu and MenuItem Creation
//-------------------------------

    private void createFileMenu()
    {
        MenuItem  item;

        fileMenu = new Menu( "File" );

        item = new MenuItem("New");         //New
        item.addActionListener( this );
        fileMenu.add( item );

        item = new MenuItem("Open...");     //Open...
        item.addActionListener( this );
        fileMenu.add( item );

        item = new MenuItem("Save");        //Save
        item.addActionListener( this );
        fileMenu.add( item );

        item = new MenuItem("Save As...");//Save As...
        item.addActionListener( this );
        fileMenu.add( item );

        fileMenu.addSeparator();            //add a horizontal separator line

        item = new MenuItem("Quit");        //Quit
        item.addActionListener( this );
        fileMenu.add( item );
    }

    private void createEditMenu()
    {
        MenuItem  item;

        editMenu = new Menu( "Edit" );

        item = new MenuItem("Cut");         //Cut
        item.addActionListener( this );
        editMenu.add( item );

        item = new MenuItem("Copy");        //Copy
        item.addActionListener( this );
        editMenu.add( item );

        item = new MenuItem("Paste");       //Paste
        item.addActionListener( this );
        editMenu.add( item );
    }


//-------------------------------
//  Action Event Handling
//-------------------------------

    public void actionPerformed( ActionEvent event )
    {
        String menuName;
```

```
        menuName = event.getActionCommand();

        if ( menuName.equals("Quit") ) {
            System.exit(0);
        }
        else {
            response.setText("Menu item '" + menuName + "' is selected");
        }
    }

}
```

File: TestMenuFrame.java

```
/**
 * Program TestMenuFrame
 *
 * A main class for testing MenuFrame
 */
class TestMenuFrame
{
    public static void main (String args[])
    {
        MenuFrame frame = new MenuFrame();
        frame.setVisible( true );
    }
}
```

Mr. Espresso: *The size of text for the response label is too small for me. Can you make it bigger?*

Dr. Caffeine: *Yes, do this:*

```
response.setFont( new Font("Helvetica", /*font name*/
                           Font.BOLD, /*font style*/
                           16 ) );    /*font size*/
```

Quick Check

1. For which object do we register as an action listener: Menu, Menu-Item, or MenuBar?

2. How do we get the text of a selected menu item in the actionPerformed method?

13.5 Handling Mouse Events

In this section we describe the handling of mouse events. Mouse events include such user interactions as moving the mouse, dragging the mouse (i.e., moving the mouse while the mouse button is being pressed), and clicking the mouse buttons.

Let's look at an example in which we display the x and y pixel coordinates of a location where a mouse button is pressed down. We will define a subclass of Frame, named TrackMouseFrame, that handles the left mouse button click events and use an OutputBox object to print out the mouse click locations. Note: For a system with a one-button mouse, we treat this button as the left mouse button.

A TrackMouseFrame object is an event source of mouse events. We will let this object be a mouse event listener also. For a TrackMouseFrame object to be a mouse event listener, its class must implement MouseListener. This interface has five abstract methods: mouseClicked, mouseEntered, mouseExited, mousePressed, and mouseReleased. The argument to all five methods is an instance of MouseEvent.

The class declaration for TrackMouseFrame will look like this:

```
class TrackMouseFrame extends Frame
                      implements MouseListener
{
    ...
}
```

In the constructor we set the frame properties and register this frame as a mouse event listener of itself. We will let a ProgramTerminator be a window event listener of the frame. The constructor is defined as

```
public TrackMouseFrame
{
    //set the frame properties
    ...

    //create an outputBox for printing out
    //the mouse click points
    outputBox = new OutputBox( this );

    //register itself as its mouse event listener and
    //a ProgramTerminator as its window event listener
    addMouseListener( this );
    addWindowListener( new ProgramTerminator() );
}
```

When the left mouse button is clicked, the mouseClicked method of its mouse event listener is called. In this method, we want to find out the x and y coordinates of the mouse click point and print out these values in an outputBox. To find the x and y coordinate values, we use the getX and getY methods of MouseEvent. So, the mouseClicked method of TrackMouseFrame is defined as

```
public void mouseClicked( MouseEvent event )
{
    int x, y;

    x = event.getX(); //return the x and y coordinates
    y = event.getY(); //of a mouse click point

    outputBox.printLine("[" + x + "," + y + "]");
}
```

This method is called every time the left mouse button is clicked, that is, the mouse button is pressed down and released. If we want to detect the mouse button press and release separately, then we can provide a method body to the mousePressed and mouseReleased methods. For example, if we define these methods as

```
public void mousePressed( MouseEvent event )
{
    outputBox.printLine("Down");
}
```

and

```
public void mouseReleased( MouseEvent event )
{
    outputBox.printLine("Up");
}
```

instead of empty method bodies, then we will see something like

```
Down
Up
[200,120]

```

when we click a mouse button.

Here's the program:

File: TrackMouseFrame.java

```java
import java.awt.*;
import java.awt.event.*;
import javabook.*;

/**
 * Class TrackMouseFrame
 *
 * This frame tracks the mouse click events. When the left mouse button
 * is clicked, the location where the mouse button is clicked
 * will be displayed in an OutputBox.
 */

class TrackMouseFrame extends Frame implements MouseListener
{
//---------------------------------
// Data Members
//---------------------------------
    private static final int FRAME_WIDTH    = 450;
    private static final int FRAME_HEIGHT   = 300;
    private static final int FRAME_X_ORIGIN=  50;
    private static final int FRAME_Y_ORIGIN=  50;

    private OutputBox outputBox;

//---------------------------------
// Constructor
//---------------------------------
    public TrackMouseFrame()
    {
        //set the frame properties
        setTitle     ( "TrackMouseFrame" );
        setSize      ( FRAME_WIDTH, FRAME_HEIGHT );
        setResizable ( false );
        setLocation  ( FRAME_X_ORIGIN, FRAME_Y_ORIGIN );

        outputBox = new OutputBox(this);

        addMouseListener( this );
        addWindowListener( new ProgramTerminator() );
    }

    public void start()
    {
        setVisible( true );
        outputBox.setVisible( true );
    }

//---------------------------------
// Mouse Event Handling
//---------------------------------

    public void mouseClicked( MouseEvent event )
    {
        int x, y;
        x = event.getX(); //return the x and y coordinates of
        y = event.getY(); //a mouse click point
```

> **TrackMouseFrame** is both a source and a listener of mouse events.

```
        outputBox.printLine("[" + x + "," + y + "]");
    }

    public void mouseEntered        ( MouseEvent event ) { }
    public void mouseExited         ( MouseEvent event ) { }
    public void mousePressed        ( MouseEvent event ) { }
    public void mouseReleased       ( MouseEvent event ) { }

}
```

File: TestTrackMouseFrame.java

```
/**
 * Program TestTrackMouseFrame
 *
 * A main class for testing TrackMouseFrame
 */

class TestTrackMouseFrame
{
    public static void main (String args[])
    {
        TrackMouseFrame frame = new TrackMouseFrame( );
        frame.start();
    }
}
```

Let's rewrite the **mouseClicked** method so that when the left mouse button is double-clicked, we will erase the contents of **outputBox**. We check the number of button clicks by calling the **getClickCount** method of **MouseEvent**. Here's the method that erases the contents of **outputBox** when a double-click occurs (a single mouse click will print out the location of a mouse click as before):

```
public void mouseClicked( MouseEvent event )
{
    if ( event.getClickCount() == 2 ) {//erase the contents
        outputBox.clear();                 //of outputBox
    }
    else {                    //print out mouse click location
        int x, y;

        x = event.getX();
        y = event.getY();

        outputBox.printLine("[" + x + "," + y + "]");
    }
}
```

Because a double-click is a sequence of two single clicks, this method is called twice when you double-click. The getClickCount method returns 1 for the first call and returns 2 for the second call.

MySketchPad

Let's try another example. This time, let's implement the SketchPad class from the javabook package. To distinguish the class we define here from the original, we will call the class MySketchPad. The basic idea of MySketchPad is to keep track of three events:

1. The left mouse button is pressed down.

2. The right mouse button is pressed down.

3. The mouse is dragged.

Notice that we are processing mouse button presses, not clicks. (Note: For the Mac platform, a mouse button press is treated as the left button press and the Command-press is treated as the right button press. For a platform that supports three mouse buttons, the middle mouse button is also treated as the left mouse button.)

To show you a variation, we will declare MySketchPad as a subclass of MainWindow so we don't have to worry about terminating the program when the window is closed. The code for handling the window closing event is inherited from MainWindow. MySketchPad will need to implement two interfaces: MouseListener and MouseMotionListener. Since we want a MySketchPad frame to process mouse button clicks, we must implement the MouseListener interface. In addition to this, we need to implement the MouseMotionListener interface in order to track the mouse dragging. The MouseMotionListener interface includes two abstract methods: mouseDragged and mouseMoved. The argument to both methods is an instance of MouseEvent.

When a mouse button, either the left or right button, is pressed, the event listener's mousePressed is called. Let's study how we should implement this method. If the right mouse button is pressed, then we have to erase the current drawing. If the left mouse button is pressed, then it means it is the start of a new mouse drag, so we have to remember the location where the left button is pressed. To determine which mouse button is pressed inside the mousePressed method, we call the isMetaDown method of MouseEvent as

```
if ( event.isMetaDown() ) {
   //the right button is pressed
   ...
}
```

The isMetaDown method returns true if the right button is pressed. We don't have a method such as isRightButtonPress in MouseEvent because not all platforms support the right mouse button. The Mac platform, for example, has only one mouse button, and for the Mac, the Command-press is treated as the right mouse button press.

The code to erase the contents of the window is as follows:

```
if ( event.isMetaDown() ) {
    //the right button is pressed
    //so erase the contents
    Graphics  g = getGraphics();
    Rectangle r = getBounds();
    g.clearRect(0, 0, r.width, r.height);
    g.dispose();
}
```

We erase the contents by drawing a filled rectangle as big as the window itself with the rectangle filled in the background color. The getBounds method returns the size of a window.

If it is not a right mouse button press, then it is a left button press, so we remember the first position to draw a line as

```
if ( event.isMetaDown() ) {
    //the right button is pressed
    ...
}
else {
    //remember the starting point of a new mouse drag
    last_x = x;
    last_y = y;
}
```

last_x and last_y are instance variables.

The position (x, y) is computed at the beginning of the mousePressed method as

```
int x = event.getX();
int y = event.getY();
```

The getX and getY methods of the MouseEvent class return the x and y coordinates of the point where the mouse button is pressed.

Now, to process the mouse drag event, we need to define the mouseDragged method. From the argument object MouseEvent, we get a new position (x, y) and draw a line from the previous position to this new position using the Graphics object g as follows:

Chapter 13

```
                g.drawLine(last_x, last_y, x, y);
```

After the drawing is done, we reset the variables as

```
        last_x = x;
        last_y = y;
```

Similar to the mousePressed method, the mouseDragged method is called whether the mouse was dragged with the left or right button. So we need to include the if test

```
        if (!event.isMetaDown() ) {
            //it's a left mouse button drag,
            //so draw a line
            . . .
        }
```

inside the method so the drawing will occur only for the left mouse button drag. Here's a complete listing of the program:

File: MySketchPad.java

```
/**
 *  Class MySketchPad
 *
 *  This class implements the SketchPad class from the javabook package.
 */

import java.awt.*;
import java.awt.event.*;
import javabook.*;

class MySketchPad extends MainWindow
                    implements MouseListener, MouseMotionListener
{

//----------------------------------
// Data Members
//----------------------------------
    private static final int FRAME_WIDTH    = 450;
    private static final int FRAME_HEIGHT   = 300;
    private static final int FRAME_X_ORIGIN = 150;
    private static final int FRAME_Y_ORIGIN = 250;

    private int last_x;
    private int last_y;


//----------------------------------
// Constructor
//----------------------------------
    public MySketchPad( )
    {
        //set frame properties
```

```
        setTitle      ("SketchPad for Your Doodle Art");
        setSize       ( FRAME_WIDTH, FRAME_HEIGHT );
        setResizable  ( false );
        setLocation   ( FRAME_X_ORIGIN, FRAME_Y_ORIGIN );

        last_x = last_y = 0;

        addMouseListener( this );          //add itself as mouse and
        addMouseMotionListener( this );   //mouse motion listener
    }

//-------------------------------
// Mouse Event Handling
//-------------------------------

    public void mousePressed( MouseEvent event )
    {
        int x = event.getX();
        int y = event.getY();

        if ( event.isMetaDown() ) {
            //the right mouse button is pressed, so erase the contents
            Graphics  g = getGraphics();
            Rectangle r = getBounds();
            g.clearRect(0, 0, r.width, r.height);
            g.dispose();
        }
        else {
            //the left mouse button is pressed,
            //remember the starting point of a new mouse drag
            last_x = x;
            last_y = y;
        }
    }

    public void mouseClicked        ( MouseEvent event ) { }
    public void mouseEntered        ( MouseEvent event ) { }
    public void mouseExited         ( MouseEvent event ) { }
    public void mouseReleased       ( MouseEvent event ) { }


//-------------------------------
// Mouse Motion Event Handling
//-------------------------------

    public void mouseDragged  ( MouseEvent event )
    {
        int x = event.getX();
        int y = event.getY();

        if ( !event.isMetaDown() ) {
            //don't process the right button drag
            Graphics  g = getGraphics();

            g.drawLine(last_x, last_y, x, y);
            g.dispose();

            last_x = x;
            last_y = y;
        }
    }
```

```
    public void mouseMoved    ( MouseEvent event ) { }
}
```

File: TestMySketchPad.java

```
/**
 *  Program TestMySketchPad
 *
 *  A main class for testing MySketchPad
 */
class TestMySketchPad
{
    public static void main (String args[])
    {
        MySketchPad frame = new MySketchPad( );
        frame.setVisible( true );
    }
}
```

Quick Check

1. Which listener object listens to mouse movements? Which listener object listens to mouse button presses and clicks?

2. What is the purpose of the isMetaDown method?

3. What is the difference between mouseClicked and mousePressed?

13.6 Other GUI Objects

Figure 13.5 shows the class hierarchy of common classes in the java.awt and java.applet packages. Notice that the Applet class is a descendant of a java.awt class called Panel. The class drawn with a parallelogram (e.g., Component and Container classes) is an abstract class. An *abstract class* contains a method called an *abstract method* that has no method body. The method body is to be defined by the descendant classes. The purpose of an abstract class is to establish the code common to all of its descendant classes for consistency and elimination of duplicate code. We will discuss further and illustrate the use of abstract classes in the next chapter.

abstract class

abstract method

As you can see from the hierarchy, the Frame class we have been using is a descendant of the Container class. We call an instance of the Container and any of its descendant classes a *container*. A Container object can contain other Component objects such as instances from the Button and Label classes. Because the Dialog and Applet classes are also descendant classes of the Container class, the

FIGURE 13.5   The class hierarchy for some of the commonly used GUI classes. Notice how the
Applet class is related to the **java.awt** package and all classes inherit from the **Object**
class.

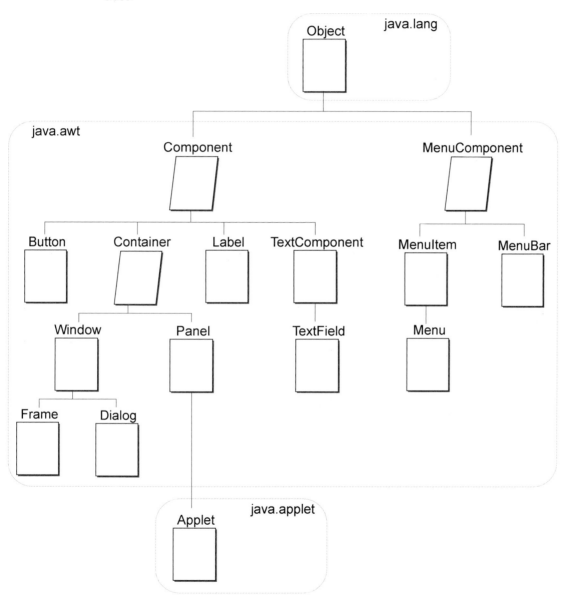

techniques we learned to place Component objects on a frame and process the generated events apply equally to a dialog and an applet. So if you know how to place a button on a frame and process the button click event, then you already know how to do the same thing with a dialog and an applet. There are, of course, differences. Otherwise, there wouldn't be three different classes. Some of the key differences are

1. Frame can have menus; the others cannot.

2. Dialog can be modal or modeless. Frame is always modeless. Modality does not apply to Applet (see item 4). We will explain the modality in this section.

3. Dialog needs an owner Frame object, that is, a dialog cannot be the main window of a program.

4. Dialog and Frame are windows. Applet is a panel that needs to be placed on a dialog or a frame like any other Component. An applet viewer is a Frame object.

Dialogs

To illustrate how much you already know about how to program a dialog, we will create a sample dialog called MyFirstDialog that supports the same functionality of MyFirstFrame. But before we start working on MyFirstDialog, we will explain the difference between the modal and modeless dialogs.

A *modal* dialog disables all other windows once it appears on the screen. This means that once a modal dialog appears on the screen, the program execution will not continue until you close this dialog. The dialog classes such as MessageBox, InputBox, and ResponseBox from the javabook package are all modal dialogs. For example, when a MessageBox object appears on the screen, you cannot click on the main window until you close this MessageBox object. A *modeless* dialog box, on the other hand, does not disable other windows. Consider the following example. Suppose dialog1 and dialog2 are dialogs, and we execute the statements

```
dialog1.setVisible( true );
dialog2.setVisible( true );
```

If these dialogs are modal, then you will not see dialog2 until you close dialog1. If, however, these dialogs are modeless, then you will see two dialogs appearing on the screen at the same time.

Using the MyFirstDialog class as an example, we will show you how to create a modal and a modeless dialog. The class extends the Dialog class as

```
class MyFirstDialog extends Dialog
{
    ...
}
```

The Dialog class defines a constructor that accepts two arguments: an owner Frame object and a boolean. The boolean argument determines the modality of the created dialog: true for a modal dialog and false for a modeless dialog. A constructor we define for the MyFirstDialog will accept the same two arguments. The first statement in the constructor is a call to the constructor of Dialog:

```
public MyFirstDialog( Frame owner, boolean modal )
{
    super(owner, modal);
    ...
}
```

If a MyFirstDialog object is most frequently created as a modal dialog, then we can define a second constructor with only one argument

```
public MyFirstDialog( Frame owner )
{
    this( owner, true ); //call the first constructor
    ...
}
```

This is basically how we defined the constructors of MessageBox, InputBox, and others.

Now, to add cancelButton and okButton to MyFirstDialog and handle the button events as we did in MyFirstFrame, we just duplicate the code we used for MyFirstFrame:

```
class MyFirstDialog extends Dialog
                    implements ActionListener
{
    //Data Members - the same as in MyFirstFrame

    public MyFirstDialog( Frame owner )
    {
        this( owner, true ); //if false, default is modeless
    }

    public MyFirstDialog( Frame owner, boolean modal )
    {
```

```
        super( owner, modal );
        //the rest is exactly the same as
        //the MyFirstFrame constructor
    }

    //the same actionPerformed method comes here
}
```

To use this MyFirstDialog in a program, we can use the following main class. Notice that we need a Frame object to create an instance of MyFirstDialog.

```
class TestMyFirstDialog
{
    public static void main( String args[] )
    {
        MainWindow    frame = new MainWindow();
        MyFirstDialog dialog
                         = new MyFirstDialog( frame, false);
        frame.setVisible( true );
        dialog.setVisible( true );
    }
}
```

Notice that when you close a MyFirstDialog object, the program is terminated because we register a ProgramTerminator object as its window event listener. If we just want to close the dialog, we can let MyFirstDialog implement the WindowListener interface and define the windowClosing method as

```
public void windowClosing( )
{
    setVisible( false ); //hide it
}
```

Applets

If you know how to program frames and dialogs, then you already know how to program applets. They are all containers, and the way to place components on them is the same. One major difference is that Applet is a panel, so it needs to be placed on a dialog or a frame like any other Component. Sample applets you have seen so far are placed on a Frame object called an applet viewer. An applet viewer is an instance of the AppletViewer class, which is a subclass of Frame. An applet viewer reads information from the applet's corresponding HTML file and adjusts its size to accommodate the applet. We can run applets without using an applet viewer; in fact, we can use any Frame object to run an applet. We will show you how in this section.

Let's say we want to run GreetingApplet from Chapter 5 without an applet viewer. We can easily do this by creating a frame and adding an instance of GreetingApplet to this frame. Here's how:

```java
import java.awt.*;

class GreetingAppletMain
{
    public static void main (String args[])
    {
        Frame myFrame;

        myFrame = new Frame("Greeting Applet in Frame");
        myFrame.setSize(300, 270);
        myFrame.addWindowListener( new ProgramTerminator() );
        myFrame.add( new GreetingApplet() );
        myFrame.setVisible( true );
    }
}
```

Quick Check

1. Name three descendant classes of the Container class?
2. What is the difference between a modal and a modeless dialog?
3. How is an applet different from a frame and a dialog?

13.7 Sample Program: A Simple Calculator

Let's build a simple four-function calculator to summarize the concepts we have covered in this chapter. Figure 13.6 shows the calculator we will develop. To implement the calculator, we will use GUI components Button and TextField, process action events generated by the buttons, and handle exceptions thrown by invalid data entry.

Problem Statement

Write a calculator that has two text fields to enter left and right operands and five operator buttons for add, subtract, divide, multiply, and clear. Clicking the CLEAR button clears both text fields. The result of the operation is displayed in the top text field. The user can continue the calculation by entering the next number in the bottom text field and clicking the desired operator.

FIGURE 13.6   A four-function calculator.

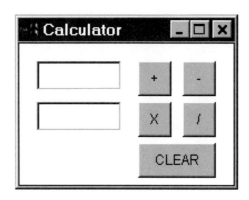

Overall Plan

What kind of an object is Calculator? Is it an application logic object? Is it a user interface object? Or is it a controller object? Since a Calculator object is intended to be a stand-alone program, it must be a controller object managing other objects such as instances from the TextField and Button class. Since the operations required for this calculator are very basic, we will let a Calculator be an application logic object also. We are therefore overloading the Calculator class with multiple tasks, but each task is short and not complex, so we will let the Calculator class handle the tasks of both controller and application logic. If we were to design a more realistic scientific or business calculator, then we would have to design a separate application object for handling numerical computations.

The key task of a Calculator is to perform the computation when an operator button is clicked and clear the entries if the CLEAR button is clicked. The buttons will be action event sources, and the Calculator object is an action event listener. Expressed in pseudocode, the actionPerformed method would look something like this:

```
if ( clickedButton == clearButton ) {
   clearEntries();
}
else { //an operator button is clicked
   compute ( clickedButton );
}
```

The clearEntries method sets the text of both TextField objects to an empty string. The compute method, expressed in pseudocode, would look something like this:

```
leftOperand = get value from the top TextField;
rightOperand = get value from the bottom TextField;

switch ( operator ) {
    case addition:
                result = leftOperand + rightOperand;
                break;

    case subtraction:
                result = leftOperand - rightOperand;
                break;

    case division:
                result = leftOperand / rightOperand;
                break;

    case multiplication:
                result = leftOperand * rightOperand;
                break;
}

display result in the top TextField;
clear the bottom TextField;
```

This pseudocode assumes that the input data are valid. We need to add an input error checking code in the final version of compute. We consider any input value that cannot be converted to a float value as invalid.

Our working design document for the Calculator class at this point is as follows:

Design Document: The Calculator Class extends Frame implements ActionListener		
Method	**Visibility**	**Purpose**
`<constructor>`	`public`	Creates and initializes a Calculator object.
`setVisible`	`public`	Inherited method. Displays and starts a Calculator object.
`actionPerformed`	`public`	Determines which type of button is clicked and, depending on it, calls either the clearEntries or compute method.

Design Document: The Calculator Class extends Frame implements ActionListener		
Method	**Visibility**	**Purpose**
`clearEntries`	`private`	Clears both TextField objects to an empty string.
`compute`	`private`	Performs the specified calculation and displays the result.

Its object diagram at this point is

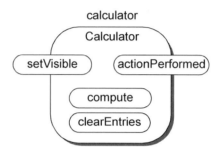

We will implement the class in the following four steps:

development steps

1. Start with a class skeleton. Define the necessary data members and constructors. Add any other methods necessary to implement the constructors.

2. Implement the actionPerformed method. Implement the private methods clearEntries and compute also. For this step, assume the input is valid.

3. Implement methods necessary to check for invalid input data.

4. Finalize the code and look for improvement.

Step 1 Development: Skeleton with Constructor

Step 1 Design

The objective of Step 1 is to identify the necessary GUI components and complete the visual appearance of the calculator. In this step, the calculator does not perform the actual computation. Let's start with data members of the class. We will use two TextField objects for the user to enter the left and right operands. We will call them leftOperand and rightOperand. We will use four Button objects for the four arithmetic operators and one Button for the CLEAR button. We declare these objects as

```
private    TextField    leftOperand,
                        rightOperand;

private    Button       plusButton,
                        minusButton,
                        multiplyButton,
                        divideButton,
                        clearButton;
```

Now, let's think about the constructors. We will support one constructor that has no parameter. We could add other constructors where the programmer, for example, can pass the window width and height as parameters. Such a constructor is meaningful if we adjust the size of buttons based on the size of the window. Since we have not covered this technique of adjusting the size of buttons using different types of layout managers, we will not support such a constructor. We will create a fix-sized calculator and use absolute positioning.

We will define the Calculator class as a subclass of Frame. We choose not to make the Calculator class the main class. The programmer must supply his own main class to derive a full calculator program. By not making the Calculator class the main class, the programmer has more flexibility in reusing a Calculator object in his program. Since the class is a subclass of Frame, we will set certain properties of Frame, such as its size and location on the screen, inside the constructor. Since it is a frame, we will include a window listener to terminate the program when the frame is closed. We will use the ProgramTerminator object defined earlier in the chapter.

To prevent the constructor from becoming too big, we will define a separate private method initGUIComponents to create and initialize the data member GUI components. We will register the Calculator object as an action listener of all five buttons in this method.

The working design document now includes this method:

Design Document:	The Calculator Class	
Method	**Visibility**	**Purpose**
. . .	. . .	. . .
initGUIComponents	private	Create and initialize GUI components. Register the Calculator object as an event listener of all five buttons.

Step 1 Code   Here's the Step 1 implementation of the Calculator class:

File: Calculator.java

```java
/**
 *   Program Calculator
 *
 *   This program provides a simple four-function calculator with
 *   two input fields to enter the left and right operands of an
 *   arithmetic operation. The program uses the JDK 1.1 event model.
 */

import java.awt.*;
import java.awt.event.*;

class Calculator extends Frame implements ActionListener
{

//--------------------------------
// Data Members
//--------------------------------

    private static final int FRAME_WIDTH    = 200;
    private static final int FRAME_HEIGHT   = 150;
    private static final int FRAME_X_ORIGIN = 300;
    private static final int FRAME_Y_ORIGIN = 200;

    private TextField    leftOperand,
                         rightOperand;

    private Button       plusButton,
                         minusButton,
                         multiplyButton,
                         divideButton,
                         clearButton;

//--------------------------------
// Data Members
//--------------------------------

    public Calculator()
    {
        //set window properties
        super        ( "Calculator");

        setSize      ( FRAME_WIDTH, FRAME_HEIGHT );
        setResizable ( false );
        setLayout    ( null );
        setLocation  ( FRAME_X_ORIGIN, FRAME_Y_ORIGIN );

        //create and lay out components
        initGUIComponents();

        addWindowListener( new ProgramTerminator() );

    }

//----------------------------------------------------
//      Public Methods:
//
//          void   actionPerformed ( ActionEvent   )
```

```
//
//-----------------------------------------------

    public void actionPerformed (ActionEvent event)
    {
        System.out.println("Inside actionPerformed"); //TEMP
    }


//-----------------------------------------------
//      Private Methods:
//
//          void   initGUIComponents    (            )
//
//-----------------------------------------------

    private void initGUIComponents( )
    {
        //create buttons
        leftOperand     = new TextField();
        rightOperand    = new TextField();

        plusButton      = new Button("+");
        minusButton     = new Button("-");
        multiplyButton  = new Button("X");
        divideButton    = new Button("/");
        clearButton     = new Button("CLEAR");


        //position buttons
        leftOperand.    setBounds ( 20,   40, 75, 25);
        rightOperand.   setBounds ( 20,   75, 75, 25);

        plusButton.     setBounds (110,   40, 30, 30);
        minusButton.    setBounds (150,   40, 30, 30);
        multiplyButton.setBounds (110,   75, 30, 30);
        divideButton.   setBounds (150,   75, 30, 30);
        clearButton.    setBounds (110, 110, 70, 30);

        //add the Calculator class as an action listener
        //to all five buttons
        plusButton.     addActionListener( this );
        minusButton.    addActionListener( this );
        multiplyButton.addActionListener( this );
        divideButton.   addActionListener( this );
        clearButton.    addActionListener( this );

        //add buttons to the calculator frame
        add( leftOperand    );
        add( rightOperand   );

        add( plusButton     );
        add( minusButton    );
        add( multiplyButton );
        add( divideButton   );

        add( clearButton    );
    }

}
```

Step 1 Test   In order to test the skeleton Calculator class, we need to write a test main class. A simple main class such as the following would suffice:

```
/**
 * Program TestCalculator
 *
 * A main class for testing the Calculator class
 */
class TestCalculator
{
    public static void main (String args[])
    {
        Calculator calculator = new Calculator();
        calculator.setVisible( true );
    }
}
```

The purpose of this test program is to verify that the constructors are executed correctly and the GUI objects appear as we expected. Also, we verify that when we click a button, a temporary output message is displayed in System.out.

Step 2 Development: Implement the actionPerformed Method

Step 2 Design   In the second step of development, we will replace the temporary output statement in the actionPerformed method with the real code to carry out the computation. This method is called when any one of the five buttons is clicked. If the clicked button is CLEAR, then we call clearEntries. Otherwise, one of the four operator buttons is clicked, so we call compute. The compute method will actually carry out the computation. Since the compute method needs to know which button is clicked, we will pass the clicked button to the compute method as an argument. To determine which button is clicked, we use the getSource method of ActionEvent. The method body of actionPerformed looks like this:

```
Button clickedButton = (Button) event.getSource();

if (clickedButton == clearButton) {
    clearEntries();
}
else {
    compute( clickedButton );
}
```

The clearEntries method sets the contents of both TextField objects to the empty string

```
leftOperand.setText( "" );
rightOperand.setText( "" );
```

In this step, we assume the input is valid and do not worry about input error checking. We first want to make sure that we can compute correctly, given a valid input. The compute method first retrieves data from the leftOperand and rightOperand objects. We will use a private method called getNumberFrom for this purpose. This method assumes the entry in the TextField object can be converted correctly to a float. Its method body is as follows:

```
return Convert.toFloat( operand.getText() );
```

where operand is a method parameter of type TextField. After the numbers are fetched from the TextField objects, the compute method determines which button is clicked and carries out the computation. To display the result, we will use another private method called displayResult. The displayResult method displays the result to the leftOperand object, the TextField object at the top.

The working design document now includes four new private methods:

Design Document:		The Calculator Class
Method	**Visibility**	**Purpose**
. . .	. . .	. . .
getNumberFrom	private	Returns a float value converted from the text in the argument TextField object.
compute	private	Computes the result.
clearEntries	private	Clears the entries in leftOperand and rightOperand.
displayResult	private	Displays the argument float value in the top TextField object.

Step 2 Code   We add a new import statement

```
import javabook.*;
```

so we can use the Convert class in the program.

The actionPerformed method is defined as follows:

```
public void actionPerformed( ActionEvent event )
{
```

```
                Button clickedButton = (Button) event.getSource();

                if (clickedButton == clearButton) {
                    clearEntries();
                }
                else {
                    compute( clickedButton );
                }
            }
```

The clearEntries method clears both TextField objects:

```
        private void clearEntries( )
        {
            leftOperand.setText( "" );
            rightOperand.setText( "" );
        }
```

The compute method is defined as

```
        private void compute (Button operatorButton)
        {
            float  leftOperandValue,
                   rightOperandValue,
                   result = 0f;

            //get the two operands
            leftOperandValue  = getNumberFrom(leftOperand);
            rightOperandValue = getNumberFrom(rightOperand);

            //compute the result
            if      ( operatorButton == plusButton ) {
                result = leftOperandValue + rightOperandValue;
            }
            else if ( operatorButton == minusButton ) {
                result = leftOperandValue - rightOperandValue;
            }
            else if ( operatorButton == divideButton ) {
                result = leftOperandValue / rightOperandValue;
            }
            else if ( operatorButton == multiplyButton ) {
                result = leftOperandValue * rightOperandValue;
            }

            displayResult(result);
        }
```

Finally, the displayResult method is defined as

```
private void displayResult( float value )
{
    leftOperand.setText( Convert.toString( value ) );
    rightOperand.setText( "" );
}
```

Step 2 Test   We run the TestCalculator class from Step 1 and verify that the calculator works correctly. Since we did not include any input error checking, we only input correct values. We test all four operations and verify that the correct results are computed. We also test the CLEAR button to make sure it works as intended.

Step 3 Development: Implement the Input Error Checking Routine

Step 3 Design   In the third step of development, we complete the class by adding an input error checking routine. We will modify the compute method so that the method first verifies the correctness of entries inside leftOperand and rightOperand. For input error checking, we will define a separate method isOperandValid. The argument to this method is TextField and the method returns true if the content of the passed TextField can be converted to a float. Using this method, the compute method becomes

```
if ( isOperandValid( leftOperand ) &&
       isOperandValid( rightOperand ) ) {
    //input okay
    //compute and display the result
    //this part is the code of compute from Step 2
}
else {
    display the error message "Invalid entry";
}
```

The isOperandValid method attempts to convert the String data in the TextField using the Convert class from the javabook package. If no exception is thrown, then the entry is valid and the method returns true. Otherwise, there's some error in the entry, so the method returns false.

Chapter 13

The working design document now includes this method:

Design Document: The Calculator Class		
Method	**Visibility**	**Purpose**
. . .	. . .	. . .
isOperandValid	private	Returns true if the argument TextField object contains a text that can be converted to a float.

Step 3 Code

The compute method is modified to the following:

```
private void compute (Button operatorButton)
{
    float  leftOperandValue,
           rightOperandValue,
           result = 0f;

    if (isOperandValid(leftOperand) &&
        isOperandValid(rightOperand) {
       //both operands okay, so
       //get the two operands
       leftOperandValue  = getNumberFrom(leftOperand);
       rightOperandValue = getNumberFrom(rightOperand);

       //compute the result
       if     ( operatorButton == plusButton )
          result = leftOperandValue + rightOperandValue;

       else if ( operatorButton == minusButton )
          result = leftOperandValue - rightOperandValue;

       else if ( operatorButton == divideButton )
          result = leftOperandValue / rightOperandValue;

       else if ( operatorButton == multiplyButton )
          result = leftOperandValue * rightOperandValue;

       displayResult(result);
    }
    else { //Error: display the message in leftOperand
       leftOperand.setText("Error: Invalid data");
    }
}
```

and the private isOperandValid method is defined as follows:

```
private boolean isOperandValid( TextField operand )
{
    boolean status;

    try {
        float number = Convert.toFloat(operand.getText());
        status = true;
    }
    catch ( NumberFormatException e ) {
        status = false;
    }

    return status;
}
```

Step 3 Test

For the Step 3 Calculator class, we test end cases, normal cases, and error cases. Try entering very large numbers, zeroes, very small numbers, invalid data, and so forth, and verify the correctness of the program.

Step 4 Development: Finalize

code
review

improving
code

As always, we will perform a critical review of the class looking for any unfinished methods. We will also review the class for any possible improvements. In fact, there are several possible improvements. First, we should display a better error message. The current calculator displays the same message Invalid Data for all types of input errors. The error message should provide more meaningful information. Second, the calculator allows a divide-by-zero operation. If you try to divide a number by zero, the calculator will display the result Infinity, because Java sets the result of divide-by-zero operation to infinity. Instead, the calculator should display an error message. Third, the ENTER key press should be processed for quick operation. For example, when the user enters the right operand and presses the ENTER key, the calculator can compute the sum of two numbers. With this feature, the user can compute the sum of N numbers very quickly without his or her hands leaving the keyboard. These improvements are left as exercises.

13.8 Exercises

1. Discuss the major difference between a frame and a dialog.

2. If you want your program to run as both an applet and an application, how would you design your classes?

3. One of the GUI objects in the java.awt package that we did not cover in this chapter is List. Look up this class in a Java reference manual and review the ListBox class from the javabook package. Do you see the similarities be-

tween the two? Identify the GUI components used in the ListBox. Read the definition of ListBox. Do you understand the code?

4. One of the GUI objects in the java.awt package that we did not cover in this chapter is TextArea. Look up this class in a Java reference manual and review the OutputBox class from the javabook package. Identify the GUI components used in the OutputBox. Read the definition of OutputBox. Do you understand the code?

5. Rewrite the Arithmetic class in the game package from Chapter 9 as a dialog. The ArithmeticDialog class uses a Label for a problem and a TextField for the user answer. When the user presses the ENTER key (while the TextField object is active) or clicks the OK button, the dialog displays a message stating whether the user's answer is correct or not. Use another Label for the message. Consider using a larger font for the Label and TextField text.

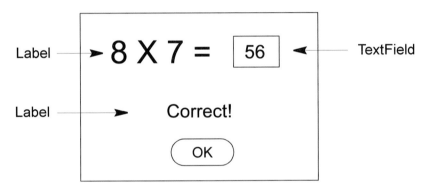

6. Rewrite the EggyPeggy class in the game package from Chapter 9 as a dialog. The EggyPeggyDialog class uses two TextField objects for entering the original text and displaying the encrypted text. When the user presses the ENTER key (while the original text TextField object is active) or clicks the OK button, the dialog displays the encrypted text in the second TextField.

Consider using TextArea objects instead of TextField objects so the user can enter multiple lines of original text. TextArea is a GUI object not covered in this chapter. See exercise 4.

7. Extend the HiLoDialog class so the user has the option of quitting the game. Add a button Give Up to the dialog. When the user clicks on the Give Up button, the dialog displays the secret number and the number of guesses the user has made. The dialog then resets itself for a new game.

8. Extend the HiLoDialog class to include the listing of guesses made by the user. Use a List object to list the user's guesses; see exercise 3.

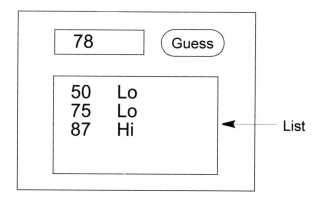

9. Modify the EggyPeggyDialog class of exercise 6 so now the dialog has three choices for encryption: Sha, Na, and Ava. The encryption methods are explained in exercise 16 on page 407.

You should design one class to handle the user interaction and another class for encrypting the original text instead of doing everything in a single class.

10. Extend the MySketchPad class to allow the user to sketch in color. Add the following menu choices.

File	Edit	Color
Quit	Erase	Red
		Green
		Blue
		Pink
		Black

When the user selects a color, set the color of a Graphics object so the subsequent sketching is made in the selected color. Selecting the menu item Erase will erase the drawing.

11. In the Calculator program from Section 13.7, an error message was displayed in the leftOperand text field. This could potentially overwrite good data (e.g., when the invalid input occurs in the rightOperand text field). Modify the class to eliminate this problem.

12. (Challenge) Write a class that implements a more realistic calculator than the one defined in this chapter.

The user enters a number using digit buttons only (see exercise 13). Some of the issues you need to consider:

- How to determine whether the user is entering a left operand or a right operand.
- How to handle the entering of multiple decimal points. A typical calculator accepts the first decimal point and ignores the rest. For example, if you press 1 . 4 . 3 . , the number entered is 1.43.
- When the display is 0 and the user enters 0, the display will not change. However, if the display is nonzero and the user enters 0, the 0 is appended to the number currently displayed.
- How to handle the operator precedence. For example, what will be the result if the user enters 4 + 3 × 2? Will it be 14 or 10? It is easier to treat all operators as having equal precedence and process them from left to right.

Study any real four-function calculator and try to implement a software calculator that simulates the real calculator as faithfully as possible, but feel free to make any reasonable changes.

13. Extend the calculator of exercise 12 to allow the user to enter a number using the keyboard. The class needs to implement the KeyListener interface and define the keyTyped method. You have to find information on KeyListener and KeyEvent from a Java API reference manual.

14. Write an application that draws a circle every time the mouse button is clicked. The position where the mouse is clicked will become the center of the circle. Set the radius of the circle to 100 pixels.

15. Extend exercise 14 by adding the following menu to let the user select the shape to draw every time the mouse button is clicked. The clicked point will be the center of the selected shape. Choose appropriate values for the dimensions of the three shapes.

Shape
Circle
Rectangle
Square

16. Modify the mortgage table program of exercise 22 on page 349. Add the following menu

File	Help
New Table	About...
Quit	

to the program. When the user selects the menu choice New Table, the program opens a dialog in which the user can enter three input values. The input dialog should look something like this:

Loan Amount:

Interest Rate:

Loan Period:

Cancel   Compute

If the user clicks on the Compute button and the three input values are valid, generate a mortgage table. If the input values are invalid, then print out an appropriate error message. Decide the range of valid values for the loan amount, interest rate, and loan period. When the user selects the menu choice About..., describe the purpose of the program using an OutputBox. You may want to use a dedicated OutputBox for this purpose instead of using the same OutputBox for displaying both the mortgage table and the program description.

17. Modify exercise 13 on page 347 using any GUI objects and techniques you learned in this chapter.

Inheritance and Polymorphism

OBJECTIVES

After you have read and studied this chapter, you should be able to

- Write programs that are easily extensible and modifiable by applying polymorphism in program design.
- Define reusable classes based on inheritance and abstract classes and abstract methods.
- Define methods using the protected modifier.
- Parse strings using a StringTokenizer object.

Introduction

In this chapter, we will describe two important and powerful features in object-oriented programming—inheritance and polymorphism. The inheritance feature of object-oriented programming was introduced in Chapter 1, and we have been using inheritance in defining classes since Chapter 2. We will provide a more detailed explanation of inheritance in this chapter. Another indispensable feature in object-oriented programming is *polymorphism*, which allows programmers to send the same message to objects from different classes. Consider the statement

polymorphism

```
account.computeMonthlyFee();
```

where account could refer to either a SavingsAccount or CheckingAccount object. If account is a SavingsAccount object, then the method computeMonthlyFee defined for the SavingsAccount class is executed. Likewise, if account is a CheckingAccount object, then the method computeMonthlyFee defined for the CheckingAccount class is executed. Sending the same message therefore could result in executing different methods. The message computeMonthlyFee is called a *polymorphic message* because depending on the receiver object, different methods are executed. Polymorphism helps us write code that is easy to modify and extend. We will explain polymorphism in this chapter.

*polymorphic
message*

14.1 Defining Classes with Inheritance

Suppose we want to maintain a class roster for a class whose enrolled students include both undergraduate and graduate students. For each student, we record his/her name, three test scores, and the final course grade. The final course grade, either pass or no pass, is determined by the following formula:

Type of Student	Grading Scheme
Undergraduate	Pass if (test1+test2+test3)/3 >= 70
Graduate	Pass if (test1+test2+test3)/3 >= 80

What kind of objects should we use to model undergraduate and graduate students? There are basically two broad ways to design the classes to model them. The first way is to define two unrelated classes, one for undergraduate students and another for graduate students. We call the two classes *unrelated* if

*unrelated
classes*

they are not connected in an inheritance relationship, that is, neither one is an ancestor or descendant class of the other nor do they share a common ancestor.[1] The second way is to model undergraduate and graduate students using classes that are related in an inheritance hierarchy.

Defining two unrelated classes for entities that share common data or behavior would make class definition ineffective because we would end up duplicating code common to both classes. Although different, graduate and undergraduate students do share many common data and behaviors, so we will design these two classes using inheritance.

We will actually define three classes. The first is the Student class to incorporate behavior and data common to both graduate and undergraduate students. The second and third classes are the GraduateStudent class to incorporate behavior specific to graduate students and the UndergraduateStudent class to incorporate behavior specific to undergraduate students. The Student class is defined as

File: Student.java

```
class Student
{

//----------------------------------
//  Data Members
//----------------------------------

    public final static int    NUM_OF_TESTS = 3;

    protected String           name;
    protected int[]            test;
    protected String           courseGrade;

//----------------------------------
//  Constructors
//----------------------------------

    public Student( )
    {
        this( "No Name" );
    }

    public Student(String studentName)
    {
        name        = studentName;
        test        = new int[NUM_OF_TESTS];
        courseGrade = "****";
    }

//----------------------------------------------------
//      Public Methods:
```

> Protected fields are visible to the descendant objects.

Chapter 14

---

1. In Java, the class **Object** is automatically set to be the superclass of a class if the class definition does not include the keyword **extends**. To be technically precise, we must say that two classes are unrelated if they do not share a common ancestor besides **Object**.

```
//
//       String getCourseGrade    (            )
//       String getName           (            )
//       int    getTestScore      ( int        )
//
//       void   setName           ( String    )
//       void   setTestScore      ( int, int)
//
//-------------------------------------------------

    public String getCourseGrade( )
    {
        return courseGrade;
    }

    public String getName( )
    {
        return name;
    }

    public int getTestScore(int testNumber)
    {
        return test[testNumber-1];
    }

    public void setName(String newName)
    {
        name = newName;
    }

    public void setTestScore(int testNumber, int testScore)
    {
        test[testNumber-1] = testScore;
    }
}
```

Notice the modifier for the instance variables is protected, making them visible and accessible to the instances of the class and the descendant classes. If you declare a data member of a class private, then this data member is accessible only to the instances of the class. If you declare a data member public, this data member is accessible to everybody. We declare them protected so they become accessible only to the instances of the class and the descendant classes. We will explore further the protected modifier later in the chapter.

We define the classes UndergraduateStudent and GraduateStudent as subclasses of the Student class. In Java, we say a subclass *extends* its superclass. The difference between the classes GraduateStudent and UndergraduateStudent lies in the way their final course grades are computed. The two subclasses are defined as follows:

extends

File: GraduateStudent.java

```
class GraduateStudent extends Student
{
    public void computeCourseGrade()
    {
        int total = 0;
```

```
        for (int i = 0; i < NUM_OF_TESTS; i++) {
            total += test[i];
        }

        if (total/NUM_OF_TESTS >= 80) {
            courseGrade = "Pass";
        }
        else {
            courseGrade = "No Pass";
        }
    }
}
```

File: UndergraduateStudent.java

```
class UndergraduateStudent extends Student
{
    public void computeCourseGrade()
    {
        int total = 0;
        for (int i = 0; i < NUM_OF_TESTS; i++) {
            total += test[i];
        }

        if (total/NUM_OF_TESTS >= 70) {
            courseGrade = "Pass";
        }
        else {
            courseGrade = "No Pass";
        }
    }
}
```

Chapter 14

Figure 14.1 shows the class diagram relating the three classes. Notice that we do not show inherited data fields and methods in the subclasses. To do so would clutter the diagram. By seeing an inheritance arrow connecting a subclass to its superclass, we know that data members and methods indicated on the superclass are applicable to the subclass also. We attach methods and data members to the subclasses only if they are defined in the subclasses or if they are overridden in the subclasses (we will discuss more on overriding later in the chapter). In Figure 14.1, both subclasses have the method computeCourse-Grade attached to them because the method is defined in the subclasses.

 Quick Check

1.   Which is the subclass and which is the superclass in the following declaration?

```
class X extends Y { ... }
```

FIGURE 14.1   A superclass **Student** and its subclasses **GraduateStudent** and **UndergraduateStudent**.

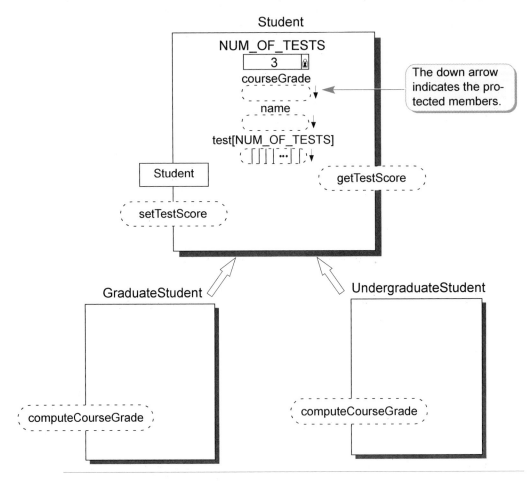

2.   Which visibility modifier allows the data members of a superclass to be accessible to the instances of subclasses?

14.2   Using Classes Effectively with Polymorphism

Now let's see how the Student class and its subclasses can be used effectively in the class roster program. Since both undergraduate and graduate students are enrolled in a class, should we declare two arrays shown below to maintain the class roster?

```
GraduateStudent        gradRoster[20];
UndergraduateStudent   undergradRoster[20];
```

We mentioned in Chapter 11 that an array must contain elements of the same data type. For example, we cannot store integers and real numbers in the same array. Following this rule, it seems necessary for us to declare two separate arrays, one for graduate students and another for undergraduate students. This rule, however, does not apply when the array elements are objects. We only need to declare a single array, for example,

```
Student roster[40];
```

Elements of the roster array can be instances of either the Student class or any of its descendant GraduateStudent or UndergraduateStudent classes. Figure 14.2 illustrates the array with both types of students as array elements.

FIGURE 14.2   The **roster** array with elements referring to instances of **GraduateStudent** or **UndergraduateStudent** classes.

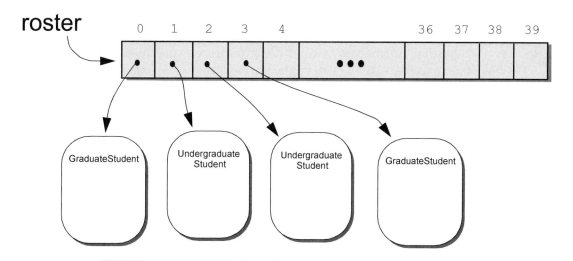

Before showing how this array is used in the program, we will explain the concept of polymorphism. In its simplest form, *polymorphism* allows a single variable to refer to objects from different classes. Consider, for example, the following declaration:

```
Student student;
```

With this declaration, not only can we say

```
student = new Student( );
```

but also

```
student = new GraduateStudent( );
```

or
```
student = new UndergraduateStudent( );
```

In other words, the single variable student is not limited to referring to an object from the Student class but can refer to any object from the descendant classes of Student. In a similar manner we can say something like

```
roster[0] = new GraduateStudent( );
roster[1] = new UndergraduateStudent( );
roster[2] = new UndergraduateStudent( );
roster[3] = new GraduateStudent( );
...
```

sibling
classes

However, you cannot make a variable of class X refer to an object from the superclass or sibling classes of X. *Sibling* classes are those that share the common ancestor class. For example, the following assignment statements are both invalid.

```
GraduateStudent grad1, grad2;
```

X NOT VALID →
```
grad1 = new Student( );
grad2 = new UndergraduateStudent( );
```

Now, to compute the course grade using the roster array, we execute

```
for (int i = 0; i < numberOfStudents; i++) {
    roster[i].computeCourseGrade();
}
```

If roster[i] refers to a GraduateStudent, then the computeCourseGrade method of the GraduateStudent class is executed, and if it refers to an Undergraduate-Student, then the computeCourseGrade method of the UndergraduateStudent is executed. We call the message computeCourseGrade *polymorphic* because the message refers to methods from different classes depending on the object referenced by roster[i]. Polymorphism allows us to maintain the class roster with one array instead of maintaining a separate array for each type of student, and this simplifies the processing tremendously.

benefits of
polymorphism

Polymorphism makes possible smooth and easy extension and modification of a program. Suppose, for example, we have to add a third type of student, say, audit student, to the class roster program. If we have to define a separate array for each type of student, this extension forces us to define a new class and a third array for audit students. But with polymorphism, we only have to define a new subclass of Student. And as long as this new subclass includes the correct computeCourseGrade method, the for loop to compute the course grade for students remains the same. Without polymorphism, not only do we have to add the new code, we have to rewrite existing code to accommodate the change. With polymorphism, on the other hand, we don't have to touch the existing code. Modifying existing code is a tedious and error-prone activity. A slight change to existing code could cause a program to stop working correctly. To be certain that a change in one portion of existing code won't affect other portions of existing code adversely, we must understand the existing code completely. And understanding code, especially the one that is long and/or written by somebody else, is a very time-consuming task.

An element of the roster array is a reference to an instance of either the GraduateStudent or UndergraduateStudent class. Most of the time, we do not have to know which is which. There are times, however, when we need to know the class of a referenced object. For example, we may want to find out the number of undergraduate students who passed the course. To determine the class of an object, we use the instanceof operator. We used this operator in Chapter 13 to determine whether an event source is a Button or a TextField object. We can use this operator here, for example,

```
Student x = new UndergraduateStudent( );

if ( x instanceof UndergraduateStudent ) {
    System.out.println("Mr. X is an undergraduate student");
}
else {
    System.out.println("Mr. X is a graduate student");
}
```

will print out Mr. X is an undergraduate student. The following code counts the number of undergraduate students in the roster array.

```
int undergradCount = 0;
for (int i = 0; i < numberOfStudents; i++) {
    if ( roster[i] instanceof UndergraduateStudent ) {
        undergradCount++;
    }
}
```

Chapter 14

Quick Check

1. Suppose Truck and Motorcycle are subclasses of Vehicle. Which of the following declarations are invalid?

```
Truck        t  = new Vehicle();
Vehicle      v  = new Truck();
Motorcycle  m1 = new Vehicle();
Motorcycle  m2 = new Truck();
```

2. What is the purpose of the instanceof operator?

14.3   Inheritance and Member Accessibility

We will describe the rules of inheritance in this and the next two sections. In this section, we will explain which members (variables and methods) of a superclass are inherited by a subclass and how these members are accessed. In addition to declaring members private and public, we can declare them protected. The protected modifier is meaningful only if used with inheritance. Consider the following declarations:

```
class Super
{
    public    int    public_Super_Field;
    protected int    protected_Super_Field;
    private   int    private_Super_Field;

    public Super()
    {
        public_Super_Field    = 10;
        protected_Super_Field = 20;
        private_Super_Field    = 30;
    }
    ...
}

class Sub extends Super
{
    public    int    public_Sub_Field;
    protected int    protected_Sub_Field;
    private   int    private_Sub_Field;

    public Sub()
    {
```

```
            public_Sub_Field        = 100;
            protected_Sub_Field     = 200;
            private_Sub_Field       = 300;
        }
        . . .
    }
```

We use instance variables for illustration, but the rules we describe here are equally applicable to other types of members (class variables, class methods, and instance methods). We use the graphical representation shown in Figure 14.3 for the three modifiers.

FIGURE 14.3   A graphical representation of super and subclasses with **public**, **private**, and **protected** members.

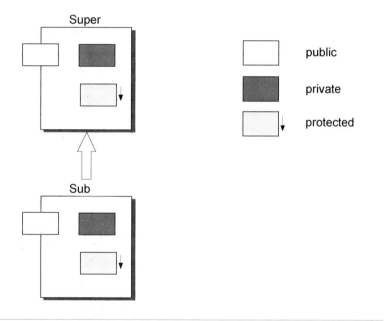

You already know the difference between the public and private modifiers. A public member is accessible to any method, but a private member is accessible only to the methods that belong to the same class. Let's illustrate this point. Consider a class that is unrelated to the classes Super and Sub:

```
    class Client
    {
        public void test()
        {
            Super  mySuper = new Super();
```

```
Sub    mySub   = new Sub();

int i = mySuper.public_Super_Field;

int j = mySub.public_Super_Field;  //inherited
                                   //by mySub
int k = mySub.public_Sub_Field;
}
}
```

VALID →

Public members of a class, whether they are inherited or not, are accessible from any object or class. Private members of a class, on the other hand, are never accessible from any outside object or class. The following statements, if placed in the test method of the Client class, are therefore all invalid:

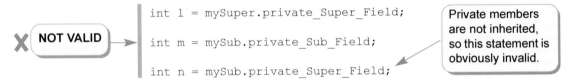

NOT VALID →

```
int l = mySuper.private_Super_Field;

int m = mySub.private_Sub_Field;

int n = mySub.private_Super_Field;
```

> Private members are not inherited, so this statement is obviously invalid.

A protected member is accessible only to the methods that belong to the same class or to the descendant classes. It is inaccessible to the methods of an unrelated class. The following statements, if placed in the test method of the Client class, are all invalid:

NOT VALID →

```
int o = mySuper.protected_Super_Field;

int p = mySub.protected_Sub_Field;

int q = mySub.protected_Super_Field;
```

Figure 14.4 summarizes the accessibility of class members from a method of an unrelated class.

Now let's study the accessibility of class members from the methods of a Sub object. A method in the Sub object can access both the protected and public members of Super, but not the private members of Super. Figure 14.5 summarizes the accessibility of members from a method of a Sub object.

Figure 14.5 shows the case where a method of a Sub object is accessing members of itself. Everything except the private members of the Super class is accessible from a method of the Sub class.

What about accessing the members of an object from another object that belongs to the same class? If a member X, whether inherited or defined in a class, is accessible from an instance of the class, then X is also accessible from all in-

FIGURE 14.4   The difference between **public**, **private**, and **protected** modifiers. Only public members are visible from outside.

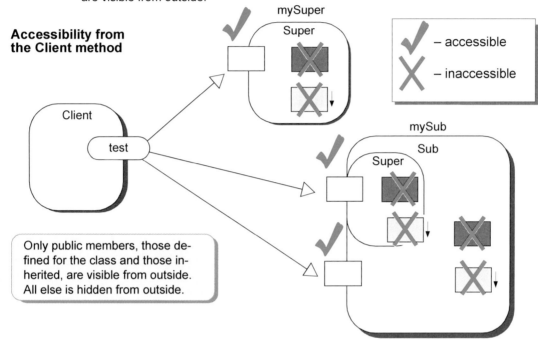

Accessibility from the Client method

Only public members, those defined for the class and those inherited, are visible from outside. All else is hidden from outside.

FIGURE 14.5   The difference between **public**, **private**, and **protected** modifiers. Everything except the **private** members of the **Super** class is visible from a method of the **Sub** class.

Accessibility from a method of the Sub class

From a method of Sub, everything is visible except the private members of its superclass.

stances of the same class. Figure 14.6 illustrates that an instance can access members of other instances of the same class.

FIGURE 14.6   Data members accessible from an instance are also accessible from other instances of the same class.

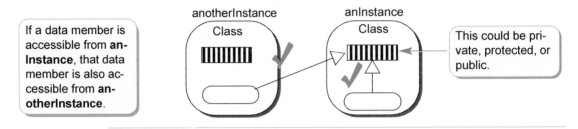

Consider the following two classes:

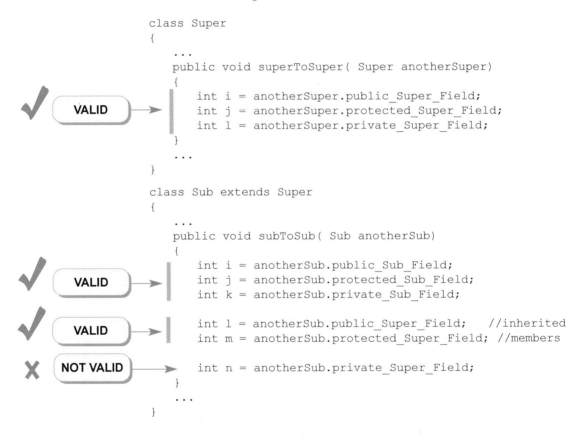

```
class Super
{
    ...
    public void superToSuper( Super anotherSuper)
    {
        int i = anotherSuper.public_Super_Field;
        int j = anotherSuper.protected_Super_Field;
        int l = anotherSuper.private_Super_Field;
    }
    ...
}

class Sub extends Super
{
    ...
    public void subToSub( Sub anotherSub)
    {
        int i = anotherSub.public_Sub_Field;
        int j = anotherSub.protected_Sub_Field;
        int k = anotherSub.private_Sub_Field;

        int l = anotherSub.public_Super_Field;    //inherited
        int m = anotherSub.protected_Super_Field; //members

        int n = anotherSub.private_Super_Field;
    }
    ...
}
```

All the statements in the two methods, except the last one in subToSub, are valid because members accessible to an object are also accessible from other objects of the same class. Now, consider the following two classes:

```
                class Super
                {
                    ...
                    public void superToSub( Sub sub)
                    {
                        int i = sub.public_Sub_Field;

                        int j = sub.protected_Sub_Field;
                        int k = sub.private_Sub_Field;
                    }
                    ...
                }

                class Sub extends Super
                {
                    ...
                    public void subToSuper( Super mySuper)
                    {
                        int i = mySuper.public_Super_Field;

                        int j = mySuper.protected_Super_Field;
                        int k = mySuper.private_Super_Field;
                    }
                    ...
                }
```

VALID →

NOT VALID →

VALID →

NOT VALID →

Chapter 14

The two methods show that only the public members of an object are accessible from another object if the two objects belong to different classes. Whether one class is a subclass of the other class is irrelevant here.

In addition to the private, protected, and public modifiers, Java supports the fourth visibility modifier called *package visibility.* Please visit our website for information on package visibility.

For information on package visibility and additional discussion on inheritance and member assessibility, please visit www.drcaffeine.com/additionaltopics.

Quick Check

1. If X is a private member of the Super class, is X accessible from a subclass of Super?

2. If X is a protected member of the Super class, is X of one instance accessible from another instance of Super? What about from the instances of a subclass of Super?

14.4 Inheritance and Constructors

In this section, we explain how the constructors of a class are affected by inheritance. Unlike other members of a superclass, constructors of a superclass are not inherited by its subclasses. This means that you must define a constructor for a class or use the default constructor added by the compiler. As we mentioned in Chapter 4, a default constructor is added to a class if you do not declare any constructor for the class. A class definition such as

```
class Person
{
    public void sayHello( )
    {
        System.out.println("Well, hello.");
    }
}
```

is equivalent to

```
class Person
{
    public Person( )
    {
        super();
    }

    public void sayHello( )
    {
        System.out.println("Well, hello.");
    }
}
```

Automatically added to the class by the compiler.

This statement calls the superclass's constructor.

The statement

```
super();
```

calls the superclass's constructor. Every class has a superclass. If the class declaration does not explicitly designate the superclass with the extends clause, then the class's superclass is the Object class.

If you declare a constructor, then no default constructor is added to the class. For example, if you define a class as

```
class MyClass
{
```

```
      public MyClass( int x )
      {
          . . .
      }
  }
```

then a statement such as

```
  MyClass test = new MyClass();
```

is invalid because **MyClass** has no matching constructor.

If the constructor you define does not contain an explicit call to a superclass constructor, then the compiler adds the statement

```
  super();
```

as the first statement of the constructor. For example, if you define a constructor as

```
  class MyClass
  {
      private int myInt;

      public MyClass( )
      (
          myInt = 10;
      }

  }
```

then the compiler will rewrite the constructor to

```
  public MyClass( )
  {
      super();
      myInt = 10;
  }
```

Let's look at another example. Consider the following class definitions:

```
  class Vehicle
  {
      private String vin;
```

```
public Vehicle(String vehicleIdNumber)
{
    vin = vehicleIdNumber;
}

public void getVIN( )
{
    return vin;
}
}
```

Since the class has a constructor, no default constructor is added to the class. This means a statement such as

```
Vehicle myCar = new Vehicle();
```

causes a compilation error because the class does not have a matching constructor. This is actually what we want because we do not want to create an instance of Vehicle without a vehicle identification number. Now let's consider a subclass definition for trucks. A Truck object has one additional instance variable called cargoWeightLimit that refers to a maximum weight of cargo the truck can carry. We assume the truck's weight limit for cargo can vary (say, depending on how much the owner pays in fees). Here's our first attempt:

```
class Truck extends Vehicle
{
    private int cargoWeightLimit;

    public void setWeightLimit( int newLimit)
    {
        cargoWeightLimit = newLimit;
    }

    public int getWeightLimit( )
    {
        return cargoWeightLimit;
    }
}
```

If you compile this definition, you will get a compiler error. Since no constructor is defined for the class, the compiler adds a default constructor

```
public void Truck()
{
    super();
}
```

This constructor calls the superclass's constructor with no arguments, but there's no matching constructor in the superclass. Thus, the compilation error results. Here's a correct definition:

```
class Truck extends Vehicle
{
    private int cargoWeightLimit;

    public Truck(int weightLimit, String vin)
    {
        super(vin);
        cargoWeightLimit = weightLimit;
    }

    public void setWeightLimit( int newLimit)
    {
        cargoWeightLimit = newLimit;
    }

    public int getWeightLimit( )
    {
        return cargoWeightLimit;
    }
}
```

You need to make this call. Otherwise, the compiler will add **super()**, which will result in an error because there is no matching constructor in **Vehicle**.

Now let's apply this knowledge to the design of the UndergraduateStudent and GraduateStudent classes. If we want a constructor that accepts the name, then we need to define such a constructor in both classes because the constructor defined for the Student class is not inherited by these classes. Notice that we can create instances of these classes by

```
student1 = new UndergraduateStudent( );
student2 = new GraduateStudent( );
```

because the default constructor is added by the compiler, not because the one defined in the Student class is inherited by the subclasses. Remember that constructors of a superclass are not inherited by its subclasses.

Here are a rule and a guideline to remember for a subclass constructor:

If a class has a superclass that is not the Object *class, then a constructor of the class should make an explicit call to a constructor of the superclass.*

Always provide a constructor for every class you define. Don't rely on default constructors.

Quick Check

1. How do you call the superclass's constructor from its subclass?
2. What statement will be added to a constructor of a subclass if it is not included in the constructor explicitly by the programmer?
3. Modify the definition of GraduateStudent and UndergraduateStudent in Section 14.1 so we can create their instances in the following way:

```
student1 = new UndergraduateStudent();
student2 = new UndergraduateStudent("Mr. Espresso");
student3 = new GraduateStudent();
student4 = new GraduateStudent("Ms. Latte");
```

14.5 Abstract Superclasses and Abstract Methods

When we define a superclass, we often do not need to create any instances of the superclass. In the previous section, we defined the Student superclass and its two subclasses GraduateStudent and UndergraduateStudent. We gave examples of creating instances of GraduateStudent and UndergraduateStudent, but not of creating instances of Student. Does it make sense to create an instance of the Student class? Depending on whether or not we need to create instances of Student, we must define the class differently. We will describe different ways of defining a superclass in this section.

Even though we can create an instance of Student if we wanted to (because of the way the class is currently defined), is there a need to create an instance of Student? If a student can be only a graduate or an undergraduate student, then there is no need to create an instance of Student. In fact, because of the way the class is defined, had we created an instance of Student and stored it in the roster array, the program would crash. Why? Because the Student class does not have a computeCourseGrade method.

In the following discussion, we will consider two cases. In the first case, we assume that a student must be either a graduate or an undergraduate student. In the second case, we assume that a student does not have to be a graduate or an undergraduate student (e.g., he could be a nonmatriculated auditing student, etc.).

Case 1: Student Must Be Undergraduate or Graduate

abstract
class

For the case where a student must be a graduate or an undergraduate student, we only need instances of GraduateStudent and UndergraduateStudent. So we must define the Student class in such a way that no instances of it can be created. One way is to define Student as an abstract class. An *abstract class* is a class defined with the modifier abstract, and no instances can be created from an abstract class. Let's see how the abstract Student class is defined.

> The keyword **abstract** here denotes an abstract class.

> The keyword **abstract** here denotes an abstract method.

> Abstract method has no method body, just a semicolon.

```
abstract class Student
{
    protected final static int NUM_OF_TESTS = 3;

    protected String          name;
    protected int[]           test;
    protected String          courseGrade;

    public Student( )
    {
        this("No name");
    }

    public Student(String studentName)
    {
        name        = studentName;
        test        = new int[NUM_OF_TESTS];
        courseGrade = "****";
    }

    abstract public void computeCourseGrade();

    public String getCourseGrade( )
    {
        return courseGrade;
    }

    public String getName( )
    {
        return name;
    }

    public int getTestScore(int testNumber)
    {
        return test[testNumber-1];
    }
```

Chapter 14

```
          public void setName(String newName)
          {
              name = newName;
          }

          public void setTestScore(int testNumber, int testScore)
          {
              test[testNumber-1] = testScore;
          }
      }
```

abstract method

An *abstract method* is a method with the keyword abstract, and it ends with a semicolon instead of a method body. A class is *abstract* if the class contains an abstract method or does not provide an implementation of an inherited abstract method. We say a method is *implemented* if it has a method body. If a subclass has no abstract methods and no unimplemented inherited abstract methods, then the subclass is no longer abstract, and thus, its instances can be created.

implementing a method

An abstract class must include the keyword abstract in its definition. Notice that the abstract class Student has an incomplete definition because the class includes the abstract method computeCourseGrade that does not have a method body. The intent is to let its subclasses provide the implementation of the computeCourseGrade method. If a subclass does not provide an implementation of the inherited abstract method, the subclass is also an abstract class, and therefore, no instances of the subclass can be created. Since an abstract class can only make sense when it is a superclass, we frequently use the term *abstract superclass*.

abstract superclass

In an object diagram, we represent an abstract class using a parallelogram. The Student abstract superclass is drawn as

Student

Case 2: Student Does Not Have to Be Undergraduate or Graduate

For the second case, where a student does not have to be a graduate or an undergraduate student, we can design classes in two different ways. The first approach is to make the Student class instantiable. The second approach is to leave the Student class abstract and add a third subclass, say OtherStudent, to handle a student who is neither a graduate nor an undergraduate student. Let's call students who are neither graduate nor undergraduate students *nonregular students*. Let's assume further that the nonregular students will receive a pass

Ms. Latte: Is the Math *class an abstract class?*

Dr. Caffeine: *It is true that we cannot create an instance of the* Math *class, but it is not an abstract class. If a class is abstract, then you cannot create an instance of the class, but not being able to create an instance does not necessarily imply that the class is abstract.*

Ms. Latte: What do you mean?

Dr. Caffeine: *The intent of an abstract class is to define common aspects of all of its subclasses and leave some portions, that is, abstract methods, to be completed by the individual subclasses.*

Ms. Latte: Then how would you classify the Math *class?*

Dr. Caffeine: *It is a noninstantiable class, a class for which we cannot create an instance. Notice that an abstract class is a noninstantiable class by definition, but the reverse is not always true. There are noninstantiable classes, for example, the* Math *class, that are not abstract.*

Ms. Latte: How do I define a noninstantiable class?

Dr. Caffeine: *Very easy. Declare a private constructor with no arguments and declare no other constructors for the class.*

grade if their average test score is greater than or equal to 50. With the first approach, we define the Student class as

Not an abstract class anymore.

```
class Student
{
    protected final static int NUM_OF_TESTS = 3;
    protected String           name;
    protected int[]            test;
    protected String           courseGrade;

    public Student( )
    {
        this("No name");
    }

    public Student(String studentName)
    {
        name        = studentName;
        test        = new int[NUM_OF_TESTS];
        courseGrade = "****";
    }
```

Not an abstract method anymore.

```java
public void computeCourseGrade()
{
    int total = 0;
    for (int i = 0; i < NUM_OF_TESTS; i++) {
        total += test[i];
    }

    if (total/NUM_OF_TESTS >= 50) {
        courseGrade = "Pass";
    }
    else {
        courseGrade = "No Pass";
    }
}

public String getCourseGrade( )
{
    return courseGrade;
}

public String getName( )
{
    return name;
}

public int getTestScore(int testNumber)
{
    return test[testNumber-1];
}

public void setName(String newName)
{
    name = newName;
}

public void setTestScore(int testNumber, int testScore)
{
    test[testNumber-1] = testScore;
}
}
```

The class is no longer abstract, and we can create an instance of Student to represent a nonregular student.

With the second approach, we leave the Student class abstract. To represent nonregular students, we define a third subclass called OtherStudent as follows:

```java
class OtherStudent extends Student
{
```

```
public void computeCourseGrade()
{
    int total = 0;
    for (int i = 0; i < NUM_OF_TESTS; i++) {
        total += test[i];
    }

    if (total/NUM_OF_TESTS >= 50) {
        courseGrade = "Pass";
    }
    else {
        courseGrade = "No Pass";
    }
}
}
```

Figure 14.7 is an object diagram that includes the third subclass.

FIGURE 14.7   An object diagram of the abstract superclass **Student** and its three subclasses.

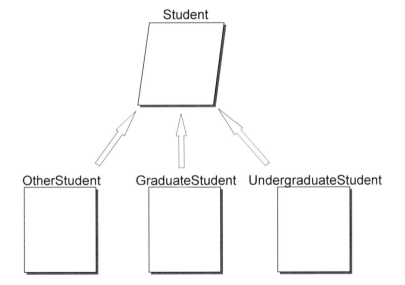

Which approach is better? There's no easy answer. It all depends on a given situation. To determine which approach is better for a given situation, we can ask ourselves which approach allows us easier modification and extension. Consider, for example, which approach will facilitate easier modification if we have to add a new type of student, say, scholarship students. Or consider the case where the rule for assigning a course grade for the undergraduate and graduate students is modified, say, they become the same.

Finally, not all methods can be declared abstract.

The following types of methods cannot be declared as abstract:

- *Private methods.*
- *Static methods.*

Quick Check

1. Can you create an instance of an abstract class?
2. Must an abstract class include an abstract method?
3. What is wrong with the following declaration?

```
class Vehicle
{
    abstract public getVIN();
    ...
}
```

14.6 When and When Not to Use Inheritance

The inheritance mechanism is a very powerful feature of object-oriented programming, and because of its power, it is open to misuse. You should keep in mind that inheritance is only one of the techniques available for code reuse. Inheritance is a technique we use if we want to design a more specialized class from an existing class. For example, suppose you want a dialog to display the text in different colors. The OutputBox class from the javabook package is capable of displaying the text in black only. So one way to create your desired object is by defining a subclass of OutputBox. Let's call this subclass ColorTextDisplay. The ColorTextDisplay will add public methods that will allow programmers to display the text in different colors. For example,

```
public void setTextColor( Color textColor )
```

Once the color is set, subsequent printing will be done in the set color. Because ColorTextDisplay is a subclass of OutputBox, the programmer can print out the text using the inherited method printLine or print.

We use inheritance also when we want to model the related entities we use in the program. This is what we did earlier in the chapter modeling different types of students. We designed the Student class and its two subclasses GraduateStudent and UndergraduateStudent. Here again, we are encapsulating a specialized functionality in the subclasses. We place common, generic information in the Student class and a specialized functionality in the GraduateStudent and

UndergraduateStudent classes. The example of Vehicle and Truck in Section 14.4 also shows this relationship.

IS-A
relationship

In all of these examples where we used inheritance, the classes are related in an *IS-A* relationship. We can characterize them as Truck IS-A Vehicle, ColorTextDisplay IS-A(n) OutputBox, and so forth. So when you declare a class A as a subclass of B, you should ask yourself, is A a B? This is not the only way to use inheritance, but for beginners, thinking in terms of an IS-A relationship is helpful.

> *If an entity A is a specialized form of another entity B, that is, A is a B, then model them by using inheritance. Declare A as a subclass of B.*

Now, let's consider another case of code reuse. This time you want to design a class for other programmers to use. You want to design an object that allows programmers to display the name of the students who either pass or do not pass the course. Let's call this class StudentList. The programmer will send the roster array to a StudentList object as

```
StudentList lister = new StudentList( );
lister.showPass( roster );
```

or

```
lister.showNoPass( roster );
```

How would you implement the StudentList class? One possibility is to use a ListBox object from the javabook package. We can make StudentList a subclass of ListBox and add needed methods to StudentList. However, this is a misuse of inheritance. Why? If we make StudentList a subclass of ListBox, then we cannot prohibit programmers from using the ListBox methods, which in this case does not make sense. We do not want the programmers to call the methods of ListBox in using an instance of StudentList. As a designer of StudentList, we want to reuse the ListBox class, but we do not want to relate them in an IS-A relationship.

code reuse
by composition

Instead of using inheritance, we design the StudentList class by including a ListBox object as its data member. We call this type of code reuse *code reuse by composition*. In other words, a StudentList object is composed of a ListBox object (and others). The relationship here is a *HAS-A* relationship; that is, StudentList HAS-A ListBox. We will give an example of code reuse by composition in the next chapter.

14.7   Sample Program: Computing Course Grades

Let's develop a program that illustrates the use of Student and its subclasses GraduateStudent and UndergraduateStudent. The program will input student data from a user-designated textfile, compute the course grades, and display the results. We assume the input textfile is created by using a text editor or another application. For example, a teacher may have kept his student grades in a notebook. Instead of manually computing the grades with a pencil and calculator, he enters data into a textfile and uses this program to compute the course grades. Another possible scenario is that the teacher uses some kind of application software that allows him to maintain student records. Suppose this application does not allow the teacher to use different formulas for computing the course grades of undergraduate and graduate students. In such case, the teacher can export data to a textfile and use our program to compute the course grades for undergraduate and graduate students using the different formulas. Using textfiles to transfer data from one application to another application is a very common technique used in software applications.

To focus on the data processing aspect of the program, we will keep its user interface very simple and leave it as an exercise to design a better user interface. We will also leave the task of saving the results back to a textfile in a different format (e.g., saving only the last name and the final course grade) or to an object-based file as an exercise.

Problem Statement

Write an application that reads in a textfile organized in the manner shown below and displays the final course grades. The course grades are computed differently for the undergraduate and graduate students based on the formulas listed on page 658. The input textfile format is as follows:

- *A single line is used for information on one student.*
- *Each line uses the format*

  <Type> <Name> <Test 1> <Test 2> <Test 3>

  where <Type> designates either a graduate or undergraduate student, <Name> designates the student's first and last name, and <Test i> designates the ith test score.
- *End of input is designated by the word* END. *The case of the letters is insignificant.*

Figure 14.8 shows a sample input textfile.

FIGURE 14.8   A sample textfile containing student names and test scores. **U** at the beginning of a line designates an undergraduate student and **G** designates a graduate student.

```
<Type>    <Name>        <Test 1> <Test 2> <Test 3>
U       John  Doe        87       78       90
G       Jill  Jones      90       95       87
G       Jack  Smith      67       77       68
U       Mary  Hines      80       85       80
U       Mick  Taylor     76       69       79
END
```

Overall Plan

We will implement a class that will

1. Read an input textfile.
2. Compute the course grades.
3. Print out the result.

To read a textfile, we will use the standard file I/O objects File, FileReader, and BufferedReader. To compute the course grades, we will use the Student, Undergraduate, and Graduate classes as defined earlier in the chapter. The formulas for calculating the course grades are defined in their respective compute-CourseGrades methods. Since the input file is a textfile, we must create either a Graduate or Undergraduate object for each line of input, so we will be able to call its computeCourseGrades method. To store the created student objects (instances of either Graduate or Undergraduate), we will use an array of Student.

To display the computed course grades, we will use an OutputBox from the javabook package. Since the OutputBox class supports the saveToFile method, it is an easy task to save the input data and the course grades back to a textfile. You just have to call the saveToFile method after all the results are displayed on an OutputBox. The task we leave as an exercise is a little more difficult than this. Often we need the capability to save the results in different format. For example, assuming the student information includes the student ID number, the teacher may want to save only the last four digits of the ID numbers and the final course grades so the results can be posted. Also, if the input data are sorted in alphabetical order by the students' last name, it would be better to save the results in a random order so the students cannot guess the other students' grades by their position in the posted listing.

Chapter 14

Let's name the class ComputeGrades and make it a subclass of the Main-Window class from the javabook package. By making ComputeGrades a subclass of MainWindow, we can add menus to it (adding menus will be left as an exercise) and let it be an owner frame of an OutputBox and possibly other dialogs. Also, MainWindow already includes the necessary code to terminate the program when the window is closed, so we don't have to worry about it. We will supply a minimal main class whose main method will create and start a ComputeGrades object.

Here's our working design document:

program
classes

Design Document:	ComputeGrades
Class	**Purpose**
ComputeGradesMain	The main class of the program.
ComputeGrades	The top-level control object that manages other objects in the program. The class is a subclass of MainWindow from javabook.
OutputBox	An OutputBox object is used to display the input data and computed course grades.
Student, Under-graduateStudent, GraduateStudent	Application logic objects for students. The Student class is an abstract superclass.
File, FileReader, BufferedReader	Objects necessary for reading data from a textfile.

Figure 14.9 is an object diagram of the program at this point.

Now let's think about the methods of ComputeGrades. What kinds of public methods should the class support? Since a ComputeGrades object is a top-level controller object, we need a single public method to initiate the operations. Let's define a method called processData that will carry out the three main tasks. The main method of ComputeGradesMain will call this method

```
ComputeGrades gradeComputer = new ComputeGrades();
gradeComputer.processData();
```

The processData method, expressed in pseudocode, will look something like this:

```
this.show();        //display itself, a main window
outputBox.show();   //and an outputBox

boolean success = readData();
```

```
if (success) {
    computeGrade();
    printResult();
}
else {
    print error message "File Input Error";
}
```

The readData method returns true if the input data are read in correctly from a textfile and the array of Student objects is properly created. The object diagram for the ComputeGrades class at this point is

FIGURE 14.9   An object diagram of the **ComputeGrades** program. **javabook** and **FileDialog** objects are not shown.

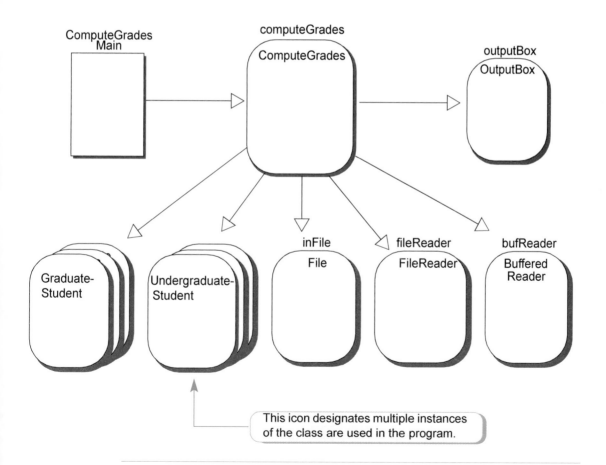

This icon designates multiple instances of the class are used in the program.

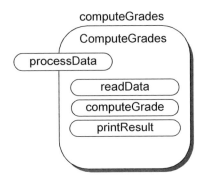

Our working design document for the ComputeGrades class is as follows:

Design Document:	The ComputeGrades Class	
Method	**Visibility**	**Purpose**
`<constructor>`	`public`	Creates and initializes the objects used by a ComputeGrades object.
`processData`	`public`	Displays itself and carries out three main tasks.
`readData`	`private`	Opens and reads data from a textfile and creates an array of Student objects from the input data. If the operation is successful, returns true.
`computeGrade`	`private`	Scans through the array of Student objects and computes the course grades.
`printResult`	`private`	Prints out the student information along with the computed grades to an OutputBox.

We will develop the program in five incremental steps:

1. Start with the program skeleton. Define the ComputeGradesMain and skeleton ComputeGrades classes.

2. Implement the printResult method. Define any other methods necessary to implement printResult.

3. Implement the computeGrade method. Define any other methods necessary to implement computeGrade.

4. Implement the readData method. Define any other methods necessary to implement readData.

5. Finalize and look for improvements.

We defer the implementation of the hardest method, readData, till the last. Some programmers prefer to deal with the hardest aspect of the program first, and there's no strict rule for ordering the implementation steps. You should order the steps in a way with which you are most comfortable. However, this does not mean you can implement the methods at random. You must always plan the implementation steps carefully so the steps follow a logical sequence. For this program, we start with the output routine so we can use the final output routine for testing other methods, instead of defining a temporary output routine for testing purposes.

Step 1 Development: Program Skeleton

Step 1 Design   Let's begin with the data members and the constructors for the ComputeGrades class. We will start with the following data members:

```
private    OutputBox         outputBox;    //for output

private    File              inFile;       //for input
private    FileReader        fileReader;
private    BufferedReader    bufReader;

private    Student[ ]        roster;       //for maintaining
                                           //student info
```

It is a straightforward operation to create the first four objects, but we need to think a little about the roster array. How big should the array be? There are several possibilities:

1. Create an array of an arbitrary size, say, 25.

2. Let the programmer pass the size in the constructor.

3. Do not create it in the constructor. Modify the input textfile to include the size of an array in the first line.

Option 3 is not attractive because it will require a change in the problem specification. Moreover, requiring the size information in the input file will put a lot of burden on the user because he must go over the textfile and count the number of lines the file contains. Such a burdensome task should be left to a computer. So we will implement Options 1 and 2. If the data cannot fit into an array of a predesignated size, then we will use the technique discussed in Chapter 9 to expand the array.

We declare a constant

```
private static final int   DEFAULT_SIZE = 25;
```

Chapter 14

and declare the two constructors as

```
public ComputeGrades( )
{
    this( DEFAULT_SIZE );
}

public ComputeGrades( int arraySize )
{
    super();   //an explicit call to the superclass constructor

    outputBox = new OutputBox( this );
    roster = new Student[arraySize];
}
```

Notice that we can't create inFile, fileReader, and bufReader until we know the actual file to open. We will create these objects in one of the methods we define later.

Step 1 Code   For the skeleton program, we include temporary output statements in the private methods to verify that they are called correctly in the right order. Here's the skeleton:

File: ComputeGradesMain.java

```
/**
 * A program that inputs a textfile containing student names and test scores,
 * computes the course grades, and displays the result.
 */

class ComputeGradesMain
{
    public static void main (String[] args)
    {
        ComputeGrades gradeComputer = new ComputeGrades();
        gradeComputer.processData();
    }
}
```

File: ComputeGrades.java

```
import javabook.*;
import java.io.*;

/**
 * This top-level object manages all other objects in the program.
 */
class ComputeGrades extends MainWindow
{

//--------------------------------
// Data Members
//--------------------------------
```

```
private static final int    DEFAULT_SIZE = 25;

private    OutputBox        outputBox;    //for output

private    File             inFile;       //for input
private    FileReader       fileReader;
private    BufferedReader   bufReader;

private    Student[ ]       roster;       //for maintaining student info

//-------------------------------
// Constructors
//-------------------------------

public ComputeGrades( )
{
    this( DEFAULT_SIZE );
}

public ComputeGrades( int arraySize )
{
    super();   //an explicit call to the superclass constructor

    outputBox = new OutputBox( this );
    roster    = new Student[arraySize];
}


//--------------------------------------------------
//     Public Methods:
//
//         void    processData       (       )
//
//--------------------------------------------------
    /**
     * Reads in data from a textfile, computes grades,
     * and displays the result in an outputBox.
     */
    public void processData ( )
    {
        setVisible( true ); //display the main window
        outputBox.setVisible( true );

        boolean success = readData();

        if (success) {
            computeGrade();
            printResult();
        }
        else {
            outputBox.printLine( "File Input Error") ;
        }
    }

//--------------------------------------------------
//     Private Methods:
//
//     void       computeGrade       (          )
//     void       printResult        (          )
//     boolean    readData           (          )
```

```
//
//-------------------------------------------------

    /**
     * Scans through the roster array and computes the course grades.
     */
    private void computeGrade( )
    {
        outputBox.printLine("Inside computeGrade");        //TEMP
    }


    /**
     * Displays the result in an outputBox.
     */
    private void printResult( )
    {
        outputBox.printLine("Inside printResult");        //TEMP
    }


    /**
     * Opens a textfile, reads in data, and constructs the roster array.
     *
     * @param return true if successful, otherwise false
     */
    private boolean readData( )
    {
        outputBox.printLine("Inside readData");        //TEMP
        return true;                                   //TEMP
    }

}
```

Step 1 Test   We execute the main class and the skeleton ComputeGrades class to verify that the classes are coded correctly. When executed, we will see the main window (ComputeGrades) and an OutputBox appearing on the screen and the following messages in the OutputBox:

```
Inside readData
Inside computeGrade
Inside printResult
```

Step 2 Development: Implement the printResult **Method**

Step 2 Design   In the second development step, we add a routine that places the result in an outputBox. To implement and test this method, we need to create the roster array. We will include temporary code inside the readData method to build a test roster array. We can use for loops such as

```
                    for (int i = 0; i < 15; i++) {
                        roster[i] = new UndergraduateStudent( );
The first half of the      roster[i].setName( "Undergrad # " + i );
array is undergrad-
uate students.             roster[i].setTestScore(1, 70 + i);
                           roster[i].setTestScore(2, 75 + i);
                           roster[i].setTestScore(3, 80 + i);
                    }


                    for (int i = 15; i < DEFAULT_SIZE; i++) {
                        roster[i] = new GraduateStudent( );
The second half of         roster[i].setName( "Grad # " + i );
the array is gradu-
ate students.              roster[i].setTestScore(1, 80 + i);
                           roster[i].setTestScore(2, 85 + i);
                           roster[i].setTestScore(3, 90 + i);
                    }
```

to create a temporary roster for testing purposes.

Now, let's design the printResult method. When this method is called, we have the roster array built. The method scans through the array and retrieves the student data using the getName, getCourseGrade, and getTestScore methods. Expressed in pseudocode, we have the following:

```
        for each element i in the roster array {

            output the name of roster[i];

            output the test scores of roster[i];

            output the course grade of roster[i];

            skip to the next line;
        }
```

How should we terminate the loop? We should realize first that the roster array may or may not be full. For example, its default size is 25, but the actual number of elements may be less than 25, so using the value of roster.length will not work. Since roster is an array of objects, one possible way to express the loop is as follows:

```
        while ( roster[i] != null ) {

            //output roster[i] information
        }
```

One problem with this while loop is that we must have at least one empty slot in the array for the loop to terminate correctly. We can improve it by using the length value as

```
while ( i < roster.length && roster[i] != null ) {
    ...
}
```

Another possibility is to keep the count, which we set in the readData method. This count will be a data member of type int. Let's call this count variable studentCount. Then the processing loop becomes

```
for (int i = 0; i < studentCount; i++) {

    //output roster[i] information
}
```

We will adopt this approach because having this count information is useful for other purposes. For example, if we want to compute the percentage of the students passing the course, we can use studentCount to compute it. If we don't have this variable, then every time we need to compute the percentage, we have to find out the number of students in the roster array.

Finally, to print out student information so the data will align properly, we will use the Format class from javabook.

Step 2 Code   We first add the declaration for a new data member studentCount:

```
//---------------------------
// Data Members
//---------------------------
private int       studentCount;
```

This data member is initialized to 0 in the constructor as

```
public ComputeGrades( int arraySize )
{
    ...
    studentCount = 0;
}
```

and incremented by one every time new student information is read inside the readData method. In this step, the readData method is temporary, so student-Count is set to the number of student objects created, which is DEFAULT_SIZE.

The printResult method is defined as follows:

```
private void printResult()
{
    for (int i = 0; i < studentCount; i++)    {

        //print one student
        outputBox.print( Format.leftAlign ( 15,
                                roster[i].getName() ));

        for (int testNum = 1;
                testNum <= Student.NUM_OF_TESTS;
                testNum++   ) {
            outputBox.print( Format.centerAlign ( 8,
                                roster[i].getTestScore(testNum) ));
        }
        outputBox.printLine( Format.rightAlign   ( 8,
                                roster[i].getCourseGrade() ));
    }
}
```

Name ──────▶

Test scores ──────▶

Course grade ──────▶

Step 2 Test   We verify two items in this step. First, the temporary readData method includes creating student objects and calling their methods. Correct execution will verify that we are including the correct student classes and using their methods properly. Second, the printResult method should display the output as intended. Since we have not implemented the computeGrade method, we will see four asterisks for the course grades. We have to run the program several times and adjust the values for the alignment methods of Format before deciding on the final values. Also, it is important to try different values for names and test scores before moving to the next step.

Step 3 Development: Implement the computeGrade Method

Step 3 Design   The functionality of computing the course grades is embedded inside the student classes, specifically, inside the respective computeCourseGrade methods of the GraduateStudent and UndergraduateStudent classes. Therefore, all we need to do in the computeGrade method is to scan through the roster array and call the element's computeCourseGrade method. This simplicity is a direct result of polymorphism.

Step 3 Code   The computeGrade method is defined as

```
private void computeGrade( )
{
    for (int i = 0; i < studentCount; i++ ) {
        roster[i].computeCourseGrade();
    }
}
```

Step 3 Test   We repeat the same testing routines of Step 2. Instead of seeing four asterisks for the course grades, we should be seeing correct values. To make the verification easy, we can set the fixed test scores for all students. Make sure you
assign test scores that will result in students both passing and not passing. Don't
forget to try out end cases such as zero for all three test scores. What about negative test scores? Will the student classes handle them correctly? If we identify
serious problems with the Student classes at this point, we may have to suspend
our development until we correct the Student class.

Step 4 Development: Implement the readData Method

Step 4 Design   We will now design the core function of the class, the readData method. We can
express the overall logic of the method in pseudocode as

```
get the filename from the user;

if (the filename is provided)
    read in data and build the roster array;
else
    output an error message;
```

We will use a FileDialog object from the standard java.awt package to let the
user specify the file. If the user cancels this dialog, then null is returned. In this
case, we print out an error message and stop. If the user specifies a file, then we
pass this information to a private method buildRoster, which will read data from
the designated file and build the roster array.

The buildRoster method will read one line of data from the designated file
at a time, and for each line of data, it creates an appropriate student object (an
instance of GraduateStudent if the type is G and an instance of Undergraduate-
Student if the type is U). The counter studentCount is incremented by one after
each line is processed. When the line contains the terminator END, the method
completes its execution. If the data in a line do not conform to the designated
format, then the line is ignored. The method, expressed in pseudocode, is as follows:

```
try {
    set bufReader for input;

    while ( !done ) {
        line = get next line;

        if (line is END) {
            done = true;
        }
```

```
                        else {
                            student = createStudent( line );

                            if (student != null) {
                                roster[studentCount] = student; //add to roster
                                studentCount++;
                            }
                        }
                    }
                }
                catch (IOException e) {
                    output an error message;
                }
```

> **createStudent** will return **null** if the **line** does not conform to the designated format.

We use the try–catch block because the creation of the BufferedReader object bufReader from a given filename could result in an exception. The createStudent method accepts a String argument, which is one line of the input file, and returns an instance of either GraduateStudent or UndergraduateStudent depending on the type specified in the line. If there's an error in the input line, then createStudent returns null. Instead of terminating the whole program, we will simply ignore the lines that do not conform to the specified format.

In a very simplied form, the createStudent method looks like this:

```
        type    = first element of inputLine;

        if (type.equals("U") || type.equals("G")) {
            student = newStudentWithData( inputLine );
        }
        else { //invalid type is encountered
            student = null;
        }

        return student;
```

> **newStudentWithData** will return **null** if the **inputLine** contains invalid data

The top statement requires us to extract the first item in the input line (String). How should we do it? The newStudentWithData method, which creates an instance of GraduateStudent or UndergraduateStudent and assigns data to it, also requires an operation to extract individual elements of data from a single line. We can write our own string processing routine to parse a given line and extract data on type, name, and test scores, but there's a better solution. We can use a standard class called StringTokenizer from the java.util package. We will take a quick detour to explain this class.

StringTokenizer   A StringTokenizer object is used to extract tokens from a given string. A *token* is a string of characters separated by *delimiter characters*, or simply *delimiters*. Any character can be designated as a delimiter, but space is the most commonly used delimiter. By default, a StringTokenizer object uses a white space (blank, tab, newline, or return) as its delimiter. Here's an example. The following code

```
String inputString
         = "I drink   100 cups of coffee every morning.";

StringTokenizer parser = new StringTokenizer(inputString);

while ( parser.hasMoreTokens() )  {
   System.out.println( parser.nextToken() );
}
```

will print out

```
I
drink
100
cups
of
coffee
every
morning.
```

The hasMoreTokens method returns true if there are more tokens remaining in parser, and the nextToken method returns the next token in parser. The nextToken method throws a NoSuchElementException if there is no token to return. Please refer to a java.util reference manual for more information on StringTokenizer.

Now let's get back to the design. Using a SringTokenizer object, we can express the createStudent method as

```
StringTokenizer  parser = new StringTokenizer( line );
String           type

try {
   type   = parser.nextToken();

   if (type.equals("U") || type.equals("G")) {
      student = newStudentWithData(type, parser);
   }
   else  { //invalid type is encountered
      student = null;
   }
}
```

Dr. & Ms.

> **Ms. Latte:** It's great if you already know about StringTokenizer, but if you don't, you're out of luck. You would end up programming the functionality of StringTokenizer yourself, redoing something that has been done already.
>
> **Dr. Caffeine:** That's a challenge for all programmers, not just for beginners. My suggestion is that whenever you encounter a situtation that seems to call for a common programming task, first look up the Java API reference manuals. You also can ask your fellow classmates, T.A., or instructor for guidance. They may know something. You should also make a habit of browsing the Java API reference manuals so you will have general knowledge about the standard classes. The key is always to look for the existing classes to reuse.
>
> **Ms. Latte:** In other words, you should avoid reinventing the wheel.
>
> **Dr. Caffeine:** Precisely.

```
catch (NoSuchElementException e) { //no token
    student = null;
}

return student;
```

A private newStudentWithData method accepts a String that specifies the type of student and a StringTokenizer object. The method creates an instance of UndergraduateStudent or GraduateStudent and assigns data to the object by calling the StringTokenizer object's nextToken method repeatedly:

```
//type and parser are the parameter
try {
    if ( type.equals("U") ) {
        student = new UndergraduateStudent();
    }
    else {
        student = new GraduateStudent();
    }

    set the student name //use parser.nextToken() to
                         //extract data from a line

    set the student test scores//use Convert.toInt()
                               //for conversion

}
```

```
catch (Exception e) { //thrown by parser.nextToken() or
    student = null;  //Convert.toInt(...)
}

return student;
```

Our design document for the ComputeGrades class now includes three more private methods:

Design Document:	The ComputeGrades Class	
Method	**Visibility**	**Purpose**
. . .	. . .	. . .
buildRoster	private	Reads one line of data from the designated file at a time, and for each line of data, it creates an appropriate student object. If the data in a line do not conform to the designated format, then the line is ignored.
createStudent	private	Creates a student object by calling **newStudentWithData** if the type in the input line is U or G. If successful, returns the created student. Otherwise returns **null**.
newStudentWithData	private	Creates an instance of **UndergraduateStudent** or **GraduateStudent** and assigns data to the object by calling the **StringTokenizer** object's **nextToken** method repeatedly.

Step 4 Code   Let's implement the methods. First, we add new import statements

```
import java.util.*;  //for StringTokenizer
import java.awt.*;   //for FileDialog
```

to the ComputeGrades class.
The readData method is defined as

```
private boolean readData()
{
    //get the file to open
    FileDialog fileBox = new FileDialog(this, "Open file",
                                          FileDialog.LOAD);

    fileBox.setVisible( true );
    String filename = fileBox.getDirectory()
                             + fileBox.getFile();
```

You need to get the full pathname.

```
            if (filename != null) {
                return buildRoster(filename);
            }
            else {
                return false;
            }
        }
```

The buildRoster method, the workhorse method of the class, is defined as

```
        private boolean buildRoster(String filename)
        {
            String   inputLine;
            Student  student;

            boolean status   = true;
            boolean done      = false;

            try {
                inFile     = new File(filename);
                fileReader = new FileReader(inFile);
                bufReader  = new BufferedReader(fileReader);

                while ( !done ) {

                    inputLine = bufReader.readLine();//read one line

                    if (inputLine.equalsIgnoreCase ("END")) {
                        done = true;                //end of file, so stop
                    }
                    else {
                        student = createStudent(inputLine);

                        if (student != null) { //ok, add it to roster
                            roster[studentCount] = student;
                            studentCount++;
                        }
                    }
                }

                bufReader.close();
            }
            catch (IOException e) {
                status = false;
            }

            return status;
        }
```

Set up the file for input.

Create a new student and add it to **roster**.

The createStudent method is defined as

```
private Student createStudent(String line )
{
    Student          student;
    StringTokenizer  parser = new StringTokenizer( line );
    String           type

    try {
        type    = parser.nextToken();

        if (type.equals("U") || type.equals("G")) {
            student = newStudentWithData(type, parser);
        }
        else { //invalid type is encountered
            student = null;
        }
    }
    catch (NoSuchElementException e) { //no token
        student = null;
    }

    return student;
}
```

And, finally, the newStudentWithData method is defined as

```
private Student newStudentWithData(String        type,
                                   StringTokenizer parser)
{
    Student student;

    try {
        if ( type.equals("U") ) {
            student = new UndergraduateStudent();
        }
        else {
            student = new GraduateStudent();
        }

        //set the student name
        String  firstName  = parser.nextToken();
        String  lastName   = parser.nextToken();

        student.setName(firstName + " " + lastName);
```

Create a graduate or undergraduate student. →

Assign the name to **student**. →

```
                                      //set the student test scores
                                      for (int testNum = 1;
```

Assign the test scores to **student**.

```
                                               testNum <= Student.NUM_OF_TESTS;
                                               testNum++) {
                                          student.setTestScore( testNum,
                                                  Convert.toInt(parser.nextToken() ));
                                      }
                                  }
                                  catch (Exception e) { //thrown by parser.nextToken() or
                                      student = null;  //Convert.toInt(...)
                                  }

                                  return student;
                              }
```

Step 4 Test

We run through a more complete testing routine in this step. We need to run the program for various types of input files. Some of the possible file contents are as follows:

Step 4 Test Data	
Test File	**Purpose**
File with 5 to 20 entries of student information with all lines in correct format.	Test the normal case.
File with 5 to 20 entries of student information with some lines in incorrect format.	Test that readData and supporting methods handle the error case properly.
File with no entries.	Test that buildRoster method handles the error case properly.
File with more than 25 entries.	Test that readData and supporting methods handle the case where the number of entries is larger than the default size for the roster array.

Step 5 Development: Finalize and Improve

program review

As always, we will finalize the program by correcting any remaining errors, inconsistency, or unfinished methods. We also look for improvement in the last step. One improvement we can always look for is the length of the methods. Although there are no hard rules for the length, a method should not be any longer than a single page. The buildRoster and newStudentWithData methods are close to the maximum. If we notice the method is getting longer in the coding stage, we may want to rethink our design. For example, if the buildRoster method becomes too big, then we can define a new method that takes care of a portion of

Chapter 14

the method, such as moving the if–then–else statement in the method to a new method.

One problem that remains (which would have been identified in Step 4 testing) is the missing method for expanding the roster array when the input file includes more student entries than the set default size of 25. We leave this method as an exercise. We also leave some of the possible improvements as exercises.

14.8 Exercises

1.   Consider the following class definitions. Identify invalid statements.

```
class Car
{
    public     String     make;
    protected  int        weight;
    private    String     color;

    ...
}

class ElectricCar extends Car
{
    private    int     rechargeHour;

    public ElectricCar( )
    {
        ...
    }

    //copy constructor
    public ElectricCar ( ElectricCar car )
    {
        this.make         = car.make;
        this.weight       = car.weight;
        this.color        = new String( car.color );
        this.rechargeHour= car.rechargeHour;
    }

    ...
}

class TestMain
{
    public static void main ( String args[] )
    {
        Car            myCar;
        ElectricCar    myElecCar;
```

```
        myCar = new Car();
        myCar.make = "Chevy";
        myCar.weight = 1000;
        myCar.color = "Red";

        myElecCar = new ElectricCar();
        myCar.make = "Chevy";
        myCar.weight = 500;
        myCar.color = "Silver";
    }
}
```

2. Consider the following class definitions. Identify which calls to the constructor are invalid.

```
class Car
{
    public    String    make;
    protected int       weight;
    private   String    color;

    private Car ( String make, int weight, String color )
    {
        this.make   = make;
        this.weight = weight;
        this.color  = color;
    }

    public Car ( )
    {
        this( "unknown", -1, "white" );
    }
}

class ElectricCar extends Car
{
    private   int    rechargeHour;

    public ElectricCar( )
    {
        this( 10 );
    }

    private ElectricCar(int charge )
    {
        super( );
        rechargeHour = charge;
    }
}
```

```
class TestMain
{
    public static void main ( String args[] )
    {
        Car         myCar1, myCar2;
        ElectricCar myElec1, myElec2;

        myCar1 = new Car();
        myCar2 = new Car("Ford", 1200, "Green");

        myElec1 = new ElectricCar( );
        myElec2 = new ElectricCar( 15 );
    }
}
```

3. In the ComputeGrades sample program, we set the default size of the roster array to 25. Modify the program so the size of the array will be increased if the input file contains more than 25 students. You need to add a method that expands the array, say, by 50 percent.

4. Extend the ComputeGrades sample program by storing the roster array using ObjectOutputStream. To allow the user to create and read the data using any text editor, add the menu choices Import and Export, which will read in a textfile (this is how the original ComputeGrades works) and write out data in ASCII format to a textfile.

5. Extend the ComputeGrades sample program to include menu choices Save, Open, and Quit. With the current program, you can open one file for each execution of the program. Extend the program so the user can open more than one file by selecting the menu choice Open repeatedly. Selecting the menu choice Save will allow the user to save the computed results to a file he or she specifies.

6. How would you modify the ComputeGrades sample program if the formula for computing the course grade is different for freshmen, sophomore, junior, and senior undergraduate students? Would you design four subclasses of UndergraduateStudent? Or would you modify the body of the compute-CourseGrade method of UndergraduateStudent? Discuss the pros and cons of each approach.

7. Write a personal finance manager program that maintains information on your bank accounts. Incorporate the following rules:

   - For the savings accounts, you can make a maximum of three withdrawals in a month without incurring a fee. The bank charges $1.00 for every withdrawal after the third.

- For the checking accounts, the bank charges $0.50 for every check you write for the first 20 checks (i.e., withdrawals) in a month. After that, there will be no charge.

You should be able to open and save account information to a file. You should be able to list all transactions of a given account or of all accounts. Include appropriate menus to select the options supported by the program. Consider using the Date class to record the date of transactions. The Date class is from the java.util package. Please refer to a java.util reference manual for information on this class.

8. Extend the address book sample program from Chapter 9. Instead of managing a single type of Person, incorporate additional types of persons such as PersonalFriend, BusinessAssociate, etc. Define these classes as a subclass of Person. Design carefully to decide whether the Person class will be an abstract class or not.

9. Consider an asset tracking program that will track four types of assets: electronic appliances, automobiles, furniture, and compact discs. What classes would you design for the program? Would you define four unrelated classes or one superclass and four subclasses? If you design a superclass, will it be an abstract superclass?

10. Implement the asset tracking program of exercise 9. Allow the user to add, modify, and delete electronic appliances, automobiles, furniture, and compact discs. Allow the user to list the assets by category and search for an asset by its serial number.

11. Extend the asset tracking program of exercise 10 by adding an object I/O capability.

12. Write an application that reads daily temperatures for 12 months and allows the user to get statistics. Support at least three options: monthly average of a given month, yearly average, and lowest and highest temperatures of a given month. Use a textfile to store temperatures. A line in the textfile contains daily temperatures for one month. The first line in the textfile contains temperatures for January, the second line for February, and so forth. Use StringTokenizer to parse a line into temperatures of type float. For a data structure, consider using either an array of Month or a 2-D array of float. Month is a class you define yourself.

15

Class Roster Maintenance Program

OBJECTIVES

After you have read and studied this chapter, you should be able to

- Develop large programs incrementally using multiple objects from object categories controller, storage, application logic, and user interface.

- Develop large programs that are extensible and modifiable by applying polymorphism and inheritance effectively in program design.

- Document how the methods in the classes are related by using method call sequence diagrams.

Introduction

In this chapter, as a culmination of what we have studied in this book, we will develop a program that is substantially larger than any of the previous sample programs. Traditionally, this program would be considered quite large and complex for an introductory programming book. We believe, however, that after studying this book, you are now conversant with object-oriented thinking and would not find this program too difficult to understand or beyond your reach. We are confident that you will be able to develop equally large programs on your own, too.

We will develop a class roster maintenance program, which requires a careful design and development plan because of its complexity. We will present the design and discuss design alternatives wherever appropriate and walk through the carefully planned incremental development steps.

15.1 Method Call Sequence Diagram

Before we start our development, we will introduce another diagramming technique called a method call sequence diagram. A *method call sequence diagram* shows the sequence of method calls starting from a given method. The object diagram is useful in showing the overall structure of a program, but it does not provide a detailed picture of how the methods are interrelated. In describing complex programs, method call sequence diagrams are very useful. We will use them extensively in this chapter.

method call sequence diagram

As an example, let's draw a method call sequence diagram for the process-Data method of the ComputeGradesMainWindow class from Chapter 14. This method reads student information from a user-designated textfile, computes the course grades, and prints out the results. The method is defined as

```
public void processData ( )
{
    this.show();       //display the main window
    outputBox.show();

    boolean success = readData();

    if (success) {
        computeGrade();
        printResult();
    }
    else
        outputBox.printLine( "File Input Error") ;
}
```

The readData method calls the buildRoster method, which in turn calls the createStudent and addStudentWithData methods repeatedly. Figure 15.1 is the method call sequence diagram of the processData method.

FIGURE 15.1   Method call sequence diagram of the **processData** method. Only the methods of **ComputeGradesMainWindow** are shown in the diagram.

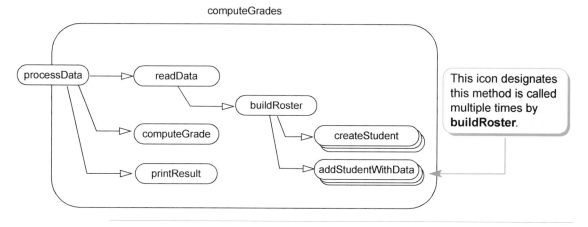

15.2 Problem Statement

Now let's start the development of the class roster maintenance program. We begin with its problem statement.

Write a class roster maintenance program that will allow the user to

- *Create a new roster.*
- *Open an existing roster (can open one roster at a time).*
- *Save the current roster to a file.*
- *Add and delete students from a roster.*
- *Change the name of students.*
- *Edit the test scores of students.*
- *Display the name, test scores, and course grade of a single student or all students in the roster.*

The program maintains both graduate and undergraduate students. For each student, we maintain his or her name, test scores, and final course grade. The final course grade is computed by using the following formula (from Chapter 14):

Type of Student	Grading Scheme
Undergraduate	Pass if (test1+test2+test3)/3 >= 70
Graduate	Pass if (test1+test2+test3)/3 >= 80

15.3 Overall Planning

What kinds of objects do we need for this program? Summarizing the tasks listed in the problem statement, we see that the program is capable of

1. Maintaining (i.e., adding, deleting, and modifying) student information.

2. Reading and writing student information to a file.

3. Displaying student information individually or as a group.

We mentioned the usefulness of classifying objects into the categories of controller, user interface, storage, and application logic. Thinking in terms of object categories, we notice that the first task calls for a storage object, the second task calls for a user interface object, and the third task calls for an application logic object. Beyond these objects, we need some kind of user interface object to accept student information from the user. We also need one or more controller objects to control these objects.

In earlier sample programs, we managed to identify almost all objects used in the programs in the overall planning stage. As this program is more complex, we will start our development by identifying only key classes and define additional classes as we progress through the development steps. Let's start thinking from the top-level controller object.

GradeRoster-
MainWindow
We will need a top-level window for this program. Instead of defining a subclass of Frame, we will make this class a subclass of MainWindow from javabook so we can reuse the functionality of MainWindow. We will call the class GradeRosterMainWindow. We use the prefix GradeRoster for naming classes instead of ClassRoster or Roster because the main purpose of this program is to maintain student grades, and it is kind of awkward to repeat the same word in a declaration, like class ClassRoster.

The role of GradeRosterMainWindow, as the top-level controller object of the program, is to display and process menu choices. For each menu selection, the actual processing is done by other objects. The task of the GradeRoster-MainWindow object is to delegate the work to subordinate objects instead of doing the work itself.

What will be the menu choices supported by the program? We want to organize the capabilities of the program into logically grouped menu choices. One possible grouping is as follows:

File	Edit	Show
New	Test Scores...	All Students
Open...	Compute Grades	One Student...
Save	Student Name...	
Save As...	Add New Student...	
Quit	Delete Student...	

The first menu is named File, and it includes operations related to opening and saving data files. It also includes the menu choice Quit. The second menu is named Edit, and it includes operations related to maintaining the student information. The third menu is named Show, and it includes operations related to displaying student information.

There are many other ways to organize menu choices, but we should try to adhere to the standard as closely as possible so the user will not get confused with an idiosyncratic menu structure. The structure of File, for example, follows the standard way of organizing the file operations.

To maintain student information, we need an application logic object. We will call the class GradeRoster. An instance of the GradeRoster class will maintain information on students in one course. The role of GradeRoster is to add, delete, and modify student information. Individual student information is kept in an instance of GraduateStudent or UndergraduateStudent. These two classes are subclasses of the abstract superclass Student. These three classes were discussed in the previous chapter.

A GradeRoster object is an application logic object for maintaining a grade roster. In the program, we need some object to control it, for example, to create a new GradeRoster object when the New menu choice is selected. Should the responsibility of controlling a GradeRoster object be given to GradeRoster-MainWindow? That is one possibility, but to do so, we will have to overload the GradeRosterMainWindow class. It is a much cleaner design to let GradeRoster-MainWindow manage the menu handling only. In other words, when a menu choice is selected, it will let other objects carry out the selected operation. We will define a class called GradeRosterControl that will manage GradeRoster objects. A GradeRosterControl object works under the control of GradeRoster-MainWindow.

Next, we need a storage object that is capable of saving GradeRoster to a file and reading it back from a file. We will call this class GradeRosterStorage.

A GradeRosterStorage object works under the control of GradeRosterMain-Window.

For the display of student information, we will define a class GradeRoster-Display. This object will be capable of displaying information of a single student or of all the students. A GradeRosterDisplay object also works under the control of GradeRosterMainWindow.

Finally, we will use various javabook objects as needed in the program. For example, we will use MessageBox to output error messages and messages from temporary output statements.

Here's our working design document:

Design Document: GradeRoster Program	
Class	**Purpose**
GradeRosterMain	The main class of the program.
GradeRosterMainWindow	The top-level control object that manages other objects in the program. The class is a subclass of MainWindow from javabook.
GradeRosterControl	An object that controls a GradeRoster object. The object works under the control of Grade-RosterMainWindow. The object manages StudentNameDialog and TestScoreDialog objects.
GradeRosterDisplay	An object responsible for displaying class rosters. The object works under the control of Grade-RosterMainWindow.
GradeRosterStorage	An object for handling the file input and output operations. The object works under the control of GradeRosterMainWindow.
GradeRoster	An object that actually maintains the roster. The object works under the control of GradeRoster-Control.
Student	An abstract class that captures common behavior and data of both undergraduate and graduate students.
GraduateStudent	An object to model a graduate student.
UndergraduateStudent	An object to model an undergraduate student.
MessageBox	A javabook object to print out error messages and messages from temporary output statements.

Figure 15.2 is the object diagram of the program at this point.

FIGURE 15.2   A simplified object diagram for the grade roster program. Primary objects are shown here. Secondary objects such as MessageBox, InputBox, and others are not shown.

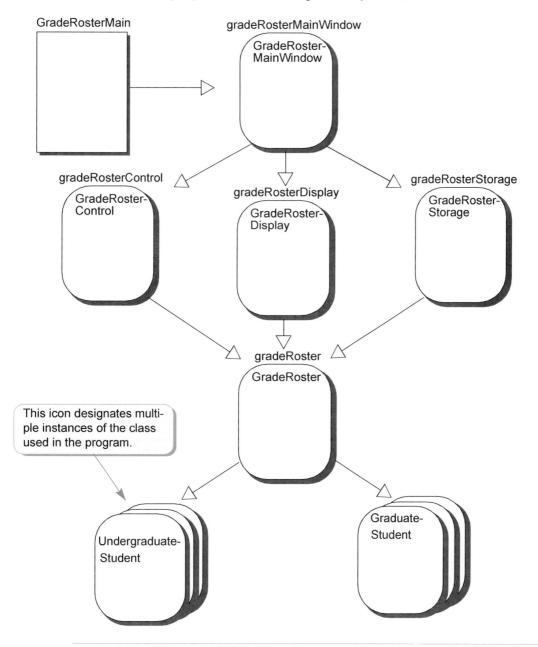

We will develop the program in nine incremental steps:

1. Start with the program skeleton. Define the GradeRosterMain and skeleton GradeRosterMainWindow classes.

2. Implement the methods to create a new roster.

3. Implement the methods to add students to a roster.

4. Implement the methods to delete students from a roster.

5. Implement the methods to edit student information.

6. Implement the methods to edit test scores and compute the final course grades.

7. Implement the methods to display the student information of a single student or all students.

8. Implement the methods to save a roster to a file and read a roster from a file.

9. Finalize and look for improvements.

There are other possible sequences of steps. For example, we could implement Step 7 or 8 after Step 3. We will develop the program in the order as presented to work on more difficult tasks early in the development. Steps 7 and 8 are pretty straightforward operations compared to others, so we will work on them at the end.

15.4 Step 1 Development: Program Shell with Menus

Step 1 Design

We start with GradeRosterMain and the shell GradeRosterMainWindow. The shell class contains all menu choices. We will include a complete actionPerformed method in the class to filter the menu choice selection. For each menu choice, we will define a corresponding method that will include the code to process the selected menu choice. The task of actionPerformed is to call a method that corresponds to the selected menu choice. The flow of the method looks like this:

```
if (menu selected is "New") {
   newRoster();
}
else if (menu selected is "Open...") {
   openRoster();
}
else if (menu selected is "Save") {
   saveRoster();

}//and so forth
```

Our working design document for the GradeRosterMainWindow class is as follows:

Design Document: The GradeRosterMainWindow Class		
Method	**Visibility**	**Purpose**
`<constructor>`	`public`	Creates and initializes the objects used by a GradeRosterMainWindow object.
`setVisible`	`public`	Displays itself. The GradeRosterMain class main method calls this method.
`actionPerformed`	`public`	Calls a method corresponding to the selected menu choice.
`createMenu`	`private`	Creates necessary objects for attaching the menu choices. This method is called from the constructor.
`newRoster`	`private`	Creates a new GradeRoster object. This method corresponds to menu choice File/New.
`openRoster`	`private`	Opens a GradeRoster object (i.e., reads the data in from a user-specified file). This method corresponds to menu choice File/Open.
`saveRoster`	`private`	Saves the currently opened GradeRoster object to the file from which it is read. This method corresponds to menu choice File/Save.
`saveAsRoster`	`private`	Saves the currently opened GradeRoster object to a file designated by the user. This method corresponds to menu choice File/Save As.
`quitProgram`	`private`	Quits the program. This method corresponds to menu choice File/Quit.
`editTestScores`	`private`	Edits the test scores of a designated student. This method corresponds to menu choice Edit/Test Scores.
`computeGrades`	`private`	Computes the course grades of all students in the grade roster. This method corresponds to menu choice Edit/Compute Grades.
`editStudentName`	`private`	Edits the name of a designated student. This method corresponds to menu choice Edit/Student Name.
`addNewStudent`	`private`	Adds a new student to the grade roster. This method corresponds to menu choice Edit/Add New Student.

Chapter 15

Design Document: The GradeRosterMainWindow Class		
Method	**Visibility**	**Purpose**
deleteStudent	private	Deletes a student from the grade roster. This method corresponds to menu choice Edit/Delete Student.
showAllStudents	private	Displays information of all students in the grade roster. This method corresponds to menu choice Show/All Students.
showOneStudent	private	Displays information of a designated student in the grade roster. This method corresponds to menu choice Show/One Student.

For each step, we will summarize the work to be done in the following format:

	Objects	To Do
Step 1	GradeRoster-Main	Implement the full class. The **main** method creates an instance of GradeRosterMain-Window and calls its **setVisible** method.
	GradeRoster-MainWindow	Implement the shell of the main class that includes menu choices and corresponding methods for processing menu choices.

Step 1 Code

The GradeRosterMain class includes the main method only. The method opens an instance of GradeRosterMainWindow:

```
class GradeRosterMain
{
    public static void main (String args[])
    {
        GradeRosterMainWindow mainWindow
                = new GradeRosterMainWindow();
        mainWindow.setVisible( true );
    }
}
```

The constructor for GradeRosterMainWindow creates and initializes the objects used in this step:

```
public GradeRosterMainWindow()
{
    createMenu( );
    messageBox  = new MessageBox(this);
}
```

The private method createMenu constructs the menu choices and attaches the GradeRosterMainWindow object as their action event listener:

```
private void createMenu()
{
    MenuItem  item;
    Menu      menu;
    MenuBar   menuBar;

    menuBar = new MenuBar();

    menu    = new Menu("File");    //File Menu
    menuBar.add(menu);

    item = new MenuItem("New");         //New
    item.addActionListener( this );
    menu.add(item);

    item = new MenuItem("Open...");     //Open...
    item.addActionListener( this );
    menu.add(item);

    item = new MenuItem("Save");        //Save
    item.addActionListener( this );
    menu.add(item);

    item = new MenuItem("Save As...");  //Save As...
    item.addActionListener( this );
    menu.add(item);

    item = new MenuItem("Quit");        //Quit
    item.addActionListener( this );
    menu.add(item);

    menu    = new Menu("Edit");    //Edit Menu
    menuBar.add(menu);

    item = new MenuItem("Test Scores...");//Test Scores...
    item.addActionListener( this );
    menu.add(item);

    item = new MenuItem("Compute Grades");//Compute Grades
    item.addActionListener( this );
    menu.add(item);

    item = new MenuItem("Student Name...");//Student
    item.addActionListener( this );         //Name...
    menu.add(item);
```

File menu

Edit menu

```
                        item = new MenuItem("Add New Student...");//Add New
                        item.addActionListener( this );          //Student...
                        menu.add(item);

                        item = new MenuItem("Delete Student...");//Delete
                        item.addActionListener( this );          //Student...
                        menu.add(item);
```

Show menu

```
                        menu    = new Menu("Show");    //Show Menu
                        menuBar.add(menu);

                        item = new MenuItem("All Students"); //All Students
                        item.addActionListener( this );
                        menu.add(item);

                        item = new MenuItem("One Student...");//One Student...
                        item.addActionListener( this );
                        menu.add(item);

                        setMenuBar(menuBar); //attach the menubar to the window
                    }
```

The actionPerformed method of GradeRosterMainWindow will filter the selected menu choice and call the corresponding private method for processing:

```
            public void actionPerformed(ActionEvent event)
            {
                String menuName;

                menuName = event.getActionCommand();

                if (menuName.equals("New")) {
                   newRoster();
                }
                else if (menuName.equals("Open...")) {
                   openRoster();
                }
                else if (menuName.equals("Save")) {
                   saveRoster();
                }
                else if (menuName.equals("Save As...")) {
                   saveAsRoster();
                }
                else if (menuName.equals("Quit")) {
                   quitProgram();
                }
                else if (menuName.equals("Test Scores...")) {
                   editTestScores();
                }
```

```
      else if (menuName.equals("Compute Grades")) {
         computeGrades();
      }
      else if (menuName.equals("Student Name...")) {
         editStudentName();
      }
      else if (menuName.equals("Add New Student...")) {
         addNewStudent();
      }
      else if (menuName.equals("Delete Student...")) {
         deleteStudent();
      }
      else if (menuName.equals("All Students")) {
         showAllStudents();
      }
      else if (menuName.equals("One Student...")) {
         showOneStudent();
      }
   }
```

The private methods for processing the selected menu choices at this step include only temporary output statements, except the quitProgram method. All of these methods are written in the following style:

```
private void newRoster( )
{
    messageBox.show("Inside newRoster");
}
```

The quitProgram method is defined as

```
private void quitProgram( )
{
    System.exit(0);
}
```

Step 1 Test

We execute the main class and the skeleton GradeRosterMainWindow class to verify that the classes are coded correctly. When we run the program, we select every menu choice and verify that the correct message for the menu choice is displayed by the temporary output statements. We select the menu choice Quit and make sure the program terminates. Once this is verified, we move on to implement one by one the private methods of GradeRosterMainWindow that correspond to the menu choices. To implement these methods fully, we may have to modify or extend existing classes or design additional new classes.

Chapter 15

15.5 Step 2 Development: Create a New Roster

Step 2 Design

The very first operation we need to implement is the capability to create a new grade roster. Without this capability, we will not be able to work on other operations. We decided that the program can open one grade roster at a time. When the user selects the menu choice New, we will create a new GradeRoster object. However, we cannot simply create a new grade roster. What will happen when there is a currently open grade roster?

Consider the behavior of a common text editor. Let's say that after you open and edit a document, you try to create a new document. What should happen to the currently open document? The text editor will ask you whether you want to save the document before creating a new one. We will make our program behave in a similar manner. When there's a currently open grade roster, we will give the user an option of saving it before creating a new grade roster.

Another behavior we model after a text editor is the labeling of the window title. When you open a document in a text editor, the window title will include the filename of the document. We will change the title of the main window to include the name of a newly created grade roster.

Since the responsibility of managing GradeRoster belongs to GradeRosterControl, the newRoster method asks GradeRosterControl whether there is currently an open grade roster. If there is no current grade roster, then we will create a new roster. Otherwise, we prompt the user and give him or her the option of saving the current roster. Here's the pseudocode:

```
if (gradeRosterControl does not have an open roster) {
    createNewRoster();
}
else {
    int answer = saveBox.prompt("Save the current roster?");

    switch (answer ) {
       case SAVE:
           saveRoster();     //save the current roster first
           createNewRoster();
           break;
       case NO_SAVE:
           createNewRoster();  //discard the current roster
           break;
       case CANCEL:            //cancel creating a new roster
           //do nothing
           break;
    }
}
```

We use saveBox, a ResponseBox object with three buttons labeled Save, Don't Save, and Cancel, to get the user's direction.

The createNewRoster method creates a new grade roster by calling the newGradeRoster method of GradeRosterControl and resets its window title by calling the private method setNewTitle. Since GradeRosterControl is the one that directly manages a grade roster, its newGradeRoster is the method that actually creates a GradeRoster object. This is the pattern we have for this program. The task of gradeRosterMainWindow is to delegate the actual work to one of the subordinate objects gradeRosterControl, gradeRosterDisplay, and gradeRosterStorage.

Inside the newGradeRoster method, we will create an instance of GradeRoster, so we need to think about a constructor for GradeRoster. What information should we pass to a constructor when creating an instance of GradeRoster? We could associate many different types of information to a grade roster; let's decide that we will maintain the title and instructor information for each course. We will pass these two pieces of information to a GradeRoster constructor. To add flexibility to the class, we also will define a second constructor that will allow the programmer to specify the enrollment size of the course. The newGradeRoster method uses the first constructor of GradeRoster and looks like this:

```
String title     = inputBox.getString("title");
String instructor = inputBox.getString("instructor");

//use the first constructor
gradeRoster = new GradeRoster(title, instructor);
```

The setNewTitle method resets the window title to reflect the course title of a newly created grade roster. To get the course title, it calls the getCourseTitle of GradeRosterControl. The course title is actually kept by a GradeRoster object, so why not call a method of GradeRoster directly from setNewTitle? We certainly could, but doing so would complicate the connection links among objects in the program. We want to maintain the connection links simple and clean, as shown in the object diagram of Figure 15.2. Increasing the number of links from a single object makes program maintenance more difficult. The method body of setNewTitle will be

```
String title = gradeRosterControl.getCourseTitle();
setTitle("C L A S S   R O S T E R  for:  " + title);
```

The getCourseTitle method returns the title by

```
return gradeRoster.getTitle();
```

where getTitle of GradeRoster returns the value of its data member courseTitle:

```
return courseTitle;
```

Figure 15.3 is the method call sequence diagram.

FIGURE 15.3   Method call sequence diagram for the **newRoster** method. Calls to standard **javabook** objects are not shown.

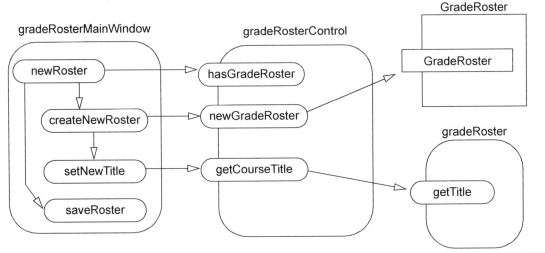

From this step, we start using an instance of GradeRosterControl, so we need to implement its constructor. In the constructor, we will create the data member objects, which include GradeRoster and InputBox at this point. We already designed an instance of GradeRoster that will be created in the newGradeRoster method, so we won't be creating it in the constructor. As for an InputBox object, we will create it in the constructor. Since InputBox is a dialog, we need a Frame object to create an InputBox object. If we create it inside a method of the MainWindow or Frame descendant class, we call the InputBox constructor

```
inputBox = new InputBox( this );
```

We cannot make such a call from the constructor of GradeRosterControl because it is not a subclass of MainWindow or Frame. We will solve this problem by passing the GradeRosterMainWindow object to the constructor of GradeRosterControl. The constructor will look like this:

```
public GradeRosterControl( Frame mainWindow )
{
    owner = mainWindow;
    . . .
    inputBox = new InputBox( owner );
}
```

We also need to implement a GradeRoster constructor. What will be the data members we need to create and initialize in the constructor? We already have decided that we will include two constructors in the GradeRoster class. The first constructor accepts the course title and instructor name, and the second constructor accepts the enrollment size as its third parameter. We will use data members to store the course title and instructor. For a roster, we will use an array of Student objects named roster. To keep track of the number of Student objects in the array, we use an int variable rosterSize. These four data members are created and initialized in the constructor. The first constructor will call the second constructor by passing the default array length of roster, which we will set to 25.

Here's the summary of work to be done in Step 2:

	Objects	To Do

Step 2	GradeRoster-MainWindow	Implement the methods
		    newRoster
		    createNewRoster
		    setNewTitle
		Modify the constructor as necessary.
		Add a ResponseBox called **saveBox** as a new data member.
		Define constants SAVE, NO_SAVE, and CANCEL.

	GradeRoster-Control	Implement the methods
		    <constructor>
		    getCourseTitle
		    hasGradeRoster
		    newGradeRoster
		Add **InputBox** as a new data member.

	GradeRoster	Implement the methods <constructor> getTitle

Step 2 Code   We will list the code modification for each class in order.

Chapter 15

GradeRosterMainWindow

Add the following data member declarations:

```
private static final int SAVE    = ResponseBox.BUTTON1;
private static final int NO_SAVE = ResponseBox.BUTTON2;
private static final int CANCEL  = ResponseBox.BUTTON3;

private    ResponseBox          saveBox;

private    GradeRosterControl  gradeRosterControl;
```

Modify the constructor to

```
public GradeRosterMainWindow()
{
    //as before

        saveBox = new ResponseBox(this,3);
        saveBox.setLabel(SAVE,"Save");
        saveBox.setLabel(NO_SAVE,"Don't Save");
        saveBox.setLabel(CANCEL,"Cancel");

        gradeRosterControl = new GradeRosterControl(this);

}
```

Define the following private methods:

```
private void newRoster()
{
    if (!gradeRosterControl.hasGradeRoster()) {
        createNewRoster();
    }
    else {
        //save current gradeRoster?
        int answer = saveBox.prompt
                        ("Save the current grade roster?");

        switch (answer) {
            case SAVE:
                saveRoster();
                createNewRoster();
                break;
            case NO_SAVE:
                createNewRoster();
                break;
```

```
                case CANCEL:
                    //do nothing
                    break;
            }
        }
    }


    private void createNewRoster()
    {
        gradeRosterControl.newGradeRoster();

        setNewTitle();
    }


    private void setNewTitle()
    {
        String title = gradeRosterControl.getCourseTitle();

        setTitle("C L A S S    R O S T E R    f o r:  " + title);
    }
```

GradeRosterControl

Add the following data member declarations:

```
        private   Frame        owner;
        private   InputBox     inputBox;
        private   GradeRoster  gradeRoster;
```

Define the constructor and methods:

```
    public GradeRosterControl(Frame mainWindow)
    {
        owner         = mainWindow;
        gradeRoster   = null;

        inputBox      = new InputBox(owner);
    }


    public void newGradeRoster( )
    {
        String title, instructor;
```

```
        title   = inputBox.getString("Enter Course Title:");

        instructor
            = inputBox.getString("Enter Course Instructor:");

        gradeRoster = new GradeRoster(title, instructor);
    }


    public String getCourseTitle()
    {
        return gradeRoster.getTitle();
    }
```

GradeRoster

Add the data member declarations:

```
    private static final int DEFAULT_LENGTH = 25;

    private String   courseTitle;
    private String   courseInstructor;
    private Student[] roster;
    private int       rosterSize; //number of students in roster
```

Define the constructor and methods:

```
    public GradeRoster(String title, String instructor)
    {
        this( title, instructor, DEFAULT_LENGTH );
    }


    public GradeRoster(String title, String instructor, int
    length)
    {
        courseTitle      = title;
        courseInstructor = instructor;
        roster           = new Student[length];
        rosterSize       = 0;
                                                          //TEMP
        System.out.println("Inside GradeRoster constructor");
        System.out.println(courseTitle);                  //TEMP
        System.out.println(courseInstructor);             //TEMP
        System.out.println("roster length: " +roster.length);
                                                          //TEMP

    }
```

```
public String getTitle( )
{
    return courseTitle;
}
```

Step 2 Test

We run the program and verify that a new grade roster object is created properly. We select the menu choice File/New and verify that correct GradeRosterControl and GradeRoster objects are created. We included temporary output statements in the constructor of GradeRoster for testing purposes.

15.6 Step 3 Development: Add Students

Step 3 Design

Once we have methods to create a new roster, we're ready to define methods to add students to and delete students from a roster. The methods corresponding to the menu choices Edit/Add Student and Edit/Delete Student are addNewStudent and deleteStudent, respectively. We will work on the addNewStudent method in this step and on the deleteStudent method in the next step.

The main task of addNewStudent is to tell gradeRosterControl to add a new student if there's an open grade roster. If no grade roster is currently open, then we will display an error message. The logic of the method is as follows:

```
if (gradeRosterControl.hasGradeRoster()) {
    gradeRosterControl.addStudent();
}
else {
    messageBox.show("No grade roster is currently open");
}
```

The method addStudent of gradeRosterControl first asks the user which type of student he or she wishes to add to a roster. Depending on the response, the method calls the private addGraduateStudent or addUndergraduateStudent. We use a ResponseBox object named selectionBox, which has two buttons labeled Undergraduate and Graduate, to prompt the user. The addStudent method in pseudocode is as follows:

```
//input student information
answer = selectionBox.prompt("Select the student type");

if (answer == GRAD_STUDENT) {
    addGraduateStudent();
}
else if (answer == UNDERGRAD_STUDENT) {
    addUndergraduateStudent();
}
```

```
//else dialog is canceled, so do nothing
```

The two methods to add a student, addGraduateStudent and addUndergraduateStudent, are almost identical except for the creation of an instance of GraduateStudent or UndergraduateStudent. In this program, we make an assumption that the names of students in the roster are unique. To maintain this assumption, we will not add a student if there's a student with the same name already in the roster. We check for a duplicate name by calling the getStudent method of GradeRoster. The method returns a Student object whose name matches the passed String parameter. The method returns null if no Student object with the given name is found. Since we want to add a new student, we expect null to be returned by the method. If the value returned is null, then we create either a GraduateStudent or an UndergraduateStudent object and add it to the roster by calling the method addStudent. Here are the two methods expressed in pseudocode:

```
//add a graduate student
studentName
    = inputBox.getString("Enter Graduate Student Name:");

student = gradeRoster.getStudent(studentName);

if (student == null) {
    newGradStudent = new GraduateStudent(studentName);
    gradeRoster.addStudent(newGradStudent);
}
else {
    messageBox.show("Duplicate name exists." +
                    " No new student is added.");
}

//add an undergraduate student
studentName
    = inputBox.getString("Enter Undergraduate Student Name:");

student = gradeRoster.getStudent(studentName);

if (student == null) {
    newUndergradStudent
            = new UndergraduateStudent(studentName);
    gradeRoster.addStudent(newUndergradStudent);
}
else {
    messageBox.show("Duplicate name exists." +
                    " No new student is added.");
}
```

The getStudent method of GradeRoster searches the roster for a student whose name matches the passed String value. If the matching student is found, then this object is returned. Otherwise, null is returned. The search routine is implemented as follows:

```
//search for student with studentName
//return null if not found

int     loc     = 0;

while (loc < rosterSize //still more elements to search
       &&
       !studentName.equals(roster[loc].getName())
                           //not a duplicate name
{
    loc++;
}

if (loc < rosterSize) {
    return roster[loc]; //return the student if found
}
else {
    return null;        //return null otherwise
}
```

To add a new student in the addStudent method, we first check to see if there is a space left in the roster array. If there is a space, we add this student to the roster array at position rosterSize. If there is no more space left in the roster array, we expand the roster array by calling the private method expandRoster before adding a new student. The logic of the addStudent method of GradeRoster is as follows:

```
//if there's no more space to add the student
//make the roster larger
if (rosterSize == roster.length) {
    expandRoster();
}
roster[rosterSize] = student;
rosterSize++;
```

The private method expandRoster expands the roster array by 50 percent:

```
//expand the roster by 50%

int newSize = (int) (roster.length * EXPAND_FACTOR);
```

The value is set to 1.5f.

```
Student newArray[] = new Student[newSize];

for (int i = 0; i < roster.length; i++) {
    newArray[i] = roster[i];
}
roster = newArray;
```

The method call sequence diagram is shown in Figure 15.4.

FIGURE 15.4   Method call sequence diagram for the **addNewStudent** method. Calls to standard **javabook** objects are not shown.

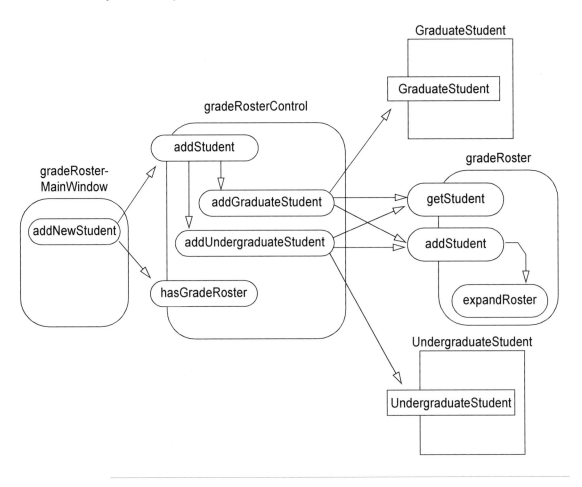

Here's the summary of work to do in Step 3:

	Objects	To Do
Step 3	GradeRoster-MainWindow	Implement the method addNewStudent

	GradeRoster-Control	Implement the methods
		    addStudent
		    addGraduateStudent
		    addUndergraduateStudent
		Modify the constructor as necessary.

	GradeRoster	Implement the methods
		    addStudent
		    getStudent
		    expandRoster

Step 3 Code

We will list the code modification for each class in order.

GradeRosterMainWindow

Define the **addNewStudent** method:

```
private void addNewStudent( )
{
    if (gradeRosterControl.hasGradeRoster()) {
        gradeRosterControl.addStudent();
    }
    else {
     messageBox.show("No grade roster is currently open.");
    }
}
```

GradeRosterControl

Add the data member declarations:

```
private static final int    GRAD_STUDENT
                                = ResponseBox.BUTTON1;
private static final int    UNDERGRAD_STUDENT
                                = ResponseBox.BUTTON2;

private ResponseBox         selectionBox;
private MessageBox          messageBox;
```

Modify the constructor to

Chapter 15

```
        public GradeRosterControl(Frame mainWindow)
        {
            ...
            selectionBox     = new ResponseBox(owner);
            selectionBox.setLabel(GRAD_STUDENT,   "  Graduate    ");
            selectionBox.setLabel(UNDERGRAD_STUDENT,
                                            "Undergraduate");
            messageBox       = new MessageBox(owner);

        }
```

Define the following public and private methods:

```
        public void addStudent( )
        {
            //input student information
            int answer
                = selectionBox.prompt("Select the student type.");

            if (answer == GRAD_STUDENT) {
                addGraduateStudent();
            }
            else if (answer == UNDERGRAD_STUDENT) {
                addUndergraduateStudent();
            }
            //else canceled, so do nothing
        }

        private void addGraduateStudent( )
        {
            String studentName
                = inputBox.getString("Enter Graduate Student Name:");

            Student student = gradeRoster.getStudent(studentName);

            if (student == null) {
                GraduateStudent newGradStudent =
                            new GraduateStudent(studentName);
                gradeRoster.addStudent(newGradStudent);
            }
            else {
                messageBox.show("Duplicate name exists." +
                            " No new student is added.");
            }
        }

        private void addUndergraduateStudent( )
        {
```

```
String studentName  = inputBox.getString
                ("Enter Undergraduate Student Name:");
Student student = gradeRoster.getStudent(studentName);

if (student == null) {
    UndergraduateStudent newUndergradStudent =
                new UndergraduateStudent(studentName);
    gradeRoster.addStudent(newUndergradStudent);
}
else {
    messageBox.show("Duplicate name exists." +
                " No new student is added.");

}
}
```

GradeRoster

Add the data member declaration:

```
private static final float EXPAND_FACTOR = 1.5f;
```

Add the following public and private methods:

```
public Student getStudent(String studentName)
{
    //search for student with studentName
    //return null if not found

    int     loc     = 0;

    while (loc < rosterSize //still more elements to search
            &&
            !studentName.equals(roster[loc].getName())
                        //not a duplicate name
    {
        loc++;
    }

    if ( loc < rosterSize ) {
        return roster[loc];
    }
    else {
        return null;
    }
}


public void addStudent( Student student)
```

```
    {
        //if there's no more space to add the student
        //make the roster larger
        if (rosterSize == roster.length) {
            expandRoster();
        }
        roster[rosterSize] = student;
        rosterSize++;

        System.out.println("Inside addStudent");        //TEMP
        System.out.println("Position added:" + rosterSize-1);
                                                         //TEMP
    }


    private void expandRoster( )
    {
        //expand the roster by 50%

        int newSize = (int) (roster.length * EXPAND_FACTOR);

        Student newArray[] = new Student[newSize];

        for (int i = 0; i < roster.length; i++) {
            newArray[i] = roster[i];
        }

        roster = newArray;

        System.out.println("Inside expandRoster");        //TEMP
        System.out.println("New length: " + roster.length);
                                                          //TEMP
    }
```

Step 3 Test

We run the program and verify that a new student can be added correctly to the roster. One possible sequence of testing operations is as follows:

1. Run the program and select Edit/Add Student. Verify that we get an error message.

2. Select File/New and create a new roster.

3. Select Edit/Add Student three or four times and add students. Verify that students are added correctly to the roster. Make sure to create both undergraduate and graduate students.

4. Select Edit/Add Student and enter a duplicate name. Verify that we get an error message.

Also, to test the expandRoster method, we change the value for DEFAULT_LENGTH to something like 4, run the program, and verify that the roster is expanded when a fifth student is added to the roster.

15.7 Step 4 Development: Delete Students

Step 4 Design

We will implement the delete operation in this step. The deleteStudent method is structurally similar to the addNewStudent method: The main task of the method is to tell gradeRosterControl to delete a student if there's an open grade roster. If no grade roster is currently open, then we will display an error message. The logic of the method is as follows:

```
if (gradeRosterControl.hasGradeRoster()) {
    gradeRosterControl.deleteStudent();
}
else {
    messageBox.show("No grade roster is open.");
}
```

The deleteStudent method of gradeRosterControl gets the name of a student to delete and checks to see if there's a student with the matching name. If there is, then it calls the deleteStudent method of gradeRoster. The method in pseudocode is as follows:

```
get studentName;

student = gradeRoster.getStudent(studentName);

if (student == null) {
    messageBox.show("Cannot delete: Student not found.");
}
else {
    gradeRoster.deleteStudent(student);
}
```

The deleteStudent method of gradeRoster locates the position of a student to be deleted in the roster array. Here's the logic of the method:

```
//search for student
int loc = 0;

while (loc < rosterSize && roster[loc] != student) {
    loc++;
```

Chapter 15

```
    }
    if (roster[loc] == student) { //student was found, so
        compactRoster(loc);          //compact the array
    }
```

Once the position loc is found, we call the private method compactRoster to fill the gap left by the deletion and decrement rosterSize by one. Its logic is as follows:

```
roster[loc] = roster[rosterSize-1];
roster[rosterSize-1] = null;

rosterSize--;
```

Figure 15.5 is the method call sequence diagram for the deleteStudent method.

FIGURE 15.5   Method call sequence diagram for the **deleteStudent** method. Calls to standard **javabook** objects are not shown.

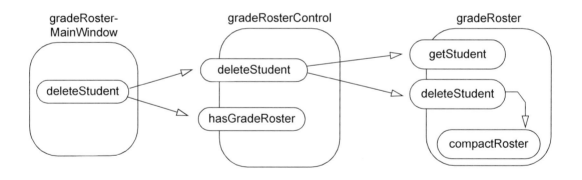

Here's the summary of work to do in Step 4:

	Objects	To Do
	GradeRoster-MainWindow	Implement the method deleteStudent
Step 4	GradeRoster-Control	Implement the method deleteStudent
	GradeRoster	Implement the methods deleteStudent compactRoster

Step 3 Code   We will list the code modification for each class in order.

GradeRosterMainWindow

Define the **deleteStudent** method:

```
private void deleteStudent( )
{
    if (gradeRosterControl.hasGradeRoster()) {
        gradeRosterControl.deleteStudent();
    }
    else {
        messageBox.show("No grade roster is open.");
    }
}
```

GradeRosterControl

Define the **deleteStudent** method:

```
public void deleteStudent(   )
{

    String studentName = inputBox.getString
                ("Enter the name of student to delete:");

    Student student = gradeRoster.getStudent(studentName);

    if (student == null) {
        messageBox.show
                ("Cannot delete: Student not found.");
    }
    else {
        gradeRoster.deleteStudent(student);
    }
}
```

GradeRoster

Define the following methods:

```
public void deleteStudent( Student student )
{
    int loc = 0;

    while (loc < rosterSize && roster[loc] != student) {
        loc++;
    }
```

Chapter 15

```
            if (roster[loc] == student) { //student was found, so
               compactRoster(loc);         //compact the array
            }
   }

   private void compactRoster(int loc)
   {
      //remove the student at position loc from the roster and
      //replace it by the element at position rosterSize-1

      roster[loc] = roster[rosterSize-1];
      roster[rosterSize-1] = null;

      rosterSize--;
   }
```

Step 4 Test

We run the program and verify that a student can be deleted correctly from the roster. One possible sequence of testing operations is as follows:

1. Run the program and select Edit/Delete Student. Verify that we get an error message.

2. Select File/New and create a new roster.

3. Select Edit/Add Student three or four times and add students. Make sure to create both undergraduate and graduate students.

4. Select Edit/Delete Student and enter a name that does not match the name of any student in the roster. Verify that we get an error message.

5. Select Edit/Delete Student and enter the name of a student in the roster. Verify that the student is deleted by trying to delete the same student again. We will get an error message if the deletion operation was executed successfully.

15.8 Step 5 Development: Edit Student Names

Step 5 Design

In the fifth step, we implement the methods that allow the user to edit student names. In what ways should we allow the user to edit student names? To change a student's name, we must have two values: the current and the new one. We use the current name to locate the student object in the roster array, and if found, we change the name to a new one, provided that the given new name is distinct from all other names in the roster. To input two names, we can use an InputBox object, as in

```
currentName   = inputBox.getString("Current Name:");
newName       = inputBox.getString("New Name:");
```

This approach works but does not support a good user interface. For instance, the user cannot go back and correct the value of currentName once it is entered. Also, the user cannot cancel the operation. Both names must be entered to continue with the program. We will support a better user interface by creating a special dialog for inputting these two values. We will call this dialog StudentNameDialog; a sample dialog is shown in Figure 15.6.

FIGURE 15.6   A **StudentNameDialog** dialog for inputting the current and new names of a student.

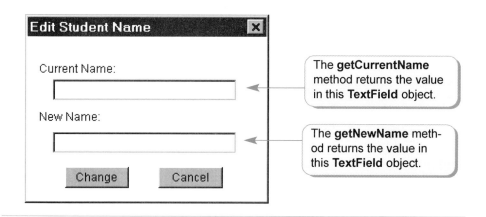

Who should manage this StudentNameDialog object? Two possible candidates are GradeRosterMainWindow and GradeRosterControl. The responsibility of GradeRosterMainWindow is the top-level interaction with the user via menu processing and the management of GradeRosterControl, GradeRosterDisplay, and GradeRosterStorage. Giving an additional object to manage to GradeRosterMainWindow will overload it and degrade the clarity of the overall program structure. Since managing a GradeRoster object is the responsibility of GradeRosterControl, we will let it manage a StudentNameDialog. The modified object diagram shown in Figure 15.7 now includes StudentNameDialog and the class is added to the program design document:

program
classes

Design Document:	GradeRoster Program
Class	**Purpose**
. . .	. . .
StudentNameDialog	A dialog used to enter the new and current names of a student. This dialog is managed by GradeRosterControl.

FIGURE 15.7   An extended object diagram for the grade roster program now includes
StudentNameDialog.

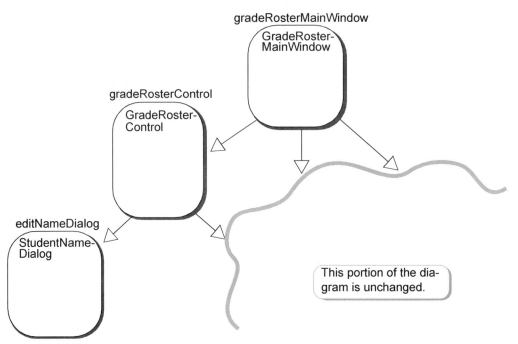

Some of you may wonder why we don't let GradeRoster control Student-
NameDialog, since the GradeRoster object is the one that maintains a grade roster. Remember, GradeRoster is an application logic object, and as a guideline,
we do not let application logic objects handle input and output. This will increase the reusability of application logic objects.

Now let's develop the StudentNameDialog class. Developing a completely
new class calls for another incremental development cycle. There are two ways
to handle the development of StudentNameDialog. The first approach is to inte-
grate the StudentNameDialog development into our current development. The
second approach is to develop the class completely separate from our current
development effort.

If we adopt the first approach, then we will initiate a sort of minidevelopment cycle, starting from a shell and gradually building up the StudentNameDialog class. We incorporate the partially completed class into the program we are
developing and test the class at each step of minidevelopment.

If we adopt the second approach, then we will either suspend the current development until we finish implementing the StudentNameDialog class or con-

tinue the development with a placeholder StudentNameDialog class. If we develop the StudentNameDialog class ourselves, then we need to suspend the current development until we complete its implementation. However, if we delegate the task of StudentNameDialog development to other programmers, we can proceed with our current development simultaneously. As long as we agree on the public methods of the StudentNameDialog class, we can continue our development by using a placeholder StudentNameDialog class.

We will use the second approach here. In order to streamline the presentation, we will develop the class in Section 15.13. We will present the design document of the class here and continue the development using the public methods listed in the design document. If you wish, you can read Section 15.13 before continuing this section. Here's the design document for the StudentNameDialog:

Design Document:	The StudentNameDialog Class	
Method	**Visibility**	**Purpose**
`<constructor>`	`public`	Creates an instance. The constructor accepts a **Frame** object as its argument.
`getCurrentName`	`public`	Returns the text value in the **CurrentName** text field.
`getNewName`	`public`	Returns the text value in the **NewName** text field.
`isCanceled`	`public`	Returns true if the dialog's **CANCEL** button was clicked.
`show`	`public`	Displays the dialog.

The role of the editStudentName method of gradeRosterMainWindow is to delegate the task to gradeRosterControl as

```
gradeRosterControl.editStudentName();
```

The editStudentName method of gradeRosterControl uses a StudentNameDialog box called editNameBox to get the current and new names. If the dialog is not canceled, then we retrieve the current and new names using getCurrentName and getNewName methods. If a student with the name matching the input current name is found, then the student's name is changed to the given new name. The logic of the method is expressed as follows:

```
editNameBox.setVisible( true );

if ( editNameBox is not canceled ) {
    currentName = editNameBox.getCurrentName();
```

```
newName      = editNameBox.getNewName();

student      = gradeRoster.getStudent(currentName);
duplicate = gradeRoster.getStudent(newName);

if (student == null) {
    messageBox.show("Cannot locate " + currentName);
}
else if (duplicate != null) {
    messageBox.show("There's already a person called "
                        + newName + "in the roster");

}
}
else {
    student.setName(newName);
}
```

> Search for the student with **currentName** and **newName**.

Figure 15.8 is the method call sequence diagram.

FIGURE 15.8 A method call sequence diagram for the **deleteStudent** method. Calls to standard **javabook** objects are not shown.

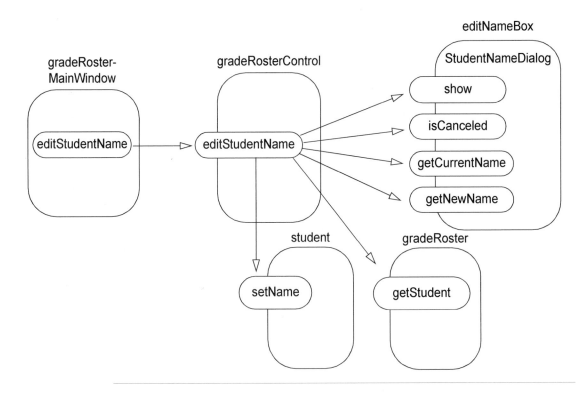

Here's the table that summarizes the work to be done in Step 5.

	Objects	To Do
Step 5	GradeRoster-MainWindow	Implement the method editStudentName
	GradeRoster-Control	Implement the method editStudentName Modify the constructor and data member declaration as necessary.
	StudentName-Dialog	Define this class fully.

Step 5 Code   We will list the code modification for each class in order.

GradeRosterMainWindow

Define the editStudentName method:

```
private void editStudentName()
{
    gradeRosterControl.editStudentName();
}
```

GradeRosterControl

Add the data member declaration

```
private StudentNameDialog    editNameBox;
```

and modify the constructor to

```
public GradeRosterControl(Frame mainWindow)
{
    ...
    editNameBox      = new StudentNameDialog(owner);
}
```

Define the editStudentName method:

```
public void editStudentName()
{
    String currentName, newName;
    Student student, duplicate;
```

Chapter 15

```
                                editNameBox.show();

                    if (!editNameBox.isCanceled()) {
                        currentName = editNameBox.getCurrentName();
                        newName     = editNameBox.getNewName();

                        student = gradeRoster.getStudent(currentName);
                        duplicate = gradeRoster.getStudent(newName);

                        if (student == null) {
                            messageBox.show("Cannot locate " + currentName);
                        }
                        else if (duplicate != null) {
                            messageBox.show("There's already a person called "
                                                + newName + "in the roster");
                        }
                        else {
                            student.setName(newName);
                        }
                    }
                }
```

Step 5 Test   We run the program and verify that the student names can be changed. One possible sequence of testing operations is as follows:

1. Select Edit/Add Student three or four times and add students. Make sure to create both undergraduate and graduate students.

2. Select Edit/Student Name and enter a current name that does not match the name of any other student in the roster. Verify that we get an error message.

3. Select Edit/Student Name and enter a new name that matches the name of a student in the roster. Verify that we get an error message.

4. Select Edit/Student Name and enter a current name that does match and a new name that does not match the name in the roster. Verify the name of this student is changed correctly.

15.9 Step 6 Development: Edit Test Scores and Compute Grades

Step 6 Design   In the sixth step, we add the methods for editing the test scores and computing the final course grades. We will design the methods for editing the test scores first. Although possible, using an InputBox object for this purpose reduces the quality of the user interface. Therefore, as we did in the previous section, we will come up with a custom-made dialog. We will call the dialog TestScoreDialog. This dialog will display the test scores of a student, and the user can add new test scores or overwrite the existing test scores. A sample dialog is shown in Figure 15.9.

FIGURE 15.9   A sample **TestScoreDialog** object for editing test scores.

The modified object diagram shown in Figure 15.10 now includes TestScoreDialog, and the class is added to the program design document:

program
classes

Design Document:	GradeRoster Program
Class	**Purpose**
. . .	. . .
TestScoreDialog	A dialog used to enter and edit the test scores of a student. This dialog is managed by GradeRosterControl.

As we did with StudentNameDialog, in Section 15.14 we will develop this class to separate it from the current development. We will present the design document of the class here and continue the development using the public methods listed in the design document. If you wish, you can read Section 15.14 before continuing this section. Here's the design document of the TestScoreDialog:

Design Document:	The TestScoreDialog Class	
Method	**Visibility**	**Purpose**
<constructor>	public	Creates an instance. The constructor accepts a Frame object as its argument.
getTestScores	public	Returns the test scores as an array of int.

Chapter 15

FIGURE 15.10   An extended object diagram for the grade roster program now includes **TestScoreDialog**.

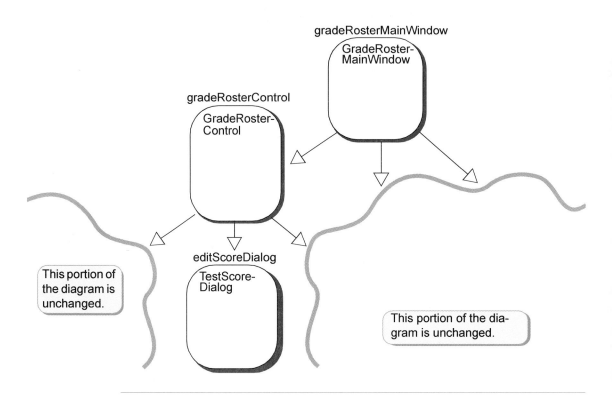

Design Document:	The TestScoreDialog Class	
Method	**Visibility**	**Purpose**
isCanceled	public	Returns true if the dialog's CANCEL button was clicked.
show	public	Displays the dialog.

The editTestScores method of gradeRosterMainWindow delegates the task to gradeRosterControl as

```
gradeRosterControl.editTestScores();
```

The editTestScores method of gradeRosterControl uses a TestScoreDialog box called editScoreBox shown in Figure 15.9 to get the test scores. First we get the name of a student whose test scores we want to edit. We search for this student, and, if found, we use editScoreBox to let the user edit the student's test scores. If the dialog is not canceled, then we retrieve the test scores using the getTestScores method. Here's the method:

```
name = inputBox.getString("Enter Student Name:");

student = gradeRoster.getStudent(name);

if (student == null) {
    messageBox.show("Cannot locate " + name);
}
else { //student found, so edit the test scores

    editScoreBox.show(student);

    if (!editScoreBox.isCanceled()) {

        int score[] = editScoreBox.getTestScores();

        student.setTestScores(score);
    }
}
```

Figure 15.11 is the method call sequence diagram for the editTestScores method.

Now, let's design the methods to compute the course grades. The compute-Grades method of gradeRosterMainWindow calls the computeGrades method of gradeRosterControl as

```
gradeRosterControl.computeGrades();
```

The computeGrades method of gradeRosterControl in turn calls the computeGrades method of gradeRoster as

```
gradeRoster.computeGrades();
```

Finally, for the computeGrades method, GradeRoster goes through its roster array and calls the computeCourseGrade method of either a GraduateStudent or an UndergraduateStudent object in the array:

```
for (int i = 0; i < rosterSize; i++) {
    roster[i].computeCourseGrade();
}
```

Chapter 15

FIGURE 15.11   Method call sequence diagram for the **editTestScores** method. Calls to standard **javabook** objects are not shown.

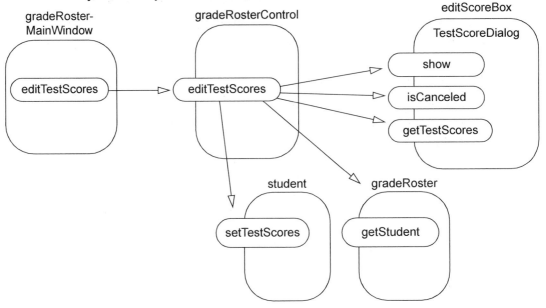

Figure 15.12 is the method call sequence diagram of the computeGrades method.

Here's the summary of the tasks to be done in Step 6:

	Objects	To Do
Step 6	GradeRoster-MainWindow	Implement the methods editTestScores computeGrades
	GradeRoster-Control	Implement the methods editTestScores computeGrades Modify the constructor and data member declaration as necessary.
	GradeRoster	Implement the method computeGrades
	TestScore-Dialog	Implement the class fully.

Step 6 Code   We will list the code modification for each class in order.

FIGURE 15.12   Method call sequence diagram for the **computeGrades** method. Calls to standard
javabook objects are not shown.

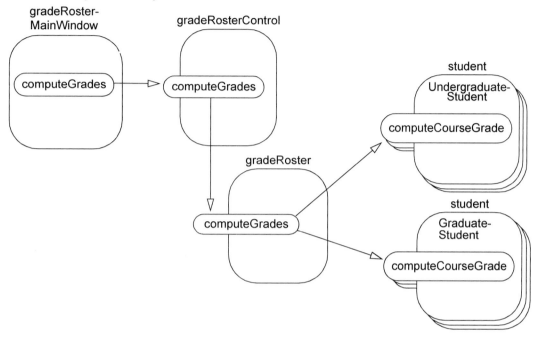

GradeRosterMainWindow
Define the following methods:

```
public void editTestScores()
{
    gradeRosterControl.editTestScores();
}


public void computeGrades()
{
    gradeRosterControl.computeGrades();
}
```

GradeRosterControl
Add the data member declaration

```
                    private TestScoreDialog    editScoreBox;
```

and modify the constructor to

```
    public GradeRosterControl(Frame mainWindow)
    {
        owner = mainWindow;
        ...
        editScoreBox      = new TestScoreDialog(owner);
    }
```

Define the following methods:

```
    public void editTestScores()
    {
        String name = inputBox.getString("Enter Student Name:");

        Student student = gradeRoster.getStudent(name);

        if (student == null) {
            messageBox.show("Cannot locate " + name);
        }
        else {

            editScoreBox.show(student);

            if (!editScoreBox.isCanceled()) {

                int score[] = editScoreBox.getTestScores();

                student.setTestScores(score);
            }
        }
    }


    public void computeGrades( )
    {
        gradeRoster.computeGrades();
    }
```

GradeRoster

Define the computeGrades method:

```
    public void computeGrades( )
```

```
        {
            for (int i = 0; i < rosterSize; i++) {
                roster[i].computeCourseGrade();

                //begin TEMP output
                System.out.print(roster[i].getName() + "   ");
                System.out.print(roster[i].getTestScore(1) + " ");
                System.out.print(roster[i].getTestScore(2) + " ");
                System.out.print(roster[i].getTestScore(3) + " ");
                System.out.println(roster[i].getCourseGrade());
                //end TEMP output
            }
        }
```

Step 6 Test

We run the program and verify that the test scores can be edited and the final course grades are computed correctly. One possible sequence of testing operations is as follows:

1. Select Edit/Add Student three or four times and add students. Make sure to create both undergraduate and graduate students.

2. Select Edit/Test Scores and enter test scores. Repeat this step to enter test scores for all students.

3. Select Edit/Compute Grades and verify that course grades are computed correctly.

4. Select Edit/Test Scores and change the test scores of a student so the student's course grade will be different. Select Edit/Compute Grades and verify that a new course grade is computed correctly. Repeat this step using different values for test scores.

15.10 Step 7 Development: Display Student Information

Step 7 Design

In the seventh step, we implement the methods that display information of all the students or a selected student. The GradeRosterDisplay class is the one responsible for displaying student information. How should we display student information? For each type of display, we can create a custom-made dialog or reuse some generic user interface object. As most of us prefer a custom-tailored outfit over off-the-rack clothing, we prefer custom-made dialogs over generic dialogs in most cases. However, designing custom-made dialogs takes time and effort. If the program can be made usable without any custom-made dialogs, we may opt for generic dialogs. Later, if the demand calls for an improvement, we may replace the generic dialogs with custom-made dialogs.

The advantage of using an object-oriented technique is the ease of replacing one implementation of a class with another implementation. For instance, we can start with one implementation of GradeRosterDisplay using a generic user interface object. Later, if the demand and budget warrant it, we can replace the first implementation of GradeRosterDisplay with a new version that includes custom-made dialogs. If the public components (constructors, constants, and methods) of GradeRosterDisplay remain the same, then the rest of the program will continue to work without modification.

We will take this approach of first using an implementation with generic objects and leaving an implementation with custom-made objects as a possible future improvement. We will implement GradeRosterDisplay using a generic OutputBox object and leave the implementation of GradeRosterDisplay that uses custom-made dialogs as an exercise.

Now let's begin our design of GradeRosterDisplay. A GradeRoster object is a controller object that manages an OutputBox object to display student information. There are two menu choices related to the display of student information: Show/All Students and Show/One Student. The showAllStudents method of GradeRosterMainWindow is executed when the first menu choice is selected, and the showOneStudent is executed when the second menu choice is selected. We will design the showAllStudents method first.

Since a grade roster is managed by gradeRosterControl and the actual task of displaying student information is done by gradeRosterDisplay, the showAllStudents method asks gradeRosterControl for a list of students and then passes this list to gradeRosterDisplay. The method expressed in pseudocode will look like this:

```
list = gradeRosterControl.getAllStudents();
gradeRosterDisplay.displayAll( list );
```

In what form should we return this list of students? One possibility is to return a GradeRoster object. Another possibility is to return an array of Student objects. Passing a GradeRoster object is more general because gradeRosterDisplay will have access to additional information beyond the list of students. For example, gradeRosterDisplay will have access to the course title and instructor information also. If a GradeRoster object is modified to keep an average for each of the three test scores, this information also will become available to gradeRosterDisplay. In contrast, if we pass an array of Student objects, then other information kept by a gradeRoster is not available to gradeRosterDisplay.

A possible disadvantage of passing a GradeRoster object is the cost of modifying the program. Suppose we pass an array of Student objects to gradeRosterDisplay, and gradeRosterDisplay does not make any call to a GradeRoster object. Since there is no direct connection link from gradeRosterDisplay to a GradeRoster object, any changes made to GradeRoster will not affect the implementation of GradeRosterDisplay. In general, we should reduce the number of connection links among program classes as much as possible. Although the larger the number of links you establish among classes, the more expensive the modification cost is potentially going to be, we can minimize it by carefully designing the classes.

Weighing the pros and cons, we choose to pass a GradeRoster object. The pseudocode for showAllStudents of GradeRosterMainWindow will then be

```
if ( gradeRosterControl.hasGradeRoster() ) {
    GradeRoster roster = gradeRosterControl.getRoster();
    gradeRosterDisplay.displayAll( roster );
}
else {
    print out an error message;
}
```

Since a GradeRoster object is a data member of GradeRosterControl, the getRoster method simply returns this data member as

```
return gradeRoster; //return its GradeRoster data member
```

Receiving this GradeRoster object as an argument, the displayAll method of gradeRosterDisplay will display the information of all students. What kind of display would be appropriate for listing student information? A common style for listing information on multiple objects, which we adopt here, is a tabular format such as the following:

```
        Name        Test1   Test2   Test 3   Grade
Mr. Espresso        76.3    88.4    92.2     Pass
Ms. Latte           76.3    88.4    92.2     Pass
Mr. Bancha          56.3    68.4    52.2     No Pass
```

The displayAll method labels each column with a heading and uses one row of OutputBox for a single student's information. We will display the column headings first and then go through the students in a roster displaying one student at a time:

```
displayHeading();

for each student in a roster {
    display this student using one line of outputBox;
}
```

```
outputBox.show();   // make outputBox visible;
```

We can get a student's name, test scores, and course grade by calling the corresponding public methods of the Student class. To access all students in a grade roster, we will define a method in the GradeRoster class called **getAllStudents** that returns an array of Student objects. The loop to access all students then becomes

```
Student[] studentList = gradeRoster.getAllStudents();

for (int i = 0; i < studentList.length; i++) {
    displayOneRow( studentList[i] );
}
```

We now have two private methods—displayHeading and displayOneRow—to add to the GradeRosterDisplay class. The displayHeading method outputs the column headings. To display information in an easy-to-read style, we need to set a field width for each column and align the values in it. How shall we set the field widths? We should not set some fixed sizes for field widths because that will limit the usability. We want the GradeRosterDisplay class to work with student names that contain a maximum of 10 characters or 20 characters. Likewise, we want the class to work with a list of students having three, seven, or any number of tests. To enable such flexibility, we will require the programmer to specify the field widths and the label for each column when a GradeRosterDisplay object is created.

We will define two data members: an integer array widthForColumn to store field widths and a String array headingForColumn to store column headings. These two arrays are set in a constructor that accepts four parameters: a Frame object owner, an integer columnCnt, a String array heading, and an int array width. Here's the body of the constructor:

```
outputBox         = new OutputBox( owner );
headingForColumn  = new String[columnCnt];
widthForColumn    = new int[columnCnt];

for (int i = 0; i < columnCnt; i++ ) {
    headingForColumn[i] = heading[i];
    widthForColumn[i]   = width[i];
}
```

Notice the for loop to assign elements of heading and width individually to headingForColumn and widthForColumn. We do not simply assign the two array arguments to the data members as

```
headingForColumn = heading;
widthForColumn   = width;
```

Do you know why? Remember that an array is an object, and only its reference is passed as a parameter. If we only assign a reference and do not create a separate local copy, any changes made to the original arrays would damage the operation of the class.

For example, to create a GradeRosterDisplay for showing student information with a name, three test scores, and a course grade, we can do the following:

```
String heading
          = { "Name", "Test1", "Test2", "Test3", "Grade" };
int fieldWidth = { 15, 8, 8, 8, 10 };

gradeRosterDisplay
    = new GradeRosterDisplay( this,  5, heading, fieldWidth );
```

With the data members widthForColumn and headingForColumn properly set, the logic of displayHeading can be expressed as

```
for (int i = 0; i < headingForColumn.length; i++) {
    outputBox.print(Format.centerAlign
                        ( widthForColumn[i],
                          headingForColumn[i] ) );
}
outputBox.skipLine(2);   //leave a blank space after
                         //the heading
```

The displayOneRow method uses one line of OutputBox to display information of one student. The number of values to display on one line varies, depending on the number of test scores kept for students. To accommodate this variation, we will define a new method named getValues to the Student class that returns student information as an array of String values. Figure 15.13 shows how the getValues method works.

Using the getValues method, the logic of displayOneRow can be expressed as follows:

```
String oneRow[] = student.getValues(); //student is one
                                       //element in the
                                       //studentList array

for (int i = 0; i < oneRow.length; i++) {
```

FIGURE 15.13   The **getValues** method returns an array of **String** that contains student information.

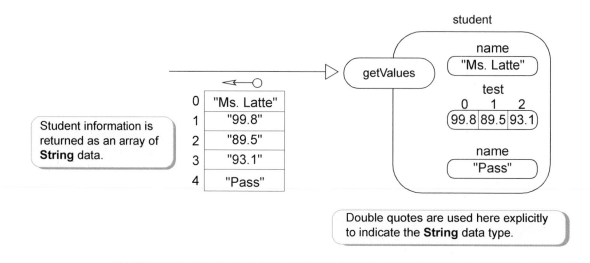

```
        outputBox.print ( Format.centerAlign
                        ( widthForColumn[i], oneRow[i] ) );
    }

    outputBox.skipLine(1); //move to the next line
```

Figure 15.14 is the method call sequence diagram for displaying student information for all the students.

The showOneStudent method of gradeRosterMainWindow displays information of a selected student. A student to be displayed will be selected by specifying the student's name. We will share most of the methods used to implement the showAllStudents method here.

The showOneStudent method of GradeRosterMainWindow calls the get-Roster method of gradeRosterControl to get a grade roster and passes this roster to gradeRosterDisplay. The logic of this method is

```
        if (gradeRosterControl.hasGradeRoster() ) {
            roster = gradeRosterControl.getRoster();
            gradeRosterDisplay.displayOne( roster );
        }
        else {
```

FIGURE 15.14   Method call sequence diagram for the **showAllStudents** method. Calls to standard **javabook** objects are not shown.

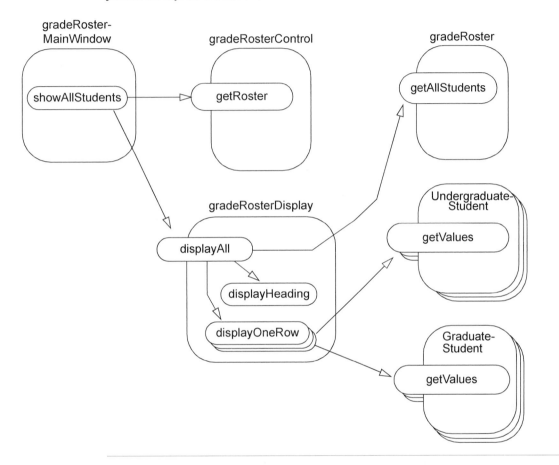

```
            print out an error message;
        }
```

The displayOne method of GradeRosterDisplay first prompts the user for the name of a student to display. It then passes the name to the getStudent method of GradeRoster. The getStudent method was defined already in Step 3. If the getStudent returns null, then we print out an error message. Otherwise, we display the column headings and the information of the student returned by getStudent. Here's the logic of the method:

```
String  name = inputBox.getString("Enter Student Name:");
Student student = roster.getStudent(name);
```

```
                    if (student == null) {
                        outputBox.printLine( "No student with the given name" +
                                             " is in the roster" );
                    }
                    else {
                        displayHeading( );
                        displayOneRow( student );
                    }

                    outputBox.show();
```

Since the method uses an InputBox object, we will add it as a new data member of the GradeRosterDisplay class and initialize it in the constructor. Figure 15.15 is the method call sequence diagram of the showOneStudent method.

FIGURE 15.15   Method call sequence diagram for the **showOneStudent** method. Calls to standard **javabook** objects are not shown.

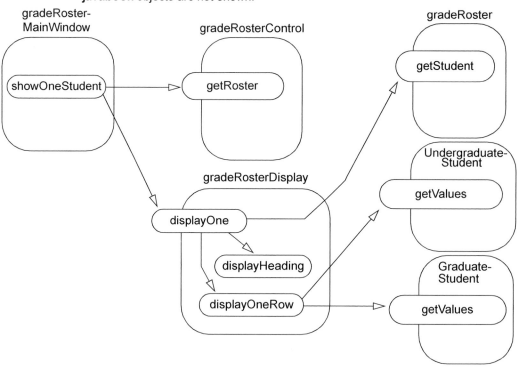

The following table summarizes the work done in Step 7:

	Objects	To Do

Step 7	GradeRoster-MainWindow	Implement the methods
		        showAllStudents
		        showOneStudent
		Modify the constructor to create and initialize an instance of GradeRosterDisplay.

	GradeRoster-Control	Implement the method getRoster

	GradeRoster-Display	Implement the methods
		        displayAll
		        displayOne
		
		Declare the data members and the constructor.

	Student	Implement the method getValues
	GradeRoster	Implement the method getAllStudents

Step 7 Code

We will list the code modification for each class in order.

GradeRosterMainWindow
We add a new data member

```
GradeRosterDisplay   gradeRosterDisplay;
```

and initialize it in the constructor:

```
public GradeRosterMainWindow( )
{
    ...
    String heading
         = { "Name", "Test1", "Test2", "Test3", "Grade" };
    int fieldWidth = { 15, 8, 8, 8, 10 };

    gradeRosterDisplay = new GradeRosterDisplay( this,  5,
                                heading, fieldWidth );
}
```

Define the following methods:

```
private void showAllStudents()
{
    GradeRoster roster;

    if ( gradeRosterControl.hasGradeRoster() ) {
        roster = gradeRosterControl.getRoster();
        gradeRosterDisplay.displayAll( roster );
    }
    else {
        messageBox.show("No roster is open.");
    }
}


private void showOneStudent()
{
    GradeRoster roster;

    if ( gradeRosterControl.hasGradeRoster() ) {
        roster = gradeRosterControl.getRoster();
        gradeRosterDisplay.displayOne( roster );
    }
    else {
        messageBox.show("No roster is open.");
    }
}
```

GradeRosterControl

We add a method that returns a grade roster:

```
public GradeRoster getRoster( )
{
    return gradeRoster; //return its GradeRoster data member
}
```

GradeRosterDisplay

We define the data members and the constructor for the class:

```
private int       widthForColumn[];
private String    headingForColumn[];
private OutputBox outputBox;
private InputBox  inputBox;

public GradeRosterDisplay( Frame     owner,
                           int       columnCnt,
                           String[]  heading,
                           int[]     width      )
```

```
{
    outputBox        = new OutputBox( owner );
    inputBox         = new InputBox( owner );
    headingForColumn = new String[columnCnt];
    widthForColumn   = new int[columnCnt];

    for (int i = 0; i < columnCnt; i++ ) {
        headingForColumn[i] = heading[i];
        widthForColumn[i]   = width[i];
    }
}
```

Define the following public and private methods:

```
public void displayAll( GradeRoster roster )
{
    Student[] student = roster.getAllStudents();

    displayHeading();

    for (int i = 0; i < student.length; i++) {
        displayOneRow(student[i]);
    }

    outputBox.show();
}


public void displayOne( GradeRoster roster )
{
    String     name;
    Student    student;

    name     = inputBox.getString("Enter Student Name:");
    student  = roster.getStudent(name);

    if (student == null) {
        outputBox.printLine( "No student with a given name"
                           + " is in the roster" );
    }
    else {
        displayHeading( );
        displayOneRow( student );
    }

    outputBox.show();
}
```

```
private void displayHeading()
{
    for (int i = 0; i < headingForColumn.length; i++) {
        outputBox.print(
            Format.centerAlign( widthForColumn[i],
                                headingForColumn[i]) );
    }

    outputBox.skipLine(1);
}


private void displayOneRow( Student student )
{
    String oneRow[] = student.getValues();

    for (int i = 0; i < oneRow.length; i++) {
        outputBox.print(
            Format.centerAlign(widthForColumn[i],oneRow[i]));
    }

    outputBox.skipLine(1);
}
```

Student

We add a method that returns student information as an array of String to the Student class (and inherited by its subclasses GraduateStudent and Under–graduateStudent):

```
public String[] getValues( )
{
    String value[] = new String[NUM_OF_TESTS + 2];
    value[0] = name;

    for (int i = 0; i < value.length; i++) {
        value[i+1] = Convert.toString(test[i]);
    }

    value[value.length-1] = courseGrade;

    return value;
}
```

GradeRoster

We add a method that returns all Student objects:

```
public Student[] getAllStudents( )
{
   return roster;
}
```

Step 7 Test   We run the program and verify that student information is displayed correctly. One possible sequence for testing operations is as follows:

1. Select Show/All Students and verify that the display works correctly when no roster is open.

2. Select Edit/Add Student three or four times and add students. Make sure to create both undergraduate and graduate students.

3. Select Show/All Students and verify the display is valid. Since no test scores are entered, the display should correctly reflect this fact.

4. Select Show/One Student and enter the name of a student in the roster. Verify that the display of this student's information is correct.

5. Select Show/One Student and enter the name of a nonexisting student. Verify the program works correctly in this case also.

6. Select Edit/Test Scores and enter test scores. Repeat this step to enter test scores for all the students.

7. Select Edit/Compute Grades and verify that course grades are computed correctly.

8. Select Show/All Students and verify that the updated student information is displayed.

15.11 Step 8 Development: Storing Grade Rosters

Step 8 Design   In the eighth step, we will complete the program by implementing the methods that handle file input and output of grade rosters. A GradeRosterStorage object is the one responsible for storing GradeRoster objects using the object file I/O technique. The methods corresponding to the menu choices File/Open, File/Save, and File/Save As are openRoster, saveRoster, and saveAsRoster, respectively. We will implement the file output operations first.

The saveAsRoster and saveRoster methods of GradeRosterMainWindow are similarly defined. The methods get a GradeRoster object to save from gradeRosterControl and call either the save or saveAs method of gradeRosterStorage. If the save or saveAs method returns false, then there was an error in saving a roster, so an error message is displayed. The logic of the saveRoster and saveAsRoster methods is

```
//saveRoster of GradeRosterMainWindow
roster  = gradeRosterControl.getRoster();
success = gradeRosterStorage.save( roster );

if (!success) {
   messageBox.show("ERROR in saving data.");
}

//saveAsRoster of GradeRosterMainWindow
roster  = gradeRosterControl.getRoster();
success = gradeRosterStorage.saveAs( roster );

if (!success) {
   messageBox.show("ERROR in saving data.");
}
```

current file

The save method of GradeRosterStorage saves a GradeRoster object to a current file. When the data are read from or written to a file, this file becomes the *current file* of the program. If there is no current file (that is, the user is working on a newly created grade roster that has not been saved yet), then save calls the saveAs method. We define an instance variable filename to Grade-RosterStorage to keep track of the current file. The save method first checks the instance variable filename. If it is a null, there is no current file, so the save method simply calls the saveAs method. If it is not null, then there is a current file, so the method calls the private saveData method instead. The method is defined as

```
//save of GradeRosterStorage
boolean status;

if (filename == null) {
   status = saveAs(roster);
}
else  { //save the data
   status = saveData(roster);
}
return status;
```

The saveAs method of GradeRosterStorage writes the data to a user designated file. If a valid file is specified, then a GradeRoster object is written to the file using saveData. The saveAs is defined as

```
//saveAs of GradeRosterStorage
boolean status;
```

```
get filename using a FileDialog;

if (filename == null) { //file dialog is canceled,
                        //so do nothing
    status = false;
}
else {
    status = saveData(roster);
}
return status;
```

When the saveData method is called from the save or saveAs method, we know the data member filename is not a null. The saveData method sets up an object output stream for filename, and if no exception is thrown, the method writes roster to the file. The saveData method is defined as

```
//saveData of GradeRosterStorage
boolean status = true;

try {
    //set up an ObjectOutputStream for filename
    outObjectStream.writeObject( roster );
    outObjectStream.close();
}
catch (IOException e) {
    status = false;
}

return status;
```

Figures 15.16 and 15.17 are the method call sequence diagrams of the saveAsRoster and saveRoster methods, respectively.

The openRoster method of GradeRosterMainWindow calls the open method of gradeRosterStorage to read a grade roster object from a file. If the open method returns a null, then there was some kind of error reading a roster object. If the method returns a GradeRoster object, then we pass the object to the setGradeRoster method of gradeRosterControl. The openRoster method is defined as

```
roster = gradeRosterStorage.open();

if (roster == null) {

    messageBox.show("ERROR: No file is opened.");
}
```

FIGURE 15.16   Method call sequence diagram for the **saveAsRoster** method. Calls to the **javabook** objects are not shown.

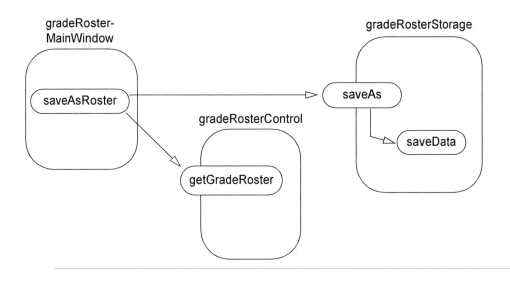

FIGURE 15.17   Method call sequence diagram for the **saveRoster** method. Calls to the **javabook** objects are not shown.

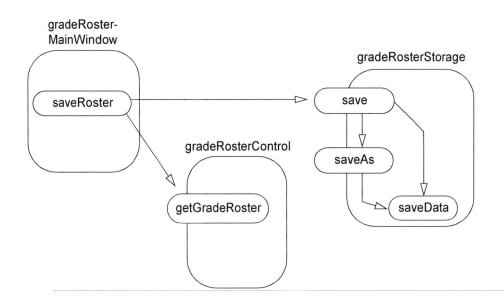

```
else {
    gradeRosterControl.setGradeRoster( roster );
}
```

The open method of gradeRosterStorage uses a FileDialog object to get the filename of a file to open from the user. If a valid filename is given, then we call the method loadData to read a GradeRoster object from the specified file. The two methods are defined as

```
//open of GradeRosterStorage
get the filename of a file to open using FileDialog

if (filename == null) { //FileDialog is canceled
    roster = null;
}
else {
    roster = loadData();
}

return roster;


//loadData of GradeRosterStorage
GradeRoster roster;

try {

    //set up an ObjectInputStream for filename
    roster = (GradeRoster) inObjectStream.readObject();
    inObjectStream.close();

}
catch (IOException e) {
    roster = null;
}
catch (ClassNotFoundException e) {
    roster = null;
}

return roster;
```

Figure 15.18 is the method call sequence diagram for reading a grade roster object from a file and assigning it to gradeRosterControl.

FIGURE 15.18   Method call sequence diagram for the **openRoster** method. Calls to standard **javabook** objects are not shown.

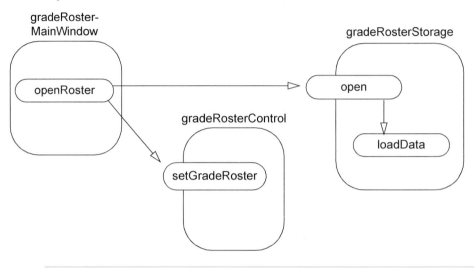

The following table summarizes the work to be done in Step 8:

	Objects	To Do
Step 8	GradeRoster-MainWindow	Implement the methods openRoster saveRoster saveAsRoster Modify the constructor to create and initialize an instance of GradeRosterStorage.
	GradeRoster-Control	Implement the method setGradeRoster
	GradeRoster-Storage	Implement the methods save saveAs saveData open loadData Define the constructor to create and initialize data members.

Step 8 Code   We will list the code modification for each class in order.

GradeRosterMainWindow

We add a new data member

```
GradeRosterStorage   gradeRosterStorage;
```

and initialize it in the constructor:

```
public GradeRosterMainWindow( )
{
    ...

    gradeRosterStorage = new GradeRosterStorage( this );
}
```

We add three methods to the class:

```
private void openRoster()
{
    GradeRoster roster = gradeRosterStorage.open();

    if (roster == null) {
        messageBox.show("Error: Open failed.");
    }
    else {
        gradeRosterControl.setRoster(roster);
    }
}

private void saveRoster()
{
    GradeRoster roster  = gradeRosterControl.getRoster();
    boolean     success = gradeRosterStorage.save(roster);

    if (!success) {
        messageBox.show("Error: No data was saved to a file");
    }
}

private void saveAsRoster()
{
    GradeRoster roster = gradeRosterControl.getRoster();
    boolean     success = gradeRosterStorage.saveAs(roster);

    if (!success) {
        messageBox.show("Error: No data was saved to a file");
    }
}
```

Chapter 15

GradeRosterControl

We define the public method setGradeRoster:

```
public void setGradeRoster( GradeRoster roster )
{
    gradeRoster = roster;
}
```

GradeRosterStorage

We define the data members and the constructor for the class:

```
private Frame      owner;
private String     filename;


public GradeRosterStorage( Frame      mainWindow )
{
    owner = mainWindow;
)
```

Define the following public and private methods:

```
public GradeRoster open( )
{
    GradeRoster roster;

    FileDialog fileDialog = new FileDialog(owner,
                                "Load Grade Roster...",
                               FileDialog.LOAD);
    fileDialog.show();

    filename = fileDialog.getFile();

    if (filename == null) {

        roster = null;
    }
    else {
        roster = loadData();
    }

    return roster;
}
```

```java
private GradeRoster loadData( )
{
    GradeRoster roster;

    try {

        //set up file and stream
        File inFile = new File(filename);
        FileInputStream inFileStream
                    = new FileInputStream(inFile);
        ObjectInputStream inObjectStream
                    = new ObjectInputStream(inFileStream);

        roster = (GradeRoster) inObjectStream.readObject();

        inObjectStream.close();
    }
    catch (IOException e) {
        roster = null;
        System.out.println(e);
     }
    catch (ClassNotFoundException e) {
        roster = null;
        System.out.println(e);
    }

    return roster;
}


public boolean saveAs( GradeRoster roster )
{
    boolean status;

    FileDialog fileDialog = new FileDialog(owner,
                                "Save Grade Roster...",
                                FileDialog.SAVE);
    fileDialog.show();

    filename = fileDialog.getFile();
    if (filename == null) {
        status = false;
    }
    else {
        status = saveData(roster);
    }

    return status;
}
```

```
private boolean saveData( GradeRoster roster )
{
    boolean status = true;

    try {
        //set up the streams
        File outFile = new File(filename);
        FileOutputStream outFileStream
                = new FileOutputStream(outFile);
        ObjectOutputStream outObjectStream
                = new ObjectOutputStream(outFileStream);

        outObjectStream.writeObject(roster);

        outObjectStream.close();
    }
    catch (IOException e) {
        status = false;
        System.out.println(e);
    }

    return status;
}

public boolean save( GradeRoster roster)
{
    boolean status;

    if (filename == null) {
        status = saveAs(roster);
    }
    else { //save the data
        status = saveData(roster);
    }

    return status;

}
```

Step 8 Test   We run the program and verify that student information is displayed correctly. One possible sequence of testing operations is as follows:

1. Select Show/All Students and verify that the display works correctly when no roster is open.

2. Select Edit/Add Student three or four times and add students. Make sure to create both undergraduate and graduate students.

3. Select Edit/Test Scores and enter test scores. Repeat this step to enter test scores for all students.

4. Select Edit/Compute Grades and verify that course grades are computed correctly.

5. Select File/Save As and save the roster to a file, say, rosterOne.dat. You can use any name you wish for the filename. Verify that the file is created and the file size is not zero.

6. Add one or two more students to the roster and save this roster to another file, say, rosterTwo.dat.

7. Select File/Open and open rosterOne.dat. List all students in the roster and verify that the information is correct.

8. Select File/Open and open rosterTwo.dat. List all students in the roster and verify that the information is correct.

9. Modify the grade roster contents by editing test scores and deleting a couple of students. Save the data to a file by selecting File/Save. Open the file and list the contents. Verify that changes are made correctly.

15.12 Step 9 Development: Finalize and Improve

We are almost done with the development. Our task in the last step is to finalize and look for any improvements. With so many classes in the program, it is very important to perform a thorough and critical review of the program. We review all classes for consistency and completeness. Some of the questions we ask ourselves while reviewing the classes are

1. Are the methods named logically and consistently over the classes?

2. Are there any overburdened classes that handle too many tasks?

3. Are the links between the classes clear and logical? Are there too many links between the classes?

4. Have we considered all possible operations? Are there any other operations we should support?

5. Is the program's user interface logical and easy to use?

To identify any remaining problem spots, we run the program through another round of testing. We basically repeat the testing procedures we performed in the earlier development steps. For a program of this size, it is also beneficial to perform a beta testing. We create a simple user manual and ask others to test

Chapter 15

the program. Beta testing is a very common way for commercial software companies to do a final testing before releasing their software to the general public.

15.13 The StudentNameDialog Class

In this section, we will implement the StudentNameDialog class identified in Step 5. We will implement this class using a separate development cycle. The design document was already created in Step 5 and, therefore, our job here is to implement it. Of course, if the given design contains any inconsistency or error, we may have to modify the design.

Problem Statement

> *Write a dialog that allows the user to enter two string values, one for the current name and another for a new name. The dialog will include* CANCEL *and* CHANGE *buttons. Its visual appearance will be as shown in Figure 15.6. The class must support the four public methods listed in the design document from Section 15.8.*

Overall Plan

What kind of behavior does the programmer who uses a StudentNameDialog expect from the class? One common behavior among the javabook dialog objects such as MessageBox, InputBox, and others is the displaying of a dialog at the center of the screen. We will incorporate this behavior into StudentNameDialog. This common behavior is programmed in the JavaBookDialog abstract class in the javabook package. MessageBox, InputBox, ResponseBox, and all other dialogs in javabook are subclasses of the JavaBookDialog class. We will make StudentNameDialog a subclass of JavaBookDialog and inherit the centering behavior from its superclass.

One condition to make a class a subclass of JavaBookDialog is to implement the abstract method adjustSize. A subclass must implement this method by including code to set the size of the dialog and the size and position of the components in the dialog. The superclass JavaBookDialog is programmed in such a way that the adjustSize method is called when an instance of its subclass is created.

In addition to implementing the required adjustSize method, we need to implement three public methods: getCurrentName, getNewName, and isCanceled. Furthermore, because we have to process the button click event, we need to implement the action-handling method actionPerformed. The object diagram at this point is

We will implement the class in the following three steps:

development
steps

1. Start with a class skeleton with the necessary data member declarations and constructors. Implement the superclass abstract method adjustSize.

2. Implement the actionPerformed method.

3. Implement the public methods getCurrentName, getNewName, and isCanceled.

Step 1 Development: Skeleton with Constructor and adjustSize

Step 1 Design

The objective of Step 1 is to identify the necessary GUI components and complete the visual appearance of the dialog. We will also implement the adjustSize method in this step. We will use two TextField objects for the user to enter the new and current names. We will call them newNameTextField and currentNameTextField. We will use two Label objects currentNameLabel and newNameLabel to label the two TextField objects. And, finally, we will have two Button objects for CANCEL and OK. These two buttons will be the only action event sources for this dialog. We declare these objects as

```
private TextField   currentNameTextField,
                    newNameTextField;

private Label       currentNameLabel,
                    newNameLabel;

private Button      changeButton,
                    cancelButton;
```

We will initialize these objects in the constructor and set their size and position in the adjustSize method. The constructor for this dialog is pretty standard:

Chapter 15

```
//set the properties of the dialog
call the super's constructor;
set title to "Edit Student Name";
set layout to null;
set resizable to false;

//create GUI objects
...

//add the created GUI objects to the dialog
add( currentNameLabel );
add( newNameLabel );
...

//set the dialog as an action listener of two buttons
cancelButton.addActionListener( this );
changeButton.addActionListener( this );
```

The adjustSize method will set the size and location of the GUI objects as

```
addNotify(); //must call this method at the beginning
Insets inset = getInsets();

//Adjust the size of the dialog
setSize(inset.left + inset.right + 250,
        inset.top + inset.bottom + 170);

//Adjust the size of components in the dialog
currentNameLabel.setBounds
              (inset.left +  13, inset.top +  25,  81, 17);
newNameLabel.setBounds
              (inset.left +  13, inset.top +  75,  81, 17);

    ...
```

We need to call addNotify before calling the insets method so the correct inset values are computed. The addNotify method actually creates a platform-dependent data structure for managing a window, and without having this platform-dependent data structure created, the getInsets method does not return the correct values.

The method getInsets returns an Insets object that contains four offset values: bottom, left, right, and top. Figure 15.19 illustrates these four values, which we use in computing the locations where we place the GUI objects.

Step 1 Code   We will list the key portions of the StudentNameDialog class source code. The import statements and class declaration will be

FIGURE 15.19   Difference between the container (window) bounds and the inset values. The inner
rectangle shows the drawing area and the outer rectangle shows the window. The area
between the two includes things such as the window title, scroll bars, window borders,
and so forth.

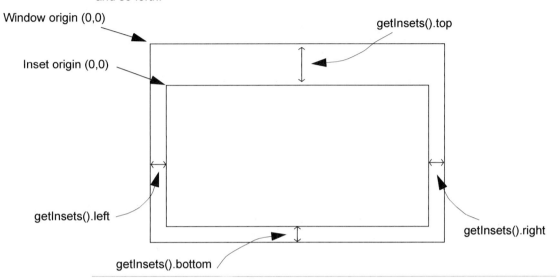

```
import java.awt.event.*;
import java.awt.*;
import javabook.*;

class StudentNameDialog extends JavaBookDialog
                        implements ActionListener {
...
```

The constructor is defined as

```
public StudentNameDialog(Frame owner)
{
    //set the properties of the dialog
    super(owner);
    setTitle("Edit Student Name");
    setResizable(false);
    setLayout(null);

    //create GUI objects
    currentNameLabel = new Label("Current Name:");
    newNameLabel = new Label("New Name:");

    currentNameTextField = new TextField("");
    newNameTextField = new TextField("");
```

```
                    changeButton = new Button("Change");
                    cancelButton = new Button("Cancel");

                    //add the created GUI objects to the dialog
                    add(currentNameLabel);
                    add(newNameLabel);
                    add(currentNameTextField);
                    add(newNameTextField);
                    add(changeButton);
                    add(cancelButton);

                    //set the dialog as an action listener of the two buttons
                    cancelButton.addActionListener( this );
                    changeButton.addActionListener( this );
                }
```

and the **adjustSize** method is defined as

```
            protected void adjustSize()
            {
                addNotify();
                Insets inset = getInsets();

                setSize(inset.left + inset.right + 250,
                        inset.top + inset.bottom + 170);

                currentNameLabel.setBounds
                        (inset.left +  13, inset.top +  25,  81,  17);
                newNameLabel.setBounds
                        (inset.left +  13, inset.top +  75,  81,  17);
                currentNameTextField.setBounds
                        (inset.left +  28, inset.top +  45, 192,  22);
                newNameTextField.setBounds
                        (inset.left +  28, inset.top + 100, 192,  22);
                changeButton.setBounds
                        (inset.left +  41, inset.top + 136,  67,  22);
                cancelButton.setBounds
                        (inset.left + 139, inset.top + 136,  67,  22);
            }
```

Step 1 Test   In order to test the skeleton **StudentNameDialog** class, we need to write a test main class because we are developing this class separate from the main development. A simple main class such as the following would suffice:

```
            import javabook.*;

            /**
             * Program TestStudentNameDialog
```

```
 *
 * A main class to test the StudentNameDialog class
 */
class TestStudentNameDialog
{
    public static void main (String args[])
    {
        MainWindow         topWindow = new MainWindow();
        StudentNameDialog testDialog
                         = StudentNameDialog( topWindow );
        topWindow.setVisible( true );
        testDialog.setVisible( true );
    }
}
```

The purpose of this test program is to verify that the constructor is executed correctly and the placement and the size of GUI objects are as we expected.

Step 2 Development: Implement the actionPerformed Method

Step 2 Design   In the second step of development, we will implement the actionPerformed method. This method is called when the CANCEL or CHANGE button is clicked. If the clicked button is CANCEL, then we close the dialog and clear any entry in currentNameTextField and newNameTextField. If we don't clear them, the entry values will still be visible when we display the dialog the next time. We will define a private method clearEntries to clear the contents of two TextField objects. In addition, we need to remember the fact that the dialog is canceled, so the object can reply correctly when the programmer calls the boolean method isCanceled. For this purpose, we will declare a boolean instance variable canceled and set this variable to true when the CANCEL button is clicked.

If the CHANGE button is clicked, then we need to remember the two String values entered in the two TextField objects and set canceled to false. To remember the two input values, we declare two String instance variables currentName and newName. We will define a private method setNames to set these String variables.

The method body of actionPerformed looks like this:

```
Button clickedButton = (Button) event.getSource();

if (clickedButton == cancelButton) {
    canceled = true;
}
else { //changeButton is clicked
    setNames();
}
```

```
setVisible( false ); //make the dialog disappear
clearEntries( );
```

The **clearEntries** method sets the contents of both **TextField** objects to empty strings

```
currentNameTextField.setText( "" );
    newNameTextField.setText( "" );
```

We will use a stub method for **setNames** in this step. What we need to achieve in this step is only the framework to process the action events. We will include temporary output statements in the stub **setNames** method. The working design document now includes this method:

Design Document:	The StudentNameDialog Class	
Method	**Visibility**	**Purpose**
. . .	. . .	. . .
clearEntries	private	Sets the contents of the two **TextField** objects to an empty string.
setNames	private	Assigns the contents of the two **TextField** objects to **currentName** and **newName**.

Step 2 Code   The **actionPerformed** method is defined as follows:

```
public void actionPerformed( ActionEvent event )
{
    Button clickedButton = (Button) event.getSource();

    if (clickedButton == cancelButton) {
        canceled = true;
    }
    else { //changeButton is clicked
        setNames();
    }

    setVisible( false ); //make the dialog disappear
    clearEntries( );
}
```

The **clearEntries** method clears both **TextField** objects:

```
private void clearEntries ( )
{
   currentNameTextField.setText ( "" );
      newNameTextField.setText ( "" );
}
```

The **setNames** method is temporarily defined as

```
private void setNames()
{
   //get data from two TextField objects
   currentName = currentNameTextField.getText();
   newName     = newNameTextField.getText();

   System.out.println("current:" + currentName); //TEMP
   System.out.println("new:     " + newName);    //TEMP
   canceled = false;                             //TEMP
}
```

Step 2 Test   We run the same TestStudentNameDialog main class from Step 1 and verify that the action events generated by the two buttons are processed correctly.

Step 3 Development: Implement the Public Methods

Step 3 Design   In the last step of development, we complete the class by finalizing the **setNames** method and defining three public methods: isCanceled, getCurrentName, and getNewName. The three public methods only need to return the value of the corresponding instance variable—canceled, currentName, or newName:

```
//isCanceled
return canceled;

//getCurrentName
return currentName;

//getNewName
return newName;
```

In the final **setNames** method, we need to incorporate some error-checking routine. What should happen when the user clicks on the CHANGE button without entering any value for the current and new names? If we do nothing, then the two instance variables remain empty strings. We could require the programmer to check the value returned by getCurrentName and getNewName, but this will put an unnecessary burden on the programmer. The task of this dialog is to input two names, current and new. If the user fails to provide either value, then it is really the same as canceling the dialog. So if either entry is an empty string, then we will set the variable canceled to true. Here's the logic of the method:

```
currentName = currentNameTextField.getText();
newName     =     newNameTextField.getText();

//make sure both are nonempty strings
if ( currentName.equals("") || newName.equals("") ) {

    canceled = true;
}
else {
    //input okay, so close
    canceled = false;
}
```

Step 3 Code   The three public methods are defined as

```
public boolean isCanceled()
{
    return canceled;
}

public String getCurrentName()
{
    return currentName;
}

public String getNewName()
{
    return newName;
}
```

and the **setNames** method is defined as

```
private void setName( )
{
    currentName = currentNameTextField.getText();
    newName     =     newNameTextField.getText();

    //make sure both are nonempty strings
    if ( currentName.equals("") || newName.equals("") ) {

        canceled = true;
    }
    else {
```

```
                    //input okay, so close
                    canceled = false;
            }
        }
```

Step 3 Test

We will modify the test program to verify the correctness of the Step 3 StudentNameDialog class. Here's the modified test program:

```
class TestStudentNameDialog
{
    public static void main (String args[])
    {
        MainWindow   topWindow = new MainWindow( );
        MessageBox   messageBox = new MessageBox(topWindow);

        StudentNameDialog testDialog
                        = StudentNameDialog( topWindow );
        topWindow.setVisible( true );
        testDialog.setVisible( true );

        if ( testDialog.isCanceled () )
            messageBox.show("Canceled");

        else {
            messageBox.show( testDialog.getCurrentName() );
            messageBox.show( testDialog.getNewName() );
        }
    }
}
```

We run the test program and do the following:

1. Click the CANCEL button without entering any value and verify that the message Canceled is displayed.

2. Enter values into TextField objects and click CANCEL. Verify that the message Canceled is displayed.

3. Enter values into one TextField object and click CHANGE. Verify that the entered values are displayed.

4. Click the CHANGE button without entering any value and verify that the message Canceled is displayed.

5. Enter values for both TextField objects and verify that the entered names are displayed correctly.

15.14 The TestScoreDialog **Class**

In this section, we will implement the TestScoreDialog class identified in Step 6. To implement this class, we repeat the process we employed in developing the StudentNameDialog class. Namely, we will implement this class using a separate development cycle with the design document already created in Step 6.

Problem Statement

> *Write a dialog that allows the user to enter test scores. Its visual appearance will be as shown in Figure 15.9. The class must support the three public methods listed in the design document from Section 15.9.*

Overall Plan

What will be the capabilities of the TestScoreDialog class? In Figure 15.9 we see a dialog for entering three test scores. Should the class we design here be capable of entering just three test scores or any number of test scores? Since the Student class can be modified to include any number of test scores, we will design the class to allow the editing of *N* test scores.

The StudentNameDialog class was designed as a subclass of JavaBookDialog. Should we do the same for TestScoreDialog? It is a possibility, but if we make it a subclass of JavaBookDialog, we need to add code to create a varying number of TextField objects, for instance. It is not difficult but time-consuming to work out all the details. Instead of doing that ourselves, is there any class for which we can make TestScoreDialog its subclass? How about the MultiInputBox class? Yes, this class from javabook has all the capabilities we need for TestScoreDialog.

We will reuse MultiInputBox to implement TestScoreDialog, but not with inheritance. We will use a technique called *code reuse by composition*. Instead of making TestScoreDialog a subclass of MultiInputBox, we will declare an instance variable that is a MultiInputBox object:

code reuse by composition

```
class TestScoreDialog
{
   ...
   private MultiInputBox   scoreBox;
   ...
```

Why do we do it this way? If we make TestScoreDialog a subclass of Multi-InputBox, then all methods of MultiInputBox will become available to the programmer who uses TestScoreDialog. If the programmer uses inherited methods in the wrong way, TestScoreDialog will not work correctly. What we want to do is to reuse the functionality of MultiInputBox but also protect the class from misuse by hiding the methods of MultiInputBox. We can do this by making MultiInputBox a part of the TestScoreDialog class.

Based on the design document from Section 15.9, the object diagram at this point is

We will implement the class in the following two steps:

development steps

1. Start with a class skeleton with the necessary data member declarations and constructors.

2. Implement the show and getTestScores methods.

Step 1 Development: Skeleton with Constructor

Step 1 Design   In Step 1 we identify the necessary data members and define a constructor. One data member will be a MultiInputBox object. We need another data member to keep track of input test scores. We will use an array of int for this purpose. We declare these objects as

```
private   MultiInputBox   scoreBox;

private   int[]           score;
```

The constructor will initialize these objects. What will be the size for the score array? This size is also the number we pass to scoreBox so the correct number of TextField objects appear on scoreBox. We will make the size an argument to the constructor. To create an instance of MultiInputBox, we need a Frame object; we will make it a second argument to the constructor. The constructor will look like this:

```
scoreBox = new MultiInputBox(owner, size);
                                      //owner is a Frame
score    = new int[size];
```

Chapter 15

```
//set the labels of scoreBox
//to Test 1, Test 2, and so forth
```

In order to make a dialog appear on the screen, we will write a temporary show method. It contains only one statement

```
scoreBox.getInputs();
```

Step 1 Code
The constructor of the TestScoreDialog class is defined as

```
public TestScoreDialog(Frame owner, int size)
{
    scoreBox = new MultiInputBox(owner, size);
    score    = new int[size];

    //set the labels of scoreBox
    String label[] = new String[size];

    for (int i = 0; i < size; i++) {
        label[i] = "Test  #" + (i+1);
    }
    scoreBox.setLabels(label);
}
```

and the temporary show method is defined as

```
public show( )
{
    scoreBox.getInputs();
}
```

Step 1 Test
As always, in order to test the skeleton TestScoreDialog class, we need to write a test main class. A simple main class such as the following would suffice:

```
import javabook.*;

/**
 * Program CheckTestScoreDialog
 *
 * A main class to test the StudentNameDialog class
 */
class CheckTestScoreDialog
{
    public static void main (String args[])
    {
        MainWindow       topWindow = new MainWindow();
        TestScoreDialog  testDialog
```

```
                        = TestScoreDialog( topWindow, 3 );
            topWindow.setVisible( true );
            testDialog.setVisible( true );
        }
    }
```

We run the program and verify that the constructor is executed correctly and the dialog has the correct number of GUI objects. We run the program again with different values of the size argument of the constructor.

Step 2 Development: Implement show **and** getTestScores

Step 2 Design

We will complete the development by finalizing the show method and defining the getTestScores method. A TestScoreDialog will allow the user to edit the current test scores of a student. This means the dialog must be able to accept the current test scores and display them. We will add one parameter to the show method to accept the test scores. This parameter will be a Student object. The values in this array will be passed to scoreBox using its setValue method. Then the show method calls the getInputs method of scoreBox. Finally, the elements in the array of String returned by getInputs are converted to float and assigned to the data member array score. Here's the logic of the method:

```
int value;
for (int i = 0; i < Student.NUM_OF_TESTS; i++ ) {
    value = student.getTestScore(i);       //student is a
    scoreBox.setValue( i, value );         //parameter
}

inputString = scoreBox.getInputs();

for (int i = 0; i < inputString.length; i++ ) {
    score[i] = Convert.toInt(inputString[i]);
}
```

The score array is set in the show method, so the getTestScores method only needs to return this score array

```
return score;
```

Step 2 Code

The final show method is defined as follows:

```
public void show( Student student )
{
    String inputString;
    int    value;
    for (int i = 0; i < Student.NUM_OF_TESTS; i++ ) {
        value = student.getTestScore(i);
```

Chapter 15

```
        scoreBox.setValue( i, value );
    }

    inputString = scoreBox.getInputs();

    for (int i = 0; i < inputString.length; i++ ) {
        score[i] = Convert.toFloat(inputString[i]);
    }
}
```

The **getTestScores** method is defined as

```
public int[] getTestScores( )
{
    return score;
}
```

Step 2 Test   We run the following modified CheckTestScoreDialog main class and verify that the values entered in the dialog are correctly displayed.

```
class CheckTestScoreDialog
{
    public static void main (String args[])
    {
        MainWindow     topWindow = new MainWindow();
        OutputBox      outputBox = new OutputBox(topWindow);
        TestScoreDialog  testDialog
                         = TestScoreDialog( topWindow, 3 );
        topWindow.setVisible( true );
        outputBox.setVisible( true );

        Student student = new Student( "Decaf Latte");
        student.setTestScore(1, 70);
        student.setTestScore(2, 80);
        student.setTestScore(3, 90);

        testDialog.show( student );
        score = testDialog.getTestScores( );

        for (int i = 0; i < score.length; i++ ) {
            outputBox.println("Test # " + i + ":   "
                             + score[i] );
        }
    }
}
```

We run the program again with different sizes and verify that the program
works for all cases.

15.15 Exercises

1. Improve the routine to get course information in the grade roster program. Instead of using an InputBox to input a course title and instructor name, define a new custom dialog class for this purpose.

2. Add import and export features to the grade roster program. Add the menu choices Import and Export to the program. Import data from and export data to a user-designated textfile. To simplify the process, use the same data format for both the import and export files.

3. Design a custom dialog for displaying information of a single student. The following is a suggested layout:

```
+-------------------------------------------+
|                                           |
+-------------------------------------------+
|                                           |
|   Name:              +-----------------+  |
|                      |                 |  |
|                      +-----------------+  |
|                                           |
|   Test Scores:    +------+------+------+   |
|                   |      |      |      |   |
|                   +------+------+------+   |
|                                           |
|   Final Grade:       +-----------------+  |
|                      |                 |  |
|                      +-----------------+  |
|                                           |
|                   (      OK      )        |
|                                           |
+-------------------------------------------+
```

4. Latte Gallery in Carmel, California, is a small gallery that specializes in selling contemporary fine art, especially lithographs and photographs. All items sold in the gallery are signed and numbered. Write an application that keeps track of:

   - Customers and their art purchases.
   - Artists and their works that have appeared in the gallery.
   - Current inventory.

   Allow the user to add, delete, or modify customer, artist, and artwork information. An inventory will include the purchase prices of the artwork and the selling price when sold. Give the user an option to list all customers or one customer. The user will specify the customer to display by entering the customer's last name and phone number.

Define at least four data members for each type of information. For customers, include the name, phone number, address, and artwork and artist preferences. For artists, include the name, speciality, whether alive or deceased, and price ranges of artwork. For artwork, include the title, date purchased, date sold, and artist. Feel free to add more data members as you see fit.

Design custom dialogs for entering and editing customers, artists, and artwork.

5. Improve the Latte Gallery Information Manager application by adding the following capabilities:

   - List all customers who bought artwork by a given artist.
   - List all artists who are still alive (so you can buy their artwork while the price is still reasonable).
   - List all artwork in the inventory that did not sell for over three months. (This requires the use of the Date class from the java.util package.)

6. Improve the Latte Gallery Information Manager application by adding a feature that allows the user to select a customer from the list of all customers by clicking on the customer he or she wants to see. The listing of all customers will include their names. When the user clicks on a name, a dialog displaying the full information of the selected customer will appear on the screen. Consider using a ListBox from javabook to list the names of all customers. For an improved user interface, consider defining a custom dialog using the List class from java.awt.

7. Write a program that plays the game of Fermi. The program generates three distinct random digits between 0 and 9. These digits are assigned to Positions 1, 2, and 3. The goal of the game is for the player to guess the digits in three positions correctly in the least number of tries. For each guess, the player provides three digits for Positions 1, 2, and 3. The program replies with a hint consisting of Fermi, Pico, or Nano. If the digit guessed for a given position is correct, then the reply is Fermi. If the digit guessed for a given position is in a different position, the reply is Pico. If the digit guessed for a given position does not match any of the three digits, then the reply is Nano.

Here are sample replies for the three secret digits 6, 5, and 8 at Positions 1, 2, and 3, respectively:

Guess	Hint	Explanation
1 2 5	Nano Nano Pico	5 matches but at the wrong position.
8 5 3	Pico Fermi Nano	5 matches at the correct position. 8 matches but at the wrong position.
5 8 6	Pico Pico Pico	All match at the wrong positions.

Notice that if the hints like the above are given, the player can tell which number did not match. For example, given the hint for the second guess, we can tell that 3 is not one of the secret numbers. To avoid this, provide hints in a random order or in alphabetical order (e.g., it will be Fermi Nano Pico instead of Pico Fermi Nano for the second reply). Design the program so that it can easily be run as an applet or an application.

8. Extend the Fermi playing program by allowing the player to

- Select the number of secret digits.
- Select alphabets instead of digits.
- Include duplicate secret digits.

9. Write a personal scheduler application. Each entry in the scheduler is either an appointment, a to-do item, or a memo. Each entry has the date and the time it is entered. An entry can be locked, and if locked, the user cannot modify it. For an appointment entry, include the person and the place of meeting. For a to-do entry, include a short description of a task and the due date. For a memo, include a text. Design a custom dialog for each type of entry. Consider using GUI components, such as Checkbox, Choice, and TextArea from java.awt. Use the Date class to record the date and the time of an entry.

10. Write a rental point tracking system for an up-and-coming Espresso's Dynamo Mopeds in Monterey, California. To compete against Ms. Latte's Moped R Us, Espresso's Dynamo Mopeds decided to install an automated points tracking system. When a customer first rents a moped, his or her information is entered into a database. For each rental, a customer receives points, and when the total points reach 100, the customer can rent a moped free for

Chapter 15

three hours or redeem a free movie rental coupon from Espresso's Majestic Movies. The points are earned in the following scheme:

Renter	Type	Points
College Student	50cc Moppi	15
	150cc Magnum	20
Adult	50cc Moppi	10
	150cc Magnum	15
Senior	50cc Moppi	20
	150cc Magnum	30

In addition to the basic operations of updating the point information for every rental, include an operation to list all customers who earned over 100 points. Also, support an operation to edit the customer information.

11. Update the rental point tracking system to support a new rental system and point awarding rules for Espresso's Dynamo Mopeds. Now the customers can rent only on an hourly basis and the points are awarded accordingly. Upon rental, the customer will state the number of hours he or she will rent in increments of one hour with a maximum of 10 hours. The rental fee is based on the following formula:

Renter	Type	Total Rental ≤ 5 hours	Total Rental > 5 hours
College Student	50cc Moppi	$3.50 per hour	$2.50 per hour
	150cc Magnum	$4.50 per hour	$3.50 per hour
Adult	50cc Moppi	$5.00 per hour	$4.00 per hour
	150cc Magnum	$6.50 per hour	$5.00 per hour
Senior	50cc Moppi	$4.00 per hour	$3.00 per hour
	150cc Magnum	$5.25 per hour	$4.00 per hour

The point-awarding rule is as follows:

Renter	Type	Points
College Student	50cc Moppi	5 points for each hour
	150cc Magnum	7 points for each hour
Adult	50cc Moppi	3 points for each hour
	150cc Magnum	5 points for each hour
Senior	50cc Moppi	4 points for each hour
	150cc Magnum	6 points for each hour

At the time of rental, record the time it is rented out and the number of hours to be rented. Upon the return, record the time, and if it is overdue, double the charge and give no award points. Keep track of the late returns, and if the customer fails to return on time for three times, he or she will not be allowed to rent.

16

Recursive Algorithms

OBJECTIVES

After you have read and studied this chapter, you should be able to

- Write recursive algorithms for mathematical functions and non-numerical operations.

- Decide when to use recursion and when not to.

- Describe the recursive quicksort algorithm and explain how its performance is better than selection and bubble sort algorithms.

Introduction

We introduced recursion in Chapter 7 and showed how to write recursive methods to implement mathematical functions. We used mathematical functions in Chapter 7 because it is easier to see how the recursion works with mathematical functions. However, recursive methods are not limited to implementing mathematical functions, and we will present several nonnumerical recursive algorithms in this chapter. We will also discuss some criteria for deciding when to use recursion and when not to. All the recursive algorithms we provide in this chapter, other than those we use for explanation, are algorithms that should be written recursively.

16.1   Basic Elements of Recursion

A *recursive method* is a method that contains a statement (or statements) that makes a call to itself. In Chapter 7, we implemented three mathematical functions using recursion. In this chapter, we will present recursive algorithms for nonnumerical operations. But before we introduce new examples, let's review one of the recursive algorithms we presented in Chapter 7.

The *factorial* of N is the product of the first N positive integers, denoted mathematically as

```
N! = N * (N-1) * (N-2) * ··· * 2 * 1
```

We can define the factorial of N recursively as

$$
\text{factorial(N)} = \begin{cases} 1 & \text{if N = 1} \\ \\ \text{N * factorial(N-1)} & \text{otherwise} \end{cases}
$$

We mentioned in Chapter 7 that any recursive method will include the following three basic elements:

1. A test to stop or continue the recursion.

2. An end case that terminates the recursion.

3. A recursive call(s) that continues the recursion.

These three elements are included in the following recursive factorial method as shown:

```
public int factorial(int N)
{
    if (N == 1) {

        return 1;
    }
    else {

        return N * factorial(N-1);
    }
}
```

Test to stop or continue.

End case: recursion stops

Recursive case: recursion continues with a recursive call.

16.2 Directory Listing

Let's try some recursive algorithms for nonnumerical applications. A first non-numerical recursive algorithm will list the filename of all files in a given directory (or folder) of a hard disk and its subdirectories. We will use a File object from the java.io package to implement the method. Assuming a Windows 9x platform, we create a File object by passing the name of a file or a directory as in

```
File file = new File("D:\\Java\\Projects");
```

Notice that we pass the full pathname. If a File object represents a directory, then the boolean method isDirectory returns true. To get an array of names of files and subdirectories in a directory, we use the list method

```
String[] fileList = file.list();
```

Let's call the method directoryListing. The argument to the method will be a File object that represents a directory. The basic idea can be expressed as follows:

```
public void directoryListing( File dir )
{
    //assumption: dir represents a directory

    fileList = an array of names of files and
               subdirectories in the directory dir;
```

```
            for (each element in fileList) {

                if (an element is a file) {
                    output the element's filename;  //end case: it's
                                                    //a file.
                }
                else { //recursive case: it's a directory
                    call directoryListing with element as
                    an argument;
                }
            }
        }
```

The complete method is as follows:

```
public void directoryListing( File dir )
{
    //assumption: dir represents a directory

    String[] fileList = dir.list();  //get the contents
    String  dirPath = dir.getAbsolutePath();

    for (int i = 0; i < fileList.length; i++) {

        File file = new File( dirPath + "\\" + fileList[i] );

        if ( file.isFile() ) {    //it's a file

            System.out.println( file.getName() );
        }
        else {

            directoryListing( file ); //it's a directory
        }                            //so recurse
    }
}
```

Test → `if ( file.isFile() ) {    //it's a file`

End case → `System.out.println( file.getName() );`

Recursive case → `directoryListing( file ); //it's a directory`

Notice the argument we pass to create a new File object inside the for loop is

```
File file = new File( dirPath + "\\" + fileList[i] );
```

where dirPath is set as

```
String dirPath   = dir.getAbsolutePath();
```

The getAbsolutePath method returns the full pathname for the directory and we need to prepend it to the name (fileList[i]) of a file or a subdirectory in this directory in order to make the testing

```
if ( file.isFile() ) ...
```

work correctly.

To give you more practice in reading recursive methods, we will remove the assumption that the argument File represents a directory and rewrite the method. If the argument File object to directoryListing can be either a file or a directory, then we need to check this first. If the argument object is a file, then we list its filename and stop the recursion. If the argument object is a directory, then we get the list of contents in the directory and make recursive calls. Here's the second version:

```
public void directoryListing( File file )
{
    //'file' may be a directory or a file

    String[] fileList;
    String   pathname = file.getAbsolutePath();

    if ( file.isFile() ) {
                                    //it's a file so
        System.out.println( file.getName() ); //print it out

    }
    else { //it's a directory, so recurse

        fileList = file.list();
        for (int i = 0; i < fileList.length; i++) {
            File file = new File(pathname+ "\\" +fileList[i]);
            directoryListing( file )); //recursive call
        }
    }
}
```

Test →

End case

Recursive case →

16.3 Anagram

anagram

Our second example of a nonnumerical recursive method is deriving all anagrams of a given word. An *anagram* is a word or phrase formed by reordering the letters of another word or phrase. If the word is CAT, for example, then its anagrams are:

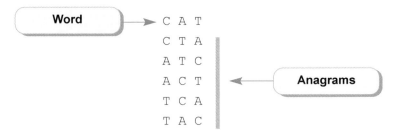

Figure 16.1 illustrates the basic idea of using recursion to list all anagrams of a word.

FIGURE 16.1   How to generate all the anagrams of a word using recursion.

Find all anagrams of a word   **H   A   L   O**

Expressing the basic idea in pseudocode, we have something like this:

```
public void anagram( String word )
{
    int numOfChars = word.length();

    if (numOfChars == 1) {
        //End case: there's only one character left,
        //              so we can't recurse anymore
    }
    else {
        for (int i = 1; i <= numOfChars; i++ ) {

            char firstLetter = word.charAt(0);

            suffix = word.substring(1, numOfChars);

            anagram( suffix );   //recurse with the remaining
                                 //letters in the word
            //rotate left
            word = suffix + firstLetter;
        }
    }
}
```

This **for** loop is illustrated in Figure 16.1.

To derive the real method that executes correctly, we must finalize a number of things. First, what will we do when the recursion stops? Hitting upon the end case means that we have found one anagram, so we will print it out. Now, this is the tricky part. When we call the method recursively, we are passing a word that has the first letter chopped off. This means the words being passed to successive recursive calls are getting shorter and shorter. But we need to access all letters in a word to print it out. We can resolve this problem by passing two parameters: the prefix and the suffix of a word. In each successive call, the prefix becomes one letter more and the suffix becomes one letter less. When the suffix becomes one letter only, then the recursion stops. Using this idea, the method now looks like this:

```
public void anagram( String prefix, String suffix )
{
    int numOfChars = suffix.length();

    if (numOfChars == 1) {
        //End case: print out one anagram
        outputBox.printLine( prefix + suffix );
    }
    else {
```

Chapter 16

```
                . . .
        }
    }
```

and this method is initially set with an empty prefix and the word being the suffix, as in

```
anagram( "", "HALO" );
```

Now, using the two parameters prefix and suffix, the for loop is written as

```
for (int i = 1; i <=numOfChars; i++ ) {

    newSuffix = suffix.substring(1, numOfChars);
    newPrefix = prefix + suffix.charAt(0);

    anagram( newPrefix, newSuffix ); //recursive case

    //rotate left to create a rearranged suffix
    suffix = newSuffix + suffix.charAt(0);
}
```

Putting everything together, we have the final anagram method:

```
public void anagram( String prefix, String suffix )
{
    String newPrefix, newSuffix;
    int numOfChars = suffix.length();
```

Test →
```
    if (numOfChars == 1) {
        //End case: print out one anagram
        outputBox.printLine( prefix + suffix );
    }
    else {
```
End case
```
        for (int i = 1; i <= numOfChars; i++ ) {
            newSuffix = suffix.substring(1, numOfChars);
            newPrefix = prefix + suffix.charAt(0);
```
Recursive case →
```
            anagram( newPrefix, newSuffix );
                                    //recursive call

            //rotate left to create a rearranged suffix
            suffix = newSuffix + suffix.charAt(0);
        }
    }
}
```

Because the ending condition for recursion is tricky, let's study carefully the test to stop the recursion. We set the test to

```
if (numOfChars == 1 ) ...
```

Is there any assumption we must make to the parameters to make this method work correctly? We mentioned earlier that the initial call to the recursive method is something like

```
anagram( "", "HALO" );
```

What would happen if we make the call initially like

```
String str = inputBox.getString();
anagram( "", str );
```

and the user enters an empty string? This is left as an exercise.

Quick Check

1. Determine the output of the following calls without actually running the method:

   ```
   a. anagram( "", "DOG" );
   b. anagram( "", "CAFE");
   ```

16.4 Towers of Hanoi

The objective of a puzzle called *Towers of Hanoi* is deceptively simple, but finding a solution is another matter. The goal of the puzzle is to move *N* disks from Peg 1 to Peg 3 by moving one disk at a time and never placing a larger disk on top of a smaller disk. See Figure 16.2.

The Towers of Hanoi puzzle can be solved very nicely using recursion. The Aha! moment to this puzzle is when you realize that you can solve the puzzle if somehow you can move the top *N*–1 disks to Peg 2. After the top *N*–1 disks are moved to Peg 2 temporarily, you move the largest disk from Peg 1 to Peg 3, and finally move the *N*–1 disks from Peg 2 to Peg 3. Figure 16.3 illustrates these three steps. The first and the third steps are of course the same puzzle with one fewer disk and the destination peg changed. So you apply the same logic recursively to the first and third steps. When the number of disks becomes one, then

FIGURE 16.2   Towers of Hanoi with *N* = 4 disks.

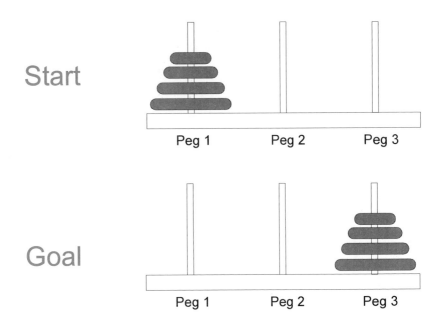

the recursion stops. Applying this recursive thinking, we can write the method as

```
public void towersOfHanoi( int N,        //number of disks
                           int from,     //origin peg
                           int to,       //destination peg
                           int spare )   //"middle" peg
{
    if ( N == 1 )
        moveOne( from, to );
    else {
        towersOfHanoi( N-1, from, spare, to );

        moveOne( from, to );

        towersOfHanoi( N-1, spare, to, from );
    }
}
```

The moveOne is the method that actually moves the disk. Here we will define the method to print out the move using an outputBox:

FIGURE 16.3   Recursive solution to the Towers of Hanoi puzzle.

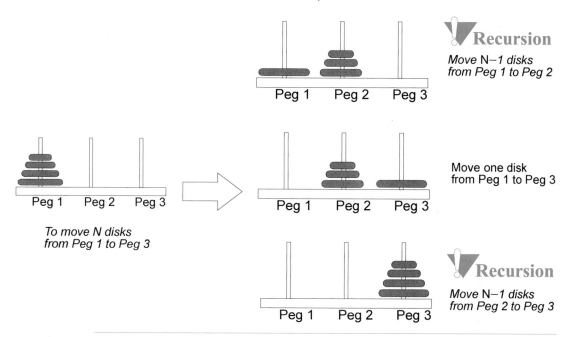

```
private void moveOne( int from, int to )
{
    outputBox.printLine( from + " ---> " + to );
}
```

When we run this method with $N = 4$, we get the following output:

```
1 ---> 2
1 ---> 3
2 ---> 3
1 ---> 2
3 ---> 1
3 ---> 2
1 ---> 2
1 ---> 3
2 ---> 3
2 ---> 1
3 ---> 1
2 ---> 3
1 ---> 2
1 ---> 3
2 ---> 3
```

The output is very difficult to read. We can improve the output considerably by padding a varying number of blank spaces to show the level of recursion. We can change the output to

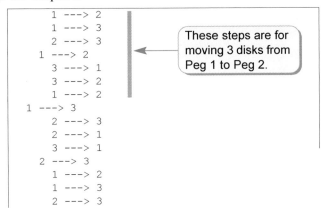

by rewriting the methods as

```
public void towersOfHanoi ( int N,        //number of disks
                            int from,     //origin peg
                            int to,       //destination peg
                            int spare,    //"middle" peg
                            int indent )  //# of leading spaces
{
    if ( N == 1 )
        moveOne ( from, to, indent );

    else {
        towersOfHanoi ( N-1, from, spare, to, indent+2 );

        moveOne ( from, to, indent+2 );

        towersOfHanoi ( N-1, spare, to, from, indent+2 );
    }
}

private void moveOne ( int from, int to, int indent )
{
    outputBox.printLine ( Format.rightAlign(indent," ") +
                      from + " ---> " + to );
}
```

16.5 Quicksort

We will present a third sorting algorithm that uses recursion in this section. This sorting algorithm is called *quicksort*, and we will compare the performance of quicksort against the previous two sorting algorithms at the end of this section to verify that quicksort deserves its name.

Figure 16.4 illustrates the core thinking of quicksort. To sort an array from index low to high, we first select a pivot element p. We can select any element in the array as a pivot, but for simplicity, we choose number[low] as the pivot. Using p as the pivot, we scan through the array and move all elements smaller than p to the lower half (left half in the figure) and all elements larger than p to the upper half. Then we sort the lower and upper halves recursively using quicksort. The variable mid points to the position where the pivot is placed. So the lower half of the array is from index low to mid-1 and the upper half of the array is from index mid+1 to high. The recursion stops when the condition low >= high becomes true.

FIGURE 16.4   The core idea of the quicksort algorithm.

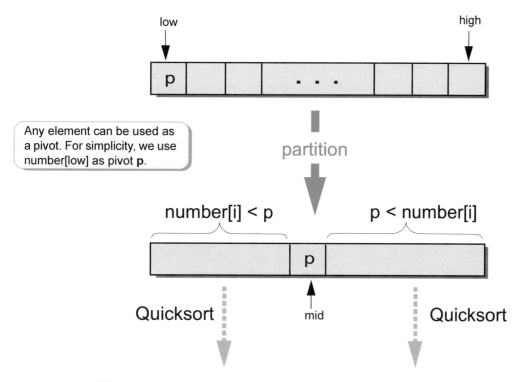

Here's the quicksort algorithm:

```
public void quickSort( int[] number, int low, int high )
{
    if ( low < high ) {

        int mid = partition( number, low, high );

        quickSort( number,    low, mid-1 );
        quickSort( number, mid+1, high  );
    }
}
```

The partition method splits the array elements number[low] to number[high] into two halves as shown in Figure 16.4. We use number[low] as the pivot element. The method returns the position where the pivot element is placed. Figure 16.5 shows the result of partitioning the array using the element 23 as a pivot.

FIGURE 16.5   Result of partitioning using 23 as a pivot.

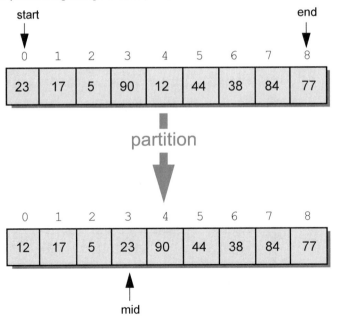

We first set the pivot to number[low]. Then we start looking for a number smaller than the pivot from position high, high-1, and so forth. Let's say the number is found at position J. Since this number is smaller than the pivot, we move it to position low. Now we start looking for a number larger than the pivot from low+1, low+2, and so forth. Let's say the number is found at position I. We move it to position J. We then repeat the process, this time looking for a number smaller than the pivot from J-1, J-2, and so forth. Figure 16.6 shows the details of the partitioning process.

Here's the partition method:

```
private void partition( int[] number, int start, int end )
{
    //set the pivot
    int pivot = number[start];

    do {
        //look for a number smaller than pivot from the end
        while ( start < end && number[end] >= pivot)
            end--;

        if ( start < end ) { //found a smaller number
            number[start] = number[end];

            //now find a number larger than pivot
            //from the start
            while ( start < end && number[start] <= pivot)
                start++;

            if (start < end) { //found a larger number
                number[end] = number[start];
        }

    } while ( start < end );

    //done, move the pivot back to the array
    number[start] = pivot;
}
```

We can avoid the nested if statement in the partition method using the break statement. We have used the break statement only with the switch statement, but we can actually use it with any loop statements. If we place a break statement inside a loop, the loop is terminated immediately when the break statement is executed. Using the break statement, we can rewrite the partition method as

```
//Second version using the break statement inside the loop
private void partition( int[] number, int start, int end )
{
    //set the pivot
    int pivot = number[start];
```

FIGURE 16.6   Details of one partitioning.

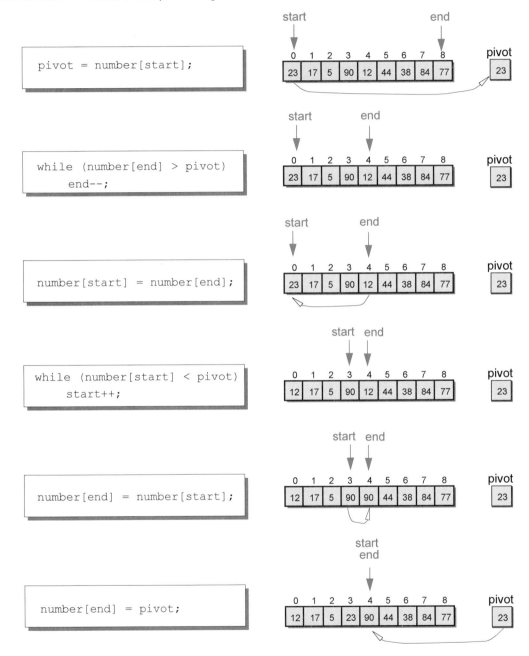

```
do {
    //look for a number smaller than pivot from the end
    while ( start < end && number[end] >= pivot)
        end--;

    if ( start = end ) break; //stop the repetition

    //move a smaller number to the lower half
    number[start] = number[end];

    //now find a number larger than pivot from the start
    while ( start < end && number[start] <= pivot)
        start++;

        if (start = end) break; //stop the repetition

        //move a larger number to the upper half
        number[end] = number[start];
    }

} while ( start < end );

//done, move the pivot back to the array
number[start] = pivot;
}
```

How good is quicksort? Does the algorithm execute a fewer number of comparisons than the selection or bubble sort? The answer is no in the worst case. Quicksort executes roughly the same number of comparisons as the selection sort and bubble sort in the worst case. When the original list is either already sorted or in descending order, then after a partition process, either the lower half or the upper half has $N-1$ elements. The effect is the same as the previous two sorting algorithms, that is, either the smallest or the largest number moves to its correct position. The worst situation can be improved somewhat if we select the median of three numbers, say, number[low], number[high], and number[(low+high)/2], as the pivot element. Even with this improvement, the number of comparisons in the worst case is still approximately the square of the size of the array.

Is the name quicksort a kind of false advertisement? Not really. On the average, we can expect a partition process to split the array into two subarrays of roughly equal size. Figure 16.7 shows how the original array is partitioned into smaller subarrays. When the size of all subarrays becomes 1, then the array becomes sorted. At level i, there are 2^i subarrays of size $N/2^i$. So there will be $N/2^i$ partition processes at level i. The total number of comparisons of all those partition processes at level i is therefore $2^i * N/2^i = N$. Since there are K levels, the total number of comparisons for sorting the whole array is

$$K \cdot N$$

but

$$N = 2^K$$

$$\log_2 N = K$$

so

$$K \cdot N = N\log_2 N$$

The total number of comparisons is proportional to $N\log_2 N$, which is a great improvement over N^2. A more rigorous mathematical analysis will show that the quicksort on the average requires approximately $2N\log_2 N$ comparisons.

FIGURE 16.7   A hierarchy of partitioning an array into smaller and smaller arrays in the quicksort.

Level No.		Number of subarrays at Level i	Size of each subarray at Level i
0		$1 = 2^0$	$N = N/2^0$
1		$2 = 2^1$	$N/2 = N/2^1$
2		$4 = 2^4$	$N/4 = N/2^2$
⋮		⋮	⋮
K		N	$1 = N/2^K$

Quick Check

1. Partition the following arrays using the partition method:

a.

0	1	2	3	4	5	6	7	8
18	19	5	77	12	14	13	84	45

b.

0	1	2	3	4	5	6	7	8
98	19	15	86	12	44	13	24	45

16.6 When Not to Use Recursion

Recursion is a powerful tool to express complex algorithms succinctly. For example, writing a nonrecursive algorithm for the Tower of Hanoi is unexpectedly difficult. Likewise, a recursive quicksort algorithm is easier to understand than its nonrecursive counterpart. For both problems, we prefer recursive algorithms because recursion is the most natural way to express their solution. However, just being natural is not the criterion for selecting a recursive solution over a nonrecursive one.

Consider a solution for computing the Nth Fibonacci number. A Fibonacci number is defined recursively as

$$
\text{fibonacci}(N) \;=\;
\begin{cases}
1 & \text{if } N = 0 \\
 & \text{or } N = 1 \\[1em]
\text{fibonacci}(N\text{-}1) & \\
\quad + \text{ fibonacci}(N\text{-}2) & \text{otherwise}
\end{cases}
$$

Because the function is defined recursively, it is natural to implement the function using a recursive method as the following:

```
public int fibonacci( int N )
{
    if (N == 0 || N == 1) {

        return 1;              //end case

    }
    else { //recursive case

        return fibonacci(N-1) + fibonacci(N-2);

    }
}
```

This recursive method is succinct, easy to understand, and elegant. But is this the way to implement it? The answer is no, because the recursive method is grossly inefficient and a nonrecursive version is just as easy to understand. The method is inefficient because the same value is computed over and over.

Chapter 16

Figure 16.8 shows the recursive calls for computing the fifth Fibonacci number. Notice that the same value, for example, fibonacci(2) is computed repeatedly.

FIGURE 16.8   Recursive calls to compute **fibonacci(5)**.

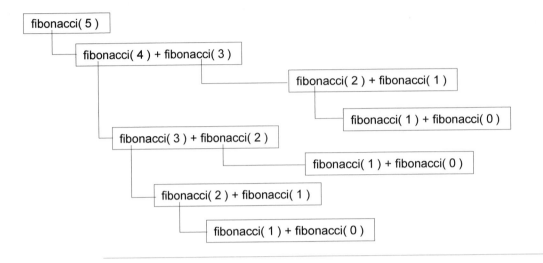

The *N*th Fibonacci number can be computed using a nonrecursive method as

```
public int fibonacci( int N )
{
    int fibN, fibN1, fibN2, cnt;

    if (N == 0 or N == 1 ) {
        return 1;
    }
    else {

        fibN1 = fibN2 = 1;
        cnt = 2;

        while ( cnt <= N ) {
            fibN = fibN1 + fibN2; //get the next Fib no.

            fibN1 = fibN2;
            fibN2 = fibN;

            cnt ++;
        }
        return fibN;
    }
}
```

The nonrecursive method is not as succinct as the recursive version, but at the same time, it is not that difficult to understand either. The nonrecursive version is much more efficient, and it is the one that should be used.

There is no clearcut rule to determine whether a routine should be implemented recursively or nonrecursively. In general, we should always search for a nonrecursive solution first. We should use recursion only when a recursive solution is more natural and easier to understand and the resulting method is not too inefficient. We repeat the guideline for using recursive methods we mentioned in Section 7.10.

> ### Use recursion if
>
> 1. **A recursive solution is natural and easy to understand.**
> 2. **A recursive solution does not result in excessive duplicate computation.**
> 3. **The equivalent iterative solution is too complex.**

16.7 Exercises

1. Write a recursive method to find the smallest element in an array. Note: This is strictly an exercise. You should not write the real method recursively.

2. Write a recursive method to compute the average of the elements in an array. Note: This is strictly an exercise. You should not write the real method recursively.

3. Write a recursive method to determine whether a given string is a palindrome or not. A string is a palindrome if it reads the same forward and backward. Ignore the case of the letters and punctuation marks.

4. Write a recursive binary search method. Should this method be written recursively or nonrecursively in practice?

5. Write a recursive method to compute the greatest common divisor of two integer values. The greatest common divisor (GCD) of two integers is derived by using the following rules:

$$GCD(i, j) = \begin{cases} i & \text{if } j = 0 \\ GCD(j, i \bmod j) & \text{if } j \mathrel{!=} 0 \end{cases}$$

6. Write a nonrecursive version of GCD in exercise 5 and compare the two solutions. Which version is the one you should use in practice?

7. The partition method of the quicksort selects the first element as its pivot. Improve the method by using the median of the values in the first, the middle, and the last element of an array. If an array number to partition has 8 elements indexed from 0 to 7, then the first element is number[0], the middle element is number[4], and the last element is number[7]. If these elements are 55, 34, and 89, for example, then the median is 55.

8. What would happen if the anagram method is called initially by passing an empty string as the second parameter:

```
anagram( "", "" );
```

Will the method work? Why or why not? If not, correct the problem. If yes, then would it be logical to leave it as is or should the method be corrected to make it more logical?

9. Another recursive sorting algorithm is called *merge sort*. The merge sort divides the array into two halves, sorts the two halves recursively using mergesort, and finally merges the two sorted halves into a sorted list. In diagram, the process of merge sort looks like this:

Write the mergesort method.

The javabook *Package*

We document the javabook classes in this appendix. You can get information on the standard Java packages from a number of sources. If you use commercial Java compilers from Borland, Microsoft, Symantec, and others, you can access desired information from their help menu. You can also access the online documentation from the website at http://developer.java.sun.com/developer/infodocs/index.shtml. Reference books on the standard Java packages such as P. Chan and R. Lee, *The Java Class Libraries, Vols. 1* and *2*, 2nd ed. (Reading, MA: Addison-Wesley, 1998), and D. Flanagan, *Java in a Nutshell: A Desktop Quick Reference*, (Sebastapol, CA: O'Reilly & Associates, Inc., 1999) are good sources of information. If you are interested in the official language specification of Java, you should get a copy of J. Gosling, B. Joy, and G. Steele, *The Java Language Specification*, (Reading, MA: Addison-Wesley, 1996).

Documentation provided in this appendix is intended for the users of the package. As such, only the public methods and constants are included (in case of JavaBookDialog, the protected method is included also). The online javadoc documentation is also available from our websites at http://www.mhhe.com/wu2 and http://www.drcaffeine.com. We plan to update the javabook package periodically, so please visit our websites occasionally. Since www.drcaffeine.com is under the author's full control, this site will be updated more frequently. Also, if you notice any discrepancy between the information provided in this appendix and the software, please visit our websites to get the most up-to-date information.

PACKAGE:	javabook
Class	**Description**
Clock	This class supports some basic clock functions such as reading the current time, getting today's date, and providing stopwatch functions. This class also provides a convenient function to pause the program execution.
Convert	The class provides methods for converting a value of one data type to another data type.
DrawingBoard	A frame window that is capable of drawing lines, circles, and rectangles.
Format	The class provides methods for formatting integers, real numbers, and strings.
InputBox	A dialog for getting an input value from the user. An InputBox object can be used to accept integers, real numbers, and strings.
JavaBookDialog	An abstract superclass that encapsulates behavior common to all dialogs in this package: InputBox, ListBox, MessageBox, MultiInputBox, OutputBox, and ResponseBox.
ListBox	A dialog for displaying a list of choices and allowing the user to select a choice in the list.
MainWindow	A frame window that serves as the main window of an application. A MainWindow object is almost as big as the screen and is displayed at the center of the screen.
MessageBox	A dialog for displaying a single line of text. A MessageBox object is intended for displaying a short warning or error message.
MultiInputBox	A dialog for getting multiple input values from the user. A MultiInputBox object can be used to accept N string values.
OutputBox	A dialog for displaying multiple lines of text.
ResponseBox	A dialog for getting a yes or no answer from the user.
SimpleInput	This class supports a simple input routine for non-GUI programs. The functionality of this class is equivalent to InputBox.
SketchPad	A frame window that allows the user to draw freeform lines using a mouse.

For each class description, we include

- The purpose of the class.
- The page and section number where the class is introduced.
- The ancestors of the class. If the superclass is also in the java-book package, then only this superclass is shown.
- The public constants of the class.
- The public methods of the class.

Class:	javabook.Clock

Purpose: This class supports some basic clock functions such as reading the current time, getting today's date, and providing stopwatch functions. This class also provides a convenient function to pause the program execution.

Introduced in: Not used in the main text. This class can be useful in some of the chapter exercises.

Hierarchy:

Public constants:
```
LONG_FORMAT

SHORT_FORMAT

TIME_12_FORMAT

TIME_24_FORMAT
```

Public methods:
```
Clock
getCurrentDate
getCurrentTime
getElapsedTime
getTotalElapsedTime
pause
reset
start
stop
```

```
public Clock    (       )
```
Creates a new Clock object.

```
public String    getCurrentDate    (                    )
public String    getCurrentDate    ( int format         )
```

The first version returns the current (today's) date in the mm/dd/yy format (short format). The second version returns the current date in either short or long format. The long format spells out the name.

```
public String    getCurrentTime    (                    )
public String    getCurrentTime    ( int format         )
```

The first version returns the current time in the 12-hr format. The second version returns the current time in either the 12-hr or 24-hr format. The 12-hr format includes the AM/PM designation.

```
public String    getElapsedTime    (                    )
```

Returns the elapsed time of the stopwatch function. The elapsed time is the time interval between the most recent start and stop. If the stopwatch is still running, then this method returns the elapsed time from the most recent call to the start method until this method is called. The unit for the elapsed time is in seconds.

```
public String    getTotalElapsedTime(                   )
```

Returns the total elapsed time of the stopwatch function. The total elapsed time is the time interval between the first start and the last stop. If the stopwatch is still running, then this method returns the elapsed time from the first time the stopwatch is started until the time this method is called. The stopwatch will keep on running. The unit for the elapsed time is in seconds.

```
public double    pause    ( double   duration   )
```

Pauses the program execution. If the clock is running, then the timer keeps on counting while the program execution is paused. If the clock is not running, then this method simply pauses the program execution.

```
public void    reset    (                    )
```

Resets the stopwatch to its initial state.

```
public void    start    (                    )
```

Starts the stopwatch. If the stopwatch is already running, then this method is ignored.

```
public void      stop        (                    )
```
Stops the stopwatch. If the stopwatch is not running, then this method is
ignored.

Class:	javabook.Convert

Purpose: This class provides methods for converting a data value of one
data type to another data type. This class is noninstantiable; all
the methods are class methods.

Introduced in: Section 9.4, page 439.

Hierarchy:

Public constants: None

Public methods:
```
toBoolean
toChar
toDouble
toFloat
toInt
toLong
toString
```

```
public static boolean  toBoolean ( String str )
```
Converts the argument str to a boolean.

```
public static char      toChar     ( String str )
```
Converts the argument str to a char.

```
public static double    toDouble  ( String str )
```
Converts the argument str to a double.

```
public static float     toFloat    ( String str )
```

Converts the argument str to a float.

```
public static int      toInt      ( String str )
```
Converts the argument str to an int.

```
public static long     toLong     ( String str     )
```
Converts the argument str to a long.

```
public static String   toString   ( boolean bool  )
public static String   toString   ( char    ch    )
public static String   toString   ( double  number )
public static String   toString   ( float   number )
public static String   toString   ( int     number )
public static String   toString   ( long    number )
```
Converts the argument to a String.

Class: javabook.DrawingBoard

Purpose: This class is used in the sample program from Chapter 6. A DrawingBoard object supports methods for drawing circles, lines, and rectangles.

Introduced in: Section 6.6, page 259.

Hierarchy:

Public constants: None

Public methods: ```
DrawingBoard
drawCircle
drawLine
drawRectangle
setColor
show
```

```
public DrawingBoard ( )
public DrawingBoard (String title)
```
A DrawingBoard object with the default title DRAWING BOARD is created. The window is not resizable and the background color is set to white.

```
public void drawCircle   (int x, int y, int r)
```
Draws a circle with radius r and whose center point is (x, y).

```
public void drawLine   (int x1, int y1, int x2, int y2)
```
Draws a line from point (x1, y1) to (x2, y2).

```
public void drawRectangle (int x, int y, int w, int h)
public void drawRectangle (Rectangle rect)
```
The first version draws a rectangle with width w, height h, and its top-left corner at position (x, y). The second version draws a rectangle with the dimension set by the Rectangle object rect.

```
public void setVisible (boolean state)
```
Overrides the superclass's setVisible to initialize the data member Graphics object so the drawing works correctly.

**See also:**     java.awt.Rectangle
Explanation of the coordinate system for the drawing is given in Section 2.6 and Section 12.1.

Appendix A
```

Class:	javabook.Format

Purpose: This class provides methods for formatting a value in a field of a given length. Three possible alignments are left, center, and right. The alignment is done by converting a value to a String with a given length and placing the value at the beginning, the middle, or the end of the String. This class is noninstantiable; all the methods are class methods.

Introduced in: Section 7.7, page 316.

Hierarchy:

Public constants: None

Public methods: centerAlign
                        leftAlign
                        rightAlign

```
public String centerAlign( int width, int decimalPlaces, double num )
public String centerAlign( int width, long   num     )
public String centerAlign( int width, String str     )
```

Returns a String that has width characters in it. The value num or str is positioned at the center of the resulting String. For the first version, the resulting String will have a decimal point and the designated number of decimal places. If the given value cannot fit into the width characters, the value converted to a String without any alignment is returned.

```
public String leftAlign ( int width, int decimalPlaces, double num )
public String leftAlign ( int width, long   num     )
public String leftAlign ( int width, String str     )
```

The same functionality as centerAlign but with the left alignment.

```
public String rightAlign ( int width, int decimalPlaces, double num )
public String rightAlign ( int width, long   num     )
public String rightAlign ( int width, String str     )
```

The same functionality as centerAlign but with the right alignment.

Class:	javabook.InputBox

Purpose: A dialog that allows the user to enter a value. An InputBox object can accept both numerical and textual values. The user cannot close the dialog until he/she enters a valid value of the designated data type.

Introduced in: Section 3.5, page 103.

Hierarchy:

Public constants: None

Public methods:
```
InputBox
getInteger
getFloat
getString
```

Appendix A

```
public InputBox ( Frame owner )
public InputBox ( Frame owner, String title)
```

Creates an InputBox object with owner as its controlling Frame object. In the second version, the title of a dialog is set to the String passed as the second argument.

```
public double getDouble (                  )
public double getDouble ( String prompt )
```

The method returns the value entered by the user as double. This method does not complete until the user enters a valid value. For the first version, the prompt is set to a default word Enter a double:. In the second version, the prompt is set to the passed String argument.

```
public int    getInteger (                     )
public int    getInteger ( String prompt )
```

The same behavior as the getDouble methods. The getInteger methods return an int instead.

```
public float getFloat   (                     )
public float getFloat   ( String prompt )
```

The same behavior as the getDouble methods. The getFloat methods return a float instead.

```
public String getString (                     )
public String getString ( String prompt )
```

The same behavior as the getDouble methods. The getString methods return a String instead.

Class: javabook.JavaBookDialog

Purpose: An abstract class that encapsulates behavior common to the other dialogs in this package. Create a subclass of JavaBook-Dialog if you want your dialog to include the common behavior of placing the dialog at the center of the screen. A subclass of JavaBookDialog must implement the abstract method adjustSize.

Introduced in: Section 15.13, page 776.

Hierarchy:

Public constants: None

Public methods: setVisible

```
public void setVisible ( boolean state  )
```
>   Overrides the superclass's setVisible. This method calls the protected
>   adjustSize method before making the dialog visible. If you create a sub-
>   class of JavaBookDialog, then you must define the adjustSize method in
>   your subclass.

**Protected
Methods:**   adjustSize

```
abstract protected void adjustSize (  )
```
>   Define this method in your subclass. You use this method to adjust the
>   size of a dialog based on the components placed on the dialog.

See also: For a sample of defining a subclass of JavaBookDialog, please
read the StudentNameDialog class in Section 15.13.

Appendix A

Class:	javabook.ListBox

Purpose: A dialog that allows the user to select an entry from a list of selections.

Introduced in: Section 6.4, page 249.

Hierarchy:

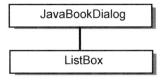

Public constants: CANCEL
NO_SELECTION

Public methods: ListBox
addItem
deleteItem
getSelectedIndex
getSelectedItem
isCanceled

```
public ListBox ( Frame owner )
public ListBox ( Frame owner, String  title )
public ListBox ( Frame owner, boolean modal )
public ListBox ( Frame owner, String  title, boolean modal )
```

Creates a ListBox object with owner as its controlling Frame object. The default title of the dialog is Select One: and the default mode is modal. Pass a String value and/or a boolean value to change the default. You pass true for modal and false for modeless dialogs.

```
public void  deleteItem      ( int  index      )
```

Deletes the entry at position index. The topmost entry is index 0, the next is index 1, and so forth.

```
public void  addItem      ( String entry   )
```

Adds an entry to the list. The newly added entry is placed at the bottom of the list, that is, the newly added entry has the highest index value.

```
public int     getSelectedIndex (                    )
```
Returns the index of the entry selected by the user. If the user clicks the CANCEL button or closes the dialog, then the public constant CANCEL is returned. If the user clicks the OK button without selecting an entry, then the public constant NO_SELECTION is returned.

```
public String getItemFromIndex( int index        )
```
Returns the value (String) of the entry at position index.

```
public boolean isCanceled (                    )
```
Returns true if the dialog was canceled or closed without an entry being selected. Returns false otherwise.

Class:	javabook.MainWindow

Purpose: A frame that serves as the main window of an application. By default, the frame size is almost as large as the screen, and it is displayed at the center of the screen.

Introduced in: Section 2.1, page 39.

Hierarchy:

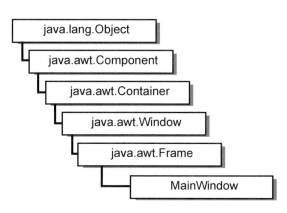

Public constants: None

Public methods:
```
MainWindow
setVisible
```

```
public MainWindow (                )
public MainWindow ( String title )
```

> Creates a MainWindow object with the text Sample Java Appliation as its default title. Use the second constructor to change the default title.

```
public void  setVisible  ( boolean  state )
```

> Displays the MainWindow object.

Class:	javabook.MessageBox

Purpose: A dialog that displays a single line of text. This dialog is suitable for displaying error or warning messages.

Introduced in: Section 2.5, page 64.

Hierarchy:

Public constants: None

Public methods: MessageBox
show

```
public MessageBox ( Frame owner )
public MessageBox ( Frame owner, boolean modal )
```

> Creates a MessageBox object with owner as its controlling Frame object. The default mode is modal. The second argument determines the modality: pass true for modal and false for modeless.

```
public void  show  ( long        number )
public void  show  ( double      number )
public void  show  ( String      str    )
public void  show  ( StringBuffer strBuf )
```

Displays the passed argument. Non-String values are converted to a String value before the display. The dialog appears at the center of the screen.

```
public void   show    ( long         number,    int x, int y )
public void   show    ( double       number,    int x, int y )
public void   show    ( String       str,       int x, int y )
public void   show    ( StringBuffer strBuf,    int x, int y )
```

Displays the passed argument. Non-String values are converted to a String value before the display. The top left corner of the dialog is set to position (x, y).

Class: javabook.MultiInputBox

Purpose: A dialog that allows the user to enter *N* input String values. TextField objects are used for accepting input values.

Introduced in: Section 9.4, page 436.

Hierarchy:

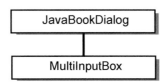

Public constants: None

Public methods: MultiInputBox
                      getInputs
                      isCanceled
                      setLabels
                      setValue

```
public MultiInputBox ( Frame owner, int      size   )
public MultiInputBox ( Frame owner, String[] labels )
```

Creates a MultiInputBox object with owner as its controlling Frame object. The second argument can be either an integer or an array of String objects. The integer value determines N—the number of input values the user can enter. If an array of String values is passed, then the value for N is determined by the length of the array. In addition, the String values will become the labels for the N TextField objects.

```
public String[] getInputs (      )
```

Returns the N input text values entered by the user. An empty String is returned for a TextField that has no entry.

```
public boolean isCanceled (      )
```

Returns true if the dialog was canceled or closed. Returns false otherwise.

```
public void  setLabels ( String[] labels )
```

Sets the labels for N TextField objects.

```
public void  setValue ( int index, String value )
```

The text of the TextField object at position index is set to value. The N TextField objects are indexed by using zero-based indexing, that is, the topmost object has index 0. This method is useful for showing the user a typically expected input value.

See also: java.awt.TextField

Class:	javabook.OutputBox

Purpose: A dialog for displaying multiple lines of text. This dialog is intended for displaying program output.

Introduced in: Section 3.6, page 106.

Hierarchy:

Public constants: None

Public methods:
```
OutputBox
appendToFile
print
printLine
saveToFile
setFont
skipLine
waitUntilClose
```

```
public OutputBox ( Frame owner )
public OutputBox ( Frame owner, String title )
public OutputBox ( Frame owner, int width, int height )
public OutputBox ( Frame owner, int width, int height, String title )
```
Creates an OutputBox object with owner as its controlling Frame object.

```
public void  appendToFile ( String   filename  )
```
Appends the contents of an OutputBox to the file whose name is filename. If no such file exists, then the method creates a new file and saves the contents of an OutputBox.

```
public void  print     ( boolean     bool   )
public void  print     ( char        ch     )
public void  print     ( double      num    )
public void  print     ( long        num    )
public void  print     ( String      str    )
public void  print     ( StringBuffer  strBuf )
```

Prints out the argument.

```
public void  printLine ( boolean       bool  )
public void  printLine ( char          ch    )
public void  printLine ( double        num   )
public void  printLine ( long          num   )
public void  printLine ( String        str   )
public void  printLine ( StringBuffer  strBuf )
```

Prints out the argument and moves the cursor to the next line.

```
public void  saveToFile ( String     filename  )
```

Saves the contents of an OutputBox to the file whose name is filename. If the file already exists, then the original contents of the file will be replaced by the contents of an OutputBox.

```
public void  setFont   ( Font newFont )
```

Sets the font to newFont. The default is size 12, plain Courier font.

```
public void  skipLine  ( int numLines   )
```

Skip numLines lines. The effect is the same as if you press the ENTER key numLines times.

```
public void  waitUntilClose (              )
```

An OutputBox dialog is always modeless. There are times, however, you want to close the dialog before continuting the execution of a program, that is, you want it to behave like a modal dialog. When this method is called, the program execution will not continue until the user closes the OutputBox object.

See also: java.awt.Font

Class: javabook.ResponseBox

Purpose: A dialog for displaying multiple lines of text. This dialog is
                       intended for displaying program output.

Introduced in: Section 7.4, page 303.

Hierarchy:

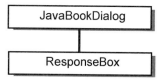

Public constants: YES
                        NO
                        CANCEL
                        BUTTON1 (== YES)
                        BUTTON2 (== NO)
                        BUTTON3

Public methods: ResponseBox
                        prompt
                        setLabel

```
public ResponseBox ( Frame owner )
public ResponseBox ( Frame owner, int buttonCount )
```
Creates a ResponseBox object with owner as its controlling Frame
object. The default ResponseBox object has two buttons labeled Yes and
No. These buttons are identified by the class constants YES and NO. You
can create a ResponseBox object with N, $1 \leq N \leq 3$, buttons by passing N
as the second argument. The buttons are identified from left to right by
the class constants BUTTON1, BUTTON2, and BUTTON3.

```
public int    prompt    ( String str)
```
Prompts the user for a response. The argument str is the query you pose
to the user. The user responds to the query by clicking one of the buttons.

```
public void   setLabel   ( int id, String label)
```
Set the label of button id to label.

Appendix A

Class:	javabook.SimpleInput

Purpose:

This class provides a simple input routine for non-GUI programs. The functionality of this class and InputBox is basically the same. One notable distinction is that all methods of SimpleInput are class methods.

Introduced in:

Not used in this book. This class is provided for those who need a quick and simple non-GUI input routine.

Hierarchy:

Public constants: None

Public methods:
```
getDouble
getInteger
getFloat
getString
```

```
public static double getDouble (         )
public static double getDouble ( String prompt )
```
The method returns the value entered by the user as double. This method does not complete until the user enters a valid value. For the first version, the prompt is set to a default word Enter a double:. In the second version, the prompt is set to the passed String argument.

```
public static int getInteger (         )
public static int getInteger ( String prompt )
```
The same behavior as the getDouble methods. The getInteger methods return an int instead.

```
public static float getFloat (         )
public static float getFloat ( String prompt )
```
The same behavior as the getDouble methods. The getFloat methods return a float instead.

```
public static String getString (            )
public static String getString ( String prompt )
```

The same behavior as the getDouble methods. The getString methods
return a String instead.

Class:	javabook.SketchPad

Purpose: A frame window that allows the user to draw freeform lines
using a mouse. You draw lines by dragging the mouse and
erase them by clicking the right mouse button (Command-
click on the Mac).

Introduced in: Section 1.6, page 31.

Hierarchy:

Public constants: None

Public methods: SketchPad

```
public SketchPad (  )
```

Creates a SketchPad object.

Index

A

Absolute positioning, 198, 219, 609
    of GUI objects, 206–208
Abstract classes, 677–682
Abstract methods, 201, 612, 676–682
Abstract superclasses, 676–682
Acceleration of gravity. *See* Gravitational constant
Access methods (accessors), 440, 594
Accessibility, inheritance and member, 666–671
Action event listeners, 611
    adding, 209, 221, 625
    setting, 200–201
Action events
    generating, 619
    sources of, 640
Action listeners, registering to menu items, 620
ActionEvent class, 202, 204, 622, 646
ActionListener, adding to an event source, 199–206
ActionListener interface, 201, 215, 612
actionPerformed method, 201–203, 205, 209–210, 214–215, 219–221, 612–613, 626, 640, 716, 720
    implementing, 646–649, 781–783

add method, 450–455
    defined, 452–453
add statements, switching, 198
Adding students, in class roster maintenance program, 729–737
addItem message, 249
Addition operators, 94
addNewStudent method, 732–733, 737
addNotify method, 778
Address book
    program for sorting, 509–514
    sample development, 446–463
AddressBook class, adding sorting routine to, 513
AddressBook object, saving, 548–556
AddressBook program, 548–556, 707
    sorting, 509–544
addSeparator method, 621
addStudent method, 729–736
adjustSize method, 777–778, 780
Age on other planets, computing, 132
Aiken, Howard, 3
Algorithms
    Anagram, 801–805
    Directory listing, 799–801

heapsort, 500
    pseudocode representation of, 322
    Quicksort, 809–814
    recursive, 797–818, 799
    searching, 786
    sorting, 488
    Towers of Hanoi, 805–808
Alignment, 198, 316
Allocation. *See* Memory
Alternatives. *See* Design alternatives
Anagrams, listing, 801–805, 818
Analysis phase, 30
Analytical Engine, 2–3
Ancestors, 27, 664
AND operators, 238–239
    Java symbols for, 242
    minimizing numbers of, 245–246
append method, 382–383
appendToFile message, 111
Applet class, 635–636
Applet skeletons, 214–218
Applet viewers, 352, 638–639
Applets, 13, 66–76, 79–81, 652
    declaration syntax for, 69
    placing GUI objects on, 192–199
    placing on dialog or frame, 638
    processing input with, 191–228
    program template for, 70–71, 192–195
    running as an application, 223–224
    writing, 80–81, 284, 406, 409
AppletViewer class, 68–70, 73–74, 638
Application logic class, 578
Application logic objects, 560, 569, 640
Applications, 13, 652
    Java, 38–48
    running applets as, 223–224
Architecture, computer, 5–11
Areas, computing, 187
Argument types, 100–102
Arguments
    key points listed, 166
    of a message, 19, 111
    passing, 43, 165–166
Arithmetic exception, 238, 254
Arithmetic expressions, 92–97
    complex, 95

data types of, 254–255
Arithmetic operators, 92–97
    addition, 92, 94
    assignment, 97
    integer division, 92–93
    modulo division, 92–93
    multiplication, 92, 94
    overloaded, 110
    precedence rules for, 94–95, 239
    subtraction, 92
    type cast, 96
    unary, 93–95
Arithmetic parentheses, 93–94, 96
Arithmetic promotion, 95
Arithmetic-logic unit (ALU), 9
Array elements, 414
    accessing, 465
    assigning, 417
    initializing, 417
    packing, 429
    removing, 458
Arrays, 411–518; *See also* Subarrays
    arrays of, 467–469
    basics of, 412–421
    and bytes, 526
    declaring, 412–413, 419–420
    defined, 412
    deletion operation for, 428–430
    dimensions of, 470
    local, 436
    not fully filled, 76
    of objects, 421–431
    one-dimensional, 463
    partitioning, 810, 814
    passing to methods, 431–436
    processing, 312
    sorting, 483–484
    specifying size of, 448, 725
    storing size of, 548
    terminating condition for, 427
    two-dimensional, 463–470
ASCII (American Standard Code for Information Interchange) coding scheme, 356–358, 367, 406, 534
    expressing in integers, 358
Assembly code, 12

Assembly languages, 11–12
Assets, tracking, 707
Assignment conversions, 96–97
Assignment operators, 97
    confusing with equality operators, 240–241
    evaluating, 97
Assignment statements, 87–88, 90–92
    dummy, 120
    with reference data type, 375–376
    syntax for, 87
    temporary, 179
    valid, 92
    writing, 99
Associativity rules, 239, 442
Asterisk (*) notation, 50–51, 55
Atanasoff, John, 3
@author tag, 145
@param tag, 148
@return tag, 149
AT&T Bell Labs, 12
Automatic Sequence-Controlled Calculator, 3

B

Babbage, Charles, 2–3
Backslash (\) symbol, 521–522
Barcode readers, 9
Base 2 numbers, 6
    scientific notation in, 127
Base 10 numbers, scientific notation in, 127
BASIC language, 12
beginIdx, 369
beginIndex, 367, 408
Bell Labs, 12
Belonging, 16–17
Berry, Clifford, 3
Binary number system, 3, 5–8, 125–128
Binary operators, 93, 95
Binary searching, 483–487
binarySearch method, 486
Binary-to-decimal conversion, 7
Bits, 6, 8, 356–359
    sign, 125–126
Bits per second (bps), 11

BMIApplet program, 213–223, 226–227
Body Mass Index (BMI), computing, 131
boolean data type, 240–241, 370
Boolean expressions, 230–232, 238–242
    avoiding complex, 245–246
    evaluating, 280, 309
    modifying, 291
    order of comparisons in, 365
    relational operators in, 231
    shortening, 363
Boolean flags, 240–241
Boolean operators, 237–239; *See also* Arithmetic operators
    precedence rules for, 239
Boolean variables, 240–241, 269, 277
    and loops, 301
    returning, 593
Braces ({ }), 233–234, 244, 254–255, 299
Brackets. *See* Square brackets ([ ])
Branching statements. *See* Selection statements
break statements, 255, 811
bubbleSort method, 491–494, 517, 813, 818
BufferedReader objects, 536–537, 685
Buffers, data, 527
buildRoster method, 696, 701, 703, 711
Button class, 208–210, 305, 634
Button events, processing, 219–221, 637
Button objects, 200, 642–643
Buttons, placing on a frame, 605–611
byte data type, 85–86, 95
Bytecode, 60, 75
Bytecode files, 60
Bytes, 356–358, 525
    arrays of, 526

C

C language, 12, 420
C++ language, 12
Caching data, 527
Caesar cipher, 408, 599
Calculator program, 654–656
Calling a method, 46
Calories needed, 131

canDraw flag, 269, 277
capacity method, 472
CardLayout class, 197
Cases, test, 336
Casting conversions, 95
    explicit, 95
    implicit, 95–96
catch blocks, 541–544, 697
    multiple, 542
Cells, 9, 12
Central processing unit (CPU), 8–9, 12
Change, calculating, 133–134
char data type, 356, 370
Character-based interface. *See* CUI
Characters, 356–359
charAt message, 360
Checked exceptions, 539
Children of a node; *See also* Sibling classes
    left and right, 495
Chinese, 357–358
Ciphers, 408–409, 599
class (reserved word), 56
Class constants, 100, 172, 253, 307, 439
    declaring public, 161–162, 251–252
Class data values
    constant, 23–24, 26
    syntax for accessing, 161
Class declarations, 55–56, 68, 144, 151–152, 195,
    216
    finalizing, 180–181
    syntax for, 55
Class definitions, 16
    invalid, 704–706
    program template for, 143
Class instances, declaring private, 161–162
Class listing convention, 150–151
Class member declarations, 55–56
Class methods, 20–22, 100, 152, 444
    declaring, 147
    declaring private, 161–162
    icons for representing, 22–23
    syntax for accessing, 161
Class names, 58, 79; *See also* Identifiers; Naming
Class roster maintenance program, 709–795
    add students, 729–737
    create a new roster, 722–729

delete students, 737–740
display student information, 753–765
edit student names, 740–746
edit test scores and compute grades, 746–753
finalize and improve, 775–776
method call sequence diagrams, 710–711
overall planning, 712–716
problem statement, 711–712
program shell with menus, 716–721
storing grade rosters, 765–775
Class variables, 23–24, 26–27, 34
    initializing, 511
Classes, 16–18; *See also* Instantiable classes; Packages; Predefined classes; Subclasses; Superclasses
    abstract, 677–682
    ActionEvent, 202
    AddressBook, 513
    Applet, 635–636
    AppletViewer, 68–70, 73–74
    application logic, 578
    Button, 208–210, 634
    CardLayout, 197
    client, 668
    Clock, 516
    ColorModel, 54
    ColorTextDisplay, 682
    container, 634, 639
    convert, 647538
    CurrencyConverter, 140–156, 478–479
    defining, 17–18, 27, 34, 61–62
    defining instantiable, 139–189
    defining with inheritance, 658–662
    designing, 273
    Dialog, 607, 634, 636–638
    Double, 212
    DrawingBoard, 259–260, 273–276
    DrawShape, 259–260
    event, 202
    exception, 541–542
    ExpandableArray, 470
    FindSum, 540
    Float, 212, 224
    FlowLayout, 197
    Font, 625
    Format, 316–322

frame, 606, 636

generality of, 570

GradeRoster, 713, 723–725, 728–733, 737–738, 748–753, 756, 764–765

GradeRosterMain, 718

graphical representations of, 18, 23

Graphics, 69–72, 75, 188–189

GridLayout, 197

grouped into packages, 53–54

Heap, 495–496, 507–508, 517–518

implementing, 273

InputBox, 84, 106, 138, 211, 249

instances of, 17–18

instantiable, 153–157, 262, 458

integer, 212

Label, 194–195, 198, 634

ListBox, 271, 652

Long, 212

maintaining integrity of, 159

MainWindow, 42–43, 55, 61, 64–66, 224, 606, 686

Math, 100–103, 115, 516, 585, 679

MessageBox, 64–66

MouseEvent, 202, 627, 631

MyFirstDialog, 636–638

MyFirstFrame, 607–617

noninstantiable, 679

OutputBox, 84, 558, 652, 682–683

Person, 422, 439, 510, 599

predefined, 38, 41, 52, 61–62, 140, 560, 595

program, 214, 259–260, 326–327, 601, 714

public, 69

redesigned, 569

ResponseBox, 303

reusable, 559–602, 699

reusable EggyPeggy and HiLo, 569–595

robustness of, 153

saving an AddressBook object, 548–556

Sibling, 664

SimpleInput, 106

skeleton, 176, 214

SketchPad, 61, 630–634

String, 359–370

StringBuffer, 379

StudentNameDialog, 741–746, 776–785

Tester, 385, 390, 458, 461

TestRandom, 338

TestScoreDialog, 786–790

TextEvent, 202

TextField, 195–195, 198

TrackMouseFrame, 626–628, 631

unrelated, 658–659

using effectively with polymorphism, 662–666

Vector, 470–475

WindowEvent, 202

wrapper, 212

ClassNotFoundException, 547

ClassRoster class, 712; *See also* buildRoster method; GradeRoster program

clearEntries method, 646–648

Client classes, 668

Clock, creating, 188–189, 227, 285, 350–351

Clock class, 516

Clock object, 81

Clock speeds, 9

COBOL language, 12

Code

assembly, 12

duplicating, 185, 576

high-level, 12

improving, 651

modifying, 251–252, 665

output from, 182–185

poorly written, 345–346

writing readable, 245–246

Code reuse, 61, 682

by composition, 683, 786

Code review, 594, 651

Coding phase, 30, 36, 66

Colon (:), 521

ColorList, 250

ColorModel class, 54

ColorTextDisplay class, 682

Comments, 48–53, 58, 78

header, 51–52, 68

javadoc, 50–51

markers for, 49

method header, 149–150

multi-line, 49

single-line, 49

uses of, 52–53
Communication devices, 11
Compact disks (CDs), 10
compareAttribute, 510–511
compareTo method, 366–367, 512, 517
Comparisons, 494
    pairwise, 492
Compilation errors, 61, 99, 675
Compilers, 12, 60
    adding default constructors, 672, 674–676
Component objects, 634
Components, program, 48–59
Composition, code reuse by, 683
Compound interest, computing, 134
Compound statements, syntax for, 235, 248
Computation, 84
Compute grades, in class roster maintenance program, 746–753
Compute loan amount, 121–124, 180
    code, 122–123
    design, 121–122
    test, 123–124
compute method, 641, 646–651
ComputeGrades program, 684–704, 706, 749–751
Computer architecture, 5–11
    simplified view of, 5
Computer chips, 3
Computer manuals, 10
Computer programming, 29; See also Event-driven programming; Object-oriented programming
    common errors in, 240–241
    computation, 84
    defensive, 257
    good style in, 245–246, 449
    incremental development, 84
    inputs, 84
    outputs, 84
    tasks comprising, 84
    testing routines, 400–401
Computers, 1–14
    generations of, 3–4
    history of, 2–4, 356
    networked, 4
    online slide show on, 4
    personal, 3–4, 9

pioneers of, 2–3
    speed of, 81
computeSum method, 540, 542
    declaring, 541–542
Computing course grades, sample program for, 684–704
Concatenation, 204
Conditional expressions, 231
Constants, 23–24, 98–100
    declaring, 266
    double literal, 99
    length, 416
    literal, 98–99, 254–255
    named, 98, 254–255
    symbolic, 98, 122
Constraints, on heaps, 495–496
construct method, 503–504, 506
Construction phase, of heapsort, 497, 508
Constructors, 153–157, 173, 195–196, 225, 543, 579
    calling, 583–584
    default, 154, 672, 674–676
    defining, 156, 444–445, 447, 572, 672–675
    explicit calls to, 675–676
    inheritance and, 672–676
    instantiable classes and, 152–157
    invalid, 157, 448–449
    limitations of, 448–449
    modifying, 451–452, 726–731
    multiple, 155, 445, 565–566, 597
    shell, 216–217
    syntax for, 153
Container class, 634, 639
Container objects, 197
continue (reserved word), 302
Control characters, 521
Control flow, 230
    nonsequential, 322
Control statements, 230; See also Repetition control
Control variables, 308–310
    declaring, 309–310
Controller objects, 273, 560–561, 640, 712
Convert class, 538, 647; See also javabook.Convert
convert method, 570, 575–577
Converting text, to a numerical value, 210–213
convertToDouble method, 222
convertToFloat method, 219–223

Count-controlled loops, 292–293, 297, 323
Counter variables, 295, 364, 581
Course grades, program for computing, 684–704
Cryptography, public-key, 409–410
CUI (character-based interface), supporting, 578
Curly braces. *See* Braces ({ })
CurrencyConverter class, 140–161, 478–479
CurrencyConverter object, 141–142, 557
Current directory, 520, 522
Current files, 766
Cycles, 9

D

Dangling else problem, 247–248
Data buffers, 527
Data caching, 527
Data members, 144, 572
Data types, 99
    matching, 211
    numerical, 83–138
    primitive *vs.* reference, 91, 370
    taxonomy of, 370
Data values
    arrays of, 412
    duplicating, 27
    saving, 534
DataInputStream objects, 533, 536
DataOutputStream objects, 532–534
Deallocation, 45, 165, 430
Debugging, 30
Decimal number system, 6–7
Decimal places shown, controlling with float data
        type, 124
Decimal-to-binary conversion, 7–8
Declarations, 55–56, 377
    invalid, 91
Decrement operators, 245–246
Decryption, 409
default (reserved word), 254–255
Default constructors, 154
    added by compiler, 672, 674–676
Defensive programming, 257
Delay, putting between setVisible messages, 81–82

Delegation-based event model, 611
delete method, 458–462
deleteStudent method, 737–740
Deleting students, in class roster maintenance pro-
        gram, 737–740
Deletion operation, for arrays, 428–430
Delimiters (delimiter characters), 697–698
Depth, of heap, 507–508
Descendants, 27, 634
describeGame method, 395, 404
describeProgram method, 181, 280, 323
Design alternatives, 63–65, 142–143, 169–171, 218–
        219, 274–276, 401–402, 435, 451,
        581–582
Design documents, 51, 63–65, 171, 215–216, 221
Design phase, 30, 36, 63–65
Destinations, of outputs, 525
Development, 29
    Address book, 446–463
    incremental, 84, 168, 259, 710
    software, 15–36
Development steps, 115, 172, 214, 259–261, 328,
        394–395, 447, 550, 582–583, 620,
        642, 777, 787
Dialog boxes, 64, 606
    modal *vs.* modeless, 636
Dialog class, 607, 634, 636–638
Difference Engine, 2
Digital video cameras, 9
Dimensions, methods for getting, 271–272
Directories, current, 520, 522
directoryListing method, 799–801
Disk drives, 9–10
Display student information, in class roster mainte-
        nance program, 753–765
displayAll method, 755
Displaying messages, sample program for, 62–66
displayOutput method, 179
displayResult method, 400, 647, 649
Divide-by-zero error, 238, 651
Division operators, 92–93
doLayout method, 204
Dot notation, 54, 158, 442
    unnecessary, 174–175
double, converting string to, 211
double data type, 85–86, 93, 95–96, 99
double literal constants, 99

double values, 99
Double class, 212
Double quotes, 43, 111, 359
Double slashes, 49, 522
doubleObject, 211
doubleValue method, 212
do-while statements, 299–303
    controlling flow of, 300
    correspondence to general format, 299–300
    syntax for, 299–300
    writing, 343
Drawing methods
    drawCircle, 274, 566
    drawLine, 72, 274, 351
    drawOval, 72, 566
    drawRect, 70–72
    drawRectangle, 274, 562–564
    drawRoundRect, 72
    drawString, 70, 72, 351
Drawing shapes, sample program for, 258–280
DrawingBoard class, 259–260, 273–276; See also
        javabook.DrawingBoard
    constructors for, 565
    methods for, 562–563
DrawingBoard objects, 348, 360, 565–566
DrawShape class, 259–260
    design documents for, 259–260, 262–263,
        266–270, 327
    object diagram for, 262
DrawShape objects, 259–260
Dummy secret number, 332–336
Duplicate computation, 343, 576
Duplicate tests, eliminating, 302

E

Earned run average (ERA), computing, 227–228
Echo printing, 117, 178
Eckert, J. Presper, 3
Edit-compile-run cycle, 59–61
Editing student names, in class roster maintenance
        program, 740–746
Editing test scores, in class roster maintenance pro-
        gram, 746–753
Editors, 60

editStudentName method, 745–746
EggyPeggy (word game) program, 392–404, 569–
        577, 652–654
Elements. See Array elements
elementsAt method, 473
Else blocks, 232–233
    rules for writing, 236, 248
Encryption, 408–409, 557, 599
End cases, 336, 340, 460
endIdx, 369
endIndex, 367, 408
Engineering, software, 29–32
ENIAC I (Electronic Numerical Integrator and Calcu-
        lator), 3
enlarge method, 453–454
    handling overflow condition with, 470
ENTER key events, 203, 208
Enumeration object, 473
EOFException objects, 543
Equality operators, confusing with assignment opera-
        tors, 240–241
Equality test, 377–379
equals method, 378–379
Equivalence test, 377
Error cases, 336
Error checking routine, 649–651
Error messages, 61, 257, 300–301, 449, 651
Errors; See also Exceptions
    compilation, 61, 99
    divide-by-zero, 238–239
    execution, 61
    identifying, 77–78
    off-by-one, 296
    out-of-bound, 365
    overflow, 294
    runtime, 238–239
Escape character, 521
Event classes, 202
Event listener objects, 200, 611
Event source objects, 200, 611
Event sources, 210
    adding ActionListener to, 199–206
Event-driven programming
    GUI objects and, 603–656
    laying out, 218–219
    supporting, 578

Event-handling code, 611
Events
    action, 200
    defined, 192
    handling, 611–617, 626–634
Exception class, 542
Exceptions, 528, 539–544
    checked, 539
    runtime, 539
    thrown, 539–544
    unchecked, 539
Exception-throwing methods, 528–529, 542
    catching, 528
    propagating, 528
Excess format, 128
Exchange rate, computing, 140–152, 157–161, 479
Execution errors, 61
Execution flow, 163
ExpandableArray class, 470
Explicit calls, to constructor of superclasses, 675–676
Exponential notation, 99
Exponentials, computing, 342
Expressions
    arithmetic, 92–97
    boolean, 238–242
extends (reserved word), 69, 660, 672
extract method, 504–506
Extraction phase, of heapsort, 497, 508

F

Factorials, computing, 339–340, 798
Fermi (game), 792–793
Fibonacci numbers, 134–135, 348, 815–816
Field width, 317
Fields, 317
    protected, 659
File I/O, 519–558
    high-level, 532–539
    low-level, 525–531
File objects, 520–526, 533, 685, 799–802
FileBox objects, opening in SAVE mode, 525
FileDialog objects, 520–525, 696
FileInputStream objects, 527–531, 533, 536, 546

fileManager objects, 549
Filenames, passing, 111
FileOutputStream objects, 526, 531–535
FileReader objects, 536, 685
Files
    closing, 527
    current, 766
    opening, 522–523
    structure of, 713
Finalizing; *See also* Program review of class roster maintenance program, 775–776
findIndex method, 459
Finding body mass index (BMI), sample program for, 213–223
FindSum class, 540
FindSum objects, 542
First generation computers, 3
Fixed-size array declarations, 419
Flags
    Boolean, 240–241
    canDraw, 269, 277
    longMessageFormat, 240–241
float data type, 85–86, 93, 95–96, 99, 210–212, 220
    arrays of, 412–415, 432–433, 476–477
    formatting, 317–320
    using to control decimal places shown, 124, 133
Float class, 212, 224
Float objects, 211–212
Floating-point format, 124, 126
floatValue method, 211, 220
Floppy disks, 9
FlowLayout class, 197, 207, 219
Font class, 625
for loops, 418, 692–693, 800, 803–804
for statements, 308–312; *See also* Nested-for statements
    controlling flow of, 309
    correspondence to general format, 308
Force between two bodies, computing, 136
Format class, 316–322, 694–695; *See also* java-book.Format
    methods for, 321
Formats. *See* ASCII; Binary number system
FORTRAN language, 12
Fourth generation computers, 4

Frame class, 606, 636
Frame objects, 636, 643, 724, 787
Frame windows, 64, 198, 605
    sizing, 607
Frames
    placing buttons on, 605–611
    placing textfield objects on, 618–619
French, 357
Fully qualified names, 54
Functions. *See* Mathematical functions
FunTime program, 33, 58, 274

G

Games. *See* EggyPeggy; Fermi; FunTime; HiLo;
    newGame method; playGame
    method
Garbage collection, 45, 430
GCD. *See* Greatest common divisor
Generality of classes, 570
Geometric functions. *See* Mathematical functions
German, 357
getAbsolutePath method, 801
getActionCommand method, 622
getCircleDimension method, 268, 271
getClickCount method, 629–630
getDouble method, 104–105
getFloat method, 104–105, 116
getGraphics method, 562–563
getInput method, 400, 438, 789
getInteger method, 103–104, 116, 211
getLineDimension method, 268, 271–272
getRandomNumber method, 590, 594
getRectangleDimension method, 268, 272
getSelectedIndex method, 250
getSource method, 646
getString method, 359, 393
getStudent method, 731, 759
getTestScores method, 789–790
getText method, 203–204, 210
getValues method, 758
Gosling, James, 13
Grade rosters, storing in class roster maintenance pro-
    gram, 765–775

GradeRoster class, 713, 723–725, 728–733, 737–
    738, 748–753, 756, 764–765
GradeRoster objects, 754–755
    creating, 722–729
GradeRoster program, 709–795
GradeRosterControl, 713, 722–728, 733–745, 748–
    755, 758, 762, 769, 772
GradeRosterDisplay objects, 714, 754
GradeRosterMain class, 718
GradeRosterMainWindow, 712–727, 733, 739–
    745, 748, 750–751, 755, 758, 761–
    762, 771–772
GradeRosterStorage objects, 713, 765–770, 772–
    775
Grades, computing in class roster maintenance pro-
    gram, 746–753
Graphical user interface. *See* GUI objects
Graphics class, 188–189
    drawing methods defined for, 69–72, 75
Gravitational constant
    computing, 136, 310–312, 350, 479, 557–558
    computing for other planets, 132
Greatest common divisor (GCD), computing, 817–
    818
GridLayout class, 197
GUI (graphical user interface) objects, 634–639
    absolute positioning of, 206–208
    class hierarchy for, 635
    and event-driven programming, 603–656
    placing on applets, 192–199

H

Handling events, 611–617
Handling exceptions, 539–544
Hard disks, 9
HAS-A relationship, 683
hasMoreElements method, 473
Header comments, 51–52, 68
Heap class
    constraints on, 495–496
    depth of, 507–508
    modifying, 517–518
    root of, 495
Heap structure, 500

Heapsort, 495–509
    performance of, 506–508
    rebuild step, 497–499
Heapsort algorithm, 500
Hertz, 9
High-level code, 12
High-level file I/O, 532–539
High-level languages, 12–13
HiLo game, 569–595, 653
    sample program for, 325–338
HTML (HyperText Markup Language) files, 217, 638
    creating, 73–75
    executing, 197
    opening, 81
    windows in, 352

I

IBM, 3
Identifiers, 41
    invalid, 48, 78
    rules for associating, 442
IEEE (Institute of Electronics and Electrical Engineers), Standard 754, 126
if statements, 230–237, 281–282; *See also* Nested-if statements
    controlling flow of, 233, 236–237
    formatting styles for, 235
    invalid, 237
    rewriting, 282–283
    syntax for, 231
If tests, 242–243
If-then statements, syntax for, 236–237, 402
If-then-else statements, syntax for, 237, 402
Implementing
    an interface, 201
    a program, 115
implements Serializable (phrase), 545, 548
import statements, 53–55, 58, 67, 78, 596
Imprecise loop counters, 295
Improving class roster maintenance program, 775–776
Increment operators, 245–246, 309
Incremental development, 84, 168

InDataStream objects, 535
Indentation, 245–248
    styles of, 247–248
Indexed expressions, 361, 414
Indexing, zero-based, 250, 360–361
inFile object, 535, 543
InFileStream objects, 535
Infinite loops, 294–297
Inheritance, 26–29, 69
    and constructors, 672–676
    defining classes with, 658–662
    guidelines for using, 672–676, 682–684
    and member accessibility, 666–671
    and polymorphism, 657–707
Inheritance hierarchies, 27–29, 36
Initialization, 86–87, 156, 395, 444–445, 584
    of class variables, 511
Inner for statements, 314
Inner loops, 323
Input, file, 519–558
Input values
    accepting, 117–118
    code, 178–179
InputBox class, 84, 103–106, 138, 211, 249; *See also* javabook.InputBox
InputBox objects, 84, 115, 178–179, 199, 259–260, 269–270, 326, 399–401, 561; *See also* MultiInputBox objects
    creating, 103
    declaring, 103
    passing text as a prompt, 104
    sending messages to, 359
inputLine, 619
Input/output (I/O) devices, 5, 9; *See also* File I/O; Object I/O
Inputs, 84
    dealing with invalid, 249, 399–401, 649–651, 697
    sources of, 525
Insertion sort, 515–516
Insets object, 779
Instance constants, 23–24, 26
Instance data values, 23, 145
Instance messages, 21–22
Instance methods, 19–22, 444, 570
    declaring, 147

declaring private, 161–162

Instance variables, 23–24, 26–27, 34, 145, 172, 441–442

declaring private, 161–162

Instance-of relationships, 17–19

instanceof (reserved word) operator, 618–619, 665

Instantiable classes, 262, 458

constructors for, 153–157, 262

defining, 139–189

introduction to, 140–152

loan calculator program with, 167–181

Institute of Electronics and Electrical Engineers. *See* IEEE

int data type, 85–86, 95–96, 133, 222, 250, 372

Integer class, 212

Integer division operators, 93

Integers, 84–86

computing the greatest common divisor (GCD), 817–818

data types for, 85–86

formatting, 317–319

initializing, 86–87

negative, 245–246

representation of, 124–126

sorting, 488–489, 515

Integrated circuits, 3–4

large-scale, 3

Integration testing, 30

Intel processors, 9–10

Interest rates, computing, 134, 137–138

Interface objects, 273; *See also* GUI (graphical user interface) objects

Interfaces

ActionListener, 201

implementing, 612

MouseListener, 626, 630

simplifying, 171

user-friendly, 249, 300

WindowListener, 614, 617

Internet, 4

finding free packages on, 64

Internets, 4

Interpreters, 61

Java, 380

intValue method, 212, 474

intVector, 474

Invalid inputs, dealing with, 249, 399–401, 649–651, 697

IOException objects, 528–529, 539, 542–543, 547, 553

IS-A relationship, 683

isMetaDown method, 631, 634

J

Japanese, 357–358

Java API reference manuals, 699

Java applets. *See* Applets

Java applications, 13, 31, 38–48, 78, 79–81

Java classes, standard, 51

Java compilers, 245–248, 372, 383, 597

Java interpreter, 380

Java language; *See also* Mathematical functions; Programs

development tools, 59–61

exponential notation in, 99

having fun with, 31–33

for the Internet, 358

introduction to, 13

programming basics, 37–82

standard libraries, 64, 403, 560, 819

translating pseudocode into, 322–323

Java packages; *See also* javabook package

java.applet, 67, 634, 636

java.awt, 55, 62, 67, 195, 197, 208, 275, 564, 595, 604–605, 620, 634, 636, 652, 823–839

java.io, 62, 520, 529, 545

java.lang, 140, 439, 823, 826, 828–829, 831

java.util, 470, 697

Java stream objects. *See* Stream objects

javabook package, 54–55, 61–62, 81, 84, 106, 115, 140, 303, 316, 437, 439, 445, 516, 538, 560, 577, 595, 604–606, 628, 649, 685–686, 694, 712, 776, 819–839

importing, 54–55

predefined classes in, 560, 595

javabook.Clock, 516, 820–823

javabook.Convert, 439, 538, 649, 820, 823–824

javabook.DrawingBoard, 259–260, 820, 824–825

javabook.Format, 316, 694, 820, 826–827
javabook.InputBox, 84, 103, 820, 827–828
javabook.JavaBookDialog, 628, 776, 820, 828–829
javabook.ListBox, 249, 604, 820, 830–831
javabook.MainWindow, 40, 712, 820, 831–832
javabook.MessageBox, 64, 820, 832–833
javabook.MultiInputBox, 437, 820, 833–834
javabook.OutputBox, 84, 106, 685–686, 820, 835–836
javabook.ResponseBox, 303, 820, 837
javabook.SimpleInput, 820, 838–839
javabook.SketchPad, 33, 820, 839
javadoc comments, 50–51, 145
javadoc tags, 145, 148–149

K

Kanji characters, 357
Keyboards, 5, 9
Korean, 357–358

L

Label class, 194–195, 199, 634
Label objects, 200, 207; *See also* setLabels method
Languages. *See* Programming languages
Layout managers, 197, 199, 609
default, 218
setting to null, 206–208
Layout of GUI objects, 218–219
Length constants, of an array, 416, 466
length method
of a File object, 391
of a String object, 416
Level, of nodes, 507
Libraries, standard, 64, 403, 560, 819
Life cycle, of software, 29–32
Linear searching, 483, 487
ListBox class, 271, 652; *See also* javabook.ListBox
ListBox objects, 249–253, 259, 600, 683
methods for, 253
Listeners. *See* Action event listeners; Mouse motion event listeners

Listing conventions, 150–151
Literal constants, 98–99, 254–255, 359, 380
Loan amount, computing, 121–124, 137–138, 180
Loan tables, 322–325, 347
LoanCalculator program, 113–124, 140, 226, 322–325, 349, 598–599, 655–656
with an instantiable class, 167–181
Local area networks (LANs), 4
Local arrays, 436
Local copies, 166, 388–389
Local variables, 162–167, 441–442
Logical operators, 238
long data type, 85–86, 95
Long class, 212
longMessageFormat flag, 240–241
longValue method, 212
Loop body, 290
Loop counters, imprecise, 295
Loop statements, 290–293
improving readability of, 404
infinite, 294–297
nested, 323–324
posttest, 299
pretest, 299
terminating, 302–303, 366, 693–694, 811
Lovelace, Ada, 2–3
Low-level file I/O, 525–531

M

Mac platform, 495, 631
Machine code, 12
Machine languages, 11–12
Magnetic strip readers, 9
Mail merge, 558
Main classes, 56, 59
defining your own, 228
invalid statements in, 181–182
main method, 140
Maintenance, 30–31, 42, 170
of class roster program, 709–795
MainWindow class, 42–43, 47, 55, 61, 64–66, 224, 606, 686; *See also* javabook.MainWindow

MainWindow objects, 107, 115, 225, 262, 712
MARK I, 3
Markers
  */, 49–50
  /*, 49–50
  //, 49
  matching, 49–50
Markup elements, 74
Matching cases, 254–255, 257
Math class, 100–103, 115, 516, 585, 679
  methods for commonly used mathematical functions, 101–102
Mathematical functions, Math class methods for commonly used, 101–102
Mauchly, John W., 3
maxChild method, 505
Member accessibility, inheritance and, 666–671
Memory
  allocation of, 44–45, 88, 163, 165, 372–375, 430
    nonvolatile, 9
    shortage of, 374
    volatile, 9
Memory locations, 11–12, 371
Memory management, 373–374
Memory usage, 91
  varying with precision, 86
Menu structure, 713
MenuFrame objects, 620–621
MenuItem objects, 620
Menus, 620–625
  in class roster maintenance program, 716–721
Merge sort, 818
Message sending, 21–22, 45–46
  syntax for, 45
MessageBox class, 64–66; See also javabook.MessageBox
MessageBox objects, 106–107, 113, 269–270, 326, 332, 381
Messages, 18–23
  displaying, 63
  errors in, 61
  naming, 19–21
  printing, 282
  sending, 46–47
Method body, 58, 678

Method call sequence diagrams, 724, 732, 744, 759, 768
  in class roster maintenance program, 710–711
Method declarations, 527–528
  syntax for, 56–57, 147
Method header comments, 148–149
Method prototypes, 565
Method signatures, 564–565, 597–598
Methods, 18–23
  abstract, 201, 676–682
  calling, 46, 174–175, 443
  duplicating, 27
  implementing, 678
  making more robust, 592
  naming, 22
  overloaded, 564
  overriding, 562–569
  passing arrays to, 431–436
  recursive, 338–343
  returning an object from, 389–392, 406
  shortening, 703–704
  throwing exceptions, 528
  verifying, 575
  writing, 406–407
Metric conversion, 84, 185–186, 226
Mice. See Mouse
Microcomputers, 3
MIDI devices, 9
Minicomputers, 3
Minimalist approach, 13
Modal dialog boxes, 636
Modeless dialog boxes, 636
Modems, 11
Modifiers, 57
  protected, 660, 666–671
  static, 147
  visibility, 146, 157–163, 662
Modulator-demodulator, 11
Monitors, 5, 9
Mortgages, computing. See LoanCalculator program
Mouse, 5, 9
  workings of, 84
Mouse events, handling, 626–634
Mouse motion event listeners, 200
Mouse movement events, 200
MouseEvent class, 202, 627, 631

MouseListener interface, 626, 630
MultiInputBox class, 436–439; *See also* java-book.MultiInputBox
MultiInputBox objects, 786–788
    methods for, 439
Multi-line comments, 49
Multimedia information, viewing, 4
Multiple constructors, 155, 445, 565–566
    and usability, 566
Multiple event listeners, 210
Multiple event sources, 210
Multiplication operators, 94
Multiplication table, 351
Musical instrument digital interface (MIDI) devices, 9
Mutator methods (mutators), 440
    avoiding naming conflict with, 441–442
MyFirstApplication program, 38–61
MyFirstDialog class, 636–638
MyFirstFrame class, 607–617
MySketchPad program, 630–634, 654

N

Named constants, 98, 254–255
Naming, 19–21, 44, 54
    standard conventions for, 42, 79
Naming conflicts, 441
Negative integers, 245–246
Nested loop statements, 323–324, 344
Nested-for statements, 312–315
    rewriting as nested do-while statements, 344–345
    rewriting as nested while statements, 344–345
Nested-if statements, 242–248, 811
    controlling flow of, 242–243
    using in switch statements, 280–282
Nestings
    minimizing, 245–246
    showing structure clearly, 245–246
Netscape Navigator, 75–76
Network interface cards (NICs), 11
Networks, 4
Neumann, John von, 3

new operation, 42
newGame method, 579–580, 589–591
nextElement method, 473
nextGuess method, 579, 582–583, 591–594
Nodes
    left and right children of, 495
    level of, 507
    root, 495
Noninstantiable classes, 679
Nonpositive numbers, 584
Nonsequential control flow logic, 322
Non-void method, 149
Nonvolatile memory, 9
NOR operators, 238–239
Normal case, 336, 460
Normalized fractions, 127–128
Notation. *See* Asterisk notation; Dot notation; Exponential notation; Scientific notation; Shorthand notation
null (reserved word), 206–208, 377
Null pointer, 377
Null reference, 377, 428–429, 458
Number systems, 6
Numbers; *See also* Standard deviation
    computing factorials of, 339–340
    computing greatest common divisor of, 817–818
    converting to Roman numerals, 283–284
    dummy secret, 332–336
    Fibonacci, 134–135, 348
    nonpositive, 584
    perfect, 346
    random, 326, 336–338, 583, 589–591
    variables for, 88–89
Numeric promotion, 95
Numerical data declaration, 89
Numerical data types, 83–138
    converting text to, 210–213
Numerical representation, 124–128

O

Object categories, 560–561
Object creation, 42–46, 377

syntax for, 42

Object data values, 371

Object declaration, 40–42, 89, 371

syntax for, 40

Object diagrams, 33, 40, 46–47, 51, 115, 169, 170–171

notation for, 44–45

Object I/O, 545–548

Object names, 79; *See also* Identifiers; Naming

Object tasks, 560

ObjectInputStream objects, 545–546

Object-oriented programming, 15–36

advantages of, 273

design principles of, 273

learning, 62

real-world, 62

Object-oriented thinking, 710

ObjectOutputStream objects, 545, 553

Objects, 16–18, 38; *See also* GUI objects

application logic, 560

arrays of, 421–431

categories of, 560, 712

controller, 560–561

definition of, 16, 19

designing, 35, 273

graphical representations of, 17, 23

interacting, 16

with multiple references, 429

passing as parameters, 384–389

passing to a method, 385–386, 406

primary, 715

referenced, 665

returning from methods, 389–392

storage, 560

storing, 544

subordinate, 712

user interface, 560

variables for, 88–89, 91

Off-by-one errors (OBOEs), 296

Offsets, 779

One-dimensional arrays, 463

openRoster method, 770

Operands, 93

Operation phase, 30

Operators; *See also* Arithmetic operators; Boolean operators; Relational operators

AND, 238–239, 242

addition, 94

assignment, 97, 240–241

binary, 93, 95

decrement, 245–246

division, 92–93

equality, 240–241

increment, 245–246, 309

instanceof, 618–619

integer division, 93

logical, 238

multiplication, 94

NOR, 238–239

OR, 238–239, 242

overloaded, 110

short-circuit, 365–366

shorthand assignment, 297–298

string concatenation, 383, 402

type cast, 96

unary, 93–95

OR operators, 238–239

Java symbols for, 242

minimizing numbers of, 245–246

outDataStream, 533

Outer for statements, 314

Outer loops, 323

outFile objects, 526, 533

outFileStream, 533

Out-of-bound errors, 365

Output devices, 5, 9

Output statements, 257; *See also* Temporary output statements

dummy, 214

Output values, 179

design, 119–121

destination of, 520

formatting, 316–321

test, 121

OutputBox class, 84, 106–112, 558, 652, 682–683; *See also* javabook.OutputBox

OutputBox methods, 112

OutputBox objects, 84, 115, 175, 259–261, 399

creation of, 107

declaration of, 107

display flexibility of, 113–114, 279–280

Outputs, 84, 182–185

file, 519–558
    making readable, 808
Outside methods, 149
outStream object, 531
Overflow condition, handling with **enlarge** method, 470
Overflow errors, 294
Overloading, 110, 562–569, 640
Overriding, method for, 562–569
Owner frames, 64

P

Package organization, 595–597
Packages, 53–54, 595; *See also* Java packages; **java-book** package
    in commercial software, 64
    creating, 601
    finding free on the Internet, 64
    putting classes into, 595–596
    reusable, 559–602
paint method, 69
Pairwise comparisons, 492
Palindromes, finding, 409, 817
Parameters, 57
    allocating memory for, 387
    declaring, 442
    key points listed, 166–167
    passing, 162–167, 384–389
Parentheses, 93–94, 96
partition method, 810–814, 818
Pascal language, 12
Pass-by-value scheme, 88–89, 91, 164, 166, 384–389
Passes, sorting, 489
Passing arrays, to methods, 431–436
Passing objects, as parameters, 384–389
Passing parameters, 162–167
Perfect numbers, 346
Person class, 422, 439, 510, 599; *See also* Address-Book
    constructor of, 444
Person objects, 422–424, 426, 429, 448–449, 471–472, 544, 546
    adding to an array, 451, 453
    comparing, 509–514

creating, 424
reading, 556
removing, 458
returning, 455–456, 520
saving, 545
verifying, 454
Personal scheduler, 793
Placeholder tags, 558
Planning, in class roster maintenance program, 712–716
playGame method, 328, 332–336
    controlling flow of, 332–333
Plus (+) symbol; *See also* Addition operators
    for concatenation of values, 110–111
Pointers
    null, 377
    self-referencing, 439–445
Polymorphic messages, 658
Polymorphism
    benefits of, 665
    defined, 658, 663
    inheritance and, 657–707
    using classes effectively with, 662–666
Population growth, computing, 136–137
Position values, 6–7
Positioning. *See* Absolute positioning
Posttest loop, 299
Precedence rules, 94–95, 239, 298
Precision
    higher, 86
    of real numbers, 295
Predefined classes, 38, 41, 52
    advantages of, 61–62
    limitations of, 140
Pretest loop, 299
Prices, printing out table of, 312–315, 347
Priming read, 293
Primitive data types, 91, 377, 538
    declaring, 371
Primitive types, *vs.* reference types, 370–379
print method, 108, 111–112, 536
Printers, 5, 9
println method, 175, 536
printLine message, 109, 112, 116, 175
    fine-tuning, 121
printResult method, 688, 692–695

printStackTrace method, 543

PrintWriter objects, 534–536, 543

private (reserved word) modifiers, 157–163, 660, 668–669, 671, 682

private visibility modifiers, 157–162

Problem statements, 63, 113, 168, 213, 258–259, 325, 393, 548, 570, 578, 639, 684, 776, 786

    in class roster maintenance program, 711–712

processData method, 686

    method call sequence of, 711

Processing input, with applets, 191–228

Program classes, 214, 259–260, 326–327, 601, 714

Program components, 48–59

Program documentation, 51; See also Comments; Design documents; Object diagrams; Programmers' work log; User manuals

Program implementation, 115

    sequence for, 115

Program readability, 235

    computing, 136

    improving, 404

Program review, 180–181, 280, 404, 463, 556, 703, 775–776

Program shell with menus, in class roster maintenance program, 716–721

Program skeletons, 116–117, 172–178, 261–265, 328–332, 394–399, 689–692

    code, 116–117, 175–178

    with constructors, 448–450, 572–575, 583–589, 642–646, 777–781, 787–789

    design, 116–117, 172–175

    test, 116–117, 178

Program structure, components of, 67

Program tasks, 113, 168, 259, 326, 393, 446, 579, 640, 685, 712

Program templates, 58–59

    for applets, 70–71, 192–195

    for class definition, 146

Program verification, 178

Programmers' work log, 51

Programming

    basics of Java, 37–82

    GUI objects and event-driven, 603–656

    introduction to object-oriented, 15–36

Programming languages, 1–14; See also individual

programming languages

    classes of, 11–12

Programs

    AddressBook, 548–556, 707

    BMIApplet, 226–227

    Calculator, 654–656

    for class roster maintenance, 709–795

    ComputeGrades, 706, 749–751

    for displaying messages, 62–66

    for drawing shapes, 258–280

    EggyPeggy (word game), 652–654

    for finding body mass index (BMI), 213–223

    FunTime, 33, 58, 274

    GradeRoster, 709–795

    HiLo (game), 325–338, 577–594, 653

    LoanCalculator, 113–124, 140, 167–181, 226, 322–325, 349, 598–599, 655–656

    MyFirstApplet, 66–76

    MyFirstApplication, 38–61

    MySketchPad, 630–634, 654

    simple calculator, 639–651

    for sorting an address book, 509–514

    word play, 392–404

ProgramTerminator objects, 622, 626, 638

Project files, 60

Projectiles. See Gravitational constant

Promotion, 95

Protected fields, 659

protected (reserved word) modifiers, 660, 666–671

Pseudocode representation, 322–323

Pseudorandom number generator, 336–338, 580

public (reserved word) modifiers, 157–163, 660, 668–669, 671

Public-key cryptography, 409–410

Punch cards, 2

Punctuation, 363, 407; See also individual marks of punctuation

Pushbuttons, 208, 608

Q

Quadratic equations, solving, 132–133

Quicksort algorithms, 809–814

quitProgram method, 721

R

Radix, 6
Random access memory (RAM), 5, 8–9
random method, 516
Random numbers, generating, 326, 336–338, 583, 589–591, 600
read method, 554–556
readData method, 687–689, 692–703, 711
readFloats method, 433–435
readIntegers method, 434–435
readLine method, 537
readObject method, 546–547
Real numbers
    data types for, 85–86
    formatting, 319–320
    in loop counters, 295
    representation of, 126–127
Rebuild steps, 497–499
    sequences of, 501
Recursion, 339–343, 353, 556, 798–799
    defined, 339–340
    guidelines for using, 342–343, 815–817
    necessary components in, 340, 798
    terminating, 340
    when not to use, 815–817
Recursive algorithms, 797–818
Recursive methods, 338–343
Redesigned classes, 569
Reference data type, 91, 370, 372, 374–375
    assigning, 389
    representing memory allocation for, 375–376
    returning, 391
    variables of, 385
Reference types, *vs.* primitive types, 370–379
Referenced objects, 665
Registers, 8–9, 11–12
Relational operators, 238–240
    in boolean expressions, 231
Relays, mechanical, 3
Removing array elements, 458
Rentals, tracking, 793–795
Repetition control, 292, 577
    checklist for, 297
Repetition statements, 289–353
    defined, 290

    pitfalls in writing, 294–298
    terminating, 366
Representation, numerical, 124–128
Requirements specification, 30
Reserved words, 47, 78; *See also individual reserved words*
resize method, 407
ResponseBox class, 303–307; *See also* java-book.ResponseBox
ResponseBox objects, 328
    methods for, 307
    uses for, 338, 394–395, 729
Result types, 101–102
return statements, syntax for, 149–150
Return types, 57
Return values, 162–167
Returning an object from methods, 389–392
Reusable classes, 559–602
    defined, 560
    making general, 577–578
Reusable EggyPeggy and HiLo, sample classes, 569–595
RGB scheme, 275–276
Root node, 495
Rosters. *See* buildRoster method; GradeRoster program
RSA cryptography system, 410
Runtime errors, 238–239
Runtime exceptions, 539

S

Sales, computing, 133–134, 186, 285–288, 346–347, 479, 599–600
SAVE mode, 524–525
saveAs method, 766–767
saveAsRoster method, 765–768
saveData method, 766
saveRoster method, 765–768
saveToFile method, 111, 558
Saving an AddressBook object, sample class, 548–556
Scanning, 463
Scientific notation, 127
search method, 455–458

Searching, 482–487

Second generation computers, 3

Secondary storage devices, 9–10

selectColor method, 267–268, 277–278

selectDimension method, 266–271

Selection control statements, 271

Selection statements, 229–288

selectionSort method, 488–491, 494, 813

selectShape method, 266–267

Self-referencing pointers, 439–445

Semicolons (;), 54, 234, 677

Sending a messages, 46–47

Sentinel-controlled loops, 293

Sequential control flow, 230

Sequential execution, 230

Sequential searching, 483

Serializability. *See* implements Serializable

setBounds method, 206–208, 609–611

setColor method, 275–276

setData method, 502–503

setExchangeRate method. *See* Exchange rate

setFile method, 549–553

setLabels method, 437

setLayout method, 207, 609

setNames method, 783

setPrefixWord method, 572, 574–576

setupArray method, 462

setVisible messages, 47
    putting delay between, 81–82

setVisible method, 628

Shapes, drawing, selecting, 266–267

Shipping cost, computing, 135

Short data type, 85–86, 95

Short-circuit evaluation, 238–239

Short-circuit operators, 365

Shorthand assignment operator (+=), 297–298

Shorthand notation, 361

show method, 562–563, 789–790

showAllStudents method, 754–755, 759

showOneStudent method, 760–761

Sibling classes, 664

Sign bits, 125–126

Signatures. *See* Method signatures

Silicon chips, 3

Simple calculator, sample program for, 639–651

Simple statements, syntax for, 235

SimpleInput class, 106

Simula language, 13

Single-line comments, 49

Single-task object (STO) principle, 273, 446, 449–451, 549, 553

size method, 472

Skeleton classes, 176, 214; *See also* Program skeletons
    testing, 265

SketchPad class, 61, 630–634; *See also* javabook.SketchPad; MySketchPad program

skipLine message, 109–110, 112, 116

Smalltalk language, 13

Software development, introduction to, 15–36

Software engineering, and software life cycle, 29–32, 62

Software maintenance, 30–31, 42
    reducing costs of, 31

sortedList array, 514

Sorting, 488–494

Sorting AddressBook, 509–544
    sample program for, 509–514

Sorting passes, 489

Source code. *See* Programs

Source files, 59
    compiling, 60

Square brackets ([ ]), 413, 431–432

Standard deviation, computing, 477

Standard libraries, 64, 403, 560
    sources of information on, 819

start method, 173, 322

Statements, 308–312; *See also* Assignment statements; Import statements; Output statements; Problem statements; Return statements
    break, 255
    compound, 233, 235
    control, 230
    do-while, 299–303
    for, 308–311
    if, 230–237
    if-then, 236–237
    if-then-else, 237
    import, 53–55, 58, 67, 78
    loop, 290
    multiple, 233–234

nested-for, 312–315

nested-if, 242–248

repetition, 289–353

selection, 229–288

sequential execution of, 230

simple, 235

single, 233

switch, 252–258

while, 290–293

writing assignment, 99

State-of-memory diagrams, 44–45, 78, 88, 92, 212, 371–372, 405–406, 477

static (reserved word) modifiers, 147, 682

STO. See Single-task object (STO) principle

Storage devices, 5, 9–10

Storage objects, 560

Stored-program scheme, 3

Storing grade rosters, in class roster maintenance program, 765–775

Stream objects, 525–526

closing, 525–526

String class, 359–363

defined, 359

String concatenation operator, 383, 402

String data values, 210–212

formatting, 318–319

specifying, 43

String objects, 360, 379

methods for, 416

returning, 390

StringBuffer class, 379–384

StringBuffer objects, 380–382, 393, 401–403

advantages over String objects, 402

creating, 386

limits on, 381

Strings, 359–370

comparing, 367

converted, 575

manipulating contents of, 359–360, 379

printing in reverse, 369, 406

StringTokenizer objects, 697–699, 707

Structural constraints, 495–496

Stub methods, 174–175, 572–573

Student information, displaying in class roster maintenance program, 753–765

Student names, editing in class roster maintenance

program, 740–746

StudentNameDialog class, 741–746, 776–785

Students

adding in class roster maintenance program, 729–737

deleting in class roster maintenance program, 737–740

Subarrays, 469

Subclasses, 27, 69, 274, 542, 545

extending their superclasses, 660–662

Subexpressions, 94

type casting, 96

Subordinate dialog boxes, 64

Subpackages, 54

substring method, 367

Subtraction operators, 92, 284

Successful searches, 482–483

Sun Microsystems, 13

Superclasses, 27, 542, 662

abstract, 676–682

defining, 676

explicit calls to constructor of, 675–676

extending, 660

switch statements, 252–258

controlling flow of, 256, 282

making readable, 257

mapping, 254

syntax for, 254–255

using nested-if statements in, 281–282, 811

Symbolic constants, 98, 122, 251–252

System.out object, 175, 542, 574, 646

T

Tables, 312–315; See also Two-dimensional arrays

formatting, 316–321

Tape drives, 9

Tasks. See Program tasks

Temperature conversion, computing, 131, 226, 305–306

Temporary output statements, 175, 179, 234–235, 266, 396, 588, 690

10BaseT, 11

Test, final, 463, 556

Test cases, 336

Test condition counter, 297

Test scores, editing in class roster maintenance program, 746–753

TestDataOutputStream, 533

TestDelete, 462

Tester class, 385, 390, 458, 461

Testing phase, 30–31, 66

    duplicate tests, 302

    posttest loop, 299

    pretest loop, 299

    priming read in, 293

TestOutputBox program, 130

TestPrintWriter, 537

TestRandom class, 338

TestScoreDialog class, 786–790

TestScoreDialog objects, 746–750

Text, converting to numerical values, 210–213

Text size, 625

TextArea objects, 652–653

TextEvent class, 202

TextField class, 194–195, 199

TextField objects, 195, 200, 210–213, 219, 287, 352, 436, 619, 641–643, 647–649, 653

    placing on a frame, 618–619

Textfiles, 534, 556–558, 684–685

Then blocks, 232–233

    rules for writing, 236, 248

Third generation computers, 3

this (reserved word), 203, 440, 443–444

Thrown exceptions, 539–544

Titles

    default, 39

    specifying, 43

Tokens, 697–699

Topmost start method, 322

toString method, 212, 381

toUpperCase method, 363, 379

Tower of Hanoi puzzle, 805–808, 815

TrackMouseFrame class, 626–628, 631

Transistors, 3

Trigonometric functions. *See* Mathematical functions

try blocks, 541–544, 697

try-catch blocks, 544

Turtle objects, 138

Two-dimensional arrays, 463–470

Twos-complement format, 124–126

Type cast operators, 96

Type casting, 95, 548

    syntax for, 96

U

Unary operators, 93–95

Unchecked exceptions, 539

Unicode Worldwide Character Standard, 357–358, 367

    lexicographical order of, 367

Unit testing, 30

U.S. Navy, 3

UNIX platform, 520

Unnormalized fractions, 127–128

Unrelated classes, 658–659

Unsuccessful searches, 482–483

User interactions, 620, 626

User interface objects, 560

User manuals, 51

User-designated words, 570

V

Vacuum tubes, 3

Validity rules, for input routines, 399

Value relationship constraints, 495–496

Value-returning methods, 149, 167

Values, dealing with invalid, 249, 257

Variable declarations, syntax for, 85

Variables, 23–25, 84–92

    assigning integer value to, 371–372

    assigning value to multiple, 97

    attributes of, 371

    boolean, 238–242

    class, 23–24, 26–27, 34

    control, 308–310

    counter, 295

    incrementing, 245

    initializing, 86–87

    instance, 26–27, 34, 145

    for numbers, 88–89

for objects, 88–89, 91
    properties of, 85
Variable-size array declarations, 420
Vector class, 470–475
    finding capacity of, 472
Vertical bar (|), 161
Vignere cipher, 409, 599
Visibility modifiers, 146, 157–163, 662
Visibility of data members and methods, guidelines in determining, 161–162
Void method, 149
Volatile memory, 9

W

waitUntilClose method, 279
Watermelons. *See* Gravitational constant
Web browsers, 4, 81
Java-aware, 75
Web documents, writing, 74
Web pages, 75, 79
Web programming language, 13
Weight, recommended, computing, 186, 227, 285
while statements, 290–293, 694
    advantage over do-while statements, 301, 328, 364
    controlling flow of, 291
    correspondence to general format, 291

for repetition control, 293
rewriting as do-while statements, 303
rewriting as for statements, 312
syntax for, 290
writing, 343
Wide area networks (WANs), 4
Window events, 614
WindowEvent class, 202
WindowListener interface, 614, 617
Windows platform, 521, 543
Word play, sample program, 392–404
Words, user-designated, 570
Wrapper classes, 212
write method, 553–554
Writing computer programs. *See* Computer programming
Writing repetition statements, pitfalls in, 294–298

Y

YesNoBox objects, 323

Z

Zero, duplicate representations for, 125
Zero-based indexing, 250, 360–361, 414, 420

Object Diagram Summary

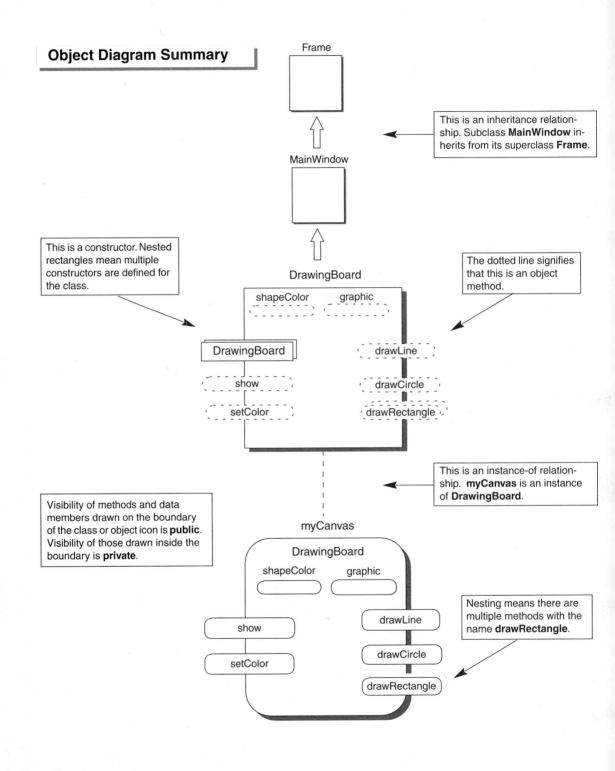

Frame

This is an inheritance relationship. Subclass **MainWindow** inherits from its superclass **Frame**.

MainWindow

This is a constructor. Nested rectangles mean multiple constructors are defined for the class.

The dotted line signifies that this is an object method.

DrawingBoard

shapeColor   graphic

DrawingBoard

show   drawLine

setColor   drawCircle

                        drawRectangle

This is an instance-of relationship. **myCanvas** is an instance of **DrawingBoard**.

Visibility of methods and data members drawn on the boundary of the class or object icon is **public**. Visibility of those drawn inside the boundary is **private**.

myCanvas

DrawingBoard

shapeColor   graphic

show   drawLine

setColor   drawCircle

                        drawRectangle

Nesting means there are multiple methods with the name **drawRectangle**.